ARIS & PHILLIPS HISI

BOOK OF ALEXANDER

(LIBRO DE ALEXANDRE)

Translated with an Introduction and Notes by

Peter Such and Richard Rabone

Aris & Phillips Hispanic Classics
are published by
Oxbow Books, Oxford

© Peter Such and Richard Rabone, 2009.
All rights reserved.
No part of this publication may be reproduced or stored in a retrieval system or transmitted in any form or by any means including photocopying without the prior permission of the publishers in writing.

ISBN   978-0-85668-864-5 cloth
ISBN   978-0-85668-863-8 paper

A CIP record for this book is available from the British Library

Printed and bound by
Short Run Press, Exeter

To Eric and Nick

CONTENTS

Acknowledgements	vii
Map of Alexander's campaigns	viii
The life of Alexander the Great – a chronology	ix
Map of the Iberian Peninsula in the early thirteenth century	x
Events of the early thirteenth century	xi

Illustrations
Alexander tells his troops the story of the siege of Troy	xiii
Alexander comes close to death after swimming in the River Cydnus	xiv
A eleventh-century map of the world	xv
The labours of the months	xvi
Notes on the illustrations	xvii

Introduction
1.	The distinctiveness of the *Libro de Alexandre*	1
2.	A novel enterprise: the poet's 'manifesto'	2
3.	The manuscripts and the questions of date and authorship	4
4.	Spain in the early thirteenth century: the background to the composition of the *Libro de Alexandre*	12
5.	Alexander the Great in history and in literary tradition: our poet's sources	23
6.	Style and structure: the poet finds his voice	33
7.	Warriors, kings and scholars – triumph but humility: the themes of the *Libro de Alexandre*	43
8.	The *Libro de Alexandre*: a synopsis	63
9.	The Spanish text	68
10.	The translation	70

Select Bibliography	75
The *Libro de Alexandre*: text, translation and notes	83

ACKNOWLEDGEMENTS

This volume has its origin in a term spent at St Peter's College, Oxford in early 2006; warm thanks are due to the Master and Fellows for their generosity, encouragement and friendship.

We have a great debt of gratitude to Jonathan Thacker, without whom the project would never have been conceived, to Jennie Williams who read the draft of the introduction, to Mary Whitby who commented on some of the notes, to the Rabone family and Katie Clifton for their support and inexhaustible patience and to Sylvia Such for her constant encouragement and for living with the *Libro de Alexandre* for the past three years.

We are also grateful to Heather O'Brien, who drew the maps.

PTS
MRKR

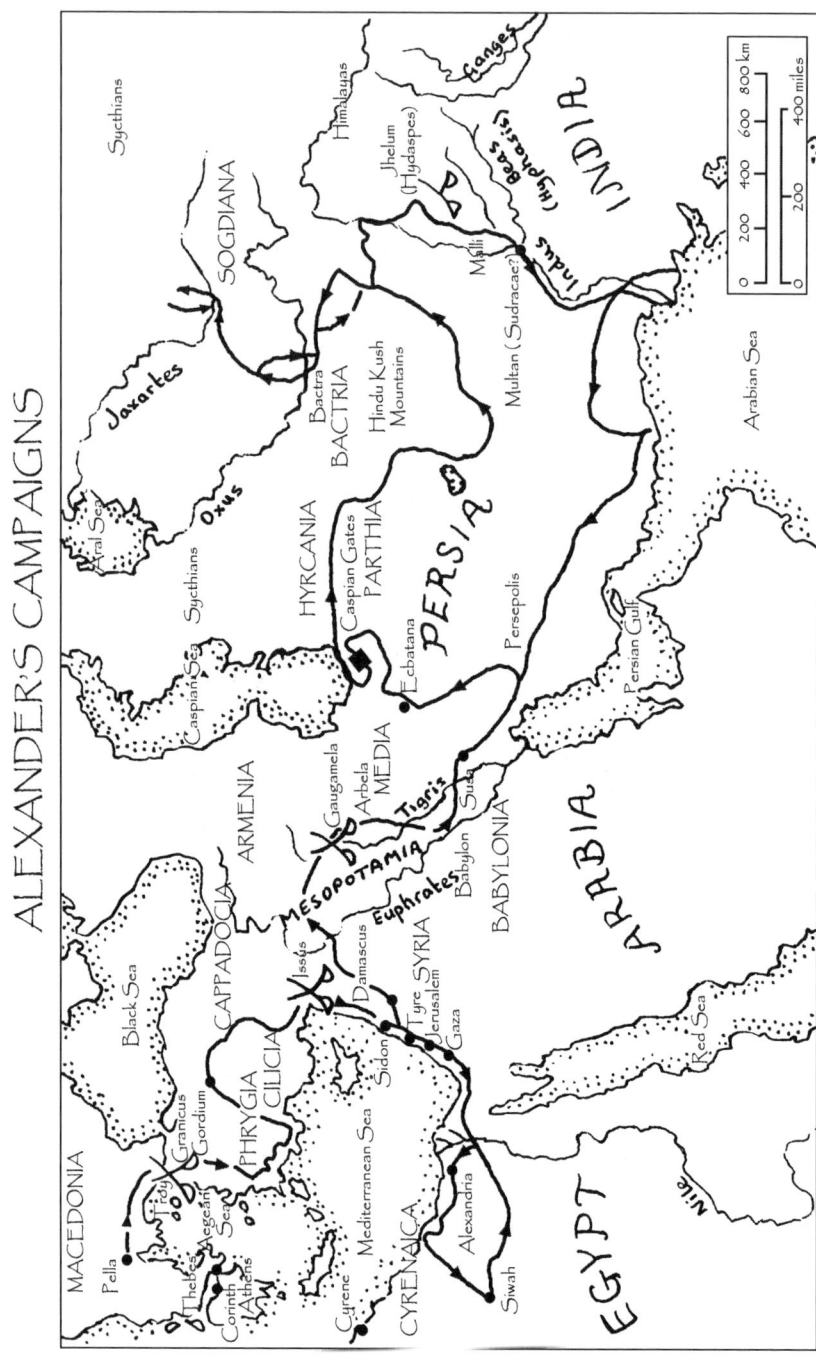

Libro de Alexandre

THE LIFE OF ALEXANDER THE GREAT – A CHRONOLOGY

359–336 BC	Reign of Alexander's father, Philip II of Macedon
356	Birth of Alexander
344	Alexander tames Bucephalus
343/342	Aristotle tutors Alexander
340/339	Alexander acts as regent during an absence of Philip
336	Accession to the Persian throne of Darius III
	Philip assassinated at Aegae
	Alexander recognised as Philip's successor and as head of the League of Corinth
335	Alexander campaigns in Thrace and against the Illyrians
	Revolt and destruction of Thebes
334	Alexander crosses into Asia Minor
	May – Battle of River Granicus, followed by extensive campaigns in Asia Minor
333	Alexander moves into Phrygia: Gordian knot episode
	November – Battle of Issus, followed by capture of Damascus by Parmenion
332	Sieges of Tyre and Gaza
	Alexander installed as Pharaoh of Egypt
331	Spring – consultation of oracle of Ammon at Siwah oasis
	1st October – Battle of Gaugamela, followed by progress through Babylonia
330	Sacking of Persepolis followed by burning of its temples
	Darius III murdered by Bessus; Alexander captures Darius' body
	Advance towards Bactria
	September – trial and execution of Philotas
	Advance as far as foot of Hindu Kush
329	Crossing of Hindu Kush
	Capture and execution of Persian pretender Bessus
329/28	Campaigns against Sogdians
328	Murder by Alexander of Cleitus "the Black"
327	Alexander marries Rhoxane, daughter of a Sogdian nobleman
	"Pages' Conspiracy"; execution of Callisthenes
	Beginning of invasion of India
326	May – Battle of the Hydaspes/Jhelum against Porus
	Death of Bucephalus
	June – advance to Hyphasis (Beas) river
	Mutiny of troops and return to Hydaspes
325	Defeat of Malli tribe; Alexander seriously wounded
	March through Gedrosian desert
324	Mass weddings at Susa
	Death of Hephaestion
323	In Babylon, Alexander prepares for Arabian campaign
	Visit of Greek envoys recognising Alexander's divinity
	10th/11th June – Alexander dies at Babylon

Libro de Alexandre

The Iberian Peninsula in the Early Thirteenth Century

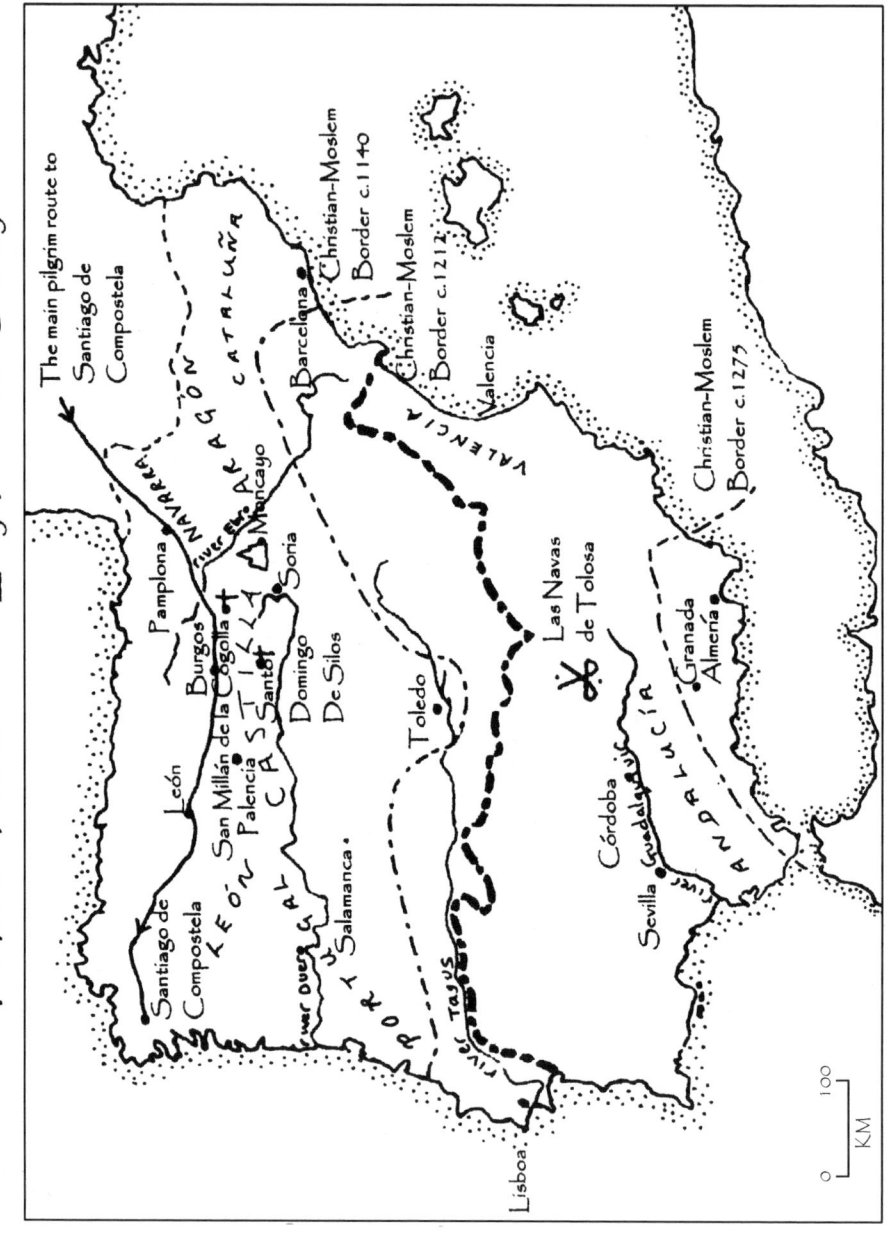

EVENTS OF THE EARLY THIRTEENTH CENTURY

	International events	*Events in Spain*	*Literature, art and culture*
1201			*Disputa del alma y el cuerpo* (fragment)
1202	Fourth Crusade begins		
1203		Balearic Islands fall to the Almohads	
1204	Crusaders take Constantinople and establish Latin empire		Death of Jewish philosopher Maimonides in Córdoba
1206		Treaty of Cabreros drawn up in Castilian and Leonese	
1207			*Poema de Mio Cid*
1208	Pope Innocent III proclaims Crusade against Cathars		Possible date of the foundation of the University of Palencia
1209		Rodrigo Jiménez de Rada confirmed as Archbishop of Toledo	
1212		Victory over the Almohads at Las Navas de Tolosa	
1213	Death of Pere II of Aragón at hands of crusaders at Muret		
1214		Death of Alfonso VIII of Castile; Jaume I succeeds to throne of Aragón at age of 5	
1215	Fourth Lateran Council Foundation of Dominican Friars		
1217	Beginning of the Fifth Crusade	Death at age of 13 of Enrique I of Castile, succeeded by Fernando III	Foundation of Salamanca University
1218		Truce between Castile and King Alfonso IX of León; Fernando faces up to Castilian nobility and begins a period of internal consolidation	*Planeta*, a compendium of clerical learning, is compiled by Alfonso VIII's chancellor, Diego García de Campos

	International events	Events in Spain	Literature, art and culture
1219	Siege and capture of Damietta	Marriage of Fernando III to Beatrice of Swebia	
1220	Frederick II is crowned emperor in Rome		
1221	Failure of the Fifth Crusade in Egypt	Birth of the future Alfonso X	Construction of Burgos Cathedral begins
1223	Franciscan order receives Pope's approval		
1225		Fernando III's first campaign in Andalusia	
1226	Louis IX (–1270) succeeds to French throne	Fernando III captures Baeza	
1227			Construction of Toledo Cathedral begins
1228	Sixth Crusade, led by Emperor Frederick II		
1229	Frederick II is crowned King of Jerusalem	Jaume I captures Mallorca; Alfonso IX of León captures Cáceres	
1230		Alfonso IX captures Mérida and Badajoz; definitive union of Castile and León on the death of Alfonso IX	(approx.) Berceo's *Vida de san Millán de la Cogolla*
1236		Fernando III captures Córdoba	Lucas de Tuy: *Chronicon mundi*

ILLUSTRATIONS

Figure 1. Alexander tells his troops the story of the siege of Troy.

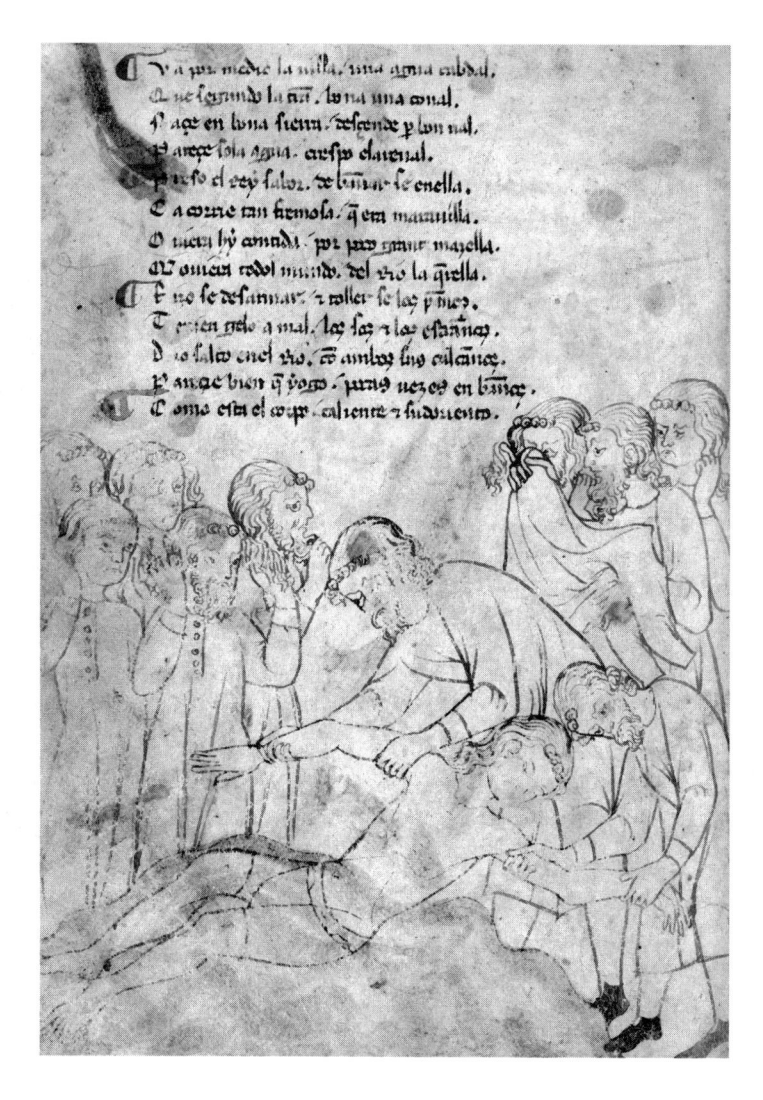

Figure 2. Alexander comes close to death after swimming in the River Cydnus.

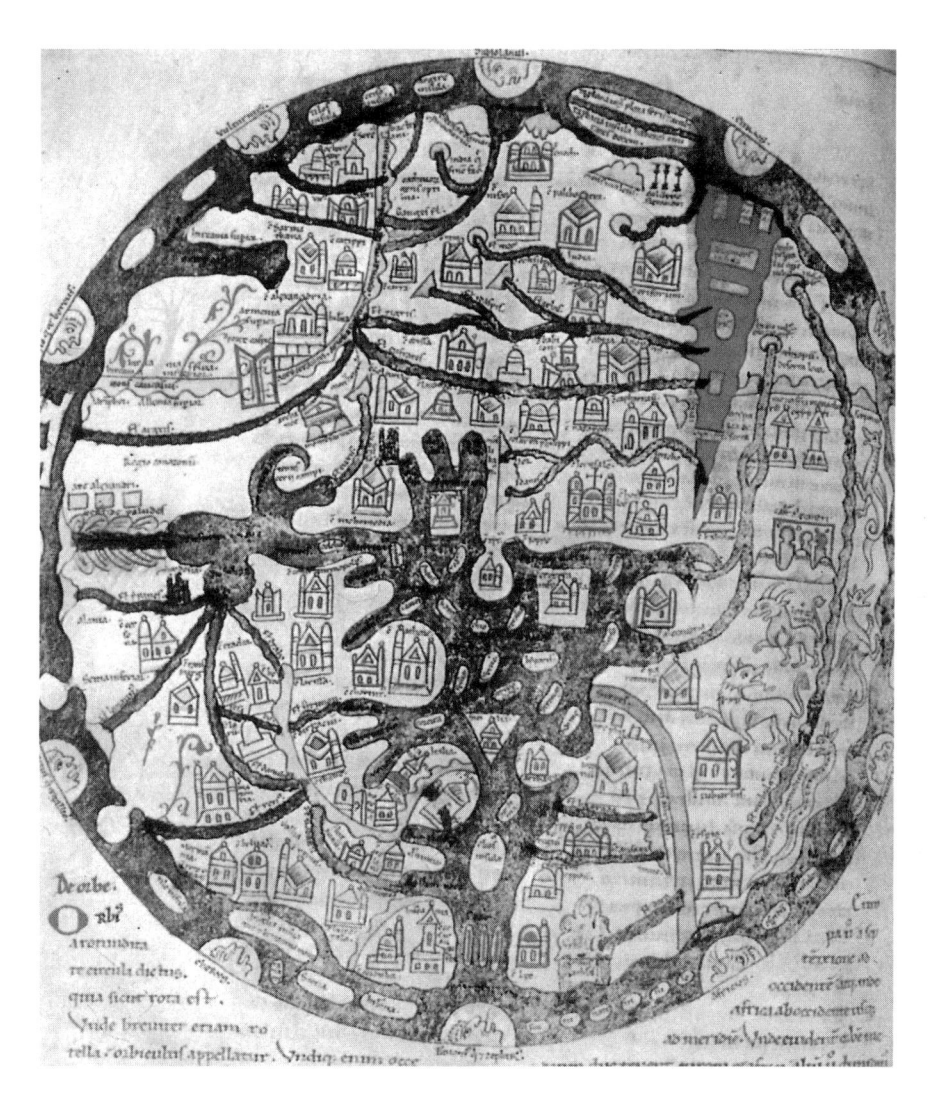

Figure 3. An eleventh-century map of the world which shows the three continents of Asia, Europe and Africa.

xvi   *Libro de Alexandre*

Figure 4. The labours of the months.

NOTES ON THE ILLUSTRATIONS

1. Of the surviving manuscripts of the *Libro de Alexandre* only *Manuscrito O*: Madrid, Biblioteca Nacional Va.5.10 contains illustrations. The vellum manuscript dates from the early fourteenth century and this drawing is mostly in the same brown ink as the text. Alexander is represented standing in front of the throne of Achilles recounting the events of the siege of Troy to his troops, who appear as medieval knights wearing chain-mail.
2. Also from *Manuscrito O* is this depiction of a strikingly Christ-like Alexander being cared for by his followers after his almost fatal swim in the River Cydnus (see stanzas 880–913). Like the previous picture, it is drawn in brown ink and has been touched up in blue-back.
3. Many copies of the *Etymologiae* of Isidore of Seville included a version of the most basic medieval world map, known as the T-O map: simply a circle divided by a T into the three continents of Asia (top half), Europe (bottom left) and Africa (bottom right). The map that appears here, however, is part of an eleventh-century manuscript and is much more elaborate; it measures 26 centimetres across. The Mediterranean with its islands occupies a dominant position and Jerusalem appears close to the central point of the world. *(Munich, Bayerische Staatsbibliothek, Clm 10058, f.154v)* See Harvey (1991, 20–23).
4. The description of visual works of art plays an important part in the *Libro de Alexandre,* and that of the labours of the months of the year (stanzas 2554–2566) is a prominent feature of the account of Alexander's tent, setting the events of Alexander's meteoric career against the backdrop of the inevitable and enduring rhythm of nature. The account given in the *Libro de Alexandre* seems not to relate exactly to any particular set of paintings or sculptures, but, to help us to envisage the kind of images that the poet had in his mind, we might look to the agricultural calendar, representing the labours of the twelve months, which is depicted in the Panteón de los Reyes in the Basílica de San Isidoro in León.

We would like to thank the Biblioteca Nacional de España (1 and 2), the British Library (3) and Edilesa (4) for their kind permission to reproduce their material.

INTRODUCTION

1. The distinctiveness of the Libro de Alexandre

There have been numerous accounts of the extraordinary life and achievements of Alexander the Great and the reader who approaches the *Libro de Alexandre* for the first time may well be inclined to wonder what a thirteenth-century Spanish cleric was able to add to this rich tradition. The following brief study will attempt to produce some answers to this question, but it nevertheless seems helpful to begin by pointing to some of the qualities which distinguish the Spanish poem, for its anonymous author did indeed produce a magnificent work which is startling in its originality.

The importance of the *Libro de Alexandre* within the context of the literature of medieval Spain has long been recognised and much attention has been paid to its significance as the most substantial poem (and almost certainly the first) composed in the learned *cuaderna vía* verse form. It draws on a wide range of sources, and the level and breadth of scholarship that its composition represents has much to tell us about the intellectual world from which it sprang. Its construction is complex and sophisticated. The poet, moreover, has direct and telling comment to make on the society and political situation of early thirteenth-century Spain. He wrestles to reconcile the ancient world with the values and beliefs of his own day; and he also seeks to produce a work which is encyclopedic in its scope, embracing material from various branches of Alexander tradition, but at the same time whose content he can put forward as credible, balanced and just. In these respects the *Libro de Alexandre* can be seen as strikingly representative of its age.

However, we should not be misled by the vastness of the poem or by any tendency to see the poet as just a conscientious compiler or tedious moraliser. The scholar who wrote that the principal value of the *Libro de Alexandre* was more archeological than poetic[1] was curiously wide of the mark. Although the *Libro de Alexandre* is recognised to be one of the most heavily didactic works in the European Alexander tradition, it in no sense constitutes a dry sermon. This is a powerful poem which conveys directly

---

[1] A. Millares Carlo (1950, 73) wrote that "la lectura del poema, cuyo principal valor más que poético es arquelógico, resulta pesada en su integridad" ("a reading as a whole of the poem, whose principal value more than poetic is archeological, proves tedious"); quoted by Bly and Deyermond (1972, 151).

and forcibly through its carefully-constructed narrative the grim message of Alexander's life, the sense of *hubris* and the horror of his fall from greatness and domination of the world to the bleak obscurity of the grave. It is a work from which we have much to learn and which richly repays the reader and the student.

2. A novel enterprise: the poet's 'manifesto'

Although the *Libro de Alexandre* is still relatively little known and studied, its opening stanzas are among the most famous of the literature of medieval Spain. They ring out a clarion call of innovation and ambition. The anonymous Spanish poet is – as we shall see – about to embark on a huge enterprise: to create in the vernacular a major poem on the life of one of the great heroes of Antiquity, welding together material from a wide range of sources into a complex literary creation which projects his own very distinctive vision of his subject. Moreover, he opens his work by making a series of claims for its formal and stylistic originality, making clear his understanding of the importance in literary and scholarly terms of his undertaking.

Given the extent to which the second stanza of the *Libro de Alexandre* has coloured so much of what has been written about the poem and also its relevance to the discussion of the work's background and authorship, it is appropriate to start by considering exactly what it tells us:

- the poet makes confident boasts for his craft (*mester*, linked to the Latin *ministerium*, which could imply a trade but could also allude to the office of the priest);
- the poet's craft is elegant or refined (the term *fermoso* is used, for example, in the works of King Alfonso X to describe language which is adorned by the skill of the rhetorician[2]);
- this is not the trade of the *juglar*, the composer of the epic poem, whose work is associated with public performance, oral tradition and improvisation;
- it is a craft without fault: a claim for the precision with which the rules for the composition of the new verse form are observed, since it is the product of the scholar's learning; equally, however, this claim can be read as meaning that it is without sin, as it is the work of the clergy;

---

[2] Montoya Martínez (1993, 77) quotes Alfonso X's definition of Rhetoric as the discipline which "essenna a ffablar ffermoso e apuesto" ("teaches speech which is refined and elegant").

- the poet is producing an elegant verse composition in a rhyming form (a feature distinguishing it from the epic which employs assonance rather than consonantal rhyme)[3];
- his poem follows a "path" based on the four-line form[4] (and in the structure of which multiples of four play an important part);
- the verse form of the poem is based on the rigorous observance of a precise syllable count; this removes it firmly from the world of the epic and tightens the association with that of Latin poetry, with the counting of feet replaced by an equivalent emphasis on that of syllables; certain principles of versification were to be carefully observed, such as the clear and complete pronunciation of each separate word, a feature which linked the composition with the world of learned composition rather than with the spoken language.[5]

We are left in no doubt by this opening declaration that the *Libro de Alexandre* has its roots in the world of the schools or of the universities and that learning and scholarship are to play a major part in its composition. The very term *cuaderna vía* (in our text spelt as *quaderna vía*), coined here to denote the four-line form, seems to carry within it an allusion to the *quadrivium*, the higher division of the medieval course of studies, and learning and scholarship are also to figure strongly in numerous other ways in the work. Indeed, the features of the *cuaderna vía* were to represent just one of the ways in which the author of the *Libro de Alexandre* was breaking new ground. In adapting a much read and studied Latin poem, the *Alexandreis*, to his own circumstances, he was – as one scholar has recently argued – contributing to "a body of work that advertises its own novelty even as it anchors it in tradition."[6]

---

[3] For a very clear and thorough analysis of the elements of the phrase "fablar curso rimado", see Arizaleta (1999, 161–174) who considers and rejects, for example, the argument that in this passage the meaning of "rimado" is connected not with rhyme but with rhythm.
[4] For the learned origins of this idea of the "path", see Arizaleta (1999, 174). M. García (1982, 210) gives a fuller analysis of the number four in the structuring of the stanzas of the poem.
[5] Scholars have emphasised, for example, how strictly the poet will have interpreted the requirement to avoid a device such as *synalepha* which involves suppressing the pronunciation of a vowel at the end of one word before another vowel at the beginning of the next. This can be associated with the firm proscription of *synalepha* by literary theorists such as Mathieu de Vendôme and Alexandre de Villedieu. See Arizaleta (1999, 177) and Rico (1985, 21–22). Rico (1985, 1 ff.) shows how the form of the *cuaderna vía* seems to have developed out of Latin poetry which demonstrates similar features of both rhyme and rhythm.
[6] Weiss (2006, 16) emphasises how the Spanish *clerecía* poets exploited the classics in such

Our poet proclaims clearly some literary principles that he intends to follow and some scholars have seen in his words a manifesto for a school of poets. During the thirteenth and fourteenth centuries the *cuaderna vía* verse form was to produce some thirty vernacular works. These include several lives of saints, poems dedicated to the Virgin and other works on religious themes by Gonzalo de Berceo, a priest associated with the monasteries of San Millán de la Cogolla and Santo Domingo de Silos and whose name twice figures in the manuscripts of the *Libro de Alexandre*. Among the other thirteenth-century *cuaderna vía* texts there are two substantial narrative poems: the *Libro de Apolonio*, the story of Apollonius of Tyre, in the tradition of the late ancient Greek romance, and the *Poema de Fernán González*, based on an earlier epic and dealing with Castile's emergence (through the deeds of the eponymous count) from domination by León. Although the last of these poems, at least, was composed significantly later than the *Libro de Alexandre*, there are evidently strong connections between the various texts grouped together as belonging to the *mester de clerecía* and it is tempting to envisage these poems as produced by a unified literary movement (see, for example, Dutton 1973, 87–90 and Uría Maqua 1981). Nevertheless, it does not seem that there is really the justification to see in the opening lines of the *Libro de Alexandre* a programme or set of principles which had been jointly elaborated and expressed by a group of poets. There are many features of the *Libro de Alexandre* that were to be taken up in the works of others, but this is surely the voice of an ambitious and exceptionally talented individual about to undertake an enterprise without precedent in the history of his nation's language and literature.

3. The manuscripts and the questions of date and authorship

There are two surviving manuscripts which contain the (more or less) full text of the *Libro de Alexandre*. One of these is known as *Manuscrito O*, named after the Osuna family to whose library it belonged in the nineteenth century, when it was acquired by the Biblioteca Nacional in Madrid. This manuscript dates from the late thirteenth or early fourteenth century. It is attributed (see stanza 2675 O) to Juan Lorenzo de Astorga who is accepted to have been a copyist, though possibly of an earlier version. This manuscript contains the

---

a way as to allow them "to adopt a dual perspective on the world, since a classic has not only a supposedly universal meaning, but also a very particular one."

apocryphal texts of two prose letters said to have been written by Alexander to his mother. The second manuscript is known as *Manuscrito P* and was acquired by the Bibliothèque Nationale in Paris in 1888. It dates from the fifteenth century. Stanza 2675 of this text attributes the poem to Gonzalo de Berceo whom it states to have been notary to Abbot Juan Sánchez of the Monastery of San Millán de la Cogolla.

There are also three surviving fragments: *Fragmento Med.* (a fourteenth-century parchment from the Archive of the Dukes of Medinaceli) contains just stanzas 1–6 and the first three lines of stanza 7; *Fragmento y* contains 19 stanzas from Aristotle's advice to Alexander and also stanza 2490cd, all transcribed as prose and included in the *Victorial* by Gutierre Díaz de Games, six manuscript versions of which survive; finally, *Fragmento B* is a printed passage from a Latin chronicle by Francisco de Bivar and contains stanzas 787–793, 851 and 1167–1168ab.

There are significant differences between *Manuscritos O* and *P*, not least that *O* is heavily marked by Leonese linguistic features whilst in *P* there is a clear Aragonese emphasis. It is generally accepted that the poet produced just one version of his poem and that the differences between the two surviving manuscripts are explained by the changes introduced by the copyists. Neither of these manuscripts represents the original version of the poem, although it is generally agreed that *P*, although later than *O*, is more directly linked to the original and represents a more reliable text.

The authorship of the *Libro de Alexandre* has provoked lively debate and continues to do so. Curiously, *Manuscrito O*, whilst mentioning Juan Lorenzo de Astorga in its final stanza, contains a remark (in stanza 1548d) addressed to Gonzalo, whilst *Manuscrito P* – which claims that the poem was written by Berceo – addresses the equivalent comment to Lorente (= Juan Lorenzo?). There have been a number of attempts to explain the contradiction between the names given in the two versions of 1548d, of which the most convincing suggests that in fact neither relates to the Spanish poet but that the remark was originally addressed, tongue in cheek, to Gautier de Châtillon, the author of his principal source, the *Alexandreis* (see Ware 1967, Dutton 1971 and, particularly, Michael 1986). The idea that Berceo was the author of the *Libro de Alexandre* is an appealing one: there are numerous stylistic and linguistic parallels between the *Alexandre* and Berceo's works and, as Dutton (1971, 30) commented, "[i]t would be nice to think that this work was his labour of intellectual love to which he devoted himself in the time left free from the composition of the pious works that we acknowledge to be his." Many consider that the evidence for this belief is thin and it is now generally assumed that both versions of the *explicit* in stanza 2675 are apocryphal. On the other hand, some scholars believe that Gonzalo de Berceo was actually the copyist of *Manuscrito P*, whilst there continues to be some convinced support for the belief that he was indeed the work's author.[7]

If there now exists a general inclination to accept that it is impossible to identify any individual as author of the *Libro de Alexandre*, there is also broad agreement that the work's origin can be found in the world of school or university studies in the first two or three decades of the thirteenth century and several scholars would go so far as to point quite confidently to the link with the University or *Studium Generale* of Palencia which enjoyed a brief but very fertile existence following its establishment by King Alfonso VIII (in collaboration with Bishop Tello Téllez de Meneses) between about 1208 and 1212. It seems significant that Palencia is not mentioned in the *Libro de Alexandre*, whilst other centres of learning are named as such in stanzas 2582–2583, but Gonzalo de Berceo certainly does display an acquaintance with the city and its surroundings. It is known that Alfonso brought scholars from Paris and Bologna to Palencia and these will certainly have included teachers of Grammar and Rhetoric, the disciplines that we can safely assume to have been the source of many of the literary teachings whose effect is much in evidence in the *Libro de Alexandre*. If the principal purpose of the new university was to train administrators for the royal chancery, the needs of such individuals (from correct accentuation of the written Castilian language to a knowledge of the history and literature of the ancient world) were certainly compatible with the literary concerns reflected in the *Libro de Alexandre*. It is in just such an environment that our poet will have encountered the *Alexandreis* which figured very prominently in the lists of texts studied under the teachers of Grammar or *auctoristas* (known in Spanish as *actoristas*, as in stanza 1197a); and likewise that he could have encountered at least some of the wealth of French influences which are heavily in evidence in the *Libro de Alexandre*. In origin the *Libro de Alexandre* could have been conceived as a kind of commentary or gloss on the *Alexandreis*, with the poet's studies helping to create his own narrative

---

[7] The strongest defender of Gonzalo de Berceo's authorship of the *Libro de Alexandre* is Dana A. Nelson. See particularly his edition of 1979 and recent studies which continue to work towards a revised edition.

style. Whether before or after the Palencia's cathedral school became a university, it is undoubtedly possible that teachings received there were the source of the poet's exciting new enterprise.[8]

Likewise, when the author of the *Libro de Alexandre* alludes to some of Christendom's great centres of learning in what has been described as "the cultural pilgrimage of an individual trained in various European cathedral schools and universities",[9] he may also be giving us a pointer to the nature of his own experience. Among other centres, he draws attention to Bordeaux, Paris ("with a rich abundance of all kinds of learning", 2582b) and Bologna ("Bologna seems outstanding above all others / and it is the fount of all laws and decrees.", 2583cd). The richness and the variety of the texts and source material that our poet knows, in some cases, like the *Roman d'Alexandre*, probably being recalled from memory – together with the breadth of his knowledge and the very nature of his literary undertaking – points clearly to a man who has travelled and come into direct contact with a wide range of cultural influences.

There have been further attempts to elaborate more specific theories with regard to the authorship of the *Libro de Alexandre*. These have included the argument that the poem was composed by a team of clerics – probably including Gonzalo de Berceo and Juan de Astorga – under the direction of an individual such as Peter of Blois (Uría Maqua 2000, 194). Some scholars have argued that the poem's author could well have been Diego García de Campos, Alfonso VIII's Chancellor and the compiler of *Planeta*, a vast compendium of clerical learning which was completed in 1218. Again, scholars are not, on the whole, convinced by the attribution, not least because it seems that Diego García was not in favour of the extension of the use of Castilian at the expense of Latin. However, surely the important point is that the author of *Planeta* was extensively travelled, representative of the

---

[8] Much work has been done in recent years on the relationship between the *mester de clerecía* and the University of Palencia; see for example Rico (1985, particularly 9–23) and Uría Maqua (2000, 57 ff.); and, for Berceo's connection with Palencia, see Dutton (1973, 80–81). Much has been made of the documented presence of teachers of grammar in Palencia: see, for example, Dutton (1973, 79–80) and Uría Maqua (2000, 64 ff.). Rico (1980, 9 ff.) discusses the likelihood that students at Palencia would have known the *Alexandreis* and Arizaleta (1999, 151 ff.) goes further by envisaging the *Libro de Alexandre* as in origin a gloss on Gautier de Châtillon's poem.

[9] Juan Casas Rigall, ed. (2007, 25): "el itinerario de las estrofas 2581–84 ... pudiera derivar del peregrinaje cultural de un individuo formado en diversas escuelas catedralicias y universidades europeas."

rapidly-developing educational world of the early thirteenth century and, as such, the possessor of a rich and encyclopedic knowledge which he seeks to pass on to his fellow clerics.[10] Like the author of the *Libro de Alexandre*, in an age of cultural renaissance he proudly combines the classical and the modern, a spirit which increasingly under Alfonso VIII, Fernando III and his son Alfonso X came to be characteristic of the royal court of Castile. A persuasive image of our author begins to suggest itself: one of a learned individual, composing a sophisticated poem for a small intellectual circle, possibly connected with the royal court.[11]

We have, then, a number of clues as to the background of our poet and it is in his education that we find several of them. A few more are to be found in the poem itself: the mention, for example, of Cogolla, in La Rioja, in stanza 2580b as one of the five great landmarks of Spain. The other peak mentioned is Moncayo, situated on the limits between the provinces of Soria and Zaragoza, which at over 2000 metres is certainly a mountain of some prominence. Cogolla, however, is no more than a hill and would certainly not normally be considered an outstanding geographical feature. On the other hand, it is very closely identified with the monastery of San Millán de la Cogolla; indeed, by the thirteenth century there were two monasteries here, Suso and Yuso, since the community had developed from one of hermits into an important Benedictine centre. It is important to bear in mind the undoubted association with San Millán de la Cogolla of Gonzalo de Berceo. It is difficult to see why, if the poet did not have some connection with this area and perhaps with the monastery itself, he would have chosen to mention Cogolla as one of Spain's five great landmarks.

There is, at the very least, then, a clear indication here that the Riojan region of northern Castile in which San Millán de la Cogolla is situated was well known to the poet. Other pointers may not be entirely reliable, but help,

---

[10] For the attribution of the *Libro de Alexandre* to Diego García de Campos, see Hernando Pérez (1992). Rico (1985, 6–8) points to the significance of the concerns expressed by Diego García as representative of the intellectual aspirations of his age.

[11] Arizaleta (1999, especially 256 and 260) argues convincingly that the ideology central to the *Libro de Alexandre* was closely linked to that of the royal court in the early thirteenth century ("l'hypothèse de l'existence de quelque lien entre le poète anonyme et la cour castillane est enrichissante, car ce n'est que dans la cour castillane que cet auteur aurait pu assister au véritable développement de l'idée de croisade et de mission chrétienne assumé par la figure royale." "The hypothesis of the existence of some link between the anonymous poet and the Castilian court is a fertile one, for it is only in the Castilian court that this author could have encountered the true development of the idea of a Crusade and Christian mission that was assumed by the royal personage.")

nevertheless, to build up a picture: even the list of grape varieties that our poet includes in stanzas 2129–2130 contain at least one variety associated with La Rioja (see note to stanzas 2128 ff.). There has been much debate as to the significance of the evidence about the poem's provenance given by the surviving manuscripts, but there is a general agreement that the dialectal features of the original are most likely to correspond to a form of northern Castilian with possibly eastern features,[12] and this would certainly not be inconsistent with the idea of an author associated with a Riojan monastery.

The poet gives one indication of his position in society, making a sharp distinction in stanzas 1824ab between "we simple clergy" and on the other hand "the greater prelates"; here and in his biting criticism of those priests who achieve advancement with no heed paid to their level of education (stanza 1825) we are given a sense of a cleric of low standing, perhaps frustrated at his failure to achieve the advancement which he considers his due. We should be wary of taking such comments at face value, however; it would be an appropriate device for the poet to feign such simplicity, as is the custom, for example, of the notary Gonzalo de Berceo, who projects the image of a simple and unlettered country priest using unsophisticated literary resources to communicate a straightforward and deeply-felt message.[13] This picture of the simple cleric is much at odds with the considerable degree of scholarship that is displayed in the *Libro de Alexandre*. It is also inconsistent with the image of the success and prosperity available to a man educated in a cathedral school or university in the burgeoning bureaucracy of the early thirteenth century.

Just as there has been much debate about the authorship of the *Libro de Alexandre*, there has been equally keen discussion of the as yet unresolved question of the date of its composition. Here too we have several clues. The

---

[12] See Casas Rigall, ed. (2007, 30–39) for an excellent survey and evaluation of this complex debate. In the context of the keen debate about the evidence for Leonese or eastern Spanish origins, he points out that we should not view these regions as linguistically-watertight compartments; rather, there is evidence for the existence in the Middle Ages of "a dialectal bridge in the northern third of the Iberian Peninsula, which takes in Galicia, Asturias, Cantabria, Burgos and La Rioja, apparent in the language of Berceo, and which, moreover, continues in an eastern line constituted by the speech of Navarre, Aragón and Cataluña." ("un puente dialectal en el tercio norte de la Península Ibérica, que abarca Galicia, Asturias, Cantabria, Burgos y la Rioja, manifiesto en la lengua de Berceo, y que, además, tiene continuidad en una línea oriental constituida por las hablas navarras, aragonesas y catalanas." (36)).

[13] See for example, the opening section of "La vida de Santo Domingo de Silos", where the poet announces that he is about to write in the plain language of the people, for he has no greater knowledge than this, and asks for a glass of wine as a reward (Dutton, ed. 1978, 35).

most conspicuous, though not necessarily the clearest, is the dating in stanza 1799 of the year of the death of King Darius III (330 BC) in relation to that in which the poem was composed. Unfortunately, the readings in the two manuscripts differ markedly; *O* has clearly been affected by scribal error and there is uncertainty as a result of the nature of the calendar employed and of possible errors made by copyists with the Roman numerals. Scholars have puzzled at length over the enigma presented by the figures. Some studies have pointed to a date of composition in the first decade of the thirteenth century, but others have suggested dates in the third decade of the century or even as late as 1233.[14]

Other details have attracted attention, such as the mention of the wealth of Damietta, a city taken during the Fifth Crusade of 1219 (stanza 860d), that of Seville as one of the outstanding cities of Christian Spain (stanza 2581b), given that the city was in Moslem hands until 1248, and the allusion to the "señor de Seçilia" (stanza 2522a), which some have interpreted as praise for Holy Roman Emperor Frederick II for the part that he played in the Crusade of 1228. There are varying levels of doubt about all of this evidence. In fact, Damietta was famous for its prosperity and its linen trade well before it fell into Christian hands. Seville is only included in *Manuscrito O* whilst *P* mentions Soria, far closer to our poet's likely homeland (although Seville does appear in both manuscripts in stanza 1787b). It has also been argued that the allusion to the Lord of Sicily lacks any historical weight: it is surprising that the poet should treat him as distinct from the ruler of Germany (2521c) and Sicily is also mentioned in the *Alexandreis* (for further consideration of these arguments, see note to stanza 2522a). Nevertheless, it is worth bearing in mind the role of Frederick II in taking up the cross following the Fourth Lateran Council in 1215: as a crusading emperor he sought to present himself as the champion of Christendom, and the Christian fleets were to assemble in Sicily. More solid evidence seems to be provided by the strong suggestion in line 279d that Jerusalem is still in Moslem hands, which would certainly mean that the poem was composed before the Holy City's recovery in 1228–1229.

It is, however, to broader aspects of the *Libro de Alexandre* that we might look to give us a more reliable pointer to the date of its composition. Mention has already been made of its possible association with the University of Palencia (founded at about the end of the first decade of the

---

[14] For a succinct summary of the work done on this much debated question, see Casas Rigall, ed. (2007, 8–30).

thirteenth century), though it must be borne in mind that there was plenty of intellectual activity centred around the cathedral school in that city before the establishment of the *Studium Generale*. Raymond Willis, the author of a number of important early studies on the *Libro de Alexandre*, argued that "the poem was most probably composed in the second quarter of the century, among other reasons because it is imbued with an attitude towards the figure of the King which reached its plenitude only in the course of the reign of Fernando III and which is, for example, reflected shortly after in the *Setenario*."[15] He goes on to affirm that the poet conceives of the monarch as the embodiment of valour, justice and nobility but also of "courtliness, erudition and saintliness". We shall see below how the *Libro de Alexandre* can be seen as offering a model for a monarch or prince and this is indeed a point to be taken into account in assessing the likely date of its composition.

It is also well worth examining the possible significance for the poem of the conclusions of the Fourth Lateran Council. There seem to be significant parallels between the moralising passages which the poet includes in the *Libro de Alexandre* and the conclusions of the Council which took place in 1215 and which was to have far-reaching consequences in many fields of life in Spain (and, indeed, throughout Christendom), notably in education, art and literature (see, for example, Lomax 1969). Although we must be cautious in any assumptions about how rapidly the effects of the Council were felt and although we must not assume that such ideas were not current before 1215, there is a good deal of evidence to suggest that, in his insistence on both the need for moral reform and the importance of scholarship, our poet is very much in tune with the ideas which emerged from it (see Section 4, below).

Although we are tantalisingly short of being able to reach firm conclusions about the date or the authorship of the *Libro de Alexandre*, quite a clear picture emerges: the *Libro de Alexandre* seems to have been composed in northern Castile; the poet's knowledge of and access to a wealth of Alexander material points to an association with an institution possessing an extensive library, such as one of the great Castilian monasteries, or perhaps a noble or even royal court; and his evident erudition and literary training mark him as a man educated to a high level, possibly at the University of Palencia or perhaps at a foreign centre of learning. Some scholars now incline strongly towards suggesting a date of composition in the first decade of the century,

---

[15] Willis (1951, 168) was the first to emphasise this point, but it has been further developed in important respects by others, notably Arizaleta (1999) and Weiss (2006).

during the reign of Alfonso VIII and in the years before the crucial battle of Las Navas de Tolosa, and in particular it has been suggested that King Alfonso himself was a direct source of inspiration for the poem which constitutes a picture of a medieval monarch devoted to the ideal of conquest in a Christian cause.[16] The argument is a very plausible one, but it is possible also to consider a later date, perhaps towards 1220, in the early years of the reign of Fernando III. Some evidence for this will be advanced in the subsequent sections of this Introduction. It is worth looking now at some of the social, political and cultural changes which marked this important period in the development of the kingdoms of Castile and León.

4. Spain in the early thirteenth century: the background to the composition of the Libro de Alexandre

The developments in the society of Spain's Christian kingdoms must, of course, be viewed against a background of the rapidly-developing reconquest of the Iberian Peninsula from Moslem control. The massively powerful Umayyad caliphate had lost its dominance some two centuries earlier and Moslem principalities (*taifas*) had gradually taken its place. The Christian rulers of the northern kingdoms (Navarre, León, Castile and Aragón) had with increasing effect exacted tribute or protection money (*parias*) and extended their territories. Rapid advances had been combined with periods of consolidation, disturbed by periodic military reverses. The capture of Toledo in 1085 by Alfonso VI of Castile had signalled a major triumph and, shortly afterwards, Pope Urban II had declared that the wars against Iberian Moslems should be seen as crusades. The ideology of the *Reconquista* was to become an increasingly important one for Spain's Christian monarchs, although there were long periods of peaceful coexistence between the Christians and Moslems of the Peninsula. In particular, two waves of invasion – by the Moroccan Almoravids, invited in by the *taifa* kingdoms after the fall of Toledo, and by the North African Almohads in the mid-twelfth century – checked the Christian advances.

It is worth bearing in mind the background of the crusading expeditions, promoted by Pope Innocent III and his successor Honorius III, which took place at the end of the twelfth century and in the early years of the thirteenth century against the Moslem domination of the Holy Land (a situation which

---

[16] See Arizaleta (1999, 255–261), who, although concentrating on the poem's possible connection with the figure of Alfonso VIII, also points out (59) that a link has been suggested with the figure of Fernando III or the future Alfonso X (Michael 1970, 86).

is lamented, for example, in stanza 279d of the *Libro de Alexandre* and again alluded to in 2510c). Their success was very limited but their effect on the psychology of their age was immense. The Third Crusade of 1189–1192 had failed to recover Jerusalem and the Fourth Crusade of 1204, originally directed at Egypt, had led to the conquest and sacking of the Christian city of Constantinople and the establishment of the eastern Latin Empire. The Fifth Crusade of 1217–21 brought about the capture of the port of Damietta but the attack on Cairo failed, with heavy Christian losses. Eventually the Sixth Crusade which began in 1228 under the Holy Roman Emperor Frederick II was to result in the short-term recovery of Jerusalem.

In the Iberian Peninsula, on the other hand, the early years of the thirteenth century were to see a sequence of extremely important developments which brought profound changes both within the Christian kingdoms and in terms of the balance of power between Christian and Moslem kingdoms. Alfonso VIII had suffered a crushing defeat by a Moslem army at Alarcos in 1195 and the hostilities among the Christian monarchs continued to reinforce the military dominance of the Almohads. Increasingly, however, the Church promoted the idea of the Iberian Crusade which was eventually preached by Innocent III. The army which gathered in Toledo under the leadership of Alfonso VIII of Castile included numerous European knights and was joined by troops led by the kings of Aragón and Navarre, together with nobles from Portugal and León. The Christian victory on the plain of Las Navas de Tolosa in 1212 was to prove immensely significant, opening the way for the conquest of the cities of Moslem Spain.

Since the mid-twelfth century, Castile and León had been separate kingdoms and relations between them had often been tense. When Alfonso died in 1214, he was succeeded as King of Castile by his young son Enrique who died in what seemed to be a freak accident three years later. Enrique's sister Berenguela, who inherited the throne, rapidly renounced it in favour of her son Fernando, although she continued to employ her considerable political skill on his behalf. The situation was complicated considerably by hostility on the part of some nobles (with the powerful Lara family playing a prominent role). With the immensely powerful and rebellious Laras supporting his claim to the Castilian throne, Fernando's father, King Alfonso IX of León, advanced as far as the very gates of Burgos, where he was turned away by Fernando and Berenguela, supported by a force led by loyal nobles. A treaty was signed with Alfonso in August 1218 and over the following years, with the Laras conciliated through a marriage alliance,

Fernando steadily imposed his authority on the Castilian nobility. In 1219 Fernando knighted himself and married Beatrice of Swabia, cousin of Emperor Frederick II.

The Leonese monarch busied himself with campaigns against al-Andalus and, on his death in 1230, Fernando was able to unite the kingdoms of León and Castile under his rule. Their union was to be permanent, and as Fernando II of Castile and later Fernando III of Castile and León – the future Saint Fernando, for he was canonised in the seventeenth century – he was to play the dominant role in the rapid expansion of the Christian kingdoms into Moslem Spain. The cousin of the French crusading monarch, Saint Louis IX, from the outset of his reign Fernando was to see his role as that of a warrior at the service of a holy cause. Baeza was conquered in 1226 and, among his numerous other conquests, Córdoba in 1236 and Seville in 1248 were the most spectacular prizes. It has been calculated that, when he died in 1252, 100,000 square kilometres had been added to the size of the territories that he possessed in Castile and León. Although the kingdom of Granada remained in Moslem hands, several cities of lower Andalucía, such as Jerez and Medina Sidonia, also recognised his authority. His son, who was born in 1221 and who succeeded him to the throne of Castile and León as Alfonso X, came to be known as *The Wise* and presided over a period of great intellectual and cultural development, whilst pursuing political ambition in the form of his candidacy to the Holy Roman Empire.

There are in the *Libro de Alexandre* no explicit allusions to the advance into Moslem Spain, although it is clear that the emphasis in the poem on conflict, on feats of war and on constant displacement and conquest reflects the spirit of such an age of dramatic military developments. If the poet writes approvingly of the draconian punishments inflicted by Alexander on his enemies, it should be borne in mind that the medieval chroniclers were just as warm in their praise for the brutal treatment meted out by rulers such as Fernando III to their enemies: "some he threw from towers, some he drowned in the sea, some he hanged, others he burned to death, or cooked in pots, or had skinned alive, and by means of various forms of torture ensured that the kingdom remained in peace and justice" (an account of Fernando's actions in 1225 given by Lucas de Tuy in the *Cronicon Mundi*, IV.86; quoted in Linehan 2008, 23). The situation faced by Alexander and his conduct as a warrior and a ruler are by no means remote from the realities of life in thirteenth-century Spain.

There are a few mentions in the poem of Moors as Alexander's enemies (we also encounter them, in a metrically convenient phrase, as in stanzas 87d and 2332b, paired with Jews) and the repeated emphasis on the tribute or *parias* brought to Alexander by the peoples of his empire recalls those paid to the Christian kingdoms by Spain's Moslems during the period of reconquest. In addition, there is certainly a significant parallel between the situation faced by the young Alexander, one of internal conflicts aggravated by treachery and foreign oppression, and that which King Fernando had to overcome: an unstable kingdom, troubled by a divided and often dangerous nobility and confronted by the threat of invasion. Fernando was not, indeed, the only Castilian monarch to have found himself in this situation, for Alfonso VIII of Castile, who in 1158 had succeeded to the throne as a minor, had had to overcome very similar threats from an unreliable nobility and Leonese invasion (see, for example, Linehan 2008, 24 ff.). The author of the *Libro de Alexandre* returns time and time again to the theme of treachery and of the fundamental importance of respect for one's lord and king. It seems highly likely that he is making a clear statement about the troubled political situation of his own age and the argument that this could well be the difficult early years of Fernando's reign – or, indeed, that of Alfonso – seems a plausible one.

The twelfth and thirteenth centuries saw the development in Spain of the chivalric ideal, offering a new social model and for the first time a secular rather than a religious one, although its religious dimension was undeniably important. The new emphasis on the military role of the heavy cavalry since the end of the eleventh century was accompanied by that on the model of the crusading knight, which spread rapidly throughout Europe. This was an ideological model which now provided a kind of justification for the new social dominance achieved by the Spanish nobility. The most powerful expression of this fusion of military skill and religious dedication was to be found in the military orders which grew rapidly in importance and wealth in the second half of the twelfth century and the early years of the thirteenth. The ideology of chivalry provided norms of conduct which extended not just to military activity but also to all areas of public and private conduct, placing special importance on loyalty and faithfulness. The chivalric model and the way of life that it inspired became increasingly popular during this period and there is ample evidence of this, for example, in the mention in both literary texts and chronicles of the increasingly widespread custom of the investiture of arms, the ceremony by which knighthood was bestowed on kings, the sons of kings and members of the nobility. The performance of this ceremony is described in a substantial early section of the *Libro de Alexandre* (stanzas 89–120) and it could well be significant that here Alexander is specifically shown as playing the active role in the ceremony, indeed girding on his own sword; for such auto-investiture of arms is precisely the act which is associated with a number of Iberian sovereigns, first among them being King Fernando in 1217.[17]

In other respects, too, the society of Spain's Christian kingdoms was evolving rapidly: in terms, for example, of the growth of administrative structures, particularly for dealing with justice and taxation; the evolving role of the nobility, reflected in the growing emphasis on the concept of chivalry; the rapid growth in the importance of the cities; and a wide variety of cultural and intellectual developments, often international in origin and which included the appearance of the first universities.

The twelfth and thirteenth centuries saw the slow development by the Castilian monarchy of the mechanism for a centralised administration. The monarchy was itinerant, with no fixed base, and the physical presence of the king was essential for the exercise of his rule – just as, indeed, the power and authority of Alexander are repeatedly shown to reside in his own immense force of character. It has been pointed out that the itinerant life and constant conflict which characterise the life of Alexander also reflect the inevitable reality of the life of the thirteenth-century king, engaged in a continuous process of war for a combination of spiritual and material profit.[18] A figure such as Alfonso VIII or Fernando III would have seen a constant process of onward movement, war and conquest as fundamental to his own role.

The monarch would be accompanied by a court or *curia* (initially small, but steadily increasing in size), made up of nobles, high officials and ecclesiastics. These clerics would be responsible not only for legal matters, but also for administrative tasks. Among these, the Chancellor would be responsible for the drawing up of official documents and would be assisted by a team of scribes. The number of chancellery officials grew rapidly and in the

---

[17] Costa Gomes (2003, 374) looks in detail at the significance of this act, which constitutes a clear statement that the monarch rules by his own right alone.

[18] See Arizaleta (1999, 230–231). Weiss (2006, 128–129) also emphasises the constant need to maintain control over conquered territories. Thus he sees Darius' murderers as representing a threat to the stability of conquest: "Alexander's desperation to pursue and destroy these individuals demonstrates how social and political chaos will continue to menace, even once frontiers have been tamed." (129)

thirteenth century there started to appear registries containing records of the various documents that had been produced (Álvarez Borge 2003, 249–253). There is a good deal of evidence in the *Libro de Alexandre* that its author was familiar with and interested in the technicalities of correspondence (see, for example, stanzas 1537b and 2525b) and it is tempting to speculate that our poet could well have worked in such an environment.

As the royal court grew in size and responsibility, it developed specialised departments staffed by professionals, often trained in law. The role of the *curia* in the dispensing of justice became increasingly prominent. There was a steady movement throughout Europe towards the formulation of a programme of legislation based on Roman law which was introduced into Spain in the thirteenth century and which was to provoke conflict between the monarchy and the nobility.[19] Moreover, from the late twelfth century there came into existence, developing out of the *curia*, assemblies of the estates or *Cortes*, which included nobles, ecclesiastics and representatives of the municipalities. The cities were growing in importance – the thirteenth century was a period of rapid urban development, often involving the growth of industry, usually based on textiles – and in many cases they became the allies of kings in political conflict with the nobility. It is not surprising, perhaps, that in describing Babylon, the author of the *Libro de Alexandre* emphasises its urban splendours or that, in creating his picture of Hell, he gives it the features of a medieval town, complete with its *real* or royal citadel and palace.

The days of greatest splendour for the monasteries had passed by the beginning of the thirteenth century and correspondence from this period shows them to have been involved in numerous wrangles which bear witness to their financial difficulties. Disputes over charters and the legal documentation for their privileges and rights are an example of the kind of work for which they clearly needed specialist legal assistance. At the same time, as the period saw a huge expansion in the use of the written word, the education of members of the clergy seeking advancement into higher positions necessarily became lengthier and more complex. Moreover, the weight of papal legislation grew rapidly and ecclesiastical administration at all levels became more complex. The very establishment of dioceses and

---

[19] Mª Eugenia Lacarra (1980, 96–102) shows how the narrative of the *Poema de Mio Cid* – written down in its existing form in the first decade of the thirteenth century – is used by the poet to communicate a clear message about the relationship between lord and vassal, in terms which relate directly to the legal and political conflicts of his own age.

ecclesiastical provinces produced a series of disputes and confrontations over the delimitation of territories and right to income.

Although in a sense the Spain of the early thirteenth century can be seen as a frontier society, in the recently conquered territories the creation of new cities was vital as a form of repopulation and as a result there was a further need for the Church to expand its organisation and for the king's delegates to exercise administrative and judicial roles. It is clear, then, that as clerics played an increasingly important part in the chancery, in diplomacy, in a wide range of administrative contexts or, indeed, in the composition of histories and chronicles, there were many paths for advancement open to a man possessing the evidently high level of learning and literary skill that characterises the author of the *Libro de Alexandre*.

At this stage it is appropriate to return to the consequences which were to be felt in Spain as a result of the deliberations of the Fourth Lateran Council of 1215. Scholars have drawn attention to the significance of Innocent III's sacramental reforms and the possible connection with the mention in stanza 2375d, further emphasised in 2384, of "true confession", *la vera confessión* (see canon 21 of the Council's conclusions).[20] There are, moreover, a number of other respects in which comments made by the author of the *Libro de Alexandre* could be seen as reflecting concerns mentioned in the canons of the Council. These comments occur principally in two major moralising passages in the *Libro de Alexandre* which constitute a sweeping and systematic criticism of the morality of the age; both of these passages, although following up details present in source material, are largely original with the Spanish poet. The parallels include the emphasis on the morality of the clergy (canons 14–17: stanzas 1822 ff.); matters concerning the bestowing of benefices (canons 29–30: stanza 1825); simony (canons 63–66: specifically mentioned in stanza 1825b and again, with emphasis on the punishment awaiting offenders, in 2366); greed in priests (canon 66: stanza 1824bc); usury (canon 67: stanza 1820); the payment of tithes (canons 53–56: stanza 1817), and various questions concerning the status and activities of Jews (canons 67–70: reflected, perhaps, in the depiction of the nature and treatment of the Jewish people in Alexander's encounter with the Lost Tribes in stanzas 2103 ff.) It may also, for example, be significant that the representation in art and literature of the Seven Deadly Sins – which

---

[20] See Casas Rigall, ed. (2007, 28) and Franchini (1997, 35–43). Franchini analyses in detail the significance of the allusion in the *Libro de Alexandre* to "true confession" but does not examine other possible parallels.

are described in a vivid and extended passage of the *Libro de Alexandre* – can be traced back to the programme of education promoted in the wake of the Council (Bloomfield 1952, 91). The Council's emphasis on clerical education (canon 11) is, as we shall see, reflected by a preoccupation with the importance of learning that is fundamental to the *Libro de Alexandre*.

There is, then, a good deal of evidence to suggest that, in his insistence on the need for moral reform, our poet is heavily influenced by the ideas which emerged from the Fourth Lateran Council. This Council was regarded as an ecumenical council by all learned and religious men of the age and was the most important such council to take place before the sixteenth-century Council of Trent. When it began in the Lateran Basilica in November 1215, there were 404 bishops present from throughout the Western Church, and from the Latin Eastern Church a large number of abbots, canons and representatives of the secular powers. The Council placed great emphasis on Church discipline and the reform of clerical morals and also on the Jewish question, obliging all Jews to wear distinctive dress at all times; and it ended by declaring a Crusade to "liberate the Holy Land from infidel hands", stating that the crusaders were to assemble in the kingdom of Sicily the following June. The delegation of twenty-three prelates from the Peninsula which attended the Council was headed by Rodrigo Jiménez de Rada, Archbishop of Toledo and seems to have included Diego García de Campos. The Spanish bishops were certainly well aware of the Council's decrees and it is very likely that they set about putting them into practice without them being formally promulgated. Whilst we must be careful about over-emphasising the immediate effects in the Spanish kingdoms of the new legislation (see, for example, Alvar 1996), there can be no doubt that the concerns that it represented were to be very live ones for the Castilian Church. Thus, in 1219 Pope Honorius III sent to Archbishop Rodrigo a harsh condemnation of the state of clerical discipline in Castile, drawing particular attention to the promotion of scoundrels to benefices. In the previous year, Diego García in his *Planeta* had directed scathing criticism at the Spanish bishops, condemning them as "the ruin of the Church, the oppressors of the poor, not only unlettered themselves but also enemies of learning". [21] Taken together, the *Planeta* and the *Libro de Alexandre* could be seen to

---

[21] For an essentially positive view of the effects of the Fourth Lateran Council on the Spanish Church, including on the development of schools and universities, and on Spanish literary culture, see Lomax (1969, 299–313). Linehan (1971, 44 ff.) paints a less encouraging picture. For Diego García's criticisms, see Linehan (1971, 12).

constitute powerful evidence that the need for moral and educational reform – as emphasised in the conclusions of the Fourth Lateran Council – was clearly recognised in Spain. Undeniably, the points that our poem's author has to make about Castilian society are very general in their application, but there is a clear indication that he is expressing concerns which were prevalent in the Spanish Church in the first three decades of the thirteenth century and which towards the end of the second decade we know to have been provoking particularly lively debate. As a highly educated and possibly widely travelled cleric, he is acutely aware of both the limitations of his fellows and the importance of education in a rapidly-evolving society.

It is also worth pausing to highlight two characteristic features of Spanish society, both of great importance and both alluded to in different ways in the *Libro de Alexandre*. Firstly, the pilgrim route to Santiago de Compostela (see also note to stanza 2535b) was, by the early thirteenth century, highly organised, with a clearly-defined route crossing northern Spain, passing through Burgos and León. This Way of Saint James, also known as *el camino francés* ("the French road"), was a channel for the entry of foreign cultural influences into Spain and as such an important indication of the internationalism of the age: numerous foreigners, many of them French, are documented as having settled in the towns along the route. There can be no doubt that with them came French cultural traditions and learning.

Secondly, attention should be drawn to the importance of the organised Jewish communities in Castile and León, which by the end of the thirteenth century were to number about 130, giving a total Jewish population of 100,000. This population had been swollen by emigration from al-Andalus and from North Africa. These Jewish communities had a political and administrative structure completely distinct from that of Christian society (although they were, of course, subject to the rule of the monarch) and were governed by councils known as *aljamas* (a term used in the *Libro de Alexandre*: see stanza 1138d). The hereditary rights (or *fueros*) granted to the Jews of Jerusalem (see, for example, stanzas 1164–1165) and the terms in which they are expressed suggest a parallel with the generous *fueros* granted to Spanish Jewish communities (Cantera Montenegro 2006, 59). Within the royal courts themselves, Jews were a conspicuous presence, making a valuable contribution as administrators, diplomats, doctors and scholars (Valdeón Baruque 2006, 15–16 and Cantera Montenegro 2006, 61–62). The history of the Jewish people plays a prominent role in the *Libro de Alexandre*, but there are also conspicuous elements which carry a strong note of anti-semitism, a feature likewise found in some of the recognised works of Gonzalo de Berceo. On occasion the Jews are mentioned as enemies alongside the Moors (as in stanza 2332b). However, the most notable anti-Semitic feature in the poem is the description of Alexander's enclosure of the lost Jewish tribes behind the Caspian mountains (stanzas 2101–2115), an episode constructed out of "medieval and much later Jewhatred" (Weiss 2006, 136). On other occasions in the poem, as has already been seen, the Jews are paired with the Moors as representing the natural enemies of a Christian warrior. There certainly seems to be a correspondence between the anti-Semitism reflected in this episode of the *Libro de Alexandre* and the hardening of the Church's attitude towards Spain's Jews in the years following the Fourth Lateran Council.[22] It is, perhaps, significant that both Fernando III in Castile and Jaume I in Aragón resisted for some time the imposition of the anti-Semitic measures determined by the Council, even persuading the Pope to grant a moratorium on their imposition on Spanish territory, in spite of considerable ecclesiastical pressure on the royal authorities to come fully into line with papal policies. It could be argued that Alexander's imprisoning of the lost Jewish tribes is a reflection of the tendency towards the segregation and social exclusion of the Jews which was already becoming increasingly common in the first half of the thirteenth century.

The early thirteenth century witnessed very significant cultural developments. Although Alfonso X, who succeeded to the throne in 1252, was to win lasting fame for his literary and scholarly achievements, his father, Fernando III, was also an important patron of the arts and of learning. His reign saw the start of the construction of the first Gothic cathedrals, arguably the supreme expression of the confident spirit of the times: work on Burgos Cathedral began in 1221 and building in Toledo, on the site of

---

[22] Álvarez Borge (2003, 284–294) analyses the changing fortunes of the Spanish Jewish communities, underlining (289) the significance of the Fourth Lateran Council as a key turning point. Weiss (2006, 132–142) looks in detail at the attitudes to the Jews which are expressed in the *Libro de Alexandre* and at the prejudices which lay behind them. "Projected onto the Jews", he argues, "are fears of various categories of disorder and pollution: physical, gender, economic, moral, religious, political, and perhaps even demographic …" They are resented, he adds, because they are "signs of imperial sovereignty, burgeoning ecclesiastical militancy, and popular urban resentment." (137)

the Great Mosque, started in 1226. Architectural influence from beyond the Pyrenees is evident. Whilst Alfonso VIII founded the University of Palencia, Fernando favoured the University of Salamanca with privileges and exemptions. Moreover, the cultural life of Fernando's court reflected his own literary interests: for example, several French troubadours were associated with it and a number of songs or *cantigas* have been attributed to Fernando himself. Certainly this was an age in which the great royal courts of Europe were becoming important centres for cultural activity: just as those of Henry II of England and his queen Eleanor of Aquitaine had done much to promote the rise of Arthurian literature in England, so, for example, in the early thirteenth century Frederick II of Sicily showed a great interest in the career of Alexander, may well have sponsored a version of the *Historia de Proeliis* and was praised by minstrels as a "new Alexander" (Stoneman 2008, 205–206; see also note to stanza 2522a). It is surely not too far-fetched to see a similar parallel being made in the court of a monarch such as Fernando III, particularly in the light of the close cultural link which is known to have existed between Frederick's court and that of Castile (Abulafia 1988, 254–255).

This was also a period in which the use of the vernacular was being rapidly extended, as much in legal documents and charters as for literary composition: a tendency which was to bear its fullest fruit in the second half of the thirteenth century under King Alfonso X whose use of the vernacular for historical and scientific works is accompanied by an insistence on its use in official documents. The *Poema de Mio Cid*, Spain's most famous epic poem and probably the oldest surviving major literary text in Spanish, seems to have been written down in its definitive form in the early years of the thirteenth century and there is a good deal of evidence that its author was a man of not inconsiderable learning, likely to have been associated with the legal profession (see, for example, Such and Hodgkinson 1987, 2, 27–28 and 36).

Culturally the monasteries continued to play an important role, but new intellectual centres had begun to spring up in a number of cities. The concentration of advanced studies in relatively few centres encouraged mobility and brought together clerics from different countries, with the most lucrative subject for study being law in any of its branches. There was a large mobile population of both students and teachers and it is important to appreciate the extent to which the world of scholarship was an international one. By the end of the twelfth century, schools and cities that could teach and accommodate large numbers of students were able to establish themselves as universities. As has been seen above, Spain's first university in Palencia came into existence by about 1212, growing out of the city's existing cathedral school, and likewise the University of Salamanca was founded around 1218. Unlike other medieval universities such as Bologna and Paris, both Palencia and Salamanca had been specifically founded by monarchs (Alfonso VIII of Castile and Alfonso IX of León respectively) in order to provide a fund of expertise to assist with the practical business of government. The possible significance of the University of Palencia for the genesis of the *Libro de Alexandre* has already been mentioned (see Section 3, above). At the same time, we should not underestimate the level of the education that our poet could have received in a cathedral school. The study of the *trivium* – Grammar, Logic and Rhetoric – was fundamental to the education imparted in all such centres and, in words which seem very appropriate to the approach of the author of the *Libro de Alexandre*, Dr Anna Sapir Abulafia (Power, ed. 2006, 153) argues that the contribution of the schoolmen was:

> their passion to examine creatively what they had inherited from the past and to reorganize it. They used the tools of the trivium to analyse all available authorities and to work out which were now the most useful. They set out to learn all there was to learn and by asking new and exciting questions to harness all the knowledge they acquired to their Christian view of the world. They sought out any possible contradictions they could find in their material in order to solve these through a careful textual analysis of their disparate sources.

Moreover, in the course of her survey of the achievements of the schools of the twelfth century, Dr Abulafia draws attention to the great popularity of the *Alexandreis*, "a grand epic in ten books" dealing with the life and achievements of Alexander the Great and composed by Gautier de Châtillon who had studied at Paris and Rheims. It was Gautier who was to provide our poet with his principal source and with his model in his vast literary undertaking.

5. Alexander the Great in history and in literary tradition: our poet's sources

It should not surprise us that Alexander the Great has exercised so great a fascination over the centuries or that he should have been the subject of such a wealth of literary and artistic creation. He lived from 356 to 323 BC and, when he died at the age of almost 33, after reigning for twelve and a half years, he had led his army to the edge of the known world and had achieved dominance over every people that he had encountered. He is the very epitome of military achievement and of worldly power, the extent of which makes all the starker his sudden death, probably through illness or, according to popular belief – and, it seems, quite plausibly – at a traitor's hand.

We might, on the other hand, be slightly surprised at the degree to which the picture of Alexander's life that is given in the *Libro de Alexandre*, for all its occasional departures into the improbable or the downright fantastic, does adhere in broad terms to what seem to be the events of history; and many of the characters who appear in the Spanish poem have a firm historical basis. The explanation for the truthfulness or otherwise of our poet's account – although admittedly this quality is very hard to define – lies, of course, in the texts that have been available to him, in the way in which he has selected his material and in how he has opted to exploit and manipulate it; but it is important to start with as clear as possible a picture of what seem to have been the essential facts of the hero's life.

Alexander was born in the Macedonian city of Pella. He was not, as the author of the *Libro de Alexandre* constantly presents him, a Greek, though Alexander saw himself as an inheritor of Greek culture and the heir both to Hercules and to Achilles and the other epic heroes of the Trojan War. Through his mother's house he could claim direct descent from Achilles and he belonged to the Macedonian royal dynasty of the Argeads, who headed their line with Hercules and thus considered themselves to be born of the line of Zeus. Alexander was to place great emphasis on this divine lineage: at his coronation the priests declared him son of Zeus and during his campaigns in Egypt he was to make a famous visit to the shrine of the god Ammon, closely identified with Zeus.

Alexander's father was Philip II who had already built up Macedon's military and political power, extending his hegemony over the Greeks to the south, within what is now known as the League of Corinth. Olympias, Alexander's mother, was a strong and, indeed, eccentric individual, one of whose more unusual habits was to keep a large collection of snakes as pets.

It is known that Alexander idolised her (Green 1991, 40). It seems that Philip was himself about to undertake a campaign against the Persian empire, by which the cities of Greece had long been oppressed – an expedition envisaged as a kind of religious crusade, to avenge the invasion by Xerxes a century and a half before – when he was assassinated in public view by a member of his bodyguard. Rumours implicated Olympias and even the prince himself. Their involvement would not, indeed, have been surprising, for Philip had already announced his attention to remarry and to repudiate Olympias, at the same time casting doubts on Alexander's legitimacy and therefore his right to succeed to the throne.

Alexander was quick to seize the throne and moved rapidly to put down resistance both in the northern borders and from some of the Greek cities: in an act which filled the Greek world with unprecedented horror and amazement, Thebes was razed to the ground. With his powerful and highly disciplined army, Alexander set sail for Asia in 334, very possibly already with the intention of establishing himself as emperor in the place of King Darius III, the immensely powerful ruler of the Achaemenid Empire of Persia.

The interest in scholarship attributed to the hero of the Spanish poem is indeed a reflection of historical fact. Having in his youth been the pupil of Aristotle, Alexander clearly absorbed a great deal of his tutor's scientific curiosity. On his campaigns he was accompanied by a large number of zoologists and botanists who collected material which formed the basis of important scientific works, among them Aristotle's *History of Animals*.[23] Among his staff there were also a historian, a geographical writer and a philosopher (Stoneman 2008, 68). We also know that Alexander had an interest in poetry, and in particular a passion for the *Iliad*, and that, as part of his rhetorical studies, he developed a considerable ability in eristics: the skill of arguing a point from both sides.

Alexander won three major battles against Darius. The first, which is alluded to only briefly in the *Libro de Alexandre*, was that of the Granicus river in May 334. The second, the Battle of Issus, took place in November 333 and the third, fought at Gaugamela, was the conclusive victory won

---

[23] Green (1991, 60–61) examines in detail the importance of Alexander's debt to Aristotle's teaching. With regard to Alexander's scientific studies, he draws attention to his life-long interest in the theory of medicine but also points out, "[p]erhaps what benefited him most in this scientific training was the observant flexibility of mind it produced, the ability to deal with any problem as it arose, on its own merits and without preconceptions. Here, indeed, we touch on his most characteristic quality as a field-commander."

on 1st October 331. Following this defeat, Darius was assassinated by his kinsman Bessus who planned to succeed him, but Alexander had the murderer executed and remained undisputed ruler of a vast empire which now stretched from Greece to the Hindu Kush mountains with the city of Babylon as its capital. Much of the toughest fighting of his campaigns was carried out over the next three years, against warrior tribes and not in the form of set-piece battles, as Alexander's army steadily subdued the inhabitants of his vast Asian territories. He pressed on into the modern Pakistan and even beyond, in May 326 winning a magnificent victory over the Paurava Rajah, known by the Greeks and also in the Spanish poem as Porus, at the River Hydaspes (now Jhelum).

Still Alexander sought to push ahead, but as his army reached the River Hyphasis (now the Beas) his troops refused to advance any further: effectively the only defeat that Alexander was ever to suffer. As he made his way back to Babylon – though sending part of his army by sea – he led many of his troops on a march in appalling conditions through the Makran desert. He now had to deal with a mixture of corruption and disloyalty among his subordinates and administrators and he was much affected by the death of his childhood friend and staunch supporter Hephaestion. Alexander died, probably at Babylon in June 323; the rumour quickly spread that his death was the consequence of poison and of a complex conspiracy. He may well have died of a fever (perhaps raging pleurisy, or very possibly malaria), but the symptoms of his final illness are also compatible with slow strychnine poisoning. In any case, advanced alcoholism combined with the effect of wounds received on his campaigns will have done much to lower his resistance.

Alexander had twice married, on both occasions for political reasons, although his second marriage – to Rhoxane – has frequently been depicted in romantic terms. After Alexander's death, Rhoxane bore him a son, also named Alexander; both mother and son became caught up in the lengthy struggle for power and both were murdered in 311. On its way back to Macedonia, Alexander's funeral cortege was intercepted and his embalmed corpse was effectively hijacked and taken to Egypt. It was put on permanent display in Alexandria, as though to legitimise the authority of Ptolemy, previously one of Alexander's most prominent generals and later king as Ptolemy I. The whereabouts of Alexander's tomb are no longer known. (For a fuller account of these events, see note to stanza 2644a.) Ptolemy's action was typical of what was to ensue, for the disputes among Alexander's generals for mastery of his vast empire were to last until the end of the century, eventually leaving it splintered into a group of separate kingdoms (see note to stanza 2664c). Effectively, the three centuries which followed Alexander's death were marked by continuing conflict and intrigue – "an unswerving policy of competitive exploitation, enabled and justified by military power"[24] – until eventually the Greek and Macedonian rulers succumbed to Roman powers and the imposition of the *Pax Augusta*. As early as 168 BC Macedonia itself ceased to exist as an independent kingdom.

The nature of Alexander's victories had demonstrated him to have been a brilliant tactician as well as a fearless warrior. He was clearly able to inspire his followers to continue their seemingly endless campaigns against hostile and dangerous enemies in often extremely unpleasant conditions; equally, by displays of extreme brutality against those who opposed him, he inspired terror in his potential enemies. Even some of his friends and seemingly close allies rapidly turned into victims of his anger or his cruelty. Just like the Alexander of the Spanish poem who repeatedly rejects the advice of his generals, Alexander exercised a personal authority rooted in his strength of character, a point whose relevance for the monarchy of thirteenth-century Spain has already been noted. Claude Mossé (2001, 133) expresses very clearly the importance of the warrior monarch as an individual whose power springs from his personal qualities as a military commander:

> Whenever it was a matter of deciding upon the right moment to engage battle, to negotiate with the enemy, to choose one route rather than another, it always seems to be the case that Alexander decided on his own. In the account of his biographer, Plutarch, the reason for this is the manner in which Alexander's character evolved, but in effect it reflects his growing personal power. The circumstances on their own suffice amply to justify that reinforcement of power: an army on the move in enemy territory needs above all to obey its commander.

Alexander seems to have had a vision of empire from the outset of his campaigns and he was steadily to adopt many of the trappings of office of the Persian Achaemenid sovereigns. It seems that he even partially adopted the dress appropriate to such office, notably the diadem. He adopted many aspects of the Achaemenid administration and absorbed Persian elements into even the most prestigious sections of his army. His marriage to Rhoxane

---

[24] Green (2007, 157). This study of the period which follows Alexander's death paints a colourful and revealing picture of seemingly endless conflict and rivalry and is fundamental to an understanding of the circumstances in which much of the vast corpus of Alexander legend was assembled.

can be seen as a calculated measure to ensure the future of his dynasty. Particularly significant is the fact that by the time of his death Alexander was being worshipped as a god in both Babylon and Egypt, just as the Persian kings had been worshipped as divine by their subjects. He was also worshipped as a living god in the Greek cities of the Asian coast and there is some evidence that he commanded that this worship be extended to mainland Greece itself. Mossé (2001, 134–135) goes on to sum up the uniqueness of the authority that, by the end of his life, Alexander had assumed:

> Alexander is no longer simply the *basileus Makedonôn*, nor is he the unqualified *Basileus* that the king of the Persians was. He is *basileus Alexandros*: his own name is all that qualifies his authority. He is somehow the incarnation of the ideal monarch whose image was constructed by the fourth-century Greek thinkers. But the question that now inevitably arises is the following: is this 'royal' Alexander simply the product of an image that his contemporaries wished to present, or did he himself knowingly construct that image, influenced by the education he had received from Aristotle and Callisthenes? Without wishing to belittle the difficulties attendant upon any attempt to get through to the real Alexander, who is obscured by all the superimposed images of him, we are bound to recognise that some of his actions during the last few months of his life do suggest that he may consciously have fine-tuned his image as a predestined leader.

Indeed, there can be no doubt that Alexander, just as the author of the *Libro de Alexandre* tells us on many occasions, was himself much concerned with the way in which his actions were to be seen both by his contemporaries and by posterity. It is partly for this reason that, in spite of the wealth of texts which recount his deeds, historians find it difficult to penetrate the enigma of his character and his intentions. It is also important to realise that, very soon after his death, his character and career were being portrayed by a host of propagandists and interested parties with specific points to make.

It was in Alexandria, Alexander's place of burial, that two of the first accounts of his life – both now lost – were produced: one of them was written by Ptolemy, the Macedonian nobleman who had fought with Alexander throughout the campaigns and who, after his death, became King of Egypt, and it was an uncritical account concentrating heavily on military matters. The second account, consisting of twelve volumes, was by Cleitarchus who had been too young to take part in Alexander's campaigns. Cleitarchus presented Alexander as a noble hero, the son of the god Ammon, pre-destined to achieve magnificent conquests. His history appealed widely, not least because of his inclusion of many colourful episodes, such as Alexander's encounter with the Amazon queen Thalestris, and it was to be extensively used as a source for later accounts of Alexander's life.

Certainly the idealised picture of Alexander was challenged and there developed a division between this image of the heroic "philosopher king" and that of a brutal and irrational individual, prone to fits of drunken rage and the very image of lack of self-control. The two views co-existed throughout the last centuries of the Roman Republic and the first two centuries of the Empire and are represented in the histories that date from that period: with an essentially negative emphasis, for example, in the case of Justin's *Philippic Histories* but much more akin to a picture of the perfect sovereign in the work of the Sicilian historian Diodorus. In the first century AD Quintus Curtius composed a biography of Alexander in ten volumes, again almost entirely laudatory in tone, whilst a very different attitude is evident in the severely-moralising tone of Lucan's *Pharsalia*, one of the most important works of Silver Latin poetry. The *Life of Alexander*, part of Plutarch's *Parallel Lives*, includes anecdotes and descriptions of incidents that appear in no other extant source and is also essentially a work of praise. However, it is the work of Arrian of Nicomedia which is generally considered to be the most authoritative of the surviving histories of Alexander's campaigns. Arrian was a Greek historian, writing in the second century AD, who seems to draw on first-hand accounts; he writes, on the whole, in praise and defence of Alexander, but he does not omit to draw attention to his failings, particular his irascibility, his anger and his pride.

If the sources considered so far are sharply divided in their judgement of Alexander, the same duality is a feature of his depiction in the writings of medieval Christendom. The starting point for the consideration of these must be the *Alexander Romance* which was a compilation – originally in Greek – of writings produced in some cases shortly after Alexander's death and in others at various stages over the following five centuries. In the body of legend contained in this work and the immense body of literature of which it formed the basis, the figure of the historical Alexander was to undergo a profound transformation into "a protean figure who is able to embody some of the deepest fears and longings of the human condition" (Stoneman 2008, 2–3).

Several late manuscripts attribute the *Alexander Romance* to Alexander's ill-fated court historian Callisthenes, but the historical figure died before Alexander and could not have written a full account of his life. The unknown author is still sometimes called Pseudo-Callisthenes. In the *Romance* Egypt plays a prominent part, for example with the presentation of Alexander as the son of Nectanebo, the last Egyptian pharaoh (transformed into a magician) and with emphasis placed on the visit to the shrine at Siwah. During Alexander's campaigns there are numerous fantastic elements: for example, he meets many strange creatures (such as centaurs, men with one foot like that of a sheep, spherical giants and animals thirty feet long); and, among his less plausible adventures, he descends to the sea-bed in a glass vessel and rises up into the sky pulled by two large birds. Some of the more fantastical elements are embedded in letters that Alexander is said to have sent to his mother Olympias in Greece. There are obviously features here which will be seen again in the *Libro de Alexandre* and together with these can be included, for example, the representation of Antipater as the traitor responsible for Alexander's death and the depiction of the Macedonian emperor himself as a Christian prince who serves the one true God. This is an image of Alexander on which medieval Christian writers were quick to seize. In short, the *Alexander Romance* presents us with a strange mixture of tales, often sensationalised or semi-mythical, but at the same time it seems to provide us with material of genuine historical value not available elsewhere.

Throughout Antiquity and the Middle Ages, the *Romance* underwent numerous expansions and revisions. Latin and Syriac translations were made in Late Antiquity. From these, versions were developed in all the major languages of Europe and the Middle East; even a late Mongol version is extant. In the West, the texts that were to be most important as sources of works on Alexander were the fourth-century AD Latin translation by Julius Valerius and that produced in the tenth century for Archpriest John III of Naples by the Archpriest Leo, known as the *Historia de Proeliis* and reworked in a number of different versions before the end of the twelfth century. In France the body of Alexander material became very well known in the twelfth century. In addition to the *Historia de Proeliis*, two Alexander texts, seemingly very different in nature and in style, were to prove extremely important as sources for the *Libro de Alexandre*: the *Roman d'Alexandre* and Gautier de Châtillon's *Alexandreis*.

The final and most complete version of the *Roman d'Alexandre* (*Li romans d'Alixandre*) is attributed to the cleric Alexandre de Bernay (also known as Alexandre de Paris). It was compiled soon after 1177 and is based on the accounts of various episodes of the emperor's life as narrated by previous poets (Lambert le Tort, Eustache and most importantly Albéric of Besançon). Partly epic poem and partly courtly romance, this work explores the contradictory features of the hero's character; it shows Alexander to be generous, loyal and courageous but excessive in his ambition and his quest for knowledge and it paints a picture of the social changes taking place in the France of the late twelfth century.

Gautier de Châtillon's *Alexandreis*, on the other hand, was – as we have already seen – a text much studied in the world of the cathedral schools of the late twelfth and early thirteenth centuries. It was, indeed, a learned work and one of the most important Latin poems of the twelfth century. Its author took his surname from the town in northern France where he headed a school; he probably went on to study law in Bologna. The *Alexandreis* was probably composed in the late 1170s and drew heavily on the history of Quintus Curtius as well as on a version of the work of Julius Valerius and the *Historia de Proeliis*. Many important features of the *Libro de Alexandre* are present in the *Alexandreis*, not least the ambivalent approach to a hero who, in many ways admirable, is also the object of sharp moral criticism and, self-obsessed, is shown to be blind to his own errors. The *Alexandreis* was extremely influential; within just over a decade of its composition, a short passage from the poem had served as a model for the epitaph of Henry II. Over two hundred manuscripts of it survive, mostly from the thirteenth century and in many cases with extensive glosses; and there is a good deal of evidence of its rôle as a standard text used in the teaching of Grammar, that is, in the literary curriculum.[25]

This, then, is the tradition on which the author of the *Libro de Alexandre* drew. He knew well the *Alexandreis* and had constant access, as he wrote, to a copy of its text. The *Alexandreis* was his principal source and most of the more colourful and fanciful episodes which had come to form part of Alexander tradition were absent from it. These were, however, readily available to our poet in the other texts to which he had access. The most important of these is what is known as Version B of the *Roman d'Alexandre*, a collection of fragments including the text by Lambert le Tort and making up a coherent whole, but not corresponding directly to the version of Alexandre de Bernay. The poet's third major source was a version, not clearly identified, of the *Historia de Proeliis*. In addition, he drew on numerous other works, among them: the *Ilias Latina* and the *Excidium Troiae*, Latin accounts (the first in

---

[25] For further information on the origins and importance of the *Alexandreis*, see Townsend, trans. (2007, 11–22).

verse, the second in prose) which were the source of his account of the Trojan War (see note to stanza 323c); other works on the life of Alexander including those of Quintus Curtius and Julius Valerius and possibly Alexander texts from Islamic literature; the *Disticha Catonis* (see note to stanza 2382c); St Isidore of Seville's compendium the *Etymologiae* (see note to stanzas 276–294); the *Physiologus* (see note to stanzas 1976–80); some works of Ovid (see note to stanza 368c) or at least some collection of classical texts or *florilegium*; and, of course, the Bible, on which he drew extensively.[26] Nor should we overlook the importance of commentaries and glosses on any of these works.

In considering the proliferation of written accounts of Alexander's exploits in the twelfth and thirteenth centuries, we should also take into account their prominence in the architecture and sculpture of the period, for this could also have exercised a significant influence on our poet. Alexander's aerial ascent is, for example, depicted in sculpture and carvings in numerous European churches: an outstanding example is Otranto Cathedral in southern Italy which possesses a vast mosaic floor – dating from the late twelfth century – in which are depicted a mixture of biblical episodes (including the Tower of Babel), the labours of the months, a variety of real and mythical beasts, scenes from the works of Ovid and Lucan and a large and commanding figure of Alexander borne by two griffins. In its compendious nature, this work has been likened to the contemporary world chronicles which included lengthy accounts of Alexander's deeds alongside a biblical narrative (Stoneman 2008, 114–120). It is evidence not only of the popularity of the story of Alexander in the twelfth and thirteenth centuries but also of the importance that by this stage was attached to him within the context of sacred history.

It is clear that the author of the *Libro de Alexandre* had access to a wide range of source material which enabled him to assemble a picture of his hero's life and deeds as comprehensive as it could possibly have been. The poet's desire to make his narrative both complete and reliable is evident in his approach to his sources and, indeed, in the comments which he makes on them. Thus, when augmenting the account which he finds in the *Alexandreis,* he marks the transition to material taken from the *Historia de Proeliis* by commenting on the need for completeness:

> But Walter the good, as he wrote his poem,
> was tired by now, and wished to be concise.

---

[26] See, for example, the thorough study of the influence of the Bible on the *Libro de Alexandre*: Bañeza Román (1994). This study concludes (183) that the Bible is "como un hilo conductor del relato" ("like a conductor wire for the story").

>   At this point he omitted much of his subject,
>   and, since he left it out, I wish to tell it.
>
>   (2098)

At the same time, although he incorporates into his poem some of the fabulous adventures from the *Historia de Proeliis* – such as the encounters with the headless men and with the trees of the sun and the moon, the submarine adventure and Alexander's flight – there are many colourful stories that he rejects, and on a number of occasions he makes it clear to us when he has doubts about the reliability of an episode that he has chosen to include. Thus, for example, he expresses reservations about the credibility of Alexander's descent beneath the seas, suggesting incidentally that he has heard rather than read the account:

>   Of one great exploit do people often tell
>   – it lies not in writing and is hard to believe –;
>   if it is true or false I cannot determine,
>   though I do not wish to let it be forgotten.
>
>   (2305)

Arguably this critical spirit was typical of the age in which our poet wrote, one in which such powerful influences as pilgrimage, the Crusades and the growth of learning in the schools, universities and the great royal courts allowed wonder at the marvels of the East to be tempered by an increasingly rational and thoughtful approach.

The author of the *Libro de Alexandre* was clearly a man of great scholarship whose aim was to choose carefully from his source materials and to adapt and rework them into a carefully crafted artefact. His poem was composed in order to convey an individual and distinctive response to texts that he had read, studied and contemplated at length. He skilfully welded together a wide range of material, but he did much more than that, employing his poetical craft to express a powerful and at times deeply moving vision of his subject and to communicate a strong and clear message about the values and principles which must govern the conduct of all men, above all those in high authority, and about the importance of scholarship and the scholar in the world in which he lived.

6. Style and structure: the poet finds his voice

When the author of the *Libro de Alexandre* set out to work his diverse source materials – as we have seen, mostly written in Latin, though some in French – into an elegant and learned poem in Castilian, he had very few vernacular models indeed on which to base his approach to composition. His poem was in all probability the first of the *cuaderna vía* texts. Moreover, it seems likely that the *Poema de Mio Cid*, the earliest of the surviving 'popular' epics composed in Castilian – in its known form, at least – dates from just a few years before the *Libro de Alexandre* and could even be preceded by it. The verse form that our poet used seems to have been based on Latin models (see Section 2 above and, for example Rico 1995, 1–23 and Arizaleta 1999, 161 ff.), but the task that he set himself as a vernacular poet was to preserve the learned tone of the scholar whilst giving written form to language which was still essentially the vehicle for the spoken word. In order to find what was to become his distinctive voice – and one which was to exercise a considerable influence on the development of Spanish poetry – he needed to combine elements from markedly different traditions.

Thus, for example, it is possible to find in the *Libro de Alexandre* numerous traces of stylistic features associated with improvisatory oral poetry (that of the *juglar* or minstrel) which are commonly encountered in epics such as the *Poema de Mio Cid*.

- epic epithets, such as the laudatory description "el caboso" (as in stanza 127a), "un cuerpo acabado" (literally "a perfect body", 1955a), "de la barva honrada" (literally "of the the honoured beard", 828a), or "en duro punto nado" (literally "born at a harsh moment"; as in 317d, 716a); (as is explained in Section 10, below, the translation has been flexible in its rendering of such phrases)
- inclusive pair-phrases, used with the meaning of "everybody", as in "mugeres e varones" ("both men and women", 1538a) or "chicos e grandes" ("small and large" or "young and old alike", 889c, 1102b, 1114b)
- "physical phrases" which combine description of some action with mention of the part of the body, as in "plorando de los ojos" (translated as "their eyes streaming with tears" 1682c, "tears streaming from his eyes", 1777a) or "rides de los dientes" ("you smile sweetly with your teeth", 478c)

There are numerous examples in the *Libro de Alexandre* of the use of such expressions, which can be useful to the poet in even making up a complete line, as in:

> Parmenio el caboso,   en duro punto nado,
> andava por las hazes como león irado;
>
> (Parmenion, the fine man, born at a cruel moment,
> moved around the battle lines like an angry lion.)
>
> (1024ab)

That is not to say that the author of the *Libro de Alexandre* is heavily influenced by the mode of composition of the epic poet. Whilst in many cases these expressions do indeed provide useful filler phrases and often a ready-made hemistich, as they might for the oral improviser, their use is not as systematic or as flexible as it would be in the hands of the *juglar*. Ian Michael's study of the use of epic epithets, for example, leads him to ponder (1961, 41) whether "we merely see in the *Alexandre* the dead remains of what had previously been a flourishing epic convention."

Undeniably present throughout the *Libro de Alexandre*, however, are numerous colourful expressions which bear the obvious mark of the spoken language.

There are several pieces of popular wisdom:

> One single wasp carries a crueller sting
> than would do a great swarm of flies;
>
> (792ab)

and several times the poet announces that he is quoting a proverb:

> The saying is a true one that fate has more speed
> than wind, wing, or saddled steed;
>
> (565ab)

There are many colourful expressions employed in the poem to denote something of low worth[27] and thus on numerous occasions striking turns of phrase are used to depict a character's lack of concern, such as Achilles

---

[27] Michael (1970, 235–38) points out that there are over fifty occurrences in the *Alexandre* of nouns denoting low value. Often occurring in the final line of a stanza and useful as 'fillers' or rhyme words, they nevertheless contribute significantly to establishing a sense of popular speech and thus of directness and freshness.

caring for it no more than a cockerel's peck.

(682d)

and, if we are to accept the reading, there is even a suggestive euphemism used when Alexander agrees to Thalestris' request:

> The King said, "I am delighted, I will willingly do it."
> He leapt into the forest, and gave the game good chase.

(1888ab)

Indeed, our poet makes extensive use of direct speech. Sometimes he introduces direct speech at points where it was not present in his source, but also, when he replaces speech already present, he medievalises the words of his characters, often to quite striking effect: thus, Aristotle lectures Alexander, showing him how to harangue his troops as might a medieval monarch (stanza 69), whilst an angry Achilles issues his challenge to Hector as to a wild and as yet untamed bull (707cd); and, as Alexander's troops close in on the Thebans, who are "bleating like sheep that are held in a pen" (230c), the poet puts into his hero's mouth a colourful comparison: "Then the King spoke: 'These lambs need some salt.'" (230d)

Ian Michael (1970), in his important study of the process by which the author of the *Libro de Alexandre* systematically medievalised the content and presentation of his source-material, shows how imaginative our poet has been in inventing direct speech and how far he has extended and added colour to the material that served as his model. Michael analyses the heavy use in the Spanish poem of allusions to animal husbandry, domestic life, business and crafts, sports and pastimes and the natural world and he shows how effectively the poet revisualises the events of Antiquity from a thirteenth-century Spanish viewpoint and popularises learned material.

A common feature of oral poetry is the direct address to the listener and certainly this, too, is a very conspicuous feature of our poet's style. On several occasions he makes reference to himself, often in a rather dismissive or slightly humorous way, for example in the description of Alexander's belt:

> The belt was worked with a craftsman's great skill,
> worked by Lady Philosophy with her own hands.
> The buckle was worth more than all of Lombardy
> – it is worth, I think, a little more than my own.

(91)

or in his criticism of the ways of some clergy:

> Neither clergy nor canons nor – of course – nuns
> act as they rightly should, by my shoes!;
>
> (1822ab)

There are numerous brief remarks addressed to his public as he guides them through the poem, often suggesting oral performance, such as "just as you have heard" (719a), and the introduction to the tale of Nicanor and Symachus:

> I want to tell a tale of two good friends,
> and we shall come to hear a little sorrow.
>
> (1992cd)

or insistence that full attention is paid to his words:

> The aged Devil, never able to sleep,
> is always scheming to lay his hands upon us;
> of all the snares he brings you have been able to hear,
> if you were willing to open your ears to it.
>
> (2398)

There are also several more detailed observations on the act of composition whose importance will be discussed at a later stage. The examples already given, however, should be sufficient to demonstrate that the author of the *Libro de Alexandre* makes extensive use of features that might be associated with oral poetry and certainly with the spoken language; and also that he quite commonly intervenes to address his public directly and to make us aware of his presence as poet and commentator on the narrative. This is an important part of the distinctive voice of our poet, which was mentioned at the beginning of this section, and a significant feature of the poem; but there are other crucial elements, conspicuously of a more scholarly nature, which exercise a fundamental influence on his form of expression and on the organisation and presentation of his work.

The early sections of this Introduction emphasised the learned origins of the *Libro de Alexandre* and its connection with the world of the schools and universities. On a number of occasions the poet directly draws our attention to the importance of the very teachings which have enabled him to construct such a work. So, in his lament to Aristotle, Alexander sets out the principal characteristics of one of the subjects that he has studied:

> I understand grammar well, I know soundly the whole art,
> I compose and write verse well and am familiar with the figures;
> I know the authors by heart, I find no book difficult.
> But I am forgetting it all, so great is my ire.
>
> (40)

Grammar meant the art of composition, of correct and elegant writing, and also involved the study of the work of a canon of authors, both classical and medieval. By the beginning of the thirteenth century, as we have seen, the latter included the *Alexandreis*. The grammatical teachings that a student was likely to encounter were closely associated with those explained in treatises written by such scholars as Matthew of Vendôme and Geoffrey of Vinsauf, which set out in detail the features of good writing.[28] These features include the use of the "rhetorical figures" or "colours". (It should be noted, by the way, that, although the distinction between the terms "Grammar" and "Rhetoric" can sometimes become a very hazy one, it is absolutely clear that the author of the *Libro de Alexandre* considers the former to deal with the art of poetic composition and the latter to be concerned with the spoken language and the art of persuasion.)

There is ample evidence that our poet is making full and conscious – it would probably be more appropriate to say self-conscious – use of the grammatical teaching that he has received, applying what he has studied in the context of composition in Latin to the new enterprise of composing an obviously erudite poem in the vernacular. The catalogue of "rhetorical" features in his poem is a lengthy one. Many of the so-called figures of thought and diction involved different forms of repetition, parallelism and contrast and there were many models for these – in sources other than classroom teaching and rhetorical treatises – that the poet could have imitated, including the *Alexandreis*, French vernacular literature and the Bible itself. Nevertheless, it is important to emphasise the extent to which these figures are used in the *Libro de Alexandre* and their effectiveness, as, for, example in stanza 2618:

> ¡Maldito sea cuerpo   que tal cosa faze!
> ¡Maldita sea alma   que en tal cuerpo yaze!

---

[28] For a clear and detailed explanation of the nature of the teaching of Grammar and Rhetoric in the Middle Ages, including summaries of the contents of the most influential of the treatises, see Murphy (1974).

¡Maldito sea cuerpo   que d'aquello le plaze!
¡Dios lo eche en lazo   que nunca se deslaze!

(Cursed be a body that does such a thing!
Cursed be a soul that lies in such a body!
Cursed be a body that delights in such a thing!
May God trap it in a snare that is never undone!)

In these lines, which give the sense of a ritual curse, *repetitio* (with *Maldito* used at the start of three lines) is complemented by the repetition of *tal*, giving almost a use of *conplexio* (repetition of both the first and the last word of each line), with the parallelism in structure producing a well-judged dramatic effect.

There is a similar highly effective use of parallelism and repetition in the stanza which signals the opening of the battle of Issus:

Ya se movién las hazes,   ívanse aplegando;
ivan los ballesteros   las saetas tirando;
ivan los cavalleros   las lanças abaxando
e ivan los cavallos   las orejas aguzando.

(Now the two armies were surging out together,
the crossbowmen letting their bolts fly out,
the horsemen lowering their lances to strike,
the horses galloping with ears pricked up.)

(1002)

These lines convey superbly the surging power of the armies' thrust forward and the sense of excited anticipation of the imminent clash. The poet is, indeed, making use of stylistic devices that he has studied, but he is also demonstrating his own acute sense of how to convey the exhilarating and the dramatic. Other easily identifiable figures include, for example, hyperbaton (an unnatural separation of words that belong together: a common feature of the *Libro de Alexandre* on account of the constraints of the verse form), hyperbole, various forms of comparison and *exclamatio* or apostrophe. Some of the poem's most powerful passages make use of *exclamatio*, for example Alexander's lament to Darius (stanzas 1777–1789) and the poet's despairing warning to Alexander which begins in stanza 2530:

King Alexander, you who are so fine a warrior,
you are going to receive great glory, but you are deceived;
your good fortune and your princely sway
are like the flower of the lily which is quick to drop.

The poet's direct address to his hero gains in intensity through the antithesis between present glory and impending loss and is reinforced by the simile of the lily.

Similarly, in another highly charged example of *exclamatio*, this time directed to Darius' murderers, the effect is increased by the use of alliteration in a form of *annominatio*: "¡El comer que comierdes   con dolor lo comades!" ("The food that you eat, may you eat it with pain!", 1744c).

Further obvious "rhetorical" features of the text include standard topics used in the introduction and the conclusion, the *locus amoenus* or description of an idealised country setting (see note to stanzas 935–940) and the idealised female portrait (see note to stanzas 1872–1879). However, a more conspicuous sign still of the poet's scholarly emphasis is his use of several technical terms from the world of the grammarian: among these figure the mentions of the "authors" ("actores", as in 40c, 1196c, 1197a, 1211b, 2390a, 2478d) and, indeed, the brief discussion of the possible interpretation of the meaning intended by these pagan writers (stanzas 2390–93); the allusion to glossing a text (1956d) and to a representative form or comparison as *figura* (280c);[29] a number of mentions of the use of *exempla* (767d, 1780a, 2360a); specific use of the terms *comparaçión* in stanza 29a and (the reading seems to be the obvious one) *descripçión* in stanza 276b. The context of the last of these seems to be particularly important, for the poet is justifying his departure from his narrative thread – on the basis that this is made necessary by his *materia* or subject-matter –, thus giving us a clear insight into the way in which he has approached the organisation of his material.

The term *materia* is in itself a significant one, for it was used by the literary theorists to signify the source material treated by a poem. It is used by the author of the *Libro de Alexandre* for the narrative line of his poem from which he departs in a digression or a description (see also, for example, stanza 1533d) as well as for his source material (1871d, 2098c); and it is likewise a term much employed by Gonzalo de Berceo in a number of his works. Our poet's approach in stanza 276 is revealing:

---

[29] For the significance of *figura* as a technique for textual interpretation and its importance in the *Libro de Alexandre*, see Bly and Deyermond (1972).

> La materia nos manda,   por fuerça de razón,
> avemos nos a fer   una descripçïón:
> cómo se part' el mundo   por triple partiçión,
> cómo faze la mar   en todas división.
>
> (My subject dictates it: by virtue of its meaning,
> here we have to include a digression
> to describe the tripartite division of the world,
> and how the sea separates the different parts.)

Our poet not only gives very careful consideration to the appropriateness of a digression from his narrative (and he makes exactly the same point, for instance, in the same terms in 2334b), but he also clearly wishes his public to be aware of just how far he is following carefully thought out artistic principles. The notion of correctness in this poem, then, goes far beyond that of the details of the verse form and the counting of syllables; it extends to the whole aesthetic basis on which his work has been constructed.

Elsewhere, we see the poet commenting on his selection of material from his sources. On one occasion he feels that the account in the *Alexandreis* is incomplete and so feels that the lacuna should be filled (see stanza 2098, quoted above). At other times he queries the reliability of his source material, as in stanza 2305:

> Of one great exploit do people often tell
> – it lies not in writing and is hard to believe –;
> if it is true or false I cannot determine,
> though I do not wish to let it be forgotten.

Finally it is important to comment on the emphasis which our poet places in some of his remarks on the need for brevity. For, although the literary theorists taught the art of amplifying a source through extensive use of the rhetorical figures, by the end of the twelfth century the theory of *brevitas* was much in vogue. In keeping with this principle, there are numerous points in the *Libro de Alexandre* where the poet announces his intention to cut an account short, as in stanzas 105b, 974ab or in the description of Alexander's wedding with Rhoxane:

> I want to say the breviary to you with brevity,

not preach a long sermon over a little:
the King seeks marriage to Darius' daughter
to Rhoxane the beautiful, a woman of great charm

(1957)

The poet wishes to leave us in no doubt with regard to just how thoughtfully the sources have been used and how carefully his poem has been crafted. Moreover, he expects us to be aware of the numerous links and relationships which are woven into it: to associate, for example, the prodigies which precede Alexander's birth with those that signal the imminence of his death; to be aware of the significance of the numerous allusions to the Tower of Babel and the rebellion of the Giants that run through the poem; to note the close parallels between the details depicted on Achilles' shield and those which appear on Alexander's tent; and to grasp just how many details there are in the poem which prefigure and explain Alexander's fall. The image of the Tower of Babel requires particular mention: fusing stories of pagan and biblical origin (see notes to stanzas 88a and 948a), which it associates closely with the worldly power and pride of both Darius and Alexander, it constitutes a potent symbol which is very skilfully worked into the fabric of the poem. It is also worth looking closely at the way in which the Trojan narrative is bound into the structure of the poem as a whole and in particular at the part that the descriptions play in this: for, just as Alexander's tent contains a panel devoted to the story of Troy, the brief description of Achilles' shield (stanzas 653–658) prefigures Alexander's observation of the marine world, alludes to the Tower of Babel and gives a brief panoramic description of the lands of the earth, before emphasising the power of the forces of nature and the irresistible onward march of the seasons. Achilles is soon to die, as is Alexander when Apelles ominously decorates his tent. Both men are great warriors who have sought by their deeds to win a fine reputation that will live long after them, but in these descriptions the poet reminds us how the careers of both men will serve equally to demonstrate the ultimate futility of earthly achievement.

Our poet's technique is a splendid example of what Eugène Vinaver calls "the poetry of interlace", in which digression constantly serves to recall details already introduced or to anticipate what is to come:

> The assumption is not only that the reader's memory is infallible, but that the exercise of such a memory is in itself a pleasurable pursuit which carries with it its own reward.

There are cases, however, where the reward is something more than the satisfaction of recognizing a familiar theme. The recurrence of a theme can confer fresh significance upon it, whether the theme is a statement of fact, or a description of an object, or an expression of feeling.[30]

In precisely this sense, the series of complex set-piece descriptions of works of art (*ecphrases*) which run through the *Libro de Alexandre* are fundamental to its appreciation and interpretation. The craftsman Apelles (whose Jewish origin is alluded to by our poet in stanza 1239a) is responsible for their creation. He becomes, by his choice of detail for inclusion, a commentator on the deeds and failings of the principal characters of the poem. Julian Weiss has recently pointed out the significance of the repeated emphasis on the seamlessness of the work that Apelles has created in Darius' tomb:

Apelles, meanwhile, crafted his funerary monument,
the tomb first of all, and the coverings to follow;
the base was in three sections, all of like proportion,
so cleverly joined that the join could not be seen.

(1791)

The faultless construction of this monument, in which the diverse elements are joined together in a perfectly harmonious whole (again emphasised in stanza 1803c), is representative of the poet's own creation: it is "a monument to the poet's own desire to forge a unified vision of events out of a varied panoply of episodes and literary sources."[31]

Here again the voice of our poet is present in his narrative as a commentator not only on the fate of his characters but also on the nature of his own art. We have seen how in creating his own highly distinctive poetic voice he has exploited many of the resources of the spoken word, but also how he has fused these with the skills and techniques that he has learned through his studies under the grammarians. He is intensely proud of his art and this pride shines through in the numerous direct comments that he makes in the course of his poem. The work that he has created is indeed a magnificent one, but

---

[30] Vinaver (1971, 68–98; see particularly 83) develops at length the parallel between the complex structure of medieval narrative, with its skilful exploitation of the digression, and that of intricate patterning and interlace in manuscript illuminations.

[31] See Weiss (2006, 40) and also Arizaleta (1999, 143–44) who comments on the way in which the Spanish poet, building on the allusions to Apelles already present in the *Alexandreis*, gives him much increased prominence and presents him as a medieval craftsman or scholar, essentially his own alter-ego.

there is, perhaps, a certain irony here, for, as we shall see, pride is also the principal cause of his hero's downfall and is one of the most prominent themes of the *Libro de Alexandre*.

7. Warriors, kings and scholars – triumph but humility: the themes of the Libro de Alexandre

The author of a recent study of the medieval romance (Brownlee 2000, 254–255) sums up the distinctive characteristics of the *Libro de Alexandre* as its didacticism and its deeply-learned nature. The presentation of the hero, she affirms, "is a hybrid one, offering a juxtaposition of the romance focus on earthly, secular achievement with the sacred, extra-textual considerations of eternity." In addition, she comments that "[i]t is, by far, the most erudite of all the European Alexander texts." Certainly, the reader will be struck by the range of learning which characterises the poem, its encyclopedic nature and the breadth of its author's vision. Moreover, set against the vast canvas of classical and biblical history, the Spanish poet's account of Alexander's career provides the basis for a moral commentary on thirteenth-century society and a profound reflection on human strengths and weaknesses and, in particular, the nature and effects of power and ambition.

The focus of the poem, of course, is provided by the figure of Alexander himself: it is a complex and many-sided figure, but at its core are his skill and overwhelming authority as a warrior. Certainly, Alexander's knightly prowess and military achievement are central to the poem. Even Aristotle's advice to the young prince, in the blue-print for the ideal lord and sovereign that he sets before him, underlines the importance of heroism, reflecting that of the heroes of the Trojan War:

> Hector and Diomedes, through their knightly exploits,
> won such fame that they are still talked about today;
> so great a litany of tales would not be told of Achilles
> if some act of cowardice were to be known of him.
>
> (70)

and the teacher has much to say about the practical matter of leading troops into battle:

> Marshal well your troops, order an unflinching advance;
> whoever tries to leave the line, order him to retake his place;
> tell them that on no account are they to break rank

until the moment comes when you order them to strike.

When the moment comes to strike, you be the first to do so;
relay the message as a good messenger would;
show your noble quality to the man who stands before you;
the blows will make clear which is the good warrior.

(75–76)

Alexander is represented as a fearsome warrior who strikes terror into any potential enemy. His depiction and that of his Greek and Trojan predecessors, it must be emphasised, also presents them as medieval knights, members of the warrior élite whose importance had grown so rapidly with the developments in cavalry warfare since the second half of the eleventh century. From the account of Alexander's dubbing (stanzas 120–126) and the description of the warrior's armour and apparel (455–57), including a coat of chain mail typical of that worn by an early thirteenth-century knight, to the description of battle scenes between Greeks and Trojans in terms which evoke the tournament or mêlée, presided over by judges (589cd), this is a picture of battle which is thoroughly medievalised. It is also clearly one of a military world which holds no little fascination for our clerical and very scholarly poet.

The accounts of warfare in the *Libro de Alexandre* are long and detailed (much more so, for example, than in the *Poema de Mio Cid*) and we must not lose sight of the fact that, for all the weight that may be placed on the poem's intellectual background, the battle scenes are approached with an evident relish and convey a strong sense of involvement on the part of the poet. A good example of a short account of a battle is that of the attack on Tyre (1104 ff.) in which the description of the savagery of the battle ("arrows that were soaked in poison soared aloft / and great clouds of stones and darts were unleashed", 1105cd) is interrupted by an impassioned harangue by Alexander and concludes with an approving description of the cruelty inflicted on the defenders:

The treasures of Tyre were heavily plundered;
young and old alike were all put to the sword;
the throats were cut of both mothers and children,
and even of babies who were born that day.

They all suffered such a fate and died such a death
except those who took sanctuary in the temples;

if they were bad people they met just as bad an end
– in faith, I am not troubled, for they well deserved it.

(1114–1115)

There is certainly no note of softness or sentimentality here and there is no hint of criticism of Alexander for his brutality; indeed, a modern reader might well find the poet's comments rather chilling. It is on rare occasions that the poet – as in stanza 1971, after the execution of Hermolaus (Ardófilo) and Cleitus – admits that Alexander has acted harshly and without due justification and in this case the emphasis is rather on the advice that he has been given. It is made abundantly clear to us that a military leader must act without sentiment when his cause is a just one, and it has already been pointed out (see Section 4, above) that equally cruel treatment of enemies could be expected of the rulers of thirteenth-century Castile.

Alexander is, we are repeatedly shown, valiant in battle, an inspiration to his troops and a brilliant strategist: there are descriptions of tactics which range from the sophisticated conduct of the siege at Tyre, involving the use of siege engines, to the cunning ploy with which Alexander combats the menace of the elephants used by Porus. The poet dwells at length and with evident approval on both Alexander's military skills and the ferocity that he shows towards his enemies and we should not lose sight of this fact.

However, there is also considerable emphasis on the motives which drive Alexander in his savage and seemingly endless campaigns. The Emperor explains to his followers the need for such achievements, for it is by them that a man will inevitably be judged. In this his models are the great Homeric heroes, and particularly Achilles, to whose deeds he saw himself as a successor. It is, indeed, to Aristotle that Alexander attributes the teaching that a man who is to achieve fame will not do so without great effort:

> I do not count my life in years or in days
> but by great deeds and acts of chivalry.
> Homer did not set down in his allegories
> the months Achilles lived, but his acts of valour. ...
>
> Men who know not how to achieve great renown
> think that this is glory: to lie in idleness;
> but the master says, and commands us to remember,
> that only through effort can valour be achieved.

(2288, 2292)

Constantly Alexander emphasises the need to ensure that his fame is not tarnished; it is partly for this reason, for example, that he rejects Parmenion's suggestion of a night attack at Gaugamela:

> people would come to tell tales of my cowardice,
> and it might cause my reputation great harm.
>
> Using tricks and traps was never worthy of a king
> and a battle in this way was never fairly won.
> Darius and his army could use it as an excuse;
> glory will be taken from our victory at once!
>
> (1322cd, 1323)

There are many mentions of the great wealth that Alexander and his followers win during the course of their campaigns. Numerous passages deal with the splendour and riches that they encounter, for example in the description of the magnificence of Darius' carriage and retinue as they prepare for battle (stanzas 855 ff.); and one of the reasons for the inclusion of the lengthy list of precious stones produced in the waters of the rivers of Babylon (stanzas 1469–1492) is clearly to emphasise the fabulous wealth of the city which has now fallen into the conquerors' hands. However, Alexander repeatedly makes it clear that, in comparison with the reputation that he passes down to posterity, all of this means nothing to him. There is an obvious parallel with the concern with reputation and honour in the poet's own day (see also the central position which this theme occupies in the *Poema de Mio Cid*) but the emphasis here is on the way in which Alexander's name is to be passed on down the centuries. The parallels with the deeds of the great Homeric heroes are constantly in Alexander's mind; both he (256a) and Aristotle (238a) point to the deeds of his ancestor Hercules and (anachronistically) the future emperor compares himself with Charlemagne (88d).

Alexander is not only a triumphant conqueror but also an imposing lord and ruler. In times of peace we see him introducing new codes of law to improve the conduct of his people (stanza 1550). He is motivated by a concern to see his people rewarded with openness and fairness (1552–1553). He introduces changes in customs, but his insight is such that they are quickly recognised to be of general benefit (1555). He is also a ruler beloved of his people, and his treatment of the people who have submitted themselves to him is praised for its moderation and fairness:

> The King was so restrained in his treatment of them all

that not a single one could be displeased with him;
with all of them he had come into a friendship so close
that if he were their father he would not have been more loved.

(1944)

The poet makes it clear that those who accept Alexander's lordship willingly (see stanza 2520) have the lightest of tributes imposed upon them. Moreover, after his death Alexander is lamented as a loving, benevolent ruler of the peoples that he has conquered:

They said, on the other side, "Alas, our Emperor!
How has the Creator been willing to suffer this,
to give such great power to an evil traitor,
and to make so many orphans of such a noble lord?"

Lord, in dying you have brought death to more people
than you and your armies killed during your life;
lord, with your death all the lands are distressed,
for with you, they would all have had pleasure and joy.

(2651, 2657)

It is, indeed, easy to see in him, in the magnificence of his achievements and the qualities that he displays, a figure against whom a medieval monarch, and particularly one who sets out to conquer, subdue and incorporate into his kingdom alien peoples, might be expected to measure himself.

Throughout the poem the contrasting themes of loyal service and treachery are to the fore. Indeed, the very frequency with which the poet returns to the theme of treachery and the punishment that it merits suggests that this is a matter much on his mind and that behind such comments there lies a preoccupation with specific contemporary circumstances or individuals. Against those whom he views as traitors (such as the people of Thebes or Tyre, Pausanias, Bessus and Antipater) the poet directs words of harsh condemnation and he is clearly appalled by the prospect in his own day of the vassal who turns against his lord (stanza 1830). The first occasion, indeed, on which the poet expresses any criticism of his hero is when he fails to mete out the appropriate punishment to the traitor Nabarzanes (stanza 1862). On the other hand we are left in no doubt that Alexander views with great sympathy the fallen figure of Darius who must – he makes abundantly clear – still be treated with the respect that is due to a ruler. The shift in the poet's viewpoint, as Darius changes from Alexander's opponent in battle to a caring and trusting lord, is very marked and it prefigures the oscillation which we shall observe in his attitude to Alexander himself; for Darius is now seen in the most positive of terms:

> he wept and forgave them, and affirmed his friendship
> – may God grant forgiveness to so merciful a man.
>
> (1683cd)

As the moment of his death approaches, like a devout Christian monarch, Darius pleads to God for forgiveness:

> I know well that I did You neither justice nor service
> as I should have, and failed to fulfil my office.
> I am a man of great sin, I am full of much vice;
> while You do not love me, I have no wish for life.
>
> (1704)

Just as the nature of the picture that we have been given of the Persian emperor changes markedly during the course of the poem, so too that of Alexander becomes increasingly complex. What does not change, however, is the sense of his natural superiority as a warrior and ruler. This is so obvious, even when he is a young man, that his fearsome steed Bucephalus bows down before him (stanza 119); but by the time that his conquests are complete, all the peoples of the known world are coming to pay homage to him, not just those who have suffered conquest but others who are in awe of his reputation. For much of the poem the epithets that the poet applies to him depict him in an unreservedly positive light: even as he reaches the final stages of his career, he is seen as "Alexander the good, a power without limits" (2496a). His great nobility is reflected in the respect that he shows for Darius' wife Stateira, before and after her death, for this is the obligation that he feels naturally to be his (stanza 1288). Moreover, as we have already seen in the case of Darius, Alexander, in a number of ways, takes on the aspect of a devout Christian. His reign begins with his coronation and knighting in a Christian Corinth (196–197). The very background to his struggle against Darius is set against a christianised scheme of the world in which the Moors hold sway over Asia (279–280) – in this sense his campaigns have the air of a Crusade – and we are told that Alexander is feared by Jew and Moslem alike (2332b). In the Battle of Gaugamela, we are told that his enemies are *aláraves* (Arabs), defeated by God's will. When he goes to visit the oracle at Siwah he adopts the dress of a pilgrim (1168a) as if following the road to Santiago de Compostela. He shows respect for Tarsus (again anachronistically, because of its association with St Paul) and, in the awe that he shows towards Jerusalem, he demonstrates the piety to be associated with a dutiful Christian monarch. In his account of his dream, he describes his encounter with a spiritual figure:

> I believe he was an angel descended from Heaven,
> for his face was unlike any man ever born. ...
>
> In every way, he had the appearance of a bishop,
> in his mitre, his shoes and all his vestments; ...
>
> I tell you, my friends, that that very messenger,
> was a sign sent from God to give me certainty;
> He is my guide, not some other soothsayer:
>
> (1153cd, 1154ab, 1162a–c)

Alexander thus seems to be charged with a divine mission to bring down the pagan Persian empire, as foretold in the prophecy of Daniel. Moreover, when he shuts away the lost Jewish tribes, God hears his prayer, although the poet comments that:

> Since God did all of this for a man who was pagan,
> for a faithful Christian, He would do as much or more;
>
> (2116ab)

In this episode God seems to endow Alexander with supernatural powers (2112–2114); and ultimately his unnatural exploits are even to be confused by Satan with the coming of Christ (2441–2442). Repeatedly he utters Christian prayers and innumerable Christian oaths and exclamations and at the moment of his death, in being lowered to the ground, he seems to be going through a ritual very similar to that which was to be followed in the final moments of two saintly thirteenth-century kings, Louis IX of France and his cousin, Fernando III of Castile.[32]

---

[32] See Michael (1969, 28–87) for a detailed analysis of the way in which Alexander's portrait as monarch has been medievalised (with regard to birth and childhood, questions of parentage, learning and education, valour, ambition and desire for fame, liberality, nobility, anger and his attitude to treachery).

Alexander thus comes to represent in many respects the embodiment of the chivalric ideal, the warrior who devotes his carefully-honed military skills to the service of God and Christendom. It has already been seen (Section 4, above) that the pursuit of this ideal, together with the adoption of its outward trappings, was becoming increasingly common among the Iberian nobility and monarchies in the late twelfth and early thirteenth centuries. It seems very justifiable to assert that the author of the *Libro de Alexandre*, through his account of the career of the pagan emperor, is giving us a model for the ideals and the undertakings of a medieval Christian monarchy and specifically the Castilian monarchy of the early decades of the thirteenth century.

However, in other respects the picture of Alexander is far from being an idealised one and the focus of the poem certainly does not remain fixed on his positive qualities and his triumphs. In spite of the many ways in which the figure and the deeds of the Emperor are christianised in the *Libro de Alexandre* and in spite, too, of the positive and laudatory comments which abound in the text, the poet makes it equally clear that ultimately rulers, like all men, must inevitably suffer the fate that God has ordained. The point is hammered home throughout the poem; it is, for example, one of the threads that run through the account of the Trojan War which is dominated by a prophecy of its predetermined course and studded with warnings that a man cannot avoid the fate that is ordained for him (as in Hector's prayer, 675ab). The poet points out to us, for example, during the Battle of Gaugamela (1390ab), that God's plan was to bring Alexander success; but later we see that both the fall of Darius (1647c) and that of Alexander himself (2491–2493) have been divinely ordained, for what God has willed to happen cannot possibly be turned aside.

The modern reader may be troubled by the apparent ambivalence of the Spanish poet's attitude to his hero.[33] On the one hand, there is warm approval and praise for Alexander's unswerving pursuit, on behalf of his people, of freedom from foreign domination and eventually great gain and prosperity through conquest; Alexander is shown to act with exemplary firmness of purpose and with all the qualities of a fine Christian knight and for this he

---

[33] Michael (1969, 282 ff.) examines this duality and argues that there was no need for the author of the *Alexandre* to choose between on the one hand praise for his hero as a man who has won fame by his deeds and on the other condemnation of him for succumbing to the sin of pride. It is, Michael shows, possible to present him as a model figure in terms of worldly achievement while lamenting his spiritual downfall.

is richly rewarded. To this extent he offers an outstanding example for the medieval monarch to follow. On the other hand, as he reaches the pinnacle of his worldly triumphs, to an increasing extent Alexander falls prey to the sin of pride and to his desire to overstep the mark of acceptable conduct laid down by God and Nature. He proves blind to the many warnings that he is given and God allows him to be punished as a result. There is surely no incompatibility here between admiration for properly-directed worldly achievement and the message that all men, even the most powerful and successful, must not lose sight of their designated place in God's creation.

When Nature descends to Hell to prepare the way for Alexander's fall, we are given an extensive picture of the sins of mankind and of the cruel punishment that awaits the sinners. This is a horrific vision through which the poet seeks to strike fear into the hearts of all those who read or hear his poem, with clear parallels, for example, in the carvings which sat above the doorways of many medieval churches and cathedrals, issuing their grim warning. All men and women must heed the teachings of the Church and overcome the failings by which great and humble alike are threatened. The poet's canvas is a broad one and his two prominent moralising digressions, systematic and searing in their intensity, make it clear that his reproaches are directed not just at kings and rulers but at all strata of society. From those who work the land to craftsmen, traders, clerics, prelates, nobles and princes, all are prone to error (stanzas 1815–1830) and Hell itself has the recognisable form of a medieval town, dominated by the figures of the vices, from whose evil influence none are free (2334–2422). Even the mightiest of rulers, whatever his worldly power and achievements, must keep in mind his own human limitations and must not forget to attend to the needs of his own soul. A king has great power to affect the lives of others and his deeds will be much more conspicuous and open to scrutiny than those of most of his fellow men, but at the same time in his strengths and in his failings he is representative of all of mankind. The author of the *Libro de Alexandre* can be seen as presenting to a prince or monarch an image of royal achievement which offers encouragement and praise and yet is deeply chastening: whatever a warrior and ruler may achieve in terms of conquest – or even, indeed, scholarship –, without Christian virtue it is worth nothing.

For there can be no doubt that Alexander commits the most serious of sins, by his pride and by a level of ambition which is a deep offence against Nature. For Nature, when she appeals to Satan, Alexander is above all "a man of great pride" (2430a), from whom not even Hell itself is safe. God's condemnation of Alexander is unambiguous:

> It troubled the Creator who had created Nature:
> He bore for Alexander great rancour and rage.
> He said, "For this lunatic who shows no restraint,
> I shall turn all his joy into bitterness.
>
> He knew how to judge the pride of the fish,
> but he could not make out the pride he had within.
> A man who knows how to pass so many judgements
> must undergo such judgement as he gave."
>
> (2329–30)

It is Pride, the sin of Lucifer himself, which, in our poet's graphic depiction of the horrors of Hell, is shown to rule over all the other mortal sins (2406–2410). It is, as this passage explains with stark clarity, the error which Alexander has seen in others (as he did when he observed the behaviour of creatures beneath the sea – 2317) but which he could not recognise in himself. Indeed, as the poet is here reminding us, there have been very many pointers in the poem to the nature of Alexander's error and to the fate which is to befall him.

It is here, moreover, in the way in which the poet has so skilfully worked his material into a complex and tightly organised whole, that lies part of the distinctiveness of the *Libro de Alexandre*. As in Eugène Vinaver's description of "poetry of interlace" (see Section 6, above), we repeatedly find in this poem that passages and details deliberately recall others, and we see that warnings given and examples observed can comment powerfully on what is to befall Alexander, but do not make it possible for it to be prevented. In their fundamental study, Peter Bly and Alan Deyermond demonstrate (1972, 167) the relevance of the work's many digressions from its central narrative thread: "the tragic downfall of greatness because of a fatal flaw, the downfall being engineered by treachery, the tool of the devil". They consider, for example, the relevance of the account of the Trojan War, drawing attention to the link established by name between the flawed Paris and Alexander (see stanza 360a), showing how the downfall of the prince of Troy prefigures that of the Macedonian emperor; they point to the many examples of treachery in the poem, often seen to be provoked by the Devil, and examine other parallels with Alexander's career, conspicuously that of Darius; they analyse the pattern of repeated allusions to the Tower of Babel and the two passages based on Bestiary tradition (those dealing with the elephant and the protection provided by nakedness against snakes); and they demonstrate how the author of the *Libro de Alexandre* has gone outside the normal Alexander sources in order to reinforce his theme. Bly and Deyermond, whilst noting the need for caution in making excessive claims for the unity of so complex a medieval text, argue convincingly that the digressions which are so prominent a feature of the poem are structurally compatible with the remainder of the work and thematically crucial. This is, indeed, exactly what we would be led to expect by the poet's self-conscious approach to his art and by his own insistence on the link between such digressions and his *materia* or central thread.

Indeed, it is worth considering further the light which is shed on the figure and role of Alexander through the links established with both biblical and classical figures. The Spanish poet, in expressing his own Christian vision of Alexander's life and achievements, combines material taken from a range of authoritative sources available to him, essentially combining two traditions of knowledge. Thus on the one hand he looks back to the ancient age of Achilles, the man whom Alexander saw as his ancestor: we see how the heroes of the Trojan War embody the pursuit of reputation and long-lasting fame through courage, perseverance and knightly qualities, but we are nevertheless reminded, as in the description of Achilles' arms (stanzas 653–659), of the futility of men's attempts to set themselves above God's natural order. On the other hand, in some of the artistic creations of Apelles (notably the tomb of Stateira, stanzas 1239–1249) there is heavy emphasis on events recounted from the Old Testament, which take us back to the earliest generations of mankind. These events are shot through with details of error, excessive conduct and conflict. In the account of Darius' arms (stanzas 989–1001) the poet draws our attention to the role of Nebuchadnezzar in carrying off the Jewish people into captivity and, in a passage which goes on to draw attention to other famous examples of fallen greatness, the link with Babylon and its Persian conquerors is established. Alexander, in turn the destroyer of the Persian empire – as the Bible had foretold – is thus presented as the most conspicuous of a long line of representatives of conquest and power stretching back to the beginnings of time. Biblical and pagan myth are intertwined, not only in the much used *exemplum* of the giants and the

Tower of Babel, but also, crucially, in the parallel established between the biblical forbidden fruit (see for example stanzas and 1240 and 2341) and the Devil's role in setting before the goddesses the fruit which is to bring about the fall of Paris and Troy (stanzas 328d, 339 and 341). Alexander is the heir to both pagan and classical traditions of military achievement and empire but also, crucially, to the human fallibility which was illustrated by the careers of so many of his predecessors. Like them, he is to become a powerful example of how Man, in aspiring to greatness, is brought down by his own excesses.

It is clear, then, that many features of the *Libro de Alexandre* prefigure Alexander's downfall through greed, lack of self-control and, above all, pride. Some further mention should be made of the second of these: for our attention is drawn to it on several occasions, notably in God's judgement in stanza 2329 (see above). *Mesura*, which can be defined as moderation or self-control (or perhaps even common sense), is a characteristic which plays an important part in the medieval epic poem: it is the principal defining characteristic of the protagonist of the *Poema de Mio Cid*, whilst in the case of Roland, the greatest of the epic heroes of medieval France, it is precisely his *démesure* or lack of moderation which is shown to bring disaster. Thus, when our poet wishes to emphasise the nature of Alexander's more noble conduct, such as the respect that he shows for Darius' mother, he describes him as being a man of great *mesura* (1590a) and Queen Thalestris comes to him because she has heard him praised as the epitome of strength, nobility and *mesura* (1885b). On the other hand, an unreliable figure like the Greek Thersites, whose conduct is badly judged, is dismissed as *desmesurado* (423b); Darius criticises the conduct of the young Alexander as overreaching himself or being without *mesura* (813b); Alexander's troops, scared by the eclipse, anticipate defeat as a punishment for being governed by pride and ignoring *mesura* (1205c); and the poet also tellingly comments that hatred can have the effect of robbing prelates of their *mesura* (2368d). This is not, then, a quality which is only important in kings and conquerors, but one which is fundamental in those who are to play their due part in a well-run and harmonious society. *Mesura* – or, in fact, the lack of it – is a crucial element in the portrait of the hero of the *Libro de Alexandre*; and, if we see the poem as offering a model of conduct for its public and perhaps for a specific noble or royal individual, then the need for moderation and good judgement is without doubt one of its essential elements.

It is important also to bear in mind, given the extent to which Alexander's failings and eventual fall are prefigured throughout the poem, the consequential heavy use of irony and particularly dramatic irony. Repeatedly there is emphasis on the blindness shown by the central characters of the poem. This is particularly striking in the case of Darius (1647 ff.) who, though he seems to have learned a bitter lesson from his fall, goes on to express his belief that his fortunes are about to improve and to thank those who are about to kill him for their loyal support. His blindness goes much further back than this, however, for, when he first went into battle against Alexander, he carried arms which depicted not only acts of cruelty committed by his Persian ancestors – for which the Bible had promised retribution – but also images of the doomed struggle of the Giants against the heavens (stanzas 990 ff.); and he proceeds to remind his troops, as they prepare for battle, that the Giants were their ancestors (stanza 948).

Earlier still, he had been warned by Alexander himself, in words which were heavily significant for both of them, had they realised their true implications:

> your fate will be as Lucifer's, who wished to climb so high
> that God abandoned him and he was doomed to die.
>
> (799cd)

Ironically, however, as Weiss points out,[34] Alexander, not only seizes Darius' empire and trappings of power and takes on the responsibility for his family, but he also assumes his destiny: the lot which he lamented in his fallen enemy now becomes his own.

In a rather different way, too, Alexander is shown to point a moral to others without, it seems, being able to act on it for himself: after the death of Darius, Alexander addresses to him a lament in which he points out the lesson to be learned from his fall and tells him that no man should ever spare a traitor:

> "Vassals who act in such a way towards their lord
> would do no better for me, if they had the chance;
> anyone who ever shows mercy to a traitor,
> may the Creator never have mercy on him!"
>
> (1789)

---

[34] Weiss (2006, 117–119) stresses not only the parallels between Alexander and Darius but also the extent to which the former is represented metaphorically as the conqueror of his own father. The implication of this is that Alexander takes on the legacy of excessive ambition and failure, as symbolised by the Giants and the Tower of Babel.

Shortly afterwards, we are told that Alexander has spared Nabarzarnes and we can only suppose that he will fall victim to his own curse.

The numerous warnings which are available to Alexander about his excessive conduct could not be clearer: for example as they are expressed by the messengers of the Scythians who explain to him the treacherous conduct that he can expect from those around him:

> You wish to climb up high – it is your lot to descend;
> you wish to run and run – it is your lot to fall;
> you are like the man with dropsy who is dying to drink
> but, the more he drinks, the more he burns with thirst.
>
> The greedy man, unable to protect himself,
> for a tiny cherry lets himself come crashing down;
> he is blinded by his greed which makes him climb to the top
> and makes him fall from the peak into a place of evil.
>
> (1924–1925)

The messengers also point out explicitly (1918d) the parallel between Alexander and the Giants who rebelled against Jupiter and who have been linked throughout the poem with the builders of the Tower of Babel. The wisdom and significance of their warnings are clear to all except Alexander who does not give for them "a miserable roast leek" (1940c) and proceeds to subdue the Scythians and devastate their lands.

The words of the defeated Porus spell out the same message:

> Anyone who wishes can set this all in writing
> and bring forward the examples of Darius and Porus
> who had great glory, but were to come to suffer:
> it is the nature of the world to rise and fall."
>
> (2214)

What is so telling here is not just that the point is made but the fact that Alexander is deeply impressed by Porus' words, to the extent that he rewards him for his wisdom. He seems to recognise the truth but then turns his back on it.

Most conspicuously of all, Alexander, after his submarine exploit, points out how his own biggest weakness is prevalent in others:

> The King said, "Pride exists in every place;
> it is a force on earth and within the seas;

likewise, birds do not see themselves as equals.
May God confound a vice that so many places have!

(2317)

He goes on to say how pride led to the fall of Lucifer and continues to lead men to betray God (here the idea of loyalty is introduced in a different context) and how those who already have much wish for more and more. The point could not be more clearly made and is driven home by the poet's telling observation:

> If, just as the King was well able to see this,
> he were willing to pass judgement rightly on himself,
> he would certainly have to hold back his tongue a little
> for he would not wish to utter such conceited words.

(2321)

There has been much discussion about how we should interpret the fate of Alexander's soul. That the poet does not, after the Emperor's death, feel that he needs to make the matter explicit is not surprising; moreover, a thirteenth-century poet might well balk at the prospect of specifically stating that a monarch has been condemned to Hell. What we certainly know is that, as the Scythians warned, Alexander has fallen suddenly from the summit of his achievement and power into "mal logar", "a place of evil". As the time of his death approached we saw him seated beneath a tent worked with an elaborate array of images. These included the heavens from which Lucifer fell, the betrayal of Darius and the death of traitors such as Pausanias and Bessus, the downfall of the Giants and the Tower of Babel and, on the other hand, a calendar of the year which marked the inevitable and immutable cycle of Nature. There are evident parallels here with a description included much earlier in the poem, that of Achilles' arms (652–659), which likewise juxtaposed the building of the Tower of Babel with a picture of the orderly and harmonious design of creation. The same points are reinforced repeatedly throughout the poem (see, for example, the description of the harmony of creation included in the account of the eclipse in stanzas 1212–1213) and all of this further reinforces the message of the narrative: that Alexander has deeply offended Nature and that for this, like others, he will be severely punished.

In the description of the tent, the poet draws together the threads of his poem but leaves us to draw our own conclusion. However, there is a further very telling passage which has to be interpreted against the background of Alexander's blindness to all that he has been told about his conduct and the

Introduction 59

end that he must expect. Knowing that his end is approaching rapidly, the Emperor anticipates the reception which awaits him in Heaven:

> I shall be warmly received by the King of Heaven,
> and when He has me, He will feel Himself protected.
> In His court, I shall be honoured and well served,
> and all will praise me, for I suffered no defeat.
>
> (2631)

In the light of all that has been said and seen about the passing nature of human triumphs and the dangers posed by pride, is there not a strong suggestion here that Alexander has still failed to grasp the message which was everywhere being made obvious to him?

However, although the author of the poem makes it abundantly clear that Alexander bears the responsibility for the excesses of his conduct, he also emphasises that the world lays many traps for the unwary and that misfortune constantly threatens even the most successful and prosperous. There is something almost malevolent about the way in which Man is deceived by the world around him:

> Never should a man put his trust in this world,
> which knows how to bring affairs to such an ill close
> and how to set its friends in exalted positions
> so as finally to crush them all the more cruelly.
>
> (999)

The poet returns on several occasions to the image of the Wheel of Fortune (see, for example, stanzas 986 and 1653–1654 and 1806–1807). In the passage which follows the account of Darius' burial he begins by condemning the unreliability of the world (stanzas 1805 ff.) but he moves on from consideration of the bleakness of Darius' fate to a bitter and extended attack on the faults of the society of his own day. Man's only defence against the ravages of Fortune is Christian humility, which enables him to pay proper heed to the warnings that he is given and guard against the traps that are laid for him. He must, above all else, keep in true perspective his own lowly place in the world, and remember that "as he comes from earth, to earth he will return" (1811c): this is the stark message, the *materia*, that he must keep in his heart.

As the work draws to its end, the poet returns to this same note and expresses a blunt message in simple worldly terms. He tells us that, although

Alexander's body is no more, his fine reputation – recorded by the scholars – will endure (stanza 2668), but almost immediately he reminds us sharply that worldly glories and the trappings of power must not be trusted:

> The glory of this world one who seeks right thought
> must value no higher than the flower of the field,
> for at the time when a man believes himself safest,
> it casts him down head first into the foulest place.
>
> For Alexander, who was a king of great power,
> and could not be contained by seas or by land,
> in the end it was his lot to fall into a grave
> which could not have been twelve feet in length.
>
> (2671–2672)

The poet has a moral to draw for his public and he spells it out to us with the greatest possible clarity. However, it would be wrong to consider that his didactic purpose reduces the intensity of his emotional response to the fall, whether it is seen in purely material terms or whether his concern is with the fate of Alexander's soul. Contemplation of the betrayal and death of Darius and of Alexander himself and of the futility of what they have sought to achieve leaves us with a powerful sense that they are victims partly of their own flawed character and partly of a destiny which has been marked out for them. Indeed we have been told many times in the course of the poem that Alexander's fall, like his triumphs, is ordained and unalterable. Just as we are told repeatedly that the events of the Troy story could not fail to conform to Calchas' prophecy and that the fate of each individual warrior was already determined (as in stanza 686), so the once mighty Darius sees the events leading to his death as preordained by God (1708) and there are indications throughout Alexander's career (as early as the assassination attempt at Tyre, see stanza 1126) that the nature of his death has already been marked out by the Fates and willed by the gods. The poem is heavy with portents, prophecies, supernatural messages and warnings, and the poet's unequivocal condemnation of Alexander's excess and error is accompanied by a strong sense of the destiny which has marked the whole of his hero's life. We see Alexander at different points as a man brought down by his own sin, as a noble figure ensnared by the Devil (see stanzas 2457–2458) and as a plaything of the Wheel of Fortune. Christian and pagan elements are interwoven and the viewpoint that our poet adopts is repeatedly – and consciously – shifted; but our response is ultimately one of horror at the sudden and chilling fall of a man whose extraordinary qualities had set him in a position of great and seemingly unshakable worldly power.

* * * *

It seems appropriate to end this brief study, as it began, with the world of scholarship. The importance of the world of the schools and universities for the genesis of the *Libro de Alexandre* has been heavily emphasised and we have also examined how the teachings of the grammarians contributed to the structure and style of the poem. What remains is a brief consideration of the significance of the world of learning within the work itself.

Indeed, the imprint of the medieval schools is clearly visible from the very start of the poem, when Alexander describes to his tutor Aristotle the studies that he has undertaken. What we see here (stanzas 38–45) is an outline, in a slightly modified form (see note to stanza 43a), of the *trivium* and *quadrivium*, the Seven Liberal Arts. The poet clearly intends from the outset to establish the importance of scholarship (or *clereçía*) in the education of a medieval nobleman or prince. More than this, however, in the course of the poem he shows us the practical application of several of the courses of study. The importance of Grammar and the art of composition is, as we have seen, fundamental to the creation of the poem as a whole, but there is also repeated insistence on the practical business of formal letter writing (as in stanzas 802, 810, 1537ab, 2450a). Rhetoric, the art of persuasion, is repeatedly in evidence in the form either of articulate presentations or of formal and carefully-constructed debates, notably those of the three goddesses (described as "formidable lawyers", stanzas 345–386) and of the prisoners at Persepolis (1614–1638). It is Rhetoric on which Alexander relies in order to ease his men's sorrow as they leave their homeland (261a), just as later he convinces them in an eloquent speech of the need to continue with the campaign (1840 ff.) and similarly wins them round to the idea of, quite literally, following him to the ends of the earth; of course, there are others who also have these skills and thus, for example, we are told that it is by means of a long rhetorical harangue that the people persuade Alexander to destroy Thebes (223a). Medicine is conspicuously represented through the life-saving services of the doctors Philip (902 ff.) and Critobulus (2250 ff.). The intervention of the astronomer Aristander (1209 ff.) plays a crucial part in allaying the fears of Alexander's troops before battle and the "musical tree" (2135 ff.) gives the poet scope to display his own musical knowledge and to emphasise the importance of the learning which lay behind its creation (2141d).

The poet loses no opportunity to draw attention to the skills of men of learning, such as the minstrel Cleadas (232 ff.), who in his appreciation of Alexander's scholarship distinguishes himself from the ordinary *juglar*, and the ill-fated scholar Zoroas (1054 ff.) whose blood Alexander refuses to shed. Indeed, we see Aristotle himself ranking among Alexander's military advisers. However, there is an even more obvious contribution made by the world of scholarship throughout the course of the poem: that of the men of great learning who produce the decorated armour, monuments and other works of art which figure so prominently. These include the creator of Achilles' shield, and Alexander's artist Apelles, the importance of whose work for our understanding of the poem has already been emphasised in the previous section of this Introduction. Apelles was an historical individual who worked in Alexander's service, but the Spanish poet took his character from the *Alexandreis* and gave it greater prominence. Like Philip, Critobulus and Aristander, he is given the title "maestro", equivalent to the Latin "magister" (see note to stanza 25a). As we have seen, Apelles, like our poet, chooses with great care the details to be included in his works and brings them together to form a harmonious, elegantly-constructed and above all coherent whole, giving a vast picture which takes in several episodes from the history of the Jewish people (conspicuously, forming the essential subject matter for the description of Stateira's tomb, included just before the decisive battle of Gaugamela), the rise and the destruction of the Persian empire and that of its conqueror. Apelles comments on the characters and events of the narrative, just as the poet through his work expresses his vision of history and, through it, of the society of his own day. Indeed, not only will Alexander's achievements always be spoken of but so too, we are told (1249d), will those of Apelles. Perhaps it is for similar lasting achievement that the poet himself longs when he ventures to compare his own enterprise with that of Homer (1504d), when he emphasises how much Alexander owes to the scholar who sets down his deeds in writing (2668) or when he describes his own ambition as being on a par with that of Alexander (2465).

However, the most important representative of scholarship in the poem is Alexander himself. We have seen how our poet established from the very outset that his hero wished his thoughts to be at least as much on his studies as on warfare and Alexander's knowledge and fascination with learning are emphasised constantly. He is articulate and persuasive and repeatedly

Introduction

demonstrates the practical skills of a rhetorician. He is well read and we see him recounting the story of Troy to his troops, who are particularly impressed by this as a feat of memory, which was understood to be an essential part of the art of Rhetoric. His learning and desire to know more extend to natural sciences; indeed, when Alexander safely sees his men through the snakes in the desert, the poet reminds us just how well he has been equipped by his education:

> As the King was a man of knowledge and learning,
> of great intellect, too, and was a fine scholar,
> he was a good philosopher, his studies extensive...
>
> (2160a–c)

However, Alexander shows that he is a scholar by doing much more than demonstrating a knowledge of Bestiary tradition: as much as to conquer he seeks to learn and to understand; it is in fact his intellectual curiosity which so goes against Nature and God and is eventually to bring about his downfall and that of his empire. What is shown to concern Nature and Satan so much is, indeed, true: Alexander seeks not only to conquer but also to discover the "Antipodes", about which he speaks with scholarly reservation:

> I shall seek out the Antipodes – I want to conquer them;
> they lie beneath the earth, or so we have heard tell,
> but I do not assert this, for I believe I might lie.
>
> (2293b–d)

Alexander, with all his strengths and weaknesses, remains a scholar. Thus he is the embodiment of the ideal of Arms and Letters and, in that sense, our poet could well be presenting him as a model for a monarch or nobleman of his own age.

This is, nevertheless, an Alexander who embodies not only many virtues to be imitated but also powerful and dangerous failings that any individual – scholar or warrior, the poet himself and his public, too – must avoid.

8. The Libro de Alexandre: *a synopsis*

Stanzas
1–6   Prologue
7–18   Alexander's birth and childhood
19–20 The death of Nectanebo

21–88	Alexander's lament about Persian domination; Aristotle's teachings and Alexander's response
89–107	Alexander determines to be knighted: description of his arms
108–119	Bucephalus
120–126	Alexander knights himself
127–141	The campaign against Nicolao
142–159	Alexander's dispute with Darius
160–168	Alexander crushes the rebellion against his father
169–195	The uprising and defeat of Pausanias and the death of King Philip
196–210	Alexander is crowned in Corinth
211–244	The uprising of Athens and Thebes; the *juglar* Cleadas tries in vain to dissuade Alexander from destroying Thebes
245–275	The expedition to Asia begins and Alexander's harangue inspires his troops
276–294	The map of the world and the description of Asia
295–310	Alexander's army arrives in Asia
311–319	Alexander names his Twelve Peers and the campaign opens
320–772	On arriving at the site of Troy, Alexander recounts to his troops the events of the Trojan War: Paris and the Apple of Discord *(335 ff.)*; the seduction of Helen and the Greeks' reaction *(388 ff.)*; the concealment and temper of Achilles *(409 ff.)*; the Greek invasion and Trojan response *(434 ff.)*; battles, duels and feats of war *(462 ff.)*; Hector's combat with Ajax *(576 ff.)*; night raid by Diomedes and Ulysses *(616 ff.)*; the death and funeral of Patroclus *(636 ff.)*; Achilles' new arms *(652 ff.)*; combat with Achilles and the death of Hector *(665 ff.)*; the death of Achilles *(720 ff.)*; Nestor's harangue *(728 ff.)*; the Trojan horse *(736 ff.)*; Alexander's conclusions and his troops' reaction *(762 ff.)*
773–827	Alexander sets off in search of Darius; they exchange correspondence and harangue their troops and news arrives of the death of Memnon
828–837	Alexander captures Sardes and solves the problem of the Gordian Knot
838–843	The capture of Ancira and Cappadocia and the advance towards the Euphrates
844–873	Description of the advance of Darius' troops and of his carriage and army

874–879	The Persians adopt a scorched earth policy but Alexander's army saves Tarsus
880–913	Alexander goes swimming in the River Cydnus, catches a serious chill and is saved by his doctor Philip
914–1001	The fall of Issus and the preliminaries to the Battle of Issus, including descriptions of *(934–40)* the *locus amoenus* or idealised landscape and *(989–1001)* Darius' arms
1002–1083	The Battle of Issus, the flight of Darius and the sharing out of booty
1084–1089	The capture of Damascus and Darius' response
1090–1091	The capture of Sidon
1092–1119	The siege and destruction of Tyre
1120–1130	The capture of Gaza and the wounding of Alexander
1131–1147	Alexander visits and spares Jersualem
1148–1163	Alexander recounts his vision
1164–1165	Alexander passes through Samaria and enters Egypt
1166–1183	The visit to the shrine of Ammon at the Siwah oasis
1184–1198	Alexander and Darius prepare for a second battle
1199–1232	The eclipse of the moon and Aristander's explanation
1233–1238	The death of Darius' wife Stateira
1239–1249	Description of Stateira's tomb
1250–1267	Darius hears of his wife's death and proposes peace to Alexander
1268–1291	In spite of Parmenion's advice to the contrary, Alexander rejects Darius' proposal
1292–1326	On the eve of battle Parmenion proposes a surprise attack but his advice is rejected
1327–1336	Alexander oversleeps and is awoken by Parmenion
1337–1347	Preparations for the battle: Alexander harangues his troops and receives a warning from a Greek deserter
1348–1433	The Battle of Gaugamela / Arbela: feats of battle; Darius' flight; some of his troops fight to the end
1434–1454	Darius' troops regroup and he tries in vain to lift their spirits
1455–1459	Alexander distributes booty and prepares to advance to Babylon which surrenders immediately
1460–1533	Description of Babylon: the surrounding region *(1461–1467)*; precious stones to be found in the waters of the rivers *(1468–1492)*; the city itself and its wealth *(1493–1504)*; the building

	of the Tower of Babel and its consequences *(1505–1522)*; the fortress and royal palace *(1523–1533)*
1534–1560	Alexander receives a triumphal reception into the city of Babylon; while his army relaxes, Alexander reorganises the army and introduces new customs
1561–1562	Alexander moves on to capture Susa
1563–1593	After a bitter siege, the city of Uxion is captured, but, after the intervention of Darius' mother Sisigambis, its inhabitants are spared
1594–1598	In pursuit of Darius, Parmenion's troops battle against hostile mountain tribes
1599–1606	The capture and destruction of Persepolis
1607–1639	An encounter with maimed Greek captives; they debate whether they should stay or return to their homeland
1640–1645	Darius endeavours to raise an army for a further battle
1646–1665	With the moment of his betrayal approaching, Darius addresses his troops on the vicissitudes of Fortune and appeals for their support
1666–1679	The traitors urge Darius to put his kingdom in the hands of Bessus
1680–1698	Nabarzanes and Bessus make their plans and Patron warns Darius
1699–1719	The traitors capture Bessus and put him in chains
1720–1738	Alexander hears of the treachery against Darius and sets off in search of him
1739–1750	Bessus and Nabarzanes leave Darius for dead and word reaches Alexander
1751–1761	Supporters of Darius fight to the death against Alexander's troops
1762–1776	Discovery of Darius' body and his funeral
1777–1790	Alexander's lament for Darius
1791–1804	Darius' tomb
1805–1830	The poet's lament: the Wheel of Fortune and the vanity of worldly ambition; survey of the evils and failings of contemporary society
1831–1839	The troops long to return home and Alexander is asked to address them
1840–1859	Alexander persuades his men to continue with the campaign

Introduction 67

1860–1862	In Hyrcania, Nabarzanes is captured but pardoned by Alexander
1863–1888	The visit of Thalestris, Queen of the Amazons
1889–1899	Hearing of Bessus' whereabouts, Alexander and his army destroy their own booty to enable faster movement
1900–1907	The execution of Philotas and the death of his father Parmenion
1908–1911	The capture, punishment and execution of Bessus
1912–1942	The attack on Scythia, the embassy of the Scythians and Alexander's response to their warning
1943–1949	Alexander imposes his authority on the peoples of Persia and plans to conquer India
1950–1954	May poem
1955–1967	Alexander's marriage to Rhoxane
1968–1972	Before setting off on the Indian campaign, Alexander has Hermolaus and Cleitus executed
1973–1975	Porus summons the peoples of his empire
1976–1980	The elephant and how it can be captured
1981–1992	Preparations for the battle of the Hydaspes
1993–2022	Nicanor and Symachus, their undertaking and death
2023–2039	Alexander's army crosses the Hydaspes
2040–2087	The battle of the Hydaspes: description of combats; the battle begins again on a second day; how Alexander overcomes the elephants; the Indian retreat begins and Porus' army is destroyed
2088–2097	Porus flees but Bucephalus dies from his wounds
2098–2100	The poet states that he intends to include material omitted from the *Alexandreis*
2101–2116	The enclosure of the Lost Tribes/Gog and Magog
2117–2142	Description of Porus' palace, including the vine of gold set with precious stones and the musical tree
2143–2154	The pursuit of Porus continues in spite of various hardships
2155–2163	A spring in the desert: Alexander explains to his men how to overcome the threat of the snakes
2164–2183	Alexander and his troops encounter a series of natural hasards and strange creatures
2184–2216	Alexander's second encounter with Porus, their duel and

                Alexander's victory
2217–2244   The attack on Sudracae, Alexander's injury and the eventual capture of the city and slaughter of the inhabitants
2245–2264   Alexander is cured by Critobulus
2265–2297   Alexander conceives his maritime adventure and, in spite of the warnings expressed by his generals, he wins them over to his enterprise
2298–2305   Alexander sets sail
2306–2323   Alexander's underwater observations and his conclusions
2324–2333   The reaction of God and Nature to Alexander's exploits; Nature goes down to Hell in search of Satan's assistance
2334–2423   Description of Hell and the Deadly Sins
2424–2435   Nature asks Satan for help
2436–2444   Satan's council meets
2445–2457   Treachery proposes making use of Antipater and prepares him for his task
2458–2468   Alexander plans further conquests
2469–2476   Alexander encounters more fabulous creatures, including the Phoenix
2477–2494   The visit to the Temple of the Sun and the Moon
2495   Encounter with the Acephali
2496–2514   Alexander's aerial adventure, including the comparison between the Earth and Man
2515–2526   The embassies of Alexander's tribute nations assemble in Babylon
2527–2537   Alexander hastens back to Babylon and is given a triumphal reception
2538–2595   Alexander's tent, including: *(2554–66)* the labours of the months of the year; *(2567–75)* deeds of Hercules and the Trojan War; *(2576–87)* the map of the world, focusing on the landmarks of Spain and the intellectual centres of Christendom; *(2588–95)* a summary of Alexander's career
2596–2601   Alexander welcomes the ambassadors and gives thanks to God
2602–2604   Heavenly prodigies signal the imminence of Alexander's death
2605–2622   Antipater and Iolaus carry out their plot to poison Alexander
2623–2631   Alexander takes his leave of his followers and anticipates his

	reception in Heaven
2632–2644	Alexander pictures the response to his death and makes his will
2645–2647	The death of Alexander
2648–2658	The lament of Alexander's followers, supporters and tributaries
2659–2662	The sorrow of Rhoxane and the ladies of the court
2663–2668	The burial and remembrance of Alexander
2669–2674	Epilogue
2675 P/O	*Explicit*

9. The Spanish text

The problems presented by the task of editing the *Libro de Alexandre* are considerable. This edition, like others produced in recent years, makes the assumption that there existed a single original from which both Manuscripts P and O and the other existing fragments derive, though there seem to have been other intermediate copies; Manuscript P, although relatively late, is believed by most scholars to be the most directly linked to the original. It is accepted that there may have been an initial version from which the "original" in turn derives, given that there seems to be evidence of at least one major passage having been moved to a new context in the poem. Some of the differences between the principal two manuscripts of the poem can be explained by simple errors and omissions, but others derive from the extensive process of modernisation and reworking of details of the text systematically carried out by each copyist, not least in introducing regional linguistic features.[35] In this sense, we are well aware of the limitations implicit in an approach which seeks to work towards (though clearly with no pretence to achieving) a lost original, given that we are providing a reconstructed text without including details of the variants which have been rejected. Our approach in this volume has inevitably been conditioned by limitations of space. It must also be pointed out that this text is based principally on the semi-paleographic edition of Raymond Willis. Comparison with recent critical editions has also been of great value, particularly in the case of the authoritative and extensively documented text produced by Juan Casas Rigall, and the transcriptions of the manuscripts and fragments produced

---

[35] Casas Rigall, ed. (2007, 114), drawing on Canfora (2002), suggests that, in view of the extent to which the copyist introduces elements of his own idiolect, culture and aesthetics, we must view him as a second author.

by the same scholar have also been consulted alongside those of Willis. Our edition cannot lay claim to novelty of approach or to offer any important new insights, but we hope that it will be clear, accurate and accessible for the reader.

As was indicated in Section 1 above, the principle of metrical regularity is fundamental to the form of the *Libro de Alexandre*, each line being divided into two hemistichs of seven syllables with an accent invariably falling on the sixth syllable: as is the rule in all Spanish verse, this final accent will always be seen to be followed by one syllable, so that, at the end of a hemistich *figura* will count as three syllables, *catar* as three and *Júpiter* as two. In accordance with the principle now generally agreed, synalepha (the merging of two vowels) is considered generally unacceptable, but the use of apocopation (shortening of a word by removal of a vowel, most commonly an *e*) is viewed as a frequent practice of our poet and adjustments as from *puede* to *pued'* and from *como* to *com'* are quite commonly made. In many cases it is possible, by reconciling the readings of the two manuscripts, to arrive at a version which is metrically regular, but it is accepted that some measure of flexibility – and of irregularity – is inevitable.

It should also be borne in mind that the scansion of individual words can vary so as to alter their syllabic value. There is considerable flexibility in the use of diaresis. Thus, for example, *traidores* can be read as containing three syllables and *traïdores* as consisting of four. A very common case occurs with *rëy*, used as a word of two syllables, and *rey*, pronounced as just one syllable. On occasions a usual diphthong gives way to hiatus, with *bueno* (two syllables) becoming *büeno* (three syllables). There is also the possibility for variation in stress, for example of the past tense, giving (more normally) *avié* as two syllables or *avie* as three, *vio* as one syllable or *vío* as two. Such flexibility is particularly the case with proper names: *Greçia* can be pronounced as two syllables or *Greçïa* as three, *Diomedes* as three syllables or *Dïomedes* as four; whilst *Menalao* can alternate with *Menálao* and it seems to be the case that *Nicanor* can be stressed on any one of its three syllables (see, for example, Casas Rigall, ed. 2007, 51).

Rhyme can also on occasion provide assistance in establishing the text. It is almost always (though not invariably) consonantal. Although the principle generally followed by the poet is that a rhyme word should not be repeated within a stanza unless with a change of meaning, this does not seem to have been invariably followed. As a general rule, the same rhyme scheme should not be used in two successive stanzas, though here too there is some flexibility.

Introduction 71

It is accepted that spelling will be marked by some inconsistency. Thus, for example, in the use of *b* and *v* and likewise *j* and *g*, our practice is to follow the usage in the manuscripts, rather than seeking regularity or to approach modern Spanish usage. With regard to the union or separation of words, we have been inclined to preserve the practice of the manuscripts rather than to adopt modern practice. Accentuation follows modern principles, but accents have been preserved on verb forms (*rogóles*, *alçóla*) when the addition of a pronoun would normally make them redundant. The elision of a vowel or apocopation has been marked by an apostrophe.

The numbering of the stanzas corresponds to the composite numbering in Willis' 1934 edition.

10. The translation

"A very pretty poem, Mr. Pope, but you must not call it Homer."

(Richard Bentley on Pope's translation of the *Iliad*,
quoted in Johnson's *Life of Pope*)

The problems of translation, and especially with translation of poetry, are widely known, and amidst the feeling that an original piece cannot survive the process wholly intact, the translator's task can seem a thankless one. Certainly, there can never be a substitute for reading any text in its original – but the act of translation is far from being without importance. Rather than as something that sets an original piece in chains, translation's force is one of liberation. What is important is not that, inevitably, it might not do all that its original does, but that it can unlock treasure-troves that are barred by language: it is to be celebrated that those without Latin can read the *Aeneid* as well as they can, before the whispers that are denied them should be bemoaned. Even for those who know the original language, a translation can open their eyes to aspects of an original text to which they had previously been blind. A perfect translation may be impossible, but the imperfect ones that we have can be of value indeed.

As we consider just what a translator does, perhaps the most obvious concern is to convey the meaning and sense of the original. To stray too far from the path that is claimed to be followed brings the danger that whatever other merits the new words may have, what they make up seems to be less a translation, more an original work, simply written on a similar theme. And yet a slavishly literal rendering that does not concern itself with the felicities of the language it is written in will not do either: it is the translator's task to find balance, to render the thoughts and words of the original author in a manner that is fitting to the language in which the translator writes. This balancing act lies at the heart of translation.

Still, though, this is not enough. There is more to a text than its meaning, and more to the author's art than conveying it. The style that the author writes in, the form that is used, the colouring that is the product of every individual choice of expression, combine to help form the reaction, the feeling that a work arouses in its reader. We do not read in a dispassionate search for meaning: literature awakens us, arouses us, and causes us to feel, and that is its greatest joy. It is the translator's hardest duty to try and awaken this feeling in the reader of the translation, too, but it is also the most exciting, and essential to this labour. The most faithful and valuable translation, it seems, is one which lets the author's own voice be heard.

This in turn throws light on the translator's practice. In order to allow a new audience to hear an alien author speak, the translator's own hearing must first be acute. To create a translation as faithful as possible to the original work, in this sense that goes beyond the literal, the translator must first be a practised reader, alert to nuance and tone, to stylistic features, to the fundamental nature of the work that the original author wrote: as far as possible, to all the possibilities that it may contain. It is important to be mindful of the feelings it arouses and listen for the voice of the author. In this, then, we see the task of the translator: to become immersed in the original, and then allow its author's own voice to be heard, by a new audience.

Mindful of this, we turn to some aspects of our present text which merit particular attention. Firstly, we have already seen (Sections 2 and 6, above) that not only is this a poem, written in verse, but that it is probably the earliest example of this poetic form, the *cuaderna vía*: it is poetry, and a new form of poetry. The regular rhythm of the Spanish gives it a sense of flow, and helps the poet to build a sense of momentum to keep the reader moving steadily through the poem, not something to be underestimated in a poem of this size. We have not attempted to set our translation in any English metre (giving it, amongst other things, a false air of familiarity, which the first readers of the original would not have felt), but our translation is line-by-line, and we hope that readers will find within these lines a sense of cadence to draw them through the English as the counted syllables do for one with eyes on the Spanish. It has seemed most fitting to try to ensure that each stanza as a whole, rather than just each line unto itself, has this sense of rhythm and flow, for so it seems, broadly, in the Spanish: that lines within a stanza are more closely tied to each other than one stanza is to the next. To this end, we have tried to avoid the disruption of over-long or excessively short lines, aiming for regularity in length, especially within each stanza, and a regular beat from the natural stresses in each line, in an effort to create an effect similar to that of the Spanish. We hope that a further benefit of this line-by-line approach may be that the right-hand pages might be of more ready assistance for one seeking to read those on the left.

The poet's range of vocabulary is wide, but if anything it is his range of expression that is most striking. He has an enormous wealth of imagery and colourful expression to draw on (see Section 6, above), and the unexpectedly vivid images provide moments of light relief in a poem that must inevitably contain lengthy passages of war; these touches are one of its greatest, and simplest, delights. These images seem neither to have been nor become standard in their use: they would strike the reader of the original as surprising, and so we have sought to preserve this imagery in the English, whilst seeking that the meaning of the phrase remains clear, and refrained from explanatory paraphrase: their unexpectedness is something to be enjoyed. Stanza 2023cd gives us this example:

> but for all the loss that they had suffered, the Greek king
> cared as much for that as for a horsefly.

In the midst of battle, the image brings a smile: the image itself is as vital as its meaning to the impression the poem gives, and to detract from it would be to steal from the reader of the translation.

The medievalisation that the poet engages in (see Section 6, above) demands similar treatment. We consider as an example the way the poet sometimes presents single combat on a battlefield in terms of a jousting match. An image so unexpected – not to mention improbable – as this serves to ground the tale very firmly in the poet's own time, despite its protagonists being historical figures long since dead. This is central to the poet's eventual aim: to use the life of Alexander as he presents it as something from which to draw examples about life and proper conduct that are relevant to the present day. It would be unwise not to reflect the medieval colouring, then, and it would undermine the poet. To keep to our example of the joust for illustration: the poet sometimes uses "torneo" to mean combat or battle, but the word could also be used to describe a jousting tournament. Thus a translation must be found that could describe battle but must not be too strongly associated with it, and could be used of a joust, too: we render it "contest".

This is not the place for a lengthy discussion of the poet's use of formal rhetorical features (see Section 6, above, especially pp. 38–39 for examples in the translation). They are an important part of the nature of the work as it is conceived, and the reader is referred to the earlier discussion for a more detailed look at some of the features which we have sought to render. We add only a further example here, to illustrate our desire to preserve these features in the translation:

> la su grant voluntad   non se li amansava;
> mas de día en día   más se encorajava.
>
> (and that great desire that he felt grew no gentler,
> but day by day did his anger grow crueller.)
>
> (1594cd)

The Spanish poet ends his lines with "amansava" and "encorajava" , the construction of his lines serving to emphasise this antithesis through the parallel placement of these words. We have sought to render this in the translation by the similar placing of the contrasting "gentler" and "crueller", to give a similar vividness to that which the Spanish poet achieves, preserving, again, as much as we are able, the effect that the original creates.

On the other hand, the use of epic epithets in the poem seems often more a case of convenience than contrivance, a tool that the poet uses to aid him in his versification rather than a feature of dramatic importance; see, further, Michael's speculation, quoted in Section 6, above, that we see in the *Libro de Alexandre* nothing more than the "dead remains" of a previously flourishing convention. It is prudent to observe, too, that the poet freely interchanges, for example, "en duro punto nado" (362d) and "en mala ora nados" (1627d) as apparent equivalents. Given that the poet allows himself such freedom in these phrases, it has not seemed appropriate to render each formula exclusively by the same translation.

Lastly, the matter of Latin. Occasionally within the Spanish text there are inserted Latin phrases, but we have felt it most appropriate to translate these, too. Latin would have been far more widely understood then than now, whereas to insert "cede majori" into a modern English translation is unlikely to be read without stumble or confusion, in contrast to the original. Thus it seems truest to the effect of the original to translate. We have made exceptions in such cases as the *benedicite* and *Paternoster*, as these are names of prayers rather than the words spoken, and for stanza 1801, entirely of Latin, the inscription of Darius' tomb. That the original is in Latin not Spanish lends the tomb an important sense of stature that it would be wrong to lose; the stanza is translated in a note to preserve the meaning.

It seems fitting to turn to Saint Isidore as we close, as our poet himself will during his poem. Isidore etymologises *interpres*, "translator", as one who stands *inter partes*, "between the two sides". We have sought to create something acceptable and not without pleasure as an English rendering, while remaining above all loyal to the Spanish poem and the feelings it arouses in the reader of the original. It must be the ideal goal of the translator to stand between these two sides and allow the original author to speak across the divide: we have endeavoured to write something we may call the *Libro de Alexandre*. It is a task that cannot be achieved with completeness, but we hope that that failure does not deprive the reader of too much.

The asterisks in the text relate to the notes on pp. 680 ff.

SELECT BIBLIOGRAPHY

1. Editions

Cañas Murillo, Jesús, ed., 1988. *Libro de Alexandre* (Madrid: Cátedra)
Casas Rigall, Juan, ed., 2007. *Libro de Alexandre* (Madrid: Castalia)
Casas Rigall, Juan, ed., 2007b. Transcripciones semipaleográficas de los manuscritos O y P, y de los principales fragmentos del *Libro de Alexandre* [online at http://web.usc.es/~fejcr/Libro_Alexandre.html]
Marcos Marín, Francisco, ed., 1987. *Libro de Alexandre* (Madrid: Alianza Editorial)
Nelson, Dana A., ed., 1979. *Gonzalo de Berceo. El Libro de Alixandre* (Madrid:

Gredos)
Willis, Raymond S., ed., 1934 (repr.1965). *El Libro de Alexandre. Texts of the Paris and the Madrid Manuscripts* (Princeton: Princeton University Press)
There is also a modern Spanish version:
Catena, Elena, ed., 1985. *Libro de Alejandro* (Madrid: Castalia, *Odres Nuevos*)

2. Medieval Latin and classical texts in translation, and related reference works

Hammond, M., trans., 1987. *Homer: The Iliad* (London: Penguin)
Rieu, E.V., trans., Rieu, D.C.H., rev., 2003. *Homer: The Odyssey* (London: Penguin)
West, D., trans., 2003. *Virgil: The Aeneid* (London: Penguin)
De Sélincourt, A., trans., Marincola, J.M., rev., 2003. *Herodotus: The Histories* (London: Penguin)
Melville, A.D., trans., 1998. *Ovid: Metamorphoses* (Oxford: World's Classics)
Rackham, H., trans., 1942. *Pliny, Natural History, II* (Loeb Classical Library) (Cambridge: Harvard University Press)
Townsend, David, trans., 2007. *The Alexandreis of Walter of Châtillon: A Twelfth-Century Epic* (Toronto: Broadview Press)
Hornblower, S. and Spawforth, A., eds, 2003. *Oxford Classical Dictionary* 3rd ed. rev. (Oxford: Oxford University Press)

3. Alexander the Great in history and in literary tradition

Bosworth, A. Brian, 1993. *Conquest and Empire: The Reign of Alexander the Great* (Cambridge: Cambridge University Press)
Cartledge, Paul, 2004. *Alexander the Great* (Woodstock and New York: Macmillan)
Cary, George, ed. D.J.A. Ross, 1956. *The Medieval Alexander* (Cambridge: Cambridge University Press)
Fildes, Alan and Joann Fletcher, 2004. *Alexander the Great: Son of the Gods* (London: Duncan Baird)
Finkel, I.L. and M.J Seymour, eds. 2008. *Babylon: Myth and Reality* (London: The British Museum Press)
Green, Peter, 1991. *Alexander of Macedon, 356–323 B.C.: A Historical Biography* (Berkeley: University of California Press)
Green, Peter, 2007. *Alexander the Great and the Hellenistic Age: A Short History* (London: Weidenfeld and Nicolson)

Heckel, Waldemar, 2006. *Who's Who in the Age of Alexander the Great* (Oxford: Blackwell)
Lane Fox, Robin, 2004. *Alexander the Great* (London and New York: Penguin)
Lida de Malkiel, Mª Rosa, 1962a. "La leyenda de Alejandro en la literatura medieval", *Romance Philology*, 15, 3, 311–318
Lida de Malkiel, Mª Rosa, 1962b. "Datos para la leyenda de Alejandro en la Edad Media castellana", *Romance Philology*, 15, 4, 412–423
Mossé, Claude, 2001. *Alexander: Destiny and Myth* (Edinburgh: Edinburgh University Press)
Stoneman, Richard, trans., 1991. *The Greek Alexander Romance* (London: Penguin)
Stoneman, Richard, trans., 1994. *Legends of Alexander the Great* (London: Orion)
Stoneman, Richard, 2008. *Alexander the Great: A Life in Legend* (New Haven and London: Yale University Press)
Vinaver, Eugène, 1971. *The Rise of Romance* (Oxford: University Press)

4. The historical and intellectual background to the composition of the Libro de Alexandre

Abulafia, David, 1988. *Frederick II: A Medieval Emperor* (London: Allen Lane, The Penguin Press)
Álvarez Borge, Ignacio, 2003. *Historia de España 3er milenio: La plena edad media. Siglos XII–XIII* (Madrid: Editorial Síntesis)
Beceiro Pita, Isabel, 2007. *Libros, lectores y bibliotecas en la España medieval* (Murcia: Nausícaä)
Bloomfield, Morton W., 1952. *The Seven Deadly Sins* (East Lansing, Michigan: Michigan State College Press)
Cantera Montenegro, Enrique, 2006. "Cristianos y judíos en la meseta norte castellana: la fractura del siglo XIII", in Yolanda Moreno Koch and Ricardo Izquierdo Benito, eds. *Del pasado judío en los reinos medievales hispánicos* (Cuenca: Ediciones de la Universidad de Castilla-La Mancha)
Costa Gomes, Rita, 2003. *The Making of a Court Society: Kings and Nobles in Late Medieval Portugal* (Cambridge: Cambridge University Press)
Curtius, Ernst, trans. Willard R. Trask, 1953, (repr. 1991). *European Literature and the Latin Middle Ages* (Princeton: Princeton University Press)
Faulhaber, Charles, 1972. *Latin Rhetorical Theory in Thirteenth and Fourteenth Century Castile* (Berkeley and Los Angeles: University of California Press)
González Jiménez, Manuel, 2004. *Alfonso X el Sabio* (Barcelona: Ariel)
Harvey, P.D.A., 1991. *Medieval Maps* (London: British Library)
Linehan, Peter, 1971. *The Spanish Church and the Papacy* (Cambridge: Cambridge

University Press)
Linehan, Peter, 2008. *Spain, 1157–1300: A Partible Inheritance* (Oxford: Blackwell)
Lomax, Derek W., 1969. "The Lateran Reforms and Spanish Literature", *Iberoromania*, I, 299–313.
Mâle, Emile, 1972. *The Gothic Image: Religious Art in the France of the Thirteenth Century* (New York, Evanston, San Francisco, London: Harper and Row: Icon)
Murphy, James, 1974. *Rhetoric in the Middle Ages* (Berkeley and Los Angeles: University of California Press)
Power, Daniel, ed., 2006. *The Short Oxford History of Europe: The Central Middle Ages* (Oxford: Oxford University Press)
Reilly, Bernard F., 1993. *The Medieval Spains* (Cambridge: Cambridge University Press)
Rodríguez López, Ana, 1994. *La consolidación territorial de la monarquía feudal castellana: expansión y fronteras durante el reinado de Fernando III*, Biblioteca de Historia, 27 (Madrid: CSIC)
Ridder-Symoens, Hilde de, ed., 1992. *A History of the Universities in Europe. I. Universities in the Middle Ages* (Cambridge: Cambridge University Press)
Vaca de Osma, José Antonio, 2004. *Grandes reyes españoles de la Edad Media* (Madrid: Espasa Calpe)
Valdeón Baruque, Julio, 2006. "Los judíos en la España medieval: de la aceptación al rechazo", in Yolanda Moreno Koch and Ricardo Izquierdo Benito, eds, *Del pasado judío en los reinos medievales hispánicos* (Cuenca: Ediciones de la Universidad de Castilla-La Mancha)
Wright, Roger, 2000. "The Assertion of Ibero-Romance", *Forum for Modern Language Studies*, xxxvi, 3, 230–240

5. Books and articles on the Libro de Alexandre *and related texts*

Alvar, Carlos, 1996. "Consideraciones a propósito de una cronología temprana del *Libro de Alexandre*", in A. Menéndez and V. Roncero, eds, *Nunca fue pena mayor. Estudios de literatura española en homenaje a Brian Dutton* (Cuenca: Universidad de Castilla-La Mancha), 35–44
Arizaleta, Amaia, 1993. "El imaginario infernal del autor del *Libro de Alexandre*", *Atalaya*, 4, 69–92
Arizaleta, Amaia, 1999. *La translation d'Alexandre. Recherches sur les structures et les significations du* Libro de Alexandre (Paris: Klincksieck)
Arizaleta, Amaia, 2000. "Alexandre en su *Libro*", *La Corónica*, 28, 2, 3–20
Alarcos Llorach, Emilio, 1948. *Investigaciones sobre el* Libro de Alexandre

Select Bibliography 79

(Madrid: *Revista de Filología Española*, anejo 45)

Alarcos Llorach, Emilio, 1981. "¿Berceo, autor del *Alexandre*?", in C. García Turza, ed., *Actas de las III Jornadas de Estudios Berceanos* (Logroño: Instituto de Estudios Riojanos), 11–18

Baldwin, Spurgeon, 1996. "Thunder and Lightning: Violence in Walter of Châtillon's *Alexandreis* and the *Libro de Alexandre*", in A. Menéndez and V. Roncero, eds, *Nunca fue pena mayor. Estudios de literatura española en homenaje a Brian Dutton* (Cuenca: Universidad de Castilla-La Mancha), 77–106

Bañeza Román, Celso, 1994. *Las fuentes bíblicas, patrísticas y judaicas* del Libro de Alexandre (Las Palmas: El Autor)

Bly, Peter A. and Alan Deyermond 1972. "The Use of Figura in the *Libro de Alexandre*", *The Journal of Medieval and Renaissance Studies*, 2, 2, 151–181

Brownlee, Marina, 2000. "Romance at the crossroads: medieval Spanish paradigms and Cervantine revisions" in Roberta L. Krueger, *The Cambridge Companion to Medieval Romance* (Cambridge: Cambridge University Press) 253–266

Canfora, Luciano 2002. *Il copista come autore* (Palermo: Sellerio)

Cañas Murillo, Jesús 1995. "Didactismo y composición en el *Libro de Alexandre*", *Anuario de Estudios Filológicos*, 18, 65–79

Casas Rigall, Juan, 2005. "La *abbreviatio* y sus funciones poéticas en el *Libro de Alexandre*", *Troianalexandrina*, 5, 63–96

Deyermond, Alan, 1965. "Mester es sen peccado," *Romanische Forschungen*, 77, 1–2, 111–116

Deyermond, Alan, 1979. "Berceo y la poesía del siglo XIII", in F. Rico, ed., *Historia y crítica de la literatura española: Vol. 1, Edad Media*, 127–40

Deyermond, Alan, 2002. "El Alejandro medieval, el Ulíses de Dante y la búsqueda de Las Antípodas", in R. Beltrán, ed., *Maravillas, peregrinaciones y utopías. Literatura de viajes en el mundo románico* (Valencia: Universitat de Valencia)

Dutton, Brian, 1960. "The Profession of Gonzalo de Berceo and the Paris Manuscript of the *Libro de Alexandre*", *Bulletin of Hispanic Studies*, 37, 137–145

Dutton, Brian, 1971. "A Further Note on the *Alexandre* Enigma", *Bulletin of Hispanic Studies*, 48, 298–300

Dutton, Brian, 1973. "French Influences in the Spanish *Mester de Clerecía*", in B. Dutton, J.W. Hassell and J.E. Keller, eds, *Medieval Studies in Honor of Robert White Linker* (Valencia: Castalia), 79–93

Dutton, Brian, 1978. *Gonzalo de Berceo, Obras completas IV: La vida de Santo Domingo de Silos* (London: Tamesis)

Espósito, Anthony: "(Re)covering the Chiasmus: Restoring the *Libro(s) de Alexandre*", *Hispanic Review*, 62, 3 (1994), 349–362

Fraker, Charles, 1988. "The Role of Rhetoric in the Construction of the *Libro de Alexandre*", *Bulletin of Hispanic Studies*, 55, 4, 353–368

Fraker, Charles, 1993. *The Libro de Alexandre: Medieval Epic and Silver Latin* (Chapel Hill: University of North Carolina)

Franchini, Enzo, 1997. "El IV Concilio de Letrán, la apócope extrema y la fecha de composición del *Libro de Alexandre*", *La Corónica*, 25, 2, 31–74

García, Michel, 1982. "La Strophe du *cuaderna vía* comme élément de structuration du discours", *Cahiers de Linguistique Hispanique Médiévale*, 7 bis (205–219)

García de Fuentes, Olegario, 1986. *El latín bíblico y el español medieval hasta el 1300. II. El Libro de Alexandre* (Logroño: Instituto de Estudios Riojanos)

García Gascón, Eugenio, 1989. "Los manuscritos P y O del *Libro de Alexandre* y la fecha de composición del original", *Revista de Literatura Medieval*, 1, 31–39

Goldberg, Harriet, 1979–80. "The Voice of the Author in the Works of Gonzalo de Berceo and in the *Libro de Alexandre* and the *Poema de Fernán González*", *La Corónica*, 8, 100–112

Grande Quejigo, Francisco Javier, 1997. "Huellas textuales indirectas sobre la difusión oral de la literatura en el *Libro de Alexandre*", *Anuario de Estudios Filológicos*, 20, 169–90

Grande Quejigo, Francisco Javier, 1998. "Huellas textuales indirectas sobre la difusión escrita de la literatura en el *Libro de Alexandre*", *Anuario de Estudios Filológicos*, 21, 119–39

Hernando Pérez, José, 1992. *Hispano Diego García – escritor y poeta medieval – y el* Libro de Alexandre (Burgos: El Autor)

Hilty, Gerold, 1997. "Fecha y autor del Libro de Alexandre", in J.M. Lucía Megías, ed. *Actas del VI Congreso Internacional de la Asociación Hispánica de Literatura Medieval* (Alcalá de Henares: Publicaciones de la Universidad de Alcalá)

Lacarra, Mª Eugenia, 1980. *El Poema de Mio Cid: realidad histórica e ideología* (Madrid: José Porrúa Turanzas)

Lacarra, Mª Jesús, 1999. "Los vicios capitales en el arrabal del Infierno: *Libro de Alexandre*, 2345–2411", *La Corónica*, 28, 1, 71–81

Marcos Marín, Francisco, 1996. "Establecimiento de la fecha del *Libro de Alexandre*", *Zeitschrift für romanische Philologie*, 112, 3, 424–437

Michael, Ian, 1960. "Interpretation of the *Libro de Alexandre*: The Author's Attitude towards his Hero's Death", *Bulletin of Hispanic Studies*, 37, 205–14

Michael, Ian, 1961. "A Comparison of the Use of Epic Epithets in the *Poema de Mio Cid* and the *Libro de Alexandre*", *Bulletin of Hispanic Studies*, 38, 1, 32–41

Michael, Ian, 1965. "The Description of Hell in the Spanish *Libro de Alexandre*", in *Medieval Miscellany presented to Eugène Vinaver* (Manchester: Manchester University Press), 220–229

Michael, Ian, 1970. *The Treatment of Classical Material in the* Libro de Alexandre (Manchester: Manchester University Press)

Michael, Ian, 1974. *Alexander's Flying Machine: The History of a Legend* (Southampton: University of Southampton)

Michael, Ian, 1982. "Typological Problems in Medieval Alexander Literature: The Enclosure of Gog and Magog", in Claire Isoz, Peter Noble and Lucie Polak, eds, *The Medieval Alexander Legend and Romance Epic. Essays in Honour of David J.A. Ross* (New York: Kraus International Publications)

Michael, Ian, 1986. "The *Alexandre* 'enigma': A Solution", in I. Michael and R.A. Cardwell, eds, *Medieval and Renaissance Studies in Honour of Robert Brian Tate* (Oxford: The Dolphin Book), 109–121

Michael, Ian, 1996. "*De situ Indiae*: las maravillas de Oriente en la literatura medieval española", in A. Menéndez and V. Roncero, eds, *Nunca fue pena mayor. Estudios de literatura española en homenaje a Brian Dutton* (Cuenca: Universidad de Castilla-La Mancha), 35–44

Michael, Ian, 1997. "Automata in the *Alexandre*: Pneumatic Birds in Porus's Palace", in I. Macpherson and R. Penny, eds, *The Medieval Mind: Hispanic Studies in Honour of Alan Deyermond* (London, Tamesis), 275–288

Michael, Ian, 2004. "Fantasía *versus* maravilla en el *Libro de Alexandre* y otros textos medievales", in Nicasio Salvador Miguel, Santiago López Ríos y Esther Borrego Gutiérrez, eds, *Fantasía y literatura en la Edad Media y los Siglos de Oro* (Madrid: Iberoamericana), 283–298

Millares Carlo, Agustín, 1950. *Literatura española hasta fines del siglo XV* (Mexico: Antigua Librería Robredo)

Montoya Martínez, Jesús, 1993. *La norma retórica en tiempos de Alfonso X. Estudio y antología de textos* (Las Gabias: Adhara)

Montoya Martínez, Jesús, 2004. "La retórica medieval en España. Breves *excursus* de la presencia de la teoría retórica en el siglo XIII español a través de testimonios de su literatura", in J.A. Sánchez Marín y Mª N. Muñoz Martín, eds, *Retórica, poética y géneros literarios* (Granada: Editorial Universidad de Granada)

Morel-Fatio, Alfred, 1875. "Recherches sur le texte et les sources du *Libro de Alexandre*", *Romania* 4, 7–90

Nelson, Dana A., 1968. "*El Libro de Alexandre*: A Reorientation", *Studies in Philology*, 65, 723–752

Nelson, Dana A., 1972a. "The Domain of Old Spanish *–er* and *–ir* Verbs: a Clue to the Provenience of the *Alexandre*", *Romance Philology*, 26, 2, 265–303

Nelson, Dana A., 1972b. "Syncopation in *El Libro de Alexandre*", *Publications of the Modern Language Association of America*, 27, 5, 1023–1038

Nelson, Dana A., 1991. *Gonzalo de Berceo y el* Alixandre: *vindicación de un estilo*

(Madison: Hispanic Seminar of Medieval Studies)

Nelson, Dana A., 1999. "El *Libro de Alixandre* y Gonzalo de Berceo: un problema filológico", *La Corónica*, 28, 1, 93–136

Nelson, Dana A., 2001. "El *Libro de Alixandre*: notas al margen de tres ediciones", *Boletín de la Real Academia Española*, 81, 283, 321–377

Nelson, Dana A., 2003. "El *Libro de Alixandre*: en marcha hacia el original", *Revista de Filología Española*, 83, 1–2, 63–92

Rico, Francisco, 1985. "La clerecía del mester", *Hispanic Review*, 53, 1–23 and 125–150

Rico, Francisco, 1986. *El pequeño mundo del hombre. Varia fortuna de una idea en la cultura española* (Madrid: Alianza)

Ross, David J.A., 1967. "Alexander Iconography in Spain: *El Libro de Alexandre*", *Scriptorium*, 21, 83–86

Ross, David J.A., 1988 (first published in 1967). *Alexander Historiatus. A Guide to Medieval Illustrated Alexander Literature* (Frankfurt am Main: Athenäum)

Sas, Louis F., 1976. *Vocabulario del* Libro de Alexandre (Madrid: Real Academia Española, Anejos del BRAE, 34)

Such, Peter, 1978. *The Origins and Use of School Rhetoric in the* Libro de Alexandre (unpublished thesis, University of Cambridge)

Such, Peter and John Hodgkinson, trans., 1987. *The Poem of My Cid* (Warminster: Aris and Phillips)

Uría Maqua, Isabel, 1981. "Sobre la unidad del mester de clerecía del siglo XIII. Hacia un replanteamiento de la cuestión", *Actas de las III Jornadas de Estudios Berceanos* (Logroño: Instituto de Estudios Riojanos), 179–188

Uría Maqua, Isabel, 1986. "Gonzalo de Berceo y el mester de clerecía en la nueva perspectiva de la crítica", *Berceo*, 110–111, 7–20

Uría Maqua, Isabel, 1987. "El *Libro de Alexandre* y la Universidad de Palencia", in *Actas del I Congreso de Historia de Palencia* (Palencia: Diputación Provincial), vol IV, 431–442

Uría Maqua, Isabel, coord., 1992. *Gonzalo de Berceo: Obra completa* (Madrid: Espasa Calpe)

Uría Maqua, Isabel, 1996. "La soberbia de Alejandro en el poema castellano y sus implicaciones ideológicas", *Anuario de Estudios Filológicos*, 19, 513–528

Uría Maqua, Isabel, 2000. *Panorama crítico del mester de clerecía* (Madrid: Castalia)

Uría Maqua, Isabel, 2001. "Ritmo, prosodia y sintaxis en la poética del mester de clerecía", *Revista de Poética Medieval*, 7, 111–130

Ware, Niall J., 1965. "The Date of Composition of the *Libro de Alexandre*: A Re-

BOOK OF ALEXANDER

(LIBRO DE ALEXANDRE)

1 Señores, si quisiéredes   mi serviçio prender,
   querríavos de grado   servir de mi mester.
   Deve de lo que sabe   ome largo seer;
   si non, podrié en culpa   e en riebto caer.

2 Mester traigo fermoso,   non es de joglaría,
   mester es sin pecado,   ca es de clereçía:
   fablar curso rimado   por la quaderna vía,
   a sílabas contadas,   ca es grant maestría.

3 Qui oír lo quisiere,   a todo mi creer,
   avrá de mí solaz,   en cabo grant plazer;
   aprendrá buenas gestas   que sepa retraer;
   averlo han por ello   muchos a coñoçer.

4 Non vos quiero grant prólogo   nin grandes nuevas fer;
   luego a la materia   me vos quiero coger;
   el Crïador nos dexe   bien apresos seer;
   si en algo pecáremos,   Él nos deñe valer.

5 Quiero leer un livro   d'un rey noble, pagano
   que fue de grant esfuerço,   de coraçón loçano:
   conquiso tod' el mundo,   metiólo so su mano.
   Ternéme si lo cumplo   non por mal escrivano.

6 El prínçep' Alexandre,   que fue rëy de Greçia,
   que fue franc' e ardit   e de grant sabïençia,
   vençió Poro e Dario,   dos reys de grant potençia;
   nunca con ávol ome   ovo su atenençia.

7 El infant' Alexandre,   luego en su niñez,
   empeçó a mostrar   que serié de grant prez;
   nunca quiso mamar   lech' de muger rafez
   si non fues' de linage   o de grant gentilez'.

8 Grandes signos contieron   quand' est' infant naçió:
   el aire fue cambiado,   el sol escureçió;
   tod' el mar fue irado,   la tierra tremeçió;
   por poco que el mundo   todo non pereçió.

9 Otros signos contieron   que son más generales:
   cayeron de las nuves   unas piedras puñales.
   Aún veyeron otros   mayores o atales:
   lidiaron un dia todo   dos águilas cabdales.

Book of Alexander

1 My lords, should you wish to engage my services,
   I would most readily serve you with my craft;
   a man must be generous with what he knows
   – if not, he might fall into blame and criticism.

2 The craft I bring is refined, it is no minstrel's work,
   a craft without fault, born of the clergy's learning:*
   to compose rhyming verse in the four-line form,
   with counted syllables – an act of great mastery.

3 Whoever wants to listen, I believe with all my heart,
   will gain from me delight and finally great contentment.
   He will learn of fine deeds of which he may tell
   and through it he will come to be known by many.

4 I wish not to offer you a great prologue or introduction,
   but to bring you without delay to my subject.
   May the Creator give us the benefit of great learning;
   if in some way we err, may He grant us His aid.

5 I want to read a book about a worthy pagan king,*
   about a great-hearted man of highest valour.
   He conquered the whole world and held it in his grip.
   If I succeed, I shall hold myself no mean writer.

6 Prince Alexander, who was the king of Greece,
   who was noble and courageous and of great wisdom,
   defeated Porus and Darius, two kings of great power;*
   never did he have friendship with any ignoble man.

7 The young Prince Alexander, right from his childhood,
   began to show that he would be of great distinction.
   Never would he suck the milk of any ordinary woman
   unless she were of lineage or great nobility.

8 Great prodigies occurred when this child was born:*
   the winds were turned and the sun grew dark.
   All the sea was angry and the earth trembled;
   the whole world stood on the brink of doom.

9 Other prodigies occurred that are better known:
   fists formed in rock did fall from the clouds.
   Others, too, were seen, as great or greater still:
   two royal eagles spent a whole day in duel.

10   En tierras de Egipto   – en letras fue trobado –
     fabló un corderuelo   que era el dia nado;
     parió una gallina   un culebro irado.
     Era por Alexandre   tod' esto demostrado.

11   Aún avino al   en el su naçimiento:
     fijos de altos condes   naçieron más de çiento;
     fueron pora servirle   todos de buen taliento.
     En escripto yaz' esto,   ¡sepades que non miento!

12   En mañas de grant preçio   fue luego entendiendo;
     esfuerço e franqueza   fue luego decogiendo.
     Íval' con la edat   el coraçón creçiendo;
     aún abés fablava,   ya lo ivan temiendo.

13   Los unos con los otros   fablavan entre dientes:
     "Est' niño conquerrá   las indïanas gentes."
     Felipo e Olimpias,   que eran sus parientes,
     avián grant alegría,   metién en esto mientes.

14   El infant', maguer niño,   avié grant coraçón,
     yazié en cuerpo chico   braveza de león.
     Mas destajar vos quiero   de la su crïazón
     ca convien' que passemos   a la mayor razón.

15   A cab' de pocos años   el infant' fue crïado.
     Nunca ome non vío   moço tan arrabado.
     Ya cobdiçiaba armas   e conquerir regnado.
     Semejava Hercules,   tant' era esforçado.

16   El padre, de siet' años,   metióle a leer.
     Diol' maestros honrados,   de sen e de saber,
     los que mejores pudo   en Greçia escoger,
     quel' sopiessen en todas   las artes emponer.

17   Aprendié de las artes   cada día liçión.
     De todas cada día   fazié disputaçión.
     Tant' aviá buen engeño   e sotil coraçón
     que vençió los maestros   a poca de sazón.

18   Nada non olvidava   de quanto que oyé.
     Non le cayé de mano   de quanto que veyé.
     Si más le enseñassen,   él más aprenderié.
     ¡Sabet que en las pajas   el cüer non tenié!

10 In the land of Egypt – as the writings testify –
    a lamb that was born that day began to speak,
    and a hen brought forth an angry serpent;
    all of this was borne out in Alexander.

11 Still more took place at the time of his birth:
    high-ranking counts sired over a hundred sons,
    who were all to serve him, and all with great pleasure
    – this lies in writing, know that I do not deceive you.

12 He quickly learned how to perform deeds of great renown,
    to take on the qualities of generosity and valour.
    As he grew in years, his heart grew greater.
    Hardly could he speak and already he was feared.

13 In hushed voices people would say to each other:
    "This child will conquer the peoples of India".
    Philip and Olympias, who were his parents,*
    were overjoyed, though it left them deep in thought.

14 The Prince, although a child, was great of heart;
    a lion's spirit lay in his small body;
    but here I want to end talk of his childhood,
    for we should pass on to the greater tale.

15 In just a few years, the prince had come of age;
    no-one had ever seen a boy so keen for war;
    already he longed to carry arms and conquer kingdoms;
    so great was his spirit, he resembled Hercules.*

16 When he was seven, his father set him to read
    and gave him honorable teachers, intelligent and wise;
    the best he could choose from all of Greece,
    that they might instruct him in all the arts.

17 He studied the arts and attended lessons every day,*
    and in all of them each day he took part in disputations.
    So sharp was his wit and so subtle his mind
    that he soon learned to overcome his masters.

18 He forgot nothing of all that he heard.
    He let slip nothing of all that he saw.
    The more he was taught, the more he would learn.
    His head, I assure you, was not in the clouds.

19   Por su sotil engeño   que tant' apoderava,
     a maestre Netánabo   dezían que semejava,
     e que su fijo era   grant roído andava;
     si lo era o non,   tod' el pueblo pecava.

20   El infant' el roído   nol' pudo encobrir;
     pesól' de coraçón,   non lo pudo sofrir.
     Despeñól' de una torre   ond' ovo a morir.
     "Fijo," dijo el padre,   "¡Dios te dexe bevir!"

21   De los quinz' años aun   los dos le mengüavan;
     en la barva los pelos   entonç' le assomavan.
     Fue asmando las cosas   del siglo cóm' andavan;
     entendió sus avuelos   quál cueïta passavan.

22   Eran los reys de Greçia   fasta essa sazón
     vassallos tributarios   del rey de Babilón;
     avián a dar a Dario   sabida enforçión;
     avién gelo a dar,   que quisiessen o non.

23   El infant' Alexandre,   quando lo fue asmando,
     camiós'le la color,   fues' todo demudando;
     maguer que blanco era,   negro se fue tornando;
     las tres partes del día   bien estido callando.

24   Comiés' todos los labros   con la grant follonía;
     semejaba enfermo   de fiera maletía;
     dizié: "¡Äy mesquino!   ¿Quándo veré el día
     que pueda restaurar   esta sobrançanía?

25   Si el mi buen maestro   non me lo devedar',
     dexaré Eüropa   e passaré la mar;
     iré conquerir Asia   e con Dario lidiar;
     aver m'a, como cuedo,   la mano a besar.

26   Sobre mí non querría   tan grant onta veer
     nin que con mi maestro   me sopiesse perder,
     ca serié fiera honta   e grant mal pareçer
     por el rey Alexandre   a ome obedeçer.

27   Alçides de la cuna,   como solemos leer,
     afogó las serpientes   que lo querién comer;
     e yo ya bien devía   en algo pareçer
     que por fil de Netánabo   non m'ayan a tener."

Book of Alexander

19 For his subtle mind which had so sharp a grasp,
    they said that he resembled Master Nectanebo*
    and a strong rumour spread that he was his son;
    whether he was or not, the whole people was at fault.

20 The prince was unable to silence the rumour.
    It grieved his heart and he could not endure it.
    He hurled Nectanebo from a tower to his death.
    "My son", said his father, "May God grant that you live!"

21 He was still two years short of his fifteenth birthday.
    The hair of his beard was now starting to appear,
    and he began to take note of the events of the world;
    he understood the sufferings his elders underwent.

22 The kings of Greece had been, up until that time,
    tributary vassals of the King of Babylon:*
    They had to give Darius the payment now accustomed,
    and had to give it to him whether willing or no.

23 As Prince Alexander turned this over in his mind,
    his colour changed, his face took on a different hue;
    although he was white, his look gradually blackened;
    for three quarters of a day he said not a word.

24 He scowled and grimaced in his great anger;
    he seemed to be stricken by a savage illness.
    "What wretchedness!" he said. "When will I see the day
    when I may fight back against this arrogance?

25 If my good master does not bar me from doing it,*
    I shall leave Europe behind and cross over the sea,
    and go to conquer Asia and do battle with Darius.
    He will, so I believe, have to kiss my hand in homage.

26 I would not want to see such great shame weigh upon me,
    nor that it should destroy my master and myself,
    for it would be a grave disgrace and great dishonour
    for King Alexander to obey another man.

27 Hercules from his cradle, as we often read,
    strangled the serpents that wanted to eat him,
    and it is right for me to bear him some resemblance,
    that I should not be taken for Nectanebo's son."

28 Contendié el infante en este pensamiento.
    Amolava los dientes como león fambriento;
    tan bien molié el fierro como si fues' sarmiento.
    Sabet que del dormir nol' prendía taliento.

29 Avié en sí el infante atal comparaçión
    como suele aver el chiquiello león
    quando yaz' en la cama e vee la venaçión;
    non la puede prender e bátel' el coraçón.

30 Revolviés' a menudo e retorçiés' los dedos.
    Non podié con la quexa los labros tener quedos.
    Ya andava partiendo las tierras de los medos,
    quemándoles las miesses, cortando los viñedos.

31 El infant' con la quexa seyé descolorido,
    triste e destemprado, de todo sabor exido,
    como si l'oviés' alguno por ventura ferido
    o si algunas malas nuevas oviesse entendido.

32 Maestre Aristótiles, que lo avié crïado,
    seyé en est' comedio en su casa çerrado.
    Avié un silogismo de lógica formado;
    essa noche nin es' dia nunca avié folgado.

33 Más era de medio día, nona podrié seer;
    exió Aristótiles a su criado veer.
    Quis quier' gelo podrié por vista coñoçer
    que veló al cresuelo do vinié de leer.

34 Los ojos tenié blancos e la color mudada,
    los cabellos en tuerto, la maxilla delgada.
    Nos' le tenié la çinta, yuso yazié colgada;
    podrié caer en tierra de poca empuxada.

35 Quando vio al diçiplo seer tan sin color,
    sabet que el maestro ovo muy mal sabor.
    Nunca pesar le vino quel' semejas' peor,
    pero ovo el niño, quandol' vio, grant pavor.

36 Empeçól' el maestro al infant' demandar:
    "Fijo, ¿vos qué oviestes o quién vos fizo pesar?
    Si yo saberlo puedo, non melo podrá lograr.
    Vos non melo devedes a mí esto çelar."

28	The Prince continued to dwell on these thoughts and ground his teeth like a hungry lion, gnawing iron as if it were a vine shoot; he did not, I tell you, have any desire for sleep.
29	The Prince, in his manner, bore such comparison with the way that a lion cub is wont to behave when it lies in its lair and sees its prey: it cannot catch it and its heart beats fast.
30	Often tossing and turning and twisting his fingers, anxious as he was, he could not keep his lips still. He was already raiding the lands of the Medes,* [ANCIENT IRANIANS] burning their harvests and razing their vineyards.
31	Anxious as he was, the Prince became quite pale, sad and out of sorts, and lost all sense of pleasure, as if someone had happened to strike him a blow or he had heard some grim piece of news.
32	Master Aristotle, who had educated him, was, at that time, shut away in his home; he had formed a syllogism using his logic* and had taken no rest on that night or that day.
33	It was after midday, perhaps the hour of None,* when Aristotle set out to see his pupil; anyone could tell, on account of his appearance, that he had been reading, sat up by an oil lamp.
34	His eyes were white and his face looked pale; his hair was dishevelled and his cheeks were sallow; the band he wore on his head hung loose; with a gentle push, he would have fallen to the ground.
35	When he saw his disciple had become so ashen-faced, I can tell you that the master was deeply upset; he did not think he had ever felt a deeper sorrow; but the youth, when he saw him, was greatly afraid.
36	The master began to question the Prince: "My son, what has ailed you? Who has upset you? If I may know what it is, it cannot trouble me. You must not keep this hidden from me."

37 El infant' al maestro   non l'osava catar;
    daval' grant reverençia,   nol' querié refertar.
    Demandóle liçençia   que le mandas' fablar.
    Otorgóla de grado   e mandól' empeçar.

38 "Maestro, tú me crieste,   por ti sé clereçía.
    Mucho me as bien fecho,   graçir non telo sabría.
    A ti me dio mi padre   quand' siet' años avía
    porque de los maestros   aviés grant mejoría.

39 Assaz sé clereçía   quanto me es mester;
    fuera tú, non ha ome   que me pudies' vençer.
    Coñosco que a ti   lo devo gradeçer
    que m'enseñaste las artes   todas a entender.

40 Entiendo bien gramática,   sé bien toda natura;
    bien dicto e versífico,   coñosco bien figura;
    de cor sé los actores,   de libro non he cura;
    mas todo lo olvido,   tant' he fiera rencura.

41 Bien sé los argumentos   de lógica formar,
    los dobles silogismos   bien los sé yo falsar,
    bien sé yo a la parada   a mi contrario levar;
    mas todo lo olvido,   tanto he grant pesar.

42 Retórico so fino: sé fermoso hablar,
    colorar mis palabras,   los omes bien pagar;
    sobre mi adversario   la mi culpa echar;
    mas por esto lo he   todo a olvidar.

43 Apris' toda la física,   so mege natural;
    coñosco bien los pulsos,   bien judgo orinal;
    non ha, fueras de ti,   ome mejor nin tal;
    mas todo non lo preçio   quant' un dinero val'.

44 Sé por arte de música   por natura cantar;
    sé fer sabrosos puntos,   las vozes acordar,
    los tonos cóm' empieçan   e cóm' deven finar,
    mas non me puede esto   un punto confortar.

45 Sé de las siete artes   todo su argumento;
    bien sé las qualidades   de cada elemento;
    de los signos del sol,   siquier' del fundamento,
    nos' me podrié çelar   quanto val' un açento.

37	The Prince did not dare look his master in the eye; he greatly revered him and would not contradict him; he asked him for permission to be allowed to speak; Aristotle gave it willingly and told him to begin.
38	"Master, you have taught me and through you I have learning; you have done me much good – I would not know how to thank you; my father entrusted me to you when I was seven years old because among all the masters you were the finest.
39	I have sufficient learning, as much as is my need; besides you there is no man who could outdo me. I recognise that I must thank you for this, since you taught me to understand all of the arts.
40	I understand grammar well, I know soundly the whole art, I compose and write verse well and am familiar with the figures;* I know the authors by heart, I find no book difficult. But I am forgetting it all, so great is my ire.
41	I know well how to form arguments from logic and am skilled in refuting double syllogisms. I know well how to leave my opponent without riposte. But I am forgetting it all, so great is my sorrow.
42	I am a fine rhetorician, I know how to speak with grace, to colour my words and give great pleasure to men, and I know how to lay blame on my adversary. Yet because of this I am going to forget it all.
43	I learnt all about medicine; I am a natural physician,* I know all about pulses and interpret urine well. There is, other than you, no man better or comparable, but I consider all of this worth not a single penny.
44	Through music's art, through nature, I know how to sing; I know how to make sweet melodies, make voices sing as one, I know how tones begin and how they have to end; but all of this cannot comfort me in the slightest.
45	I know the full explanation about the seven arts; I know well the qualities of each one element; about both the signs of the sun and those of the earth* what could be hidden from me is not worth a straw.

46   Grado a ti, maestro,   assaz sé sapïençia;
     non temo de riqueza   aver nunca fallençia;
     mas bivré con rencura,   morré con repentençia,
     si de premia de Dario   non saco yo a Greçia.

47   Non serié pora rëy   vida tan aontada;
     ternía por mejor   en morir muert' honrada;
     mas, si tú lo vïeres   por cosa aguisada,
     contra Poro e Dario   irié una vegada."

48   Pagós' don Aristótiles   mucho de la razón;
     entendió que non era   en vano su missión;
     "Oíd", dixo, "infante,   un poco de sermón
     por que podedes más   valer toda sazón."

49   Respuso el infante   – nunca viestes mejor – :
     "Yo so tu escolar,   tú eres mi doctor;
     espero tu consejo,   como del Salvador;
     aprendré lo que dixierdes   müy de buen amor."

50   El niño man' a mano   tolióse la capiella,
     posó çerca'l maestro   a los pies de la siella;
     dava grandes sospiros   ca tenié grant manziella;
     pareçiés'le la rencura   del cuer en la maxiella.

51   Empeçó Aristótiles   com' ome bien letrado:
     "Fijo," dixol', "a buena   hedat sodes llegado;
     pora seer ome bueno   tú lo as aguisado,
     si levarlo quisierdes   com' lo as empeçado.

52   Fijo eres de rëy,   tú as grant clereçía;
     en ti veo aguçia   qual para mí querría;
     de pequeño demuestras   muy grant cavallería;
     de quantos öy biven   tú as grant mejoría.

53   Siempre faz con consejo   quanto que fer ovieres;
     fabla con tus vassallos   quanto que fer quisieres;
     seránte más leales   si assí lo fizieres;
     sobre todo te guarda   de amor de mugeres:

54   desque se buelve ome   en ellas una vez,
     siempre más va arriedro   e más pierde su prez;
     puede perder su alma   e Dios lo aborrez';
     pued' en grant ocasión   caer muy de rafez.

46	Thanks to you, master, I have wisdom in abundance;
	I do not fear ever having a shortage in my store;
	but I shall live with rancour and die in repentance
	if I do not free Greece from the oppression of Darius.
47	Such a shameful life would not be right for a king,
	I would think better of myself if I died a noble death.
	But if you were to judge it a fitting thing for me to do,
	I would ride once and for all against Porus and Darius."*
48	Aristotle took great pleasure from what he said
	and understood that his effort was not in vain.
	"Listen," he said, "my Prince, to a few words of guidance,*
	through which you may always be of greater worth."
49	The Prince replied – you have never seen a better student –:
	"I am your scholar and you my learned teacher,
	I await your advice like that of the Saviour,
	and shall learn from what you say with the greatest affection."
50	The youth straight away took his cap from on his head
	and sat near the master, at the foot of his chair.
	He was sighing deeply for he felt great shame;
	the bitterness of his heart could be seen in his cheeks.
51	Aristotle began, as a man of great knowledge:
	"My son," he said to him, "you have reached a good age;
	you have equipped yourself well to become a fine man,
	if you strive to carry on just as you have begun.
52	You are the son of a king and possess great learning;
	in you I see a sharpness I would wish for as my own;
	in your youth you display great qualities of chivalry
	and are outstanding among all men alive today.
53	Always act with advice in all you have to do
	and talk through with your vassals all you wish to undertake;
	they will be more loyal to you if you act in this way;
	above all, be very wary of love for women:
54	as soon as a man once turns towards them,
	he slips ever backwards and loses his renown;
	he may lose his soul and be hated by God
	and all too easily he may fall into great harm.

55   En poder de vil ome   non metas tu fazienda
      ca dart'a mala çaga,   nunca prendrás emienda;
      falleçert'a a la cueita,   como la mala rienda,
      echart'a en lugar   onde Dios te defienda.

56   El vil ome, quand' puja,   non se sabe seguir;
      Com' se teme de todos,   a todos quier' premir;
      quien vergüença non tiene   non dubda de fallir;
      veémoslo muchas vezes   todo est' avenir.

57   Pero, si tú le vieres   que puja en bondat,
      non mostrar que le amas   serié deslealtat,
      ca los omes el seso   non l'han por heredat,
      si non en quien lo pone   Dios por su pïedat.

58   Nin seas embrïago   nin seas venternero,
      mas sey en tu palabra   firme e verdadero;
      nil' ames nin escuches   al ome lisongero;
      si aquesto non fazes,   non valdrás un dinero.

59   Quando fueres alcall',   siempre judga derecho:
      non te vença cobdiçia   nin amor nin despecho;
      nunca mucho non quieras   gabarte de tu fecho,
      que es grant liviandat   e non yaz' y provecho.

60   Fijo, a tus vassallos   non les seas irado;
      nunca comas sin ellos   en lugar apartado;
      e nunca sobre vida   les seas denodado;
      si tú esto fizieres,   serás d'ellos amado.

61   Fijo, quando ovieres   tus huestes a sacar,
      los viejos por los niños   non dexes de levar,
      ca dan firmes consejos   que valen en lidiar;
      quando entran en campo   non se quieren rancar.

62   Si quisieres por fuerça   todo'l mundo vençer,
      non te prenga cobdiçia   de condesar aver;
      quanto que Dios te diere   pártelo volenter;
      quando dar non pudieres,   non çesses de prometer.

63   El prinçip' avariento   non sabe quel' contez';
      armas nin fortaleza   de muert' non lo guarez';
      el dar le vale más   que armas nin fortalez';
      el dar fiende las peñas   e lieva todo prez.

55	Do not place your affairs in a base man's power, for he will repay you ill and you will never gain your right. In hard times he will let you down like untrustworthy reins and may God defend you from the place where he will cast you!
56	When the dishonourable man prospers, he cannot hold back; being fearful of all, he wants to oppress everyone. A man who has no shame does not shrink from deceit. All of this we see happen with great frequency.
57	However, if you see him growing in goodness, not to show your love for him would be great disloyalty, for men do not gain wisdom through their inheritance but it is given them by God through His own mercy.
58	Do not be a drunkard and do not be a glutton, but in your words be firm and always speak the truth; do not listen to the flatterer and do not hold him dear; unless you follow this advice you will not be worth a thing.
59	When you sit in judgement, take care always to be just; may you not be overcome by greed or love or spite. Never give in to the desire to boast of your deeds, for this is most unseemly and no benefit lies there.
60	My son, do not show anger towards your vassals, and never eat without them, in a separate place; never on your life take out your feelings on them. If you do as I say, you will be loved by them.
61	My son, when you come to lead out your armies, do not leave older men behind for those in their youth, for they give sound advice which is valuable in battle and when they enter the field they do not countenance defeat.
62	If you wish to overcome the whole world by force, do not be gripped by desire to build a store of wealth. All that God gives you, you should willingly share; when you cannot give, do not fail to promise.
63	The greedy prince knows not what is happening to him: neither arms nor fortresses protect him from death; giving is worth more to him than either of these; giving splits open rocks and carries off every honour.

64 Si bien quisieres dar,   Dios te dará qué des;
si non ovieres öy,   avrás d'oy en un mes.
Qui es franc' e ardit,   ésse tienen por cortés;
qui pued' e non quier' dar,   non vale nulla res.

65 Fijo, si de ventura   buena as a seer,
o si en este siglo   algo as a valer,
en muchas grandes cueitas   te avrás a veer;
el seso e el esfuerço   te avrá menester.

66 Qui los regnos agenos   cobdiçia conquerir,
menester ha que sepa   d'espada bien ferir;
non deve por dos tantos   nin por demás fuïr
mas ir cab' adelante   o vençer o morir.

67 Quando los enemigos   a ojo los ovieres,
asma su cabtenença   quanto mejor pudieres;
mas atrás non te fagas   del logar que sovieres
e diles a los tuyos   que semejan mugeres.

68 Si ellos muchos fueren,   tú di que pocos son;
di, si son treinta millia,   que son tres mill o non;
di que por todos ellos   non dariás un pepión.
Sepas que a los tuyos   plazrá de coraçón.

69 Entrante de la fazienda,   muestra grant alegría.
Diles: 'Oíd, amigos,   siempr' esperé est' día.
Est' es nuestro mester,   nuestra merchantería
ca tavlados ferir   non es barraganía.'

70 Éctor e Dïomedes,   por su cavallería,
ganaron prez que fablan   d'ellos öy en dia.
Non farián de Aquiles   tan luenga ledanía
si sopiessen en él   alguna covardía .

71 Dizen que buen esfuerço   vençe mala ventura;
meten al que bien lidia   luego en escriptura.
Un día gana ome   preçio que siempre dura;
de fablar de covarde   ninguno non ha cura.

72 Pues que de la muert' ome   non puede estorçer,
el algo d'este mundo   todo es a perder.
Si ome non gana prez   por dezir o por fer,
valdriá más que fues' muerto   o fuesse por naçer.

64	If you truly wish it, God will grant you enough to give; should you not have it today, it will be yours a month from now. A noble and courageous man is held to be polite; but one who can yet will not give is worth nothing at all.
65	My son, if you are to enjoy good fortune, or if you are to be of any worth in this world, you will have to experience many great difficulties and you will have need of both intelligence and valour.
66	A man who desires to conquer foreign kingdoms needs to know well how to strike with a sword; he must not flee men twice his number or more but press on forwards, to victory or death.
67	When you have your enemies within your sight, study their tactics as well as you can, but do not move back from the place that you hold and tell your men they are acting like women.
68	Should there be many of them, say that they are few; if there are thirty thousand, say three or even fewer; say that you would not give tuppence for them all. This, I tell you, will gladden your men's hearts.
69	As you go into battle, give a display of great joy. Say to them: 'Listen, friends, I have always longed for this day; this is our craft, this is how we earn our living, for the sport of training is not an act of valour.'
70	Hector and Diomedes, through their knightly exploits,* won such fame that they are still talked about today; so great a litany of tales would not be told of Achilles* if some act of cowardice were to be known of him.
71	They say that great valour overcomes misfortune and the good warrior is later remembered in writing; in one day a man wins everlasting glory, but nobody desires to speak of a coward.
72	Since death is a fate from which no man can escape, and the possessions of this world are all to be lost, if a man does not win fame through his actions or his words, better that he were dead or never had been born.

73   Los que tú entendieres que derecho farán,
di que fagan su debdo, ca bien lo entendrán;
promete a los logados quanto ellos querrán,
ca muchos avrá y d'ellos que nunca lo prendrán.

74   A los unos castiga, a los otros falaga;
que dar, que prometer, a todos apaga;
afuerça los delante, sí faz a los de çaga.
Con esta medeçina, guarirás esta plaga.

75   Cabdilla bien tus hazes, passo las manda ir;
qui derramar quisiere, fazlo tú referir;
diles que se non quieran por nada desordir
fasta que venga l'ora que los mandes ferir.

76   Quand' vinier' al ferir, tú sé y el primero;
recabda el mensaje como buen mensajero;
seméjal' bien fidalgo al que sovier' frontero;
los colpes lo dirán: quál es el cavallero.

77   Ferrán sobre ti todos, bolvers'a la fazienda;
grant será el roído, grant será la contienda.
Al que ferir pudieres, nulla res nol' defienda;
de todas las tus ontas allí yaz' la emienda.

78   Allí es el lugar do es a pareçer
cad'uno cóm' se preçia o qué deve valer.
Allí paresca tu fuerça e todo tu poder;
si as a enflaqueçer más te valdrié morrer.

79   Maguer colpado seas, non des por ello nada;
torna en la fazienda e fier' bien de espada.
miémbrete cómo peches a Dario la soldada
de las ontas quet' fizo en la su encontrada.

80   A los de más de lexos tiren los ballesteros
e a los de más çerca fieran los cavalleros;
a los algareadores e a los adargueros
déveslos toda vía meter más delanteros.

81   Feritlos muy apriessa, non les dedes vagar,
tanto que non les vague las espaldas tornar;
qui en fazienda quiere a otro perdonar,
él mesmo se quïere con su mano matar.

73	Those men that you are confident will do what is just, tell them to do their duty, for they will fully understand; promise those that you have hired as much as they demand, for there will be many of them who will never receive it.
74	Lay rebuke on some, lavish others with praise; all can be pleased with a gift – or a promise. Encourage those in your front line and likewise those at the rear; using this medicine you will remedy this affliction.
75	Marshal well your troops, order an unflinching advance; whoever tries to leave the line, order him to retake his place; tell them that on no account are they to break rank until the moment comes when you order them to strike.
76	When the moment comes to strike, you be the first to do so; relay the message as a good messenger would; show your noble quality to the man who stands before you; the blows will make clear which is the good warrior.
77	They will all rush upon you, the battle's course will turn; great will be the noise and fierce will be the conflict. Whoever you may strike, let there be nothing to defend him. For all your dishonour, there redress is to be found.
78	That is the place where it is to become clear how each man is valued and what his worth must be. Let all your strength and power be seen in that place; should you falter, it would be better for you to die.
79	Even if you are wounded, pay it no regard; return to the fray and strike well with your sword. Remember how you are to pay Darius back for the shame he piled upon you when you met.
80	Let the crossbowmen aim at those in the distance and the horsemen attack those closer at hand. The light-cavalrymen and those who bear shields – always must you set these men further forward.
81	Be quick to strike them, allow them no respite, so that they do not have a chance to turn tail. Anyone who wants to spare another in the fight wants death for himself by his own hand.

82   Quando – ¡que Dios quisiere! –   la lid fuer' arrancada,
       non te prenga cobdiçia   a ti de prender nada;
       parte bien la ganançia   con la tu gent' lazrada;
       en ti lleva el prez,   que val' raçión doblada.

83   Con esto otro día   vernán más encarnados;
       por amor de ganar,   serán más denodados;
       los unos verás muertos   e los otros colpados;
       non te cal', ca, si vençes,   not' menguarán vassallos.

84   Si, lo que Dios non quiera,   los tuyos se movieren,
       tú finca en el campo   maguer ellos fuyeren;
       ternánse por fallidos   quando a ti non vieren,
       tornarán sobre ti,   maguer que non quisieren.

85   Camiars'a la ventura   e mudaredes fado;
       ganaredes el campo;   Dario será rancado.
       Sallirá Greçia de premia,   tu fincarás honrado,
       e será el tu preçio   fasta la fin contado."

86   El infant' fue alegre,   tovos' por consejado;
       non olvidó un punto   de quantol' fue mandado.
       Perdió el mal talento   e tornó tan pagado
       como si ya oviesse   tod' esto acabado.

87   Ya tornava las treguas   a Poro e a Dario;
       ya partié a quarteros   la plata e el oro;
       mayor tenié la gorga   que si fuesse un toro;
       non treguava en el siglo   a judío nin moro

88   Ya contava por suya   la torre de Babilón,
       India e Egipto,   la tierra de Sión,
       África e Marruecos   quantos regnos y son,
       quanto que Carlos ovo   bien do el sol se pon'.

89   El diziembre exido,   entrante el janero
       – en tal día naçiera,   era día santero –
       el infant' venturado,   de don Mars compañero,
       quiso çenir espada   por seer cavallero.

90   Allí fueron aduchos   adobos de grant guisa;
       bien valié tres mill marcos   e demás la camisa.
       El brïal non serié   bien comprado por Pisa;
       non sé al manto dar   preçio por nulla guisa.

82	When (God willing!) the battle has been won,
	let no greed lead you to take anything for yourself.
	Share the booty fairly among your men who have suffered.
	Take the fame for yourself, which is worth twice as much.
83	After this, another day they will return yet fiercer;
	for the love of victory they will be more committed.
	You will see some men dead and others wounded.
	Fear not, for, if you win, you will not lack vassals.
84	If – may God forbid! – your men should turn and run,
	stay on the field of battle even though they have fled.
	They will realise they were wrong when they do not see you
	and will return to you even if they are unwilling.
85	Fortunes will change and you will shift your destiny:
	you will take the battlefield and Darius be defeated.
	Greece will be freed from oppression, you will be left with honour,
	and men will tell tales of your glory for ever."
86	The Prince was delighted, he heeded the advice
	and forgot not one detail of his master's instructions.
	He lost his bad humour and was filled with such joy
	as if he had already completed the whole of his task.
87	He was already shunning peace terms from Darius and Porus
	and dividing into quarter shares the silver and the gold;
	his throat was so swollen that he had the look of a bull.
	In the whole world he would make peace with neither Jew nor Moor.
88	He already counted as his the Tower of Babylon,*
	India and Egypt and the land of Sion,*
	Africa and Morocco and all the kingdoms they contain,
	all that belonged to Charles as far as the setting sun.*
89	With December ended, at the beginning of January,
	– he had been born at that time, and it was a saint's day –
	the youth favoured by fortune and companion of Mars
	determined to gird on his sword to become a knight.
90	Fine-quality apparel was brought to him there.
	The shirt was worth three thousand marks or even more.*
	The tunic could not be bought for all the wealth of Pisa*
	and I do not know a way to set a value on the cloak.

91 La çinta fue obrada a muy grant maestría;
    obróla con sus manos doña Filosofía.
    Más valié la fiviella que toda Lombardía;
    más vale, segunt creo, un poco que la mía.

92 Qual quier' de los çapatos valiá una çibdat,
    las calças poco menos tanto avián grant bondat.
    Quisquier' querriá las luas más que grant heredat;
    nunca qui las oviere caeriá en mesquindat.

93 Est' adobo toviera la madre condesado;
    al rey Felipo fuera en presente embiado,
    ca les fue muchas vezes en sueños demostrado
    que non fuesse nul ome de vestirlo osado.

94 La espada fue rica, ca fue muy bien obrada;
    fízola don Vulcán, óvola bien temprada;
    avié grandes virtudes, que era encantada;
    la part' do ella fuesse nunca serié rancada.

95 Non es ningunt mercádor nin clérigo d'escuela
    que pudies' poner preçio a la una espuela:
    oviera Alexandre d'allén mar una avuela;
    a esa gelas dieron quando fuera moçuela.

96 La obra del escudo vos sabré bien contar:
    y era debuxada la tierra e el mar,
    los regnos e las villas, las aguas de prestar,
    cascuno con sus títulos por mejor devisar.

97 En medio de la tabla estava un león
    que tenié yus' la grafa a toda Babilón;
    catava contra Dario, semejava fellón,
    ca vermeja e turvia teniá su visïón.

98 Tant' echava de lumbre e tanto relampava
    que vençiá a la luna e al sol refertava.
    Apelles, que nul ome mejor d'él non obrava,
    por mejor lo tenié quanto más lo catava.

99 Que no digan que bafo, aún quiero tornar,
    la virtud de los paños de cad'uno contar,
    e, si me bien quisieren a derechas judgar,
    dirán aún que poco las sope preçïar.

91	The belt was worked with a craftsman's great skill, worked by Lady Philosophy with her own hands. The buckle was worth more than all of Lombardy* – it is worth, I think, a little more than my own.
92	Either of his shoes was worth as much as a city, his hose little less, so fine was its quality. Anyone would want his gloves more than a great inheritance, and their owner would never fall into poverty.
93	This apparel had been kept for him by his mother and had been sent as a gift to King Philip. For it was made clear to them many times in dreams that no man should have the boldness to wear it.
94	The sword was ornate, for it was finely worked, and wrought and finely tempered by Lord Vulcan.* It had great qualities, for it had been enchanted: whichever side carried it would never be defeated.
95	There is no merchant or scholar from the schools who could put a value on one of the spurs; Alexander had had a grandmother from a distant land to whom they had been given when she was still a girl.
96	I shall be able to tell you all about the shield's decoration: on it were depicted both the land and the sea, the kingdoms and the cities, the rivers of great importance, each with its own inscription to make it all the clearer.
97	In the middle of the shield there was a lion that held Babylon entire beneath its claws; it was gazing at Darius, and had a look of fury, for its eyes were red and cloudy in appearance.
98	The shield blazed and flashed so brightly that it outdid the moon and rivalled the sun; Apelles – whom no man surpassed in his craft –* grew ever more pleased the more he gazed upon it.
99	Let them not accuse me of excess! I still wish to return to describe the qualities of each of the garments, and, if my public are prepared to judge me fairly, still they will say that I could not do these justice.

100   Fizieron la camisa   dos fadas so el mar;
dieron le dos bondades   por bien la acabar:
quis quier' que la vistiesse   nos' pudiés' embebdar
e nunca lo pudiesse   luxuria retentar.

101   Fizo la otra fada   terçera el brïal;
quando lo ovo fecho   diole muy grant señal:
quis quier' que lo vistiesse   fuesse siempre leal;
frío nin calentura   nuncal' fiziesse mal.

102   Quis quier' que fizo el manto   era bien mesurado:
non era grant nin chico   nin liviano nin pesado;
tod' ome quel' vistiesse   non serié tan cansado
que non fuesse lüego   en su virtut tornado.

103   Demás, qui lo toviesse   perdrié toda pavor;
siempre andarié mucho   en todo su sabor;
manto de tan grant preçio   e de tan grant valor
bien convinié que fuesse   de tal emperador.

104   Óvol' el Rey Felipo,   como dizen, ganado
otro tiempo, quand' ovo   a Serses arrancado;
perdiólo él enante,   como ome mal fadado;
si non, de tan mal guisa   non serié aontado.

105   Quiero de la correa   un poco renunçiar;
en pocas de palabras   lo cuedo destajar:
qui la toviesse çinta,   segunt oí cuntar,
de postema nin gota   non podrié peligrar.

106   Quiérovos esponer   la bondat del escudo:
fecho fue de costiella   d'un pescado corpudo;
nol' passarié fierro,   non serié tan agudo;
cavallero quel' toviesse   non serié abatudo.

107   Si lo avié el braço   sí l'avié la espada,
era la maledita   de guisa adonada
que quien ella colpava   sola una vegada
en escudo ajeno   nunca darié lançada.

108   La bondat del cavallo   vinçiá todo lo al:
nunca en este siglo   ovo mejor nin tal;
nunca fue enfrenado   nin preso en dogal;
mucho era más blanco   que nieve nin cristal.

| 100 | The shirt was made by two goddesses beneath the sea
who, as a finishing touch, gave it two special qualities:
that whosoever wore it could not become drunk,
and lust would never again be able to tempt him. |

| 101 | It was a third goddess who made Alexander's tunic
and on its completion she gave it a great power:
that whosoever wore it would be forever loyal
and neither cold nor heat would ever do him harm. |

| 102 | Whoever made the cloak was a person of fine judgement:
it was neither great nor small, and neither light nor heavy;
any man who wore it would never have been so tired
that he would not be able quickly to regain his strength. |

| 103 | Moreover its possessor would lose all sense of fear,
would always be joyful and take pleasure in everything.
It was a cloak so great in value and in worth
that it was right for it to belong to such an emperor. |

| 104 | King Philip – so they say – was the one who had won it
when in other times he had defeated Xerxes;*
Philip had already lost it, as a man whom fortune shunned,
for otherwise, he would not have suffered so much shame. |

| 105 | I want to tell you just a little about the belt,
but I intend to cut my words to just a few:
whoever wore the belt, as I have heard tell,
would not run the risk of abscesses or gout. |

| 106 | I want to set out for you the merits of the shield:
it was made from the bones of a vast fish;
no weapon of iron would be sharp enough to pierce it,
nor would any knight who held it be brought down. |

| 107 | All that the arm could reach was within the sword's range;
the enchanted sword was endowed with the power
that anybody who felt its force just once
would never drive his lance into another's shield. |

| 108 | The merits of the horse exceeded all else:*
never in this world was there one as good or better;
never was he mastered by reins or by a bridle;
his white was more brilliant than either snow or crystal. |

109　　En tres redes de fierro　　estaba ençerrado;
　　　　y fuera con pan cocho　　e con vino crïado.
　　　　De part' llegarse ome　　sól' non era osado,
　　　　que aviá grant pavor　　e grant dubdo echado.

110　　Avié rotos a dientes　　muchos fuertes calnados,
　　　　muchos fuertes çerrojos　　a coçes quebrantados;
　　　　avíe muchos omes　　comidos e dañados,
　　　　dond' eran fiera mente　　todos escarmentados.

111　　Un rey de Capadoçia,　　el nombre he olvidado,
　　　　óvol' al rey Felipo　　en present' embïado.
　　　　Domar nuncal' pudieron,　　ca assí fue adonado
　　　　quis quier' quel' cavalgasse　　serié rey venturado.

112　　Fízol' un elefante,　　com' diz' la escriptura,
　　　　en una dromedaria　　por muy grant aventura;
　　　　viníel' de la madre　　ligerez' por natura,
　　　　de la parte del padre　　fortalez' e fechura.

113　　Quando avié el rëy　　a justiçiar ladrón,
　　　　dávalo al cavallo　　en lugar de prisión;
　　　　ant' lo avié comido,　　tanto era glotón,
　　　　que veint' e quatro lobos　　non combrién un moltón.

114　　De manos e de pies　　ante él más yazién
　　　　que diez carros o más　　llevar non los podrién;
　　　　avién fuerte pavor　　quantos que lo oyén
　　　　que sabién, si furtassen,　　que por tal passarién.

115　　El infant' sopo nuevas　　del cavallo tan fiero.
　　　　Dixo: "Nol' prendrá ome　　si yo non lo prisiero;
　　　　creo que será manso　　luego que yo l'oviero;
　　　　perderá toda braveza　　quando en él subiero."

116　　Priso maço de fierro,　　quebrantó los berrojos.
　　　　Buçifal, quand' lo vío　　enclinó los inojos;
　　　　encorvó la cabeça　　e abaxó los ojos;
　　　　catáronse los omes　　todos ojos a ojos.

117　　Entendió el cavallo　　que era su señor;
　　　　perdió toda braveza,　　cogió todo sabor.
　　　　Dexós'le manear　　todo a derredor;
　　　　todos dizién: "Aquéste　　será emperador.".

| 109 | He was enclosed within three cages made of iron; there had he been raised on baked bread and wine. No man, from any place, even dared approach him, for he had spread great terror and alarm. |

| 110 | With his teeth he had broken many strong padlocks and many firm bolts he had shattered with his hooves. He had bitten and injured a great many men, from which they all learned a harsh lesson. |

| 111 | A king of Cappadocia – whose name I have forgotten –* had sent him as a present to King Philip; no-one could ever tame him, for thus he had been blessed: that whosoever rode him would have good fortune as king. |

| 112 | According to the writings, he was fathered by an elephant, from a dromedary, by very great good fortune; from his mother he inherited a natural turn of speed; from his father's side, appearance and strength. |

| 113 | When the King had to pass sentence on a thief, instead of imprisonment he gave him to the horse; so great was its appetite, the horse had eaten him faster than twenty-four wolves would consume a sheep. |

| 114 | More hands and feet now lay before him than could be carried in ten carts or more. All those who heard of this were filled with fear, for they knew that if they stole then this would be their fate. |

| 115 | The Prince found out about the horse that was so fierce and said: "No man will master him unless I do so; I believe he will be tamed the moment he is mine; he will lose his wildness when I am mounted on his back." |

| 116 | He took an iron mace and broke the bolts; Bucephalus, when he saw him, knelt before him, and bowed down his head and lowered his gaze; the men all turned their eyes upon each other. |

| 117 | The horse understood that this was his lord, he shed all his wildness and took on a gentle nature; he allowed the prince to handle him from all around. All the men were saying: "This man will rule an empire." |

118   Fue luego bien guarnido   de freno e de siella,
        de fazquía de preçio,   de oro la feviella;
        prísole las orejas   d'una cofia senziella.
        Valié, quand' fue guarnido,   más que toda Castiella.

119   El infant' el caballo   nol' quiso cavalgar
        ant' que fuese armado   e besas' el altar.
        Graçiólo Buçifal   e fues'le inclinar;
        non fuera menester   que lo oviesse por far.

120   El infant' fue venido   por las armas prender,
        mas, como fue de seso   e de buen coñoçer
        antes quiso a Dios   una oraçión fer;
        como era costumbre   sus donos ofreçer.

121   "Señor," dixo, "que tienes   el mundo en poder,
        a qui çielo e tierra   deven obedeçer:
        Tú guía mi fazienda,   sit' cae en plazer,
        que pueda lo que asmo   por mí acabeçer.

122   Tú da en estas armas,   Señor, tu bendiçión,
        ca sin Ti non val' nada   ninguna guarniçión,
        que pueda fer con ellas   atal destruçïón
        por que saque a Greçia   de grant tribulaçión."

123   Quand' la oraçión ovo   el infant' acabada,
        enclinó los inojos   e besó en la grada.
        Desent' alçós' un poco   e çiñós' la espada.
        Ese dia dixo Greçia   que era arribada.

124   Ante que se moviesse   el infant' del logar,
        armó más de quinientos   omes de prestar;
        a todos dio adobos   muy graves de preçiar,
        ca todos eran tales   que lo querién pechar.

125   Cavalgó su cavallo   e salló al trebejo.
        El cavallo con él   fazié gozo sobejo;
        viniénlo sobre sí   veer cada conçejo;
        dizién: "El Crïador   nos ha dado consejo."

126   Tant' corrié el cavallo   que dizián que bolava;
        si un mes le durasse,   él nunca se quexava;
        al señor en fazienda   muy bien le ayudava;
        non tornava la rienda   quien se a él llegava.

Book of Alexander

118   The horse at once was harnessed, with reins and saddle,
with girths of great value and buckles of gold;
and over his ears was placed a simple cap.
His worth, when he was harnessed, was more than all Castile.

119   The Prince did not want to ride the horse
until he was armed and had kissed the altar;
Bucephalus was grateful and went down before him;
it had not been necessary for him to do such a thing.

120   The Prince had come to take up arms,
but, as he was a man of good sense and judgement,
his first desire was to say a prayer to God,
and, as custom demanded, to offer up his gifts.

121   "Lord," he said, "who hold the world in Your power,
whom Heaven and Earth are obliged to obey,
guide my actions, if so it should please You,
that I may bring my plans to fulfilment.

122   Grant, Lord, Your blessing to these arms,
for without You no protection has any worth,
that I may wield them to such deadly effect
that I might free Greece from her trials so great."

123   When the Prince had finished his prayer,
he kissed the altar steps on bended knee,
then rose a little and girded on the sword.
That day Greece could say her fortunes improved.

124   Before the Prince had moved on from that place,
he knighted over five hundred men of valour.
He gave all of them apparel of value hard to reckon
for all of them were such as wished to pay him tribute.

125   He mounted his horse and set off to the joust;
the horse was overjoyed to be under his hand.
From every town came councillors to look upon him closely,
and all said: "The Creator has given us His guidance."

126   The horse galloped so fast that they said he could fly;
if they rode for a month he would never complain;
he was of great assistance to his lord as he fought;
no man's approach could make him pull at the reins.

127 Non quiso essa vida   el caboso durar:
fue buscar aventuras,   su esfuerço provar.
Non quiso cavalleros   si non pocos llevar:
lo que valié con pocos   se querié ensayar.

128 Fízolo mayor mente   por las tierras veer,
los passos e los puertos   de las tierras saber,
e por los cavalleros   noveles emponer,
ques' fuessen abezando   guerra a mantener.

129 Falló en luengas tierras   un rey muy estrevudo
que mandava grant regno   e era muy temudo.
Quando vio estas gentes   y el rey tan argudo,
do nol' comiá se iva   rascando a menudo.

130 Demandó al infante   de quáles tierras era,
qué andava buscando   o de quál manera.
Respuso Alexandre,   luego de la primera,
mesturas de su nombre   e de su alcavera.

131 Dixo: "Yo so llamado   por nombre Alexandre.
Felipo, rey de Greçia,   aquél es el mi padre.
Olimpias la reína,   sepas que es mi madre.
Quien a mí con mal viene   de mí con mal se parte.

132 Andamos por las tierras   los cuerpos delectando,
por yermos e poblados   aventuras buscando,
a los unos parçiendo,   a los otros robando;
quien nos trebejo busca   nos' va d'ello gabando."

133 Dixo Nicolao: "¡Andas con grant locura!"
Respuso Alexandre: "¡Non ayas de nos cura!
Mas consejar te quiero   yo a toda cordura:
si de nos non te partes,   avrás mala ventura."

134 Fellón fue Nicolao,   compeçó a dezir:
"Entiéndote por loco,   non lo puedo sofrir;
sim' fazes en tu rostro   a sañas escopir,
sin fierro e sin fuste   te faré yo morir."

135 El infant' Alexandre   un poco fue irado,
mas por esso non quiso   dezir desaguisado.
Dixo a Nicolao: "Eres mal razonado,
mas aún este dicho   te será calomiado.

127	But our noble hero could not endure that life. He set out to seek adventure and prove his valour. He wanted to take but a few knights with him, to see what he could achieve with a small force.
128	He did it above all in order to explore the land, to discover the passages and pathways through the mountains, and to train the men that he had recently knighted, that they might grow accustomed to the ways of waging war.
129	He encountered in a distant land an audacious king,* who ruled a great kingdom and was feared indeed. When he saw these people and their king who was so shrewd he felt a deep and inexplicable irritation.
130	The King asked the Prince from what lands he came, what he was seeking and in what spirit. Alexander replied with no hint of a delay and told him of his name and lineage.
131	He said: "I bear the name of Alexander; the famed Philip, King of Greece, is my father; you should know that Queen Olympias is my mother. He who comes to me with ill intent will leave with ill reward.
132	We are travelling across the land at our pleasure, seeking adventure in territory of all kinds, sparing some and taking from others; whoever takes us on will have no cause to boast."
133	King Nicolao said: "You are acting with great folly." Alexander replied: "Do not be troubled by us; but I want to give you advice, as wisely as I can: if you do not leave us be, it will go ill with you."
134	Nicolao was enraged at this; he began to speak: "I can see you are irresponsible. I cannot stand for this. If you cause me to spit in your face in anger, without either sword or staff I shall put you to death."
135	Anger rose a little in Prince Alexander, but this did not make him speak unreasonably. He said to Nicolao, "You talk with little sense, but these words will yet count against you.

136 Treguas te do agora   fasta'l otro mercado,
que escusa non ayas   porque estás desarmado.
Mas non te metrás es' día   en tan chico forado
que d'estos moços locos   non seas bien buscado."

137 El infant' çierto vino   al día siñalado.
Reçebiólo Nicolao,   non a guisa de covardo;
las azes fueron fechas,   el torneo mezclado;
si pudies', Nicolao   repentiérase de grado.

138 Los golpes eran grandes,   firmes los alaridos;
de cornos e de trompas   ivan grandes roídos;
d'ella e d'ella parte   avié muchos caídos;
exién a todas partes   los cavallos vazíos.

139 El infant' a Nicolao   tant' lo pudo buscar
d'aquí a que se ovo   con él a fallar;
dixo: "Don Nicolao,   pensat de vos guardar,
ca lo que me dixiestes   vos quiero demandar."

140 Abaxaron las lanças   e fueron se golpar;
errólo Nicolao,   non lo pudo tomar.
El infant' fue artero,   sópolo bien sestar;
ayudól' su ventura   e óvol' a matar.

141 Quand' Nicolao fue muerto,   el campo fue rancado,
desbarató la hueste,   ganó tod' el regnado;
tornós' pora su casa,   rico e much' onrado;
fue desí adelante   Buçifal alabado.

142 Falló en cas' del padre   mensagerios de Dario
que venián demandar   el çenso tributario.
Quando ovo leídas   las cartas el notario,
dixo el infant': "Çesso   este aniversario.

143 Ide dezir a Dario,   esto sea aína:
quand' non aviá Felipo   fijo en la reína,
poniá ge ovos d'oro   siempre una gallina;
quando nació el fijo,   morióse la gallina."

144 Fueron los mensageros   fiera mient' espantados;
fazián se d'este dicho   todos maravillados,
que sól' por catarlo   non eran osados;
ya querrián, si podiessen,   seer d'él alongados.

136	I am now giving you a respite until our next meeting, so you have no excuse for being unprepared for battle. But on that day you will find no hole so small that you will not be hunted out by these furious young men."
137	The Prince came punctually on the agreed day and Nicolao met him with no hint of cowardice. The battle lines were drawn up, the contest was begun; if Nicolao could, he would have willingly backed down.
138	The blows were hard, the cries of war were loud, great blasts burst forth from horns and trumpets; all around there were many who fell and riderless horses galloped off in all directions.
139	The Prince did all he could to seek out Nicolao until, at last, he managed to locate him. He said to him: "Nicolao, make ready your defence; I now wish to call you to account for what you said."
140	They lowered their lances and moved in on the attack; Nicolao missed his aim and could not strike a blow. The Prince was skilful and knew well how to strike. With fortune at his side, he was able to kill him.
141	With the death of Nicolao, the battle was won. The army was routed and the whole kingdom conquered. Alexander turned for home, rich and honour-laden; Bucephalus was revered from that day on.
142	In his father's palace he found messengers from Darius* who had come to demand the payment of the tribute. When the letters had been read by the notary, the Prince said, "I now halt this yearly obligation.
143	Go and tell Darius, and let this be done quickly, that when Philip had no son by the Queen a hen always used to lay golden eggs for him; but at the birth of his son, the hen died."
144	The messengers were filled with great terror and all astounded at the Prince's words, for they were not even bold enough to look upon him; they would have wished, if they could, to be now far away.

145 Ant' que fuessen a Dario   las cartas allegadas,
fueron por toda India   las nuevas arramadas;
las gentes se fazién   todas maravilladas
de quál fue quïen dixo   atales palavras.

146 Quando fueron plegados   los mensageros a Dario,
entendió del infante   que le era contrario.
Dixo: "Yo non terniá   que so fijo de Arsanio
sil' non fago que prenga   de mí un mal escarnio."

147 Non avía el rëy   acabada su paravla,
dixeron ge por nuevas   que aviá lit rancada;
a nul ome del siglo   non preçïava nada;
aún querrié sobr' él   venir en cavalgada.

148 Demandó del infante   qué fechuras aviá,
de qué sintido era   o qué mañas traiá.
Dixo un escudero   que bien lo coñoçiá
que fechuras e mañas   él gelas cuntariá.

149 "Non es grant cavallero,   mas ha buenas fechuras;
los miembros ha bien fechos,   fieras las conjunturas;
los braços ha lüengos,   las presas muy duras.
Non vi a cavallero   tales camas yo nuncas.

150 El un ojo ha verde   e el otro bermejo;
semeja osso viejo   quando echa el çejo.
Ha un muy gran tavlero   en el su pastorejo;
como fortigas ásperas,   atal es su pellejo.

151 Atales ha los pelos   como faz' un león,
la boz como tronido,   quexoso'l coraçón;
sabe de clereçía   quantas artes y son,
de franquez' e esfuerço   más que otro varón.

152 Quand' entra en fazienda   assí es adonado
que quien a él se aplega   luego es delibrado
e qui es una vez   de su mano colpado,
sil' pesa o sil' plaze   luego es aquedado."

153 Fizo en una carta   Dario fer la figura
por veer de quál cuerpo   ixié tal travessura;
pero fue muy quexoso   quand' sopo la natura,
mas sopos' encobrir   com' ome de cordura.

145 Even before the letters had reached Darius,
the news spread throughout the whole of India;
the people there were all filled with wonder
at who it was that spoke such words.

146 When the messengers had reached Darius,
he realised that the Prince had set himself against him,
and said, "I would not think myself Arsanes' son*
unless I make sure to teach him a harsh lesson."

147 The King had not reached the end of his speech
when he was given news that war had been declared;
he set no store by any man in the world
and now he wanted to ride against Alexander.

148 He asked about the prince: what his features were like,
how keen his understanding and what ways he had.
A squire told him – who knew Alexander well –
that he would describe his features and his ways:

149 "He is not a very large man, but he is strongly built;
he has well-formed limbs and a warrior's joints;
his arms are long and his grasp very firm.
I have never seen a knight with such sturdy legs.

150 He has one green eye and the other is vermilion.
When he frowns he has the look of an old bear.
The back of his neck is formed like a great board
and his skin resembles a bunch of rough nettles.

151 He has hair that is like a lion's mane;
a voice like the thunder and a raging heart.
He knows about scholarship and all of the arts,
and of nobility and valour more than any other knight.

152 When he enters into battle he has such a gift
that anyone who assails him is quickly dispatched;
and if a man is dealt a blow by his hand,
like it or not, he is swiftly laid low."

153 Darius had his likeness drawn on parchment
to see from what body such fearsomeness came,
but he was sorrowful indeed when he realised his nature
– though, in his wisdom, he managed to disguise his thoughts.

154 Dixo, "Dezir vos e   verdat, ¡sí Dios me vala!
    Sodes caídos todos   en una razón mala,
    mas que quïer' que diga   a mí poco m'encala,
    que yo aquí non veo   mata ond' lobo sala.

155 Siempre son orgullosos   los chicos por natura,
    siempre trahen sobervia   e andan con locura;
    mas, si con él me fallo   por su mala ventura,
    yo sabré tajar capa   de toda su mesura."

156 Embïól' en sus letras   menazas con castigo
    quel' dava buen consejo   como a su amigo,
    que traher non quisiesse   tal liviandat consigo
    e non quisies' buscar   mejor de pan de trigo.

157 Díxol' que recordasse   las cosas fazederas,
    que las palabras viejas   siempre son verdaderas:
    que nul ome a juegas,   nin encara a veras,
    con su señor non quiera   nunca partir peras.

158 Non preçió Alexandre   tod' esto un dinero.
    Dixo, "Yo nunca dubdo   de ome muy verbero.
    Qui por y gelo llevasse,   assaz es él bozero,
    mas non gelo llevaré   por aquel sendero."

159 Non es pora varón   mucho relevar;
    puede quien muchos' gaba   aína empegar.
    Fasta que venga tiempo   quiero me yo callar,
    mas aún verná ora   quel' veré al cantar."

160 El regno de Felipo,   como avedes oído,
    era müy mal puesto,   todo destroído.
    Levantós' le Armenia   en aqueste roído;
    empeçó a guerrear   contra el rey Felipo.

161 El rëy fue en cueita,   qué farié o qué non,
    que sele iva todo   poniendo en mal son,
    ca, si ellos lograssen   atán grant traïçión
    irié por allí el regno   todo a perdiçión.

162 Quando vio Alexandre   cóm' iva la fazienda,
    dixo: "¡Non vos cuitedes   por tan poca emienda!
    Sól' que Dios d'ocasión   a mí solo defienda,
    yo faré que non les valga   el escudo nin la rienda.

154 "I will tell you the truth," he said, "may God assist me!
You have all fallen into a false way of thinking;
but, whoever may say otherwise, it does not trouble me,
for here I see no thicket from which a wolf might spring.

155 Arrogance lies always in the nature of the young;
always are they proud, forever irresponsible;
but if, by his misfortune, I should come upon him,
I shall know how to cut a cloak to suit his measure."

156 He sent in his letter threats and warning,
that he was giving good advice as to a friend:
that Alexander should not carry such impudence in his heart
nor seek to go beyond the lot of those whom bread sustains.

157 He told him to remember the things that can be done
and that the old sayings forever ring true:
that no man either in jest or in earnest
should ever wish to be at odds with his lord.

158 Alexander did not think all of this worth a penny,
and said, "I never fear any talkative man;
whoever acts the way he does is fine enough with words
but that is not the path along which I shall go.

159 It is not the place of a knight to speak at such length;
one who brags a lot can come quickly to be mocked.
Until the moment comes, I want to keep my silence,
but the hour will yet come when I see him sing a different song."

160 Philip's kingdom, as you have already heard,
had suffered much harm and great destruction.
Armenia rose up on hearing this rumour,*
and began to wage war on King Philip.

161 The King was troubled as to what to do or not,
as everything was starting to go against him.
For if they succeeded in such great treachery,
throughout the kingdom all would go to ruin.

162 When Alexander saw how matters were going, he said,
"Do not be concerned over so little damage done;
provided that God protects me alone from harm,
I shall not let their swords or their reins give them aid.

163 Aun sobre todo esto al vos quiero dezir:
    sólo que quinze años me dexe Dios bevir,
    faré que tod' el mundo me aya a servir."
    "Fijo," dixo su padre, "¡déxet'lo Dios complir!"

164 Despidiós' de su padre, salliés' de la posada;
    non lo metió por plazos, moviós' con su compaña.
    Fízol' Dïos buen tiempo, falló la mar pagada,
    ovieron la aína a l'otra part' passada.

165 Armenia, maguer sopo la nemiga asmar,
    de la mala ventura non se sopo guardar;
    mas ella lo cuidó sobre otro echar,
    todo lo ovo ella en cabo a lazrar.

166 Ante que lo sopiessen, el infant' fue con ellos;
    alçar no se pudieron e ovo a vençerlos;
    fizo tal escarmiento e tal daño en ellos
    que a los nietos öy se alçan los cabellos.

167 Quand' los ovo vençido a todo su taliento,
    estorpó más de mill, enforcó más de çiento;
    juraron por jamás todos su mandamiento
    e que nunca farián otro tal fallimiento.

168 El infant', quando ovo su cosa acabada,
    tornós' pora su tierra, su barva much' onrada.
    Falló de otra guisa la cosa aparada
    que él quando fue dende non la aviá lexada.

169 Un ric' ome – ¡que pueda mal siglo alcançar! –
    óvos' de la reína fuert' a enamorar;
    por nul seso del mundo non la pudo ganar,
    ca ella era buena e sabiés' bien guardar.

170 Pausona le dizián, al que Dios dé mal poso;
    óvol' fecho Felipo rico e poderoso;
    mas, por su ocasión, enloqueçió'l astroso,
    e asmó un consejo malo e peligroso.

171 Asmó que, si pudiesse a Felipo matar,
    casarié con la reina, a todo su pesar;
    avriálo tod' el regno por señor a catar;
    non osarié el fijo nunca y assomar.

163	One thing more I want to add to all this: may God allow me but fifteen years more and I shall oblige the whole world to serve me." "My son," spoke his father, "may God allow this to be!"
164	He took leave of his father and went out from the house; admitting no delay, he set off with his men. God granted him good weather and he found the sea calm. In just a short time they completed the crossing.
165	Armenia, although she knew how to scheme for ill, was unable to protect herself against her misfortune; although she meant to inflict it on another, in the end it was she left with suffering to endure.
166	Before they knew it, the Prince was among them. They could not take refuge and victory was his. He taught them such a lesson and did them such harm that to this day their descendants bristle with fear.
167	When he had overcome them and gained his satisfaction, he mutilated over a thousand, hanged a hundred and more. They all swore forever to obey his command and that never again would they make such a mistake.
168	The Prince, when he had completed the task at hand, set off back to his homeland, having won himself great honour.* He found things there in a very different state from how they had been before his departure.
169	A nobleman – may he come to an evil end! –* came to fall deeply in love with the Queen. By no worldly trick could he win her for his own for she was a good woman and could protect herself well.
170	Pausanias was his name, may God grant him no rest! Philip had given him both wealth and power but, to his misfortune, the wretched man lost all sense and devised a plan full of evil and danger.
171	He considered that if he could bring death to Philip he would marry Olympias all against her wishes; the whole kingdom would have to look upon him as lord and their son would never dare to show his face.

172   Bolvío con él guerra   por non seer reptado;
        andava por el regno   a todo su mal grado.
        Tovos' el rey Felipo   d'esso por desonrado;
        fue a lidiar con él,   levól'y el pecado.

173   Como sabiá el falso   que, si fues' arrancado,
        nol' valdrié tod' el mundo   que non fues' justiçiado,
        bastió tod' enemiga   com' ome perjurado,
        ca Satanás andava   en él tod' encarnado.

174   Diol' salto en un puerto,   un lugar apartado,
        como se lo teniá   d'ant' el traidor asmado.
        El logar fue estrecho   e él apoderado;
        fue el rëy Felipo   muy mal desbaratado.

175   Golpes ovo de muerte;   fincóse espantado;
        fue, quando esto vío,   Pausona esforçado;
        el que mal siglo aya   füe tan alegrado
        como si lo oviessen   sus parientes ganado.

176   Dexó el rey por muerto,   que tanto se valié;
        füe pora la villa   do Olimpias yazié,
        mas el mal venturado   agrimar non sabié
        la su mala ventura,   tan çerca le vinié.

177   Si vino en las nuves   o l'aduxo el viento
        o l'aduxo la fada   por su encantamiento,
        abés fue él entrado   con su pendón sangriento,
        sobrevino el infante   lasso e sudoriento.

178   Quand' lo sopo Pausona,   tovos' por afollado,
        vío que lo aviá   traído el pecado,
        pero mísos' en armas   e cavalgar privado;
        ixió contra'l infante,   justa le demandando.

179   Assaz trayé compañas,   todas bien aguisadas,
        mas fueron con el infante   todas muy mal quexadas.
        Tajava les los braços   e fuyán querelladas;
        temián lo que les vino,   que serián malfadadas.

180   El infant', quand' los vio,   luego los fue ferir,
        empeçóles afirmes   luego a desordir.
        Pausona, si pudiesse,   querríes' referir,
        mas lo que mereçió   ovo lo a padir.

172	Lest he be challenged, he waged war against Philip
and moved around the kingdom doing harm at will.
King Philip considered himself dishonoured by this
and went against him in combat; the Devil led him into error.
173	As the perjurer knew that, if he were defeated,
nothing in the world could stay his execution,
he plotted all kinds of hatred, as a traitorous man,
for Satan was in him, fully incarnate.
174	The traitor ambushed Philip in a remote mountain pass,
according to the careful plan that he had made.
The way was narrow and Pausanias' force was strong.
King Philip suffered a very heavy defeat.
175	Deadly blows were struck and terror took hold;
Pausanias, when he saw this, was emboldened.
The accursed man was as full of joy
as if the battle had been won by his ancestors.
176	He left the King for dead – the valour of the man! –
and set off for the city where Olympias had her home;
but the unfortunate man was unable to foresee
how close his grim fate had come.
177	Whether it came in the clouds or was carried by the wind
or it was brought by the mysteries of fate,
hardly had he entered with his bloody pennant
when the Prince came upon him, wearied and bathed in sweat.
178	When Pausanias realised this he knew that he was lost
and he saw that the Devil had brought him to that place.
Still, he girded on his arms and rapidly rode out
confronting the prince and demanding a joust.
179	Pausanias brought a good many troops, all well equipped,
but they all met with great suffering at the Prince's hands.
He sliced off their arms and they fled from him in grief.
Their fear had come to pass: that they would meet an evil end.
180	When the Prince saw them he rode to strike them
and firmly began to break up their ranks.
Pausanias, if he could, would have liked to resist
but he had to suffer the fate that he deserved.

181 Óvol', por su ventura,   el infant' a veer;
    desque lo ovo visto   nos' pudo retener;
    aventurós' con él   e óvol' a vençer;
    lo que buscó el falso   óvolo a prender.

182 Assaz fizo Pausona   quanto que fazer pudo,
    dío a Alexandre   grant colp' en el escudo.
    Rajas fizo la lança   que tenié en el puño;
    cuidó el desleal   quel' avié abatudo.

183 Golpólo el infante   a guisa de varón;
    non l'açechó en al   si non al coraçón.
    Nol' prestó nin migaja   toda su guarniçión;
    por medio las espaldas   le echó el pendón.

184 Mandól' luego prender,   fízolo enforcar
    y lo comieron aves;   nol' dexó enterrar;
    desí fizo los huessos   en un fuego echar
    que non pudies' del falso   nunca señal fincar.

185 Murió el traïdor   como lo mereçié.
    Por y passaron todos   quantos que él trayé;
    nada non acabó   de lo que él querié.
    La tierra al infante   toda l'obedeçié.

186 Todos los traïdores   assí devién morir;
    ningunt aver del mundo   non les devié guarir;
    todos, com' a merçed,   devién a ellos ir;
    nunca les devié çielo   nin tierra reçebir.

187 Quand' esto fue librado,   com' avedes oído,
    el infant', com' estava,   de sus armas guarnido,
    fue saber de su padre   qué l'avié contido
    e falló que yazié   fascas amorteçido.

188 Ya tornava los ojos   e passar se queriá;
    contendiá con el alma,   ca transido yaziá,
    pero quando entendió   que su fijo veniá,
    recobró la memoria   que perdida aviá.

189 Abrió luego los ojos,   començó a plorar;
    cató contra'l infante   e nol' podié fablar;
    signóle con los braços   que lo fues' abraçar;
    obedeçiól' el fijo,   non lo quiso tardar.

181	It happened that the Prince caught sight of him; once he had seen him he could not hold himself back. He took him on in battle and managed to defeat him. The traitor was forced to suffer what he sought.
182	Pausanias fought hard and did all he could; he struck Alexander a heavy blow on his shield; the lance held in his hand shattered into splinters. The traitor believed that he had brought him down.
183	The Prince struck truly, as a good knight should, and aimed at nothing but his opponent's heart. All Pausanias' armour proved of not the slightest worth and the pennant burst through the centre of his back.
184	Then he ordered his body to be taken and hung out and the birds came to eat it – he allowed him no burial. He commanded the bones to be cast into a fire so that no sign should remain of the traitor.
185	The treacherous man died the death he deserved; all those he had with him met a similar fate and he achieved nothing of what he desired. The whole land obeyed the Prince's command.
186	All traitors should die in such a way as this; all the wealth in the world should not give them protection; all should pursue them as they would pursue God's mercy; never should Heaven or Earth give them rest.
187	When all this all been dealt with, just as you have heard, the Prince, as he was, still wearing his armour, went to find out what had befallen his father and discovered him lying wounded, on the edge of death.
188	He was rolling his eyes and wanted to die. He struggled with his soul as he lay there lifeless; but when he understood that his son was coming he recovered the memory he had lost.
189	At once he opened his eyes and began to weep. He gazed at the Prince but could find no words. He gestured with his arms for him to come and embrace him. His son obeyed without a moment's delay.

190   Diol' Dios mano a mano   ya quanta mejoría;
      recobró la palabra   con la grant alegría.
      Díxol': "Yo, fijo, mucho   cobdiçié este día;
      desaquí que yo muera   una nuez non daría.

191   Fiera ment' vos honrastes   e en grant preçio soviestes,
      quand' Nicolao matastes,   Armenia conquisiestes;
      mas todas vuestras bondades   agora las cumpliesteis,
      quando a nos acá   ad acorrer viniestes.

192   Galardón d'est' serviçio   el Crïador vos lo rienda;
      fijo, Él vos reçiba   en la su encomienda;
      Él vos sea pagado   e guie vuestra fazienda;
      de mano de traidores,   fijo, Él vos defienda.

193   Fijo, yo vos bendigo,   ¡sí faga el Criador!
      ¡Él vos dé sobre Dario   vitoria e onor!
      ¡Él vos faga del mundo   seer emperador!
      Con tanto me despido,   vom' a la cort' mayor."

194   El regno de Felipo   fuera muy mal traído
      si el infant' non fuesse   por ventura venido;
      mas quando a él vieron   çessó tod' el roído
      e todo el fervor   que era somovido.

195   Murió a poca d'ora   el su padre honrado;
      fue con los otros rëys   a Corintio llevado;
      como él mereçié,   assí fue soterrado.
      En poder del infante   fincó tod' el regnado.

196   Era esta Corintio   atán noble çibdat;
      convertióla sant Paulo   después a la verdat.
      Sobre todas las otras   aviá grant potestat:
      cabeça fue de todas   bien de antigüedat.

197   Quando avién en Greçia   rëy a ordenar,
      allí l'avién a fer,   non en otro lugar;
      el infant' non lo quiso   en sí desaforar;
      y fuera cavallero   e fues' y coronar.

198   El rëy Alexandre,   quando fue coronado,
      pavor aviá tod' ome   que lo viesse irado.
      Su amo Aristótiles   estava bien pagado
      que tan grant alegría   veyé de su crïado.

190	At once God granted him a measure of recovery;
he recovered his speech with a surge of joy.
He said to him, "My son, how I longed for this day;
henceforth I would not give a fig for my death.
191	You have won yourself great honour and gained great esteem,
for killing Nicolao and conquering Armenia
but now you have shown the finest of your qualities
in coming here to give us your aid.
192	May the Creator give you reward for this service;
my son, may He take you under His protection;
may you win His favour and He guide you in your actions.
May He protect you, my son, from the hands of traitors.
193	I bless you, my son, and may the Creator do so too!
May He grant you victory and honour at Darius' expense!
And may He make you emperor of the whole world!
But now I take my leave, for I am going to God's court."
194	The kingdom of Philip would have come to great harm
if the Prince had not arrived by good fortune.
But when he was seen there, the trouble was over,
so too all the disturbance that had arisen.
195	A short while afterwards his honoured father died
and was taken to Corinth to be with the other kings.*
He received the fine burial that he had deserved
and the whole of the kingdom was in the Prince's power.
196	This city of Corinth was of the highest nobility,
and Saint Paul was later to convert it to the Truth.
Over all other cities it held great authority:
it was the capital of all others from great antiquity
197	When there was a king to be crowned in Greece,
it had to be done there and in no other place.
The Prince did not want to infringe its rights in this.
There he had been knighted and there he was crowned.
198	Once King Alexander had been crowned,
any man who saw him angered was struck with fear.
His master Aristotle was filled with delight
that he saw his pupil become so joyful.

199 Fueron por tod' el regno los pregones echados,
los unos con menazas, los otros con falagos,
que a cab' de tres meses fuessen todos plegados:
peones, cavalleros, todos bien aguisados.

200 Quand' oyeron las gentes tan cuitados pregones,
esperar non se quisieron, merinos nin sayones;
venián los cavalleros, sí fazién los peones;
en Roma más apriessa non van a los perdones.

201 La corte fue bastada quanto el rey mandara;
semejava que todos vinién a fust' o a vara;
quando los vio el rëy, alegrós' le la cara;
quis quier' ge lo verié que la tenié más clara.

202 Sedién çerca del rëy todos los ançïanos,
los de las barvas saras, de los cabellos canos;
estavan más alexos los niños más livianos;
los de media edat pusieron los medianos.

203 Los pueblos eran muchos, grandes las peonadas;
non les cabién los campos, sedién más alongadas;
tant' estavan las órdenes a razón assentadas
como si fuessen siempre en aquello crïadas.

204 Maestre Aristótiles, viejo e decaído,
con sus manos timblosas, luenga capa vestido,
sedié çerca del rëy, leyendo en un libro;
nunca tan rica corte vío ome naçido.

205 El rey sedié en medio, a cada part' catando;
quanto más los catava más se iva pagando.
Todos oreja escucha estavan esperando
qué fablariá el rëy que estava callando.

206 Quando vío su ora, empeçó su sermón:
"Oít me, fijos d'algo, un poco de razón;
hevos yo que gradir mucho toda sazón
porque obedeçistes tan bien el mi pregón.

207 Sabedes vuestros padres en quál vida finaron;
ellos a sus avuelos en tal se los fallaron;
en grant premia bivieron, nunca dend' se quitaron;
qual ellos la ovieron a nos tal la lexaron.

199	Proclamations were made throughout the whole kingdom, some bearing threats and others promising rewards, to tell all to assemble within three months, foot-soldiers and knights, and all fully equipped.
200	When the people heard such an urgent proclamation, neither administrators nor officials were willing to wait. The knights came and the foot-soldiers too – no faster do people seek pardon in Rome.
201	The court was assembled in great numbers, as the King had ordered. By hook or by crook, it seemed all had arrived. When the King saw them his face became brighter and anyone could see that his heart had lightened.
202	All of the elders took their place near the King, yellow of beard and with grey heads of hair. Furthest away stood the most agile youths and those in middle age occupied the middle ground.
203	The people were vast in number, the groups of soldiers great; the fields could not take them – they stretched far into the distance; the ranks were arranged in such careful order it seemed they had always been trained that way.
204	Master Aristotle, old and growing weak, with quivering hands and wearing a long gown, sat near to the King, reading from a book. No man ever born has seen so rich a court.
205	The King was in the centre, looking all around; the more he looked upon them, the more his pleasure grew. With their ears pricked up, they were all waiting for the King to speak, although he still kept silent.
206	When he saw the time was right, he began his speech: "Listen a little, my noblemen, to what I have to say. I shall always be full of gratitude to you for such a ready answer to my summons.
207	You know in what conditions your parents ended their life; they had found their own grandparents in the same position; they lived in great hardship from which they never escaped; just as they endured it so they left it to us.

208   Avián al rey de Persia   por debdo a servir;
        quanto él les mandava   avién lo a complir;
        aviénse cada año   todos a redemir.
        Del mal sabor que he   non lo puedo dezir.

209   Los nietos non podemos   d'essa red ixir
        si do ellos bivieron,   queremos nos bevir;
        mas, si esto quisierdes   una vez aborrir,
        faré venir a Dario   a merçed vos pedir."

210   Calló el rey con tanto,   respuso el senado:
        "Señor, nos prestos somos   por complir tu mandado;
        do tú nunca quisieres,   iremos nos de grado
        e pornemos los cuerpos   e quant' avemos ganado."

211   Atenas en tod' esto   un seso malo priso:
        enfestóse al rëy,   obedeçer nol' quiso.
        El conde don Demoste,   que en esto los miso,
        fuera, si non por poco,   dura mente repriso.

212   Non gelo llevó'l rëy   por plazo nin por maña.
        Mandó luego mover   la su bella compaña.
        Semejavan quand' ivan   una fiera montaña;
        ya queriá començar   a reverter su saña.

213   Fue, quando vio la seña,   represo el conçejo;
        reptavan a Demoste   que les dio el consejo;
        por poco le ovieran   fecho muy mal trebejo,
        mas prisieron acuerdo   mejor un poquillejo.

214   Embïaron al rëy   omes entremedianos
        que coñoçiessen culpa,   metiénse en sus manos;
        e que él non catasse   a los sus fechos vanos
        que siempre con aquesto   serién escarmentados.

215   Quando los vio el rëy   con tan grant umildat,
        non les quiso mostrar   ninguna crüeldat;
        perdonó al conçejo,   deçercó la çibdat;
        dixeron: "¡Viva rëy   de tan grant pïedat!"

216   En enfoto de Dario,   la çibdades de Greçia
        non querién a su rëy   dar nulla reverençia,
        ond' aviá Alexandre   con Tebas mal querençia,
        ca biviera su padre   con ellos en entençia.

208	They had an obligation to serve the King of Persia,
	and all that he ordered they had to observe;
	each year they had to pay the ransom that was due;
	I cannot speak the words for the foul taste in my mouth.
209	We descendants cannot escape from that trap
	if we too wish to live as they lived;
	but if you want deliverance once and for all,
	I shall make Darius come to beg you for mercy."
210	With this, the King fell silent and the senate then replied:
	"Sire, we are ready to carry out your commands;
	even where you would never ask, we will most willingly go
	and risk our bodies there with all that we have won."
211	Athens at this point took a very bad decision:*
	it went against the King and was unwilling to obey him.
	Count Demosthenes, who encouraged them in this,
	could very easily have suffered harsh reprise.
212	The King would not entertain any delay or trick,
	but ordered his fine army to strike out from camp.
	As they marched, they resembled a mighty mountain
	– now he wanted to begin to vent his anger.
213	When his standard was seen the people blamed the city council
	and they criticised Demosthenes who gave them such advice.
	It would have been so easy for them to treat him harshly,
	but they came to a decision which showed rather better judgement.
214	They sent men to act as intermediaries with the King:
	they had accepted their guilt and placed themselves in his hands,
	begging him to ignore their foolish conduct,
	for from this they had learned their lesson for ever.
215	When the King saw them standing so humbly before him
	he did not wish to inflict any cruelty upon them.
	He pardoned the council and lifted his siege.
	They said, "Long live a king who shows such mercy!"
216	Too much trusting in Darius, the cities of Greece
	did not wish to pay due homage to their King,
	and thus Alexander was at odds with Thebes,*
	for his father had lived in conflict with this people.

217   Mas él non enduró   por y gelo llevar;
        cavalgó sobre Tebas   e fuela a çercar;
        empeçóla lüego   a firmes a lidiar;
        los de dentro e todo   non se davan vagar.

218   Plenos eran los muros   de omes lorigados;
        las puertas eran presas,   los postigos çerrados;
        mas con tod' el esfuerço   eran mal desmayados,
        ca los que tuerto tienen   non son tant' esforçados.

219   Mandava el buen rëy   a los embäidores:
        "¡Feritlos! ¡Non ayades   dubda de los traidores!
        Ellos son vuestros siervos;   nos somos sus señores.
        ¡Non escapen los chicos   nin fagan los mayores!"

220   Ya se iva veyendo   Tebas en estrechura,
        ca el rey Alexandre   dávales grant pressura;
        mostrávales a firme   que era con rencura
        de la onta que avián   fecha en su natura.

221   Era müy mal quista   Tebas de su frontera
        ca biviera con ellos   siempre en grant dentera.
        Como diz' que mal debdo   a mal tiempo espera,
        conteçïól' a Tebas   d'essa misma manera.

222   Las gentes de las tierras   todas al rey vinién,
        maldiziendo a Tebas   todas quanto podién;
        de muy malas fazañas   muchas le retrayén;
        ençendido era'l rëy   mas más lo ençendién.

223   Dizién luenga retórica   de muchas traïçiones,
        de muchas malas fembras,   muchos malos varones,
        por do toda la villa   devié seer carvones
        que de tan malas vides   non sallessen murgones.

224   Fue contra los de Tebas   el rëy muy fellón,
        ca la palabra mala   metiél' mal coraçón.
        Moviós' pora lidiar   toda la crïazón
        com' si oviessen todos   venidos a perdón.

225   Ya querián los de fuera   al adarve plegar,
        mas bien gelo sabién   los de dentro vedar,
        que tan muchas pudieron   de las galgas echar
        que los fazién sin grado   un poco a quedar.

217	But he would not endure it or accept the situation. He rode against Thebes and laid siege to the city and began to wage war against it in earnest. Those within the walls were given no respite.
218	The walls were lined with men in armour, the gates were held fast and the doors tightly shut; but for all their courage many still felt fear, for those who are in the wrong lack valour.
219	The good King was giving orders to the attackers: "Strike them down! Have no fear of the traitors! They are your slaves, and we their lords. Be they aged or young, let none escape!"
220	Now Thebes came to see it was in a dangerous position, for King Alexander was pressing hard upon them, showing them clearly the depth of his anger at the affront that they had made to his blood.
221	Thebes was borne great ill-will by its neighbours, for it had always lived in deep dispute with them. They say that a bad debt will lead to bad times, and it happened to Thebes in just that way.
222	The peoples of those lands all came to the King cursing Thebes as bitterly as they knew how. They accused the city of committing evil deeds and stoked the King's anger into even greater fury.
223	They told persuasive tales of many acts of treachery, of many wicked women and many evil men, such that the whole city deserved to be turned to charcoal, lest fresh shoots emerge, rooted in such evil lives.
224	The King felt great fury towards the people of Thebes, for such talk of evil had filled his heart with anger. All of his vassals moved out into battle as if they had all come in search of God's pardon.
225	Now the attackers were trying to reach the inner wall but the defenders knew just how to prevent the assault, for they were able to hurl down so many lumps of rock that there was no choice but to halt for a time.

226   "Esto", dixo el rëy,   "non val' una arveja;
      non sabe esta liebre   con quál galgo trebeja;
      ca me terné por malo   e por fijo d'oveja
      si yo nol' despüello   otra ment' la pelleja."

227   Fizo fer una capa   de muy fuertes maderos
      que bien cabrién yus' ella   quinientos cavalleros.
      Tiravan la por tornos   tres cavallos señeros;
      allí non temién galgas   nin temién ballesteros.

228   Llegaron a la çerca   a todo lur pesar;
      socavaron el muro   por a ellos plegar;
      ya temblava la tapia,   queriá se acostar;
      querriá lo que fiziera   Tebas aver por far.

229   Fue en poca de ora   el muro trastornado;
      ovieron a tollerse   del portillo sin grado.
      Dieron consigo dentro   los griegos muy privado;
      a los que alcançavan   diziénles mal mandado.

230   Quando vieron que iva   su fazienda a mal,
      acogiéronse todos,   metiérons' al real;
      balaban com' ovejas   que yazen en corral.
      Diz' el rey: "Estos borros   cobdiçia han de sal."

231   Non les ovo provecho   esso más que lo al.
      Tebas fue barreada,   ellos idos a mal.
      Mató entre sus piedes   mas de mill Buçifal.
      Devié aver tal cabo   siempre el desleal.

232   Un juglar de grant guisa   – sabiá bien su mester –
      ome bien razonado   que sabiá bien leer,
      su vïola tañiendo,   vino al rey veer.
      El rey, quando lo vío,   escuchól' volenter.

233   "Señor," dixo al rëy,   "eres de grant ventura.
      Semejas a los dios,   que ende as natura.
      Tod' el siglo se teme   de la tu amargura;
      quando estás irado,   as fiera catadura.

234   Oviste buen maestro,   sópot' bien castigar;
      tú bien lo decogiste   como buen escolar.
      Bendita fue la madre   quet' pudo engendrar;
      bien se puede tu padre   de buen fijo gabar.

226	"This," said the King, "makes not a bean of difference; this hare does not know the greyhound that pursues it; I will see myself as feeble and the child of a lamb if I find no other way to shear it of its fleece."
227	He had them build a shelter made of stout wood panels that five hundred knights would easily fit within, and which was dragged in turn by three single horses. There they had no fear of rocks or crossbowmen.
228	They reached the defences much to their foes' dismay and undermined the walls so that they could break through. The wall was now trembling, it was about to fall; Thebes wished that its actions could now be undone.
229	In very little time the wall was brought to the ground. Unwillingly, the defenders had to abandon the gateway and the Greeks very rapidly forced their way inside;* those who came within their reach were given deadly news.
230	When the defenders saw how badly things were going, they rallied together in the royal camp, bleating like sheep that are held in a pen. Then the King spoke: "These lambs need some salt."
231	That served them no better than anything else. Thebes was sacked and they all went to their doom, a thousand and more beneath Bucephalus' hooves – a disloyal man should always meet with such an end.
232	A minstrel of great talent, a master of his craft, a man of subtle tongue who had mastered reading too, playing his vihuela, presented himself to the King. The King, when he appeared, listened to him willingly.
233	"My Lord," he said to the King, "you have great good fortune. You resemble the gods, for you are of their line. The whole world is afraid of incurring your wrath, for when you are moved to anger your gaze is cruel.
234	You had a good master, well able to instruct you; you learned your lessons well, as a good scholar does. Blessed was your mother, the one who brought you forth, and your father can indeed boast of having a good son.

235 En ti son ayuntados   seso e clereçía,
     esfuerço e franqueza   e grant palaçianía;
     semeja la tu lengua   la de filosofía;
     pareçe en tus mañas   que el Criador te guía.

236 Pero, non te gravesca,   dezirt'e mi mandado:
     si Tebas mal mereçió,   bien lo ha alcançado;
     nuncas' gabará ella   de aqueste mercado.
     ¡Dios curie mis amigos   de prender tal mudado!

237 Pero, rëy, bien deves   otra cosa asmar:
     non deves por mal ome   desfer tan buen lugar;
     omes d'aquí salleron   que te sabré cuntar,
     por que al terretorio   deves tú perdonar:

238 Alçides, tu abuelo,   d'aquí fue natural,
     Dïomedes el noble,   Aquiles otro tal;
     villa do tales ixen   non devié ir a mal;
     si las gentes destruyes,   non desueles lo al.

239 Aquí naçió don Bacus,   un cuerpo venturado,
     que conquistó a India   ond' es hoy adorado;
     e muchos otros buenos   de qui sabes mandado,
     por que este lugar   fue sïempre dubdado.

240 Aquí merçet te clamo: si tu lo destruyeres,
     nunca acabarás   todo lo que quisieres;
     mas, si a los vençidos   tu merçet les ovieres,
     guiarse ha tu fazienda   sólo com' tu quisieres.

241 Si los que rëys sodes   e los regnos mandades,
     por vos unos a otros   honra non vos portades;
     d'esto seet seguros,   nunca en al creades,
     que de los otros pueblos   tan dubdados seades."

242 Cleor finó su cántica;   fue el rey su pagado;
     diol' quanto él se quiso   de aver monedado.
     Mas perdonar non quiso   a Tebas el pecado;
     mandó que le pusiessen   fuego de cab' a cabo.

243 Tebas fue destroída   e fue toda cremada.
     Fizo luego el rëy   a Corintio la tornada.
     Un tebano y vino   por que fue restaurada;
     por tres saltos que fizo   gela dio en soldada.

235	In you there are united intelligence and learning, and with them valour, nobility and great courtesy. Your tongue seems to be that of a philosopher and it seems that in your actions the Creator is your guide.
236	But let it not offend you that I give you my message. If Thebes deserved ill, I can see that it has suffered; it will never boast of this piece of business. May God preserve my friends from going down this path!
237	But, my King, you really must bear another point in mind. You must not destroy so fine a place for one evil man. Men have sprung from this city whose tales I shall tell you and on account of whom you must pardon the land.
238	Hercules, your ancestor, was a native of this place,* the noble Diomedes and Achilles likewise. A city whence such men come should not be brought to ruin; if you wipe out the people, do not destroy the rest.
239	Here Bacchus was born, one who had good fortune, who conquered India, for which he is worshipped today, and many other good men of whom you have learned, for whom this place has always been held in such awe.
240	Here I beg you for mercy: if you destroy this place, you will never be able to achieve all that you wish; but if you show mercy to those you have defeated your deeds will all bring the success you desire.
241	If you who are kings and the rulers of kingdoms act with no honour in your dealings with each other, – be sure of what I tell you, never believe otherwise – then in other peoples you will inspire only fear."
242	Cleadas finished his song and the King was greatly pleased; he offered him as much money as he wished to take but still he would not forgive Thebes for its error. He ordered the whole city to be put to the torch.
243	Thebes was destroyed and burned to a cinder. The King set off immediately back to Corinth. A Theban came there who caused the city's restoration;* he received it in reward for his acrobatic show.

244 Tanto avié el rëy   echado grant pavor
que non osava nadie   entrarle fïador;
mató toda la guerra   e todo el fervor;
empeçó a mandarse   Greçia por un señor.

245 Quando todas las tierras   ovo en paz tornadas,
las naves fueron prestas,   de conducho cargadas.
El rëy Alexandre   ensembló sus mesnadas,
todas fasta diez años   rica ment' adobadas.

246 Non eran tanto muchas   com' eran bien guarnidas;
eran, lo que más vale,   por mano escogidas;
todas, una mejor d'otra,   en esfuerço complidas.
Sabet, non semejavan   que eran desmarridas.

247 Quiérovos de las naves   quántas eran contar,
onde podades quántas   serién las gentes asmar.
Como lo diz' Galter,   en su versificar,
de dos vegadas çiento   doze podién menguar.

248 Ya podedes veer   de qué esfuerço era,
que con tan pocas gentes   iva en tal carrera;
ca el poder de Dario   era en tal manera
que plegarié diez tantos   a una boz señera.

249 Mas el rey Alexandre   sabié una costumbre:
que ome nunca puede   vençer por muchedumbre;
ca más valen los pocos   que han la firmedumbre
e les vien' por natura   de cuer la fortedumbre.

250 Mandó mover las naves   a los naveadores;
desbolvieron las velas   de diversas colores;
mandó cómo guïassen   a los governadores;
pora bogar aína   dio muchos remadores.

251 Andava por moverlas   el rey muy fazendado;
diziá a los maestros   que librassen privado;
dixo: "¡Quánto tardades!   Prengo yo menoscabo,
ca m'está la victoria   ya al puerto clamando."

252 Ya ivan de la tierra   las naves despegando;
ivan los remadores   los remos aguisando;
ívanse a los griegos   los cueres demudando;
pocos avié y d'ellos   que no fuessen plorando.

244 The King had instilled such great fear
     that nobody had the confidence to oppose him.
     He put an end to all the war and all the dissent
     and Greece was for the first time ruled by a single lord.

245 When all the lands were restored to peace,
     the ships were made ready and laden with provisions.
     King Alexander assembled his armies,
     all richly rewarded with a full ten years' payment.

246 They were not so great in numbers as they were well equipped;
     what is most important, they were chosen by hand;
     all were rich in valour, each greater than the last;
     I tell you, they did not seem lacking in spirit.

247 I want to tell you just how many ships there were,
     from which you can tell the number of his troops;
     for, as the poet Walter tells us in his verse,*
     there may have been twelve short of two hundred.

248 Now you can see the valour of the man,
     to set off on such an enterprise with so few troops;
     for the power of Darius was of such a kind
     that ten times as many would answer a single call.

249 However, King Alexander knew one established truth:
     no man ever wins victory through sheer strength of numbers,
     for a few men are worth more who have firmness of purpose
     and whose nature it is to have strength in their hearts.

250 He ordered the sailors to cast off from the land
     and the ships unfurled their many-coloured sails.
     He gave orders to the helmsmen on how to steer the ships
     and provided many rowers to ensure they travelled quickly.

251 The King busied himself with hastening their exit,
     telling the masters of the ships to be quick about their task:
     "How greatly you delay! It ails my reputation,
     for victory is already calling me to port."

252 Now the ships were moving away from the sands
     and the oarsmen were working hard at the oars.
     Greek hearts were now beginning to sink;
     few of them were without tears in their eyes.

253   Ellos ploravan dentro,   las mugeres al puerto,
      como si cada una   su marido tovies' muerto.
      El rëy Alexandre   dávales grant confuerto,
      diziéndoles: "Amigos,   tenedes me grant tuerto.

254   Si nos d'aquí non imos,   en paz nunca bivremos;
      de premia e de cueita   nunca escaparemos;
      por tres meses o quatro   que nos y lazraremos,
      atamaña flaqueza   demostrar non devemos.

255   Qui quisier' a sabor   de su tierra catar,
      nunca fará bernaje   nin fecho de prestar,
      mas es en una vez   todo a olvidar;
      si ome quisier' preçio,   ¡que aya a prestar!

256   Alçides, si non oviesse   a España passado,
      maguer era valiente,   non serié tan contado.
      Bacus, si non oviesse   el su lugar lexado,
      non oviera el regno   de Indïa ganado.

257   Nos, por aquesto todo,   dos razones avemos:
      la una que los regnos   de Dario ganaremos,
      la otra que de cueita   por siempre ixiremos.
      ¡Esforçadvos amigos,   ca alegres tornaremos!

258   El sabor de la tierra   faze muchos mesquinos
      e que a grant repoyo   biven de sus vezinos.
      Jasón si non oviesse   abiertos los caminos
      non avría ganado   tan ricos velleçinos.

259   Yo lexo buena madre   e buenas dos hermanas,
      muchas ricas çibdades   e muchas tierras planas;
      mas, tant' en cor me yazen   las tierras persïanas,
      tod' esto non lo preçio   quanto tres avellanas.

260   Si supiéssedes las tierras   quántas han de bondades,
      veriedes qué perdedes   porque tanto tardades.
      ¡Esforçadvos, amigos,   en vuestras voluntades!
      Por poco non vos digo   que mugeres semejades."

261   El rey non pudo tanta   retórica saber
      que les podiés' la dolor   del coraçón toller;
      quanto más ivan yendo   más se querién doler;
      e non podién por nada   las lágremas tener.

253	They wept in the ships as did the women in the harbour as though each one had a husband now dead. King Alexander gave great comfort to his men, saying to them: "My friends, you do me great injustice.
254	If we do not sail from here, we shall never live in peace, we shall never escape from oppression and sorrow. For the three or four months that we shall suffer hardship there we must not show such weakness as this.
255	For whoever wants to linger on the pleasure of his homeland will never bring noble deeds or knightly exploits to fulfilment, but he is to be forgotten for once and for all time; if a man desires glory he must lend his service.
256	If Hercules had not travelled across to Spain,* valiant though he was, he would not have such fame. If Bacchus had not left his homeland behind, he would never have won the kingdom of India.
257	We have two reasons for doing all of this: the first: we shall conquer the kingdoms of Darius; the second: misfortune we forever shall escape. Have courage, my friends; we shall be happy on our return.
258	The love of land leaves many men unhappy and makes them live despised by their neighbours. If Jason had not opened the ways overseas he would not have won fleeces so rich.*
259	I leave a good mother and two good sisters,* many rich cities and many flat lands. But the lands of Persia lie so deep in my heart that, for me, all of this is worth nothing.
260	If you knew what qualities those lands possess, you would see what your great delay costs you. Be strong, my friends in your hearts and wills! How close am I to saying that you behave like women!"
261	The King could not have enough command of Rhetoric to be able to remove such pain from their hearts; the further they travelled, the deeper their grief; they could find no way to hold back their tears.

262 Grant cosa fue del rëy   e de su coraçón,
    nunca tornó cabeça   nin dexó su razón,
    o serié tan alegre,   en su tierra o non;
    non semejó en cosa   a nul otro varón.

263 Desque perdieron tierra   fueron más aquedando,
    e fueron contra Asia   las cabeças tornando;
    e fueron de los ojos   las lágremas mondando;
    e fueron poc' a poco   las razones mudando.

264 Maguer fazié tal viento   que las naves bolavan,
    semejava al rëy   que nada non andavan;
    todos a maravilla   catando lo estavan,
    mas por esso el duelo   aún non l'olvidavan.

265 De la mayor partida   del mar eran passados
    e en cara del puerto   eran alongados.
    Sedién en sus lugares   cad'uno assentados;
    fueron apareçiendo   de Asia los collados.

266 Víolos Alexandre   de todos más primero;
    antes lo vío él   que ningunt marinero.
    Dío salto de piedes   en un alto madero
    por veer si eran ondas   o si era otero.

267 En pie se levantaron   todos los marineros,
    subién a grant prïessa   en los bancos someros,
    que si era verdat   querién seer çerteros;
    por veer mas alexos   tolliénse los sombreros.

268 Fue por todas la naves   el roído entrando;
    en pie se fueron todos   apriessa levantando.
    Fueron se poc'a poco   todos çertificando;
    tenían que avía   ganado el su vando.

269 Plogo a Alexandre   con esta alegría,
    ca nunca otra tal   ovo él en un día;
    fizo luego remar   toda la mançebía;
    fazién correr las naves   con muy grant alegría.

270 Nos' cuidava veer   de las naves sallido;
    dizié, si fuera fuesse,   ques' ternié por guarido.
    Dava con alegría   bozes e apellido;
    nol' cabié el pellejo   tant' era ençendido.

262	There was something extraordinary about the King and his emotions: he never once turned his head or abandoned his convictions, wherefore he would be as joyful, whether in his land or not; in the way he acted he was like no other man.
263	Once they left the land behind, their emotions became calmer; steadily their thoughts began to turn toward Asia; steadily the tears began to dry from their eyes and steadily their thoughts began to dwell on other things.
264	Although the wind was strong enough to make the ships fly, it seemed to the King that they scarcely moved at all. Everyone was gazing upon him in wonder but still that did not stop them from thinking of their grief.
265	Most of the sea crossing was now behind them, and yet they were still far from the harbour; and as each of them sat in his place the heights of Asia came into view.
266	It was Alexander who was first of all to see them – he did so before any of the sailors –; he jumped to his feet and stood on a high beam to see if they were waves or if it was a hill.
267	All of the sailors bounded to their feet and were quick to leap onto the highest benches, for they wanted to know for sure if it was true; they removed their hats so they could see a greater distance.
268	A great roar spread throughout all of the ships, and with a rapid movement they were all on their feet, all of them gradually making it out for themselves. They felt as though they had won victory in battle.
269	Alexander was pleased at this show of great joy, for he had never before seen the like in one day. Then he had all the young men row the ships – they made them skip over the waves with great joy.
270	He never thought that he would disembark from the ships and said that if he did so his troubles would be over. In his joy he yelled out, screaming loud war cries. His excitement could scarcely be contained within his skin.

271　　Quando fueron al puerto　a piedra echadura,
　　　　priso una ballesta,　parada a tesura;
　　　　echó una saeta,　tinta con amargura,
　　　　dio con ella en Asia　pora prender ventura.

272　　Ovieron ge los griegos　d'esto müy grant grado,
　　　　que todo su negoçio　serié bien acabado,
　　　　que ganarién a Persia,　Dario serié rancado,
　　　　aünque le pesasse　a todo su fonsado.

273　　Una cosa cuntió　ond' les plogo derecho:
　　　　como dizen, un cuervo　mató en este trecho.
　　　　"Assí," dixieron todos,　"Dios nos dará consejo
　　　　de Dario, que nos fizo　siempre mucho despecho."

274　　Tantas eran las bozes　que al çielo bolavan,
　　　　allá sobre los çielos　a los dios enojavan;
　　　　firién palmas de gozo,　reían e sotavan;
　　　　las naves con las coçes　quedar non las dexavan.

275　　Fueron en arenal　las áncoras echadas,
　　　　fueron por la ribera　las tiendas assentadas;
　　　　posavan ad anchura,　a luengas e a ladas;
　　　　com' en su heredat,　assí prendién posadas.

276　　La materia nos manda,　por fuerça de razón,
　　　　avemos nos a fer　una descripçïón:
　　　　cómo se part' el mundo　por triple partiçión,
　　　　cómo faze la mar　en todas división.

277　　El que partió el mundo　fízolo tres partidas:
　　　　son por braços de mar　todas tres divididas;
　　　　la una es mayor,　las otras dos más chicas;
　　　　la mayor es caliente　e las dos son mas frías.

278　　La una meatad　es contra Orïente;
　　　　fizo la una suerte　el Rey Omnipotente;
　　　　las otras dos alcançan　por medio Occidente;
　　　　fiende la mar por medio　ad ambas igualmente.

279　　Es clamada por nombre　Asïa la primera,
　　　　la segunda, Europa,　África la terçera.
　　　　Tiene el cristianismo　a Europa señera;
　　　　moros tienen las otras　por nuestra grant dentera.

271   As they approached the harbour, just a stone's throw away,
       Alexander took a crossbow, which was wound tight and ready,
       and fired a bolt that was soaked in bitterness;
       he sent it flying into Asia to secure them good fortune.

272   At this the Greeks were filled with great joy,
       seeing that their deeds would all end in success,
       that they would win Persia and Darius be defeated,
       even if all his army should wish it otherwise.

273   One thing happened which brought them deep pleasure:
       it is said that with this very bolt he killed a crow.
       And so they spoke with one voice: "God will grant us His aid
       against Darius, who has always done us great harm."

274   So great were the cries that rose up to the sky
       that there in the heavens the gods grew irate.
       The men beat their palms, they laughed and leapt for joy,
       and made the ships rock with the stamping of their feet.

275   The anchors were dropped into the sands
       and the tents were pitched on the shore.
       Freely they camped over the length and breadth of beach
       and they took up their quarters as if in their own land.

276   My subject dictates it: by virtue of its meaning,
       here we have to include a digression*
       to describe the tripartite division of the world,
       and how the sea separates the different parts.

277   He who made the division split the world in three parts,
       which are all three kept separate by arms of the sea:
       one is larger than the others, which do not extend as far,
       the largest is hot and the other two are cooler.

278   One of the parts is located in the East
       and the Almighty King gave it special favour.
       The other two each make up half of the West
       and the sea divides them in equal proportion.

279   The first of them bears the name of Asia,
       the second is Europe and Africa the third.
       Christianity is master only of Europe;
       the Moors hold the others, to our great sorrow.*

280   Qui asmare cóm' yazen   las mares, de quál guisa,
        la una que comedia, la otra que quartiza,
        verá que tien' la cruz   essa figura misma,
        ond' vienen los incrédulos   prender la mala çisma.

281   Dexemos de las otras,   de Asïa contemos:
        a lo que començamos   en esso nos tornemos;
        el uno que leyemos,   el otro que oyemos,
        de las mayores cosas   recabdo vos daremos.

282   Asïa de sí misma   ave bondat estraña:
        ave mucho buen río,   mucha buena montaña,
        de pan e de vino   non ha tierra calaña,
        el bien que d'ella dizen   non es si non fazaña.

283   Tanto tien' esta sola   como todo lo al;
        aún un poquïello   passa de la señal;
        ond' asmó Alexandre,   un seso natural,
        que si prisiesse éssa,   avrié todo lo al.

284   Es más rica de todas   Asïa, e mayor;
        aún como es buena   devié seer mejor;
        deviénle reverençia   todas dar, e onor,
        ca y naçió don Christus   el nuestro redemptor.

285   Dent' son los patrïarcas,   omes de santa vida;
        otrossí los profetas,   una gent' escogida;
        fue del Fi de la Virgen   la su sangre vertida,
        por ond' fue la fallençia   de Adam redemida.

286   Toda Santa Iglesia   d'allí priso'l çimiento;
        dent' fueron los apóstolos,   un honrado conviento.
        Pero a Eüropa   Dios le dio alçamiento,
        ca es Roma cabeça   de tod' ordenamiento.

287   Ixen del paraíso   las quatro aguas santas:
        y son las buenas piedras,   jaspes e dïamantes.
        En India es do son   los grandes elefantes,
        do sembran dos vegadas   e cogen otras tantas.

288   Cáucaso, un mont' alto,   li yaz' en un rencón;
        como dizen, a parte   yaze de Septentrión;
        náçenle muchos ríos   cabdales en fondón,
        mas Indus es más frío   de quantos que y son.

280	Anyone who contemplates the form of the seas – one divides into halves; the other makes two quarters – will see that the cross has exactly the same form, such that unbelievers are thrown into confusion.
281	Let us leave aside the others and tell of Asia; let us return to what we had begun. From, in part, our reading, in part what we have heard, we shall tell you about the things of most importance.
282	Asia in itself has great and strange qualities: it has many fine rivers and many fine mountains; for bread and for wines no other land compares; the good things they tell of it are no less than wondrous.
283	This land alone has as much as all the others and even by a little exceeds their mark; from this Alexander, intelligent by nature, saw that if he won this land all the rest would be his.
284	Asia is richer than the others and the best, but fine though it is, it should be finer still; all the world should pay it honour and reverence for it was there that Christ, our Redeemer, was born.
285	From there came the patriarchs, men of holy life, and also the prophets, a chosen people, and there was shed the blood of the Son of the Virgin, through which Adam's Fall was redeemed.
286	All the Holy Church laid its foundation there and from there came the Apostles, an honoured community; but God raised Europe into the highest position, for Rome is the head of all the religious orders.
287	The four holy rivers spring from Paradise,* and there lie precious stones, jasper and diamonds; it is India where mighty elephants are to be seen, where they sow twice a year and reap as often.
288	Caucasus, a lofty mountain, stands in a corner of Asia. It is, so they say, to be found in the northern part; many mighty rivers are born at its foot, but the River Indus is the coldest of them all.

289 En Asia yaz' Asiria, tierra muy abondada,
Frigia e Panfilïa, que non le deven nada;
y son Persia e Media, regnos de fuert' entrada;
non merez' Mesopótamia que sea olvidada;

290 Babilonia la magna, que todo el mundo val',
que val' más que un regno, ca es emperïal;
Caldea, que es tierra del todo comunal;
y son Saba e Siria, buenos uno con al;

291 Arabia, do a Cristo vinieron en pitança,
quand' fizo en los niños Herodes la matança;
Armenia, que al çielo tañe por demostrança,
el arca de Noé, do fizo la folgança;

292 Egibto do los fijos de Israel ixieron;
el mont' de Sinaí do la Lëy prisieron;
el desierto do muchos años estovïeron,
do muchas sorrostradas e porfaçio ovieron;

293 la tierra de Judea, que es mejor de todas,
do con Santa Iglesia Cristo fizo las bodas,
ésta, con Palestina, deve çercar las otras;
contra ésta las otras devién seer devotas.

294 Otras y ave muchas que contar non sabría;
aún si las supiesse, nunca lo cumpliría,
ca serié grant estoria e luenga ledanía;
mas tornemos al curso mientras nos dura'l día.

295 Alegre fue el rëy quando fue arribado;
rindía a Dios graçias quel' aviá aliñado;
confortava sus gentes, andava esforçado;
dizié que su negoçio serié bien recabado.

296 Adobaron cozinas, fazién grandes missiones;
a guisa de sages omes, estableçién razones;
avián ya ordenado en los sus coraçones,
asmava cado uno dó farién poblaçiones.

297 Avién buenos agüeros e buenos encontrados;
ovieron noche buena; durmieron segurados;
avién lo menester, ca eran muy cansados,
ca los que del mar ixen son cochos e assados.

289	In Asia lie Assyria, a land of great abundance, Phrygia and Pamphylia, comparable in every way; there too Persia and Media, kingdoms of vast wealth; nor does Mesopotamia deserve to be forgotten;
290	Babylonia the great, equal to any place in the world, worth more than any kingdom, for it is an empire; Chaldea, a land similar in every respect, and Sheba and Syria are there, as fine as each other;
291	Arabia, from where they came bearing gifts to Christ, when Herod committed the massacre of the children; Armenia, whose heights can be seen to touch the sky: this is the place where Noah's ark came to rest;
292	Egypt, from where the sons of Israel set out, Mount Sinai, where they were given the tablets of law, the desert in which they saw many years pass by and where they suffered much insult and harm;
293	the land of Judea, which is the finest of all, where Christ brought about the marriage with the Holy Church; this, with Palestine, must enclose all the others; the others must show their devotion to this land.
294	There are many other lands there of which I could not tell; even if I had the knowledge, I would never fulfil the task, for it would be a vast tale and a long litany. Let us, rather, return to our course while our daylight lasts.
295	Joyful was the King, when he had arrived, thanking God for having brought him to this point. Full of good cheer, he gave encouragement to his men, saying that their business would be brought to a good end.
296	They cooked their food, made careful preparations and worked out with prudence what their plans were to be. They had composed themselves now in their hearts and each one considered where towns should be established.
297	They had good auguries and fortunate encounters, they spent a good night and they slept secure; they had great need of this, for they were deeply tired: those who have crossed the sea are weary and exhausted.

298 Ya iva aguisando doñ' Aurora sus claves;
tolliá a los cavallos don Febo los dogales.
Despertós' Alexandre al canto de las aves
que fazién por los árboles los cantos muy süaves.

299 Tant' avié grant sabor que nada nol' membrava;
sól' nol' vinié en miente en quál tierra estava,
nil' membrava de Dario a qui él guerreava,
nin que en imperïo ajeno alvergava.

300 Quand' apuntó el sol, cató contra la mar;
vío luzir las ondas e las naves andar.
Començó el buen ome en su cuer a tornar;
fuera salló del lecho, luego se fue armar.

301 Cavalgó man' a mano su cavallo ligero;
furtós' del almofalla, non clamó compañero;
subió en una sierra, en un alto otero,
pero Festino fue con él, su escudero.

302 Cuando fue en el poyo, en un alto lugar,
començó d'y las tierras todas a mesurar;
quanto más las catava más se podié pagar;
dixo: "En estas tierras me quiero yo morar."

303 Vío muchas çibdades, todas bien assentadas,
montañas muy fermosas e bien vallejadas;
muchas buenas riberas e todas bien pobladas,
de fuentes e de prados todas bien abastadas.

304 Semejól' que de caças nunca tan buenas vío,
nin tan buena de fruta nin de tanto buen río.
Dixo entre su cuer: "Como creo e fío,
antes de pocos días, será tod' esto mío."

305 Tornó a l'alvergada, contra ora de nona;
mató en la tornada una fiera leona;
aduxo'l coraçón Festino en la azcona
por mostrar a los griegos que avián entrada bona.

306 Adiesso que plegó, dixo a sus fonsados:
"Dezir vos quiero nuevas ond' seredes pagados;
suéltovos Eüropa con todos sus condados,
ca yo he muy mejores emperios barruntados.

Book of Alexander

298   Now Aurora made ready to unlock her doors,*
and Phoebus removed the halters of his horses.
Alexander awoke at the sound of the birds,
whose song spread sweetly through the trees.

299   So great was his satisfaction that he remembered nothing:
he could not even think what land he was in,
nor remember Darius, on whom he was waging war,
nor that he spent that night in a foreign empire.

300   When the sun appeared, he looked out to sea
at the sparkling waves and the ships as they swayed.
Gradually the good man's thoughts returned;
he leapt from his bed and went to don his armour.

301   He mounted his swift-footed horse without delay
and slipped away from the army, summoning no comrade.
He rode off into the hills and scaled a lofty peak;
only Festinus, his squire, went with him.*

302   When he stood at the top, from a lofty view-point
he began to take stock of all the lands.
The more he gazed upon them, the more he grew content
and said, "In these lands, I wish to remain."

303   He saw many cities, all well established,
very beautiful mountains, and many fine vales,
many rich river valleys, all full of people,
and all of them abounding in springs and in meadows.

304   He did not think that he had ever seen
either game, fruit, or rivers so fine;
he said to himself: "As I believe and I trust,
within just a few days all this will be mine."

305   He returned to the camp towards the hour of None,
and on the way back he killed a fierce lioness.
Festinus brought back its heart on his lance
to show the Greeks that they had made a good beginning.

306   As soon as he arrived he said to his armies,
"I wish to give you news that will delight you;
Europe I cede to you with all of its counties,
for I have espied much finer empires.

307 Sabet que yo he vista   tanta buena ventura,
que non ha la bondat   nin cabo nin mesura;
qui non lo oviés' visto,   terniélo por locura;
el que aquí morasse   nunca verié rencura."

308 Tant' avié grant feüza   e firme voluntad
que nos' le defendié   castillo nin çibdat;
partió a sus varones   Greçia por heredat
et fizo fazer luego   cartas de salvedat.

309 Fizo otro esfuerço   que era más estraño.
Dizía a sus gentes: "Non fagades nul daño,
ca el que lo fiziesse   verá que me ensaño,
ca lo tengo por mío   a la fe, sin engaño."

310 Las gentes de la tierra   por que esto fazié
tornávansele todos   do quiere que vinié;
sabet que este seso   grant pro le aduzié,
ca si fuesse muy crudo   peores los avrié.

311 Dos vassallos del rëy,   ambos sus naturales,
Clitus e Tolomeo,   dos varones leales,
apartaron al rëy   fuera de los tendales;
fuéronlo cometiendo   con palabras atales.

312 Dizién: "Rëy, tú as   mucho de delibrar:
acabdellar tus hazes,   los judiçios judgar,
quándo han a mover   cómo han de posar;
Rëy, sufres grant pena,   non lo podrás durar.

313 Grant es la tu fazienda,   as mucho de veer,
non lo podrás por ti   todo acabeçer;
podrié por aventura   tal falta conteçer
que a ti e a nos   podrié empeeçer.

314 Mas, segunt nuestro seso,   si por bien lo toviesses,
una cosa de nuevo   queriemos que fiziesses:
que escogiesses doze,   quales tú más quisiesses,
alcaldes e cabdillos,   a éssos nos pusiesses.

315 Después iriés seguro,   seriés más sin ardura;
avrié ante derecho   la gent' de su rencura;
e esto serié seso   e de todos cordura;
irié toda la cosa   en mejor derechura."

307	I tell you that I have seen such great good fortune that its splendour has no limit and no reckoning; anyone who had not seen it would consider this madness; but any man who stayed here would never feel regret."
308	He had such great confidence and strength of will that he kept back for himself no castle or city; he divided up Greece among his men as their inheritance and then he gave them letters of guarantee.
309	He performed another – and a stranger – noble deed, saying to his followers, "Do not do any harm, for anyone who does so will clearly see my anger, for I hold it my affair, in faith; I do not deceive you."
310	The peoples of the land, because he had done this, all surrendered to him, wherever he went; I tell you that this tactic brought him great advantage: had he been very harsh he would have found them less compliant.
311	Two vassals of the King, both relatives of his, Cleitus and Ptolemy, two loyal men,* took the King aside, away from the tents, winning him over with such words as these:*
312	"My King, there is much that falls to you to resolve: you have troops to command, and judgements to make, when they are to move off and when they should pitch camp: a great burden, my King; you cannot bear it all.
313	Great are your tasks, you have much to oversee, and alone you will not be able to deal with it all. Misfortune might cause such a problem to arise as could do great harm, to you and us alike.
314	But, in our opinion, and if you were in agreement, there is one further step we would like you to take: to choose twelve men, the ones you thought best, and give them to us as officials and leaders.
315	Then you would be more certain and would have fewer problems, and people would more readily have redress for their grievances. It would be wise to take this course and sensible for all, and in everything there would be greater justice."

316 Dixo el rëy: "Veo que bien me consejades;
otorgo leal mente que buen seso me dades;
los dos primeros quiero que vos amos seades."
Dixieron ellos: "Plázenos, señor, pues lo mandades"

317 Desent' clamó el rëy Elier el su privado;
maestre Aristótiles, que le ovo crïado,
púsolo con los otros en esse mismo grado;
Parmenio fue el quinto, ¡en duro punto nado!

318 El sesto fue Euménides e Sansón el seteno;
Festino el octavo, Filotas el noveno;
el dezeno fue Nícanor, Antigón el onzeno;
Pérdicas fue metido en el lugar dozeno.

319 Éstos puso el rëy que fuessen mayorales;
non los podría ome escoger más cabdales;
pusieron les después nombre los doze pares;
en Roma otros tanto avié de cardenales.

320 Quando ovo el rëy sus cosas assentadas,
puesto sus doze pares, sus leyes ordenadas,
mandó mover las huestes, prender otras posadas,
ca querié contra Dario meters' a denodadas.

321 Fizo por media Frigia la primera entrada;
nin castillo nin villa non sele tovo nada;
óvola much' aína conquista e ganada;
fue cogiendo esfuerço la greçisca mesnada.

322 Desent' vino a Troya la mal aventurada,
la que los sus parientes ovieron assolada.
Veyé fiera labor toda desbaratada;
faziés' maravillado de cosa tan granada.

323 Maguer que yerma era, desfecha e quemada,
pareçién los çimientos por do fuera poblada;
veyé que don Omero non mintiera en nada,
todo quanto dixiera fuera verdat provada.

324 Mostráronle el soto do parava sus redes,
quando robó el águila al niño Ganimedes;
vertiólo ante Júpiter sobre unos tapedes,
dio a la cort' del çielo tal honra qual veedes.

316	The King said, "I can see that you give me sound advice. I grant you in truth that you are making a wise suggestion. I want the two of you to be the first among them." They said, "Willingly, lord, since it is your command."
317	Next, the King called on Elier, his trusted knight;* Master Aristotle, who had educated him, he placed with the others, on the same standing; Parmenion was the fifth, a man ill-starred from birth.*
318	The sixth was Eumenes and Samson the seventh,* Festinus the eighth and Philotas the ninth, Nicanor was tenth, Antigonus eleventh and Perdiccas included as the twelfth.
319	These the King appointed as his chief officers; he could not have chosen men of greater worth; later they were given the name of the Twelve Peers; in Rome there was just the same number of cardinals.
320	When the King had settled all his affairs, appointed his Twelve Peers and put in place his laws, he ordered his armies to move out to a new position, for he wanted to strike a forthright blow against Darius.
321	He began by pushing through the heart of Phrygia and no castle or city gave him any resistance. Very quickly it was conquered and defeated; the morale of the Greek force was now on the rise.
322	Next he came to Troy, the city of ill fortune,* the one that his ancestors had razed to the ground; he could see a great creation totally destroyed and he wondered at such mighty events.
323	Although it was a wilderness, destroyed and burned, the foundations it was built on were clearly to be seen, and he could see that Homer had not lied in any way;* there was ample proof that all he said was true.
324	They showed him the grove where the young Ganymede* was putting out his nets when the eagle carried him off and cast him down onto rich rugs before Jupiter; he paid the court of Heaven such honour as you see.

325 Contóles a los suyos   cómo fue destroída,
cómo oviera Paris   a Elena rabida,
cómo ovo Diomedes   a Venus mal ferida,
cómo murió don Éctor,   una lança ardida.

326 Dixo cóm' fue Ulixes   sossacador d'engaños,
cómo vistió Aquiles   en la orden los paños,
cómo avián yazido   en la çerca diez años,
cómo ellos e ellos   prisieron grandes daños.

327 Tanto pudo el rëy   la cosa acuçiar
fasta que él ovo   el árbol a fallar
do escrivió Oenone   de viersos un buen par
quando dizién que Paris   la avié de dexar.

328 Aprés falló un val,   un lugar apartado,
do Paris el juïçio   malo ovo judgado,
quand' avién las tres dueñas   el pleito afincado
sobre una mançana   que les dio el pecado.

329 Falló en un bel campo   una grant sepultura
do yazié soterrada   la gent' de su natura,
que tenié cada uno   de suso su escritura,
e dizié cada uno   qui fuera su mestura.

330 Falló entre los otros   un sepulcro honrado,
todo de buenos viersos   en derredor obrado.
Qui lo versificó   fue ome bien letrado
ca puso grant razón   en poco de dictado.

331 "Aquiles so, que yago   so est' mármol çerrado,
el que ovo a Éctor,   el troyano, rancado.
Matóme por la planta   Paris el perjurado,
a furto, sin sospecha,   seyendo desarmado."

332 Quando ovo el rëy   el pitafio catado,
dizié que de dos viersos   nunca fue tan pagado;
tovo que fue Aquiles   ome aventurado,
que ovo de su gesta   dictado tan honrado.

333 Echaron grant ofrenda,   dieron grant oblaçión,
ençensaron las fuessas,   fizieron proçessión.
Orava cada uno   con grant devoçión
por aquellos que fueron   de su generaçión.

325	He told his people how it was destroyed, how Helen had been stolen away by Paris, how Diomedes had inflicted a cruel wound on Venus and how the valiant warrior Hector met his death.
326	He told of how Ulysses was a weaver of deceptions, how Achilles was clothed in the dress of a holy order; how they had kept up the siege for almost ten years and how both sides suffered great losses.
327	The King was able to persist in his search until he discovered the very tree where Oenone composed a fine pair of verses* when told that Paris was going to leave her.
328	Then he found a valley, a remote spot, where Paris had made the fatal judgement when the three ladies had taken part in the contest over an apple which was given them by the Devil.
329	In a beautiful field, he found a great tomb where lay buried the fathers of his line; above each one of these was found an inscription which explained the lineage of each.
330	He found among the others an honoured grave, decorated all around with fine verses; whoever composed them was learned indeed, for he infused his few words with great meaning:*
331	"I am Achilles, who lie enclosed beneath this marble, the man who vanquished the Trojan Hector. The treacherous Paris killed me through my heel, in secret, when I, unsuspecting, lay unarmed."
332	When the King had finished gazing on the epitaph, he said that no two lines ever delighted him so. He held Achilles to be a man of great fortune for having won such noble words through his exploits.
333	They laid out great offerings and made great oblations,* they sprinkled incense on the graves, as they passed in procession, each and every one of them praying with great devotion for those who had been of their own line.

334 La proçessión andada,   fizo el rey sermón
     por alegrar sus gentes, ferles buen coraçón.
     Empeçó la estoria   de Troya de fondón:
     cómo fue destroída   e sobre quál razón.

335 Consagráronla dos reys,   como diz' la leyenda;
     fazián, com' eran ricos,   bodas de grant fazienda;
     todos avién abondo   en paz e sin contienda,
     qui quiere en palaçio,   qui quiere en su tienda.

336 Fueron allí clamados   los dios e las dehessas,
     rëys muchos, e condes,   reínas e condessas,
     dueñas e cavalleros,   e duques e duquessas;
     avié y un grant pueblo   sólo de juglaressas.

337 Avié muchos conçejos,   muchas gentes balderas,
     juglares de tod' el mundo,   de diversas maneras;
     aún, por más buscar,   ixién a las carreras,
     ca non podién dar cabo   a vaziar las calderas.

338 Sedié, com' es derecho,   cad'un' con su igual;
     assí sedién a tabla,   e mantenién ostal;
     duraron essas bodas   un mes, en tal señal
     que nunca y sintieron   escándalo nin mal.

339 El pecado, que siempre   andido en follía,
     cogió en essa paz   una mal' enconía;
     asmava, si pudiesse,   sembrar su zizanía,
     meter algunt escándalo   en essa cofradía.

340 Comién por aventura   tres dehessas en uno:
     por nombre les dizién   Venus, Palas e Juno;
     todas eran cabdales   e de linaje uno;
     nunca tan rica tabla   vío ome ninguno.

341 El pecado, que siempre   sossaca travessura,
     buscó una mançana   fermosa sin mesura.
     Escrivióla el malo   de mala escriptura,
     echósela en medio,   ¡atán en ora dura!

342 Ésta fue la materia,   es verdadera cosa:
     "Prenga esta mançana   de vos la más fermosa."
     Ellas, quando vidieron   fazienda tan preçiosa,
     estava cada una   por ganarla golosa.

334	The procession completed, the King made a speech to cheer his people and make them of good heart. He began from its origins the story of Troy, of how it was destroyed and for what reason.
335	The story tells of marriage between king and queen and the elaborate ceremonies held by the wealthy pair, with abundance for all in peace and without conflict, some in the palace and some apart in their tent.
336	Gods and goddesses were summoned there, many kings and counts, queens and countesses, ladies and knights, dukes and duchesses; there was a great crowd there made alone of lady minstrels.
337	There were many groups of people and many at leisure – from all over the world, performers of different kinds – and even then they went out to search the streets for more, for they could not finish eating what the cauldrons contained.
338	Each one, as is right, sat with his equal; thus they sat at table and kept rank in the hall; those celebrations lasted for a month in such a way that there was never any sense of dispute or harm.
339	The Devil, who has always been involved in wickedness, took a dislike to this peace and harmony; he planned, if he could, to sow his seed of darnel and create some discord amidst that brotherly gathering.
340	Three goddesses chanced to be eating together, Venus, Pallas and Juno by name; all were powerful and of the same descent; no man ever saw a table so rich.
341	The Devil, incessant weaver of mischief, sought out an apple, its beauty beyond measure; the evil one wrote on it in an evil script and cast it into their midst at an ill-fated hour.
342	This was the substance – it is a true account –: "Let the most beautiful among you take this apple." They, when they saw so attractive a prize, were each of them eager to win its sweet taste.

343   Dixo doña Juno: "Yo la devo aver."
      Respuso doña Palas: "Non lo puedo creer."
      "¡A la fe!", dixo Venus, "Non pued' esso seer,
      ca yo so más fermosa;   mía deve seer."

344   Entró entre las dueñas   baraja e entençia;
      non las podié nul ome   meter en abenençia;
      en cabo abiniéronse,   diéronse atenençia,
      que Paris el de Troya   diesse esta sentençia.

345   Quando plogo a Dios   que fueron abenidas,
      fueron delante Paris   al judiçio venidas;
      fueron de cada parte   las razones oídas;
      semejavan las dueñas   unas fieras legistas.

346   Quiérovos un poquillo   sobre Paris fablar,
      ond' podedes creer   e podedes firmar
      que lo que Dios ordena   cómo ave d'estar
      por nul seso del mundo   nos' puede estorvar.

347   Príamo era rëy   de Troya la çibdat;
      como dizen, estonçe   era grant heredat;
      su muger era Écuba,   fembra de grant bondad;
      ellos eran entrambos   muy buenos, por verdat.

348   Écuba la reína   fue de Paris preñada;
      soñó un fuerte sueño,   ante que fues' librada,
      que ixié de su cuerpo   una flama irada:
      quemava toda Troya,   tornávala en nada.

349   Despertó con el sueño   Écuba mal espantada;
      non cuidava que era   del fuego escapada.
      Luego que assomó   la luz del alvorada,
      dixo al rey Príamo   quál noch' avié llevada.

350   Quando ovo el rëy   el sueño entendido,
      perdió toda la sangre   e parós' estordido;
      veyé que era signo   müy malo complido;
      dixo: "Sea aquello   que Dios ha establido."

351   Alçó a Dios sus manos   e fizo un pedido:
      "Rey, Padre e Señor,"   dixo, "merçet Te pido,
      si este lugar ha   de seer destroído,
      ¡que mates a mí ante,   que assaz he bevido!

343 At this, Juno said: "It is I that must have it."
Pallas replied, "This I cannot believe."
"In faith," said Venus, "it cannot be so,
for I am most beautiful; it must be mine."

344 Among the ladies there arose such discord and dissent
that no man could bring them into agreement,
but at last they reached accord, and showed each other amity,
that Paris, the man from Troy, should make this judgement.

345 When it was God's will that they had reached this accord,
they went before Paris, coming to him for justice.
The cases were heard, put forward from each side;
the ladies seemed to be formidable lawyers.

346 I would like to talk to you just a little about Paris,
from which you can see and draw a firm conclusion
that all things whose working is ordained by God
cannot be hindered by any earthly design.

347 Priam was king of the city of Troy
– which, as they say, was a great inheritance –;
his wife was Hecuba, a woman of great goodness;
in truth they were a very fine king and queen.

348 When Queen Hecuba was pregnant with Paris,
she dreamed a compelling dream, before she gave birth:
that an angry flame issued forth from her body
which was burning all of Troy and reducing it to nothing.

349 Hecuba awoke in terror from her dream;
she did not think she had escaped from the fire;
as soon as the light of dawn began to show
she told King Priam of the night she had spent.

350 When the King had learned about the dream,
the blood drained from his face and he stood there bewildered.
He saw that a very grim sign had come about
and said: "Let it be as God has determined!"

351 He raised his hands to God and made a request:
"My King", he said, "and Father, my Lord, I entreat You
that if this place is to be destroyed,
You should kill me first, for I have lived long enough.

352 Por caridat, reína, que fagades un ruego,
que quiere que vos nasca que lo matedes luego.
Podredes por ventura amatar este fuego
si quisierdes fazer esto que vos yo ruego.

353 Menos de mal será que un fijo perdades
que de tan grant peligro vos carrera seades."
Respuso la reína: "Rëy, bien lo sepades,
faré muy volenter lo que vos me mandades."

354 Quando vino el tiempo que ovo de parir.
Écuba fue en cuita que cuidava morir;
mandó a las parteras quel' avién de servir
que quiere quel' naçiesse nol' dexassen bevir.

355 Naçió ge por pecado e por mala ventura
un infant' muy querido, apuesta crïatura;
furtáronlo las amas por su grant fermosura;
mintiéronle a Écuba ¡que les dé Dios rencura!

356 Como ant' vos dixiemos, lo que Dios ha parado
non podié ser por seso de ome estorvado:
mintieron a Ecuba, falsaron su mandado,
dieron lo a pastores que curiavan ganado.

357 Dávanle muy grant viçio, fue aína crïado;
luego que andar sopo vinos' pora'l poblado;
atant' era fermoso el que non fuesse nado
que se faziá el pueblo mucho maravillado.

358 Niño era ardido e müy sabidor,
en cara palaçiano e muy doñeador;
non ha rëy en mundo nin tal emperador
que si toviés' tal fijo nos' toviés' por mejor.

359 Fue aína sabida toda la poridat;
al rëy con su fijo plógol' de voluntat;
heredól' en su mueble e en su heredat,
camiól' encara el nombre con grant proprïedat.

360 Soliénlo Alexandre de primero clamar,
mas óvole el padre el nombre a mudar.
Paris le puso nombre, si lo oyestes contar,
ca egual lo fazié de los otros e par.

352	And, for pity's sake, my Queen, grant me this request, that you kill at once any child you bring forth. With good fortune you will be able to put out this fire, if you are willing to perform this act I ask of you.
353	It will do less harm that you should lose a son than that you should be the path to such great peril." The Queen replied, "My King, you know well that I will most willingly do what you command."
354	When the time came for her to give birth, Hecuba was so distressed that she feared she might die and she ordered the midwives who were to serve her that whatever child was born should not be allowed to live.
355	Through sin and through misfortune there was born a very dear child and a fine-looking baby; on account of his great beauty, the midwives stole him away and lied to Hecuba – may God send them bitterness!
356	As we said to you before, what God has determined cannot be prevented by the scheme of any man. They lied to Hecuba and did not carry out her orders, but gave the child to shepherds looking after their flocks.
357	They looked after him fondly and quickly did he grow; as soon as he could walk he went down into the city; so good-looking was this boy who should not have been born that the people were filled with wonder.
358	He was a child of courage and great intelligence, who also was courteous and full of great charm; there is no king or emperor in the world who would not feel himself the better for having such a son.
359	The whole of the secret was quickly disclosed. The King was truly delighted with his son and made him the heir to his possessions and lands; he also changed his name, as he was right to do.
360	At first people used to call him Alexander, but his father decided to change his name and gave him that of Paris, as you have heard tell, for it set him on a par with the others as their peer.

361   Apriso de retórica,   era bien razonado;
        en cara de sus armas   era muy esforçado.
        Por que les semejava   ome tan acabado,
        lo pusieron las dueñas   por su adelantado.

362   Quand' fueron ante Paris   dixieron sus razones,
        afincavan sus bozes   commo si fuessen varones;
        fazién, maguer mugeres,   fuertes alegaçiones;
        maravillosas eran   las sus conclusïones.

363   Començó doña Juno,   fabló la más primera;
        dieronle avantaja   por que reína era.
        Entró en su razón   como buena bozera,
        cuidóles a las otras   tomar la delantera.

364   Semejava que era   reína muy sabrosa;
        tenié en su cabeça   corona muy fermosa;
        luzié en derredor   mucha piedra preçiosa.
        Començó su razón   a guisa de cabosa.

365   "Oyas me," dixo, "Paris,   qué te quiero dezir;
        plógome quando ove   ante ti a venir;
        ca sé yo bien que amas   derecho departir
        e sé que non querrás   en judiçio fallir.

366   Muger so e hermana   del grant emperador,
        de Júpiter, que es   de los çielos señor;
        si él oviés' fallada   más genta o mejor
        a mí non escogiera   por seer su uxor.

367   De mi beldat non quiero   luenga mente contar;
        lo que parez' por ojo   non ha mester provar;
        la mi beldat a muchos   fizo e faz' lazrar;
        d'esto puedo, si mandas,   muchos testigos dar.

368   Por que es tan fermosa   la rueda del pavón,
        fue a mí aparejada   por atal razón;
        esto yaze en libro   que escrivió Nasón;
        devo con la mançana   ir a toda sazón.

369   Si esto otorgares,   que esto es derecho,
        fallart' as bien en ello   e avrás end' provecho;
        nunca te verás pobre   nin te verás mal trecho;
        e si tú al fizieres,   farás a mí despecho."

Book of Alexander

361 He learned about Rhetoric and constructed speeches well
and he was also skilled in the use of arms.
Because he seemed a man of such accomplishment,
the ladies settled upon him as their judge.

362 When they stood before Paris they set out their cases,
speaking resolutely as though they were men;
although they were women they produced strong arguments
and their conclusions were marvellously well drawn.

363 Juno began, it was she who spoke first
– they gave her precedence because she was queen –
and she began her speech like a first-rate lawyer,
thinking to gain an advantage over the others.

364 She had the appearance of a most elegant queen
and wore on her head a very beautiful crown;
about her she displayed a wealth of precious stones.
She began to speak as a fine and noble woman.

365 "Paris," she said, "hear me, and what I wish to say to you.
I was pleased it was you before whom I had to come,
for I know well that you love to dispense justice
and I know you will not want to err in your judgement.

366 I am the wife and sister of the great Emperor,
of Jupiter, who is lord of all the heavens.
Had he found a woman who was better or more beautiful,
he would not have chosen me to be his wife.

367 I do not want to tell you at length about my beauty,
for what is evident to the eye need not be proved.
Because of my beauty, many had and have to suffer;
of this, if you so order, I can bring many witnesses.

368 Because the peacock's tail is so beautiful,
for just that reason it is linked with me;
this is to be found in a book from Ovid's hand.*
The apple must be mine to have forever.

369 If you should grant that what I say is right
you will come out of this well and reap the reward;
you will never see yourself in poverty or hardship;
but if you act otherwise, you will waken spite within me."

370   Quand' ovo doña Juno   su razón acabada,
      Palas se levantó,   çinta la su espada.
      "Oyas me," dixo, "Paris,   diré mi dinarada;
      assaz ha dicho Juno. ¡Escuche su vegada!

371   De grant linaje viene,   assí com' ella diz'.
      Otrossí me so yo   d'essa misma raíz;
      so más genta que amas,   d'ojos e de nariz;
      çiertas, nom' preçio menos   d'una emperadriz.

372   So ligera de pies   e sé bien cavalgar;
      sé bien tener mis armas,   de ballesta tirar;
      quando de correr monte   vengo o de caçar,
      éstas non serién dignas   ante mí se parar.

373   Prosérpina me dizen;   de Febus so hermana;
      sin éste he dos nombres: Minerva e Dïana.
      Yo alumbro la noche,   adugo la mañana;
      sólo por esto devo   ir yo con la mançana.

374   Aún ay otra cosa   que deves tú asmar:
      tú por cavallería   as preçio de ganar
      e yo so la maestra   que te he de guïar;
      e puedes me tú öy   pora siempre adebdar.

375   Aún sobre tod' esto   al te quiero dezir:
      si yo esta vegada   en ti he de fallir,
      avert'has dura mente,   Paris, a repentir,
      e si tú as orejas,   deves esto oír."

376   Venus dio luego salto,   ixió del diversorio;
      paróse ante Paris   en medio'l consistorio.
      Más genta non ixió   a aquel parlatorio,
      que quanto de linaje   eran d'un avolorio.

377   Dueña era de preçio,   de cuerpo bien tajada;
      quanto tañié en mañas,   era bien enseñada;
      sobre todas las otras   era bien razonada;
      non devié a ninguna   por fermosura nada.

378   Por mostrar que non eran   las otras sus parejas
      alcofoló los ojos,   tiñó las sobreçejas;
      cubrióse de colores   blancas e bermejas,
      cargó sortijas d'oro   en ambas sus orejas.

370	When Juno had finished and given her speech, Pallas rose to her feet and girded on her sword. "Paris," she said, "hear me, and I shall give my arguments; Juno has said enough; it is her turn to listen.
371	She comes from noble lineage, just as she says; I likewise have exactly those same roots; my eyes and my nose are lovelier than theirs, and for certain I prize myself as highly as any empress.
372	I am light of foot and can ride horses well; I am skilled in wielding arms and firing a crossbow; and when I return from riding in the hills or from the hunt these two would not be worthy to stand before me.
373	I am known as Proserpina and am sister of Phoebus;* I have two names besides this: Minerva and Diana. I light up the night and I bring on the morning; for this alone I must be awarded the apple.
374	There is one more thing that you must take into account: you are to win your reputation through your skills as a horseman; I am the teacher who will always be your guide and you today can put me forever in your debt.
375	There is yet one more thing that I wish to say to you: if on this occasion I am to lack support in you, in the future, Paris, you will regret it bitterly and if you have ears you must listen to what I say."
376	Venus then leapt up and left the waiting chamber;* she stood before Paris in the centre of the courtroom; no more beautiful woman entered that locutory, and with regard to lineage their ancestry was alike.
377	She was a very noble lady, with a body finely formed. In concerns of conduct she was very well taught and eloquent in speech, more so than the others, neither of whom surpassed her in beauty.
378	To show that her rivals could not compare with her, she darkened her eyes and tinted her eyebrows; she made herself up with white and with red and in both her ears she wore rings of gold.

379 Descubrióse el boço   quand' ovo de fablar;
     catava contra Paris,   començó de çeñar;
     dixo: "Si quieres, Paris,   el derecho judgar,
     ya lo vees por ojo   qui la deve levar.

380 De un linaje somos,   como ellas dixeron.
     Quanto tañe en eso,   en nada non mintieron;
     mas, como en lo al   dixeron que pudieron,
     falsaron de la regla quand' donas prometieron.

381 En las ondas del mar füi yo engendrada,
     quando dio a su padre   Júpiter la colpada;
     non ovi otra madre,   por que so más honrada;
     tovos' don Mars por rico   quandom' ovo ganada.

382 Quanto en el judiçio   sé que non falsarás,
     mas quiérote dezir   el pro que ganarás;
     si tú esta mançana,   Paris, a mí la das,
     tal don avrás de mí   que siempre gozarás.

383 Quit' promete riqueza   non te faz' nul amor;
     ca tú as assaz d'ella,   merçed al Crïador;
     e por cavallería   Éctor non es mejor,
     ond' pareçe que Palas   es baratador.

384 De lo que non as mengua   ellas assaz prometen;
     non lo fazen por al   si non que te abeten;
     qual que les es contrario   ellas aquesso temen;
     si lo tú bien entiendes,   mucho te escarneçen.

385 Lo que pora ti es,   ond' as tú de pujar,
     lo que fijo de rey   ha siempre de buscar,
     todo yaz' en mi mano   de toller e de dar,
     ca, si por mí non fuere,   non podrás bien casar.

386 Dart'he yo casamiento   muger qual tú quisieres,
     por casar o casada,   qual quier' que me pidieres;
     yo non te fallecré   si tú non me falleres."
     A esto dixo Paris: "Judgo que tú la lieves."

387 Venus fue con el preçio,   las otras con rencura,
     desafiaron a Paris   con toda su natura;
     toviéronlo por falso   e por sin derechura
     e que devrié aver   toda mala ventura.

379	She revealed her face when it came to her to speak. Looking into Paris' eyes, she began to wink; she said "Paris, if you want to give the right verdict, you can see with your own eyes who must win."
380	We are of one lineage, as they have said. In that respect, all that they told you was true; but whilst in all else they spoke things within their power, they deceived you when they promised you gifts.
381	I was given life in the waves of the sea when Jupiter struck the blow against his father.* I had no other mother and so I am more honoured. Mars felt rich indeed when he had won me for his own.
382	As for the judgement, I know that you will not err, but I want to tell you what advantage you will gain: if you, Paris, award this apple to me, you will earn a reward that will bring you joy forever.
383	The one who promises riches is doing you no favour, for you have enough of these, thanks be to God; and in the art of horsemanship, Hector is no better, and so Pallas, it seems, is engaged in deceit.
384	They are promising you plenty of what you do not lack and they do this for no purpose other than to deceive you, for they fear whatever goes against their own interests. If you see this clearly, greatly do they mock you.
385	What is for your own good and by which you will prosper, what the son of a king is always compelled to seek, to give or take away lies entirely in my hand, for without my aid you will not marry well.
386	I shall grant you marriage with a woman of your choice, married or unmarried, whoever you ask of me; I shall not fail you, provided you do not fail me." To this Paris replied, "I judge that you win the contest."
387	Venus carried off the prize; the others were filled with fury. They protested against Paris from the bottom of their hearts; they considered him fickle and with no sense of justice and thought that he deserved all possible ill fortune.

388   Avié oído Paris   d'una dueña famada,
      muger de Menalao,   ¡en fuerte punto nada!
      Era por tod' el mundo   la su beldat contada;
      demandógela Paris   a Venus en soldada.

389   Dixo Venus a Paris: "Grant cosa as pedida;
      éssa que tú demandas   otra vez fue rabida;
      tienen la – por es' miedo –   agora escondida,
      mas sepas que en el mundo   no sé yo tan vellida.

390   Pero lo que demandas   es a mí a complir;
      non te puedo, que quiera,   Paris, contradezir;
      podremos en la cosa   a duro abenir,
      mas avremos a ella,   como que quiera, ir.

391   Quiérote demostrar   cómo ha de seer,
      que vayas aguisando   lo que avrás de fer;
      piensa de aguisar   abtezas e aver;
      métete en las naves   e véla a veer.

392   Faz te camiar el nombre,   vé como mercadero;
      non t'entienda ninguno   que eres cavallero;
      el prínçip' Menalao   non será tan artero
      que a entrar non ayas   tú en el su çillero.

393   En la cort' poc'a poco   ferte as conosçer,
      a chicos e a grandes   a todos faz plazer;
      avrás como que sea,   la dueña a veer;
      yol' metré en coraçón,   avert'ha a querer.

394   Dali de tus abtezas,   como ome granado;
      avrás de la reína   algunt solaz privado;
      como tú bien pareçes,   eres bien razonado;
      podrás, como que sea   recabdar tu mandado.

395   Pero a la reína   dili tu poridat;
      fazle entender bien   toda tu voluntat;
      las mugeres son febles,   olvidan lealtat;
      avrá de ti cordojo,   fazert'a caridat.

396   Yol' traeré consejo,   darl'e mis medeçinas,
      las que yo suelgo dar   a las otras reínas;
      todas nos entendemos,   como somos vezinas;
      creo que te querrá   meter so sus cortinas."

388	Paris had heard of a lady of great fame, Menelaus' wife, ill-starred at her birth.* Her beauty was renowned throughout the whole world; Paris asked Venus for her as his reward.
389	Venus said to Paris, "You have made a great request. This woman that you ask for was carried off once before; now for fear of this they keep her hidden away, but I tell you that in the world I know of no greater beauty.
390	Yet it falls to me, Paris, to do what you ask; even if I wish, I cannot go against your word. We may find this task a hard one to perform, but we shall succeed in it come what may.
391	I want to explain to you just how it is to be, so that you may prepare for what you will have to do; set about readying treasures and goods, embark on your ships and set off to see her.
392	Have your name changed and travel as a merchant; let nobody find out that you are a knight; Prince Menelaus will not be so clever as to stop you making your way into his granary.
393	In court you are gradually to make yourself known; curry favour with all people, young and old; in one way or another you will get to meet the lady; she will fall in love with you – I shall set it in her heart.
394	Give the King some treasure, as a wealthy man might; you will have a chance to be alone with the Queen; as you have good looks and have a way with words, one way or another you will gain what you seek
395	But to the Queen you should disclose your secret and explain to her fully all your heart's desire. Women are fickle and their loyalties forget; she will be moved by you and will treat you with affection.
396	I will persuade her and give her my medicine, the one I am accustomed to give to other queens. We all understand each other, because we are of equal rank; I think that she will want to slip you beneath her curtains."

397 Paris, con la cobdiçia de la dueña ganar,
    entró luego en barcas e travessó la mar;
    fasta que fue en Greçia, non se dio a vagar;
    ovo a la reína el su prez a plegar.

398 Óvol' en grant privança el rey a acoger,
    non le mandava puerta ninguna retener.
    Ovo todos los pleitos la dueña a saber;
    en cabo otorgóse a todo su plazer.

399 Ovo'l rëy a ir en una cavalgada.
    Fizo el mercadero a riedro la tornada;
    tant' ovo a bollir quel' robó la posada;
    tornós' pora Troya con su dueña ganada.

400 Fueron al rey las nuevas e sopiéronle mal;
    tovo al mercadero por falso desleal.
    Tornóse pora Greçia, dexó todo lo al;
    falló de mala guisa barrido su ostal.

401 Plegó sus ricos omes e toda su natura,
    plorando de los ojos, diziendo su rencura:
    "Oíd," dixo, "amigos: naçí en ora dura;
    terném', si non me vengo, por de mala ventura.

402 Parientes e amigos, por el Nuestro Señor,
    de tamaño quebranto ¡que vos prenga dolor!
    ¡Vayámonos vengar del falso traïdor!"
    Respusiéronli todos: "¡Müy de buen amor!"

403 Todos por una boca, como si fuessen hermanos,
    juráronle al rey en amas las sus manos,
    que nunca le faldrién, nin enfermos nin sanos,
    ata que destruyessen los adarves troyanos.

404 Con esta segurança creçiól' el coraçón;
    vertié fuegos e flamas, como puerco verrón;
    plegó huestes sobejas de su generaçión;
    por amor de vengarse nol' dolié fer missión.

405 Cataron por agüeros; ovieron a veer
    que ante de diez años non la podrién prender;
    fasta'l onzeno año y avrién de yazer;
    mas serié mucha sangre primero a verter.

397	Paris, in his keen desire to win the lady, immediately embarked and sailed across the sea; he did not break the journey until he was in Greece; now his reputation reached the ears of the Queen.
398	The King came to take him into his confidence and ordered that no door be barred against him. The Queen came to know about all of his dealings and finally yielded to him just as he desired.
399	The King then had to ride out on campaign and the merchant turned and retraced his steps, so able to intrigue that he robbed the palace and returned to Troy with the lady he had won.
400	The news reached the King and he was filled with anger, condemning the merchant as disloyal and false. He returned to Greece and forsook all other cares; he found that his home had been cruelly plundered.
401	He gathered his nobles and all those of his line; with tears falling from his eyes, he told them of his rancour. "Listen to me, my friends; I was ill-fated at birth; I shall hold myself ill-starred if I do not take my vengeance.
402	My relatives and friends, in the name of our Lord, you must be grieved at so great an affront. Let us go and take vengeance on that treacherous deceiver." Every one of them replied: "With the greatest of pleasure."
403	All, with one voice, as if they were brothers, swore to the King on both of their hands that never would they fail him, with sick or healthy body, until they had destroyed the walls of Troy.
404	With this assurance, his heart swelled up large, and he spat out fire and flame like a wild boar. He assembled a vast army from his people; desiring vengeance, he felt no grief at its cost.
405	They interpreted the omens and they came to see that they could not take the city in under ten years, that they would have to stay there into the eleventh* but that first much blood was to be shed.

406 Calcas, un agorero, que sabié bien catar,
vío una serpiente con dos aves lidiar;
avién ocho fijuelos, querié gelos matar,
mas non gelos pudieron en cabo emparar.

407 Desque mató los fijos, tornó en los parientes,
e óvolos a ambos a degollar a dientes.
Estonçe dixo Calcas a las greçiscas gentes:
"Avedes grant agüero. ¡Meted en todo mientes!

408 A los griegos demuestra la sierpe ravïosa,
las aves los troyanos, que son gent' deliçiosa;
la cuenta son los años de la çerca lazrosa;
provaredes que esto es verdadera cosa."

409 Fízoles otro fado, sin éste, entender,
que Aquiles avrié a Éctor a vençer;
en cabo él avrié y a remaneçer;
ca, menos de atanto, non la podrién prender.

410 La madre de Aquiles era müy artera,
que era adevina e encara sortera;
sopo que, si su fijo fues' en esta carrera,
avriá y a morir por alguna manera.

411 Quando era chiquiello, fízolo encantar
que non pudiesse fierro en él nunca entrar;
e fízolo en orden de sorores entrar
que, maguer lo buscassen, nol' pudiessen fallar.

412 Fue por todas las órdenes don Aquiles buscado;
nunca fincó rincón que non fues' demandado;
mas, como ponié tocas e era demudado,
fallar non lo pudieron ca non era guisado.

413 Y sossacó Ulixes una grant maestría
por saber si Aquiles era en la mongía;
dizen que si non fuesse por la su artería
non salliera Aquiles enton' de la freiría.

414 Priso çintas e tocas, camisas e çapatas,
espejos e sortijas, otras tales baratas;
en la buelta, escudos, e ballestas e astas;
diógelas en presente a las toquinegradas.

406	Calchas, a soothsayer skilled in reading omens, saw a serpent locked in battle with two birds; they had eight chicks, which it wanted to kill, but in the end they were unable to protect them.
407	Once it had killed the chicks it turned on the parents and it managed to pull the head off each one. Then Calchas said to the people of Greece, "You have a great augury. Take heed of all I say:
408	the angry snake represents the Greeks and the birds are the Trojans, a people fond of pleasure; the number is the years that the grim siege will last; you will prove all of this to be true."
409	As well as this, he told them of another prophecy, that Achilles would have victory over Hector, but in the end he would have to remain there in death, for unless all this happened, they could not take the city.
410	Achilles' mother was a very artful woman, for she was a sorceress and could see into the future; she knew that if her son took part in this expedition he would meet his death there in some fashion.*
411	When he was very young she cast a spell on him such that no iron could ever enter his body and she had him enter an order of holy sisters so that even if sought, he could not be found.
412	They looked for Achilles throughout every convent and no corner remained where they did not hunt for him, but, as he wore a nun's wimple and his appearance was changed, they were unable to find him, for it was no easy task.
413	Ulysses devised there a masterful trick to discover if Achilles was in the convent. They say that were it not for his cunning Achilles would not have left the nunnery.
414	He took ribbons and wimples, undershirts and shoes, mirrors and rings and other such trinkets and, on the other hand, crossbows, shields and lances. He gave them, as a present, to the ladies dressed in black.

415   Escogié cada una   de lo que le plazié;
Aquiles de las armas   los ojos non tollié;
meneava las astas,   los escudos prendié.
Luego dixo Ulixes   que aquél ser podrié.

416   Travaron luego d'él,   diéronle otros paños,
pensaron mucho d'él,   metiéronlo en baños.
Su madre de Aquiles   dava grandes sossaños,
mas nol' valieron nada   todos sus engaños.

417   Avié una amiga   que él mucho querié;
teniéla por fermosa   qui quier' que la veyé;
el rey Agamenón,   por que bien pareçié,
tollióla a Aquiles,   que mal non mereçié.

418   Pesól' de voluntad,   tovos' por desonrado,
ca lo avié el rey   mala ment' aontado.
Non lo quiso sofrir,   partióse d'él irado,
començó darle guerra   com' ome despojado.

419   Tant' denonada mente   lo pudo guerrear,
tantos muchos le pudo   de vassallos matar,
que, como diz' Omero,   que non quiere bafar,
quántos eran los muertos   non los podién contar.

420   Assí yazién los muertos   com' en restrojo paja;
non los podién cobrir   nin meter en mortaja;
levávanlos como lieva   los pelos la navaja;
ermarse ie la hueste   si duras' la baraja.

421   Fizieron los varones   conçejo general;
dixéronle al rëy: "Señor, estáte mal.
La huest' es mal andante   e a ti non t'encal'.
Si la dueña non riendes,   tornaremos en al."

422   Rindió el rey la dueña   a todo su mal grado;
quand' la ovo Aquiles,   fue todo amansado.
Tornó en paz la guerra,   que pesó al pecado.
Fue desí adelante   don Aquiles dubdado.

423   Avié y un mal ome   ávol e mal lenguado,
desleal e sobervio,   vil e desmesurado.
Tersites avié nombre,   ¡el que aya mal fado!
Dixo una palabra   que nol' ovieron grado:

415	Each one was allowed to choose just as she wished but Achilles could not take his eyes off the weapons, brandishing the lances and taking up the shields; then Ulysses said that he might well be the one.
416	They took hold of him and dressed him in other clothes, they gave him every attention and they bathed him; Achilles' mother was loud in her complaints but all her deceptions did nothing to help her.
417	He had a friend whom he greatly loved;* all who saw her considered her beautiful. King Agamemnon, because of her great beauty, snatched her from Achilles, who deserved no such wrong.
418	It weighed heavy on him and he felt himself dishonoured, for the King had grievously shamed him. He would not endure it and left him, in a temper. Like a man despoiled, he began a war against him.
419	So furiously was he able to wage war, and so many vassals was he able to kill, that, as Homer says – I do not want to overstate it –, the dead were so numerous that they could not be counted.
420	The dead lay scattered like straw in a field of stubble, they could not cover them or dress them in shrouds; they were cut down as a razor cuts through hair; if the conflict were to last the army would be ruined.
421	The barons of the kingdom held a general council and said to the King, "Lord, things are ill for you: the army is in a poor state and you pay no heed. If you do not return the lady we shall take a different path."
422	The King returned the lady, all against his will, and when Achilles had her with him he was completely calmed; the war turned to peace, to the sorrow of the Devil, and from this point on Achilles inspired fear.
423	There was a wicked man there, base and vile of tongue, treacherous and arrogant, evil and fond of excess. Thersites was his name – may he meet a cruel fate! – the words that he spoke were the cause of great trouble.

424 "Varones," dixo él, "¿en qué nos contendemos?
Otri avrá el pro e nos y lazraremos;
en cabo galardón ninguno non avremos.
Si creer me quisierdes, quiero que nos tornemos."

425 Como diz' la palabra que suelen retraer,
que más pued' en conçejo un malo cofonder
que non podrién diez buenos assentar nin poner;
ovier' allí por poco assí a conteçer.

426 Creyeron a Tersites la más mayor partida;
era pora tornarse toda la gent' movida.
Ulixes fue irado, diol' una grant ferida;
la gent' de su natura tovos' por escarnida.

427 Partiéronse los vandos, quisiéronse matar;
grand' era la rebuelta, non los podién quedar;
todos clamavan armas, todos querién lidiar;
querié la su simiente el dïablo sembrar.

428 Avié un ome bueno, viejo e de grant seso;
era de grandes días, blanco como el queso;
do quier' que uvïava, siempre fue bien apreso;
era en los judiçios tan igual com' el peso.

429 Néstor era su nombre, avié mucho bevido;
escuchávanlo todos e era bien oído.
Pesól' de voluntat quando vio el roído,
metióseles en medio con un bastón bronido.

430 Maltrayélos a firmes, dava les bastonadas;
todos por su verguença escondién las espadas.
Diziéles a las gentes que soviessen quedadas
que fazién desaguisado, eran mal acordadas.

431 Maltrayé a Tersites que dixiera locura;
rebtava a los otros que fazién desmesura;
diziéles: "¡Ay, amigos, mal vos miembra la jura
que jurastes al rëy quand' vos dixo su rencura!

432 Calcas el agorero sabié bien terminado;
avemos, *Deo graçias*, a Aquiles fallado;
de vengar nuestra onta era bien aguisado;
mas quiere destorvarnos agora el pecado."

424	"My lords," he said, "for what do we fight? Another will gain while we find hardship there; in the end, we shall be rewarded with nothing. Should you wish to believe me, I wish us to return home."
425	According to the saying, which is often repeated, in a council one bad member can cause harm greater than the progress and accord ten good ones can achieve; it very nearly happened there in just that way.
426	The majority of them did believe Thersites and all the people were moved to favour a return. Ulysses was angered and struck him a sharp blow; those of Thersites' line felt themselves insulted.
427	The groups divided up, ready to kill each other; great was the uproar; they could not be calmed down. All were calling for arms, all eager to fight; the devil now sought to sow his seed.
428	There was a good man there, old and of great wisdom – in great old age, he had hair as white as cheese – whatever place he came to, he was always well received, and in his judgements he was as just as the balance.
429	Nestor was his name and he had lived for many years. They all listened to him and his words were heeded. It weighed heavy on him when he saw the disturbance and he made his way into their midst with his burnished staff.
430	He criticised them roundly and struck blows with his staff; all of them felt shamed and hid their swords away. He told the men to be still, that they should be at peace and that they were acting foolishly, forgetting their accord.
431	He criticised Thersites, whose words had been folly, and rebuked the others for their excessive conduct. He said to them, "Oh, my friends, you are forgetting the oath that you swore to the King when he told you of his grievance!
432	As Calchas the prophet wisely foretold, we have found Achilles, thanks be to God! He was well capable of avenging our shame; but now the Devil wants to stand in our way."

433　　El dicho de don Néstor　　fue tan bien adonado
　　　　que el fervor del pueblo　　fue todo amansado.
　　　　Fue tenido por ome　en seso acabado;
　　　　fue d'allí adelante　　temido e amado.

434　　Otro día mañana,　aprés de los albores,
　　　　el rëy por la hueste　　mandó ferir pregones:
　　　　que rancassen las tiendas,　moviessen los peones,
　　　　entrassen en la mar　　con naves e pontones.

435　　Si me el Crïador　　quisiesse ayudar,
　　　　los nombres de los prínçipes　　vos querría contar:
　　　　los que con Menalao　　fueron Troya çercar
　　　　e cada uno quántas　　naves pudo llevar.

436　　El prínçipe Peneleus　　e el varón Laeretes,
　　　　Arquesilao el fuerte,　　Pretenor e Boetes,
　　　　todos eran parientes　　e de grandes averes;
　　　　trayén çinquenta naves,　　plenas de sus poderes.

437　　Otro rëy de Greçia,　　por nombre Agamenón,
　　　　llevava dos atantas　　plenas de grant missión.
　　　　Por que de todas era　　prínçipe Menalón,
　　　　trayé sesenta naves,　　tantas Agapenón.

438　　Néstor el ançïano,　de los cabellos canos,
　　　　el que dixe que dava　　los consejos muy sanos,
　　　　con dos fijos que bien　　semejavan hermanos,
　　　　trayé seis vezes quinze　　por fer mal a troyanos.

439　　Ascladus e Pistopus,　dos cuerpos muy honrados,
　　　　en treguas muy leales,　　en guerras muy dubdados,
　　　　levavan treinta naves　　de omes adobados;
　　　　non avié entre todos　　omes más denodados.

440　　Plipetas e Leontas,　　ambos buenos braçeros,
　　　　trayén treïnta naves　　de buenos cavalleros.
　　　　Esténelus e Surípilo,　　Dïomedes con ellos,
　　　　otras tantas trayén　　éstos solos señeros.

441　　Escálapus con Télamon,　　su leal compañero,
　　　　éstos trayén treïnta,　　como lo diz' Omero.
　　　　Áyaz cargó quarenta　　él solo señero;
　　　　levava otras tantas　el fi del Ulixero.

433	The words that Nestor spoke were so well judged that the anger of the people was completely calmed; he was held to be a man of consummate wisdom and from then on he was both feared and loved.
434	The following morning, as soon as dawn broke, the King ordered that it be proclaimed throughout the army that the tents should be dismantled and the troops prepare to move, and that with ships and pontoons they were to set sail.
435	Should the Creator be willing to give me His aid, I would like to tell you of the names of the princes* who went with Menelaus to lay siege to Troy and how many ships each one was able to take.
436	Prince Peneleus and Baron Laërtes, strong Arcesilaus, Prothoënor and Boetes. All these were relatives and men of great wealth, and brought fifty ships full of their troops.
437	Another king of Greece, Agamemnon by name,* took twice as many ships, all packed with equipment, and Menelaus, because he was prince of all of them, brought sixty ships, and Agapenor just as many.
438	The elderly Nestor with his head of grey hair – the man who, as I told you, gave wise counsel –, with two sons who had in every way the look of brothers, brought six fifteens of ships to inflict harm on the Trojans.
439	Schedius and Epistrophus, two men of highest honour, loyal in times of peace and much feared in war, took with them thirty ships of well equipped men – in the whole force there were none of greater spirit.
440	Polypoetes and Leonteus, fine warriors both, brought thirty ships that were full of good knights; Sthenelus, Euryalus, and Diomedes with them, these leaders brought just as many by themselves.
441	Ascalaphus and Ialmenus, his loyal companion, as Homer says, brought with them thirty ships. Ajax contributed forty – all of these by himself –,* and just as many were taken by Ulysses' son.*

442 Inchió çinquenta naves   Aquiles el claustral,
en todos non avié   uno mejor nin tal.
Éste fue de las aguas   crïado natural;
non le fazián los vientos   nin contrario nin mal.

443 Antifus e Peliofus,   dos niños de Tesalia,
ivan con treinta naves   contra la gent' d'Italia.
Térçer e Tritolemus   embiavan doz' en paria;
querién a los de Troya   buscar toda contraria.

444 Rodius e Eumelenus,   dos vassallos leales,
plenas de cavalleros   llevavan onze naves.
Áyaz el Telamón,   un de los mayorales,
non trayé más de doze,   éstas bïen cabdales.

445 Astrofus e un otro   que era fijo de Téstor,
Rubëus e Mejés,   Duliquius e Alpénor,
Télamus e Ascálapus,   Doas, fi de Anténor:
éstos trayén diez naves   bien guisadas d'onor.

446 Levava doze naves   Ulixes el artero;
iva con otras tantas   Áyaz el Telamero.
Ordifineus, un cuerpo   de fuerça sobrançero,
aguisó veint' e dos;   ést' era buen guerrero.

447 Idomenes e Merion   ambos eran de Creta;
trayán en su quinón   éstos solos sesenta.
Iva con otras tantas   el fijo de Moneta;
de Atenas fue éste,   como lo diz' la letra.

448 Anfimacus, Alpinus,   Políxenes e Otas;
éstos avién treïnta,   bien adobadas todas;
traye Protesilao   con Podarco siet' solas;
otras tantas llevava   el fijo de Fetontas.

449 Maguer todos dixiemos,   aún Áyaz fincava,
que de cavallerías   quatro naves llevava.
Polidarius, el mege   que enfermos sanava,
con Macaón a bueltas,   con treinta naveaba.

450 Éstos fueron los prínçipes   que de Greçia ixieron;
mas otros ovo y   que nombre non ovieron
ca, que una que dos,   tantas naves trayeron
que de mill e dozientas   catorze falleçieron.

442	Achilles of the convent filled fifty ships full, in the whole fleet there were none as good or better; this man was a natural child of the seas; the winds bore him neither opposition nor harm.
443	Antiphus and Pheidippus, two sons of Thessaly, sailed with thirty ships against the people of Italy; Nireus and Tlepolemus sent twelve as their tribute, wanting to cause every hindrance to the people of Troy.
444	Rhodius and Eumelus, two loyal vassals, took eleven ships that were filled full of knights; Ajax son of Telamon, one of the leading nobles, brought no more than twelve, but these of great quality.
445	Prothous and one other, the son of Tenthredon, Eubeus and Meges, Dulichius and Elephenor, Ialmenus and Ascalaphus, Thoas, son of Antenor: these brought ten ships, well and honourably equipped.
446	The crafty Ulysses took twelve ships with him. Ajax son of Telamon went with just the same number; Phineus, a man of towering strength, prepared twenty-two; he was a fine warrior.
447	Idomeneus and Meriones were both from Crete; these two alone brought sixty ships to contribute, and Menestheus' son with just as many more – this man was from Athens, as the text recounts.
448	Amphimachus, Thalpius, Polyxinus and Diores, these had thirty, all fully equipped. Protesilaus, with Podarces, brought just seven and the son of Poeas came with just as many.
449	Though we have mentioned them all, still Ajax was left, who brought with him four ships full of cavalry; Podalirius, the doctor who cared for the ill, and with him Machaon, sailed with thirty ships.
450	These were the princes who sailed from Greece but there were others who went without name, for, in their ones and twos, they brought so many ships that of one thousand two hundred, they were short fourteen.

451 Arribaron al puerto,   bien alegres e sanos,
     ancoraron las naves,   posaron por los planos;
     rindién graçias a Dios   e alçavan sus manos;
     pensaron de folgar,   ca eran quebrantados.

452 Aún ellos non eran   del puerto levantados,
     al buen rëy de Troya   llegaron los mandados
     que avién grandes pueblos   de Greçia arribados,
     que vinién sobre Troya   sañosos e irados.

453 Membról' al rey del sueño,   ovo miedo sobejo;
     el grant cuer que aviá   fízos'le poquillejo.
     Mandó ferir pregones   que fiziessen conçejo,
     sobre tan grant fazienda   que prisiessen consejo.

454 Dixo Éctor al padre: "¡Vos fincadvos en paz!
     Avedes buenos fijos   e vassallos assaz.
     Nos iremos a ellos,   ferremos les de faz;
     nunca se encontraron   con tan crudo agraz."

455 Armóse el buen cuerpo,   ardient' e muy leal.
     Vistióse a carona   un gambax de çendal,
     de suso la loriga   blanca como cristal.
     "Fijo," dixo su padre,   "¡Dios te curie de mal!"

456 Calçó sus brafoneras   que eran bien obradas,
     de sortijas d'açero   sobre bien enlaçadas;
     assí eran bien presas   e tan bien assentadas
     que semejavan calças   de la tienda sacadas.

457 Pues fincó los inojos   e çiñós' la espada.
     Qui tollerla quisiesse   avriála bien comprada.
     Cubrióse d'un almofre,   una cofia delgada;
     de suso puso un yelmo   de obra adïana.

458 Cavalgó su cavallo   fermoso e ligero,
     sobra bien enfrenado,   de fuerça sobrançero.
     Priso lança en mano,   en braço el tavlero;
     qui dubda nol' oviesse   serié buen cavallero.

459 El buen pueblo de Troya   fue luego aguisado;
     ixieron con don Éctor   de amor e de grado.
     Assentaron las tiendas   de fuera en un prado
     fasta que fue el pueblo   todo y aplegado.

| 451 | They reached the harbour, joyful and safe,
| | they anchored the ships and camped on the plains.
| | They raised their hands and gave thanks to God;
| | they were eager to rest, for they were greatly wearied.

| 452 | They had not yet left the harbour
| | when word reached the good King of Troy
| | that great forces had arrived from Greece,
| | bearing down on Troy in anger and wrath.

| 453 | The King remembered the dream and was deeply afraid;
| | his great heart shrank to a tiny size.
| | He ordered it to be proclaimed that there would be a council,
| | so that they could take counsel on a matter so important.

| 454 | Hector said to his father, "You can be at peace,
| | you have good sons and a good number of vassals.
| | We shall go against them, take them on in open battle;
| | never have they encountered a grape so bitter."

| 455 | The fine warrior armed himself, a valiant and loyal man;
| | next to his skin he wore a padded doublet of fine cloth,
| | and over that, his body armour, which was as white as crystal.
| | "My son," said his father, "may God keep you from harm!"

| 456 | He put on greaves and arm-guards, which were finely worked
| | and elegantly adorned with steel rings;
| | they were so securely fastened and neatly fitting
| | that they seemed like hose that had been cut from cloth.

| 457 | Then he knelt down and girded on his sword;
| | whoever wished to take it would have paid a high price.
| | He put on a mail hood and a fine cap
| | and on top he put the helmet of great worth.

| 458 | He mounted his beautiful and swift-footed horse,
| | richly saddled and of towering strength.
| | He took his lance in his hand and his shield on his arm.
| | It would be a fine knight who had no fear of him.

| 459 | The good people of Troy at once made ready,
| | and with love and good will they rode out with Hector.
| | They set up camp in a field outside the city
| | until all of the people had arrived.

460 Con él ixió don Paris, de la grant fermosura,
el que pora sus gentes naçió en ora dura.
Otros y ovo muchos, com' diz' la escriptura:
prínçipes acabados, todos de grant natura.

461 Tanta de buena gente y era aplegada,
que, si non por que era contra ellos la fada,
ovieran de los griegos a Troya emparada
e non fuera su cosa atán mal aguisada.

462 El pecado, que nunca en paz pudo seer,
tanto pudo el malo bollir e rebolver,
que ovo de tal guisa las huestes a poner
que bien podién los unos a los otros veer.

463 Paris, por demostrarse de quál esfuerço era,
e por far pagamiento a la su compañera,
partióse de los suyos, priso la delantera,
como si él oviesse a tener la frontera.

464 Violo por aventura – mostrógelo el pecado –
Menalao el biudo, al que ovo robado.
Tornó el mal astrugo tan mal escarmentado
com' si fierro caliente lo oviesse quemado.

465 Quando lo vío Éctor venir cabez' tornando,
cuidó que lo vinién los griegos segudando;
ixió a reçebirlo apriessa aguijando;
fuese un grant roído por la huest' levantando.

466 Mas quando entendié de quál guisa vinié,
que por la vista sola de Menalao fuyé,
airós' de fiera guisa, ca piedá lo avié.
Por poco que con ira a él nos' remetié.

467 Començól' mal traer con palabras airadas;
díxol': "Tus bondades as las bien acabadas;
busqueste la nemiga, fuyes de las lançadas,
as todas tus gentes mala ment' aontadas.

468 Quand' corriés la palestra, a todos nos vençiés;
bien cuidavas que nunca tu igual fallariés;
quand robeste la dueña, esso non comediés;
estonçes delant' ella grandes nuevas faziés.

460	With him rode out Paris, a man of great good looks, the man whose hour of birth was ill-fated for his people. There were many others there, as the writings say: princes of great standing, all of noble line.
461	So many fine people had come together there that, had fate not been standing in their way, they would have protected Troy from the Greeks and things would not have ended so badly for them.
462	The Devil, who was never able to be at peace, the evil one, was so able to agitate and intrigue that he managed to bring the armies so close that they were now in full sight of each other.
463	Paris, to show the extent of his valour, and in order to please her who was his companion, left his own troops and rode out ahead of them as if to hold the boundary between the armies.
464	He saw by chance – the Devil pointed him out – Menelaus the widower, the man he had robbed; the ill-fated man turned, so cruelly shamed as if he had been burned by hot iron.
465	When Hector saw him coming, looking back over his shoulder, he thought that the Greeks were coming after him in pursuit. He spurred on rapidly and went out to meet him and a great roar gradually spread throughout the army.
466	But when he understood the manner of his coming, that he was fleeing at the mere sight of Menelaus, he grew deeply angry, for he felt contempt for him and in his fury was not far from striking out at him.
467	He began to chastise him with angry words and said: "You have clearly put an end to your good deeds. You went in search of combat but fled from the lance blows; upon all your people you have brought deep shame.
468	When you competed in the arena you got the better of us all, and you believed that you would never encounter your equal; when you stole the lady you did not have this in mind and then in her presence you put on a great show.

469 Nos' faze la fazienda   por cabellos peinados,
     nin por ojos fermosos,   nin çapatos picados;
     mester ha puños duros,   carrillos denodados,
     ca lanças nin espadas   non saben de falagos.

470 Non lo querrié nul ome   por derecho judgar:
     por tú dormir con ella   nos aquí lo lidiar.
     ¡Mas lidiat lo vos amos!   ¡Pensat de lo livrar!
     ¡Ésse lieve la dueña   que la debe levar!"

471 Dixo Paris a Éctor: "Mal me as porfaçiado;
     creo que assaz deves   de mí seer vengado.
     Non quiero al dezir;   de tu dicho me pago;
     reçibo el judiçio   que tú aves judgado."

472 Embïó a los griegos   Éctor este mandado.
     Plaçiól' a Menalao,   tóvose por pagado;
     fue de ambas las partes   el pleito otorgado;
     fue luego el lugar   e el dia atajado.

473 A todos plogo mucho   con esta abenençia:
     tovieron que avién   librada su entençia;
     dieron unos a otros   verdat e atenençia
     que non fuesse falsada   por nada la sentençia.

474 Seyén ambas las huestes   sobre sendos collados,
     nin mucho açerca   nin mucho alongados;
     cada uno, por fer   los sus santos pagados,
     por fazer holocaustos   matavan los ganados.

475 Yaziéles entre medio   un fermoso vallejo,
     rico de mucha liebre   e de mucho conejo;
     otorgáronse todos   que era buen consejo
     que Menalao e Paris   y fiziessen trebejo.

476 Antuvïós' el griego,   com' ome sabidor,
     que vergüença e ira   le tollié el pavor;
     bien guarnido de armas   de müy grant valor,
     dio salto en el campo   com' buen campeador.

477 Ixió del otro cabo   Paris galopeando,
     de unas armas frescas   su pendón meneando;
     iva a Menalao   justa le demandando;
     seyén todas las dueñas   de los muros mirando.

469	Our business is not done with neatly styled hair, with handsome eyes or with gilded shoes; for this we require hard fists and angry faces, for lances and swords know nothing of sweet words.
470	No man would want to judge that it was right that we should fight here so that you may sleep with her. So fight it out you two; see about setting things in order. Let him who ought to have the lady carry her away!"
471	Paris said to Hector, "You have insulted me deeply; I think that your vengeance on me must be complete; I wish to say nothing else; I am content with your words; I accept the sentence that you have devised."
472	Hector sent this message to the Greeks. Menelaus was pleased and felt satisfied; on both sides the agreement was accepted and then both the day and the place were settled.
473	They were all greatly pleased at the striking of this deal, and they held that their dispute had been resolved. They gave each other a firm and binding promise that the pact would not be broken by anyone.
474	Each of the armies took its place on a hill, neither too close by nor too far away. Each of them, in order to satisfy their own saints, killed their animals to make a full sacrifice.
475	Between the armies lay a beautiful valley, richly stocked with many hares and rabbits. They all granted that it was a good decision that Menelaus and Paris should do battle there.
476	As a wise man, the Greek moved forward to the fight, for shame and anger took away his fear; well equipped with arms very great in value he charged onto the battlefield as a good battler does.
477	From the other side emerged Paris at a gallop, with brand new weapons and fluttering pennant; he was demanding a joust against Menelaus and all the ladies were watching from the walls.

478   Quando lo vio el griego,   díxol' a altas bozes:
      "Aquí eres mal huéspet,   plaga de tus alfoçes.
      Bien rides de los dientes   e lanças malas coçes;
      de lo que me feziste,   non creo que te gozes.

479   Reçebít' en mi casa   e fiz'te grant onor;
      tal galardón me diste   que non pudist' peor.
      Mas bien creo e fío   en el Nuestro Señor
      que me dará derecho,   don falso traïdor."

480   Encobriós' del escudo,   endereçó la lança;
      cuidó aver de Paris   derecho e vengança;
      fue ferir se con él   sin ninguna dubdança;
      cuidó, sis' le fiziesse,   darle mala pitança.

481   Quando lo vío Paris   venir tan denodado,
      sabié que, si pudiesse,   quel' matarié de grado;
      endereçó por darle   del pendón señalado
      mas non lo quiso Dios,   ca non era guisado.

482   Dieron se tales colpes   en medio los escudos,
      quebrantaron las lanças   que tenién en los puños;
      amas cayeron rajas   e pedaços menudos;
      dieron las albergadas   alaridos agudos.

483   Como avié a Paris   Palas desafïado,
      andava a Menálao   siempre cab' el costado;
      maguer nol' ovo dono,   Venus, del otro cabo,
      querrié quanto pudiesse   valer a su crïado.

484   Qual quier' de los escudos   fincó pedaços fecho;
      Vistién buenas lorigas,   que les ovo provecho.
      Ixieron a dos partes   cad'un' en su derecho;
      pareçié en los colpes   que se avién despecho.

485   Membról' a Menalao,   quel' dieron pescoçada:
      si perdiesse la lança   quel' membras' del espada.
      Prísola sobre mano   e fizo la tornada;
      Paris tenié la suya,   quand' él vino, sacada.

486   Fue por darle con ella   por somo del almofre;
      non lo priso en pleno   e deslayó el colpe;
      como firió en bago   engañós' el buen ome;
      ixiós'le de la mano   e fincó él muy pobre.

478	When the Greek saw him, he roared out these words, "You are unwelcome here, a plague on your peoples! You smile sweetly with your teeth while aiming cruel kicks. I do not believe you will rejoice in what you did to me.
479	I welcomed you into my home and I paid you great honour. The way that you repaid me could not have been worse. But I have good faith and trust in our Lord that He will grant me justice, O you treacherous deceiver."
480	He lowered himself behind his shield and held his lance steady. He believed he would have justice and vengeance over Paris. He went to meet him in battle without the slightest fear. If possible, he thought to repay him in mean measure.
481	When Paris saw him coming towards him, so steadfast, he knew that, if he could, he would willingly kill him; he steadied his decorated lance to strike him, but God did not will it so, for the moment was not right.
482	They struck each other such blows to the middle of their shields and shattered the lances that they grasped in their hands; both of these fell broken into splinters and small pieces and the two camps uttered shrieks of high emotion.
483	As Pallas had uttered her challenge to Paris she rode with Menelaus, ever a guardian at his side; on the other hand, Venus, although she had no power, as much as she was able, wished to help the one who served her.
484	Both of the shields were broken into pieces but they wore body armour, which did them great service. The two moved apart, each one to his own side; their hatred showed in every blow they struck.
485	Menelaus remembered – it had been drummed into him – that if he lost his lance he should take up his sword. He took it in his hand and returned to the fight. When he reached him, Paris had already drawn his own.
486	He went to strike him on the crown of his helm, but did not catch him on the full: he missed his blow. As his sword struck empty air the good man made an error. His sword slipped from his hand and he was left with nothing.

487 El pueblo de los griegos   tovos' por afollado;
     metieron todos bozes   plorando su mal fado.
     Paris con el roído   paróse desarrado;
     non le sopo dar priessa   el mal aventurado.

488 Non sopo con la cueita   Menalao qué fer,
     pero asmó un seso,   quel' quiso Dios valer:
     que, sil' pudiés' la mano   so el yelmo meter,
     con ayuda de Dios   quel' cuidava vençer.

489 Aguijó contra él,   entról' so la espada;
     echól' por aventura   mano en la laçada;
     embargól' fiera guisa   tanto que li pesava;
     Paris, maguer querié,   non li podié fer nada.

490 Comol' tenié en pleno,   fuelo luego tirando;
     íval' poco a poco   los laços sossacando;
     quanto más lo tirava,   más se iva quexando,
     ques'le ivan toda vía   los laços apretando.

491 Oviera Menalao   buen derecho tomado,
     ca lo oviera muerto   o l'oviera llevado;
     mas acorrióle otro,   sacógelo de mano,
     tornaron lo a Troya   mal trecho e lazrado.

492 Quando lo vio Elena   sossañólo un poco;
     díxol' que lo tenié   fiera mente por loco
     e que fue engañado   e ella non lo sopo;
     si non, non lidiarié   con él uno por otro.

493 Díxol': "Si tú supiesses   cómo es buen cavallero
     mucho te dubdariés   de ir a él fazero;
     mas deves le en medio   poner un grant otero,
     ca es de grant esfuerço   e sobra buen cabero."

494 Dixo Paris a Elena: "Yo te juro, hermana,
     qu'él nunca me vençiera   por fuerça nin por maña;
     mas Palas me vençió,   que me tenié grant saña,
     por que dixe que Venus   mereçié la mançana.

495 Mas como yo fío   en Venus la leal,
     a la que yo bien sé   quel' pesa de mi mal,
     yo faré en su cuerpo   un exemplo atal
     que siempre fablen d'ello   en Greçia por señal."

487	The Greek people, who thought that they were lost, all cried out, bewailing their ill fate. Paris stopped in confusion at the noise: the ill-fated man could not strike with any speed.
488	Menelaus, in dire straits, did not know what to do, but an idea came to him, for God wanted to help: that if he could get his hand beneath his helmet, with God's aid, he thought Paris could be defeated.
489	He rushed towards him, ducked under his sword and managed to get his hand on the strap; he pulled it so tight that it caused him pain; Paris, for all his efforts, could do nothing about it.
490	As he had a firm grip he then dragged him along and little by little, pulled the strap ever tighter; the further he dragged him, the more Paris groaned, for the strap drew ever closer round his throat.
491	Menelaus would have achieved what was due to him for he would have killed Paris or taken him prisoner, but another came to Paris' aid and took him from his hands* and he was returned to Troy in a sorry state.
492	When Helen saw him she chided him a little, telling him she thought his conduct very foolish, that he had made a mistake of which she was unaware; otherwise he would not have been fighting in single combat.
493	She said to him: "If you had known how fine a knight he is, you would have been very hesitant about going to face him; rather you must put a vast hill between you, for he is very valiant and an extremely good fighter."
494	Paris said to Helen, "I swear to you, my sister, that he would not have vanquished me, through either strength or skill, but Pallas defeated me, for she bore me great anger for saying it was Venus who deserved to have the apple.
495	But as I put my trust in loyal Venus, who I know well is troubled by my plight, I shall make of his body such an example that in Greece they will always tell of it for its fame."

496   Andava en tod' esto   Menalao irado,
      que era de verdat   malament' soberviado.
      Dizié que le tuviessen   lo que fuera parado;
      si non, les caerié   en mal desaguisado.

497   Salleron los troyanos,   metiéronlo por razón:
      los unos dizién, "¡Démosgela!";   los otros dizién "¡Non!"
      Quando Dïos non quiere,   non val' composiçión;
      pudo más el dïablo;   metié y división.

498   Ant' que fuesse el pleito   de sí o non librado,
      ellos faziendo tuerto,   él seyendo forçado,
      Pándarus, un arquero   – ¡a qui dé Dios mal fado! –
      oviéralo por poco   a Menalao matado.

499   Tiról' d'una saeta,   fincógela al costado.
      Dixo don Menalao: "Esto es mal mandado."
      Tornó pora los griegos,   dura ment' espantado;
      non cuidavan los suyos   que lo avién cobrado.

500   Toviéronse los griegos   todos por mortiguados;
      tenién que los avién   troyanos aviltados.
      "¡Vía!", dixieron todos,   "Más vale que muramos
      que atantas de vezes   seamos aontados."

501   Movieron para ellos   todos a denodadas,
      todos señas arechas   e las haçes paradas;
      grandes eran los polvos   e las bozes tamañas
      que oyén el roído   a cab' de dos jornadas.

502   Vinién a denodadas   por la villa entrar,
      por enforcar a Paris,   a Elena quemar,
      prender todos los otros   e la villa hermar,
      que nunca y pudiessen   ningunos habitar.

503   Dixieron los de Troya: "Esto non pued' seer;
      allá somos de fuera   primero a veer."
      Ixió Éctor a ellos   con todo su poder;
      óvose el torneo   por y a rebolver.

504   De cada part' aviá   mucha seña cabdal;
      bolvieron un torneo   que valié lit campal;
      assí manava sangre   todo el arenal
      como si fuesse prado   o fuente perenal.

496	Menelaus raged, stirred to fury at all this, for he was in truth a man filled with anger; he said that they should honour what had been agreed; otherwise they would fall into grave error.
497	The Trojans left their homes to discuss the matter, some saying, "Let us hand her over," and others saying, "No"; when God is not willing, trying to agree is fruitless: the Devil managed better at inciting dissent.
498	Before the issue was resolved one way or the other – the Trojans were in the wrong and he had suffered offence – Pandarus, an archer – may God grant him an evil fate! – had very nearly taken the life of Menelaus.
499	He fired an arrow at him and it went into his side. King Menelaus said, "This is an evil message." He rode back towards the Greeks, deep in shock. His men did not believe they had recovered him from death.
500	The Greek forces were all sorely afflicted and considered that the Trojans had dishonoured them. "Onward!", they all cried; "it is better that we die than that we should suffer shame so many times."
501	The Greeks moved towards them, all full of menace, with their standards erect and battle lines drawn; there were great clouds of dust and the roars were so loud that the noise could be heard two days' journey away.
502	They came, full of menace, to enter Troy's city, with intent to hang Paris and set Helen aflame, to capture all the others and desolate the city so that nobody could ever live there again.
503	The people of Troy said, "This cannot be; first we shall see about this outside the city." Hector rode out towards the Greeks with all his troops; the combat was to take place out there.
504	On both sides were the standards of many fine warriors; a contest took place, the size of a pitched battle, such that blood flowed over all the sands as though it were a water meadow or permanent spring.

505 Que muertos que colpados,   cayén a bolodrones;
a piedes de cavallo   murién muchos peones;
bien lidiava don Éctor,   bien las sus crïazones;
semejavan y todos   los griegos bien varones.

506 Avié en los troyanos   un ome de linaje:
fue fijo de Alfión,   ome de grant paraje.
Éste entre los griegos   fazié muy grant domaje,
que querié recabdar   afirmes su mensaje.

507 Ajuntóse con él   Áyaz el Telamón;
travessóli la lança   por medio'l coraçón;
nol' prestó nin migaja   toda su guarniçión;
ixiól' luego el alma   a poca de sazón.

508 Esto pesó a Ántifo   e cuidólo vengar;
echó de cuer la lança   por a Áyaz matar;
guardósele el otro,   nol' pudo açertar;
firïó en Culcón   e fízolo quedar.

509 El prínçip' Menalao,   como fuera colpado,
andava tan ravioso   com' un león irado;
trayé en su cabeça   un yelmo señalado,
el que ovo a Paris   en el campo robado.

510 Membrával' cóm' avié   presa mucha grant honta,
cómo se avié visto   en müy grant afronta;
dio de mano a la lança,   mató a Demofonta,
un valiente cavallero   e ome de grant conta.

511 Demofonta yazié   sobre sus armas muerto;
tenié, como cayera   las çervizes en tuerto;
aplegós'le Umbrásides   por despojarl' el cuerpo,
mas al mal astrugo   ixióle a mal puerto.

512 Estaba cabez' tuerto   por toller la loriga;
vino sobr'él un asta   tamaña com' una viga;
echóla por amor   Toás de su amiga;
cosiólo con la tierra   al fijo d'enemiga.

513 De los pueblos de Troya   muchos avié caídos;
de los griegos e todo   muchos y avié perdidos.
Los ríos de la sangre   bien aluent eran idos;
non dubdavan morir,   tant' eran ençendidos.

| 505 | Both dead and wounded fell in their masses;
many foot soldiers died beneath a horse's hoof.
Hector fought valiantly and likewise all his vassals
and the Greeks could all be seen to be fine men indeed. |

| 506 | Among the Trojans was a man of noble descent,
the son of Antemion, a man of fine heritage.
This man was wreaking untold harm among the Greeks
for he wanted to leave his mark firmly written. |

| 507 | Ajax son of Telamon took him on in battle
and thrust his lance through the centre of his heart;
all his armour was, for him, of not the slightest use,
and it was little time before his soul was lost to him. |

| 508 | This was grief to Antiphus, who determined to avenge him;
he put all his strength behind his lance to kill Ajax
who managed to dodge it so that it missed him,
although it did strike Leucon, and it left him dead. |

| 509 | Prince Menelaus, as he had been struck,
moved around raging like angry lion,
wearing on his head a distinctive helmet
which he had taken from Paris on the field of battle. |

| 510 | He could not forget how he had suffered great shame
and how he had been victim to a cruel insult;
he took his lance in his hand and wounded Democoön,
a brave knight and man of great renown. |

| 511 | Democoön lay dead on his weapons;
as he fell down he had twisted his neck.
Imbrasides went up to him to strip him of his armour
but it worked out badly for this man of ill fate. |

| 512 | He was bending over to remove the body armour
when he was hit by a spear the size of a beam,
thrown by Thoas, for the love of his lady,
which pinned his wretched foe to the ground. |

| 513 | Of the people of Troy, many men had fallen
and many of the Greeks had also been lost.
The rivers of blood flowed into the distance;
they did not fear to die, so great was their passion. |

514 Los unos e los otros,   por amor de vençer,
    tanto podién fer cabo   que avién a caer;
    pero tanto ovieron   los troyanos a fer
    que ovieron los griegos   las riendas a bolver.

515 Quando vio Dïomedes   fuïr sus compañeros,
    firió en los troyanos   e mató muchos d'ellos;
    si les plogo o non,   fízoles seer quedos;
    assí los delibrava   como lobo corderos.

516 Rebolvié bien los braços,   dava colpes mortales;
    mató una partida   de prínçipes cabdales;
    si oviesse ayuda   com' él era de tales,
    oviera en los troyanos   fecho malas señales.

517 Andava tan ravioso   com' un león d'ayuno
    quand' lo cuita la fambre,   si falla brusco alguno;
    destruye e degüella   sin cosimén ninguno;
    fazién gozo sobejo   Palas e doña Juno.

518 Ovieron los troyanos   a bolver las espadas;
    siguiélos Dïomedes   dándoles grandes colpadas;
    dizién que avién visto   en mal punto a Palas;
    las nuevas de Elena   que non fuessen sonadas.

519 Toás, que a Umbrásides   mató, como sabedes,
    avié tales dos fijos   que valién dos paredes;
    por su mala ventura   víolos Dïomedes;
    aguijó contra ellos,   dixiéndoles: "¡Morredes!"

520 Endereçó la lança,   firmós' sobre la siella;
    dio al mayor hermano   por medio de la tetiella;
    por medio las espaldas   echóli la cuchiella;
    en Greçia oy en día   lo traen por fabliella.

521 Quando vío aquesto   el hermano menor,
    tirósele delante   al toro lidiador;
    si un poco quisiesse   refertar al señor,
    fiziéral' esso mismo   que fizo al mayor.

522 Fazié como corneja   quandol' roban el nido:
    defender non lo puede,   da bozes e apellido;
    assí estava Idus,   que andava esmarrido;
    con ravia del hermano   andava enloquido.

514	Men of both sides, in their desire for victory, fought with such zeal that they met their death, but in the end the Trojans fought so fiercely that the Greeks had no choice but to turn their horses back.
515	When Diomedes saw his companions in flight, he struck out at the Trojans and killed many of them. However much they struggled, they were quietened by him, for he slaughtered them as a wolf does lambs.
516	Swinging his arms freely, he struck deadly blows, killing a group of powerful princes. If he had had the help of others like himself he would have done the Trojans notorious harm.
517	He moved around raging like a starving lion stricken by hunger, which, if it finds a lamb, rips apart and destroys it with no sign of mercy. Great was the rejoicing of Pallas and Juno.
518	The Trojans were forced to turn tail and run; Diomedes pursued them, dealing heavy blows. They said it was to their ill when they saw Pallas and that the tale of Helen should never have been told.
519	Thoas who killed Imbrasides, as you have heard, had two sons who were built like strong walls. To their misfortune, they were seen by Diomedes, who rode in pursuit of them, saying, "You will die."
520	He steadied his lance and sat still in the saddle and dealt the elder brother a blow through his breast, thrusting the weapon right out through his back. In Greece today they still tell the story.
521	After seeing that happen, the younger brother got out of the way of the fighting bull. Had he made any attempt to stand up to Diomedes, he would have done to him what he did to the elder.
522	He acted like a crow when its nest is being robbed: it cannot prevent it but cries out and screeches. Idaeus, in his sorrow, was just the same, crazed by his anger at the death of his brother.

523 Veyélo mal prender, non le pudo prestar,
que, aun que lo quisiesse, non le podié uviar.
Toás, que a Umbrásides fizo quedo estar,
toda su alegría tornós'le en pesar.

524 El rey Agamenón, maguer tan alto era,
nin quiso tener çaga nin ir en costanera;
metióse en la priessa, en la muebda primera;
a qual parte que iva dávanli la carrera.

525 Rodeüs, un troyano que fue mal avorado,
por ferir se con él vino muy denodado;
diole el rey tal colpe por el diestro costado,
quel' echó muerto frío en la yerva del prado.

526 Sin éste, mató çinco, todos omes valientes,
todos de grant poder e de nobles parientes;
en cabo, a Eurípilo diol' por medio los dientes;
fazié tales trebejos en las troyanas gentes.

527 Pándarus, el que ovo a Menalao golpado,
andava el maliello con su arco parado;
iva a Dïomedes por las hazes buscando,
ca fazié fiera guisa grant mal en el su vando.

528 Óvolo a veer, ¡al que dé Dios rencura!
do estava lidiando a una grant pressura;
tiról' a la tetilla, mas erról' por ventura;
fincógela en el ombro mas por su amargura.

529 Quando sintió Diomedes que lo avién ferido,
com' non sopo quién era, tovos' por escarnido;
ovo tan fiera ira e fue tanençendido
como osso ravioso que anda desfambrido.

530 Buscando el arquero quel' tiró el quadriello,
fazié mucha carniça e mucho mal mançiello;
el que por su pecado cayé en su portiello
nunca iva jamás tornar a su castiello.

531 Mató çinco viscondes, todos omes granados:
todos los diz' Omero por nombres señalados.
En cabo, a Toás, de quien ante fablamos;
creo que, en comedio, otros ovo colpados.

523   He saw him come to harm, but could not be of any help,
      for even if he wanted, there was nothing he could do;
      Thoas, the man who had laid low Imbrasides,
      saw all his joy turned into deep grief.

524   King Agamemnon, in spite of his high rank,
      did not want to go in the rear or on the flank,
      but placed himself amidst the fray, in the front line,
      and wherever he turned a path was opened.

525   Odius, an ill-starred man of the Trojans,
      approached him with menace to engage him in battle.
      The King struck him such a blow to his right-hand side
      that he left him cold dead on the battlefield.

526   He killed five more besides him, all men of valour,
      all of great power and all of noble stock;
      in the end he struck Euryalus right in his teeth;
      such havoc he wrought on the people of Troy.

527   The wicked Pandarus, who had wounded Menelaus,
      roamed over the battlefield with his bow at the ready;
      he was seeking out Diomedes among the troops,
      who was savagely causing his side great harm.

528   Pandarus caught sight of him – may God make him suffer! –
      where Diomedes fought in the thick of battle.
      He aimed at his breast but missed it by chance;
      he hit him in the shoulder, to his great anguish.

529   When Diomedes realised that he had been wounded,
      not knowing by whom, he was filled with shame
      and felt such wild anger and a fury so great
      as does an enraged bear driven wild with hunger.

530   Looking for the bowman who had fired the arrow,
      he inflicted great slaughter and many grave wounds.
      Any man who, for his sins, strayed across his path
      would never again return to his own castle.

531   He killed five viscounts, all men of importance
      – Homer talks of all of them with distinguished names –
      and finally Thoas, of whom we spoke before.
      I believe he had struck down others in the meantime.

532 Fincó ojo a Pándarus, violo en un corral;
aguijó contra él, dexó todo lo al;
diol' una espadada por medio'l çervigal;
fízole dos toçinos partidos por igual.

533 Avié el maledito tal escarmiento fecho,
pareçer non osava ningún en su derecho;
non era bien vengado aún de su despecho;
non avié olvidado el mal sabor del trecho.

534 Por lo que avié fecho non se querié alçar;
non era bien çevado, aún querié caçar.
Buscaba día malo si gel'oviés' quien dar,
mas non osava nadi ante él se parar.

535 Óvose con Eneas en cabo a fallar:
fijo del rey Anquises, un cuerpo de honrar;
cuidóselo aína o vençer o matar;
respúsole Eneas: "Mucho a y que far."

536 Diéronse de las lanças, mas non sintieron nada;
esso mismo fizieron a la quarta vegada.
Diomedes, quando ovo la lança quebrantada,
tiró de la vaína la su mortal espada.

537 Eneas por tod' esto non quiso enflaquir;
espada sobre mano, pensó sobre él ir.
Sabiénse rica mente guardar e encobrir;
por ninguna manera non se podién ferir.

538 Semejavan entrambos pecados maleditos
que estaban refaçios uno contra otro fitos;
todos, de cada parte, davan bozes e gritos;
las narizes de los cavallos semejavan solvitos.

539 Quando vio Dïomedes que nol' podié colpar,
nin por ninguna guisa a él podié passar,
víose embargado; asmó qué podrié far,
cal' semejava onta pora sí lo dexar.

540 Vio cabo un ribaço un grant canto yazer,
que doze cavalleros non lo podrién erzer;
deçendió del cavallo e fuelo a prender;
bien se cuidava Eneas que nol' podrié mover.

532	He caught sight of Pandarus amidst a ring of people. He spurred on towards him and ignored all else. He made a deep cut into his neck with his sword and sliced him in two parts, each equal in size.
533	This accursed man had done such damage that no man dared to step forward to face him. He had not yet avenged the slight done to him nor forgotten the hurt the arrow caused.
534	Diomedes had no wish to withdraw because of what he had done – he was not so well fed that he did not still want to hunt –; he was looking for battle, if anyone would face him, but nobody dared to step out and come to meet him.
535	Finally he came face to face with Aeneas,* the son of King Anchises and a knight of worthy honour. He thought that he would very quickly inflict defeat or death, but Aeneas replied to him: "You have a long fight on your hands."
536	They clashed lances but neither felt a thing, and now it was the fourth time that they had done just that. Diomedes, once he had shattered his lance, drew out his deadly sword from its scabbard.
537	Aeneas, through all of this, did not lose heart and determined to go after him sword in hand; they were expert in how to give themselves protection and there was no way that either could land a blow.
538	They both had the look of accursed devils each one constantly threatening the other, with everyone on both sides shouting and yelling. The horses' nostrils were whistling like bellows.
539	When Diomedes saw that he could not strike him and that he could not find any way to reach him, he felt disconcerted and wondered what he could do, for it seemed shameful for him to abandon the fight.
540	He saw a large stone lying near a steep slope, which would be too heavy for twelve knights to lift. He jumped off his horse and went to pick it up. Aeneas was confident that he could not move it.

541 Alçólo Dïomedes   müy ligera mente;
     dio con él a Eneas   un palmo sobr'el vientre;
     echólo de la silla   tan aontada mente;
     oviéralo por poco   quedado pora siempre.

542 Luego que fue Eneas   caído en el campo,
     dio salto Dïomedes   por recobrar el canto;
     erçiólo tan rafez   como erçrié un manto;
     si ferido l'oviesse, nol' valdrié nul encanto.

543 Su madre dona Venus   sabié encantamientos,
     que turbava las nuves e rebolvié los vientos;
     vío los pestorejos   de su fijo sangrientos
     e andar sus cabellos por tierra polvorientos.

544 Ante que lo uviasse   Dïomedes colpar,
     óvolo la dïabla   de Venus a encantar;
     óvol' con una niebla los ojos a çegar.
     Eneas por tanto   ovo de escapar.

545 Maguer que non veyé,   com' era muy liviano,
     palpava si pudiesse   ferir algunt troyano;
     firió por aventura   a Venus en la mano;
     aquel colpe aduxo   a muchos a grant daño.

546 Venus por la ferida   tovos' por aontada;
     rencoróse a Júpiter,   e mostróli la plaga.
     Si non fuesse por Juno, la greçisca mesnada
     oviera sines dubda   tomada mala çaga.

547 Fue a pocos de días   Eneas bien guarido;
     non echó el quebranto   que priso en olvido;
     más irado que nunca   tornó al apellido;
     rebolvié la fazienda   com' ome desfaçido.

548 Todos como de nuevo   movieron a lidiar;
     ovieron de los griegos muchos y a fincar;
     recudién las espadas   que no podién tajar,
     pero, quales que eran, non se davan vagar.

549 Eneas, con la saña   del colpe que prisiera,
     tan ravioso andava   com' una sierpe fiera,
     buscando por el campo el griego quel' firiera;
     tovo que, sil' fallasse, vengado se oviera.

541   Diomedes picked it up and did so with great ease;
        with it he struck Aeneas a hand's span above the stomach;
        he threw him from the saddle in such ignoble fashion
        that it very nearly laid him low forever.

542   As soon as Aeneas lay fallen on the ground,
        Diomedes leapt down to retrieve the stone.
        He lifted it as easily as he would lift a cloak;
        if it had struck him, no spell would have saved him.

543   His mother Venus had knowledge of enchantments,
        – she disturbed the clouds and whipped up the winds –,
        and she saw her son with his neck bathed in blood
        and his dust-defiled hair spread out on the ground.

544   Before Diomedes had the chance to strike,
        the cunning Venus managed to cast a spell:
        she managed to blind his eyes with a cloud,
        in such a way that Aeneas was able to escape.

545   Although he could not see, Diomedes was so sharp
        that he felt around in case he could strike some Trojan;
        it happened that he did strike Venus on the hand;
        many were those whom that blow brought to great harm.

546   Venus felt humiliation on account of the blow;
        she complained to Jupiter, showing him the wound.
        Had it not been for Juno, there can be no doubt:
        the Greek army would have suffered dire consequence.

547   Aeneas' full recovery took just a few days,
        but he did not let the hurt he had suffered be forgotten.
        More angry than ever he rejoined the fray
        and heightened battle's frenzy like a man outraged.

548   They all moved into battle as men renewed;
        for many of the Greeks, this was where they would remain;
        they hurled their swords that could no longer cut
        but none of them at all allowed himself to rest.

549   Aeneas, in his anger at the blow that he had suffered,
        went about with the fury of a fierce serpent,
        searching the battlefield for the Greek who had struck him
        and sure that, if he found him, vengeance would he his.

550	Todos estavan firmes,	grant era la refierta;
	de los muertos la tierra	toda yazié cubierta;
	andavan en la sangre	fasta la media pierna;
	nunca fue en un día	Belona tan espierta.

551	Andava entre todos	Éctor flamas vertiendo,
	a los suyos cabdellando,	a los otros firiendo;
	quantos que lo veyén	ivan ant'él fuyendo;
	el que prender podié	nol' iva bendiziendo.

552	Andava tan ravioso	com' una sierpe brava;
	el que delant' prendié	d'allí non escapava.
	La su bella mesnada	que él acabdellava
	todos cogién esfuerço	sólo que él fablava.

553	Mal andavan los griegos	– non lo podien durar –;
	ovieron sin su grado	las cuestas a tornar;
	firié Éctor en ellos,	non les dava vagar;
	querrién una jornada	luen' de Troya estar.

554	El rëy de los griegos,	maguer era cansado,
	quando vido aquesto,	fue muy desaborado.
	Dixo: "Non pued' seer;	¡que pese al pecado
	que, maguer que lazremos,	nos rancamos el campo!"

555	Entró esto diziendo	por medio de las hazes,
	llamando "¡Dios, ayuda!",	firiendo colpes grandes;
	a los que non tornavan	cofondiéles las fazes,
	diziéndoles: "Amigos,	¿por qué me desonrades?"

556	Pesó a los troyanos	con el su encontrado,
	ca los fizo quedar	a todo su mal grado.
	Aforçaron los griegos,	tornaron y de cabo;
	era de fiera guisa	rebuelto el mercado.

557	Andava el buen rëy	las emiendas cogiendo,
	a los unos matando	a los otros firiendo.
	Ivan com' de pecado	todos ant'él fuyendo;
	al que alcançava	non iva muy riyendo.

558	Éctor del otro cabo	firié con los troyanos;
	non tenié toda ora	embargadas las manos.
	Él e don Eneas,	dos cuerpos adïanos,
	tan bien se ayudavan	como unos hermanos.

550	They all stood firm and the fighting was hard; everywhere the land was strewn with the dead; men waded through blood that was halfway up their legs; never in one day was Bellona so alert.*
551	Hector moved among them with flames pouring from him, marshalling his own men and striking their opponents. All who caught sight of him ran in flight before him but any whom he caught laid no blessings on him.
552	He went about with the fury of a ferocious serpent: any man he caught before him did not get away; the fine army which he had under his command all took great heart at the mere sound of his voice.
553	The Greeks were in a sorry state, unable to resist him, and unwillingly they had to turn their backs on their foe. Hector struck against them and gave them no respite – they would have wished to be a day away from Troy.
554	The King of the Greeks, tired as he was, was deeply displeased when he saw this, and said, "It cannot be! Let it weigh heavy on the Devil, that, even though we suffer, we shall win the battle."
555	With these words he rushed in amidst the troops, calling on God's help and striking mighty blows; those who failed to turn he insulted to their faces, saying to them, "My friends, why do you bring me dishonour?"
556	It was to the Trojans' sorrow that they encountered him for he brought them to a halt, all against their wishes; the Greeks were emboldened and in the end rejoined the fray; the market was set into ferocious upheaval.
557	The good king moved around exacting vengeance, bringing death to some and inflicting wounds on others; they all fled before him as they might flee the Devil; anyone that he caught up with had no cause for mirth.
558	In the other army Hector fought on the Trojan side and at no time was there anything that could hold back his hands. He and Aeneas, two men of great qualities, supported each other as though they were brothers.

559   Todos, unos e otros,   fiera priessa se davan,
pero ellos e ellos   rancar non se dexaban.
Las aguas e los prados   todos sangre manavan;
recudién los valleros   a los colpes que davan.

560   Sedié de cada parte   la fazienda en peso;
ningunos non podién   rancar se por nul seso.
Ay ovo Menalao   a don Adastro preso,
que avié la cabeça   tan blanca como queso.

561   Çarpedon el troyano,   cavallero novel,
fijo era de Júpiter,   semejava a él;
abatió a Tritólano,   firiól' por el budel;
Ulixes, por vengarlo,   firió luego sobr'él.

562   Çarpedon fue colpado;   fuese pora su tienda.
Ulixes el artero   rebolvió la fazienda;
mató çinco mançebos,   todos de grant contienda;
non fue éste peor,   como diz' la leyenda.

563   Éctor e Dïomedes,   entrambos porfaçados,
estavan en el campo   firmes e denodados;
esforçavan sus gentes   como omes senados;
dezir quál fue mejor   seriemos embargados.

564   Sedién como verrones   que están porfidiosos:
colmillos amolados,   los labros espumosos,
las sedas levantadas   e parados los ombros,
dándose grandes colpes   los unos a los otros.

565   Como diz' la palabra   que más corre el fado
que nin viento nin pluma   nin roçín ensellado,
aforçaron los griegos,   fizieron un remango;
ovieron los troyanos   a dexar les el campo.

566   Allí entendió Éctor   que eran engañados,
que eran a los griegos   todos los dios passados;
ellos, como que era,   avién los despagados;
si non fuesse por esso,   non serién tan afollados.

567   Entró por a la villa,   fizo conçejo fer,
fízoles cómo era   la cosa entender;
mandó por las iglesias   las vigilias tener,
e que diessen ofrenda,   ca era menester.

559	On either side, everyone was fierce in the fighting, but neither of the armies would see itself defeated. The rivers and the fields both ran with blood and the valleys echoed to the blows that they struck.
560	Everywhere the battle hung in the balance and neither side was able to find a way to conquer. There Menelaus took Adrastus as his prisoner, a man who had hair that was as white as cheese.
561	Sarpedon, a newly dubbed Trojan knight* – the son of Jupiter, whom he resembled –, brought down Tlepolemus, wounding him in the gut, and Ulysses, in vengeance, then struck at the attacker.
562	Sarpedon was wounded and retired to his tent. Ulysses, the artful, increased the battle's heat and killed five young men, all of them fine fighters; he was far from worst in battle, so the account tells us.
563	Hector and Diomedes, the two of them moved to anger, were both full of strength and tireless in battle, encouraging their troops like men of great good sense; we would be at a loss to judge the better warrior.
564	They were like two unrelenting wild boars, with sharp-pointed tusks and foaming at the mouths, their bristles erect and their shoulders poised still, striking fierce blows, the one against the other.
565	The saying is a true one that fate has more speed than wind, wing, or saddled steed; the Greeks took heart and launched an attack and the Trojans were forced to give way before them.
566	At that point Hector saw that they had been deceived, that all the gods had passed to the side of the Greeks and that the Trojans had somehow displeased them; were it not for this, things would not have been so ill.
567	He rode back into the city and had councils called, explaining to them the situation they were in; he ordered that vigils be held in the churches and offerings made, for there was great need.

568 Las madronas de Troya   fizieron luego çirios,
    vistieron todas sacos   e ásperos çiliçios;
    ornaron los altares   de rosas e de lirios;
    pora pagar los santos,   todos cantavan quirios.

569 La muger de don Éctor   – Androna le dizién –
    todos bien dizién d'ella   quantos que la veyén;
    temiés' de su marido   que gelo matarién,
    que unos malos sueños   siempre la perseguién.

570 Priso Astemïata   en braços, su fijuelo,
    adúxol' ant'el padre   e ploró él de duelo;
    quísolo saludar,   refusó el moçuelo;
    tovieron tales y ovo   que era mal agüero.

571 Esto pesó a Éctor;   ovo muy mal sabor;
    alçáronsel' los pelos,   pero non por pavor.
    Díxole la muger   – com' era sabidor –
    que oviera el niño   de las armas pavor.

572 Tolliós' luego el yelmo   e descubriós' la faz;
    coñoçiólo el niño,   e fuel' ya a dar paz.
    "Assí,", dixo don Éctor,   "fijo, esto me plaz';
    Dios te faga buen ome,   que vome yo al haz."

573 Glaucas, en est' comedio,   buscó abze mala.
    Fallós' con Dïomedes   en medio la batalla.
    Cuidó que lo podrié   derrocar sines falla
    e dioli un grant colpe   en medio de la tabla.

574 Dïomedes fue bueno   e müy mesurado;
    non dio por ello nada   e estido pagado.
    Dixo: "Creo, amigo,   que fueste engañado,
    que, si me conoçiesses,   non m'ovieras colpado.

575 Mas perdónote ésta   e fágot' grant amor
    por que de mí non fueste   quién era sabidor;
    si jamás te conteçe,   prendrás mala sabor."
    Díxol' Glaucas: "Non plega   esso al Crïador."

576 Despidióse don Éctor   de toda su compaña;
    esto tovieron todos   non por buena fazaña;
    su hermano con él,   Paris de la montaña,
    tornaron a las hazes   lidiando muy a saña.

568 Then the matrons of Troy lit votive candles,
they all dressed in sackcloth and rough hair shirts;
they decked the altars with roses and lilies
and everyone sang Kyries to win round the saints.*

569 The wife of Hector, who bore the name of Andromache,*
of whom all who saw her spoke only in praise,
feared for her husband, that he was to meet his death,
for she was constantly tormented by troubling dreams.

570 She took in her arms Astyanax, her young son,
and brought him before his father, who wept in grief;
he tried to talk to him but the child would not respond;
all those who were there judged it an ill omen.

571 This troubled Hector and he was filled with sorrow;
his hair stood on end, but it was not in fear.
His wife said to him – for she could read the signs –
that the child had been frightened by his armour.

572 Then he took off his helmet and revealed his face;
the child recognised him and now showed its love for him.
Hector spoke these words: "My son, I am pleased at this.
May God make a good man of you, for I now leave for battle."

573 Glaucus, at this point, went in search of ill fortune:
he encountered Diomedes in the midst of the battle;
believing that he could strike him down without fail,
he dealt him a heavy blow to the centre of his shield.

574 Diomedes was a fine man and one of great restraint;
he was not troubled by this and even showed pleasure.
He said, "I think, my friend, you have made a mistake,
for, had you known me, you would not have struck that blow.

575 But I forgive you this and offer you my warm affection,
for you were without knowledge as to who I was.
If this befalls you again, the taste will not be sweet."
Glaucus replied, "May it not please the Creator so!"

576 Hector took his leave of all of his household
and all of them took this to be a troubling sign.
He and his brother, Paris of the mountain,
returned to the battle lines, great fury in their fighting.

577 Començó a ferir luego   Éctor como solié,
derrocar de las sillas   quantos prender podié;
el que de la su punta   una vez estorçié
quanto más de su grado   ant'él non pareçié.

578 Afrontóse con él   Áyaz el Telamón,
de quien fiziemos ante   de suso la mençión:
cavallero de preçio   e de grant coraçón;
fuese ferir con él   sobre puesta missión.

579 Entendiólo Éctor   e fuele atendiendo;
qui quier' gelo verié   que él non avié miedo.
A poder de cavallo   vino Áyaz corriendo,
firiól' en el escudo   tod' su poder metiendo.

580 Quedo estido Éctor,   cuidólo travessar;
entendiógelo Áyaz,   súpose bien guardar.
Quando vio esto Éctor,   non quiso dar vagar;
derrancó por a él,   cuidól' descabeçar.

581 Tornó contra él Áyaz   – nol' quiso refoír –,
espada sobre mano   por a Éctor ferir.
Tan bien se sabién amos   guardar e encobrir,
por ninguna manera   non se podién nozir.

582 Lo que Éctor asmava   Áyaz bien lo sabié;
nin Áyaz podié más   nin don Éctor fazié;
nin a Áyaz su engaño   nada non le valié.
Non podié ningún d'ellos   complir lo que querié.

583 Áyaz era artero   e de mala raíz;
cuidóle dar a Éctor   por medio la çerviz.
Mas encubrióse Éctor,   como Omero diz',
pero rompiól' un poco   de la loriga terliz.

584 Diol' en somo del ombro   una poca ferida,
pero quatro sortijas   rompiól' de la loriga;
plególe a la carne,   sacól' la sangre biva.
Dixo Éctor: "Aquésta   te será bien vertida."

585 Condesó el espada   dentro en su vasera;
dexó correr un canto   grant de fiera manera;
cuidóle dar ad Áyaz   en medio la mollera,
mas púsol' el escudo   Áyaz en la carrera.

577	Then Hector began to attack, as was his custom, and strike down from the saddle all those he could find, and if any man once managed to avoid his thrust he would wish all the more never to stand before him.
578	Ajax, son of Telamon, stood against him – we have already made mention of this man, a knight of great distinction and nobility of heart; he went to engage him as was his part to play.
579	Hector saw his intention and awaited his attack: it was clear to any man that he felt no fear; Ajax galloped towards him at full tilt and struck him on the shield with all his force.
580	Hector remained still, planning to run him through, but Ajax saw his intention and knew well his defence. When Hector saw this he strove to grant him no respite but charged straight at him with mind to strike off his head.
581	Ajax turned towards him with no attempt to avoid him, sword in hand ready to strike Hector a blow; but so well did both of them know how to defend and parry that there was no way for either to inflict a wound.
582	Ajax knew well what Hector intended; neither Ajax nor Hector could gain the upper hand; Ajax's sleight was of no value to him and neither of them could achieve what he sought.
583	Ajax was a cunning man, born of noxious roots, and he tried to strike Hector clean through the neck, but, as Homer tells us, Hector gave himself protection, though a part of his mail-coat was cut through.
584	He was slightly wounded in the tip of his shoulder but four rings were broken off from the coat of mail. The blow reached his flesh and drew life-giving blood; Hector said, "This debt of blood you shall repay in full."
585	He plunged his sword back into its scabbard and hurled a stone with savage force, aiming to hit Ajax in the middle of his head; but Ajax placed his shield in its path.

586 Luego fue presto Éctor, prísolo otra vez;
     como era valiente, tomól' muy de rafez;
     diol' en somo del yelmo, do la calba fallez';
     cayó Áyaz en tierra, más negro que la pez.

587 Fue a prender el canto Éctor otra vegada
     por aquedar a Áyaz, una barva honrada;
     fuera, si lo fiziesse, la cosa delibrada,
     que dava atal virto com' una algarrada.

588 Ya quería don Éctor el canto ajobar;
     Áyaz alçó los ojos, vido quel' querié dar;
     como dizen que cuita faze vieja trotar,
     esforçó con el miedo; fue del canto travar.

589 Començaron entrambos a firmes a luchar;
     Áyaz con el mïedo nos' dexava echar;
     plogo a Dios e ovo la noche a uviar;
     mandaron las justiçias que quedas' el lidiar.

590 Ovieron a quedar los toros lidiadores;
     corriénles filo a filo a ambos las sudores;
     tovieron los a ambos siempre por más mejores;
     mas la lucha a Áyaz membróli todas sazones.

591 Preguntóli a Áyaz Éctor a la partida:
     "Digas me, cavallero, sí Dïos te bendiga,
     de quál linaje vienes, ¡sí ayas buena vida!
     Querría tu fazienda aver bien entendida."

592 Dixo Áyaz: "D'aquesto te daré razón;
     parientes ove muy nobles, maguer müertos son;
     mi madre fue Esiona, mi padre Telamón.
     Las tierras do naçí en medio Greçia son.

593 Fallaron se que eran parientes muy carnales;
     camiaron las espadas, tajaron amistades;
     firieron se las diestras por seer más leales;
     partiéronse un' d'otro, fueron se a sus lugares.

594 Otro día mañana, a ora maitinal,
     mandó pregonar Éctor conçejo general.
     Fizieron se los omes todos muy grant corral;
     las armas non dexavan por uno o por al.

586	Hector was quickly ready: he picked up the stone again – a powerful man, he picked it up with ease – and hit him atop the helmet, right at its tip; Ajax fell to the ground, blacker than pitch.
587	Hector went to take up the stone once more, to finish off Ajax, a knight of high honour; had he let it fly, the fight would have found its end, for the force of a catapult was in his throw.
588	Now Hector made ready to lift the stone and Ajax looked up and saw the blow he meant to land; as they say trouble makes an old woman run, spurred on by fear he went to grasp the stone.
589	Then they both began to fight with all their force. Ajax did not, in fear, allow himself to be thrown down. So it pleased God and the hour of nightfall came and the judges decreed that the combat should cease.
590	It was time for the two fighting bulls to take rest; drop by drop the sweat ran down them both. Both were always held to be the finest of men, but Ajax remembered the combat for ever.
591	Hector asked of Ajax as they parted from each other: "Tell me, my knight, may God grant you His blessing, from what line are you sprung? May you enjoy a good life; I would have liked to learn all about your heritage."
592	Ajax said, "This I shall recount to you in full: I had noble parents, although they are now dead: Hesione was my mother and my father Telamon; the land of my birth is in the centre of Greece."
593	They discovered that they were of very close kinship, they exchanged their swords and established bonds of friendship. They joined right hands as a pledge of loyalty, parted from each other, and went each to his own side.
594	On the next morning, at the hour of morning prayer, Hector ordered a general council to be summoned and the men all came together to form a great assembly, though for no reason did they lay down their arms.

595 Dixo Éctor: "Varones, por seso lo veía
que diéssemos la dueña e irs'ien éstos su vía;
que non siempre biviéssemos en esta azedía,
que peor se nos pone la cosa toda vía."

596 "Veemos lo", dixieron todos, "por aguisado;
terniemos lo a vos a merçed e a grado."
Embïaron con esto a los griegos mandado
que el pueblo de Troya que era acordado.

597 Respondieron los griegos que non podié seer,
que ora non era por abenençia fer;
si non que mensajeros non devién mal prender,
pudiérase Idëus en grant cueita veer.

598 Los griegos en tod' esto estavan desarrados,
que avién muchos menos de los omes honrados;
pero juraron todos, tant' eran esforçados,
que se non fuessen dende fasta seer vengados.

599 Tornó el mensajero que fue con el mandado;
díxoles cóm' avié muy poco recabado;
estonçe dixo Éctor: "Tengo me por afollado;
pero, como yo creo, dizía aguisado.

600 Por todas las sus bafas non perderé el dormir;
el mal que me farán bien lo cuido sofrir;
e, si Dïos me dexa algunt día bevir,
avrán d'estas grandías pesar a reçebir."

601 Mandó todas sus gentes, otro día, guarnir,
a prender les el campo e ir los a ferir;
desque avié la cosa toda a mal a ir,
ellos que nos' echassen a luengas a dormir.

602 Si bien lo mandó Éctor, ellos bien lo fizieron;
quand' apuntó el sol, en el campo sovieron;
las huestes de los griegos, quando esto vidieron,
por meter se en armas ningunt vagar nos' dieron.

603 Los troyanos, com' eran fellones e irados,
pensaron de ferir com' eran castigados.
Yazién ante don Éctor muchos descabeçados;
los griegos en un rato fueron desbaratados.

595	Hector said, "My lords, I would consider it most wise if we handed back the lady, for these men would then depart, that we might not live always amidst this bitterness, for our situation is becoming ever worse."
596	All of them said, "We think this judgement sound, and for it would be deeply grateful to you." With this agreed they sent word to the Greeks that the people of Troy had reached an accord.
597	The Greeks replied that it could not happen so, that it was no longer time for a compact to be made. Were it not that messengers must not come to harm, Idaeus could have found himself in great difficulty.
598	The Greeks in all of this were greatly disheartened, for they had now lost many honourable men; but they all swore – so great was their valour! – that they would not depart until they had their vengeance.
599	The herald who had borne the message returned and told them of how he had achieved very little. Then Hector said, "I feel that I have been insulted, but I do believe that what I said was right.
600	For all their boasting, I shall lose no sleep: I think I can well endure the harm that they will do me. If God grants me any length of time to live, they will meet with sorrow in payment for this bluster."
601	The next day, he ordered all his men to take up arms, to occupy the battlefield and go to wound their foes. Since all that lay before them would turn to toil, they should not allow themselves to lie in sleep for long.
602	If Hector gave sound commands, so too were they enacted, and when the sun rose his men stood on the battlefield. The army of the Greeks, when they saw this happen, lost no time in girding on their arms.
603	The Trojans, as they seethed with fury and anger, launched their attack in the manner they were taught. Many lay at Hector's feet with their heads hewn away and the Greeks in but a short time were in disarray.

604   El pros de Dïomedes,   firm' en todo lugar,
      ovo, quando lo vío,   ira e grant pesar;
      y ovo, como dizen,   Ageo a matar;
      aforçó a los griegos   e fízolos tornar.

605   Tan grant fue la fazienda   que nunca fue mayor,
      mas cayén los de Greçia   toda vía peor;
      don Éctor sobre todos   semejava señor;
      avié de fiera guisa   echado grant pavor.

606   Avién los griegos fecho   un firme valladar
      ques' pudiessen a ora   de cuita emparar;
      ovieron los de Troya   essa vez a rancar;
      fizieron los sin grado   allá dentro entrar.

607   Fazién los seer quedos,   assí non les vagaba;
      ixir a la batalla   ninguno non osava.
      Tod' el poder de Greçia   embargado estava;
      maldizién a Aquiles   que tan mal les uviava.

608   Los varones de Greçia   seyén acorralados;
      los troyanos de fuera,   fuerte encarniçados,
      matándoles los omes,   fazién les grandes daños;
      por que non pleitearan   tenién se por errados.

609   La çerca en tod' esto   avié mucho durado;
      avié que empeçara   bien un lustro passado;
      mas non avién aún   más d'esto recabado
      ca el término puesto   non era aplegado.

610   Aquiles en comedio,   como fuera irado,
      del despecho que priso   non avié olvidado;
      sediés' con su amiga   en los montes alçado;
      por todas estas nuevas   non avía cuidado.

611   Embïaron los griegos   cartas e mensajeros,
      los unos tras los otros,   en cara los terçeros;
      dezién, "Si tú non uvias,   por todos los braçeros
      non se tomará Troya   segund los agoreros.

612   Los unos son ya muertos   e los otros cansados;
      an nos los de Troya   muy sobra cavalgados;
      tienen nos fiera guisa   de la villa redrados.
      Por campear a ellos   sól' non somos osados.

604	The worthy Diomedes, nowhere giving ground, when he saw this, felt both anger and great sorrow. At his hands, so they say, Agelaus met his death; he urged on the Greeks and made them turn back.
605	So great was the clash of battle, never on a bigger scale, but the slaughter of the Greeks was even worse than before. Hector seemed as if he was lord over them all; with such ferocity he had instilled great terror.
606	The Greeks had constructed a strong palisade so that they might seek shelter in times of need. Now it was the Trojans who were putting them to flight: they forced the Greeks behind it, unwilling though they were.
607	They kept them pinned there and gave them no respite. None of the Greeks dared to go out to the battle. All the might of Greece was being overwhelmed, and now they cursed Achilles who gave so little help.*
608	The noblemen of Greece were backed into a corner, and outside the palisade with fury unabated the Trojans killed their men and brought on them great harm. They thought that they had erred in turning down the truce.
609	With all of this the siege had gone on at great length and a good five years had passed since it had begun. But so far they had achieved nothing more than this, for the allotted end had not yet arrived.
610	Achilles, at this point, being in a state of fury – he had not yet forgotten the slight that he received – was with his lady friend, away in the mountains, and had little care for the news of all this.
611	The Greeks sent letters and messengers to him; second followed first and then came the third as well. They said, "If you do not help us, in spite of all our warriors Troy will not be taken, so the soothsayers foretell.
612	Some of our men are dead and others are exhausted and the men of Troy have us completely overrun; fiercely they hold us far away from the city and we dare not even go to meet them in battle.

613 Tiempo serié e ora que nos vengas valer,
que todos ¡mal pecado! avremos y qué fer.
Non dexes a tus gentes tan grant daño prender,
de que esta fazienda por ti s'ha a vençer."

614 Aquiles con las nuevas ovo grant alegría;
plógol' quel' conoçiessen los griegos mejoría.
Luego se vino d'essa de la ermitanía,
por acabar el preçio de su cavallería.

615 Los griegos con Aquiles fueron todos guaridos;
cogieron coraçones e fueron más ardidos.
Fueron del viento malo los troyanos feridos;
fuéronse acogiendo con sus braços caídos.

616 Dïomedes el bueno, un mortal cavallero,
valient' e de buen seso e leal consejero,
do se querié dormir, en el sueño primero,
asmó fer una cosa él solo señero.

617 Asmó ir prender lengua o palabra çertera
de las huestes de Troya que lis tenién frontera;
fablólo con Ulixes: díxoli que bien era;
metieron se entrambos solos a la carrera.

618 El adalil de Troya – avié nombre Delón –
sabidor e argudo, bivo de coraçón;
ixiera otrossí, solo como ladrón,
por saber de los griegos qué fazién o qué non.

619 Abés podié en medio la carrera seer,
al cabo d'una cuesta que querié deçender;
ovieron lo los griegos primero a veer;
ambos a sendas partes fueron se esconder.

620 Delón passa non passa echaron en él mano,
estorçer non les pudo, non era tan liviano.
Supieron por él todo el esfuerço troyano,
pero non le quisieron en cabo dar de mano.

621 Des qu'ovo la verdat toda manifestada,
rogóles quel' dexassen, mas non le valió nada.
Ovo luego la tiesta de los ombros tajada,
que nunca más pudiesse descobrir tal çelada.

613	It is high time now that you come to our assistance,
	for we shall all – by the Devil! – have a part to play in this.
	Do not let your people come to such great harm,
	since it is through you that this conflict shall be won."
614	Achilles was filled with great joy by this news
	and pleased that the Greeks recognised his valour.
	He emerged without delay from his solitude,
	to gain the crowning glory that his knightly worth deserved.
615	Achilles brought salvation to all of the Greeks;
	their hearts were emboldened and their courage grew.
	The Trojans were shaken by this ill wind
	and with shoulders sloping they began to withdraw.
616	The good Diomedes, a death-dealing knight,
	valiant, prudent, and a loyal counsellor,
	as he was falling asleep, in the first of slumbers,
	thought of acting alone and unaccompanied.
617	He thought of gaining information or accurate reports,
	about the Trojan armies that were drawn up before them.
	He talked it through with Ulysses, who gave him his approval,
	and together those two set off alone on their way.
618	The spy from Troy, who had the name of Dolon,
	who was a man of wisdom, of cunning, and stout heart,
	had also set out, alone, as if he were a robber,
	to find out what the Greeks were doing, and what they were not.
619	He could scarcely have been halfway down the path,
	at the top of a hill that he meant to descend,
	when the Greeks managed to catch sight of him first
	and the two split up to hide, each in a different place.
620	Caught in two minds, Dolon fell into their hands;
	he could not escape them, to do so was beyond him.
	From him they learned all about the army of the Trojans
	but they would not after all let him go on his way.
621	Once he had revealed the whole truth to them,
	he begged them let him go but it availed him not at all;
	then his head was cut asunder from his shoulders
	so that never might he tell of such an ambush.

622   Maguer que avién lengua,   nos' quisieron tornar
d'aquí a que pudiessen   a las gentes llegar.
Ovieron en la tienda   de Reso a entrar
assí que los non pudo   can nin ome ventar.

623   Cortáronle la tiesta   luego en las primeras;
alçóla Dïomedes   luego en las troxeras;
prisieron dos cavallos,   dos bestias tan ligeras,
que, fuera Buçifal,   non avién compañeras.

624   Tornaron con grant preda   e con fiera ganançia;
fízoles Dios en ello   merçed e grant pitança.
Más plogo a los griegos   que ganar toda Françia;
pero los fazedores   non cogieron jactançia.

625   Des que sonó la cosa   cómo eran sallidos,
sovieron en grant miedo   fasta fueron venidos.
Fueron con alegría   sobeja reçebidos.
Dixo Néstor: "Agora   son troyanos vençidos."

626   "D'esto", dixo Aquiles   "non vos maravilledes:
Ulixes fer tal cosa,   si quiere Dïomedes;
que mayor cosa fizo   éste que vos veedes
quando sacó a mí   dentro de las paredes."

627   Éctor e los de Troya   fueron mal quebrantados;
tovieron que Aquiles   los avié estrenados.
Maguer se encubrién   eran mal desbalçados;
dizién: "Naçió est' ome   por los nuestros pecados."

628   Las trompas otro día   fueron luego tocadas,
d'ella e d'ella parte   las hazes assentadas,
el torneo rebuelto,   las feridas mescladas;
de la sangre las aguas   todas ivan cuajadas.

629   El rey Agamenón   firié en los troyanos;
luego de las primeras,   derrancó dos hermanos,
amos valientes omes,   braçeros adïanos;
otros y ovo muchos,   todos primos cormanos.

630   Ya ivan su fazienda   los griegos bien poniendo,
ca ivan los troyanos   fiera ment' enflaquiendo;
ívanles poc'a poco   la mudada rindiendo;
sedié, man' a maxilla,   Venus, duelo faziendo.

622	Though they had information, they would not turn back, until they had gone right up to the Trojan armies. They managed to enter the tent of Rhesus with neither dog nor man catching their scent.
623	Their first act, then, was to sever his head and Diomedes lifted it up into his saddlebag. They stole two horses, two fleet-footed animals, with which, except Bucephalus, no others would compare.
624	They returned laden with fine booty and rich gains; it pleased the Greeks more than would winning all of France. In this God granted them mercy and great favour, but the authors of the deed did not boast of it.
625	As soon as news had spread of how those two were gone, the Greeks were in great fear until their return. They were welcomed back with the greatest rejoicing and Nestor said, "Now the Trojans are defeated."
626	Then Achilles spoke: "Do not let it surprise you that Ulysses or Diomedes should do such a thing. For this man you see before you did something even greater when he brought me out from within the convent walls."
627	Hector and the Trojans were deeply alarmed and thought that Achilles had given the Greeks fresh heart. Though disguising what they felt, they were in disarray and said, "It was through our sins that this man was born."
628	The next day the horns issued forth their cry, and on both sides the battle lines were drawn. Combat was rejoined and blows were exchanged and all the rivers ran thick with blood.
629	King Agamemnon struck out against the Trojans and right at the beginning he overcame two brothers, both men of valour and outstanding in the fight. There were many others there, all of them kinsmen.*
630	Now the Greeks were steadily turning things their way for bit by bit the Trojans were growing much weaker. Little by little, they were repaying them in kind; her head in her hands, Venus was weeping in grief.

631 Uviaron en tod' esto   Éctor e su hermano,
     escudos embraçados,   lanças a sobre mano;
     el que delant' fallavan   non veyé el verano;
     ofreçién muchas almas   al infierno yusano.

632 Fizieron les tornar   las cuestas sin gradiello,
     fizieron les entrar   sin grado al castiello;
     non ayuda al clérigo   mejor el monaziello
     que ayudava a Éctor   Paris, su hermaniello.

633 Fueron de fiera guisa   los griegos embaídos,
     las puertas quebrantadas,   los sotos ençendidos;
     si non por que serién   los fados desmentidos,
     fueran en mala ora   de sus tierras exidos.

634 Los días e las noches   non les davan vagar,
     fizieron les sin grado   en las naves entrar.
     Tanto les pudo Éctor   de guerra afincar
     quel' ovo, como dizen,   Áyaz a derrocar.

635 Mas, por essa caída,   fue después más espierto;
     lidiava más afirmes   e firié más en çierto;
     al que, por aventura,   firié en descubierto
     tan rafez lo llevava   como a un enxierto.

636 Un alférez de Aquiles,   Patroclo lo llamavan,
     quando vio sus parientes   que tan laidos andavan,
     pesól' de coraçón,   ca por verdat lazravan;
     maldiziá a los fados   que tan mal los guïavan.

637 Armóse de las armas   de su señor dubdado;
     salló a los troyanos   e fuelos rodeando;
     conoçieron las armas   e fuerons' assemblando;
     dixieron: "Este diablo   nuestro mal va buscando."

638 Éctor el estrevudo   ixió luego a él
     e dixo, "Torna a mí,   si quieres justar, donzel;
     si demandas a Éctor,   sepas que yo so él;
     el campo sólo sea   entrambos por fïel."

639 Patroclo contra Éctor   por en dubda lo meter,
     nil' tornó la cabeça   nil' quiso responder.
     "A la fe," dixo Éctor,   "esso non pued' seer,
     que en otro recabdo   es esto a poner."

631	Hector and his brother arrived amidst all this, shields on their arms and lances in hand; any man they found before them did not see the summer; they made offerings of many souls to Hell, which lies below.
632	They made the Greeks turn tail in spite of their wishes and forced them to retreat within the palisade; the little altar boy gives the priest no greater aid than that given to Hector by his young brother Paris.
633	The Greeks were under the most ferocious of attacks, their gates were broken down and the thickets set aflame. Were it not that the Fates would be proven to lie they would have made an untimely exit from their lands.
634	By night and by day they gave them no respite and made them unwillingly withdraw to their ships. With ferocity did Hector carry the fight to them until – they say – Ajax managed to strike him down.
635	But because of that fall Hector was later more alert; he fought more stoutly and struck with truer aim. Any man that he chanced to catch without protection was cut down as easily as the shoot of a vine.
636	An officer of Achilles, Patroclus by name,* when he saw the sorry plight that afflicted his kinsmen, it weighed heavy on his heart, for they were truly in torment, and he cursed the Fates which guided them so ill.
637	He girded on the arms of his feared master Achilles, and set out to meet the Trojans and went about them. They recognised the arms and began to crowd together; "This devil," they said, "is seeking to bring us harm."
638	Hector, the man of daring, hastened towards him; "Turn to me," he said, "if you wish to joust, young man. If you ask for Hector, then know that I am he. Let the battlefield alone serve as judge for us two."
639	Patroclus, in order to strike fear within Hector, neither turned his head nor deigned to answer. "By my faith," said Hector, "such a thing cannot be; for this shall come to a very different close."

640   Endereçó la lança   e fuelo a colpar;
        súpoli bien Patroclo   el colpe desechar;
        nol' pudo de la punta   en derecho tomar;
        Patroclo por tanto   ovo de escapar.

641   Entendiélo Patroclo   en la espolonada
        que, si en él tornasse   Éctor otra vegada,
        tantol' vadrié loriga   quanto queça delgada;
        quísose defuïr,   mas non le valió nada.

642   Pero, por desmayado   con miedo e con quexa,
        por ferir se con él   fizo una remessa;
        nol' dio vagar don Éctor,   fuelo a ferir d'essa;
        atendiólo Patroclo,   fue buelta la contessa.

643   Lidiaron un grant día,   non se podién vençer;
        non podién un'a otro   en carnes se prender;
        pero dubdava Éctor   de bien se demeter;
        si non, oviéral' dado   venino a bever.

644   Membról' que le dixieran   que encantado era,
        que nol' fariá mal fierro   por ninguna manera;
        aliñó contra él,   a rienda muy soltera,
        por darli grant porrada   en somo la mollera.

645   Nol' valió a Patroclo   todo su algazar;
        coñoçiólo el otro,   óvol' a derrocar;
        sil' pesó o sil' plogo,   óvolas a baldar;
        ovo se el troyano   las armas a llevar.

646   Aquiles e los griegos   fueron todos pesantes,
        que ya de tod' en todo   se veyén mal andantes.
        Éctor e los troyanos   fazién depuertos grandes;
        fueron muy más alegres   que nunca fueran antes.

647   Aquiles por Patroclo   fazié sobejo duelo
        como si fues' su padre   o fuesse su abuelo;
        los ríos de las lágremas   corrían por el suelo;
        dizién que avié Éctor   plantado mal majuelo.

648   Tirava de sus pelos,   rompiése las mexiellas;
        con ambos los sus puños   batié las mançaniellas.
        Los griegos en sus caras   fazién malas maziellas;
        rasgadas las capas,   descosién las capiellas.

640	He lowered his lance and moved into combat, but Patroclus was well able to deflect the blow so that Hector could not catch him fully with the point, and Patroclus in this way managed to escape.
641	Patroclus understood from the force of the charge that, were Hector to strike him one more time, his armour would have the value of a sliver of cheese. He attempted to flee but it was to no avail.
642	Although weighed down with fear and sorrow he rode against him, looking to strike. Hector gave him no respite and aimed a blow at once; Patroclus faced up to him and battle was joined.
643	They fought for a full day and neither could gain victory or manage to strike the other in the flesh. But Hector feared he might not emerge safely; if so, he would by now have given him his poison.
644	He remembered being told that Achilles was enchanted and that nothing made of iron could do him any harm. He sped towards him with the reins held slack to strike a blow to the top of his head.
645	All Patroclus' war-cries were of no use to him; his foe recognised him and managed to unseat him. Whether willing or no, he had suffering to endure and the Trojan was able to carry off his arms.
646	Achilles and the Greeks were all stricken with grief, for now they saw themselves in the depths of misfortune. Hector and the Trojans were wild in rejoicing and were more exultant than ever before.
647	Achilles went into great mourning for Patroclus, as though he were his father or his grandparent. The rivers of his tears flowed across the ground; they said Hector had planted a vine of ill fruit.
648	He ripped out his hair and scratched at his cheeks and with both fists pounded the sides of his face. The Greeks left ugly bruises on their features, tore at their clothes and unstitched their hoods.

649　　Firié a su cabeça　Aquiles con su mano,
　　　　llamando: "Compañero,　amigo e hermano,
　　　　si yo algunos días　duro e bivo sano,
　　　　lo que fizo a ti　faré yo al troyano."

650　　Fizieron a Patroclo　todos su complimiento,
　　　　balsamaron el cuerpo　d'un fermoso ingüento;
　　　　metieron grant missión　en el soterramiento;
　　　　querién fazer ad Aquiles　sabor e pagamiento.

651　　Fue con grandes obsequios　el cuerpo soterrado,
　　　　de los rëys de Greçia　plañido e honrado.
　　　　Los setenarios fechos,　el clamor acabado,
　　　　fue en est' comedio　el sepulcro obrado.

652　　Maguer era el planto　e el duelo quedado,
　　　　Aquiles non avié　el pesar olvidado;
　　　　fizo fazer otras armas　a maestro ortado;
　　　　nunca durmié buen sueño　fasta que fue vengado.

653　　En pocas de palabras　vos quiero destajar
　　　　la obra de las armas　qu'Aquiles mandó far,
　　　　que, si por orden todo　lo quisies' end'notar,
　　　　serié un breviario　que prendrié grant logar.

654　　Ome que por espaçio　lo quisiesse asmar,
　　　　y verié los pescados　quantos son en la mar;
　　　　las unas naves ir　e las otras tornar;
　　　　las unas pereçer,　las otras arribar.

655　　Y estavan las tierras　por poblar e pobladas,
　　　　los montes e las aguas　e las villas çercadas;
　　　　la torre que fizieron　las gentes perjuradas,
　　　　las aves e las bestias　por domar e domadas.

656　　Y estavan contrarios　los vientos prinçipales,
　　　　cada unos cómo corren　e quáles temporales;
　　　　cómo naçen los truenos　e los rayos mortales,
　　　　cómo son en el año　quatro tiempos cabdales.

657　　Estava don Ivierno　con vientos e geladas,
　　　　el Verano con flores　e dulçes mañanadas;
　　　　el estivo con soles　e miesses espigadas;
　　　　Atupno vendimiando　e faziendo pomadas.

649	Achilles beat at his head with his hands, crying out "My companion, friend and brother, if for some days I live on in good health, what he did to you I shall do to the Trojan."
650	They all paid fine compliments to Patroclus and embalmed his body with a rich unguent. They went to great effort over his burial, wanting Achilles to be pleased and content.
651	The body was buried with great ceremony and wept for and honoured by the kings of Greece; with the week of prayer over and the cries subdued,* now the decoration of the tomb was carried out.
652	Although the weeping and laments had died down, Achilles had not forgotten about his sorrow. He had a master craftsman make him new weapons and never slept soundly until he was avenged.
653	I want to reduce for you to just a few words the decoration of the weapons ordered by Achilles; for if I were to try to set it all out in order it would make a breviary that would fill a vast space.
654	A man who wished to contemplate it with care would see there all the fish to be found in the sea, some ships setting sail, others coming back to port, some perishing and others arriving in safety.
655	There lay the lands, both deserted and well peopled, the heights and the rivers and the cities ringed by walls, the tower built by those treacherous people,* the birds and the beasts, both wild and tamed by man.
656	There, in opposition, the main winds were to be seen, how each one blows and the times at which they do, how the thunderclaps are born, and the deadly lightning, too, and how in the year there are four great seasons.
657	There was Winter, with his winds and his frosts; Spring, with flowers and gentle early mornings; Summer, with sun and crops now fully grown; Autumn, picking grapes and making cider.

658 Eran y los doz' signos   del sol bien compassados,
     los unos de los otros   igual mente tajados;
     e las siete planetas   cómo tienen sus grados:
     quáles son más raviosos o quáles más pagados.

659 Non es ome tan neçio   que vidiés' el escudo
     que non fuesse buen clérigo   sobra bien entendudo;
     el maestro quel' fizo   fue tan mientes metudo
     que metió en las armas   granado e menudo.

660 Maguer nol' fazié mengua,   ca era encantado,
     vistió una loriga   de azero colado;
     terliz e bien texida,   el almofre doblado;
     que del maço de Éctor   non oviesse cuidado.

661 Por defender las cambas calçó las brafoneras,
     fízolas enlaçar   con firmes trabugueras;
     calçaronli espuelas   del cavallo guerreras,
     quando fues' en alcançe,   por livrar las carreras.

662 Pusieron le un yelmo   firme e bien obrado
     que por oro nin por plata   non sería comprado.
     Fue a grant maestría   preso e enlazado;
     como estava fellón,   semejava pecado.

663 Después de todo esto,   çiñó una espada
     que diez vezes fue fecha   e diez vezes quebrada;
     el que la ovo fecha,   quand' la ovo temprada,
     dixo que nunca vío   cosa tan esmerada.

664 Cavalgó el fidalgo,   luego que fue armado,
     uno de los cavallos   que ovieron furtado.
     Provólo por veer   si era bien mandado,
     mas nunca en sus días   fue tan escarmentado.

665 Embraçó el escudo   que oyestes contar;
     endereçó la lança,   començó de fablar:
     "Creo que, si los fados   non quisieren falsar,
     Éctor esta vegada   non me pued' escapar."

666 Echó la lança al cuello   como buen cavallero;
     fue yendo pas' a passo   de fuera del sendero.
     Violo la atalaya   que sedié en otero;
     embïó a la hueste   luego el mensajero.

658	There were the sun's twelve signs in harmony,* each one of them equally finely carved, and the seven planets and the qualities of each, and which are more disruptive or calmer by nature.
659	There is no man so foolish that, should he see the shield, he would not become a learned scholar of great wisdom; the master who created it used such fine scholarship that he depicted on it all things, both great and small.
660	Although he did not need it, for he was enchanted, Achilles put on body armour made of pure steel, a thrice-woven mail coat, with a hood of double thickness, so that he need not have any fear of Hector's mace.
661	To protect his legs he fastened on his greaves and had them tied securely with firm straps; his men put on his spurs to drive his horse in battle so that in the chase he could sustain the gallop.
662	They placed on him a helmet that was strong and finely worked and which neither gold nor silver would be able to acquire. It was tightened and fastened with a great amount of skill; in his fury he seemed like the Devil himself.
663	After all of this, he girded on a sword, which had been made and broken ten times over. The man who had made it, when he had tempered it, said he had never seen anything crafted with such care.
664	As soon as he was armed, the nobleman mounted one of the horses they had stolen from the Trojans. He tested it out to see if it had been well trained but never in its days was such a lesson learned.
665	He took on his arm the shield of which you have heard tell, he held straight the lance and began to speak: "I believe that, if the Fates do not wish to play me false, this time there is no way that Hector can escape me."
666	As a good knight, he held the lance upright to his neck and made his way gradually out along the path. He was sighted by the watchman posted on a hill top, who promptly dispatched a herald to the army.

667   Ante que el mensaje   a Éctor fues' venido,
　　　　　ante plegó el miedo   que non el apellido,
　　　　　ante ovo a todos   el mal viento ferido;
　　　　　fue entre los troyanos   el furor ençendido.

668   Quand' assomó Aquiles   a unos campos planos,
　　　　　conoçiéronlo luego   en los gestos loçanos;
　　　　　assí se quebrantaron   Éctor e los troyanos
　　　　　como fazen los pollos   quando sienten milanos.

669   Quando los vio Aquiles,   enfestó el pendón;
　　　　　quando lo vío Éctor,   quebról' el coraçón;
　　　　　pero misso en medio   luego otra razón:
　　　　　dixo que nol' preçiava   quanto un gorrïón.

670   Ovo y cavalleros   ques' quisieron provar;
　　　　　ixieron a Aquiles   por torneo le dar,
　　　　　mas assí él los sopo   referir e redrar
　　　　　que todos de su mano   ovieron a finar.

671   Éctor nin los troyanos   nol' pudieron durar;
　　　　　oviéronle sin grado   el campo a dexar;
　　　　　faziendo grandes daños,   óvolos a rancar;
　　　　　óvolos en la villa   todos a embarrar.

672   Fue comediendo Éctor   ant' que fuesse entrado;
　　　　　asmó de tod' en todo   que era engañado;
　　　　　dixo entre su cuer: "Yo so amortiguado;
　　　　　más me valdrié seer   muerto e soterrado.

673   Señor, si de los fados   assí es ordenado
　　　　　que yo por la su mano   sea desbaratado,
　　　　　nin me defendrá Troya   nin castillo çerrado;
　　　　　que assí es a ir   como es destinado.

674   Firme seré en aquesto;   nunca en al credería,
　　　　　nunca escusa muerte   ome por covardía;
　　　　　non morrá por Aquiles   Éctor ante del día;
　　　　　Paris fue qui por miedo   falsó cavallería.

675   De que ome bien sabe   que ave de morir
　　　　　– todo es escripto   cómo es de complir –
　　　　　por miedo de la muerte   nunca deve füir,
　　　　　ca gana y mal preçio   e non puede guarir.

667	Before the message had reached Hector's ears, fear arrived ahead of the battle-cry, and already the ill wind had struck them all; frenzy was set aflame among the Trojans.
668	When Achilles appeared on a low-lying plain, he was quickly discerned for his proud demeanour. Hector and the Trojans were thrown into panic like chicks on sensing the presence of kites.
669	When Achilles saw them, he raised his pennant high and when Hector saw him his heart burst open, but he quickly expressed a different opinion, saying Achilles meant less than a sparrow to him.
670	There were knights there who wished to prove themselves and rode out towards Achilles to engage him, but he was able to repel them and drive them back and there they all met their end at his hand.
671	Hector and the Trojans could not resist his attack and unwillingly they had to yield the battlefield to him; as he struck firm blows he managed to put them to flight and force them all to take refuge in the city.
672	Before entering the city, Hector took careful thought, and reached the firm conclusion that he was in error, and he spoke within his heart: "I am mortified by this; death and burial would be preferable for me.
673	Lord, if it be so ordained by the Fates that I am to be defeated at his hand, Troy will not save me, nor castle enclosed by walls, for it will come to pass just as destiny demands.
674	I shall be firm in this, for I would always be so minded; no man ever avoids death by means of cowardice; Hector will not die by Achilles' hand before his time; it was Paris who, in fear, brought dishonour upon chivalry.
675	Once a man knows well that he has to die – the form it is to take is already written – for fear of death he must never flee, for he thus shames himself yet cannot be saved.

676 En que assí fuyamos, mayor preçio li damos
que si fuéssemos todos muertos a las sus manos;
mejor es que en campo ranquemos o muramos
que por nuestro porfaçio tan grant onta prendamos.

677 Quiçá, por aventura, Dios mejor lo fará:
a nos dará vitoria, a él quebrantará.
Dios nunca lo defiende, qui en Él dubda ha;
¡faga de mí aquello que Él por bien verá!"

678 Éctor, asmando esto, perdió el mal espanto;
por lo que avié fecho teniés'lo por quebranto;
acomendó su alma a Dios, el Padre Santo,
tornó contra Aquiles, esforçado ya quanto.

679 Palas contendié siempre – nunca en al andava –
por fer matar a Éctor, mas nos' le aguisava,
ca entendié que Troya por él se emparava.
Si non, que serién todos caídos en la trava.

680 Asmó la maledita una grant travessura:
priso forma de Paris, essa misma figura,
armas quales las suyas e tal cavalgadura,
e vino contra Éctor a müy grant pressura.

681 Cuidó Éctor que era Paris el su hermano;
dio con grant alegría a la lança de mano;
cuidó sobre Aquiles emplear bien la mano,
mas nunca en sus días aguijó tan en vano.

682 Fue ferir a Aquiles a poder de cavallo;
asmó, sis'le fiziesse, de voluntad matarlo;
firme estovo Aquiles, non dubdó esperarlo;
non dio por ello más que sil' picas' un gallo.

683 Cuidó que ferrié luego Paris del otro cabo,
quel' farién con la priessa cuestas tornar privado;
cató e non lo vío, tovos' por engañado,
quebról' el coraçón e parós' deserrado.

684 Entendié de su vida que era acabada,
la rueda de su fado que era trastornada;
sopo que nol' valdrié nin lança nin espada,
que, quando Dios non quiere, todo non vale nada.

676	By fleeing in this way we give him greater fame than if we had all met our death at his hands; it is better that we conquer or we die on battle's field than incur such great dishonour for our humiliation.
677	Perhaps by our good fortune God will treat us better, grant victory to us and destruction to Achilles. God never defends a man who doubts in Him; let Him do with me just as He thinks fit."
678	Hector, as he thought this through, lost his deep terror; he was feeling remorse for what he had done; he commended his soul to God, the Holy Father, and turned back towards Achilles with his courage reinforced.
679	Pallas strove always – she thought of nothing else – to cause Hector's death, though she could not achieve this, for she understood that he was Troy's protector and but for him they would all have come to grief.
680	The accursed woman conceived a cruel trick: she took on precisely the exact form of Paris, with arms just like his and an identical mount, and came riding up to Hector in great haste.
681	Hector thought that she was his brother Paris, and with great joy he took his lance in his hand. He meant to use his hand to good effect against Achilles, but never in his life did he ride in such vain cause.
682	He moved to strike Achilles, mounted on his horse, thinking that, if he struck him, he would with pleasure kill him; Achilles sat firm, not afraid to await him, caring for it no more than a cockerel's peck.
683	Hector thought that Paris would at once attack from the other side and that they would quickly force Achilles into flight; he looked but could not see him, and knew he had been tricked; shock ran through his heart and he stopped in dismay.
684	He understood that his life had reached its end and that the wheel of his fate had spun round. He knew neither lance nor sword would be of use to him, for when God is not willing, all things are worth nothing.

685 Alçó a Dios las manos,   premió el coraçón;
vertiendo bivas lágremas,   fizo su oraçión:
"Señor," dixo, "que sabes   quantas cosas y son,
"Tú non me desampares   a tan mala sazón.

686 Mas, si esta sentençia   de Ti es confirmada,
que escapar non pueda   Éctor esta vegada;
Señor, piensa de Troya   la mal aventurada;
si es de mí, non sea   de Ti desamparada.

687 Bien sé yo que Aquiles,   por su barraganía,
nin me vençrié por armas   nin por cavallería;
mas, de que Tú as puesto   la ora e el día,
contra lo que Tú fazes   venir yo non podría.

688 Por todo su esfuerço   nin por todo su seso,
non serié sobre mí   öy tan bien apreso,
mas Tú eres señor   e Tú tienes el peso;
el tu poder me ha   embargado e preso."

689 Aquiles en comedio   pensó por lo que vino;
membról' cómo muriera   Patroclo su vezino;
endereçó la lança   de nervio e de pino,
assí fue por a él   como a vaso de vino.

690 Éctor, maguer veyé   que non podié guarir,
el su grant coraçón   non sabié enflaquir.
Sallól' a la carrera   quando lo vio venir;
quál fue mejor colpado   non lo sabriá dezir.

691 Cad' un' en su derecho,   estos colpes passados,
salleron a dos partes,   ambos escarmentados.
Maguer entrambos eran   firmes e afforçados,
eran uno con otro   fiera ment' embargados.

692 Éctor, con el sabor   que avié de lidiar,
nol' membrava la muerte   que avié de llevar;
tan afirmes queriá   la fazienda buscar
como si fuesse çierto   que lo ovies' a matar.

693 Faziés' mucho Aquiles   ende maravillado
por ome mortal   seer tan esforçado;
dizié entre su cuer,   "Est' ome, mal pecado,
ante fará nemiga   que non sea rancado."

Book of Alexander

685 With heavy heart, he raised his hands to God,
and, shedding bitter tears, said his prayer:
"Lord," he said, "You who know all things that are,
do not forsake me at so cruel a moment.

686 But if this sentence is passed by Your will,
that on this occasion Hector cannot escape,
Lord, think of Troy in all its misfortune:
let it not be forsaken by You even if it is by me.

687 I know well that Achilles, for all of his valour,
could not vanquish me by force of arms or knightly virtue;
but since You have set the hour and the day,
I could not set myself against what You bring to pass.

688 In spite of all his courage and all his good sense
he would not, on this day, have such fortune at my expense,
but You are Lord and the authority is Yours;
by Your power I am confined and constrained."

689 Achilles meanwhile thought about his purpose
and remembered how his companion Patroclus had died.
He steadied his lance, made of fine pine wood,
and made for Hector as for a glass of wine.

690 Although Hector saw that he could not be saved,
his great heart did not know how to grow enfeebled
and he rode out to meet him when he saw him come;
I could not say which man was struck the better blows.

691 When these blows had been dealt, each one for his part
moved away to one side, both having suffered pain;
although both were staunch and valiant fighters,
each one was very much hindered by the other.

692 Hector, with the pleasure that he took in fighting,
remembered not the death which was to befall him;
so keenly did he want to seek out this duel,
as though he were certain that he was to win the day.

693 Achilles was made to wonder greatly at these events,
that a mortal man should display such valour.
He spoke within his heart: "This man, who has the Devil in him,
will do great harm before suffering defeat."

694   Dixo Éctor, "Agora   viene la nuestra vez;
       ¡Vayamos lo ferir!   ¡Nol' tengamos belmez!
       Si él me acomete,   él se lleva el prez;
       ternién todos que fui   de coraçón rafez."

695   Aún abés avié   la cosa bien asmada,
       fizo contra Aquiles   una espolonada;
       tornól' todas las oras   rica ment' la mudada,
       mas el otro dïablo   non dio por ello nada.

696   Aquiles toda vía   iva escalentando;
       ívalo poc' a poco   Palas encorajando;
       ívanli con la ira   las narizes finchando;
       diz': "Semejamos moços   que andamos trebejando.

697   Semeja que viniemos   aquí por trebejar,
       ir e revenir como   qui juega al azar;
       mas, por la mi cabeça,   esto non pued' estar,
       que yo le mostraré   el gato cóm' assar."

698   Assí fue por a Éctor,   el pendón aleando,
       como rayo que viene,   grandes fuegos echando;
       fues' Éctor un poquillo   a diestro acostando;
       dio passada al griego   que vinié flameando,

699   Aquiles por el yerro   tovos' por aontado;
       tovos' por mal apreso,   fue fiera ment' irado;
       dixo a altas bozes: "¡Que pese al pecado
       Non se gabará Éctor   öy d'este mercado!

700   Bien sé e bien entiendo   toda su joglaría;
       anda por lo fer maña,   sólo que passe'l día,
       mas por a mí non era   tan fiera bavequía;
       si non, a las mis gentes   oy nunca tornaría."

701   Dio tornada con ira,   la lança sobre mano,
       cuitando el cavallo,   maguer era liviano;
       tornós'li de cara   lüego el troyano;
       nol' dava avantaja   quanto seriá un grano.

702   Començól' a dar priessa   dándol' grandes feridas;
       aviél' del escudo   quatro tablas tollidas;
       aviél' de la loriga   quatro machas rompidas;
       pero non tenié Éctor   las manos adormidas.

694	Then Hector spoke: "Now our time is coming; let us move to strike him and show him no mercy. If it is he who now attacks me, he carries off the fame; I would be seen by all as a weak-hearted man."
695	Hardly had he thought all of this through when he spurred on to attack Achilles. He repaid in full every blow he was given but the other devil cared nothing for it.
696	Achilles was still growing steadily in spirit and bit by bit taking encouragement from Pallas; his nostrils were steadily swelling with his anger and he said, "We seem like young boys at play.
697	It seems that we have come here just to play, bobbing about as though in a game of chance, but, I swear on my head, such a thing cannot be: I shall show him how this cat must be skinned."
698	So he made for Hector with rippling pennant like a flash of lightning casting out great flames. Hector moved aside slightly to his right and dodged the Greek who burned with rage as he attacked.
699	Achilles considered himself shamed by his error; convinced of his ill-fortune, he was wild with anger and he shouted loudly: "Let it grieve the Devil! Hector will not boast today of this piece of business.
700	My knowledge and my grasp of his scheming are sound; he wants today to pass and this to last till tomorrow, but tomfoolery as great as this appeals not to me; I would never rejoin my people today without victory."
701	He spun round in anger, his lance in his hand, spurring on the horse, though it was swift already; the Trojan quickly turned to look him in the face, conceding to him not the slightest advantage.
702	Achilles launched an attack and struck him heavy blows. He had rent four panels of Hector's shield and had broken four links of his coat of mail; but neither did Hector's hands lie in sleep.

703 Firmes eran los colpes e grandes los roídos,
como, quando los vientos andan desabenidos,
fazen bolar las nuves e echan los tronidos;
los cavallos y todos eran fuert' ençendidos.

704 Firm' era e sobeja e dura la fazienda;
amos eran cansados e fartos de contienda.
Bien prendrié uno d'otro entrega e emienda;
non tomarié a Éctor tod' ome por la rienda.

705 Fazién de todas partes los niños e los viejos
candelas e limosnas, oraçiones e priegos;
los troyanos por Éctor, por Aquiles los griegos;
veyén que los caídos serién por jamás çiegos.

706 Cómos'iva la ora a Éctor aplegando,
íval' el cuer fallendo, los braços apesando;
fue perdiendo la fuerça, los colpes apocando;
el otro ¡cosa mala! iva gelo ventando.

707 Entendiólo Aquiles cómo era desmayado.
Dixo entre su cuer, "Esto es delibrado."
Clamó ad altas vozes: "¡Don toro madrigado,
öy será el día que vos veré domado!"

708 Firmóse el caboso sobre las estriberas;
dexó correr la lança ca lo avié a veras.
Éctor, como aviá çerradas las carreras,
nol' valieron sus armas quanto tres cañas veras.

709 Escudo nin loriga non li valieron nada;
metióli la cuchiella por medio la corada;
sallól' del' otra parte más de una braçada.
Ovo a caer Éctor, essa barva onrada.

710 Los varones de Troya, quando aquesto vidieron,
todos por do estavan amortidos cayeron.
Los griegos con el gozo todos palmas firieron;
todos por una boca Deo graçias dixieron.

711 El buen muro de Troya yazié mal trastornado;
el que lo trastornara andava muy pagado,
echando el boforê, firiendo al tablado,
que avié su negoçio rica ment' acabado.

703	Hard were the blows and great the noise they made, just like when the winds howl in discord, speeding on the clouds and unleashing roars of thunder. All the horses there were burning with excitement.
704	The battle they kept up was hard, intense and cruel; both men were exhausted and tired of fighting. Each one gave and was given as much as the other; no man could have put Hector under the reins.
705	On all sides, both the young and the old were preparing votive candles and alms, prayers and pious words, the Trojans for Hector and the Greeks for Achilles; they could see that those who fell would be forever blind.
706	As Hector's hour was steadily drawing near, his heart was slowly failing and his arms growing heavy; his strength ebbed away and his blows became fewer; it is a sad tale, but his foe could sense his weakness.
707	Achilles realised that his spirits were sinking and spoke within his heart: "This is all at an end." He cried out to him: "Fine-bred bull that you are, this will be the day when I shall see you mastered."
708	The fine warrior made himself secure on the stirrups and attacked with his lance, now indeed in earnest; and as Hector's ways of escape were closed off his arms were not worth as much as three reeds to him.
709	Neither shield nor armour could be of any use and Achilles plunged his sword straight through his innards, so that it emerged more than an arm's length behind. It was the hour of Hector's fall, that knight of great honour!
710	All the men of Troy, when they saw what had happened, fell down where they stood, all stricken with sorrow. The Greeks in their great joy all beat their palms and all with one voice cried out "Thanks be to God!"
711	The fine wall of Troy was cruelly laid to ruin and the man who brought this ruin was filled with pleasure, hurling forth his lance and striking the mock castle,* for he had brought his business to a fine conclusion.

712 Aquiles, desque fue   pagado del depuerto,
    vino veer si era   Éctor bivo o muerto.
    Falló la alma ida   e finado el cuerpo,
    l'escudo abraçado,   las çervizes en tuerto.

713 Fizo con el despecho   una grant crüeldat;
    por vengarse de la ira,   olvidó pïedat.
    Veyéndolo por ojo   toda su hermandat,
    rastrólo tres vegadas   redor de la çibdat.

714 Non se tovo por esto   Aquiles por pagado;
    levólo do yazía   Patroclo soterrado.
    Fue de todos los griegos   alta ment' correado,
    que vedién que su pleito   era ya acabado.

715 Los unos tenién armas,   quebrantavan tablados,
    los otros trebejavan   açedrejes e dados;
    los otros fazién juegos   menudos e granados;
    non preçiavan un figo   los lazerios passados.

716 Príamo el mesquino,   en duro punto nado,
    yazié amorteçido,   todo desacordado;
    la barva polvorienta   e el rostro rascado,
    yazié el pecador   a guis' de mal fadado.

717 Androna nunca más   recobró su sentido;
    nol' membró de su fijo   tan dulç' e tan querido.
    Destajárvoslo quiero: quand' Éctor fue caído,
    el buen pueblo de Troya   fue luego abatido.

718 Maldixieron a Paris   e al día que nasco,
    maldixieron al vientre   que a Elena trasco,
    maldixieron las tetas   e la leche que pasco,
    maldixieron a Venus   que los fizo por asco.

719 Éctor murió, amigos,   com' avedes oído;
    nunca finó en siglo   fidalgo mas complido;
    su preçio nos' podreçe,   maguer él es podrido;
    mientres omes oviere   non caerá en olvido.

720 La fazienda de Troya,   tant' era de granada,
    la çerca fuert' e alta,   de gentes bien poblada,
    que, maguer que tenién   que la avién ganada,
    non podién y los griegos   aver nulla entrada.

712	Achilles, for he was rejoicing at this celebration, approached to see if Hector was dead or alive and found his soul departed and his body without life, his shield on his arm and his neck twisted round.
713	In his spite he committed an act of great cruelty and angrily put pity from his mind to gain vengeance: before the very eyes of all of his kinsfolk he dragged Hector three times around the city.
714	Achilles did not consider himself satisfied by this but took him to the place where Patroclus lay interred. He was warmly applauded by all of the Greeks who could see that his dispute was now at its end.
715	Some took up arms and broke down mock castles, others were at play in games of chess or dice, others were making entertainments, great and small: they cared not a fig for their past hardships.
716	The wretched Priam, ill-starred from birth, lay half dead with sorrow, a broken man, his beard thick with dust and his face covered with scratches; the sinner had the manner of a man of ill fate.
717	Andromache, who nevermore regained her wits, remembered not her son, so gentle and beloved. I want to cut this short for you: when Hector was fallen, the good people of Troy were immediately brought down.
718	They cursed Paris and the day he was born, they cursed the very womb that carried Helen, they cursed the breasts and the milk from which she fed, they cursed Venus who made their people hated.
719	Hector died, my friends, just as you have heard; no finer nobleman ever met his worldly end. Though his body rots, his fine name does not decay; as long as men exist, he will not fall into oblivion.
720	The defences of Troy were of such formidable size, the walls vast and tall and well stocked with defenders, that, although they considered it already to be theirs, the Greeks could not manage to force their way inside.

721 Nunca tanto pudieron   bollir nin trebejar
que por nula guisa   la pudiessen entrar.
Estavan en grant cuita   e en fiero pesar;
si non por el porfaçio,   ya se querrién tornar.

722 Paris andava muerto   por a Éctor vengar,
mas nunca lo podié   complir nin aguisar;
pero ovo en cabo   un seso a fallar;
mostrógelo'l pecado   que non sabe bien far.

723 De suso, si vos miembra,   lo oviemos contado:
cómo avié Aquiles   el cuerpo encantado;
que nol' entrarié fierro   andava segurado;
vino en contra Éctor,   ende, tan denodado.

724 Por su mala ventura   non quisieron las fadas
las plantas de los piedes   que fuessen encantadas.
Oyera estas nuevas   Paris muchas vegadas,
mas con el grant desarro   avié las olvidadas.

725 Asmó quel' non podrié   otra guisa matar
si non por aventura,   por aquel lugar.
Quando yazié a priezes   óvol' a desechar;
tiról' una saeta   ond' ovo a finar.

726 Vínoles a los griegos   grant pesar sin sospecha;
andavan aüllando   todos con la contrecha;
muchos dizién que Paris   fizo cosa derecha
e nunca en sus días   fizo tan buena trecha.

727 Eran de tod' en todo   los griegos deserrados;
de conquerir a Troya   eran desfeüzados.
Los gozos en tristeza   eran todos tornados;
dizién que los de Troya   eran se bien vengados.

728 Néstor el ançïano   fízoles buen sermón
on' li ovieron siempre   en Greçia oraçión.
Dixo pocas palabras   e müy grant razón;
nunca les dio consejo   a tan buena sazon.

729 "Varones," dixo Néstor,   "sodes mal acordados.
Veo que los agüeros   avedes olvidados.
De diez años los nueve   aún non son passados
e vos antes con antes   sodes desfeüzados.

721	However energetically they worked at their task, by no means were they able to make their way inside; they were in deep distress, their sorrow a weighty burden; were it not for loss of honour, they would gladly now turn back.
722	Paris was dying to avenge the death of Hector but he could not achieve it or even form a plan; but in the end he managed to devise a clever scheme – it was shown him by the Devil, he who cannot do good.
723	We had already explained to you, if you recall, how Achilles came to have a body enchanted; he went about sure that no iron could break his skin – his boldness when he went against Hector came from this.
724	To his ill fortune, the Fates had not willed that the soles of his feet be also enchanted. Paris had heard tell of this many times but in his anguish it had slipped from his mind.
725	He judged that he could kill him in no other way except by the good fortune to hit him on that spot. As Achilles knelt at prayer, he managed to strike him down: he pierced him with a arrow which was to cause his death.
726	There came to the Greeks a weighty sorrow unforeseen, and all of them wept loudly at this cruel blow. Many said that Paris had done what was right and that never in his days had he performed so great a deed.
727	The Greeks were thrown into utter disarray, now despairing of ever conquering Troy. At this their joy had all turned to sorrow for they said that the Trojans were avenged in full.
728	Old Nestor set such wisdom in his address to them that for it in Greece he would always be remembered in prayer; he used only a few words but spoke great good sense; never did he give them advice at such a crucial time.
729	"My lords," said Nestor, "you are acting unwisely. I can see that you have forgotten the auguries. Of the ten years prophesied, nine are not yet passed, and before the time is up you are already losing heart.

730   Si ventura oviermos,   en poco lo tenemos;
      los mayores lazerios   passados los avemos.
      ¡Por un año que finca   flaqueza non mostremos!
      Si non, mientre biviermos   siempre nos repintremos.

731   Dirán que semejamos   al que nada en la mar;
      afógase en cabo   en un rafez lugar.
      Más valdrié que la cosa   fuesse por empeçar
      que non por nuestra onta   en cabo la lexar.

732   Si nos perdiemos uno,   ellos otros perdieron;
      ellos con esti cambio   ганançia non ovieron.
      Si nos fizieron mal,   ellos peor prisieron.
      Dirán, si nos tornamos,   que ellos nos vençieron.

733   Pesará a los fados   por esto que dubdamos:
      si dubdamos en ellos   dura mente pecamos.
      Yo vos fago seguros   que con Troya vayamos,
      sólo que fasta'l plaço   de Colcas atendamos.

734   Dios en poca de ora   faze grandes merçedes;
      estonç' acorrerá   quando non cuidaredes.
      Varones, seet firmes   por la fe que devedes;
      Dios vos fará merçed   sólo que aturedes."

735   Del consejo de Néstor   fueron todos pagados.
      Tovieron se sin dubda   por bien aconsejados.
      Todos, chicos e grandes,   fueron asaborgados
      por esperar el plazo   que pusieron los fados.

736   Andavan los diez años   en cabo de passar;
      nin la podién prender,   nin la podién dexar.
      Ovo, quando les quiso   el Crïador prestar,
      Ulixes el artero   un seso ad asmar.

737   Asmó fer un cavallo   de grandes maderos
      que pudiessen caber   quinientos cavalleros;
      en somo fer castiello   e en medio çilleros
      e ençerrar y dentro   los mejores braçeros.

738   Asmava de poner   en somo batalleros
      que lidiassen la villa   quatro días señeros.
      Entrarién en comedio   de yus' los cavalleros
      e pegarién el arca   de fuera los ferreros.

730	If we have good fortune, we think nothing of it. We have already endured the greatest hardships. For one year that remains, let us not show weakness, or we shall always repent, as long as we live.
731	They will say we are like a man swimming in the sea who ends up drowning in the shallow waters. It would be better that this were still to be begun than for us to abandon it at its end, to our shame.
732	If we have lost one man, they have lost others, and from this exchange they have emerged with no gain. If they did us harm, they have suffered still worse, and, if we return home, they will say they overcame us.
733	The Fates will be unhappy that we hesitate over this; if we fail to trust them we are severely at fault. I can give you an assurance that we shall conquer Troy if we only wait for the time specified by Calchas.
734	In but a little time, God grants men great mercies; He will come to our aid when you do not expect it. My lords, by the faith that you owe, stand firm: God will grant you His mercy if you only persevere."
735	All the Greeks were delighted with Nestor's counsel and saw that without doubt they had been soundly advised; all of them – both young and old – were encouraged to await the moment determined by the Fates.
736	Now, at last, the ten years were nearly at an end; the Greeks could neither take Troy nor abandon it. When the Creator chose to give them His aid, the crafty Ulysses devised a clever scheme.
737	He thought of building a horse of thick wooden beams,* which would be able to fit five hundred knights inside, fortified at the top and with compartments in its middle, within which the finest fighters would be enclosed.
738	He planned to position fighters at the top who would attack the city for just four days and meanwhile the knights would enter from below and from outside the smiths would close the ark up tight.

739 Asmava, en pues esto,   ques' dexassen vençer,
    desemparar las tiendas   e todo el aver;
    todos por do podiessen   foír a grant poder
    e de toda la vista   de Troya trasponer.

740 Con sabor del encalço   derramarién troyanos;
    por encalçar, los viejos   se tornarién livianos.
    Por amor que sangrienten   en los griegos las manos,
    non fincarié en Troya   ninguno de los sanos.

741 "Sólo que los pudiéssemos   un poco sossacar,
    encarnars'ien en nos,   pensarién de robar,
    cuidarién el cavallo   que era castellar;
    non se catarién d'él   e darle ien vagar.

742 Desque fuessen un poco   de Troya apartados,
    ixirién los del castillo   que serién ençerrados;
    fallarién los postigos   todos desemparados;
    serién, quando catassen,   en la villa entrados.

743 Tornarién en comedio   los que irién fuyendo;
    ir se ien a la çibdat   los otros acogiendo;
    yr les ien los de dentro   a fuera refiriendo.
    Quando esto vidiessen   perdrién sabor e tiento."

744 Quando ovo Ulixes   esti seso asmado,
    fablólo con don Néstor,   un ome muy senado.
    Asmaron que serié   consejo aguisado
    e que Dios les avié   esti seso mostrado.

745 Metieron en consejo   los prínçipes cabdales;
    vidieron lo por seso   todos los mayorales.
    Dieron todos a Néstor   las fees por señales:
    los que se retrayessen   que fuessen desleales.

746 Fueron luego sacados   e en carta metidos
    quáles serién por nombre   en el arca encloídos.
    En cabo, quando fueron   en todo abenidos,
    fizieron encubierta   ques' partién desmarridos.

747 Fue luego la madera   aducha e labrada;
    fue el engeño fecho,   el arca aguisada;
    el castillo en somo   con mucha algarrada,
    que asmavan con esso   encobrir la çelada.

739	He planned that after this they would give up the fight, abandoning the tents and everything they owned, fleeing in all haste and by whatever route, and putting themselves out of sight of Troy.
740	In their desire to give chase, the Trojans would flock out, old men now fleet of foot again to pursue the Greeks. In their desire to stain their hands with Grecian blood, not one of the healthy men would stay behind in Troy.
741	"If only we could lure them a little way out, they would rage against us, trying to take our possessions; believing that the horse was just a tower for the siege, they would pay it no heed and leave it alone.
742	As soon as they had gone some distance from Troy, the men enclosed in the horse would break out and find the city gates completely unprotected; they would have entered the city before anyone knew.
743	Meanwhile, those who were in flight would turn about and the Trojans would retreat back into the city. The men who were within would then drive them back outside and when they saw this they would lose heart and strength."
744	Once Ulysses had thought up this scheme, he discussed it with Nestor, a man of fine judgement, and they concluded it would be a wise plan and that it was God who had revealed it to them.
745	The most important princes were gathered in council and the leaders all saw that the plan was wise. They all gave pledges of their support to Nestor; any who drew back would be seen as traitors.
746	At once, the men were chosen and a record was made of the names of those to be set inside the ark. Finally, when they were completely in agreement, they made pretence of departing in great sorrow.
747	Immediately the wood was brought and shaped, the trick was prepared and the ark closed shut; the tower at the top was well equipped with catapults, for thus they intended to conceal the deception.

748 Pusiéronlo en ruedas   por rafez lo traer,
que non lo podién omes   otra guisa mover.
Tanto pudo Ulixes   andar e contender
fasta que l'ovo çerca   del muro a poner.

749 Pesó a los troyanos   mucho con el castiello;
tajávanles las tejas   com' farié un cuchiello.
Dizién entre sus cueres,   "¡Mal aya tal potriello
que non quiere por bozes   tollerse del portiello!"

750 Diéronle grant prïessa   en el día primero;
en el otro, non menos,   mayor en el terçero.
Fízose cada uno   al quarto más ligero,
que era bien afirmes   bastido el çillero.

751 Fuéronles poc' a poco   las pajuelas echando;
faziendo torna fuye,   fueron los sossacando.
Fueron les los averes   e las tiendas dexando.
Troyanos mal fadados   fuéronse encarnando.

752 Derramaron los griegos,   dieron se a guarir;
como si non pudiessen   esperar nin sofrir;
los troyanos astrosos,   com' avién a perir,
todo lo olvidavan   por en pues ellos ir.

753 Los unos por robar,   los otros por ferir,
ovieron los troyanos   de Troya a exir.
Aquellos del cavallo   pensaron de salir;
ovieron sin batalla   Troya a conquerir.

754 Quando vieron su ora   los que ivan fuyendo,
tornaron las cabeças,   fuerte los refiriendo.
Tornaron pora Troya   los troyanos corriendo,
mas fues' les la entrada   en dos e as poniendo.

755 Dávanles los de fuera   de cuesta e de lado;
ívanles segudiendo   lo que avién tomado.
Quand' a las puertas fueron,   oyeron mal mandado,
que avié el potriello   leones abortado.

756 Huéspedes non rogados   mandavan las posadas,
que fazién mal mercado   e malas dinaradas.
Dezién "¿Quién vío nunca   rencuras tan dobladas
por todas nuestras cosas   seer tan anebladas?"

748	They set it on wheels to transport it more easily for men could not move it in any other way. Ulysses strove and struggled with the task until he managed to set it up against the wall.
749	The Trojans encountered great problems with the tower: their roof-tiles were sliced off as if by a knife. They spoke within their hearts: "A curse on this colt, for not even our shouting makes it leave the gate."
750	The Greeks launched a great assault on the first day, no less on the second and greater on the third. They all reduced the scale of their attack on the fourth, for the compartment was now very soundly built.
751	Little by little, they carried out their deceit, and, feigning flight, they lured them from the city, abandoning their tents and the riches they had gained; the ill-fated Trojans grew steadily bolder.
752	The Greeks scattered and made to flee for safety as though they could not stand to wait or suffer more. The ill-starred Trojans, doomed as they were to perish, forgot everything to go in pursuit of them.
753	Some in search of booty, others seeking combat, the Trojans decided to go out from their city. Those men in the horse now looked to emerge; they were to conquer Troy without a battle.
754	When those who were in flight saw that their moment had come, they turned about and began to drive the Trojans firmly back; turning for Troy, the Trojans ran towards their city, but to gain entry was now a hard hand to play.
755	Those outside attacked them from the rear and from the sides, taking back from them the booty they had gained, and when they reached the gate they learned the bad news that the horse had miscarried and given birth to lions.
756	Unwanted guests now had charge of the lodgings, which were doing bad business and bringing scant profit. They said, "Who has ever seen sorrow so immense that all our affairs are under so thick a pall?"

757 Los varones de Troya   fueron mal engañados.
     Por el seso de Ulixes   fueron desbaratados;
     fueron en la çibdat   griegos apoderados;
     otorgaron que fueron   verdaderos los fados.

758 Todos murién de buelta, mugeres e varones;
     retrayén les los griegos las muchas traïçiones;
     posiéronli en cabo   de cada part' tizones;
     tornó Troya la magna   çeniza e carbones.

759 Dizen una fazaña,   pesada de creyer,
     que diez años duró   la villa en arder.
     Qué conteçió d'Elena   non podemos saber;
     non lo quiso Omero   en su libro poner.

760 Desque fue tod' ardida   ante que dend' partiessen,
     destruyeron los muros   que nunca pro toviessen,
     que, quant' el mundo dure,   quantos que lo oyessen
     de guerrear con Greçia   nunca sabor oviessen.

761 Pero, com' eran muchos,   todos non pereçieron;
     por qual guisa que fue,   muchos end' estorçieron.
     Éssos poblaron Roma   los que ende ixieron.
     A qual parte que fueron,   porfidia mantovieron.

762 Quando ovo el rëy   complido su sermón,
     más plogo a los griegos   que si les dies' grand don.
     Fueron todos alegres   que siguié bien razón
     e que tenié los nombres   todos de coraçón.

763 Pero, com' es costumbre   de los predicadores,
     en cabo del sermón   adobar sus razones,
     fue aduziendo él   unos estraños motes
     con que les maduró   todos los coraçones.

764 "Amigos," diz', "las gestas   que los buenos fizieron,
     cascunos quáles fueron   e quál preçio ovieron,
     los que tan de femençia   en libro las metieron,
     algund pro entendién   por que lo escrivieron.

765 Los maestros antiguos   fueron de grant cordura;
     trayén en sus faziendas   seso e grant mesura.
     Por esso lo metién   todo en escriptura
     por a los que viniessen   meter en calentura.

757	The men of Troy had been sorely deceived and had been defeated by Ulysses' wiles. The Greeks had taken possession of the city and they granted that the Fates had spoken truly.
758	All died as one, both women and men, as the Greeks repaid their many betrayals. Finally, they cast firebrands everywhere and Troy's great city was reduced to ash and charcoal.
759	They tell of a wonder that is hard to believe, that the city stayed aflame for a full ten years. We have no way of knowing what became of Helen* for Homer did not want to include this in his book.
760	Once the city was burned down, before they departed, they demolished the walls lest they ever be of use, and so that, while the world endured, any who heard of it should never desire to wage war against Greece.
761	But, the Trojans being many, not all of them perished and, in whatever way they might, many saved themselves from there. They were the founders of Rome, those who escaped from Troy; wherever they travelled, dogged fighters they remained.
762	When King Alexander had reached the end of his address, the Greeks were more pleased than had they received a great gift; they were all delighted that he told the tale so well and that he knew every single name by heart.
763	But, as it is the usual custom of the preacher to set out his points carefully at the end of his address, so he began to draw original conclusions with which he enriched the minds of all his men.
764	"My friends," he said, "these deeds done by good men, who each of them was and the fame that he won – those who with such vigour set these things to words saw in them some quality that drove them to write.
765	The masters of old were men of great learning and went about their work with wisdom and fine judgement; it is for this reason that they set it all in writing – to stir to burning passion those men yet to come.

766 Ulixes e los otros   que fueron tan lazrados,
si tanto non lazrassen   non s'ovieran vengados;
mas, por que fueron firmes   e fueron denodados,
fizieron tales cosas   por que son oy contados.

767 Siempre qui la grant cosa   quisier' acabeçer,
por pérdida quel' venga,   non deve recreer;
el ome que es firme   todo lo pued' vençer;
podemos d'esta cosa   pro de enxemplos veer.

768 Los nuestros bisavuelos,   por solo un pesar,
por una mala fembra   que se dexó forçar,
por vengar su despecho   e por preçio ganar
sufrieron tal lazerio   qual oyestes contar.

769 Parientes e amigos,   si vos preçio amades,
sólo que vos entiendan   firmes las voluntades,
esto será verdat   – bien seguros seades –
ganaredes tal preçio   qual nunca lo perdades.

770 Tant grant será el preçio   que vos alcançaredes
que quant' éstos fizieron   por poco lo ternedes;
salvaredes a Greçia,   el mundo conquerredes;
orar vos han buen siglo   los que vos dexaredes.

771 Desque ome de muerte   non puede estorçer,
el bien d'aqueste mundo   todo es a perder;
si non ganare presçio   por dezir o por fer,
valdriéle mucho más   que fuesse por naçer."

772 "Señor," dixieron todos,   "as nos bien confortados;
de quanto tú as dicho   somos mucho pagados;
de fer quanto mandares   somos aparejados;
nunca d'esti propósito   non nos verás camiados."

773 Quand' entendió el rëy   que estavan ardientes,
los cueres saborgados,   ençendidas las mientes,
fizo rancar las tiendas,   mandó mover las gentes
por ir buscar a Dario   a las tierras calientes.

774 Echaron las algaras   a todas las partidas;
quand' las unas tornavan   las otras eran idas;
conquirién los castillos,   las villas enfortidas;
non fallavan contrasto   ond' fuessen embaídas.

766   Ulysses and the others who underwent such trials,
        had they not endured so much, would not have been avenged,
        but because they were steadfast and showed great daring,
        for the feats they performed, their names are sung today.

767   Whenever someone tries to achieve great renown,
        whatever setback may befall him, he must not lose heart;
        the man whose resolve is strong can conquer all
        and we can see a wealth of examples of this fact.

768   Our ancestors, because of just one sorrow-bringing act,
        because of one wicked lady who let herself be taken,
        to avenge their anger and to win themselves fame
        endured such trials as you have heard described.

769   My kinsmen and friends, if you are lovers of fame,
        provided only that men can see your hearts are firm,
        this will be true – you may be in no doubt –:
        you will win such fame as you will never lose.

770   So great will be the fame that you will secure
        that you will hold the achievements of these men as little.
        You will save Greece, you will conquer the world
        and those you leave behind will pray for your eternal life.

771   Since a man is unable to save himself from death,
        the wealth of this world is all to be lost;
        if fame is not won by words or by deeds
        it would be much better not to have been born."

772   "Lord," they all said, "you have given us great heart
        and by all that you have said we are delighted;
        we are ready to do anything that you order of us
        and you will never see us swayed from this intent."

773   When the King saw their fiery zeal,
        their hearts impassioned and minds aflame,
        he ordered camp to be struck and his men to move off
        that they might seek out Darius in warmer lands.

774   They sent off raiding parties in all directions;
        when some returned home, others were already gone.
        They conquered castles and fortified cities
        and they found no opposition able to repel them.

775 Todo lo conquirién   quanto delant' trobavan;
     quanto más ivan yendo   más se encarnavan;
     mas la justa de Dario   tanto la cobdiçiavan
     que toda la conquista   nada non la preçiavan.

776 Tanto pudo la fama   por las tierras correr
     fasta que ovo Dario   las nuevas a saber;
     empeçós' el buen ome   todo a contorçer,
     pero dixo en cabo: "Non lo puedo creer."

777 Dario era de días   de guerra desusado;
     avié con la grant paz   el lidiar olvidado,
     ca desque rëy fuera   non avié guerreado;
     si entonçes fues' muerto   serié bien venturado.

778 Si, quanto era rico   e era poderoso,
     sisquiere de vassallos,   sisquiere de tesoro,
     assí fuesse ligero   e fuesse venturoso,
     non fuera Alexandre   a India tan gozoso.

779 Pero, que non toviessen   que era recreyente,
     empeçó de baldir   menazas alta mente:
     jurava con la ira   al Rey Omnipotente
     que los farié colgar   a él e a su gente.

780 Mandó fer unas letras   que avién tal tenor:
     "Dario, rey de los rëys,   igual del Crïador,
     diz' a ti, Alexandre,   nuevo guerreador,
     que si non te tornares   prendrás mala onor.

781 Eres niño de días,   de seso bien menguado;
     andas con grant locura,   serás y mal fallado.
     Si te fuesses tu vía   seriés bien acordado;
     si te guías por otro,   eres mal consejado.

782 El árbol que temprano   comiença a floreçer,
     quémalo la elada,   non lo dexa creçer;
     avert'ha otrossí   a ti a conteçer
     si en esta follía   quisieres contender.

783 Embío te pitança   bien qual tú la mereçes:
     correuela quet' çingas,   pello con que trebejes,
     bolsa en que los tus   dineros condeses.
     ¡Tien te por de ventura   que tan bien me guareçes!

775   They conquered all that they found before them
      and the further they ventured the bolder they became;
      but the encounter with Darius they desired so much
      that, without it, the whole conquest meant nothing to them.

776   So far did their fame spread through the lands
      that Darius came to hear news of them.
      The good man began to be wrung with worry
      but in the end he said, "I cannot believe it."

777   Darius had been for some time unused to conflict;
      with the long peace he had forgotten the art of battle,
      for since he had been king he had not had to go to war
      – had he been dead by then, great would have been his fortune.

778   If, just as much as he possessed wealth and power –
      in both the vassals and the treasure he possessed –,
      Darius likewise were active and enjoyed good fortune,
      Alexander would not have gone to India so content.

779   But, lest he be thought to be lacking in courage,
      he began to give vent to threats, crying loud,
      in his fit of anger swearing to God Almighty
      that he would have Alexander and his men hanged.

780   He ordered a letter to be composed to this effect:
      "Darius, King of Kings, and equal to the Creator,
      says to you, Alexander, a warrior of no experience,
      that, if you do not turn back, dishonour will be yours.

781   You are just a child in age and lacking in sense;
      you are committing great folly and will suffer here for it.
      If you went on your way you would be very prudent;
      if you take another's guidance, you are ill advised.

782   The tree which begins to flower early in the year
      is burnt up by the frost and not allowed to flourish.
      Exactly the same thing will happen to you
      if you wish to persevere in this folly.

783   I am sending you the little gift you well deserve:
      a belt for you to wear, a ball with which to play,
      a bag in which you can keep your money;
      think yourself fortunate that you escape me.

784   Mas si en tu porfidia   quisieres aturar,
        non porná en ti mano   nul ome de prestar;
        fert'he a mis rapazes   prender e enforcar
        como mal ladronçillo   que anda a furtar.

785   Non sé con qué esfuerço   buelves tú tal baraja,
        que más he yo de oro   que tú non aves paja;
        de armas e de gentes   he mayor avantaja
        que non es marco d'oro   en contra una meaja."

786   Quando fueron las letras   ant' el rëy rezadas,
        quexaron se las gentes,   mal fueron espantadas;
        por poco con el miedo   non tremién las quexadas;
        querrián seer en Greçia   todos en sus posadas.

787   Entendió Alexandre   luego las voluntades;
        dixo les: "Ya, varones,   quiero que me oyades;
        muchas vezes vos dixe,   si bien vos acordades:
        de can que mucho ladra   nunca vos d'él temedes.

788   Una cosa que dixo   devedes bien creer:
        que ave rica tierra   e sobra grant aver;
        ca nunca fizo al   si non sobre poner,
        ca nunca se cuidó   en aquesto veer.

789   Mucho más vos devedes   por esto alegrar
        como omes que aven   tal cosa a ganar,
        que puesto an los fados   todo a vos lo dar,
        sólo que vos querades   un poco aturar.

790   Que tod' esto avremos,   maguer es cosa puesta,
        Dios non vos lo dará   yaziendo vos en cuesta.
        ¡Esforçad, fijos dalgo!   ¡Tornemos le repuesta!
        Ca en quanto que dixo   a sí mismo denuesta.

791   Muchas ave de gentes   más de las que él diz',
        mas todas son gallinas   e de flaca raíz;
        tant' osarién alçar   contra nos la çerviz
        quanto contra açor   podrié fer la perdiz.

792   Más trae una viespa   de cruda vedegambre
        que non farié de moscas   una luenga exambre;
        tant' avrién ante vos   esfuerço nin estambre
        quant' bruscos ante lobos   quando aven grant fambre."

784	But if you wish to persist in your stubbornness, it will be no man of worth who lays a hand on you; I shall have my young boys capture and hang you like a wicked little thief who goes around stealing.
785	I do not know with what forces you seek this fight, for I possess more gold than you have straw; in both arms and men I hold a greater advantage than a gold mark does against a halfpenny."
786	When the letter was read out before the King, his men cried out in sorrow and were filled with fear; very nearly did their teeth chatter with the terror – they all wished to be back in their homes in Greece.
787	Alexander quickly understood what they desired and addressed them: "Now, my lords, I wish you to hear me; many times have I said to you, if you remember well, that you should never be afraid of a dog that barks a lot.
788	One thing that he said must you take as certain: that he has rich lands and immense wealth besides; for he has never done anything but take for himself, never thinking that he would see himself in this position.
789	You must rejoice much more over this, as men who have such wealth to gain, since the Fates are going to give you it all if only you are willing to persevere a little.
790	All this we shall have. But although it is determined, God will not give it to you if you lie at rest. Take heart, my nobles, let us give him back his answer! For in every word he said he brings dishonour on himself.
791	He has very many men, more even than he says, but they are all chickens and of poor descent; they would dare to raise up their heads before us as much as the partridge might do before a hawk.
792	One single wasp carries a crueller sting than would do a great swarm of flies; before you they would have as much courage or strength as little goats before starving wolves."

793 "Señor," dixeron todos, "en todo te creemos;
de aquí adelante nunca más dubdaremos;
sólo que tú nos bivas por ricos nos tenemos;
por las bafas de Dario un figo non daremos."

794 Mandó luego el rëy prender los mensajeros;
mandólos enforcar sobre sendos oteros.
"Señor," dixeron todos, "por tuerto lo avemos,
ca nunca deven mal prender los mandaderos."

795 Dixo el rey: "Bien veo que esto es razón,
mas, desque su señor dixo que so ladrón,
quiero salvar su dicho, como de tal varón:
que quier' que ladrón faga nol' cae a traición."

796 "Señor," dixieron ellos, "si Dario falleçié,
non era maravilla, que non te coñoçié;
mas, si tú lo mandasses, en preçio te cayé
que non prisiesse mal qui non lo mereçié."

797 Segurólos el rëy e mandó los dexar,
dioles de su aver quant' quisieron levar;
rendién graçias a Dios que lis quiso prestar.
Dezién: "Rey Alexandre, ¡Dios te faga durar!"

798 Mandó luego fer letras escriptas en tal son:
"El rey Alexandre, fijo del dios Amón,
embía a ti, Dario, atal responsïón,
lo que has de veer, que quieras o que non.

799 A todas tus palabras te quiero recodir.
Dixiste grant falençia; avert'ha a nozir;
contert'ha com' a Lúçifer que tant' quiso subir:
desemparólo Dios e ovo a perir.

800 Los donos que me diste te quiero esponer;
maguer loco me fazes, sélo bien entender:
la bolsa sinifica todo el tu aver
que todo en mi mano es aún a caer.

801 La pella, qu'es redonda, tod' el mundo figura;
sepas que será mío, est' es cosa segura.
Faré de la correa una açota dura
con que prendré derecho de toda tu natura."

793	"Lord," they all said, "we believe your every word and from now on shall never again be afraid; if only you still live, we consider ourselves rich and we shall not give a fig for Darius' boasts."
794	Then the King ordered them to seize the messengers and to hang them, each from different hilltops. "Lord," they all said, "we consider it wrong, for envoys must never be allowed to suffer harm."
795	The King said, "I can well see that this is right, but, since their lord said that I am a thief, I wish to uphold his words, as befits such a man: whatever a thief does, it is not so base as treason."
796	"Lord," they said, "if Darius spoke in error it was no wonder, for he knew you not. But it would bring you honour if you were to order that a man not deserving of harm should meet with none."
797	The King reassured the messengers and told them to go free, and gave as much of his wealth as they wished to take; they gave thanks to God, since He was willing to protect them, and said, "King Alexander, may God grant you long life!"
798	Then he ordered that a letter be drawn up of this kind: "King Alexander, son of the god Ammon,* is sending you, Darius, this answer to your letter, which you have to see, whether you wish to or no.
799	To all your words I wish to give an answer: you spoke great blasphemy, which will bring you ill; your fate will be as Lucifer's, who wished to climb so high that God abandoned him and he was doomed to die.
800	I wish to explain for you the meaning of your gifts – although you call me foolish, I understand them well –: the bag is a sign of all the wealth that you possess, which will all one day fall into my hands.
801	The ball, which is round, represents the whole world: you should know it will be mine, there can be no doubt. From the belt I shall fashion a cruel whip and with it take my vengeance over all your line."

802 Quando fueron las letras   escriptas e dictadas
con tales palabras   e otras más pesadas,
fueron presas en çera   con sello ençerradas;
fueron al rëy Dario   de Persia embïadas.

803 Dario, en est' comedio,   com' ome perçebido,
mandó por toda Persia   andar el apellido:
el ome que non fuesse   a cab' d'un mes sallido
del aver e del cuerpo   sería encorrido.

804 El rëy era ome   complido de bondat,
ledo e de justiçia   e de grant caridat;
las gentes eran buenas   e de grant lealtat;
vinién al mandamiento   de buena voluntat.

805 A cab' de pocos días   fueron todos plegados,
una enfinidat   de pueblos devisados,
de diversas naturas,   todos sobreseñados;
los que vinién más tarde   tenién se por errados.

806 Vinién de luengas tierras,   de diversas fronteras;
fablavan los lenguajes   de diversas maneras;
vinién noches e días   muy plenas las carreras;
vinién como a bodas   las gentes plazenteras.

807 Grandes eran las gentes,   los adobos mayores,
señas e coberturas   de diversas colores;
semejavan las tierras   arboladas de flores;
querién se demostrar   por buenos defensores.

808 Quando fue el poder   en uno ajuntado,
fue el emperador   alegre e pagado;
rindié a todos graçias   ca les avié grant grado
por que obedeçieran   tan bien el su mandado.

809 En medio de la hueste   seyé un grant otero;
subió el rëy Dario   allí con su terçero;
cató a todas partes,   vío pueblo plenero.
Dixo: "Darm'ha las parias   el infant' refertero."

810 Mandó una grant manga   de lienço aduzir;
de simient' de papáver   fízola bien fenchir.
Mandó al chançeller   las letras escrevir;
embïó a los griegos   tales cosas dezir:

802	When the letter had been composed and written with such words as these and others harsher, it was sealed with wax and fastened with thread* and it was sent to Darius, King of Persia.
803	Darius, meanwhile, being a man of sense, sent out the call to arms through all of Persia: the man who had not set out within a month would suffer penalty in goods and to his person.
804	The King was a man filled with goodness, well-disposed and just, and of great charity. His people were good and intensely loyal, and willingly they came at his command.
805	Within a few days they had all arrived, a myriad of differing peoples, of diverse lineage, all bearing standards; the latecomers knew they were in error.
806	They came from distant lands and far-flung frontiers and they spoke a wealth of different tongues. Night and day the roads were filled as they came, like people coming happily to a wedding.
807	Great were the people, their apparel finer still, their standards and their livery many-coloured; the whole land seemed to be carpeted with flowers; they all wished to show that they were worthy defenders.
808	When the whole army was together as one, the Emperor was pleased and contented; he gave thanks to them all in his great gratitude for so dutifully obeying his command.
809	In the middle of the host there stood a large hill which King Darius ascended with his steward; he gazed all around and beheld his whole people, and said, "The irksome prince will pay me the tribute."
810	He ordered a great sack of canvas to be brought and had it filled quite full with watermelon seed. He ordered the chancellor to compose the letter and sent it to the Greeks to give this message:

811   "¡Meted, varones, mientes! Quiérovos consejar;
      esti vuestro señor,   veed qué quiere far;
      tanto podrié nul ome   el mi poder asmar
      quanto esta simiente   podriedes vos contar.

812   Oyemos por fazaña   que varones de Greçia
      de aver fueron pobres,   ricos de sapïençia;
      mas vos sodes caídos   en loca estrevençia
      ond' sé que vos veredes   en mala repentençia.

813   Varones que andades   en tan fiera locura,
      escuchades un moço   loco e sin mesura;
      caeredes vos todos   en grant mala ventura;
      como vos preçia poco,   él non avrá end' cura."

814   Reçibieron los griegos   los mensajes de Dario;
      entró luego en ellos   un roído contrario.
      Díxoles Alexandre: "¿Quién vio tal escarnio
      qual faze de vos todos   aquel fi de Arsanio?"

815   Priso luego la manga   e sacó de los granos;
      metiélos en su boca,   empeçó de mascarlos.
      "Dulçes son", diz', "e muelles,   de comer livïanos;
      sabet que tales son   los pueblos persïanos."

816   Desent' priso la manga,   finchóla de pimienta.
      Escrivió unas letras   con tinta sangrïenta.
      Dixo: "Aquel parlero   que tanto nos refierta,
      pesarm'ha si non fago   que sobre sí lo sienta.

817   Quiero que lo sepades   la materia quál era;
      a ti lo digo, Dario   de la lengua parlera:
      embiésteme grant cuenta   de menuda çivera;
      nunca pora comer   vi cosa tan ligera.

818   Un grano de pimienta   tiene más amargura
      que non toda la quilma   d'aquella tu orrura;
      assí fazen los griegos   que son gent' fuert' e dura
      que más val' de nos uno   que mill de tu natura."

819   Pagó bien los troteros,   embïólos su vía;
      vedó que non viniessen   más con mensajería,
      ca qual que y viniesse   tornarié con mal día,
      ca non avié qué fer   de tal allegoría.

811	"Hearken, knights, I wish to give you some advice; behold what this lord of yours has in mind to do. No man could reckon the extent of my power any more than you could count the number of these seeds.
812	We have heard tell of how the knights of Greece were poor in possessions but rich in wisdom; but you have fallen into foolish excess, for which I know you will have bitter regret.
813	You knights who are behaving with such wild folly and heed a foolish boy wanting in judgement, you will all fall into very great misfortune; since he cares little for you, this will not trouble him."
814	The Greeks received the message from Darius and at once a rumble of disquiet arose in them. Alexander said, "Whoever saw such mockery as that son of Arsanes is making of you all?"
815	Straightaway he took the sack and removed some seeds, he put them in his mouth and began to chew. "They are sweet and soft and easy to eat; be assured that the Persian peoples are the same."
816	Next he took the sack and packed it full of pepper and he wrote a letter with blood-coloured ink.* He said, "That prattler who is so rude to us – I will be aggrieved if I do not make him regret this.
817	I want you to know the real meaning – this is to you, Darius, of prattling tongue: you sent me a large amount of tiny seed – never did I see a thing easier to eat.
818	One grain of pepper has more sharpness in it than the whole bag of that rubbish of yours; the Greeks are like that too: a people strong and tough, one of us worth more than a thousand of your kind."
819	He paid the envoys well and sent them on their way, but forbade them to return with any further message for any who came there would return the worse for it since he had no more use for such allegory.

820   Quando entendió Darío que nol' prestava maña,
      mintrié quien vos dixiesse que non avié grant saña;
      como Sersis fiziera, requerié su compaña
      e mandó que moviessen otro día mañana.

821   Sobr' Éufrates el río los mandó ir posar:
      un agua de grant guisa, fascas semeja mar.
      Allí prendié consejo cómo avié de far,
      si irién adelante o querrién esperar.

822   Mas, ante que moviessen, vínoles mal mandado,
      que avié Alexandre a Mémnona matado;
      de quantos que llevava non avié ren fincado.
      "El juego," dixo Darío, "en veras es tornado."

823   Ménona era de Media, un mortal cavallero;
      non avié en su corte Darío mejor braçero.
      Gabós' que a los griegos él querié ir frontero,
      e que cuidava dar treinta por un dinero.

824   Diole el rëy Darío quantas quiso de gentes,
      sesenta vezes mill de nobles combatientes;
      todos de grant esfuerço, todos omes valientes;
      devrién vençer el mundo sola mente a dientes.

825   Maguer que tantos eran e tan bien adobados,
      vençiólos Alexandre, fueron desbaratados;
      el cabdiello fue muerto, los otros desbalçados.
      "¡Par Dios!" dizen los bárbaros, "¡Mal somos emprimados!"

826   Semeja fiera cosa, mas diz' lo la leyenda:
      que tres días complidos duró esta fazienda;
      el sol, por el grant daño, perdió de su luzienda;
      de la lumbre cutiana más perdió de la terçia.

827   Darío por esto todo non quiso desmayar;
      como que mejor pudo, encubrió su pesar.
      Dixo: "Rafez se suele la ventura camiar,
      ca por los omes suelen tales cosas passar."

828   El rëy Alexandre, de la barva onrada,
      quand' ovo la fazienda de Ménona arrancada,
      çercó una çibdat; Sardis era clamada;
      entraron la por fuerça, con mucha sorrostrada.

820	When Darius understood that his scheme did not avail him, whoever told you he was not enraged would tell a lie. Just as Xerxes had done, he now sent for his men* and ordered that camp be struck the very next morning.
821	He ordered them to camp on the banks of the Euphrates – a very great river, it seems almost like a sea – and there he took counsel on how they should proceed, whether to move on or whether they should halt.
822	But before they could move from there, ill news arrived, that Alexander had killed the warrior Memnon* and that of those in his company none now remained. "What was a game," said Darius, "is now played in earnest."
823	Memnon was from Media and a death-dealing knight; Darius had had no finer fighter in his court. He boasted that he wanted to be first to fight the Greeks and that he reckoned to trade thirty for a single coin.
824	Darius gave him all the men that he wanted; there were sixty thousand noble warriors, all of great courage, all valiant men, who should conquer the world with just their teeth.
825	Although they were so numerous and so well equipped, Alexander defeated them, their army overwhelmed; their leader was killed and the others overcome. "By God," said the barbarians, "we have made an ill beginning."
826	It seems hard to believe – though the text recounts it – that this battle lasted for three full days;* before such great strife, the sun's brilliance waned, and more than a third of the day's light was lost.
827	Darius would not be disheartened by all this and covered up his concern as best he could. He said, "Fortune is wont to be fickle in her changing, for such things as these often happen among men."
828	King Alexander, the honourable warrior, once he had won the battle with Memnon, encircled a city that bore the name of Sardes,* stormed it by force and wrought great devastation.

829 Allí do estava, Asia   fázese un rencón;
     dos mares la ençierran   que yazen envirón;
     de fruente va Sagario   que nol' saben fondón;
     non podrié y ninguno   plegar sin pontón.

830 Todas aquellas fuerças   non li valieron nada;
     óvola Alexandre   aína quebrantada.
     Ovo y padre Midas   una rica posada,
     por ond' "Casa de Midas"   era toda clamada.

831 Estava en un templo   un laço enredado;
     fuera bien en el tiempo   de Midas enlaçado;
     era de fiera guisa   buelto e encantado:
     el imperio de Asia   y era figurado.

832 Assí eran los ramos   entre sí embraçados,
     non podié saber ome   dó fueran ajuntados.
     Semejava que eran   los filos adonados,
     mas era fiera cosa   cómo eran travados.

833 Assí era fadado,   qu'en escripto yazié:
     qui soltar lo pudiesse   emperador serié;
     los emperios de Asia   todos los mandarié;
     ome en tod' el mundo   contrastar nol' podrié.

834 Alexandre, con gana   de tal preçio ganar,
     contendió quanto pudo   por el laço soltar;
     mas tanto non se pudo   el señor esforçar
     que pudiesse la puerta   de los nudos fallar.

835 Paráronse los griegos,   todos mal desarrados,
     de conquerir a Asia   eran desfiuçados;
     dizién entre sus cueres: "¡Mal somos engañados!
     Por ojo lo veemos   que somos aojados."

836 El rey Alexandre,   com' era perçebido,
     dixo les: "¡Ya, varones,   yo vos tolré el dubdo!"
     Sacó la su espada,   fízol' todo menudo.
     Dixo: "Como yo creo,   soltado es el nudo.

837 Yo otra maestría   non sabría qué far;
     como quiere que fuesse,   óvelo a soltar."
     "Señor," dixieron todos,   "¡Dios te faga durar!,
     ca nunca lo podriés   más mejor aguisar."

829	Where Sardes stood, Asia narrows to a corner,
	enclosed by two seas which flank its shores.
	On the other side flows the Sangarius, its depths unknown;*
	no man could reach the city without using a pontoon.
830	All those forces could do nothing to protect it:
	and it was quickly overwhelmed by Alexander.
	There did father Midas have a rich dwelling,
	because of which it was all called the House of Midas.
831	In a temple was a thread fastened in a knot,
	which had been firmly tied in the time of Midas;
	so was the knot secured and enchanted
	that the empire of Asia was depicted there.
832	The strands of the knot were so interlaced
	that no man could tell where they were joined;
	it seemed that they were imbued with some power
	for it was a mystery how they were bound together.
833	It was so determined – it was set down in writing –
	that the man who could undo it would be emperor
	and would reign over all the empires of Asia:
	no man in all the world could go against him.
834	Alexander, eager to earn such honour,
	strove in every way he could to untie the knot,
	but, for all the effort the good lord exerted,
	he could not find the way to pull the knot apart.
835	At this, all the Greeks were left deeply disheartened,
	and despaired of being able to conquer Asia.
	In their hearts they said, "We have been cruelly deceived;
	we can see with our own eyes that our auspices are ill."
836	King Alexander, as a man who had good sense,
	said to them: "Now, my lords, I shall remove your doubt."
	He drew out his sword and cut the knot into small pieces,
	and said, "As I believe, the knot has been undone.
837	I could not have done this by any other skilful act,
	but, however it was to be, I was to undo the knot."
	"Lord," they all said, "may God grant you long life,
	for you could never have found a better answer to this."

838 Desque, con Dios a una, esto fue delibrado,
mandó el rey mover el su real fonsado;
çercaron ad Arquira, un castillo ortado,
mas fue en poca d'ora el pleito destajado.

839 Embïó end' poderes de gentes escogidas
conquerir Capadoçia, unas gentes ardidas;
mas todo su esfuerço non les valió tres figas;
fueron, si les pesó, aína conqueridas.

840 De las huestes de Dario vino lengua çertera:
qu'en Éufrates yazién çerca de la ribera;
ya se querién con ellos veer en una era
por provar cada uno qué valié o quién era.

841 Las sierras eran altas e las cuestas enfiestas,
las carreras angostas, las passadas aviessas,
pobladas de serranos, unas gentes traviessas;
temiéns' que les darién algunas malas priessas.

842 Por miedo quel' farién contraria en la vía,
que non podrié llegar a la gent barbaría,
fizo tal trasnochada que fue sobrançaría:
setenta e tres millas cavalgó en un día.

843 Cuitavan se los griegos, ca barruntes avién
que las huestes de Dario otro día movrién;
por end' ivan a priessa quanto más se podién,
ca en al non dubdavan si non ques' les irién.

844 Súpolo luego Dario cómo eran passados;
nol' pudieran venir mensajes más pesados.
Fízolo saber luego a sus adelantados;
quis quier' que al vos diga, fueron mal aquexados.

845 "Pero," dixo el rëy, "quexar non nos devemos;
somos más e mejores, rafez los vençeremos;
encara, sin tod' esto, otra razon avemos:
que sabe tod' el mundo que derecho tenemos.

846 Por que vençió a Ménona es assí enfotado,
cuídase que será siempre en tal estado;
si supiesse el loco cómo es engañado,
fers'ie de su locura mucho maravillado."

838　　As soon as this matter was resolved, with God's aid,
　　　　the King ordered his royal army to set out;
　　　　they laid siege to Ancira, a castle of note,*
　　　　but their business there was rapidly completed.

839　　From there he sent out forces of carefully chosen men
　　　　to conquer Cappadocia, its people full of courage
　　　　though all their bravery was not worth three figs to them;
　　　　to their sorrow, they were quickly defeated.

840　　Of Darius' armies there now came certain news,
　　　　that they were camped on the banks of the Euphrates,
　　　　intending to meet them on the field of battle
　　　　that each man might prove his name and his worth.

841　　High were the mountains, the hills soaring skywards,
　　　　narrow the paths, the passes full of danger,
　　　　this the land of mountain-dwellers, a rebellious people:
　　　　the Greeks were afraid lest they launch an attack.

842　　For fear of being caught in ambush on their path
　　　　and not managing to reach the barbarian peoples,
　　　　Alexander's troops marched overnight, a striking feat,
　　　　and seventy-three miles did they ride in one day.

843　　The Greeks were concerned, for they had reports
　　　　that Darius' armies would move out any day,
　　　　and for this reason they made haste all they could,
　　　　for they feared only lest their enemy escape them.

844　　Darius soon learned how they had moved so quickly,
　　　　and he could not have received less welcome news.
　　　　Without delay he gave the information to his generals
　　　　– whoever might tell you otherwise, they were greatly troubled.

845　　"But," said King Darius, "we must not make complaint:
　　　　greater in strength and numbers, quick victory shall be ours;
　　　　we have another reason, too, besides all of this:
　　　　the whole world knows that we are in the right.

846　　Because he vanquished Memnon, he is so puffed up with pride
　　　　that he thinks that he will always be in this position.
　　　　If the fool knew just how deceived he is,
　　　　he would be amazed at his own folly."

847 Ya querié en tod' esto   apuntar el albor;
     querié tornar el çielo   de bermeja color.
     Mandó mover las huestes   el buen emperador,
     ca non podié de sí   partir el baticor.

848 Las trompas e los cuernos   allí fueron tanidos;
     fueron los atambores   de cada part' feridos;
     tanto eran de grandes   e fieros los roídos;
     semejavan las tierras   e los çielos movidos.

849 Ordenó su fazienda   por ir más acordados
     que, si les aviniesse,   fuessen aparejados;
     mandó que de tal guisa   fuessen todos armados
     como si de fazienda   fuessen asegurados.

850 Levavan por reliquias   un fuego consagrado;
     siempre estava bivo,   nunca fue amatado;
     éssi iva delante   en un carro dorado,
     sobre altar de plata   e bien encortinado.

851 La estoria de Júpiter,   con otros çelestiales,
     iva aprés del fuego   con muchos capellanes;
     andava es' convento   en diez carros cabdales,
     que eran de fin' oro   e de piedras cristales.

852 Doze pueblos que eran   de sendas regïones,
     de diversos vestidos,   de diversos sermones,
     que serién a lo menos   bien doze legïones;
     éstos dio que guardassen   a essas religiones.

853 Bien avié diez mill carros   de los sabios señeros,
     que eran por escripto   del rëy consejeros;
     los unos eran clérigos,   los otros cavalleros;
     qui quier' los coñoçrié   que eran compañeros.

854 Ivan en pues aquéllos   quinze mill escogidos;
     todos eran de Dario   parientes conoçidos;
     todos vistién pretextas,   muy nobles vestidos;
     semejavan que fueran   en un día naçidos.

855 En medio iva Dario,   un cuerpo tan preçioso;
     semejava profeta,   tant' era de sabroso;
     el carro en que iva   tant' era de fermoso
     que quil' podié veer   teniés' por venturoso.

847	At this point, the dawn was about to break and the sky beginning to take on a reddish hue. The good Emperor ordered his armies to move out, for he could not cast off his own anxiety.
848	Now the trumpets and the battle horns were sounded and on both sides the crash of drums was heard; so loud and so fierce rang the din of battle that land and sky seemed split asunder.
849	Darius ordered his troops to march in tighter order, that they might be prepared if anything befell them, and he commanded that they all be equipped as though they were certain of battle ahead.
850	As a holy relic, they took a consecrated fire – it always burned with life and was never extinguished –; this was carried on ahead, in a gilded cart, set on a silver altar, well protected by a curtain.
851	The image of Jupiter, with other heaven-dwellers; went behind the fire, with many chaplains; ten large carts carried that gathering of priests, carts of fine gold and gemstone-adorned.
852	Twelve peoples each coming from a different region, who were different in dress and different in speech, and who formed at the least a good twelve legions; these he set to guard those men of religion.
853	A good ten thousand chariots bore only wise men, all named in writing as advisers of the King; some were men of learning and others were knights, but anyone would know that they were companions.
854	After these there went fifteen thousand chosen men, all of them known to be kinsmen of Darius; all of them wore gowns, which were noble garments; and they all seemed to have been born on one day.
855	At their centre rode Darius, such a fine figure: he resembled a prophet, such was his elegance. The chariot that carried him was of such great beauty that anyone who saw it thought himself of good fortune.

856 Los rayos eran d'oro, fechos a grant lavor,
    las ruedas esso mismo davan grant resplandor;
    el ex', de fina plata, que cantasse mejor,
    el ventril de çiprés, por dar buena olor.

857 El cabeçón del carro nol' tengades por vil;
    era todo ondado de muy buen amarfil;
    todo era lavrado de obra de grafil;
    de piedras de grant preçio avié y más de mill.

858 Las puntas de los rayos eran bien cabeadas,
    de bestiones bien fechos e de piedras preçiadas;
    eran tan sotil mente todas engastonadas,
    semejavan que eran en uno ajuntadas,

859 Digamos vos del yugo, si quier' de la laçada:
    obra era greçisca, nueva mente fallada;
    toda una sirpiente la tenié embraçada,
    por cadena de oro que era muy delgada.

860 El escaño de Dario era de grant barata:
    los piedes de fin' oro e los braços de plata;
    mas valién los anillos en que ome los ata
    que non farié la renta de toda Damïata.

861 Tenié puestos los pies sobre quatro leones
    que semejavan bivos, tanto eran lidones;
    tenién en las cabeças otros tantos grifones
    e tenién so las manos todos sendos bestiones.

862 Venié sobre el rëy, por temprar el calor,
    un águila bien fecha de preçiosa lavor,
    las alas espandidas por fer sombra mayor;
    siempre tenié al rëy en temprada sabor.

863 Eran en la carreta todos los dios pintados:
    e cómo son tres çielos e cómo son poblados;
    el somero muy claro, lleno de blanqueados,
    los otros más de yuso, de color más delgados.

864 Ivan, sin todo esto, de cuesta e delante
    diez mill aguardadores çerca el emperante;
    todos avién astas de argent' blanqueante
    e cuchillas bruñidas de oro flameante.

856	The struts were made of gold and elaborately worked
and the wheels, also golden, shone out brightly;
the axle was fine silver, to sing a sweeter note,
the platform made from cypress wood, that its smell be pleasing.
857	Do not overlook the headpiece of the chariot:
it was gently curving, made from ivory of high worth,
all of it delicately worked with a chisel,
and inlaid with more than a thousand precious stones.
858	The ends of the struts were capped with carvings
of finely formed beasts, and with precious jewels
which were all so cleverly set in their place
that they seemed to be joined together as one.
859	Let us talk of the yoke and even the fastenings,
work of Greek origin, newly devised;
a serpent held it entire in its coils,
formed from a very fine golden chain.
860	Darius' seat was of very great value,
with feet of fine gold and silver arms;
the rings securing them were of greater worth
than the income of all of Damietta.*
861	The feet of the seat were placed atop four lions,
so convincing that they seemed to be alive;
on their heads they held just as many gryphons
and a monstrous beast beneath each paw.
862	Over King Darius, to temper the heat,
was a finely made eagle, elaborately worked,
its wings outstretched to give greater shelter,
to keep the King always in cool comfort.
863	All of the gods were depicted on the chariot;
it showed the three heavens and those who dwell in them,*
the highest very bright, full of figures clad in white,
the lower ones painted in more subdued colours.
864	In addition to all this, ahead and at his back,
ten thousand guards accompanied the Emperor,
all bearing lances of shining silver
and burnished blades of flaming gold.

865 Levava más de çerca   dozientos lorigados,
    todos fijos de rëys   e a ley engendrados;
    todos eran mançebos,   todos rezién barvados,
    de pareçer fermosos   e de cuerpos granados.

866 Aún fizo al Dario   por las huestes salvar
    e que las non pudiessen   los griegos desbalçar:
    sacó treinta mill otros,   varones de prestar,
    por governar la çaga   e las huestes guardar.

867 Vinié çerca del rëy   su muger la reína,
    en preçiosa carreta   so preçiosa cortina:
    un fijo e dos fijas,   mucha rica vezina,
    más cabera la madre   e con muy grant cozina.

868 Avié y cinqüenta carros,   todos bien adobados;
    de mugeres de rëys   todos vinién cargados.
    Por guardar essas dueñas   avié y dos mill castrados;
    quando eran chiquillos,   fueron todos cortados.

869 Los rëys de Oriente   avién todos tal maña
    de ir en apellido   con toda su compaña;
    bien de antigüedat   tenién esa façaña,
    mas pora Dario fue   más negra que la graja.

870 Levavan de tesoros   tres vezes çient camellos
    e seisçientas azémillas   cargadas en pos ellos;
    de más ivan cargados   assí todos aquéllos
    que salién las sudores   por somo los cabellos.

871 Más avié de çient mill   de omes lorigados
    que eran de ballestas   e de fondas usados.
    De otra gent' menuda   de pueblos aledanos
    non vos podrién dar cuenta   tales diez escrivanos.

872 Assí llevava Dario   sus hazes ordenadas;
    cómo avién de fer   eran bien castigadas;
    todas de buenos omes   eran bien cabdelladas;
    eran de todas armas   todas bien arreadas.

873 Tan grant era la cosa,   los pueblos tan largueros,
    que a la part' que ivan   tenién quinze migeros;
    las nuves de los pueblos   cobrién los oteros;
    ensordién las orejas   al son de los tromperos.

865	Closest to him he had two hundred armoured men,
	all sons of kings, born legitimate heirs;
	all were young men with their beards newly grown,
	handsome in appearance and large in limb.
866	Darius did one thing more to protect his forces,
	so that the Greeks would be unable to defeat them:
	he chose another thirty thousand knights of worth
	to protect the rear and guard the army.
867	Near to the King went his wife and queen,*
	in a cart of great beauty, behind a fine curtain,
	his son and two daughters, a train of comely attendants.
	and finally his mother with a great retinue.
868	There were fifty carts, all with exquisite decoration,
	and all of them were laden with the wives of kings;
	to guard these ladies there were two thousand eunuchs,
	all of them castrated when they were young boys.
869	It was the custom of the kings from the East
	to ride out to battle with all their court.
	This had been their practice since ancient times
	but for Darius it was blacker than a rook.
870	Their treasures were borne on three hundred camels
	and six hundred laden mules that traced their steps;
	indeed, all those beasts were so heavily burdened
	that sweat poured out over all their hair.
871	There were over a hundred thousand men in armour,
	practised in the use of crossbows and slings;
	to the other rank and file from neighbouring countries,
	ten such writers could not do full justice.
872	Darius had his troops drawn up in just this way
	and they were well trained in what they must do;
	they were all led well by excellent men
	and all were well equipped and fully armed.
873	This was all on such a scale and the numbers so vast
	that the army stretched a full fifteen miles;
	the people were like clouds covering the hills
	and men's ears grew deaf at the sound of the horns.

874 Con todas estas nuevas e tod' este roído,
iva el rëy Dario fiera ment' esmarrido,
ca la muerte de Ménona le avié desmaído,
ca avié por verdat estraño braço perdido.

875 Que sin miedo non era qui quier' lo podrié asmar;
ca fazié a los suyos las fronteras robar;
fazié las fortalezas destroír e quemar,
ca non se las trevié, creo, a mamparar.

876 El rëy Alexandre, que no sabié foír,
nin se querié echar a luengas a dormir,
nol' membrava de cosa ninguna conquerir
ca por veer a Dario querié todo morir.

877 Pero, como tenié por suyas las çibdades,
castillos e aldeas e otras heredades,
nula ren non robava en ningunos lugares;
dávales, por do ivan, firmes seguridades.

878 Oyó cómo avién a Tarso ençendida:
una villa real, de todo bien complida,
ond' sallió el apóstol, una lengua fardida;
embió a amatarla ante que fues' ardida.

879 Fue aína Parmenio, por'en todo argudo;
metióse por la villa, amató quanto pudo;
desent' plegó el rëy, un cuerpo estrevudo,
sí que non le vagó; fue el fuego vençudo.

880 El rey, con la priessa, era escalentado,
era de la calor del fuego destemprado;
e provó una cosa que non avié provado:
que la salut non dura siempre en un estado.

881 El mes era de julio, un tiempo escalentado,
quando en el León ave el sol su grado;
aviá a lo de menos quinze días andado;
segunt esto, pareçe que era bien mediado.

882 El tiempo era fuerte e el sol muy ferviente;
querié de calentura morir toda la gente.
Çiliçia, sobre todas, ave aire caliente,
ca el ardor del sol l'aquexa fiera mente.

874	Amidst all this splendour and all the great din, King Darius was feeling deeply troubled for he had been dismayed by the death of Memnon, as he had truly lost a knight of great valour.
875	That he was not without fear, anyone could tell, for he had his men make raids on the borders and had fortresses destroyed and burned to the ground for, as I believe, he did not dare to defend them.
876	King Alexander, who knew not how to flee nor wanted to lie in sleep for any length of time, now had no thoughts of making any conquest, for to meet Darius he was quite prepared to die.
877	But as he considered the cities as his own, as well as castles, villages, and other estates, he stole nothing at all from any of these places but gave out firm assurances everywhere they went.
878	He heard how they had set Tarsus aflame* – a royal city, well possessed of every quality, home of the apostle Paul, of persuasive tongue – and sent help to quench the fire before the city was burned.
879	Parmenion, gallant in all things, went quickly and entered the city, quenching all the flames he could, and when the King arrived, that man of great valour, the fire was overcome without any delay.
880	The King was both stoked to elation by the struggle and feeling uncomfortable from the heat of the fire, and he learnt something he had never known before: that health does not remain forever constant.
881	It was the month of July, a time of great heat, when beneath the lion's sign the sun has its wish; Leo had been abroad for at least fifteen days so it seems to me this was the middle of its term.
882	The weather was fierce and the sun burned with power, and the people were ready to die with the heat. Cilicia, above all lands, is used to being hot,* for the sun's ardour beats down on it with fury.

883 Va por medio la villa   una agua cabdal
que es, segunt la tierra,   buena uno con al;
naçe en una sierra,   deçiende por un val;
pareçe so el agua   crespo el arenal.

884 Priso el rey sabor   de bañarse en ella,
ca corrié tan fermosa   que era maravella;
oviera y por poco   contido tal manziella
que oviera del río   tod' el mundo querella.

885 Fízose desarmar   e tollerse los paños,
tenién gelo a mal   los sos e los estraños;
dio salto en el río   con ambos sus calcaños;
pareçié bien que yogo   pocas vezes en baños.

886 Com' estava el cuerpo   caliente e sudoriento,
era el agua fría   e contrario el viento.
Priso en aquel baño   un tal destempramiento
que cayó fascas muerto,   sin seso e sin tiento.

887 Los varones de Greçia,   quando esto vidieron,
todos en sus cabeças   con sus manos firieron;
sacaron lo del río   quanto ante pudieron;
nunca quantos y eran   tan mal día ovieron.

888 Como muerte de rëy   de leve non se calla,
sopo luego las nuevas   toda la almofalla;
allí fueron veyendo   los grïegos sin falla
que tenién mal consejo   por ir a la batalla.

889 Fueron en fiera cueita,   fue grande el espanto;
nunca quantos y eran   prisieron tal quebranto;
todos, chicos e grandes,   fazién duelo e planto;
bozes e alaridos   ivan de cada canto.

890 Davan a sus cabeças,   diziendo su rencura:
"Mesquinos, ¿cómo somos   de tan mala ventura?
Fuemos de nuestras madres   nados en ora dura;
viniemos a pardernos   un año d'andadura."

891 Dezién: "Señor, ¿quién vío   omes tan deserrados?
Somos en sazón mala   de ti desamparados;
somos de tod' el mundo   por ti desafïados
e nos por defendernos   somos mal aguisados.

883	A large river flows through the middle of the city, a river as fine as the land is full of goodness; born in a mountain range, it flows down through a valley, and, beneath the water, appear the ridges of the bed.
884	The King took delight in bathing in the river, for its flow was so beautiful that it was a wonder, but something so awful very nearly occurred there* that the whole world would have laid curses on it.
885	He removed his armour and stripped off his clothes – to the concern of both his own men and outsiders – and, with heels together, he plunged into the river; it was clear that he had little experience of bathing.
886	As his body was hot and bathed in sweat and the water was cold and a hostile wind blew, through that swim in the river he caught so severe a chill that he fell almost lifeless, unconscious, without feeling.
887	The men of Greece, when they saw this happen, all struck themselves in their faces with their fists and dragged him from the river as soon as they could; none of those there present ever had so bad a day.
888	As the death of a king is not easily kept secret, the news spread throughout the whole army at once; there the Greeks could see beyond any doubt, that they would be ill advised to go into battle.
889	They were in terrible distress and great was their terror: those men who were there never felt so cruel a blow; young and old alike, the men all grieved and lamented, and from every rock were echoed their cries and their howls.
890	They beat at their heads, giving vent to their sorrow: "We are wretched men – how can we suffer such ill fortune? We were born to our mothers at an ill-fated hour and have come to meet our doom after a year of travel."
891	They said, "Lord, who ever saw men in such distress? We are forsaken by you at the worst of times, when because of you the whole world is set against us, and we are ill prepared to defend ourselves from them.

892 Darío nos yaz' açerca, escapar non podremos;
     sin ti, en la batalla entrar non osaremos;
     las sierras nos han presas, tornada non avemos.
     Por malos de pecados aquí las baldaremos.

893 Aún maguer pudiéssemos a la tierra tornar,
     sin ti non osaremos en ella assomar;
     vassallos sin señor saben se mal guardar.
     Señor, ¿a quáles tierras iremos nos poblar?

894 Señor, la tu ventura, que te solié guïar,
     tóvote mal fe, dexót' en mal lugar.
     Nunca devié en ella ome bivo fïar;
     sabe a sus amigos galardón malo dar."

895 Tovos' doña Fortuna mucho por denostada;
     vío que eran neçios, non dio por ello nada.
     Fue tornando la rueda que yazié trastornada;
     fue abriendo los ojos el rey una vegada.

896 Fuel' viniendo el seso, recobró su sentido;
     fue del mal mejorado pero non bien guarido.
     Díxoles: "¡Ya varones, pueblo tan descosido!
     Non vi tan grant conçejo sin feridas vençido.

897 Aún seyendo bivo, judgádesme por muerto;
     de buena gent' que sodes, traedes mal confuerto.
     Veo que mal sabedes avenir en depuerto;
     por verdat vos dezir, tenedes me grant tuerto.

898 Nuestro vezino Darío, si fuesse buen guerrero,
     levárseme podrié como a un cordero;
     en las tierras agenas lazraría señero;
     todo nuestro lazerio non valdrié un dinero.

899 Mas si algunos meges me pudiessen guarir,
     aún esta vegada non querría morir;
     e non lo fago tanto por amor de bevir
     mas por que me querría con Darío combatir.

900 Sólo sobr' el cavallo me pudiesse tener
     e ante mis vassallos en el campo seer,
     avriénse los de Persia sin grado a vençer
     e fariedes los míos lo que soliedes fer."

892	Darius lies close to us, escape we shall not manage; without you we shall not dare to enter battle; they have barred the mountains to us and we have no way back: here we shall be made to pay for all our sins.
893	Even if we were able to return to our own land, without you we would not dare appear in it: bereft of their lord, vassals cannot protect themselves. What lands shall we go to, lord, to make our own?
894	Lord, your good fortune which used to be your guide has betrayed you and left you in a dreadful plight. No man alive should ever put his trust in it for it knows how to give a poor reward to its friends."
895	Lady Fortune thought herself grievously insulted but saw that they were foolish and cared nothing for it. The wheel that had spun round began to turn again, and the King slowly opened his eyes once more.
896	Gradually, his senses and his mind returned to him: he was starting to recover though not yet fully cured. He said to them, "My knights, you people in despair, I have never seen so great a host vanquished without a wound.
897	When I was still alive you gave me up as dead, although men of noble line, you give little cheer. I can see you do not know how to unite in joy. To tell you the truth, you do me great wrong.
898	Our neighbour Darius, if he were a good warrior, could carry me off as if I were a lamb, and I would find suffering alone in foreign lands; all of our hardship would not be worth a penny.
899	But if some doctors were able to cure me, even now I would not want to die; and this is not the case so much for love of living but because I would like to do battle with Darius.
900	If only I were able to sit astride my horse at the head of my vassals on the battlefield, the Persians would unwillingly have to endure defeat and you, my men, would act as you have grown accustomed."

901 Andava por las huestes   una grant alegría
     por que en el señor   entendién mejoría;
     pero dubdavan muchos   que con la osadía
     farié por aventura   de cabo recadía.

902 Felipo, un su mege,   que lo avié en cura
     – físico delantero,   coñocié bien natura –
     prometié quel' darié   una tal purgadura
     que lo darié guarido,   esto cosa segura.

903 Fue en este comedio   el mege acusado
     que lo avié el rëy   Darïo engañado,
     que li darié su fija   con müy grant condado,
     sólo que por él fuesse   d'este ome vengado.

904 Mintié el mesturero   en quanto que dizié;
     aviél' muy grant enbidia,   por esso lo fazié;
     non lo creyé el rëy,   que bien lo coñocié:
     siempre lo quiso bien,   ca él lo merecié.

905 Quál fue el mesturero,   non lo quiero dezir:
     ome fue de grant preçio,   quiérolo encobrir;
     sopo en todas cosas   al rëy bien servir
     pero ovo en cabo   mala muert' a morir.

906 Sacó sus melezinas   el mege del armario;
     de todas las mas finas   tempró su lectüario;
     non y mescló un punto   del gingibre de Dario,
     ca non fuera vezado   de prender tal salario.

907 Quando ovo el rëy   la yerva a bever,
     ovo un poco dubdo,   quísose retener.
     Entendiólo Felipo,   fízolo descreer;
     ovo su melezina   el rëy a prender.

908 El rëy, quando ovo   la espeçia tomada,
     dio al mege la carta   quel' avién embïada.
     Felipo, quand' la vío,   non dio por ello nada;
     echóla en el fuego,   toda despedaçada.

909 "Señor," dixo, "non dubdes   en esta melezina;
     nunca en esti siglo   bevrás otra más fina.
     Si sovieres quedado,   serás sano aína;
     mas el mesturador   es de mala farina.

Book of Alexander

901   Great rejoicing spread through Alexander's armies
for they saw that the health of their lord had improved,
but many were afraid that through his daring conduct
in the end he might happen to suffer a relapse.

902   Philip, one of his doctors, under whose care he was,
– a noted physician, well versed in nature's ways –
promised to purge him to such good effect
that, without the slightest doubt, he would leave him cured.

903   At this point the doctor met with the accusation
that he had received a bribe from King Darius
who offered him his daughter and immeasurable estates
if only he had vengeance on Alexander by his hands.

904   The slanderer lied in all the things he said
– he felt great envy and did it for that reason –;
the King did not believe him for he knew his doctor well
and always loved him dearly, as he thoroughly deserved.

905   Who the slanderer was, I do not wish to say
– he was of great distinction, whose name I would conceal.*
In other matters he was able to serve the King well
but in the end he was to die a sorry death.

906   The doctor took his medicines out from his cupboard
and tempered his remedy with the finest of them.
He mixed into it nothing of Darius' ginger
for he would not have been so base as to accept such pay.

907   When it was time for the King to drink the potion,
he hesitated briefly in his reluctance;
Philip understood this and made him change his mind:
the King was to take his medicine in the end.

908   When the King had drunk the herbal potion
he gave to the doctor the letter sent to him.
Philip, when he saw it, gave it not a second thought:
he tore it into pieces and cast it in the fire.

909   He said, "Be not afraid of this medicine, my lord:
never in your life will you drink any finer.
If you remain at rest now you will be quickly cured,
but the author of those lies is of evil stock.

910 Señor, aquel que quiso tu salut estorvar
queriéte, si pudiesse, de buen grado matar;
esto que yo te digo as aún a provar,
que algunt mal serviçio te ave a buscar.

911 Ca de mí ha enbidia o tu muerte querrié;
si non, atal nemiga nunca sossacarié;
señor, en él non fíes, ca fe non te ternié;
o por sí o por otri la muert' te buscarié."

912 El dicho de Felipo non lo levó el viento;
entró al rey en cuer, ovo grant pagamiento;
tóvoli a Parmenio siempre muy mal taliento
e bien gelo mostró en el acabamiento.

913 A cab' de pocos días el rëy fue guarido;
ixió que lo vidiessen de sus armas guarnido;
todos le rindién graçias al maestro Felipo;
dizién todos que fuera en buen tiempo naçido.

914 Fueron a pocos días las comarcas corridas;
las que se non rindieron fueron todas ardidas.
Embïó a Ismón muchas gentes guarnidas;
fallaron la vazía e las gentes fuïdas.

915 Ya estavan los rëys fascas en un tablero,
avié del un' al otro assaz poco migero.
El rey Alexandre, un natural guerrero,
quiso poner su cosa en recabdo çertero.

916 Fabló con sus vassallos cómo s'acordarién,
si irién contra ellos o si los atendrién.
Escusólo Parmenio que por bien lo veyén
de ir a cometer los bien allá do seyén.

917 Sísenes, un ric' ome, por que non dixo nada,
tovieron que de Dario avié presa soldada.
Fue luego la sentençia por conçejo judgada
que por al non passase si non por la espada.

918 Otro, un alto prínçipe de los reyes de Greçia,
con el rey Alexandre ovo desabenençia;
con aquellos que eran de su atenençia,
passóse pora Dario, mas non por su fallençia.

910	Lord, that man who strove to do harm to your health, had he been able, would have been glad to bring you death. What I tell you now you will yet see proved, for he will find some way to do you wrong.
911	Either he envies me or he would have wished your death, otherwise he would never have devised such a plot. Lord, do not trust him: he would not return your faith; in one way or another he would seek out death for you."
912	The words that Philip spoke were not lost to the wind: the King took them to heart and they delighted him; always towards Parmenion he was so ill-disposed, and gave full evidence of this in his demise.
913	It was a matter of days before the King was cured and he went out to be seen, arrayed in his armour. Everybody gave thanks to Master Philip saying he had been born at a favoured hour.
914	The neighbouring regions were overcome within a few days; those that did not surrender were all set ablaze. Against Issus, Alexander sent many men in arms,* but they found it deserted and all the people fled.
915	Now the two kings were almost pieces on one board, each one but a little distance from the other. King Alexander, a warrior by nature, wished to leave nothing of his affairs to chance.
916	He discussed with his vassals their plan for battle, whether to make the attack or await the enemy. Parmenion argued – and his words received support – against moving to attack them just where they were.
917	The nobleman Sisenes, because he said nothing,* was believed to be in Darius' pay; the sentence was promptly passed by the council that he receive nothing but death by the sword.
918	One other prince, eminent among the kings of Greece,* had a disagreement with King Alexander and together with those men who made up his train he went over to Darius, but not through his fault.

919 Plogo con él a Darío, ca fazié grant derecho;
prometiól', si vençiesse, quel' farié grant provecho;
mas, por quanto al rëy consejó de su fecho,
ovieron le los medos saña e grant despecho.

920 "Señor," dixo el griego, "téngom' por tu pagado;
de la merçed que dizes riéndote graçias e grado;
pero, quando vassallo tuyo me so tornado,
dezirt'he un consejo que tenía asmado.

921 Del rëy Alexandre dezirt'he yo sus mañas;
es firme cavallero, trae firmes compañas.
Non son tanto de muchas como son de estrañas;
bien creo qu'en el siglo non ave sus calañas.

922 Como son segurados que non han de fuïr,
en uno lo han puesto de vençer o morir.
Demás, son se parientes, non se quieren partir;
es una fiera cosa a tales omes ir.

923 Demás, son en faziendas omes aventurados
que andan con agüeros e guían los los fados;
e, si fueren los tuyos por ventura rancados,
y ten que son en Asia todos apoderados.

924 Por ende, lo vería por cosa aguisada
que fincas' la batalla fasta otra vegada,
ca tomarás grant daño ant' que sea rancada;
e si al te contiere, será mala plomada.

925 Rëy, de mi consejo bien veo que non te pagas;
o tienes que non era seso que te retrayas.
Aún consejaría otra cosa que fagas;
escusa muchas vezes que se guarden las plagas.

926 Traes grandes averes en uno aplegados,
azémillas e carros e camellos cargados.
Non lo tengo por seso averes tan granados
meterlo a ventura a un echo de dados.

927 Sí tú fer lo quisieres, yo por bien lo vería,
que de tantos tesoros toda la mejoría,
con una grant partida d'esta mançebía,
fincasse en Damasco fasta otro día.

919	Darius was pleased and judged his actions good, / and promised him great profit, if victory were his; / but, because of the advice that he gave to the King, / the Medes felt great anger and resentment for him.
920	"My lord," said the Greek, "I am grateful to you; / for the favour you grant me I thank you in full, / but I shall give you, now I have become your vassal, / a piece of advice that I have carefully thought through.
921	I shall tell you of the ways of King Alexander: / he is a brave knight and has courageous troops, / great not in number, but in the deeds they have performed, / and – so I believe – without rival in the world.
922	As they are determined that they will not flee, / as one they are decided to conquer or die; / moreover, they are kinsmen who will not be divided; / it is a hard task to go to battle with such men.
923	They are also men of good fortune in battle, / with favourable omens, who have the Fates to guide them, / and, if it should happen that your troops be defeated, / be sure that they will be masters of all Asia.
924	So in my opinion it would be a wise plan / for you to delay the battle for another time, / for you will suffer great harm before you see him worsted; / should something else befall you, it will be a savage blow.
925	My King, I can see you are not pleased by my advice, / or consider it unwise for you to withdraw. / I would still give you one further piece of counsel: / it is often best to guard against danger.
926	You are bringing with you an assemblage of great wealth, / mules and carts and camels, all with heavy loads. / I do not consider it wise for such great riches / to be gambled thus on one throw of the dice.
927	If you were to be willing, I would think it right / that the best part of so great a store of treasure, / with a good section of this warrior youth, / should stay in Damascus until a later day.

928 Si – ¡lo que Dios non quiera! – se torçiere el viento,
en esto, si al non, avrás abastamiento.
Señor, ¡lieva tu cosa a maña e a tiento!
Lo al non será seso por mi coñoçimiento."

929 Seso fabló Timoda, mas non fue escuchado;
fue de tales y ovo por desleal rebtado;
pero, quando el pleito fue todo acabado,
vidieron que dixera el griego aguisado.

930 Quisieron al grïego afirmes mal meter;
dizién que con la alma non devié estorçer;
ca dava mal consejo, devía mal prender;
mas al emperador non pudieron mover.

931 Diz' Dario: "¡Ya, varones, fablemos ya en al!
Los que en mí fïaron por mí non prengan mal;
quando logro non lievan non pierdan el cabdal;
ca ya non so en tiempo por seer desleal."

932 Partieron se los griegos, fueron se su carrera,
veyén que la fincança muy sana non les era,
ca todos los de Dario les tenián grant dentera;
pesól' mucho a Dario, cosa fue verdadera.

933 Pero en es' consejo ovieron a tornar;
fizieron los tesoros a Damasco llevar;
mas ovieron las dueñas con el rey a fincar;
non quisieron la lëy antigua quebrantar.

934 Çertero era Dario que, den' al otro día,
avrién el medianedo sobre tuya e mía;
pagarién el escote, farién la cofradía.
Verién quáles a quáles coñoçrién mejoría.

935 En medio de las huestes avié un colladiello,
d'ella e d'ella parte, más alto un poquiello;
era en la cabeça plano e verdeziello;
era un logarejo por verdat apostiello.

936 Estávali en medio un laurel muy anciano,
las ramas muy espessas e el tronco muy sano;
cubrié toda la tierra un vergel muy loçano;
siempre estava verde, ivierno e verano.

928 If, may God forbid, the wind should blow against you,
in this respect, if not in others, you will be well set.
My lord, govern your affairs with cunning and with care,
for to act otherwise will not be prudent, to my mind."

929 Timodes spoke wisely but his words were not heeded:
he was denounced as disloyal by those present;
but when the whole affair had come to its end,
they saw that the Greek had spoken with insight.

930 They wished to mete out punishment firmly on the Greek,
saying that he should not escape with his life,
and as he gave bad advice he should gain ill in turn;
but they were unable to sway the Emperor.

931 Said Darius, "Now, my knights, let us talk of other matters:
let those who put their trust in me not suffer on my account;
when I prevail, let them neither gain nor lose possessions,
for I am not in a position to act disloyally."

932 The Greeks departed and set off on their way,
seeing that it was not safe for them to remain,
for Darius' troops nursed great hatred for them.
It weighed heavy on Darius, it is true to tell.

933 But they decided to accept one piece of advice
and they took the treasures back to Damascus.
However, the ladies were to stay with the King,
for they did not want to break the ancient law.

934 Darius was confident that just a day from then
the fate of the battle would be in the balance;
men would pay their tribute and form their brotherhood
and it would be seen which of them came out the stronger.

935 Between the two armies there stood a small hill,
just a little above the land they each occupied;
at its peak it was flat and pleasantly green:
this was indeed a most beautiful spot.*

936 In the middle of the hill stood an ancient laurel tree,
the branches densely crowded and the trunk in rude health;
all the land was covered by a rich, lush orchard,
forever green, in winter and in summer.

937   Manával' de siniestro   una fuent' perenal;
       nunca se mengüava,   ca era natural;
       avié so el rosario   fecho un regajal;
       por y fazié su curso   com' por una canal.

938   Ixié de la fontana   una blanda frïor;
       de la sombra del árbol   un temprado sabor;
       dava el arbolario   sobre buena olor;
       semejava que era   huerto del Crïador.

939   Que por la buena sombra,   que por la fontana,
       allí vinién las aves,   tenién la meredïana;
       alli fazién los cantos   dulçes cada mañana,
       mas non y cabrié ave   si non fues' palaçiana.

940   El agua de la fuente   deçendié a los prados;
       teniélos siempre verdes,   de flores colorados;
       avié y grant abondo   de diversos venados,
       de quantos en el siglo   podrién seer fallados.

941   El emperant', vestido   de un xamit' bermejo,
       asmó de apartarse   en aquel logarejo;
       de solos ricos omes   fizo un grant conçejo;
       començó de tratar   con ellos su consejo.

942   Sólo en el aseo   del su buen contenente
       fazié grant pagamiento   a toda la su gente;
       podriégelo quis quiere   coñoçer vera mente
       que él era el rëy   de todo Orïente.

943   Sola ment' de la vista   qui quier' que lo vidiesse
       lo podrié entender   maguer nol' coñoçiesse;
       non es ome naçido   que grado nol' oviesse
       e de la su palabra   grant sabor non prisiesse.

944   Movió gent' su palabra,   començó de dezir.
       Dixo: "Mi cuer vos quiero,   parientes, descobrir:
       esto he sobre todo   a los dios que gradir,
       que entre tales omes   me dieron a bevir.

945   Saben esto los dios,   que lisonja non digo:
       non preçio contra vos   todo lo al un figo,
       ca ant' falleçe regno   que non el buen amigo.
       Qui amigos non ha   pobre es e mendigo.

937	On the left-hand side ran an ever-flowing stream, which never dried up, for it was nature-made; a little brook had formed near a bed of roses, through which it traced its course as if down a canal.
938	The spring exuded a soothing air of freshness and the shadow of the tree gave a gentle warmth; from the grove there was shade and balmy perfume; it seemed like the very Creator's garden!
939	Whether because of the shade or the spring, it was there that the birds came to rest at midday; there did they sing their sweet song every morning, and there only the finest of birds could be found.
940	The water from the spring flowed down to the meadows; it kept them always green and decked with bright flowers; the place had an abundance and variety of game, every species that can be encountered in the world.
941	The Emperor, wearing a robe of ruby silk, decided to seclude himself in that fine spot; he held a great assembly of just his highest nobles and began his discussions in council with them.
942	Through the mere look of his goodly appearance he gave great delight to all his people and any man at all could tell for certain that this man was the king of all the Orient.
943	Merely from his appearance, anyone who saw him could have known this even without ever having met him: no man born would not have looked on him with pleasure nor would he have failed to be delighted at his words.
944	He began to speak, his words elegantly crafted; he said, "I want to open my heart for you, my kindred; for this above all I must be grateful to the gods, that they allowed me to live among such people.
945	The gods know this: it is no lip-service I pay; against you I do not care a fig for all else; for a kingdom will fail you before a good friend; the man with no friends is a beggar and poor.

946　　Ond' creo que los dios　grant merçed me fizieron
　　　　e pareçe por ojo　que grant bien me quisieron
　　　　quando tales vassallos　tan leales me dieron
　　　　por defender los regnos　en que a mí pusieron.

947　　Si supiessen los griegos　de quál raíz venides
　　　　o vuestros bisavuelos　quáles fueron en lides,
　　　　non vos vernién buscar　en qual tierra bevides;
　　　　mas aún non provaron　cómo vos referides.

948　　Los gigantes corpudos,　unos omes valientes
　　　　que la torre fizieron,　fueron vuestros parientes.
　　　　Torpe es Alexandre　que tan mal para mientes;
　　　　si non, non volverié　guerra con tales gentes.

949　　El prez de los parientes　vos debe despertar;
　　　　demás que se vos vienen　mala ment' aontar;
　　　　de vassallos que son　querrién señorear;
　　　　mas fío bien en vos　que est' non pued' estar.

950　　Demás, non veo cosa　en que dubdar devamos
　　　　que nos con Dios aína　non los vençamos;
　　　　sólo que ellos vean　que nos non los dubdamos
　　　　dexarnos han el campo　ante que los firamos.

951　　Un sueño yo soñava　que vos quiero contar,
　　　　por onde so seguro　que serán a rancar;
　　　　pero fasta agora　quíseme yo callar,
　　　　que non dixies' alguno　que quería bafar.

952　　Veía que estávamos　todos hazes paradas,
　　　　los unos a los otros　todos caras tornadas;
　　　　deçendién unos fuegos,　unas iradas flamas,
　　　　quemávanles las tiendas　e todas las posadas.

953　　Departién se las flamas　como rayos agudos;
　　　　quemávanles las lanças　que trayén en los puños;
　　　　ivan ellos fuyendo,　los cavallos perdudos,
　　　　todos en sus cabeças　firiendo grandes puños.

954　　Alexandre, el loco,　que me es tan esquivo,
　　　　por ferli mayor honta　faziále prender bivo;
　　　　cadena en goliella,　levávalo cativo,
　　　　lo que será de vero,　segunt que yo fío."

946	Therefore I believe the gods did me great favour, and I can see that they showed me great love when they presented me with such loyal vassals to defend the kingdoms they had set into my hands.
947	If the Greeks knew of the roots from which you come or the feats that your ancestors performed in battle, they would not come to seek you out in your own land; but they are yet to see how you defend yourselves.
948	The huge-bodied giants, men of great valour* who built the tower – they were your kinsfolk; Alexander is foolish and a muddled thinker, otherwise he would not make war on such men.
949	You must be inspired by your ancestors' glory, and because these men come to bring you great dishonour, although they are vassals they wish to act as lords; I trust in you to ensure that this cannot come to pass.
950	Besides, I see nothing which should cause us to doubt that with God's help we can quickly conquer. Let them only see that we have no fear of them: they will flee the field of battle before we strike a blow.
951	I have dreamed a dream of which I wish to tell you, by which I am certain that they are to be defeated; but until now I have wished to keep my silence, lest anyone should say that I wanted to make boasts.
952	I saw that we all stood with battle lines drawn, and both armies looked each other in the face; angry-burning fires descended from the sky, and consumed all their dwellings and their tents.
953	The flames spread as sharp lightning-flashes, burning the lances that they carried in their hands; they all went in flight with their horses uncontrolled, all striking firm blows to their own heads.
954	The madman Alexander, who treats me so rudely, I had captured alive, to cause him greater shame, and led him in captivity chained by the neck. All of this shall come true, so do I have faith."

955 Aún non avié Dario   su razón bien complida,
     vínol' un mensajero, ¡que aya mala vida!
     Díxol' que Alexandre avié su huest' movida;
     ivan todos fuyendo   quis quier' por su partida.

956 Mucho plogo a Dario   e mandó cavalgar;
     por cuestas e por planos mandó los alcançar.
     Al rëy Alexandre   mandávalo tomar;
     querriélo a Babilonia en presente embïar.

957 Toda su alegría   nol' valdrié un dinero,
     ca de quanto que dixo mintió el mensajero;
     ca non querién fuïr   nin un passo señero
     – ante morrían todos, fasta el postrimero.

958 Ya eran los primeros çerca de la çelada;
     por poco non firieron dentro en la alvergada;
     vieron que estava   su cosa mal parada;
     fuéronse reteniendo   con mala espantada.

959 Ya avién esto todo   los griegos entendido,
     qu'avié el atalaya   echado apellido.
     El rëy Alexandre   tóvose por guarido,
     mas fue del otro cabo Dario mal cofondido.

960 Las mesnadas de Dario fueron mal espantadas;
     non se podién llegar, tant' eran desmayadas,
     ca vedién que las nuevas que les avién contadas
     eran, por mal pecado, otra guisa tornadas.

961 El rëy Alexandre   vos quiero enseñar
     – verdat quiero dezir, non cuido y pecar –
     quál cabtenençia ovo, qué empeçó a far,
     quando vío las huestes de Dario assomar.

962 Tendió a Dios las manos, cató a suso fito.
     "Señor," dixo, "que prestas a toda cosa vito:
     ¡el tu nombre laudado sea e bendito!
     De toda cueita tengo que me as öy quito.

963 Señor, yo gradeçértelo aquesto non sabría,
     que me das a veer   tamaña alegría;
     siempre Te pedí esto e fago oy en día
     ca por esto sallí de Corintio la mía."

955	Darius had not yet reached the end of his speech
when a messenger approached him – may his life turn to ill! –
and told him that Alexander had moved his army out
and the men were all fleeing in their separate directions.
956	Darius was greatly pleased and bade his men ride out
and hunt down their enemy on the plains and the hills.
He commanded that they capture King Alexander,
wanting to send him as a trophy to Babylonia.
957	All his joy would not be worth a penny to him,
for in everything he said the messenger had lied:
the Greek troops did not want to flee a single step
but all would rather die, to the very last man.
958	Now the first men were drawing near the place of ambush
on the point of striking the enemy lines;
there they saw that they were in a dangerous position
and in their great fear they slowed to a halt.
959	The Greeks were well aware of all that was happening,
for the watchtower had sounded the call to battle.
King Alexander realised that he was out of danger;
Darius, however, was filled with deep consternation.
960	Darius' troops were filled with utter terror
and could not move forward, paralysed by fear,
for they saw the information that they had been given,
through the Devil's work, had proved completely false.
961	I wish to explain to you about King Alexander
– I mean to tell the truth and do not think I err –,
what his tactics were and the actions that he took
when he saw Darius' armies appear.
962	He raised his arms to God and fixed his gaze skywards.
"Lord,' he said, 'You who sustain all creation,
may praises and blessings be spoken of Your name,
as You have rid me of all my anxiety this day.
963	Lord, I would not know how to give thanks to You for this,
that You allow me to experience such great joy.
I always prayed to You for this and still do so today,
for this was why I departed from my city of Corinth."

964 Tornó a sus vassallos   quel' sedién derredor;
empeçó a fablar   a una grant sabor:
"Amigos," diz', "¿veedes?   Grado al Crïador,
pone se nuestra cosa   toda vía mejor.

965 Todos nuestros contrarios   vienen nos a las manos;
han de fincar con nusco,   sól' prender los queramos;
todo nuestro lazerio   aquí lo acabamos;
nunca contrast' avremos   si esto quebrantamos.

966 Lo que doña Victoria   nos ovo prometido,
ávelo *Deo graçias*   leal ment' atenido.
Fizo nos buen compieço   quand' Ménona fue vençido,
mas aquí yaz' el cabo   e el preçio complido.

967 De oro e de plata   vienen todos armados,
todos relampaguean   tant' vienen afeitados.
Éstos, con Dios a una,   tenedlos por rancados,
ca por fer buen bernaje   están mal aguisados.

968 Non traen guarnimientos   de omes de prestar;
semejan se mugeres   que se quieren preçiar;
fierro vençe fazienda,   com' l'oyestes contar,
e coraçones firmes   que lo saben durar.

969 Miembre vos la materia   por que aquí veniemos;
miembre vos las soberbias   que de Dario prisiemos;
nos nin nuestros parientes   nunca desque naçiemos
por vengar nuestra onta   atal sazón toviemos.

970 Sé bien que por aquesto   todos sodes pagados:
la una, por que todos   sodes omes granados;
la otra, por que fuestes   de mi padre crïados;
la terçera, que sodes   comigo desterrados.

971 Mientes metré en cascuno   de quál guisa me quiere;
aquél me querrá más   el que mejor firiere,
el que pedaços fecho   el escudo trayere,
e que con l'espada bota   fuertes golpes firiere.

972 A los que fueren ricos   añadiré riqueza;
a los que fueren pobres   sacaré de pobreza;
quitaré a los siervos,   que bivan en franqueza;
non daré por el malo   una mala corteza.

964	He turned to his vassals who were at his side and with great relish he began to speak to them. "My friends," he said, "you see, thanks to the Creator, how our affairs are ever turning for the better.
965	Our enemies are all falling right into our hands and are to meet their end here if we only will it. We are here putting an end to all our hardship and shall never have rivals if we crush this threat.
966	What the goddess Victory had promised to us, thanks be to God, she has loyally fulfilled. She gave us a good beginning when Memnon was defeated but here lies the conclusion and untarnished fame.
967	They are all coming here armed in gold and silver, so brilliantly attired that light flashes from them all. With God's help, consider them already vanquished, for they are ill prepared for great exploits in battle.
968	The apparel that they wear is not that of valiant knights, but they look like women who want to be thought fair. It is iron that wins battles, as you have heard tell, and stout hearts that know how to endure the fight.
969	Recall the real purpose for our coming here; recall the arrogant insults we suffered from Darius. Since we were born, neither we nor our parents have ever had such a chance to avenge our honour.
970	I know well that you are all delighted at this, firstly because you are all men of great stature, secondly because you were brought up by my father, and thirdly because you are in foreign lands with me.
971	I shall look closely at each, to see how well he loves me: the fiercest fighter will be he who loves me most – the one who brings back his shield broken into pieces still striking the hardest blows with a blunted sword.
972	Onto those already rich I shall heap further wealth and those who are poor I shall lift from poverty. I shall free the slaves that they may live in freedom and for the bad man I shall not give a rotten crust.

973　Lo que a mí vïerdes　non quiero qu'al fagades;
　　　si delant' yo non fuere,　non quiero quem' sigades;
　　　mas quando yo firiere,　quiero que vos firgades;
　　　mientes querré meter　cómo me aguardades.

974　Quiérovos breve mente　la razón estajar,
　　　ca non tenemos ora　por luengo sermón far;
　　　de toda la ganançia　me vos quiero quitar;
　　　assaz he yo del prez,　non quiero más levar."

975　Aviélos con sus dichos　mucho escalentados;
　　　sól' non lo entendién　tanto eran corajados;
　　　todos por a ferirlos　estavan amolados;
　　　non cuidavan en ellos　aver sendos bocados.

976　Paró el rey sus hazes　como costumbre era:
　　　costaneras estrañas　e firme delantera.
　　　Mandó que cada uno　guardasse su frontera;
　　　mandó que non oviesse　vagar la doladera.

977　Puso en las primeras　un muro de peones
　　　que non lo derromprién　picos nin açadones;
　　　todos sus naturales　de puras crïazones
　　　ant' perdrién las cabeças　que non los coraçones.

978　La diestra costanera　fue a Nicánor dada,
　　　con muchos ricos omes,　mucha barva honrada,
　　　Clitus e Tolomeo,　quisquier' con su mesnada;
　　　Pérdicas con tres otros　de fazienda granada.

979　Governava Parmenio,　un preçiado cabdiello,
　　　con su fijo Filotas,　el siniestro portiello;
　　　terçero fue Antígonus,　que valié un castiello;
　　　Craterus, de grant nombre　e de cuerpo chiquiello.

980　Las hazes de los griegos　assí eran bastidas,
　　　de armas e de gentes　sobra bien enfortidas;
　　　eran unas con otras　fiera mente cosidas,
　　　pero priso el rëy　las primeras feridas.

981　Dario fue en grant cueita,　tovos' por engañado;
　　　batiél' el coraçon,　maldizié al pecado.
　　　Demandó por el ome　quel' levó el mandado;
　　　fuera mal escorrido　si l'oviesse fallado.

973	What you see me do, I would have you do the same: if I do not move forward, I do not want you to advance, but when I strike the enemy I want you to strike them too; I shall keep a careful eye on the support you give to me.
974	I want to bring my speech to you swiftly to a close, for there is no time for me to speak at length; I want to give up all the booty to you; the fame is enough for me; I wish to take no more."
975	With his words he had set their spirits aflame; they did not even comprehend, so greatly were they roused. They were all now ready to strike the enemy and thought they would prove but a mere morsel.
976	The King drew up his forces as was his custom – élite troops at the flanks, steadfast men at the fore – and commanded that each one defend his own position and that none give the enemy any respite.
977	He set a wall of foot soldiers at the front line which could not be broken down by picks or mattocks; all Alexander's countrymen and loyal vassals would lose their lives before betraying their hearts.
978	To Nicanor was the right flank entrusted, with many noblemen and honoured warriors, Cleitus and Ptolemy, each with his troops, and Perdiccas, with three more of illustrious deeds.
979	Parmenion, a distinguished knight, was in charge of the left-hand side, with his son Philotas; Antigonus was third, strong as a castle,* and Craterus, great in renown, but small in body.*
980	Thus were the battle lines of the Greeks laid out, with such powerful protection of arms and men and each individual firmly bonded to the whole, but the King claimed the right to strike the first blows.
981	Darius was greatly troubled and thought himself deceived; his heart throbbed powerfully and he cursed the Devil. He sent for the man who had brought him the message; he would have suffered great harm had he been discovered.

982 Mandó todas las gentes en un campo fincar;
empeçólas él mismo por sí a rodear;
mandólas seer quedas, la çaga esperar,
ca avién un portiello traviesso a pasar.

983 Díxoles grant esfuerço quando fueron plegados:
"Varones, tengámosnos por omes venturados.
Sabet que, si non fuéssemos tan aína uviados,
fueran en tod' en todo idos e derramados.

984 Mas el Nuestro Señor faz' nos grant caridad:
oy nos faze señores de nuestra heredat;
faremos en los griegos una tal mortaldat
que nunca en est' mundo ganarán enguedat.

985 Cómo ha de seer, quiérovos lo dezir:
çerquemos los en medio que non puedan fuïr;
non sabrán, maguer quieran, a qüál parte ir;
o dar s'han a prisión o avrán a morir."

986 Assaz dixiera Dario consejo aguisado,
mas era otra guisa de los dios ordenado.
Por su ventura dura non li fue otorgado,
ca el ex' de la rueda yazíe trastornado.

987 El cuidar de los omes todo es vanidat,
los pensamientos nuestros non han establidat;
ca non es nuestro seso si non fragilidat,
fuera que nos contiene Dios por su pïedat.

988 Nin poder nin esfuerço nin aver monedado
nol' valen al que es de Dios desemparado;
aquel que a Él plaze ésse es bien guïado;
él que Él desempara es del todo afollado.

989 Conviene que fablemos, entre las otras cosas,
de las armas de Dario, que fueron muy preçiosas;
de obra eran firmes, de pareçer fermosas,
pora traer livianas, mas non bien venturosas.

990 Avié en el escudo mucha bella estoria,
las gestas que fizieron los reys de Babilonia;
yazié de los gigantes y toda la memoria
quando de los lenguajes prisieron la discordia.

982	He ordered all his troops to halt in a field and began to make a review of them himself, commanding them to stay there and await the rearguard for they had a difficult obstacle to clear.
983	When they had arrived he gave them heart with his words: "My knights," he said, "let us consider ourselves fortunate; I can tell you that had we not arrived so quickly they would have fled and scattered in all directions.
984	But our Lord is doing us a great favour making us lords of our inheritance this day. We shall commit such slaughter of the Greeks that never in this world shall they gain their freedom.
985	How it is to be done, I shall tell you now: let us encircle them, that they may not break out; even should they try, they will nowhere find escape; they will be forced to surrender or die."
986	The plan that Darius had set out was wise but events were not thus ordained by the gods; to his cruel misfortune this was not granted him, for Fortune's wheel had spun on its axis.
987	Man's intentions are naught but vanity; our thoughts have no substance to them, for our plans have nothing if not fragility, unless God sustains us through His mercy.
988	Neither power nor valour nor riches are of worth to a man forsaken by God; the man pleasing to God is soundly guided but the one He abandons is utterly lost.
989	It is right that we speak, among other matters, of Darius' arms, which were of great splendour, sound in construction, a delight to behold, and light to wear, but they did not bring him fortune.
990	On his shield were many and elegant stories: the feats that the kings of Babylonia performed; the whole account of the giants was there to be found, when they came to be divided through language.

991 Seyé del otro cabo   el rëy de Caldea,
    Nabucodonosor,   que conquiso Judea;
    quántas ontas fizo   sobre la gent' ebrea,
    cómo priso Sión,   Trípol e Tabarea;

992 cóm' destruyó el templo   en la santa çibdat,
    cómo fueron los tribos   en su cabtividat;
    cómo sobre el rëy   fizo tal crüeldat
    que li sacó los ojos,   ca assí fue verdat.

993 Por amor que las armas   non fuessen manzilladas,
    unas estorias bueltas   non fuessen entecadas;
    non quiso el maestro   que fuessen y pintadas,
    que serién las derechas   por éssas desfeadas.

994 Non lo vío por seso   que fuesse y metido
    Nabucodonosor   cómo fue enloquido,
    cóm' andido siet' años   de memoria sallido,
    pero tornó en cabo   en todo su sentido.

995 Non quiso y poner   al fijo perjurado
    que fue sobre su padre   crudo e denodado;
    lo que peor li sovo,   óvolo desmembrado,
    ca querié regnar solo   el que aya mal fado.

996 Mas en cabo estava   sotil mente obrado
    el buen regno de Persia   cómo fue empeçado;
    la mano que fazié   el obscuro ditado,
    lo que don Baltasar   ovo determinado.

997 La estoria de Çiro   fue derredor echada,
    qué grant conquista fizo   todo por su espada;
    cóm' ovo la compaña   de Israel quitada;
    Cresus en la su guerra   cómo non ganó nada;

998 cómo fue a escuso   en los montes crïado
    e de quál guisa fue   aducho a poblado;
    pero, quando en cabo   todo fue delibrado,
    óvolo en batalla   una dueña matado.

999 Nunca en esti mundo   devrié ome fïar,
    que sabe a sus cosas   tan mala çaga dar;
    sabe a sus amigos   poner en grant lugar
    por que peor los pueda   en cabo quebrantar.

991	In another part was the King of Chaldea and Nebuchadnezzar who conquered Judea* and all the disgraces he inflicted on the Hebrews, how he conquered Sion, Tripoli and Tabarea;
992	how he destroyed the temple in the Holy City, how the tribes came into his captivity, and how, in an act of such cruelty to the King, he put out his eyes – for this was indeed true.
993	In his desire that the arms not be dishonoured, there were some troubling and harmful stories that the master did not wish to be depicted on them for they would serve to spoil those rightfully portrayed.
994	He did not think it right that it be included how it was that Nebuchadnezzar lost his mind and for seven years lived out of his wits, although at the end he returned to sanity.
995	He wished not to depict there the treacherous son,* who treated his father with such cruelty and anger, and had him mutilated, which grieved the master most, for the accursed man wanted to reign without rival.
996	But in one part there lay, worked with much subtlety, the origin of the great kingdom of Persia, the hand which wrote the obscure message,* and what Belshazzar had brought about.
997	The story of Cyrus was laid out near to this:* the great conquest that he made by his own sword, how he had given the people of Israel their freedom and how Croesus could achieve nothing in his war;*
998	how Cyrus was secretly raised in the hills* and how he came to be brought to the city but, when his life at last came to its end, it was a woman who killed him in battle.*
999	Never should a man put his trust in this world, which knows how to bring affairs to such an ill close and how to set its friends in exalted positions so as finally to crush them all the more cruelly.

1000 Çiro, tan poderoso en tierra e en mar,
      dioli Dios grant ventura, diol' mucho a ganar;
      pero tod' su ganançia nol' pudo emparar;
      óvolo una fembra en cabo a matar.

1001 Por ninguna riqueza que pudiesse seer,
      nunca devié nul ome lo de Dios posponer,
      ca qui rafez lo da rafez lo pued' toller;
      pierde a Dios en cabo e todo el aver.

1002 Ya se movién las hazes, ívanse aplegando;
      ivan los ballesteros las saetas tirando;
      ivan los cavalleros las lanças abaxando
      e ivan los cavallos las orejas aguzando.

1003 Fueron en tal manera mescladas las feridas
      que eran con los colpes las trompas ensordidas;
      bolavan las saetas por el aire texidas;
      al sol tolién la lumbre assí ivan cosidas.

1004 De piedras e de dardos ivan grandes nuvadas,
      com' si fuessen abejas en exambre juntadas;
      tant' eran las feridas firmes e afincadas
      que eran de los cuernos las bozes enfogadas.

1005 Com' sedié Alexandre mano al coraçón,
      aguijó delantero, abaxó el pendón;
      más irado que rayo, más bravo que león,
      fue ferir do estava el rey de Babilón.

1006 Fendió todas las hazes que fronteras estavan;
      parárseli delante ningunos non osavan.
      Firié entre los rëys que a Dario guardavan;
      pocos y avié d'ellos que d'él non se dubdavan.

1007 Querié a todas guisas a Dario allegar,
      ca non querié su lança en otro emprimar;
      desdeñava los otros, non los querié catar,
      ca toda la ganançia yazié en es' lugar.

1008 En medio de las hazes abés era huviado,
      fevos un cavallero, Areta fue llamado;
      señor era de Siria; escudo embraçado,
      dioli ad Alexandre un buen colpe provado.

| 1000 | To Cyrus, so powerful on land and on sea,
God gave great good fortune and winning of wealth,
but all that he had won could bring him no protection,
and in the end he was to die at a woman's hand. |

| 1001 | By no human riches that could ever exist
could any man ever put off God's will,
for He who quickly gives can quickly take away;
in the end a man parts from both God and all his wealth. |

| 1002 | Now the two armies were surging out together,*
the crossbowmen letting their bolts fly out,
the horsemen lowering their lances to strike,
the horses galloping with ears pricked up. |

| 1003 | With such ferocity were the blows exchanged
that the horns were silenced by their crash;
the arrows were flying through the air, tightly-woven,
so closely joined they stole the light from the sun. |

| 1004 | There flew thick clouds of stones and darts,
as if they were densely-packed swarms of bees;
so heavy and insistent were the blows men struck
that the cries of the horns were drowned beneath them. |

| 1005 | Alexander waited there, hand on his heart,
then spurred on his horse and lowered his pennant;
angrier than lightning and braver than a lion,
he rode to do battle with the King of Babylon. |

| 1006 | He split apart all the battle lines that were before him
and no man dared to stand against him face-to-face.
He cut his way through the kings who guarded Darius;
there were few among them who were not afraid of him. |

| 1007 | He desired to reach Darius at whatever cost,
for he did not wish to use his lance first on another;
he scorned other men and did not wish to look upon them
for all of his winnings lay in that place alone. |

| 1008 | Hardly had he come into the midst of all the troops
when here was a knight, a man called Arethas,
a nobleman from Syria, his shield on his arm,
who struck Alexander with a good firm blow. |

1009   Firme se ovo'l rëy,   non dio por ello nada;
        tornó contra Areta,   firiólo su vegada;
        metióli la cuchiella   por medio la corada;
        echólo muerto frío   en medio la estrada.

1010   Bozes dieron los griegos,   fueron del rey pagados;
        tenién que los avié   sobra bien emprimados.
        Fueron de la victoria   muy bien assegurados,
        com' si en Babilonia   fuessen apoderados.

1011   Vassallos de Areta,   una haz de caldeos,
        por vengar su señor   fizieron sus asseos.
        Mas fueron luego prestos   Clitus e Tolomeos;
        fizieron los foïr   con la ira de Dios.

1012   Andavan estos ambos   entre los enemigos,
        como unos leones   que andan desfambridos;
        los dientes regañados,   dando bozes e gritos;
        bien les venié emiente   por qué eran venidos.

1013   Y fizo Tolomeos   sin tiesta a Dodonta;
        Clitus a don Ardófilus,   prínçipe de grant conta;
        mas esto a lo al   fascas nada non monta,
        tant' fazién en los medos   grant daño e grant onta.

1014   Ardófilus e Clitus   tales colpes se dieron
        qu'ellos con sus cavallos   amortidos cayeron;
        antuvïós' primero   Clitus, quand' recudieron;
        las nuevas de Ardófilus   todas y pereçieron.

1015   Lo que Dario asmava,   en medio lo çercar,
        non ovieron poder   d'ello bien acabar,
        ca assí los supieron   los otros arredrar
        que sól' de acordarse   non ovieron vagar.

1016   Tan mal fueron corridos   luego de la primera
        que sofrir non pudieron   jamás la delantera;
        por mudar ventura,   que suel' seer vezera,
        fueron acometer   la siniestra costanera.

1017   Un vassallo de Dario,   ome de grant beldat,
        firme e esforçado,   de primera hedat;
        Maçeos lo dizién,   avié grant heredat;
        dolava en los griegos   sin toda pïedat.

1009	The King stood firm, untroubled by the blow, turned to Arethas, and struck him in his turn;* he drove his sword through the middle of his heart and left him cold dead in the middle of his path.
1010	The Greeks roared their pleasure at the victory of their king, believing he had started things very well for them. They felt such confidence that they would gain victory as if they were already masters of Babylonia.
1011	Vassals of Arethas, a company of Chaldeans, made ready to avenge the death of their lord, but Cleitus and Ptolemy were ready for them quickly and, spurred by the wrath of God, turned them to flight.
1012	These two men moved among their enemy as if they were a pair of starving lions, with snarls on their faces and ferocious roars; they had not forgotten the reason they had come.
1013	There it was that Ptolemy beheaded Dodontes as Cleitus did Ardophilus, a prince of great renown; but this scarcely mattered next to all else that happened, such great harm and disgrace did they inflict on the Medes.
1014	Ardophilus and Cleitus struck each other such blows that, with their horses, they fell down almost dead. When they recovered, Cleitus was first to his feet and Ardophilus' achievements all perished in that place.
1015	What Darius had planned, to encircle his foes, his men did not have the power to effect, for the Greeks were so successful in driving them back that they did not even have the chance to regroup.
1016	So fiercely driven back from the very start, they were never able to withstand the vanguard; to try to change their fortune, which is often inconstant, they mounted an attack against the left flank.
1017	A vassal of Darius, a very handsome man, steadfast and brave, in the prime of his youth, Mazaeus by name, and heir to great wealth,* wrought havoc without pity among the Greeks.

1018 Ovo y el infante a Yolos a matar,
cavallero de preçio, si lo oyestes contar;
mas presto fue Filotas por luego lo vengar;
oviéral' mal julgado sil' podies' alcançar.

1019 Alongóse Maçeos, non lo pudo tomar;
afrontós' con otro, óvolo a matar.
Prestóli a Maçeos ques' ovo ad alongar;
si non, por essa misma oviera a passar.

1020 Çercaron a Filotas cavalleros ircanos,
unos omes valientes e de piedes livianos;
cuidaron sines dubda prendérselo a manos;
mas mal se y fallaron, non fueron tan loçanos.

1021 Teniénlo en grant cueita e en grant estrechura,
Querién le fer sin grado pechar la moledura.
D'ella e d'ella parte seyén en grant pressura;
todos avién abonda de la mala ventura.

1022 Avié por día negro Filotas embïado,
ca ellos eran muchos e él era cansado;
mas acorriól' Parmenio quel' ovo engendrado,
Craterus e Antígonus con Çenus, su crïado.

1023 Çenus mató a Midas, dioli fiera lançada;
Antígonus a Filax diol' mortal espadada.
Craterus a Anfíloco diol' una tal porrada
quel' sallién los meollos e la sangre cuajada.

1024 Parmenio el caboso, en duro punto nado,
andava por las hazes como león irado;
avié mucha cabeça echada por el prado;
al que prender podié non era su pagado.

1025 Delibró a Isanes, un mortal cavallero,
otro que dezién Dimus diol' él por compañero;
Dimus venié de cuesta e Isanes fazero,
mas entrambos ovieron a ir por un sendero.

1026 Aún por todos éssos non amansó la ravia;
mató ad Aguilón, una cabeça sabia;
Eleón, otro quinto que era de Arabia;
mas en cabo, por todo, priso mala ganançia.

1018	There it was that the Prince managed to kill Iollas – he was a worthy knight, if you have heard tell of him –, but Philotas went quickly to take his vengeance; he would have inflicted a harsh sentence had he caught him.
1019	Mazaeus moved away and could not stand to face him, he squared up to another and managed to kill him; this helped Mazaeus, who managed to get away, for otherwise he would have suffered the same fate.
1020	Philotas was surrounded by knights from Hyrcania – they were valiant men and fleet of foot – who without doubt thought that they could capture him but they came off less well and did not have such joy.
1021	They had him in in dire straits and very hard pressed; they wanted to make him pay his dues against his will; the Greeks were coming under attack from all sides. In all their hearts lay a deep sense of foreboding.
1022	Philotas had encountered a black day, for they were many and he was tired, but his father Parmenion came to his aid, with Craterus, Antigonus and Coenus, his vassal.
1023	Coenus killed Midas, lunging hard with his lance, and Antigonus struck Phylax a deadly sword-thrust, while Craterus dealt Amphilocus a blow so firm that out flowed his brains and congealed blood.
1024	Parmenion, the fine man, born at a cruel moment, moved around the battle lines like an angry lion. He had cast many heads down onto the field and any man he caught was far from happy.
1025	Parmenion slew Isannes, a death-dealing knight, and another, called Dimus, he gave as his companion. Dimus came from behind and Isannes from the front but both were to leave by a single path.
1026	Despite all those deaths his anger did not lessen: he killed Agilon, who was a wise man, Helon and a fifth man who came from Arabia, though in spite of it all, in the end he made no gain.

1027 Andava Eüménides, un' de los doze pares,
con derecho despecho firiendo los quexares;
de cabeças de muertos finchó los valladares;
non sallieron de Greçia mejores dos pulgares.

1028 Nicánor, que tenié la diestra costanera,
a diestro e siniestro vertié mala felera.
Avié mucho buen ome fecho sin calavera;
ívalos raleando de estraña manera.

1029 Dávanli a grant priessa colpes en el escudo;
pedrisco sobre techo non darié más menudo.
Mas estava'l caboso firme e perçebudo;
maguer fue grant la priessa, nunca moverlo pudo.

1030 El infant' don Eclimus, cavallero cosido,
de beldat e linaje, de mañas bien complido,
por ferir a Nicánor vino muy demetido,
mas fue a riedra parte rica ment' referido.

1031 Con la saña del colpe dio Nicánor tornada;
por el ojo siniestro daval' muy grant lançada;
tanto fue la ferida cruda e enconada
que los perdió entrambos, ¡Dios, qué mala mudada!

1032 Un rey de los de Dario, que Nínive mandava,
– qui nombrar lo querié Negusar lo clamava –
andava más ravioso que una ossa brava;
a qual parte que iva todo lo delivrava.

1033 Firié a todas partes, rebolvié bien el braço;
el colpe de su mano valié fascas d'un maço;
al que prender podié nol' cubría pelmaço;
querrié que fuesse Dario bien ixido del plazo.

1034 Mató tres ricos omes, uno mejor de otro,
a Elin por los pechos, a Dolit por el ombro;
fendiól' a Ermógenes la cruz con el escopro;
mas escorriél' en cabo Filotas con mal logro.

1035 Óvolo a veer Filotas el caboso;
endurar non lo pudo, ca era corajoso.
"Señor," diz', "Tú me valas, Padre, Rëy glorioso,
que pueda desmanchar este dragón ravioso."

1027	Eumenes, one of the Twelve Peers, was there, splitting open men's jaws with righteous anger and filling valleys with the heads of the dead; never did two hands with more power leave Greece.
1028	Nicanor, in command on the right flank, to his left and his right, was inflicting great harm. He had hewn the skull from many a good man and was wreaking a remarkable devastation.
1029	The blows were raining down thick on his shield – hail striking a roof would not be heavier –, but the noble man was steadfast and shrewd; however thick the storm of blows, he could not be moved.
1030	Prince Eclimus, who was a knight of courage, a man excellent in looks, in lineage and his ways, came forward, in a rage, to fight with Nicanor, but with great force he was driven far away.
1031	With the fury of the blow Nicanor spun round and struck him hard in the left eye with his lance; the blow that he dealt was so cruel and so savage that the man lost them both; Lord, what a grim bargain!
1032	A king in Darius' army, the ruler of Nineveh,* – whoever wished to name him would call him Negusar – moved around with more anger than a wild she-bear and wherever he went he slew all before him.
1033	He smote men on all sides, swung his arms freely, and a blow from his hand was like a mace; a padded doublet brought no aid to anyone he reached; his desire was that Darius be delivered from his trial.
1034	He killed three noblemen, each better than the last, wounding Helim in the chest and Dolit in the shoulder; he split asunder Hermogenes' frame with his dagger, but at last, to his ill, Philotas crossed his path.
1035	The fine warrior Philotas had watched all this, and because of his valour was unable to endure it. He said, "Lord, give me strength, Father and glorious King, that I may pierce the armour of this frenzied dragon."

1036 Aguijó contra él, maguer era cansado,
su espada en puño, escudo embraçado;
cuidól' fender la tiesta, mas era bien armado;
non pudo acabar lo que tenié asmado.

1037 Non lo priso en pleno, óvol'a deslayar;
contra'l braço siniestro óvolo a dexar;
alçólo Negusar por el colpe redrar;
ovo gelo al cativo en medio a cortar.

1038 Negusar fue en cueita, querrié seer más muerto,
que ya avié perdido todo el medio cuerpo;
pero a don Filotas fiziéral' mal depuerto,
si non fues' por Amintas que li tovo grant tuerto.

1039 Ajobó con la diestra una fiera plomada;
avrié y una bestia carga desaguisada.
Cuidó dar a Filotas una grant mollerada,
mas destorvóli antes Amintas la colpada.

1040 Ante que fues' el braço al cuerpo destendido,
argudóse Filotas, barón entremetido;
diole una espadada por l'otro cobdo mismo;
perdié el diestro braço quel' avié remanido.

1041 Negusar en sus pechos firió con sus tucones,
sallié d'ellos la sangre como por albollones;
sangrentavas' las barvas, la fruent' e los grinones;
querié e non podié travar a los arzones.

1042 Maguer que pora vida non era aguisado,
el su buen coraçón non avié abaxado.
Andava por las hazes, maldiziendo al pecado:
"¡Ferid los, cavalleros, ca avedes rancado!"

1043 Quando otro destorvo non les podié buscar,
a un prínçip' de Greçia, que solié bien lidiar,
echós'le de delante, fízol' entrepeçar;
ovieron y entrambos lüego a fincar.

1044 Bien avié la fazienda medio día durado;
yazié mucho buen ome muerto e desangrado;
los ríos de la sangre fascas non avién vado;
non avié tan donzel que non fuesse cansado.

1036	He spurred on against him, although he was tired, his sword in his hand and his shield on his arm. He sought to cleave his head, but Negusar was so protected that he could not carry out what he had intended.
1037	He did not catch him on the full but at an angle, and it was on his left arm that he struck him. Negusar raised it to fend off the blow and the wretched man's arm was severed in two.
1038	Negusar was in distress; he would rather have died, for he had lost a great part of his body, but he would still have made cruel sport of Philotas, had it not been for Amintas who did him great harm.
1039	In his right hand he carried a savage mace – it would have been a hard burden for beast to bear – looking to strike Philotas hard about the head, but Amintas was able to block the blow first.
1040	Before Negusar had raised his arm to strike the blow, Philotas, a battle-hardened warrior, got in first and struck him with his sword on his other elbow; he lost his right arm and last remaining defence.
1041	Negusar beat his breast with the stumps of his arms, the blood gushing out from them as if from a sewer, bloodying his beard, his brow, his matted hair; he longed but was unable to hold on to the pommels.
1042	Although his life was drawing to a close, his valiant heart had still not weakened and he roamed the battle lines, cursing the Devil: "Strike them my knights, for the battle is yours."
1043	When he could find no other way to trouble his foes, he came across a Greek prince, who was a fine fighter, threw himself in his path, and brought him to the ground. It was there that both men were soon to meet their end.
1044	The battle had now lasted for a full half-day and many fine men were now lying dead and bloodless. The rivers of blood were almost impassable, and there was no young man who was free from fatigue.

1045   La fada que quebranta   los filos de la vida
non podié tener cuenta,   tajava sin medida;
avié de cansedat   la memoria perdida;
la dueña en un día   non fue tan de servida.

1046   Las otras dos mayores   que ordenan los fados
tenién de cansedat   los inojos plegados;
juravan todas tres   sobre los sus quexados,
que nunca vieran tales   poderes ajuntados.

1047   Todos, padres e fijos,   sobrinos e hermanos,
todos avién un cuer   pora traer las manos;
murién de los de Greçia,   mas plus de los ircanos;
eran los valladares   todos tornados planos.

1048   Todos y eran buenos,   Alexandre mejor;
como en al, en esso   semejava señor;
tanto avié abierto   en la priessa mayor
que estava ya açerca   del otro emperador.

1049   Oviera li a Dario   su razón rencurada;
toda su derechura   oviera recabdada;
mas un fraire de Dario   quel' yazié en çelada
fízole grant estorvo,   mas él non ganó nada.

1050   Dario en est' comedio   en balde non estava;
ninguno en el campo   más de cuer non lidiava;
nunca fazié tal colpe   que ome non matava;
demás, ninguna vez   el colpe non errava.

1051   Mas, como diz' la letra   e es verdat provada
que en la fin yaz' todo   el prez e la soldada,
non le valió a Dario   todo su fecho nada,
ca Dios avié la cosa   cóm' fuesse ordenada.

1052   Avié y un ric' ome   que era de Egibto;
sabié todas las cosas   que yazen en escripto;
aviélo ante noche   en las estrellas visto
que l'avié a matar   cavallero greçisco.

1053   Aviélo entendido,   ca sabié bien catar,
que avié esse día   en la lit a finar;
por es' querié al rëy   Alexandre trobar,
ca querrié, si pudiesse,   de su mano finar.

1045   The Fate who severs the threads of life*
        could not keep count and cut without measure,
        having lost her memory in her exhaustion;
        on no day did the lady ever have so heavy a task.

1046   The other two noble ladies and ordainers of fate
        had fallen now onto bended knee in exhaustion;
        all three of them were swearing by the men who suffered
        that they had never seen such forces come together.

1047   Fathers and sons, nephews and brothers:
        all men were wielding their arms with all their heart;
        many Greeks died, but many more from Hyrcania,
        and all of the valleys were turned into plains.

1048   All present were fine men, Alexander the finest;
        as in all else, so in combat, he was seen to be the lord.
        So much space had he cleared in the thick of battle
        that he was now standing near the other emperor.

1049   He would have gained vengeance for Darius' words
        and would have achieved all that was his right,
        but a brother of Darius who lay in ambush for him*
        barred his way – though it brought the man no good.

1050   Darius, meanwhile, had not had idle hands
        and no man was ever braver in the fight on battle's field;
        no blow that he unleashed did anything but kill,
        and on no occasion did he fail to find his mark.

1051   But, as the text says, and it is proven to be true,
        everything lies still in the end, both fame and profit:
        all of Darius' feats were worth nothing to him,
        for God had ordained how matters should be.

1052   There was a nobleman there, who came from Egypt,
        and knew everything that is set down in writing;
        he had seen, the night before, written in the stars,
        that a Greek knight would come to bring him death.

1053   He had understood, for he knew how to read the signs,
        that on this day he was to meet his end in the battle,
        because of which he wanted to find King Alexander,
        for he wanted, if he could, to die at his hand.

1054 Zoreas avié nombre   e era bien letrado;
avié de las siet' artes   escuela governado;
por' en cavallería   era bueno provado;
por tales dos bondades   avié preçio doblado.

1055 Zoreas fincó ojo   do andava el rey,
faziendo lo que fazen   los lobos entre grey.
Fuelo a conjurar   por Dios e por la ley
que quisiesse su lança   emplearla en él.

1056 Maravillós' el rëy,   fue fuerte espantado.
Díxole: "Eres loco   o miembro de pecado.
Serié mi preçio todo   aquí menoscabado
si yo contra'l vençido   fuesse tan denodado.

1057 Mas ruégote quem' digas   por la lëy que tienes
de quáles tierras eres,   de quál linaje vienes;
ca tú eres sin seso   o engañarme quieres,
o por alguna guisa   cosa nueva entiendes."

1058 Zoreas le respuso: "Dezirt'he la verdat:
en Egibto fui nado   e vin' a tal hedat;
ond' ovi los parientes   e he grant heredat;
allí apris' sapiençia   a muy grant plenedat.

1059 Sé bien todas las artes   que son de clereçía;
sé mejor que todo ome   toda estremonía:
cómo laudan a Dios   en santa armonía;
de entender leyenda   sól' fablar non querría.

1060 Yazen todos los sesos   en esta arca mía;
aquí fizieron las artes   toda su cofradía;
demás, por todo esto   por' en cavallería
non coñosco a ome   naçido mejoría.

1061 Conoçílo anoche   por mi sabiduría
quem' sacarién el alma   oy, en aqueste día.
Sepas bien por verdat   que, por ende, querría
morir de la tu mano,   gradeçértelo ía."

1062 "Serié," dixo el rëy,   "cosa desaguisada
tirarles a las artes   tan preçiosa posada;
non lo querrién los dios   que ésta mi espada
en tan santa cabeça   fuesse ensangrentada."

1054 Zoroas was his name and he had great learning:
he had taught the seven arts in the schools;
as in knighthood he was a man of proven ability,
with two such qualities he was of double worth.

1055 Zoroas fixed his eyes on where the King was passing,
doing just what wolves do among a flock of sheep,
and he went to beseech him by God and by the law
that he might be willing to use his lance on him.

1056 The King was filled with wonder and lost in amazement,
and said to him: "You are mad, or a limb of the Devil;
my reputation would be greatly lessened by this,
were I to show such cruelty towards a conquered man.

1057 But I ask you to tell me, by the law that you obey,
from what lands you come and of what line you are;
for you are acting in folly or you wish to deceive me,
or in some way possess some new understanding."

1058 Zoroas replied to him, "I shall tell you the truth:
I was born in Egypt, where I reached my present age,
where my parents are from and I have a great inheritance;
it was there that I gained the full measure of my knowledge.

1059 I know well all the arts that learning comprises;
I know all about astronomy best of all men
and how the stars praise God in blessed harmony;
of understanding books, I would not even speak.

1060 Every type of knowledge lies within this frame of mine,
and there the arts have established their brotherhood;
but besides all this, in terms of chivalry,
I know of no man alive superior to me.

1061 Through this wisdom of mine, I discovered last night
that today, this day, would be when my soul is taken;
in truth, you should know that thus it was my wish
to die at your hand, for which I would be grateful."

1062 "It would be," the King said, "a wrongful act
to deprive the arts of so fine an abode;
the gods would not wish this sword of mine
to be stained with the blood of so saintly a head."

1063 Quando entendió Zoreas que nol' podié mover,
començól' un dicho malo a retraer:
díxol' que non devié rëy nunca seer,
ca era fornezino e de rafez aver.

1064 Por amor de moverlo todavía en saña,
retróxole que era fijo de mala nana;
que mató a su padre ascuso en la montaña
e que nunca ome fizo atán mala fazaña.

1065 El rey por todo esto non quiso recodir,
ca vío que andava cuitado por morir;
sorrendó su cavallo, començóse de ir;
en la punta de Dario començó de ferir.

1066 El fol de su porfidia non se quiso toller;
fue pora Alexandre a todo su poder;
do suele la loriga con la calça prender
diole tal ferida quel' fizo contorçer.

1067 El rey fue del colpe de Zoreas plagado
de müy mala plaga onde fue embargado;
pero nol' tornó mano, tanto fue mesurado,
mas escusólo otri que lo libró privado.

1068 Meleáger fue presto e diol' por el costado;
fue luego abatido el loco endiablado;
fue luego fecho pieças, en las lanças alçado;
¡qui a rëy firiere non prenga mejor grado!

1069 Ya fincava la priessa sobre Dario señero;
era desemparado de tanto buen braçero;
veyés' en grant porfaçio, ca tenié fuert' guerrero;
veyé el mal por ojo en medio del tablero.

1070 Los unos veyé muertos e los otros perdidos;
en los que más fïava todos eran caídos;
veyése fascas solo entre los enemigos.
"Mesquinos," dizié, "fuemos en mal punto naçidos."

1071 Non sabié ques' fiziesse, tanto era deserrado;
si muries' o fuyesse, todol' era pesado;
su regno veyé perdido, su pueblo estragado;
"¡Mesquino," dizié, "fui en duro punto nado!"

1063	When Zoroas realised that he could not move him, he began to provoke him with wicked words: he said that he should never have the right to be king, for he was born of adultery and of lowly origin.*
1064	In his desire to rouse the King to greater anger, he accused him of being a wicked mother's son, who brought death to his father in secret, on the mountain, a more terrible deed than any man has ever done.
1065	The King, with all of this, did not wish to respond, for he could see that his desire was to die. He gave rein to his horse and began to move away, and he started to attack those surrounding Darius.
1066	The fool did not want to give up his struggle and made for Alexander with all his force and, where it is normal that chain-mail meets hose, he gave him such a blow that he made him shudder.
1067	The King was hurt by the blow that Zoroas struck, and wounded so badly it impeded his movements, but did not turn his hand on him, so great was his restraint, but another came to help him, and quickly killed Zoroas.
1068	Meleager moved quickly and hit Zoroas in the side;* the Devil-guided madman was quickly cut down, and hacked into pieces, and raised up on lances, for a man who strikes a king deserves no better reward.
1069	Now the pressure of battle fell on Darius alone, for he had lost the protection of so many fine fighters. He saw himself in deadly combat, for he had a strong foe, saw his misfortune with his eyes, in the middle of the board.
1070	He could see some dead and others in despair; all those on whom he most relied had fallen. He could see himself almost alone among his enemies. "What wretches we," he said, "born at a cruel hour!"
1071	He was so disheartened that he knew not what to do; were he to die or flee, he felt equal sorrow. He could see his kingdom lost, his people now in ruin. "What a wretch am I," he said, "born at an ill-fated hour."

1072 Sedié en esti dubdo   el buen emperador:
el morir era malo   e el fuïr peor;
asmava de los males   quál sería mejor,
mas qual si quiere d'ellos   le faziá mal sabor.

1073 Mientre que él asmava   qué farié o qué non,
Pérdicas, de los doze,   acabado varón,
remetió una lança   tan grant com' un timón;
diole en las çervizes   çerca del cabeçón.

1074 Dario fue desbalçado,   non lo pudo sofrir;
desemparó el campo,   començó de fuïr;
apeós' el buen ome   por mejor se encobrir,
por que non lo pudiessen   los griegos perçebir.

1075 Uno de sus vassallos,   quel' dizíen Ausón,
tóvogel' su ventura   pora buena sazón;
diole el su cavallo   – ¡dél' Dios buen galardón! –
passó en Eüfrates,   fues' por a Babilón.

1076 Quando lo entendieron   los que avién fincado
que avía el campo   Dario desemparado,
cayeron les los braços,   fueron cuestas tornando;
onraron a los griegos   a todo su mal grado.

1077 Tornaron las espaldas,   dieron se a guarir;
los otros en pues ellos   sabién los bien seguir;
los que podién lidiando   honrada ment' morir
murieron en mal preçio   por amor de bevir.

1078 Ivan d'ellos e d'ellos   lo más peor asmando;
ívanseles los cueres   con el miedo camiando;
sintiélo Alexandre,   fuelos más acuitando;
fueron a las espaldas   los escudos echando.

1079 Quand' ovo Alexandre   la fazienda rancada,
e fueron encalçados   Dario con su mesnada;
mandó toller las armas   a la su gent' lazrada
e coger la gananchia   que Dios les avié dada.

1080 Cargaron a su guisa   quanto nunca quisieron;
más averes trobaron   que a Dios nunca pidieron;
maletas e perçintos   quantos sacos ovieron;
assí fueron calcados   que más non pudïeron.

1072	The good Emperor found himself in this doubt: to die was bad and to flee was worse still; he wondered which of the ills would be greater but either of them caused him great distaste.
1073	While he was considering what action to take, Perdiccas, of the Twelve, an accomplished knight, attacked him with a lance, the size of a beam, and hit him in the neck, just missing his head.
1074	Darius was defeated, he could not endure it, he abandoned the battlefield, turning in flight; the good man dismounted, to conceal himself better, and so that the Greeks could not track him down.
1075	One of his vassals, who was known as Auson, through Darius' good fortune, being there at the right time, gave his horse to the Emperor – may God reward him well! – who then crossed the Euphrates and made for Babylon.
1076	When those who had remained behind realised this, that Darius had abandoned the field of battle, with their shoulders slumped they turned tail in retreat and paid honour to the Greeks, all against their will.
1077	Turning about, they began to run for safety; the Greeks, at their backs, were skilled in pursuit: those who could have died with honour in battle died with ill repute because they wished to stay alive.
1078	Everywhere the Persians were thinking the worst and their hearts were sinking with the fear they felt. Alexander sensed this and harassed them more fiercely; they were starting to set their shields on their backs.
1079	When Alexander had the battle in his power, and Darius with his army had been put to flight, he ordered his exhausted men to down their arms and collect the booty that was given them by God.
1080	They gathered up at will more than they ever desired and found greater wealth than they ever asked of God: chests and bundles and every bag left on the field; they weighed themselves down till they could carry no more.

1081　Quando fue lo del campo　todo bien abarrido,
　　　　tornaron en las dueñas,　un pueblo desmedrido;
　　　　fueron luego robadas　de todo su vestido
　　　　e de quantos adobos　en sí avién traído.

1082　Quando de sus adobos　fueron despoderadas,
　　　　prisieron peor onta,　fueron todas forçadas;
　　　　por tal passaron todas,　por casar e casadas,
　　　　mas non fue a su grado,　por do non son culpadas.

1083　La compaña de Dario,　la muger e la madre,
　　　　el fijo e las fijas　guardólas Alexandre;
　　　　non las honrarié más　si él fuesse su padre.
　　　　¡Bien aya qui a Dario　fueli leal cofadre!

1084　Supiera Alexandre　por barrunte çertera
　　　　cómo tornó sus tesoros　Dario de la carrera;
　　　　en Damasco fincaron,　cosa fue verdadera.
　　　　Fue Parmenio por ellos,　una lança señera.

1085　El señor de Damasco　asmó grant malvestat;
　　　　asmó con Alexandre　de poner amistat;
　　　　bastió a traïçión　de omes la çibdat;
　　　　mas él non ganó calças　en essa falsedat.

1086　Quand' sintieron los pueblos　que eran engañados,
　　　　más quisieron morir　que non seer rebtados;
　　　　mataron al perfecto　que los avié sossacados;
　　　　lidiaron con Parmenio,　fueron desbaratados.

1087　Más plazió a Darïo　la muert' del traïdor
　　　　que nol' pesó la pérdida　nin la su desonor.
　　　　Contra la otra cueita,　fuel' esto grant sabor;
　　　　rindió con alegría　graçias al Crïador.

1088　Dixo: "¡Ay Dios, bendito　seas Tú e laudado!
　　　　Aún de Ti nom' tengo　yo por desemparado;
　　　　téngome d'esto sólo,　Señor, por tu pagado
　　　　quando del traïdor　me has tan bien vengado.

1089　Aún en pues aquesto,　mayor merçet espero:
　　　　que merçed me farás　veo signo çertero;
　　　　desque me has vengado　del mi falso guerrero,
　　　　que quiere que me venga　non darié un dinero."

1081	When the booty from the battlefield had all been carried off, they turned to the women, who were waiting in terror; they were immediately robbed of all their clothes and all the adornments that they carried with them.
1082	When they had all been stripped of their apparel they received still worse shame: they all suffered rape; they all met the same fate, be they married or no, but it was against their will, so they bear no blame.
1083	Darius' household, his wife and his mother, his son and his daughters, Alexander protected, and honoured them as much as if he were their father.* May he fare well, that loyal brother to Darius!
1084	Alexander had received definite information about how Darius had sent away his treasures: they remained in Damascus – this was the true account –, and Parmenion set off for them, a singular knight.
1085	The lord of Damascus devised a wicked scheme:* he planned to form a friendship with Alexander, and treacherously filled the city with his men, but he did not gain any reward from this deception.
1086	When the people saw that they had been deceived, they would rather have died than be held to blame; they killed the prefect – for he had plotted against them – fought with Parmenion, and met with defeat.
1087	Darius felt more pleasure at the death of the traitor than regret at the defeat or at his own dishonour; this was a great delight to set against the other sorrow and in his joy he gave thanks to the Creator.
1088	"O Lord, praise and blessing unto You!" he said; "I do not yet think myself abandoned by You; for this alone, Lord, I hold that I am in Your favour: that You have granted me such vengeance on the traitor.
1089	After this I still hope to receive a greater mercy – that You will grant me grace I can see a sure sign –: since You have avenged me on my false warrior, for whatever now befalls me I would not give a penny."

1090   Quand' ovo Alexandre   los averes partidos,
        los septenarios fechos,   los clamores complidos,
        mandó mover sus pueblos,   de lazerio usados,
        fue çercar a Sidón,   que fuessen bien guisados.

1091   Como eran encarnados,   non dubdavan morir;
        pensaron a porfidia   en los muros sobir;
        tanto non los podieron   los otros referir;
        ovieron la por fuerça   muy tost' a conquerir.

1092   Quando Sidón fue presa,   fueron Tiro çercar:
        çibdat de grant fazienda   que tenié fuert' lugar;
        bien más de las tres partes   çercávala la mar;
        nunca fue quien por fuerça   la pudiesse ganar.

1093   Embïó Alexandre   si gela querrién dar;
        dixieron ellos non,   ca serié mal estar.
        Plaçiól' ad Alexandre   e fuela a lidiar;
        pensáronse de mientre   ellos de aguisar.

1094   Bastieron bien los muros,   çerraron los portiellos;
        mandaron fer apriesa   saetas e quadriellos;
        lanças e segurones,   espadas e cuchiellos;
        perpuntos e lorigas,   escudos e capiellos.

1095   Partieron los lugares   a medidas contadas;
        bastïeron las torres   de firmes algarradas;
        metieron y conducho,   mas de çient mill carradas;
        eran, si Dios quisiesse,   gentes bien adobadas.

1096   Quando vido Alexandre   que en esso andavan,
        dixo que los de Tiro   grant serviçio le davan,
        ca ellos todavía   mayor preçio sacavan
        quando por pura fuerça   lo ageno ganavan.

1097   La çibdat fue çercada,   nol' dieron nul vagar;
        fue luego combatida   por tierra e por mar;
        sabiénles de saetas   tan fiera priessa dar
        que sól' non les dexavan   la cabeça rascar.

1098   Era les Alexandre   fiera guisa irado,
        ca avién ellos fecho   un grant desaguisado;
        los entre medïanos   avién gelos matado
        que entraron en treguas   a ellos con mandado.

1090	When Alexander had distributed the riches, with the week of prayer over and the cheering grown quiet, his troops, now used to hardship, he bade set out that they be well prepared to lay siege to Sidon.*
1091	Emboldened by their fury, they had no fear of death and were eager to scale the walls in conflict; their enemy were not able to put up firm resistance, so they quickly managed to conquer the city by force.
1092	When Sidon was captured, they brought siege to Tyre,* a very wealthy city on a formidable site: on more than three sides it was surrounded by sea, and there never was a man who could take it by force.
1093	Alexander sent messengers to invite them to surrender; the people cried "No!" for that would be an error; this pleased Alexander and he moved to attack, while the inhabitants began to make ready to resist.
1094	They fortified the walls and firmly closed the gates; they ordered arrows and bolts to be made with haste, lances and axes, with swords and knives, doublets and mail-coats, shields and helmets.
1095	They divided up the stations, all measured precisely, equipped the towers well with powerful catapults, and brought in stocks of food, over a hundred thousand cartloads; as long as God was willing, they were well provided for.
1096	When Alexander saw that they were taking these measures he said that the Tyrians were doing him great service, for his men were thus winning even greater fame by gaining others' property through sheer force.
1097	The city was besieged and given no respite and attacked at once both by land and by sea; they were able to unleash such a hail of arrows that the defenders had not even time to scratch their heads.
1098	Alexander was wild with fury at them for they had committed a great transgression and killed the emissaries that they had been sent, who bore his message into Tyre beneath a truce.

1099   Ivan los mandaderos   por la paz assentar;
        ovieron los de Tiro   traïçión a asmar;
        por sus graves pecados   ovieron a çegar;
        mataron a los omes   que los querién salvar.

1100   End' era Alexandre   e todos sus varones
        en contra los de Tiro   sañosos e fellones;
        ende juraron todos   por los suyos griñones
        que posiessen en ella   todos sendos tizones.

1101   Por agua e por tierra   los fueron combatiendo;
        fueron el miedo todos   con la saña perdiendo;
        los de dentro, con todo,   fueron se ençendiendo;
        fues' derredor de la villa   la rebuelta faziendo.

1102   Bien sabién los de Tiro   que, si fuessen vençidos,
        serién, grandes e chicos,   a espada metidos;
        querrién morir lidiando   más que seer rendidos;
        ya ivan conoçiendo   que fueran deçebidos.

1103   Fuéranse los de Tiro   por leales provados
        si los entre medianos   non oviessen matados;
        mas fueron en aquesso   dura mente errados;
        mientre dure el mundo   siempre serán rebtados.

1104   Alexandre, que nunca   perdonó a traidores,
        mandólos combatir   a los embaïdores;
        dioles tan fiera priessa   de lit a los señores,
        quantos pelos avién   vertién tantos sudores.

1105   D'ella e d'ella parte   batién las algarradas;
        artes de muchas guisas   que avién sossacadas;
        bolavan las saetas   en venino tempradas;
        de piedras e de dardos   vinién grandes nuvadas.

1106   Con los almañaneques   davan grandes colpadas
        que avién de las torres   las demás aplanadas;
        mas las gentes de Tiro   eran tan denodadas
        que las tenién de fuera   de la villa redradas.

1107   El rëy Alexandre   aplegó su conçejo.
        Díxoles: "Ya, varones,   caemos en trebejo;
        perdemos nuestros días   en un mal castillejo;
        mester es que busquemos   otro mejor consejo.

1099	Although the envoys went to agree terms of peace the Tyrians had conceived treachery towards them; they came to be blinded by their own grave sins and they brought death to the men who sought to save them.
1100	For this reason, Alexander and all his knights felt a raging anger against the people of Tyre and for this reason they all swore by their beards that each one of them would set firebrands to the city.
1101	On both sea and land they waged war on them and in their fury they all lost their sense of fear; the Tyrians at this were aflame with anger; the frenzy of battle began to spread around the city.
1102	The Tyrians knew well that, if they were defeated, young and old alike would be put to the sword; they preferred to die fighting rather than surrender, but now began to recognise that they had been in error.
1103	The people of Tyre would have proved themselves loyal had they not put the emissaries to death; but in this action they were gravely at fault: they will always be condemned while the world endures.
1104	Alexander, who never gave forgiveness to traitors, ordered the attackers to go into battle, and roused his knights to action with such intensity that all their hair was running thick with sweat.
1105	The catapults were hurling stones on all sides using many different tactics that they had devised; arrows that were soaked in poison soared aloft and great clouds of stones and darts were unleashed.
1106	With the siege engines they struck tremendous blows which had already flattened most of the towers but the people of Tyre fought with such ferocity that they kept those attacking the city at bay.
1107	King Alexander called together his council and said, "Now, my knights, we have our work cut out; we are wasting our days on a wretched little castle; we must find another plan that suits us better.

1108 Si assí nos escampan éstos esta vegada,
      quantos esto supieren por nos non darán nada;
      la nuestra buena fama que ya es levantada
      a nada e a vilta será luego tornada.

1109 Mas quiero que fagamos todos un paramiento;
      acostemos nos todos, demos atendimiento;
      vayamos los ferir todos de buen taliento;
      faremos que las menas egualen el çimiento.

1110 Demos les todos priessa, quis quier' por su lugar;
      de noche nin de día non les demos vagar;
      non dexen por los muertos los bivos de lidiar;
      por cansedat derecha se nos avrán a dar."

1111 Non lo dixo a sordos; fueron los combater;
      por mar e por terreño, a müy grant poder;
      por que veyén los unos a los otros caer
      por esso non dexavan su camino tener.

1112 Todos, altos e baxos, lidiavan bien de veras;
      a mía sobre tuya ponién las escaleras;
      trayén descalavradas muchos las calaveras;
      el rëy toda vía tomava las primeras.

1113 Que mucho vos digamos, tod' aquí se ençierra:
      el buen muro de Tiro fue aína en tierra,
      que les avién tomado los de fuera la sierra;
      ívanles demostrando rica mente la yerra.

1114 Los tesoros de Tiro fueron bien abarridos;
      fueron chicos e grandes a espada metidos;
      degollaron las madres, sí fizieron los chicos,
      encara los que eran aquel día naçidos.

1115 Por tal passaron todos e tal muerte prisieron;
      fuera si en los templos algunos se metieron;
      si malos fueron ellos tan mala fin fizieron;
      por fe, a mí non pesa ca bien lo mereçieron.

1116 Desque fue de los omes la villa tod' hermada,
      ençendieron las casas, fue aína quemada;
      tornaron en la çerca: fue toda derrocada;
      fue la çibdat de Tiro por suelo aplanada.

Book of Alexander

1108   If these people escape us on this occasion,
       all those who hear of it will pay us no heed;
       our fine reputation which is already well formed
       will quickly be as nothing, and turned to scorn.

1109   But I want us all to set this plan into action:
       let us all approach, but let us go with care;
       let us all go against them, being of stout heart;
       we shall level their battlements to the ground.

1110   Let us all attack them, each man from his own station;
       by night and by day let us give them no respite;
       the living must not cease to fight on the dead's account;
       out of sheer exhaustion they will have to yield to us."

1111   He spoke not to deaf ears; they went into battle
       with a huge assault, made by land and by sea;
       the fact that some men saw their companions fall
       did not make them hesitate in their advance.

1112   Great and small, they were all fighting in earnest,
       setting up ladders, one after the other;
       many of these men had their skulls split open,
       the King always among the first in the attack.

1113   However much we might tell you, the crux lies here:
       Tyre's valiant defence was soon laid low;
       those coming from outside had taken their city
       and set about making their error quite clear.

1114   The treasures of Tyre were heavily plundered;
       young and old alike were all put to the sword;
       the throats were cut of both mothers and children,
       and even of babies who were born that day.

1115   They all suffered such a fate and died such a death
       except those who took sanctuary in the temples;
       if they were bad people they met just as bad an end
       – in faith, I am not troubled, for they well deserved it.

1116   Once the city had been purged of its people,
       they torched the houses and it was quickly burned down;
       they turned to the walls, and it was all brought to ruin:
       the city of Tyre was razed to the ground.

1117   Siempre devián tal çaga   prender los traïdores;
          non devién escapar   por nulos fïadores;
          ca nin guardan amigos   nin escusan señores;
          ¡mala fin prengan ellos   e sus atenedores!

1118   Assí fue destroída   Tiro la muy preçiada;
          la que ovo Genor   a grant missión poblada;
          mas en tiempo de Cristo   fue después restaurada;
          a las otras çibdades   fue por cabeça dada.

1119   El buen rëy Irán   d'esta Tiro era,
          el que a Salamón   embïó la madera
          quando fazié el templo,   rico de grant manera;
          e de y fue Martol,   una bestia ligera.

1120   Çerca era de Tiro,   en essa vezindat,
          Gaça era su nombre,   una rica çibdat;
          de seso e de obra   e de toda bondat
          era villa complida   e de grant plenedat.

1121   Non li membró de Tiro   nin del su emperant',
          cómo ante los griegos   fuera tan mal andant';
          cogió un mal enojo,   ond' fue después pesant';
          dezié que a los griegos   nos' lis toldrié delant'.

1122   Cuidaron se por fuerça   la çibdat defender;
          plazió́l' ad Alexandre,   fue los a combater,
          maguer de todas partes   era grant el poder;
          los unos e los otros   avién pro que veer.

1123   Bien querién los de fuera   a las menas sobir;
          mas sabiénlos los otros   rica ment' referir.
          Avién en es' comedio   grant priessa de morir;
          abés uviava Átropos   los filos desordir.

1124   Vino en est' comedio   un ome endiablado,
          en guis' de peregrino   todo muy demudado.
          Avién lo los de dentro   asmo que embïado;
          oviera ad Alexandre,   si por pocas, matado.

1125   Trayé yus' el vestido   cubierta la espada.
          Açercóse al rëy,   cuidó́l' dar grant golpada;
          mas enflaquió́l' la mano   que non fue bien osada;
          erró́lo, que non era   la ora uvïada.

| 1117 | Traitors should always meet just such an end:
they should never escape through any guarantor,
for they aid not their allies and spare not their lords;
may they meet an evil end, and their followers too. |

| 1118 | Thus was destroyed the famed city of Tyre,
which Agenor had toiled hard to found;*
but it was later restored in the time of Christ,*
and placed at the head of all other cities. |

| 1119 | The good King Hiram was from this city of Tyre,*
he who had sent the wood to King Solomon
when he was building the magnificent temple;
Melqart came from there, too, a fleet-footed beast.* |

| 1120 | There was another near Tyre, in that same region:
its name was Gaza, and the city was rich,*
in learning, fine works and all kinds of quality:
an outstanding city and one of great wealth. |

| 1121 | The city was not mindful of Tyre or its emperor
or how great were its mistakes in its dealings with the Greeks,
but acted with hostility it would later regret,
and said it would not open its gates before the Greeks. |

| 1122 | They planned to make defence of the city by force;
this delighted Alexander and he moved to attack,
although the force assembled on both sides was great;
both armies had a great battle before them. |

| 1123 | The Greeks were attempting to scale the battlements
but the defenders were well able to repulse their attack.
In doing this they rushed headlong to their deaths:
Atropos could scarcely unravel the threads. |

| 1124 | Meanwhile a man arrived, a servant of the Devil,
in the guise of a pilgrim, his appearance transformed;
it seems to me that the defenders had sent him,
and he could so easily have killed Alexander. |

| 1125 | He wore his sword concealed, underneath his clothing,
and approached the King, aiming to land a heavy blow,
but his hand wavered, for it lacked the calm of courage,
and he missed his target, for the hour had not yet come. |

1126 Non lo querién los fados   que muriesse colpado,
que otra guisa era   de los dios ordenado:
ya era el venino   fecho e destemprado
que avié de sus omes   a seer escançïado.

1127 Fue preso el mal ome;   ovo a manifestar
cómo era venido   pora'l rëy matar;
mandól' la mano diestra   el rey luego cortar
e non si non por quanto   nol' pudo açertar.

1128 El rëy contra Gaça   fue fiera ment' irado;
por a lidiar la villa   fue muy mal denodado;
querríeles entrar   en la villa sin grado,
mas retovos' un poco,   ca fue muy mal colpado.

1129 Diéronle en el ombro   una grant venablada;
diéronle en la pierna   otra fiera pedrada;
quedó un poquillejo,   mas non les valió nada.
Fueron ellos vençidos   e la villa entrada.

1130 Sojornaron en Gaça,   ca eran muy cansados;
fue el rëy guarido,   los otros, esforçados.
Com' de tod' en todo   eran a guerra dados,
fueron fer su mester   en que eran usados.

1131 El rëy Alexandre   e toda su mesnea,
desque prisieron Gaça   fueron por a Judea;
fueron mal espantadas   tierras de Galilea,
ca tenién que avién   a sovar la correa.

1132 El rëy de los griegos,   tan cosido barón,
oyó cómo tenién   la ley del Crïador;
embióles a dezir,   en paz e en amor,
que catassen a él   por su emperador.

1133 Por a Jerusalén   embïó su notario
que li diessen la renta   que solién dar a Dario.
Demás, qui contra esto   le viniesse contrario,
darl'ie mala fiesta   e peor ochavario.

1134 Jadus, que de la ley   era el mayoral,
respuso que con Dario   avié puesta señal:
si a otri la diessen   que pareçerié mal
e por ninguna guisa   non demandasse al.

Book of Alexander

1126 The Fates did not wish him to die bearing wounds,
for it was ordained otherwise by the gods:
the poison was already prepared and dissolved
which he was to be served by his men.

1127 The evil man was captured and forced to confess
how he had come there to murder the King.
Alexander ordered that his right hand be severed,
if only because it had failed to strike truly.

1128 The King was in a terrible rage against Gaza
and utterly determined to attack the city.
He wanted them to enter the city uninvited,
but held back a little, for he was gravely wounded.

1129 He had suffered, in his shoulder, a deep lance-wound,
and been badly injured by a stone in the leg;
he delayed a little, but it did not help his foes,
for they were defeated and the city was taken.

1130 They passed some time in Gaza, for they were very tired;
the King was cured and the others' strength restored.
Since they were completely given over to warfare,
they returned to the craft to which they were accustomed.

1131 King Alexander and the whole of his army,
once they took Gaza, marched on Judea.
The lands of Galilee were in great terror,
thinking that they would come under his lash.

1132 The King of the Greeks, so valiant a knight,
heard how they observed the Creator's Law,
and sent them a message in peace and goodwill
telling them to look on him as their emperor.

1133 To Jerusalem he sent his notary and his command
that they pay him the tribute they used to pay to Darius,
adding that, should anyone go against him in this,
he would give them the blackest week of observance.

1134 Jadus, who was the city's foremost man of law,*
replied that, as they had made their pledge to Darius,
they were not willing to make payment to another
and that in no way should he ask otherwise.

1135   El rey fue irado   e mandó cavalgar;
        mandó luego que fuessen   Jerusalén çercar,
        que, quando querién ellos   en esso se parar,
        él les mostrarïé   a quién lo devién dar.

1136   Quando entendió Jadus   e toda la çibdat
        que vinié Alexandre,   pesól' de voluntad;
        fizieron rogaçiones   por toda santidad
        que les fiziesse Dios   alguna pïedat.

1137   Vínole en visión   a Jadus do durmié
        que, quando Alexandre   supiesse que vinié,
        sallese contra él   qual la misa dezié
        e pornié su fazienda   tan bien como querrié.

1138   Otro día mañana,   hevos los apellidos
        que era Alexandre   con los griegos venidos,
        e vinién a la villa   irados e guarnidos;
        ya dizié el aljama: "¡Somos mal confondidos!"

1139   Vistióse el obispo   de la ropa sagrada:
        puso en su cabeça   una mitra preçiada;
        en la fruent' una carta   que era bien ditada,
        que de nombres de Dios   era toda cargada.

1140   Fizo aparejar   toda la clereçía;
        los libros de la lëy   aver por mejoría;
        fueron ad Alexandre   reçebir a la vía;
        nunca mejor consejo   prisieron en un día.

1141   Cubrieron las carreras   de rosas e de flores
        que pareçién fermosas,   davan buenas olores;
        todos llevavan ramos,   los moçuelos, menores;
        querién ad Alexandre   darle grandes onores.

1142   Quando vio Alexandre   tan noble proçessión,
        membról' por aventura   de una visïón;
        fizo ant'el obispo   su genuflecçïón;
        prostrado sobre tierra,   fizo grant oraçión.

1143   Mandó fincar de fuera   todas sus crïazones;
        entró él en la villa,   fizo sus estaçiones;
        como la ley mandava,   ofreçió oblaçiones;
        confirmóles su lëy   e todas sus acçiones.

1135	Enraged, the King ordered his men to ride out, and commanded them at once to besiege Jerusalem, for, since the city's people wanted it to come to this, he would make it clear to them whom they would have to pay.
1136	When Jadus, and all of the city, understood that Alexander was coming, he was deeply anxious and offered up prayers by every saint in order that God might show them some mercy.
1137	One night, a vision came to Jadus as he slept, that, when he knew Alexander was coming, he should go out to meet him as if saying Mass, and thus would order his affairs as well as he could wish.
1138	The morning of the next day, the war cries rang out to proclaim that Alexander and the Greeks had arrived, and they came to the city irate and battle-ready; all the Jews now said, "We have come to ruin."*
1139	The bishop put on his sacred vestments and placed on his head a precious mitre. On his brow was a parchment with words clearly written, which was heavily embellished with names of God.
1140	He had the whole of the clergy ready themselves, and bring the books of the Scripture to strengthen their position. They went out to receive Alexander as he came – on no day did they ever take a sounder decision.
1141	They covered the roads with roses and flowers, the sight of them beautiful, their aroma sweet; they all carried garlands – the children, smaller ones – wanting to pay Alexander great honour.
1142	When Alexander saw so noble a procession, he chanced to remember a vision he had seen and went down on bended knee before the bishop; he lay prostrate on the ground and spoke in prayer.
1143	He ordered all his vassals to wait outside the city, while he went inside and set up his stations of prayer, he offered his oblations just as the Law commanded, and confirmed his law for them, and his way of acting.

1144 Soltólos de tributos e de todas las pechas,
mandóles que toviessen la lëy a derechas;
mandó todas sus gentes ques'tornassen derechas,
ca avié por jamás con ellos pazes fechas.

1145 Leyó en Danïel en una profeçía
que tornarié un griego Asia en monarquía;
plaziól ad Alexandre, ovo grant alegría.
Dixo: "Yo seré ésse, por la cabeça mía."

1146 Entró un grant escándalo entre la su mesnada
que fiziera el rëy cosa desaguisada
e toda su nobleza avié menoscabada,
ond' se tenié su corte por müy desonrada.

1147 Parmenio el caboso non lo pudo sofrir;
acostóse al rëy e fuégelo dezir;
llamó el rey a todos quel' viniessen oír,
ca a esta pregunta les querié recodir.

1148 "Quando el rey Felipo, mi padre, fue passado
e fue el traïdor de Pausona enforcado,
estava, como sabedes, el regno mal parado;
yo, como era nuevo, estava desmayado.

1149 Estava en mi cámara en un lecho yaziendo,
de las cosas del regno yazía comidiendo;
fue con la grant anxïa el sueño trasponiendo;
yazía en grant cueita, grant lazerio sufriendo.

1150 Era la noche lóbrega e la casa obscura;
corrién de mí sudores, ca era en ardura;
semejava la cóçedra que era tabla dura;
ca yaz' quien ave cueita siempre en estrechura.

1151 Mientre que yo estava en esti pensamiento,
movióse un relámpago e levantós' un viento;
descuñó las finiestras, como ome sin tiento;
yo espantém' un poco, com' ome soñoliento.

1152 Levanté la cabeça, ca fui espantado,
paréme sobr' el cobdo, que estava pesado;
vi el palaçio todo fiera ment' alumbrado,
como si fues' grant día, el sol escalentado.

1144	He set the people free from all their tributes and payments but ordered them to give full obeisance to his laws. He ordered all his men to leave, walking tall with pride, for he had made an everlasting peace with them.
1145	He read in a prophecy from the Book of Daniel* that a Greek would turn all Asia into a monarchy. Alexander was pleased at this and filled with great joy; he said, "By this head of mine, that man will be me."
1146	A great sense of outrage ran through his army that the King had done such an extravagant thing: he had brought disrepute on all of his nobles, for which his court thought itself gravely dishonoured.
1147	The valiant Parmenion could not endure it; he approached the King and went to tell him so; the King called them all to come and listen to him as he wished to give them an answer to this question.
1148	"When King Philip, my father, met his death and when the traitor Pausanias was hanged, the kingdom, as you know, was in a poor state; newly crowned as king, I felt ill at ease.
1149	I was in my chamber, lying in my bed, and lay with my thoughts on the kingdom's affairs; with my great anxiety my sleep abandoned me, and I lay there, deeply worried, deeply troubled.
1150	In the gloom of the night and the dark of the house, the sweat poured from me for I was greatly disturbed; the mattress felt to me as if it were a hard board, for the worried man lies always in discomfort.
1151	While my mind was thinking on all these matters, there was a flash of lightning and the wind rose up and threw open the windows as a man in the dark; I felt a little fear, as a man half-asleep.
1152	I raised up my head, for I was very afraid, and leant upon my elbow in my torpor. I saw that the palace was all ablaze with lights as if in broad daylight with the sun burning down.

1153   Paróseme de suso   un ome revestido:
        porque ome lo llamo,   téngome por fallido;
        creo que era ángel   del çielo deçendido;
        ca non avrié tal cara   ningunt ome naçido.

1154   Obispo semejava   en toda su figura,
        en mitra e en çapatas   e en su vestidura;
        vistié una dalmática,   toda de seda pura;
        cubriél' todos los pies   tanto avié largura.

1155   Tenié quatro caractas   en la fruent' debujadas,
        de obscura materia   obscura ment' dictadas;
        non las sope leer   ca eran muy çerradas;
        de oro fino eran;   semejavan sagradas.

1156   Quando vi tal nobleza,   persona tan honrada,
        fuile yo preguntar   – non quiso dezir nada –
        qué era o dónt venié   o dó era su andada;
        acuçïós' él ante;   dixo esta bocada:

1157   'Entiende, Alexandre,   qué te quiero fablar;
        salte de Europe,   passa a ultra mar;
        avrás todos los regnos   del mundo a ganar;
        nunca fallarás ome   quet' pueda contrastar.

1158   Quiérote toda vía   mostrar una cordura:
        quando vieres a ome   que trae mi figura,
        dale grant reverençia,   muéstral' toda mansura;
        irá siempre pujando   la tu buena ventura.'

1159   Quand' ovo dicho esto,   començos' a desfer;
        sallós' me de los ojos,   non lo pude veer;
        tornós' la casa lóbrega,   qual solía seer;
        podrié un ome muerto   del olor guaresçer.

1160   Essa misma figura,   esse mismo vestido
        que en es' ome santo   ovi estonç' veído,
        en est' obispo lo he   vera ment' coñosçido;
        por end' non me devedes   tener por falleçido.

1161   Yo a ést' non adoro   nin cato por señor,
        mas so la su figura   adoro al Criador,
        al que me prometió   de fer emperador,
        que es rey e obispo   e abat e prior.

1153	There appeared above me a man of rich adornments, though I think myself wrong to call him a man; I believe he was an angel descended from Heaven, for his face was unlike any man ever born.
1154	In every way, he had the appearance of a bishop, in his mitre, his shoes and all his vestments; he wore a dalmatica, a garment of pure silk, so long as to cover his feet completely.
1155	He had four characters drawn on his forehead,* difficult in meaning, in a difficult script; I could not read them, for they were very complex; they were of fine gold and seemed to be sacred.
1156	When I saw such nobility, such an honourable figure, I tried to question him but he did not want to speak: who he was, where he came from or where his path led; he spoke with care before me and uttered these words:
1157	'Understand, Alexander, what I wish to tell you: take your leave of Europe and go beyond the seas; you will come to conquer all the kingdoms of the world; you will never find a man who can stand against you.
1158	I wish still to give you one piece of wise advice: when you see a man who bears my appearance, treat him with reverence and show him restraint; he will always cause your good fortune to grow.'
1159	After he had said this, he began to disappear; he faded from my eyes, I could no longer see him; the house was filled with gloom again, as it was wont to be, yet the sweet smell could have raised a man from death.
1160	That same appearance, those same vestments that I had seen at that time on that holy man, truly I have recognised them in this bishop, and because of this you must not think me in error.
1161	I do not worship this man, nor see him as my lord, but in his appearance I worship the Creator, who made a firm promise to make me emperor, and who is King and Bishop, and Abbot and Lord.

1162 Bien sepades, amigos, que aquel mandadero
mensaje fue de Dios, por fer a mí çertero;
a mi Ésse me guía, non otro agorero;
vos lo veredes todos que será verdadero."

1163 Entendieron ya todos que fizo aguisado;
fueron bien fiuçantes de ganar el regnado;
vieron en tod' en todo que era bien guisado,
que non fue maravilla si Dario fue rancado.

1164 Desent' fue a Samaria, fue luego reçebido;
pidieron le los pueblos un general pedido
que les diesse tal fuero todo tan bien complido
qual en Jerusalén avié estableçido.

1165 Demandó de su vida; sopo çertenidat
que les dizién ebreos, ca assí fue verdat.
Díxoles: "Yo, amigos, tamaña enguedat
a los judíos solos la di por heredat."

1166 Puso en buen recabdo lo que avié ganado;
entró para Egibto como rayo irado;
el rëy fue de seso, el pueblo acordado,
reçibieron lo luego, juraron su mandado.

1167 Sobjudgada Egibto en toda su grandía,
con muchas otras tierras que dezir non sabría,
al rëy Alexandre, señor de grant valía,
entról' en voluntad de ir en romería.

1168 Priso su esportilla e priso su bordón;
pensó por ir a Libia a la sied' de Amón
– do Júpiter a Bacus ovo dado grant don –
por dar y su ofrenda e fer su oración.

1169 Marras, quand' ovo Bacus a India sobjudgada,
escaeçió en Libia con toda su mesnada;
avié por unos yermos fecha muy grant andada;
era toda la hueste de sed mal cuïtada.

1170 La tierra era seca, de fuentes muy mañera;
non podién aver agua por ninguna manera;
rogó Bacus a Júpiter que les diesse carrera
por do oviessen agua, ca menester les era.

1162	I tell you, my friends, that that very messenger, was a sign sent from God to give me certainty; He is my guide, not some other soothsayer: you will all see that this will become true."
1163	Now they all understood that he had acted correctly and their confidence of gaining the kingdom was high; they could see that he was prudent in everything he did and that it was no wonder if Darius had been defeated.
1164	He went next to Samaria and was welcomed at once;* all the peoples together made a collective request: that he grant them such privilege, and on the same scale, as he had established in the city of Jerusalem.
1165	He asked about their life and found out for certain that they were called Hebrews, for this was the truth. He said to them: "My friends, I gave liberty so great to the Jews alone, and as an inheritance."*
1166	The booty he had won he put into safe stores and he entered Egypt like an angry flash of lightning;* the King was wise and the people in agreement: they welcomed him at once, and swore their allegiance.
1167	Now that Egypt had been conquered in all its grandeur, with many other lands I would not know how to list, King Alexander, who was a lord of great worth, was filled with the desire to go on a pilgrimage.*
1168	He took up his basket and picked up his staff; he thought to go to Libya and the shrine of Ammon,* where Jupiter had given his great gift to Bacchus, to make his offering there and to say his prayer.
1169	In other times, when Bacchus had mastery of India,* he met suffering in Libya with all of his army; he had made a great journey across deserted lands and all his men were suffering badly from thirst.
1170	It was a dry land, with a great dearth of springs, and they could find no way of obtaining water. Bacchus begged Jupiter to show them a means* for them to find the water of which they were in need.

1171 Pareçió yus' un árbol, çerca d'una costana,
un cabrón todo blanco, bien cubierto de lana;
firié con el pie diestro sobre la tierra plana;
asmaron que podrié allí aver fontana.

1172 Mandó allí cavar, sallió luego la vena;
los que cavar querién non sufrieron grant pena;
salló grant abastança, llenava el arena;
fueron todos alegres, ovieron buena çena.

1173 Consagró la fuent' Júpiter que fuesse perenal,
de la virtud de Bacus que fuesse por señal;
ivierno e verano manasse comunal:
en verano fues' fría, caliente en lo al.

1174 Con todas éstas buenas avié otra natura:
de día era fría, quando fazié calura;
tibia era de noche a la mayor frïura;
ome que beviés' d'ella serié de grant ventura.

1175 Avié çerca la fuente una grant santidat;
sanava de cutiano mucha enfermedat;
non pidrié atal cosa ome de voluntat
que oído non fuesse de su neçessidat.

1176 Oviera Alexandre d'esti logar oído;
ya lo querié aver de su grado veído,
ya querié su ofrenda aver y ofreçido
e avrié de su grado d'aques' agua bevido.

1177 Durava el camino grandes quatro jornadas;
por a bestia ligera serién assaz tiradas;
non eran tanto muchas como eran airadas,
ca avié en comedio muchas malas passadas.

1178 Nunca cayén y nieves nin pluvia nin roçío,
nin fallavan y fuentes nin çisterna nin río;
de toda cosa verde era lugar vazío;
creo que por a mí non serié muy sanío.

1179 Quand' el sol escalienta, com' es todo arena,
non sofririé en forno ome más fuerte pena;
demás, quando el polvo las sus algaras mena,
non yaze mayor pena do canta la serena.

| 1171 | Beneath a tree there appeared, near to a hill,
a spotless white goat, with a fine coat of wool,
which beat its right hoof upon the flat ground;
they thought that there might be a spring in that spot. |

| 1172 | He bade them dig there, and the water gushed forth at once,
but those who wished to dig did not suffer great hardship;
such a quantity appeared that it filled the sand;
they were all overjoyed and consumed a fine meal. |

| 1173 | Jupiter blessed the fountain to make it perennial,
that it might be a sign of Bacchus' power
and its water flow freely in winter and in summer,
cold in the summer and warm at other times. |

| 1174 | Besides all these fine qualities it had yet one more:
that amidst the day's heat the stream ran cold,
but at night's coldest hour, the water was warm;
and a man who drank from it would enjoy good fortune. |

| 1175 | Around the spring was an air of great sanctity:
each day it brought cures to many illnesses;
no man of good will would ever ask for anything
such that in his need he would go unheard. |

| 1176 | Alexander had heard a great deal of this place,
and was now very keen to see it for himself,
and longed to make his own offering there;
he was filled with desire to drink of that water. |

| 1177 | The journey there lasted a full four days,
which would be long enough for any swift-footed beast;
but the journey was not so long as it was hard,
with many gruelling stretches on the way. |

| 1178 | No snow ever fell there, no rain and no dew,
nor did they find springs or pools or rivers;
the place was without any trace of green;
I believe that for me it would be no healthy spot. |

| 1179 | When the sun grows hot, as this land is all of sand,
a man would not endure worse torment in a furnace,
and, furthermore, when the dust makes its onslaughts,
there would be no greater torment where the siren sings. |

1180   El rëy Alexandre,   guerrero singular,
       que non dexó por dubda   cosa de ensayar,
       metiése en carrera   por veer es' logar;
       mas ante ovo mucho   lazerio a passar.

1181   Perdió en la carrera   muchos de sus varones,
       si quier' de cavalleros,   si quier' de peones;
       dañávales el polvo   e sed en los polmones;
       yendo por la carrera   cayén a bolodrones.

1182   A cab' de quatro días,   seyendo muy lazrados,
       fueron al santüario   los griegos aplegados;
       pensaron de folgar,   ca eran muy cansados;
       creo, a lo de menos,   que eran bien diezmados.

1183   Tovieron sus vegillas   con grant devoçïón,
       de çirios e d'ofrendas   fizieron grant missión;
       pensó fer cada uno   a Dios su petiçión,
       qual asmó cada uno   entre su coraçón.

1184   Quand' a toda su guisa   ovieron sojornado,
       por ir a Eçiopía   era todo fablado,
       veer dó el sol naçe,   do nunca fue poblado;
       mas vínole en tanto   un mensaje cuitado.

1185   Dixiéronle que Dario   era aparejado;
       por batalla le dar   estava aguisado;
       aún que lo avié   por la tierra buscado
       e retrayén que era   por a Greçia tornado.

1186   Plaçió ad Alexandre;   pensó de cavalgar,
       ca murié el dïablo   por amor de lidiar;
       tornó por a Egibto,   fue a Dario buscar,
       d'aquí a que se ovo   con él a fallar.

1187   El emperant' de Persia,   después que fue rancado,
       nunca folgar pudo   ca non era aguisado;
       allegó sus poderes   que le avién fincado
       por lidiar con el rëy   Alexandre de cabo.

1188   Fizo de tal manera   el regno acotar
       que non fuesse ninguno   osado de fincar;
       mandó cómo viniessen   todos a un lugar,
       ca querié morir   o se querié vengar.

1180	King Alexander, a singular warrior, who never shrank for fear from any endeavour, set out on his journey that he might see that place, but first he had great hardship to endure.
1181	Many of his men did he lose on the way, many knights and foot soldiers alike; the dust and the thirst were damaging their lungs, and as they went along they fell out in droves.
1182	After four days, having suffered great distress, the Greeks had arrived at the sanctuary; their thoughts were of rest, for they were deeply tired, and I think they had been cut by a tenth at least.
1183	They held their vigils with great devotion; they made great display with candles and offerings. Each man sought to make his requests to God just as he conceived them within his heart.
1184	When Alexander's men had had their fill of rest, all the talk was of going to Ethiopia, to see where the sun rises and where men never dwelt, but meanwhile ill tidings were brought to the King.
1185	They told him that Darius had made preparations and readied himself to do battle against him, and had even searched throughout the lands for Alexander; he was told that the King had turned for Greece.
1186	Delighted, Alexander determined to ride off: the devil in him was dying for love of battle; he headed for Egypt and went in search of Darius until finally he managed to catch up with him.
1187	The Emperor of Persia, after suffering defeat, could never be at rest, for to be so was not right; he gathered the forces which he still had left to meet King Alexander in battle once more.
1188	He had an edict set forth in his kingdom that no man should dare not to answer his call. He ordered that they should all meet in one place, for he wanted to die or gain his vengeance.

1189   Plegó grandes poderes, muy más que los primeros:
        aláraves e turcos, otros que dizen seros;
        los bactros e los bárbaros que yazen más caberos;
        los çitas, que en mundo non ha tales guerreros.

1190   Y eran los eçiopes, otrossí los cananeos,
        tierras de Babilonia con todos los caldeos;
        Media, con los de Persia, de barones sabeos,
        los partos, que bien saben abenir en torneos.

1191   Las dos Indias menores, con la otra mayor,
        avién sól' en su cabo prínçep' emperador:
        Poro era en ella mayoral e señor:
        ome de grant esfuerço, rico e sabidor.

1192   Poro, sin todo esto, embióle de sus gentes,
        plus de çient vezes mill de nobles combatientes,
        todos bien adobados, todos barva ponientes,
        todos de buen linaje e de nobles parientes.

1193   Muchos pueblos y ovo de que vos non dixiemos,
        tierras grandes e muchas, que contar non podriemos;
        pero a los ircanos en tuerto les yaziemos
        quando de tales omes mençïón non fiziemos.

1194   Assí lo mandó Dario en toda su onor
        que non fincasse ome, rabadán nin pastor,
        nin fincasse burgués nin ningunt labrador,
        nin ningunt menestral de ninguna lavor.

1195   Quando vido Alexandre pueblos tan sobejanos
        que todo yazié lleno, las cuestas e los llanos,
        diz': "Mester es, amigos, que traigamos las manos,
        ca sobre nos son estos indïos e paganos.

1196   Por uno que matamos, más de çiento naçieron;
        resuçitaron todos quantos nunca morieron;
        creo que los actores esto tal entendieron
        quando de las cabeças de la sierpe dixieron.

1197   Contan los actoristas, que dizen muchas befas,
        que fue una sirpiente que avié siet' cabeças;
        quando le tollién una, siet' le naçién espessas;
        semeja que es esto aquessas nuevas mesmas.

1189   He assembled great armies, much greater than his first:
there were Arabs and Turks, some they call Orientals,
Bactrians, Barbarians from far out on the frontier,*
and Scythians, warriors without equals in the world;

1190   there, too, the Ethiopians, and others from Canaan,*
the lands of Babylonia, with all the Chaldeans,
Medians, Persians, and warriors from Sheba,
and Parthians, who acquit themselves well in contest.

1191   The two lesser Indies, with the third and the greatest,*
had a prince and emperor only in their eastern part.
It was Porus who was India's lord and ruler,
a man great in valour, in wealth and in wisdom.

1192   Besides all these troops, Porus sent from his people
a hundred thousand and more noble fighters,
all well equipped, and all fresh-faced with youth,
all of fine lineage and born of noble stock.

1193   Many peoples were there of whom we have not spoken
and many vast territories which we could not number;
but we have done the Hyrcanians a wrong
in not making mention of such men as these.

1194   Darius commanded this be done in his honour:
that no man stay behind, be he steward or goatherd,
that the townsman stay not, nor any farmer,
nor any craftsman, whatever his trade.

1195   When Alexander saw such a vast array of men,
and that all the land was filled, both the hills and the plains,
he said, "We, my friends, must apply ourselves well,
for these men are upon us, Indians and pagans.

1196   For every one we killed, over a hundred were born;
all the men who ever died have come back to life.
I think that the authors had just such a thing in mind
when they spoke of the heads of the serpent.*

1197   The grammar teachers, who recount many wondrous things,
tell us that there once was a seven-headed serpent
and when one was cut off, a seven-strong cluster sprouted;
this seems to be the same story exactly.

1198 El luchador Anteo esta virtud avié:
quanto más lo echavan mayor fuerça cogié;
mas vedógelo don Ércules, que con él contendié;
semeja que agora Dario esso querrié."

1199 Ya avién en tod' esto Eüfrates pasada;
yazié cab' una sierra: Arbela es llamada.
Dario yazié bien çerca, quanto una jornada,
mas la plaça d'en medio era bien defesada.

1200 El sol era entrado, querié escureçer;
la luna era llena, querié apareçer;
començaron se todas las gentes a bolver,
las unas por dormir, las otras a comer.

1201 Aún por a dormir non eran bien quedados;
d'ellos seyén en çena, d'ellos eran çenados.
Vidieron en la luna colores demudados;
ende, baxos e altos eran mal espantados.

1202 Salló primero negra, non dava claredat,
duróle un grant rato la obscuridat;
después tornó bermeja, en otra calidat.
Dezién: "De plan' es esto signo de mortandat."

1203 Eran baxos e altos mal escandalizados;
eran de sus cabeças todos desfïuzados.
Dizíen: "¡Ay mesquinos! ¡Cómo somos malfadados!
Por aquí nos troxieron nuestros grieves pecados."

1204 Dizién: "Rey Alexandre, nunca devriés naçer,
que con todo el mundo quieres guerra tener;
los çielos e las tierras quieres yus' ti meter;
lo que Dïos non quiere tú lo cuidas aver.

1205 Tant' avemos ganado quanto nunca cuidamos;
quanto más conquerimos tanto mas cobdiçiamos;
traemos grant sobervia, mesura non catamos;
avremos a prender aún lo que buscamos.

1206 Tanto avemos fecho que los dios son irados;
nin el sol nin la luna non son nuestros pagados;
todos aquestos signos son por nuestros pecados,
quando los dios son contra, nos seremos lazrados."

Book of Alexander

1198   The wrestler Antaeus possessed this quality:*
the more he was thrown, the more he gained in strength,
though Hercules prevented it, when he fought with him;
it seems that Darius has now sought this too."

1199   By now they had crossed the River Euphrates;
the city called Arbela stood at the mountains' foot.*
Darius' camp was near, a day's journey away,
but the land between them was heavily fortified.

1200   The sun was setting and dark was falling;
the moon was full and about to rise;
all the people began to return to the camp,
some coming to sleep and others to eat.

1201   They had not yet settled down to sleep:
some were still eating, others had eaten;
they saw that the moon was changing in colour,*
at which men both great and small were terrified.

1202   First it turned black and gave out no light;
that darkness lasted for no short time;
next it turned crimson, a very different hue,
and they said, "This for certain is a sign of death."

1203   Great and small alike, they were deeply disturbed
and now they were all in despair of their lives,
saying, "Oh, wretches we are, our fate is against us;
it is our evil sins that have brought us to this place.

1204   King Alexander, you should never have been born,
for you want to wage war against the whole world
and set Heaven and Earth beneath your power;
what God does not will, you seek to make yours.

1205   We have won more than we ever thought we could,
but the more we conquered the more we craved;
we have great arrogance but no sense of measure;
we shall still take what we seek for ourselves.

1206   We have come so far that the gods have grown angry;
neither sun nor moon is pleased with our conduct;
all these signs are the result of our sins:
as the gods are against us, hardship will be ours."

1207 Alexandre el firme, de los rëys dubdado,
que por ningunt peligro nunca fue desmayado,
entendió el murmurio que era levantado,
cómo era el pueblo mal escandalizado.

1208 Mandó venir los sabios que sabién las naturas,
que entendién los signos e las cosas escuras;
mandóles que mostrassen segunt las escripturas
qué signos demostravan estas tales figuras.

1209 Avié entre los otros un maestro ortado:
diziénle Aristánder; en Egibto fue nado.
Escusó a los otros, ca era más letrado;
fue sobra bien apreso quando ovo fablado.

1210 Començó de dezir, fue bien escuchado.
"Varones," dixo, "fágome mucho maravillado
pueblo de tan grant preçio, por natura senado,
en cosa tan abierta seer tan embargado.

1211 Saben lo los pastores que en el monte biven,
los actores en cara assí nos lo escriven,
que todas crïaturas a su Crïador sirven
e, teniendo su curso, su mandamiento siguen.

1212 Sol, luna nin estrellas non sallen de sendero
en el que fueron puestas en el tiempo primero,
nin alçan nin abaxan un punto señero,
nin cambian su natura valor de un dinero.

1213 Si quiere en sallidas, si quiere en entradas,
en tornos, en retornos, en todas sus andadas,
la estrellas del çielo, menudas e granadas,
en esse curso andan en que fueron crïadas.

1214 Pero de todas éssas el sol es el mayor;
d'allí prenden las otras lumbre e resplandor;
a las que más alcança echan lumbre mayor,
e son, a las que menos, de claredat menor.

1215 Cueido a esto dar aún razón çertera:
luego que el sol salle a la ora primera,
la luna e las estrellas pierden toda lumbrera
e sólo non pareçe una d'ellas señera.

1207   Alexander the resolute, a man feared by kings,
       who remained undaunted in the face of any danger,
       learned that a murmur of discontent had arisen
       and of how the people had been so disturbed.

1208   He sent for the wise men who knew the ways of nature,
       who understood signs and matters dark in meaning;
       he commanded they interpret, according to the writings,
       what was the meaning to be seen in these portents.

1209   There was, among the others, a learned scholar,
       by the name of Aristander, born in Egypt;*
       he surpassed the others through his greater learning,
       and, when he had spoken, his words were well received.

1210   He began to speak and held everyone's attention:*
       "My lords," he said, "it causes me great amazement
       that a people so worthy, and wise by nature,
       is so troubled by a matter with a meaning so plain.

1211   It is known by the shepherds who dwell on the mountain
       – and the authors set it in writing for us, too –
       that all creatures render service to their Creator
       and follow His commandments in keeping to their course.

1212   Sun, moon and stars do not sway from the path
       on which they were set at the dawn of time,
       nor rising nor falling to the slightest degree,
       nor changing their nature by a penny's worth.

1213   Whether moving away or coming close,
       as they turn and turn about, in their every movement,
       the stars of the heavens, regardless of their size,
       move along that path on which they were created.

1214   Yet of all of them it is the sun that is greatest
       and from this the others take their light and splendour,
       and those closest to its rays cast out the brightest light
       while those at greatest distance shine least clearly.

1215   I intend to give a sure account of this:
       as soon as the sun rises at the day's dawn,
       the moon and the stars lose all their brilliance
       and not a single one of them can then be seen.

1216 Non por cosa que ellas sean más ençerradas,
mas la lumbre del sol las tiene apremiadas;
e, non él se traspone, luego son abivadas;
pareçen e relumbran, semejan argentadas.

1217 Esto en la candela lo podedes veer;
la mayor a la chica tírale el poder;
non está çerca d'ella, fázela recreer;
mas ella en su cabo cumple su menester.

1218 Aún vos quiero ir a otro argumente:
quando parez' la luna prima en Ocçidente,
si quier' quando pareçe menguant' en Orïente,
todol' viene del sol que le está presente.

1219 Ésta, çerca del sol, pierde la valentía;
los omes que la veen dizen que es vaçía;
desent' vas'le redrando, descubres' cada día,
d'aquí a que es llena, en toda su grandía.

1220 Vas'le, de que es llena, el sol más acostando;
vali con la grant fuerça la lumbre embargando;
va de día en día ella menoscabando;
cuidan los omes neçios ques' va adelgazando.

1221 Quiero vos toda vía una dubda soltar
en que a las vegadas suelen muchos dubdar:
quando va so la tierra el sol a su lugar,
de noche a la luna cóm' puede alumbrar.

1222 Es mayor que la tierra la luna vera mente,
ond' en todas las tierras pareçe egualmente;
el sol es siet' atanto – esto sin fallimente –
e está de la luna más alto luenga mente.

1223 Segunt esta razón, podemos entender
que la luna al sol nos' puede esconder;
do quiere que sean, bien se pueden veer;
non les puede la tierra nul embargo fazer.

1224 Entr'el sol e la tierra faz' ella su andada;
caen en un derecho amos a la vegada;
la claredat del sol es estonç' replegada.
Esa defecçïón eclipsis es llamada.

1216	The reason is not because their light has faded, but the light of the sun keeps them subservient, and when it moves off, they grow brighter at once: they appear and they sparkle and seem to be of silver.
1217	This you can see in the light of a candle: the larger flame draws the strength from the smaller; even when not near, it makes the smaller pale, but in its place this one is fulfilling its role.
1218	I wish to move on to yet another proof for you: when the moon, as it waxes, is sighted in the West, or even is in view on the wane in the East, its light comes all from the sun, which does not fail it.
1219	When the moon nears the sun it loses its strength and the men who see it say it has no substance; then it separates from it, growing clearer each day, until the full moon appears in all its grandeur.
1220	Once the moon is full, the sun gradually draws near, steadily weakening its glow with its great strength; day by day the moon begins to wane and weaken and foolish men believe it is becoming thinner.
1221	I still wish to resolve a mystery for you about which sometimes many incline to doubt: when the sun dips to its place below the earth, how can it then, at night, light up the moon?
1222	It is true that the moon is larger than the earth, and so in every land it has the same appearance. The sun is seven times as big – there is no doubt of this– and it is above the moon, at a far greater height.
1223	For this reason, it is possible for us to understand that the moon is unable to hide itself from the sun; wherever they may be, they can see each other clearly, and the earth cannot be any hindrance to this.
1224	The moon makes its journey between sun and earth; the sun and the moon fall sometimes into line and then the brilliance of the sun is hidden, and the name for this want is an eclipse.

1225   Lüego que el sol   d'es' punto es passado,
es en toda su fuerça   luego apoderado;
el pueblo que es neçio   faz'se maravillado;
non sabe la natura   e es mal espantado.

1226   Esto mismo devedes   de la luna asmar,
quand' quier' el sol so tierra   a Oriente tornar:
cae en su derecho,   non lo puede durar;
de la su resplandor   hase a demudar.

1227   Ond' luego que el sol   passa de la señal,
luego torna la luna   en su color cabdal;
cuidan los pueblos neçios   que sinifica mal,
e vos sodes caídos   en espanto atal.

1228   En cara suele esto   venir d'otra manera:
quando cae el sol   e va so la ribera;
la sombra de la tierra   yes entre medianera,
ond' un poco de rato   la tiene sin lumbrera.

1229   Aún dezirvos quiero   otra soluçïón
por que non vos temades   de nula lisïón:
el sol es de los griegos   – diré por quál razón –
la luna de los bárbaros   que en Oriente son.

1230   Quand' se cambia la luna   por signo demostrar,
a ellos amenaza   que les viene pesar;
si el sol se turbasse,   devriemos nos dubdar,
mas por esto devemos   letiçia demostrar.

1231   La negrura demuestra   los quebrantos passados,
los que de nos prisieron   onde son fatilados;
la bermejura demuestra   que cras serán rancados;
perderán mucha sangre,   nos seremos honrados."

1232   Fueron todos pagados,   çessó el mal roído;
maestre Aristánder   fue de todos creído;
fue por la fazïenda   el pueblo ençendido;
creçióles grant esfuerço   por lo qu'avién oído.

1233   El rey Alexandre,   de los fechos granados,
quando vio que estavan   todos encorajados,
mandó mover las gentes,   los sus pueblos dubdados,
e ir a la fazienda   a guisa d'esforçados.

1225	As soon as the sun has passed on from that point, it is at once endowed with all its force. People of ignorance appear bewildered; not knowing nature, they are filled with terror.
1226	You must consider this very point about the moon: when the sun wants to dip below the earth in the East the moon falls into line and cannot endure this, and thus does it come to lose its brilliant light.
1227	Then, as soon as the sun has passed beyond the mark, the moon returns at once to its full and normal colour; ignorant people think this a sign of evil and you have fallen into such terror as this.
1228	This is also wont to happen in a different way: when the sun comes low and dips below the shore, the shadow of the earth is cast between them, which can leave the moon briefly without light.
1229	I want to give you yet one more explanation so you will not fear that some harm may come. The sun belongs to the Greeks – I will tell you why –, the moon to the Barbarians, who live in the East.
1230	When the moon is in change, to give us a sign, it threatens that sorrow is coming to them; if the sun were disturbed, the fear should be ours, but in this case we must express our joy.
1231	The darkness shows the hardships already endured, inflicted by us, which have brought them anguish; the crimson that tomorrow will bring their defeat: they will lose much blood as we gain in honour."
1232	They were all delighted and the ill rumours ceased: Master Aristander was believed by them all; the passion of the people was stoked by this account, and great courage grew in them for what they had heard.
1233	King Alexander, the man of great feats, when he saw courage rising high in them all, ordered his men, his feared troops, to strike camp and, as valiant men, to march to the battle.

1234   Todos eran movidos, ivan señas arechas;
ivan hazes paradas a Dario a derechas;
queriénle ofreçer ofreçiones a pechas
que de lüengo tiempo ge las tenién privechas.

1235   La muger de Darïo, que yazié en prisión,
con cueita del marido e su generaçión,
quando aquesto vío creból' el coraçón;
sallól' luego el alma a poca de sazón.

1236   Pesól' a Alexandre e fizo muy grant planto;
por su madre misma non faría atanto;
alimpiával' apriessa la cara con el manto;
entardó la fazienda por aquexo ya quanto.

1237   Tan bien e tan apuesto sabié duelo fazer
que non podién los otros las lágremas tener;
plañién los varones de Greçia a poder;
non podrié en su tierra más honrada seer.

1238   Fue el cuerpo guardado de mucho buen convento;
fue luego balsamado de preçioso ungüento.
Fizo el rey sobr'ella tamaño complimiento
que duró quinze días el su soterramiento.

1239   Apelles el ebreo, un maestro contado,
que de lavor de manos non ovo tan ortado,
entalló el sepulcro en un mármol preçiado;
él se maravillava quando lo ovo obrado.

1240   Allí pintó las estorias quantas nunca cuntieron:
los ángeles del çielo de quál guisa cayeron;
los parientes primeros cómo se mal metieron,
por que sobre deviedo la mançana comieron.

1241   Estava más adelante Noel el patrïarca;
los montes de Armenia do arribó el arca;
Sem, Cam e Jafet, cadaun' en su comarca;
los gigantes confusos, la torre que es alta.

1242   Abraham el católico, Isac çerca él;
todos los doze tribos, fijos de Israel;
las plagas de Egibto e el ángel crüel;
el taü en las puertas de sagne del añel;

1234	They had all moved out and, with standards aloft and battle lines formed, marched straight for Darius, eager to offer him such payments and tributes as had been due to him for a long time.
1235	King Darius' wife, who lay in Alexander's prison, in her anxiety for her husband and children, when she saw these events, her heart burst and in but a little time her soul flew out.
1236	This grieved Alexander and he wept bitterly; for his own mother he would not have felt so much. He was quick to wipe his face clean with his cloak, but because of this the battle was delayed for a time.
1237	So fittingly and nobly did he express his grief; that his people were unable to hold back their tears: the knights of Greece wept with great emotion; in her own land she could not have been more honoured.
1238	Her body was watched over by many fine clerics and was embalmed at once with precious ointment; the King paid her such great respect and honour that her burial lasted a full fifteen days.
1239	Apelles the Hebrew, a renowned master craftsman, who was never rivalled for the skill of his hands, sculpted her tomb from a precious piece of marble, and he himself marvelled at his finished work.
1240	There he painted all the histories that ever took place: the angels from Heaven and in what way they fell; the first parents of men and how they met misfortune because they ate the apple forbidden to them.
1241	Further on could be seen Noah the patriarch, the hills of Armenia where the ark came to rest, and Shem, Ham and Japheth, each in his own land,* the confounded giants and the lofty tower;
1242	Abraham the Catholic and Isaac near him, and all the twelve tribes, the sons of Israel;* the plagues of Egypt and the cruel angel;* the Tau on the doors, in lamb's blood marked;

1243 las carreras del mar, la muerte de Farón;
cómo pidién los pueblos rëy a Aarón;
cómo prendié la ley Moïsés el varón;
cómo se consumién Datán e Abirón;

1244 de quál çevo bivieron por todo el desierto;
quál fue el tabernáculo, de quál guisa cubierto;
todo era notado tan bien e tan ençierto
que lo verié tod' ome com' en libro abierto.

1245 En la otra estoria, don Moïsés finado,
tenié en su lugar Josüé el ducado;
metiólos en la tierra e fue bien adonado;
es de Santa Iglesia oy en día plorado.

1246 Y eran los profetas, convento general,
todos tablas en manos, todos con su señal;
cada uno qué dixo o en quál temporal;
quisque en su escripto de dó era natural.

1247 David con su salterio, sus salmos acordando;
Salamón faz' el templo, justos judiçios dando;
Roboas en el regno metié çisma e vando;
en es' día fue su obra Apelles ençerrando.

1248 Las otras inçidençias de las gentes paganas,
como non son abténticas, yazién más orellanas.
Tant' eran las estorias muchas e adïanas
que sedién sobr' el túmulo las gentes paüsanas,

1249 Quando ovo Apelles lo que sopo labrado,
fue en quatro colupnas el sepulcro alçado;
fue con grandes obsequios el cuerpo condesado;
el seso de Apelles será siempre contado.

1250 Fue en esti comedio a Dario un castrado;
loco e dolorido levóli el mandado.
Dario, quando lo vío venir tan demudado,
entendió que avié algunt daño tomado.

1251 Mandóle que dixesse con qué nuevas andava,
ca sabié que el daño todo en él quebrava;
pero el mensajero dezir non lo osava
ca sabié que por ello albriçias non ganava.

1243	the paths through the sea, the death of the Pharaoh and how the peoples asked for Aaron as their king;* the handing of the Law to their leader Moses and how Dathan and Abiron were swallowed up;*
1244	the manna which they lived on all the way through the desert, the nature of the tabernacle and how it was covered; it was all depicted with such fidelity and skill, that every man could see it as in an open book.
1245	In the other history, Moses was now dead, and Joshua held the dukedom in his place; he led them to the Promised Land and received great gifts, and is mourned today by the Holy Church.
1246	The general assembly of the prophets was there, all with tablets in their hands and their own emblem, what each one said and the age in which he lived; and in the inscription was the native land of each.
1247	There is David with his psaltery and singing his psalms;* Solomon builds his temple, making just judgements; Rehoboam sets discord and faction on his kingdom. Apelles gradually brought his work to its end on that day.
1248	The other episodes of the pagan peoples, as they are not authentic, lay towards the edge. So many were the scenes, and of such quality, that the people were amazed at the tomb.
1249	When Apelles had depicted all that he knew, the tomb was raised up and set upon four columns and the body was laid in it with great ceremony; men will always tell of Apelles' great skill.
1250	Meanwhile, a eunuch made his way to see Darius; wild with grief, he brought him news of what had happened. Darius, when he saw him coming so disturbed, understood that he had suffered some misfortune.
1251	He commanded that he tell him the news that he brought, for he knew all the ill news was bursting to escape him, but the messenger did not dare tell him these things, knowing he would gain no reward for his service.

1252 Maguer, non gelo pudo en cabo encobrir,
la muerte de la reina óvola a dezir.
Dixo Dario: "Non quiso nemiga consentir;
bien se ovo por esso, non por al, a morir."

1253 Dixo el mensajero: "Señor, sepades verdat,
nol' fizo ningund ome ninguna crüeldat;
ant' le fizo el rëy tamaña pïedat
que tu non li fariés mayor umanidat.

1254 Endrona, mientras bivió, nunca fue sossañada;
nil' dixo nin le fizo cosa desaguisada;
de quanto ella quiso nunca fue denodada;
dentro en Babilonia non serié más honrada.

1255 Ploróla a la muerte tanto que maravella;
fizo grant complimiento e grant duelo sobr' ella;
fízole sepultura rica e mucho bella.
Señor, mala ment' pecas si d'él aves querella."

1256 De que entendió Dario la cosa cómo era
e fue el ome bueno entrado en carrera,
vertiendo de los ojos a medida plenera,
alçó a Dios las manos, oró en tal manera:

1257 "Señor, en cuya mano somos muertos e bivos,
que los sueltos cativas e sueltas los cativos
e los ricos aprimes e alças los mesquinos,
Tú non me desampares, que he fuertes vezinos.

1258 Mas si en Tu secresto assí es ordenado
que yo e mi natura perdamos el regnado,
Señor, merçed Te pido como desventurado,
¡otórgalo a ésti, que es rey acabado!"

1259 Clamó diez de sus prínçipes, honrados cavalleros;
embiólos al grant rëy, fízolos mensajeros:
que querié con él pazes, adobos verdaderos,
e darli por los presos almudes de dineros.

1260 Aquilas, de los otros mayor e más honrado,
de fermosa persona, de hedat bien mediado,
prospuso su razón ant' el rey aguisado;
mas recabdó muy poco quando ovo fablado.

1252	However, in the end he could not hide it from him: he had to tell Darius of the death of the Queen; he replied, "She wished that there be no further conflict; for that reason, and no other, it was her lot to die."
1253	The messenger said, "Lord, you must know the truth; no man committed any act of cruelty to her, but rather the King treated her with such compassion that even you would not have done her greater kindness.
1254	As long as she lived Stateira never suffered insult: he neither spoke nor did to her any improper thing and in all she desired she was never denied: in Babylonia she would not have been more honoured.
1255	He wept over her death with wondrous feeling; he paid her rich honour with a great display of grief; he had a tomb built for her, rich and very fine; my lord, your fault is grave if you have complaint of him."
1256	When Darius understood the state of affairs and the good man had gone on his way, with tears in his eyes and streaming down his face, he raised his hands to God and spoke thus in prayer:
1257	"Lord, in whose hands we find death or life, You who capture the free and free the captive, who cast down the wealthy and raise up the poor, do not abandon me, for my neighbours are strong.
1258	But if it is so ordained by Your judgement that I and my line should lose the kingship, my Lord, I beg Your mercy, in my ill fortune: grant it to this man, who is a king complete."
1259	He summoned ten of his princes, knights of honour, and sent them as messengers to the great king to say he sought peace and true concord with him, and offer him a vast sum of money for the captured.
1260	Achillas, the eldest and most honoured of them all, handsome in appearance and in life's middle years, set out his arguments before the wise king but won little reward when he had spoken.

1261 Dixo: "Rey Alexandre, señor de grant valía,
eres de grant ventura, el Crïador te guía;
si Dios puso en ti tan grant cavallería
devriés a los mejores conoçer mejoría.

1262 Dario quiere contigo sus pazes afirmar;
non lo faze por miedo, mas por su bien estar.
Él pide lo que tu devrías demandar,
por que a la reína quesiste tant' honrar.

1263 Quiere te dar su fija, e es buen casamiento;
deves de tal entrega tú aver pagamiento.
Dart'ha de su imperio çibdades más de çiento;
d'esto pornà contigo estable atenimiento.

1264 La madre e los fijos quiéretelos quitar;
quiere te de fino oro çient mil tallentos dar.
Mejor te es a ti los dineros tomar
que de gentes cativas embargado estar.

1265 Mucho nos has vençido con el tu cosimente
quando a la reína onrest' tan alta mente;
adebdado nos as a toda la su gente;
todos son tus pagados, segunt mi oçïente.

1266 Si por esso non fuesse, bien somos çerteros,
en el campo seriedes tu y tus cavalleros
e farié Buçifal los saltos ligeros;
iriemos refiriendo los pesares primeros.

1267 Si quisieres fer al, serás mal consejado,
ca es de fiera guisa Dario apoderado.
Tiene todo un mundo de gentes assemblado;
fert'ha prender el preçio que ovieste ganado."

1268 Quando ovo Aquilas su sermón acabado,
sacó el rey a fabla el su noble senado:
demandó que le diessen consejo aguisado,
quál respuesta darién contra aquel mandado.

1269 Calló toda la corte, todos los doze pares;
todos tenién silençio, como monjes claustrales;
non osavan ningunos dezir sus voluntades
por que los avié turrados sobre cosas atales.

1261	He said, "King Alexander, lord of great valour, you enjoy good fortune and the Creator guides you. If God endowed you so greatly with knightly virtue, you should recognise the qualities of the best of men.
1262	Darius wishes to confirm his peace with you; he acts not through fear, but through his goodness; he is requesting what you should yourself be seeking, because you were willing to pay such honour to the Queen.
1263	He wants to give you his daughter, a fine match indeed; you should be delighted that he makes you such an offer; he will give you of his empire a hundred cities and more, and so establish between you a firm understanding.
1264	He wants to ransom from you his mother and children and give you a hundred thousand talents of fine gold; it is better for you to accept the money offered than to have the concern of captive people.
1265	You have won much from us through your compassion, in honouring the Queen in so illustrious a fashion. You have placed the whole of his people in your debt and I believe that every one of them is grateful to you.
1266	If it were not for this – we can be in no doubt – you and your knights would be on the field of battle, Bucephalus would now be showing his speed and we would be repelling the first attacks.
1267	Should you not wish so to act, you will be ill advised, for Darius has an immense force at his command: he has brought together a whole world of troops and will make you pay the price for what you have won."
1268	When Achillas had finished what he had to say, the King invited his noble council to speak out; he asked them to give to him prudent advice and the response that they would give to that proposal.
1269	The whole court was quiet, among them all Twelve Peers: all were in silence, like monks in the cloister; no-one had the boldness to speak his opinion, for he had sharply rebuked them for such things.

1270 Fuert' cosa es e dura   consejar a señor,
ca, quando non se paga,   recude sin sabor;
demás, si por ventura   viene algunt error,
torna todo el riebto   sobr' el consejador.

1271 Recudióle Parmenio,   cuidó algo fablar,
mas nol' valdría menos   en silençio estar;
ca mejor abinié   en armas menear
que en dezir razones   nin en consejo dar.

1272 "Señor," dixo Parmenio,   "tan mucho te dubdamos
que lo que entendemos   dezir non lo osamos;
ca, quando non te pagas,   dasnos malos sossaños,
que quantos aquí veyes   por esso nos callamos.

1273 Pero, segunt mi seso   te quiero consejar:
con dueña mas de preçio   nunca podriés casar;
demás, en paz bien era   tan grant tierra ganar
que siempre non oviéssemos   en guerra a durar.

1274 De la razón segunda   te quiero motejar:
qui pazes te demanda   nos' treve guerrear;
si bien quisieres fer   tu deves gelas dar,
ca cae en tu preçio   e en tu bien estar.

1275 De las gentes cativas   que nos aquí traemos,
missión e grant embargo,   otro pro non avemos;
que muertos, que fuïdos,   nos pocos tenemos;
ante de poco tiempo   aún menos seremos.

1276 Andamos de mugeres   e de niños cargados;
los otros andan libres,   nos somos embargados;
creo que en esto   grant amor les buscamos,
si de tan embargosa   cosa los escusamos.

1277 Señor, si tú quisieres,   semejava razón
que diesses los cativos   por esta redempçión
e, como as de fer   sobra grant missïón,
avriás ayuda buena   pora tu quitaçión.

1278 Los que se nos murieron   e los que son fuïdos,
si fuessen de tal guisa   por aver remedidos,
non los avriemos todos   tan en balde perdidos;
ende, tenemos todos   que somos deçebidos.

1270	It is a hard and tricky business to advise a lord, for, when he disapproves, he replies with irritation; and besides, if by chance an error is made all the criticism will fall back on the adviser.
1271	Parmenion answered him and made to speak; but silence would have served him at least as well, for he was more skilled in the use of arms than in making speeches or giving counsel.
1272	"My lord," said Parmenion, "such is our awe of you that we dare not express the thoughts that we have; for when you are dissatisfied you speak so harshly that all of us you see here remain in silence.
1273	But from my own judgement I want to give you counsel: you could not make a marriage to a more worthy lady; besides, we would do well to win such great land while at peace, so that we might not have to remain at war for ever.
1274	I wish also to tell you of the second of my reasons: a man who seeks peace with you dares not make war; if you wish to act rightly, then grant it him you must, for it adds to your glory and to your good standing.
1275	From those captive people that we are bringing here, we gain labour, a great burden, but no advantage; our losses are not few, to death or to flight, and in a short time we shall be fewer still.
1276	We are heavily laden with women and children; our enemies move freely but we are encumbered; I believe that in this we deserve great affection since we free them of such a weighty burden.
1277	Lord, if you so wish, it seems to be right to hand over the captives for this ransom; and, as the labour they bring you is excessive, you would gain great benefit in setting them free.
1278	Those we lost to death and those who have fled, if they had thus been exchanged for wealth our loss of them all would not have been so vain, for in this we all think ourselves ill served.

1279   Señor, el mi consejo   todo lo as oído;
           sepas que te consejo   de coraçón complido;
           si a ti al semeja,   ca as mejor sentido,
           presto so de seguirte   calçado e vestido."

1280   El consejo del conde   non fue bien escuchado.
           Sossañólo el rëy,   óvoli poco grado.
           Díxol' "Tal como vos   sería yo tornado
           si en esse consejo   m'oviesse yo fallado.

1281   Grant honra me acreçe   en tal dona tomar,
           la que ante quisieron   con Maçeos casar.
           Varón que tal consejo   sabe a señor dar
           devrié aver vergüença   ante otros fablar.

1282   La tierra que me manda   yo me la he ganada
           con todos vos a una,   con derecha espada.
           Ant' le costarié mucho   que la ovies' ganada;
           de quanto me promete,   él non tiene nada.

1283   Demás, si por su mano   tomasse nin migaja,
           suyo serié el preçio   e tod' la avantaja;
           serién todas mis nuevas   caídas en la paja,
           por do vuestro consejo   non valdrié una meaja.

1284   Si todo su imperio   me quisiesse dexar,
           yo non gelo querría   de tal guisa tomar;
           ca, como en Dios fío,   a todo su pesar,
           a mejor nuestro preçio   lo podremos ganar.

1285   El fijo e las fijas   e la madre de Dario,
           en darlos por dineros   seméjame escarnio;
           ca non so mercadero   nin so de tal salario;
           rëy so por natura,   de los de grant donario.

1286   Nobleza nunca quiso   entender en mercado,
           non ha ninguna graçia   sobre pleito tajado;
           plus gent' nos pareçrá   en dárgelas en grado,
           ca non seré mas rico   por aver monedado."

1287   Mandó los mensajeros   ante sí venir;
           dioles de su aver,   mandóles bien vestir.
           "Entendet", diz, "amigos,   qué vos quiero dezir:
           a lo que me dixestes   vos quiero recodir.

1279	My lord, you have heard all the advice I have to give; you must know that I give you my counsel sincerely; but if you choose otherwise, as you have greater wisdom, I am ready to follow you in heart and soul."
1280	The count's advice did not meet a warm response; the King spoke sharply, and held him with displeasure: he said to him, "Just like you, I would have given in had I found that I, too, held such an opinion.
1281	I gain great honour from accepting such a wife, the lady they once tried to marry to Mazaeus: a man capable of giving such advice to his lord should be ashamed to speak in the presence of others.
1282	The land that he offers me I have already won, with all of you together and a sword that strikes true; it would cost him dearly to win it back from me; he is the owner of none of what he promises.
1283	Besides, if from his hand I were to take a single crumb his would be the honour and all of the gain; all of my fame would be fallen into nothing: for this reason your advice is not worth a halfpenny.
1284	If he were willing to give over all his empire to me, I would not want to take it from him in that way, for, as I trust in God, to Darius' great regret, we shall be able to win it to our greater renown.
1285	The son and the daughters and the mother of Darius – to give them up for money seems to me humiliation: for I am no merchant and make no profit in that way; I am a king by my line and one of great distinction.
1286	Nobility never sought a part in commerce, nor takes any pleasure when a deal is done. The hostages' free return will win us more support, for I shall never gain riches by accepting payment."
1287	He summoned the messengers to appear before him making gifts of money and commanding they dress well. "Listen," he said, "my friends, to what I wish to tell you; I wish to make response to what you said to me.

1288   Si yo a la reína   fiz' alguna onor,
        non lo fiz' por su miedo   nin por el su amor;
        por complir tales cosas   téngome por debdor;
        si esto non fiziesse,   faría grant error.

1289   De lo qu'él me promete   yo non gelo gradesco;
        él me quiere premir,   yo cada día cresco;
        cotiano se me faze   el coraçón tan fresco;
        aún él non entiende   con quál ançuelo pesco.

1290   Quant' que Dario me manda,   yo téngolo por mío;
        qui me non obedeçe   téngolo por sendío.
        Mas, si Dios lo quisiere,   como en Él fío,
        yo le faré levar   el gato d'aquí al río.

1291   Todas sus crïazones   que yazen en prisión,
        embïarlas quïero   sin aver end' perdón;
        del mi aver non quiero   prender redempçïón;
        tornad vos por a Dario   con tal responsïón."

1292   Dario en est' comedio   aguisava su cosa;
        tenié plegada hueste   grant e maravillosa;
        mas su aventura   estava çegajosa
        ca s'iva açercando   la ora peligrosa.

1293   Andava esforçado   que quiere quel' viniesse;
        nol' pesarié la muerte   sólo que bien muriesse;
        buena le fuera la muerte   si Dios le reçibiesse
        ante que tan grant cuita   nin tan grant mal le viniesse.

1294   El rëy Alexandre,   de la otra partida,
        la su bella mesnada   teniéla bien bastida;
        de cueres e de armas   estava bien guarnida;
        serié por nula fuerça   a duro desordida.

1295   Mandó luego mover   e ir a las feridas,
        mandó taner las trompas   e ferir las bozinas.
        De sí mismos las gentes   eran tan ençendidas
        que serién de su grado   mucho ante movidas.

1296   Las huestes de los griegos,   con sabor de lidiar,
        como avién grant feuza   que avién de rancar,
        non fincaron las tiendas   nin quisieron posar,
        fasta çerca los otros   ovieron a plegar.

1288	If I have paid any kind of honour to the Queen,
	I did so not fearing or with feelings for her;
	I believe I have a debt to fulfil such obligations
	and if I did not do this I would be gravely in error.
1289	For the promise that he makes me, I feel no gratitude;
	he wants to put me down but each day I grow taller;
	with every day that passes, my heart grows so much stronger,
	but he does not yet understand the hook I use to fish.
1290	All that Darius offers me I hold as mine already;
	whoever gives me not obeisance I hold to be a fool;
	but, if God should will it, as I trust in Him,
	I shall make him take this kitten to the river.*
1291	All the members of his household who lie in prison
	I wish to send to him with no payment in return;
	I do not wish to receive recompense for what is mine:
	go back to Darius and take him this as my reply."
1292	Darius, meanwhile, was making his preparations:
	the force he had assembled was huge, it was a marvel;
	but his fortune was one that brings tears to the eyes,
	for the hour of danger was slowly drawing near.
1293	He strutted in confidence, whatever might befall him,
	death would be no burden, if only he died well;
	death he would welcome, were God to receive him,
	before such great misfortune or sorrow came upon him.
1294	But King Alexander, on the other side,
	had his own fine army well equipped for battle,
	men with hearts steeled and a rich supply of arms;
	any other force would find it hard to rout them.
1295	He told them to move out at once and go to strike the blows,
	commanding that the horns and the clarions cry out;
	the hearts of Alexander's men burned with such fire
	that their pleasure would have been to move off long before.
1296	The armies of the Greeks, in their desire for battle,
	and unshakeable belief that they were to conquer,
	did not pitch their tents and were unwilling to delay
	until the forces of Persia drew near to them.

1297 Ya se veyén a ojo   ambos los emperantes;
bien se conoçién ambos,   que se vïeran antes.
Más traía entonçe   Dario de elefantes
que él la vez primera   non trayé cavalgantes.

1298 Los pueblos de los griegos,   com' eran encarnados,
aún que por natura   eran muy esforçados,
por ir luego ferir los   eran muy denodados;
mas fizo los el rëy   seer müy quedados.

1299 Más era de medio día,   el sol querié entrar;
non era aguisado   d'en fazienda entrar,
ca prender los ia la noche,   fer los ia derramar;
aún que los rancassen,   non podrián encalçar.

1300 Fazién de cada parte   sobejanos roídos
de cuernos e de trompas   e de alaridos;
semejavan los montes   e los çielos movidos
e que los elementos   eran desabenidos.

1301 El sol cumplió su curso,   ya era en el mar;
revolviénse los omes,   pensavan de çenar;
querién a los cavallos   la çevada echar,
ca avién de mañana   en la lit a entrar.

1302 Alexandre el claro,   luego el sol entrado,
çercó todas las huestes   con el su buen cavallo;
mandó que velassen   cada uno por su cabo,
ca dend' a otro día   serié todo librado.

1303 Tornó para su lecho   de que ovo andado;
non serié tan fuert' ome   que non fuesse cansado;
querié dormir un poco,   por seer más temprado,
mas non lo podié fer,   ca era pressurado.

1304 Tenié de pensamiento   el coraçón çercado;
non fallava en él   el sueño nul forado;
non pegava los ojos,   atant' era embargado;
com' ome que non duerme,   yazié fuert' quebrantado.

1305 Yazió de tal manera   d'aquí a gallos cantados;
fueli dona Vitoria   tollendo los cuidados;
aquedaron los miembros   que yazién muy cansados;
fueron de muy buen sueño   los ojos megeados.

1297	Now the emperors could both look each other in the eye: they knew each other well – this was not their first encounter –; but this time Darius was bringing more elephants than he had brought horsemen at the first time of asking.
1298	The Greek troops, among whom the fury was rising, as well as being men of great courage by nature, were eager to go out and strike them at once, but the King commanded that they remain still.
1299	Midday was now passed, and the sun began to set – this was not a prudent time to enter into battle: they would be overtaken and scattered by the night and, even with victory, could not pursue their foes.
1300	From every direction there rose tremendous roars, from horns and clarions and the cries of men; it seemed that the hills and the heavens had been moved and that discord reigned over the elements themselves.
1301	The sun had run its course and come to meet the sea; the men made their way back and set about their meal; they were eager to provide their horses with fodder, for the next day they were to enter into battle.
1302	The renowned Alexander, right after the sunset, rode around all his armies on his fine horse, commanding that each man remain on the alert since the very next day it would all be at an end.
1303	Once he had ridden round them he turned for his bed: there could never be a man so strong he did not tire; he sought to sleep a little, so as to feel more rested, but he could not do so, so great was his impatience.
1304	His mind was besieged by the thoughts that beset him and sleep could find no opening in these through which to pass; so anxious was he, he could not even close his eyes, and, like any man who does not sleep, he grew unsettled.
1305	He lay there in this way until the cocks had crowed, when Lady Victory gradually took away his cares and his exhausted limbs now began to feel at rest; he felt his eyes be soothed by a very deep sleep.

1306   Ya querié ser ora   de maitines tañer,
       la estrella del çielo   quería pareçer;
       querié un día malo   e negro amaneçer
       en que mucha de sangre   se avié a verter.

1307   Assaz querié el sol,   si pudiesse, tardar,
       por amor que pudiesse   tan grant mal destorvar;
       mas la obedïençia   non pudo traspassar,
       flaco e desmaído,   començó de assomar.

1308   Dario el emperante,   como aviá estado
       de la primera junta   muy mal escarmentado;
       ante del sol sallido   fue en armas entrado;
       por ferir en los griegos   estava aguisado.

1309   Avié toda la noche   redor la huest' velado,
       que, si le diessen salto,   non fuesse engañado;
       todo lo barruntava   lo que avrié estado
       si al conde Parmenio   oviessen escuchado.

1310   El rëy Alexandre,   un ome tan dubdado,
       oviera ante noche   con sus duques fablado;
       del pleito de la batalla   les avié preguntado,
       cómo irién a ella   que pusiessen recabdo.

1311   Como de otras vezes   eran escarmentados,
       non recudió ninguno,   estudieron quedados;
       pero a grant ora,   bien tres ratos passados,
       respondióli Parmenio   biervos bien assentados.

1312   "Rëy, por mi ventura,   assí so adonado,
       por bien que te consejo   nunca so escuchado;
       so, en cabo de cosa,   de ti mal sossañado,
       pero quiérote dezir   lo que teniá asmado.

1313   Son las huestes de Dario   grandes a desmesura;
       temiendo la primera,   passaron a anchura,
       ca engañóles ante   mucho el angostura;
       traen en su fazienda   recabdo e cordura.

1314   Çiento son para uno,   çercar non los podriemos;
       aún que non tornassen,   matando cansaremos;
       com' están perçebidos,   non los descosiremos.
       En lo que nos cuidamos,   a duro aberniemos.

| 1306 | Now the hour of Matins was beginning to draw near;
in the sky the morning star was about to appear;
a day black and grim was coming to its dawn,
in which the blood of many would come to be shed. |

| 1307 | The very sun wanted to delay, had it been able,
in its desire to turn aside misfortune so great,
but it could not transgress its duty of obeisance,
and it began to show itself, thin and watery. |

| 1308 | The Emperor Darius, as he had already learned
the cruellest of lessons from their first encounter,
before the sun had risen had already donned his armour
and made his preparations to do battle with the Greeks. |

| 1309 | All night long his army had remained there on the watch,
so that, if they were attacked, it would not take them unawares;
he imagined everything that would have come to pass,
if they had taken heed of Count Parmenion. |

| 1310 | King Alexander, a man who inspired such fear,
had spoken with his commanders on the night before:
he had asked them questions about the plan for the battle
and told them to be careful in their approach to it. |

| 1311 | As they had learned their lesson from other occasions,
no-one spoke in answer, but they all remained in silence;
but in a pregnant moment, as the minutes passed by,
Parmenion replied to him with well thought-out words: |

| 1312 | "My King, by my fortune, the lot granted me was such
that though I give you good counsel, my words are never heeded;
when all is said and done, I incur your great displeasure;
nonetheless, I wish to tell you what has occurred to me. |

| 1313 | Darius' armies are of immeasurable numbers;
mindful of their first defeat, they spread their forces wide,
for then the confined space greatly caught them out;
now they bring prudence and wisdom to their tactics. |

| 1314 | They are a hundred to our one, we could not surround them;
even if they did not flee, we would tire ourselves with killing;
as they are well organised, we shall not break their forces;
we would find it difficult to achieve our aim. |

1315 Demás, vienen y gentes   que han fiera grandez';
      caras han como canes,   negros como la pez;
      que con la valentía   que con la legirez',
      espantarán a muchos;   esto será rafez.

1316 La otra: como saben,   si fueren arrancados,
      non les han a prestar   yermos nin poblados;
      más querrán en el campo   seer descabeçados
      que de gentes estrañas   seer tan ahontados.

1317 Mas, diría un seso,   si a todos plaçiesse,
      de dar salto en ellos   luego qu'anocheçiesse;
      serién desbaratados,   cad'un' por do soviesse;
      tomarién a fuïr   cad' un' por do pudiesse.

1318 Vienen de muchas tierras   e de muchos rincones;
      non han unas costumbres   nin han unos sermones;
      non podrán entender   entre sí las razones;
      caerán como puercos,   todos a bolodrones.

1319 Non avrán acüerdo   nin nul cabdellamiento;
      uno solo de nos   sagudirá más de çiento;
      faremos nuestra cosa,   segunt nuestro talento,
      por seso vos lo digo,   sabe Dios que non miento."

1320 El dicho de Parmenio   plogo mucho al senado:
      todos tovieron qu'era   consejo aguisado.
      Mas el rey Alexandre   non gelo tovo en grado;
      demostrógelo luego   que non fue su pagado.

1321 Dixo: "Non me semeja   d'esta tal razón,
      ca esti tal engaño   maña es de ladrón
      o de ome covarde   que es sin coraçón;
      aún semeja fascas   maña de traïçión.

1322 Tan poco lo querría   de tal guisa vençer
      quanto ser vençido   o grant onta prender;
      de la mi covardía   avrién que retraer,
      podría en mi preçio   grant menoscabo fer.

1323 Nunca por a rey fue   engaño nin çelada;
      fazienda de tal guisa   nunca fue bien rancada;
      meterl'ie por escusa   Dario e su mesnada.
      ¡Henos nuestra victoria   luego menoscabada!

1315	Moreover, in their midst come men of fearsome size, who have faces like dogs and are as black as pitch; men who, through their valour and through their agility, will strike terror into many, which can easily happen.
1316	And further, as they know that, should they be defeated, no land will be of worth to them, peopled or deserted, they will prefer to die, their heads hewn off, on battle's field, than be so put to shame by men from foreign lands.
1317	But I would propose a plan, if it were pleasing to all, to launch an attack on them as soon as night fell: they would be defeated, each caught wherever he stood, and they would take to flight, each in whatever way he could.
1318	They come from many lands and from many distant parts; they do not have common customs nor share a common tongue; they will be unable to understand each other's words and they will all be slaughtered as pigs would be, in droves.
1319	They will have no accord, nor obey the same command: one of us will account for over a hundred of them; we shall carry out our plan just as we ourselves desire; I tell you this scheme is wise; God knows I do not lie."
1320	What Parmenion said gave great pleasure to the council and all considered that it was indeed sound advice, yet King Alexander did not give it his approval and promptly made it clear that this was not his pleasure.
1321	He said, "I do not believe that what you say is right, for deception such as this is the trick of a thief or a cowardly man who is without courage, and this trick even seems one of treachery.
1322	Just as little would I wish to defeat him thus as I would to suffer defeat or great dishonour; people would come to tell tales of my cowardice, and it might cause my reputation great harm.
1323	Using tricks and traps was never worthy of a king and a battle in this way was never fairly won. Darius and his army could use it as an excuse; glory will be taken from our victory at once!

1324 Demás, es otra cosa: están muy perçebidos;
todos andan escudos e lorigas vestidos;
adieso que moviéssemos, seriemos entendidos;
férsenos ian lenguados maguer serían mudos.

1325 Mas cras al día claro ¡vayamos por a ellos!
El que manos oviere, allí gelas veremos.
Cada uno qual fuere, allí gelo entendremos;
iremos sin retrecha, que sé que rancaremos."

1326 Dario, si por tod' esto oviesse a passar,
mas perçebida mente nunca podrié estar;
non lo podrié nul ome de esfuerço rebtar,
mas la mala ventura non la podié redrar.

1327 El sol era sallido, el pueblo levantado;
el rëy Alexandre aún durmié quedado;
del velar de la noche era mal quebrantado;
aún durmiera más si l'oviessen dexado.

1328 Maguer veyén que era ora de despertar,
non osava ninguno a la tienda entrar.
Consejóles Parmenio que fuessen a almorçar;
después serién más prestos pora en armas entrar.

1329 Sopearon aína, fueron luego tornados;
ante de media ora fueron todos armados;
esperavan al rëy; estavan aquexados;
por que tanto durmié estavan embargados.

1330 Ya eran los de Dario, hazes puestas, movidos;
eran de las tïendas grant migero ixidos.
Metién bozes e gritos, fazién grandes roídos;
non osavan sallir, seyén mal apremidos.

1331 Sin mandado del rëy temién de cavalgar;
despertar non l'osavan nin a él aplegar;
estavan en grant dubdo, non sabién dó tornar;
temién algunos d'ellos que los querrié provar.

1332 En tod' esto, Parmenio ovo a demudar;
entró por a la tienda, óvol' a despertar;
"Señor," diz', "es grant día; terçia quiere passar;
ya quieren los de Dario a las tiendas llegar.

1324	There is one thing more: they are very well prepared and all carry shields and wear their coats of mail; as soon as we moved, they would be aware of us; mute though they would be, our men would gain tongues.
1325	But at the break of day tomorrow, let us attack them; any man who has hands, we shall clearly see them there, and there we shall learn what each man is truly like, and not waver in attacking, for I know we shall win."
1326	Had Darius been forced to endure all this, he could never have been more prudently prepared, and no man could accuse him of lacking in courage; yet he could not repel the ill fortune that assailed him.
1327	The sun had risen and the troops had stirred, but King Alexander still lay in peaceful slumber, set in deep discomfort by his sleepless night; he would have slept still longer had they left him.
1328	Although they could see that it was time to wake, there was no man who dared to go into the tent; Parmenion advised them to go to take their meal, for after that they would be readier for battle.
1329	They took repast quickly and came back at once; within half an hour they were all fully armed. They waited for the King, and they were uneasy, and troubled that he was sleeping for so long.
1330	Darius' troops had now moved out, his battle lines drawn up, and had moved a good mile away from their camp; the Greeks uttered shouts and cries, letting out fierce roars, but they dared not attack, though they were hard to restrain.
1331	Without the King's order, they were afraid to ride out, but they dared not wake him, or even approach him; in their great confusion, they knew not which way to turn, and some feared that he wanted to put them to the test.
1332	Amidst all this, it fell to Parmenion to act: he went into the tent and managed to rouse the King. "It is broad daylight, lord," he said; "the hour of Terce draws near;* Darius' troops are now eager to attack our tents.

1333 Non es sazón nin ora   de tan mucho dormir;
¡piensa de cavalgar   e mándalos ferir!
Tienen que non osamos   contra ellos sallir.
Señor, lo que he fecho   deves melo parçir."

1334 Sonriyós'le el rëy,   tornóle a dezir:
"Sepas verdat, Parmenio,   non te devo mentir:
fasta çerca del día   yo non pude dormir,
por ende non podía   tan rafez recodir.

1335 Demás, non veo cosa   por que nos acuitemos,
quando al rëy Dario   tan çerca lo tenemos;
que, maguer fuïr quiera,   nos non lo dexaremos;
lo que ante perdimos   aquí lo cobraremos.

1336 Ante era la ora   de mucho nos quexar;
quand' andava alçado,   non lo pudiemos fallar.
Mas, en nombre de Dios,   pensat de cavalgar;
¡Vayamos los ferir!   ¡Non les demos vagar!"

1337 Fueron puestas las hazes   como en la primera:
costaneras espessas   e çaga cabdallera.
Mas era por a tanto   mejor la delantera.
por que iva el rëy   Alexandre en ella.

1338 El mes era de mayo,   quando sallen las flores,
quandos' vistién los campos   de diversas colores;
juntarons' en el campo   los dos emperadores;
nunca se ajuntaron   tales dos nin mejores.

1339 Danïel, el profeta,   niño de Dios amado,
dentro en Babilonia   l'ovo profetizado:
que vernié en la sierra   un cabrón mal domado;
quebrantarié los cuernos   al carnero doblado.

1340 Ésti fue Alexandre   de los fechos granados;
Dario fue el carnero   de los regnos doblados,
que Persïa e Media,   tan buenos dos regnados,
ambos él los mandava,   mas fueron quebrantados.

1341 Quando vio Alexandre   tal fazaña de gentes,
começó con cuer malo   de amolar los dientes.
Dixo a sus varones: "Amigos e parientes,
quiérovos dezir nuevas,   meted en ello mientes.

1333	This is not the moment or the hour to sleep so long;
	prepare to ride out and command them to attack;
	they believe that we do not dare move out against them.
	My lord, you must forgive me for what I have done."
1334	The King gave him a smile, and turned to speak to him:
	"You should know the truth, Parmenion; I must not lie to you.
	Until just before daybreak, I was not able to sleep
	and so I found it difficult to regain my senses.
1335	Besides, I see no reason why we should be uneasy
	when we have King Darius so close at hand;
	for, even if he wished to flee, we shall not allow it;
	what we lost the last time, here we shall regain.
1336	The time for us to feel great regret was earlier,
	when he went in flight and we could not track him down,
	but in the name of God, think now of riding out:
	let us go and strike them and give them no respite!"
1337	The battle lines were drawn up as in the first encounter
	with reinforced flanks and a strong force at the rear,
	but the vanguard was most powerful of all
	for King Alexander formed a part of it.
1338	It was the month of May when flowers bloom,*
	when they clothed the fields in varied hues;
	the two emperors met on the field of battle:
	never did two such fine men come together.
1339	Daniel the prophet, the beloved child of God,
	had made the prophecy in the land of Babylonia,*
	that an untamed goat would come to the mountains
	which would shatter the twin horns of the ram.
1340	This was Alexander, the man of great deeds;
	Darius was the ram, with his twin kingdoms,
	for Persia and Media, two very fine dominions,
	were both beneath his rule – but they were shattered.
1341	When Alexander saw such a force of soldiers,
	he began to grind his teeth and his heart grew black;
	he spoke to his knights: "My friends and kinsmen,
	I want to tell you something – pay heed to my words!

1342	Assaz avedes fechas faziendas muy granadas;
	ya son por tod' el mundo vuestras nuevas sonadas;
	son todas sobre nos las tierras acordadas,
	onde es menester que traigamos las espadas.

1343	Agora nos devemos por varones preçiar,
	quand' con todo el mundo avemos a lidiar;
	nos pocos, ellos muchos, podremos nos honrar;
	avrán *per cuncta secula* de nos que fablar.

1344	Traen grandes riquezas, tesoros sobejanos;
	todos andan por nuestros, ¡si oviéremos manos!
	Non vos y quiero parte, amigos e hermanos;
	nunca avrán pobreza los que salieren sanos."

1345	Quand' ovo Alexandre la razón acabada,
	por ferirse con Dario avié cara tornada;
	vínole un barrunte de l'otra encontrada;
	fízolo perçebir d'una fuerte çelada.

1346	Díxol' que avié Dario las carreras sembradas
	de clavos de tres dientes, las puntas azeradas,
	por matar los cavallos, dañar las peonadas;
	si non metiessen mientes avrién malas passadas.

1347	Díxoli otra cosa: que en la delantera
	aduzié çient mill carros de espessa madera
	que corrién por engeño más que rueda trapera;
	todos eran tajantes como foz podadera.

1348	Quando sopo el rëy toda la antipara,
	mandó prender a diestro la su mesnada clara;
	guïólos él mismo por medio una xara;
	quando cató Dario, parósele de cara.

1349	Sepades non les quiso lüengo plazo dar;
	endereçó la lança, ovo a derranchar;
	a poder de cavallo fuelos a vesitar;
	tan mal por al primero que pudiesse fallar.

1350	El prínçip' Aristómones en India fue crïado;
	quando lo vio venir tan fuert' e tan irado,
	sallól' a la carrera firme e denodado;
	colpól' en el escudo, fízoli grant forado.

1342	Numerous are the great battles you have fought and your reputation has rung out through all the world; people of all lands are united against us, and so it is necessary for us to wield our swords.
1343	Now we must indeed value ourselves as men when it is the whole world with whom we have to fight; we are few, they are many and we can gain great honour: they will have great tales to tell of us throughout the ages.
1344	They are bringing with them great wealth and vast treasures and all will be ours if we have hands to take them; I want no share in this, my friends and brothers; those who emerge alive will never see poverty."
1345	When King Alexander had finished his speech, he looked towards Darius, in desire for battle; there came to him a spy from his enemy's side, to inform him that a dangerous trap had been laid.
1346	He told him that Darius had sown the pathways with three-toothed nails bearing points of steel to kill the horses and injure the foot soldiers; were they not careful, their passage would be cruel.
1347	He said one thing more: that among the vanguard he had placed a hundred thousand carts of thick wood with deceptive speed quicker than a fulling-wheel, and all as sharp-cutting as a harvesting scythe.
1348	When Alexander found out all about the trick, he ordered his illustrious army to veer right, guiding them himself across an area of rockrose, and when Darius realised, Alexander was upon him.*
1349	I can tell you he was willing to allow him no truce; he held his lance steady and moved to attack; he went to meet his foes with his horse at full gallop; so much the worse for the first man he encountered.
1350	Prince Aristomenes, who was raised in India, when he saw him coming, so great in strength and anger, went to meet him on his path, resolute and bold: he struck him on his shield, and left a deep hole.

1351   Fiziera la loriga   maestro natural;
           era de fin' azero,   blanca com' un cristal;
           com' avié buen señor,   ella fue muy leal;
           defendióli el cuerpo   que non prisiesse mal.

1352   Com' era Aristómones   por natura gigante,
           venía cavallero   sobr' un grant elifante,
           çercado de castillos   de cuesta e delante;
           nunca ome non vio   tan fiero abramante.

1353   Súpoli bien el otro   el pleito destajar:
           quando vio que al cuerpo   non li podié llegar,
           firió al elefante   por el diestro ijar;
           óvol' al otro cabo   la lança a echar.

1354   Como era la bestia   mortal mente ferida,
           fue luego man' a mano   en tierra abatida;
           cayo el filesteo   con toda su bastida;
           semejava que era   una sierra movida.

1355   Quando vio Alexandre   que era trastornado,
           perdonar non li quiso,   e fue bien acordado.
           Dio de mano a la sierpe   que trayé al costado,
           cortóle la cabeça   ant' que fues' levantado.

1356   Orcánides, un rëy   – en Egibto naçiera –
           otro, un peón fiero,   que de Siria viniera,
           dieron ad Alexandre   una priessa tan fiera;
           maguer que muchas fizo   en tal nunca se viera.

1357   Pero, en cab' de cosa,   que vos mucho digamos,
           ayudól' su ventura,   matólos a entrambos;
           y fizo Alexandre   colpes tan señalados,
           mientre omes oviere   siempre serán contados.

1358   Ya andavan las hazes   todas entre mescladas;
           bolavan las saetas,   retinién las espadas;
           las plaças de cabeças   todas eran cuajadas;
           andavan muchos cavallos   con las riendas cortadas.

1359   Los de parte de Dario,   com' eran castigados,
           por dar en Alexandre   andavan acordados;
           mas, como eran todos   firmes e denodados,
           nol' podién coñosçer   entre los sus crïados.

| 1351 | His armour had been made by a skilled master craftsman,
and was of fine steel and as white as crystal;
as it had so fine a lord, it was a loyal guard,
and it kept his body safe from any harm. |
|---|---|
| 1352 | As Aristomenes was a giant by nature,
this knight was mounted on an enormous elephant,
enclosed by towers to the rear and to the fore;
no man ever saw so formidable a titan. |
| 1353 | Alexander knew well how to solve his problem:
when he saw he was unable to reach his body,
he wounded the elephant in its right flank,
and managed to thrust his lance through its other side. |
| 1354 | As the beast had suffered a mortal wound,
it was immediately brought to the ground,
and the Philistine fell with all his towers;*
it was as if a mountain range had moved. |
| 1355 | When Alexander saw he had been thrown down,
he did not wish to let him escape and rightly so;
he let loose the serpent that he carried at his side
and severed his head before he was able to rise. |
| 1356 | Orcanus' son, a king who had been born in Egypt,
and another, a fierce foot soldier, hailing from Syria,
engaged Alexander in a most ferocious fight;
though he had had many, there was never one like this. |
| 1357 | But at the end of it all, however much we tell you,
fortune served him well: he brought death to both men;
in that fight Alexander struck such memorable blows
that they will be forever told of, as long as men live. |
| 1358 | The armies were now altogether mixed in battle,
arrows were flying as the clash of swords rang out;
severed heads lay everywhere, strewn over the ground,
and many horses galloped with sundered reins. |
| 1359 | Those on Darius' side, as they had been instructed,
together sought to make an attack on Alexander;
yet as all his troops were determined and courageous,
they could not pick him out from among his vassals. |

1360 Tan afirmes lidiavan   todos, fijos e padres,
      que semejavan todos   que eran Alexandres:
      sabet, non semejavan   fijos de sendas madres;
      todos se demostravan   por leales cofadres.

1361 Oviéronlo en cabo,   pero, a coñoscer
      en los colpes que dava   a sobra grant poder;
      oviéronse sobr' él   mas de mill a verter;
      valiera seles más   en sus tiendas seer.

1362 Ya lo tenién en cuita,   en una grant pressura;
      querriénle fer sin grado   pechar la moledura;
      mas al que el prendié,   por su mala ventura,
      nunca otra vegada   le fazié travessura.

1363 Acorrióli Filotas,   un su leal braçero,
      por'en tales faziendas   un estraño bozero;
      abatió a Enos   con otro cavallero;
      fueron desbaratados   en poco de migero.

1364 De la parte de Dario,   entr' essa gente tanta,
      avié un filesteo   – el escripto lo canta –
      fijo de padre negro   e de una giganta;
      bien avié treinta cobdos   del pie a la garganta.

1365 Traíe una porra   de cobre enclavada;
      avié muerto con ella   mucha barva honrada;
      que al que él podié   colpar una vegada
      non li valié capillo   nin almofre nada.

1366 Vinié endïablado,   com' era estrevudo,
      por dar ad Alexandre   grant colp' en el escudo;
      mas estido el rëy   firme e perçebudo;
      el otro lo que quiso   acabar non lo pudo.

1367 Ant' que a él plegasse,   como era sobervio,
      compeçó a dezir   mucho de mal proverbio.
      Dixo: "Don Alexandre,   non sodes tan estrevio
      que non quitedes öy   a Dario el emperio.

1368 Pero por de ventura   vos devedes tener
      que tan honrada muerte   avedes a prender;
      morredes de tal mano   que vos debe plazer,
      ca non so de los moços   que soledes vençer.

1360	They all fought with such resolve, both sons and fathers, that each one of them seemed to be an Alexander; I tell you they did not seem sons of different mothers and they all proved themselves to be loyal brothers.
1361	But, at last, they were able to recognise him by the blows he struck with his immense force; over a thousand men launched themselves upon him but they would have done better to stay in their tents.
1362	They had him in a difficult and dangerous position and wished to make him pay his dues, against his will, but whoever he encountered, to their misfortune, would never again attempt harm towards him.
1363	Philotas, his loyal warrior, went to his aid, an outstanding advocate in such disputes: he struck down Enos and another knight, overcoming them in but a short time.
1364	On Darius' side, amidst that force so great, there was a Philistine – the text tells of him –, son of a black father and a giant mother; he measured a full thirty cubits, foot to throat.*
1365	He carried a club inset with copper nails, and with it he had killed many men of honour, since for any man that he could strike just once, neither helmet nor mail-cap would be of any worth.
1366	He came, the Devil's force in him, for he was a bold man, to deal Alexander a heavy blow on his shield; but the King stood waiting both firm and alert and his opponent was unable to achieve what he sought.
1367	Before reaching him, as he was an arrogant man, he began to insult him with many base words and said to him: "Alexander, you are not so daring that today you will be able to seize Darius' empire.
1368	But you must hold yourself a man of good fortune, that you are to die such an honourable death: you will die by such a hand that it must give you pleasure, for I am no young boy such as you usually defeat.

1369   Yo soy de los guerreros   que la torre fizieron,
       que con los dios del çielo   guerra mantovieron;
       vuestros grieves pecados   mala çaga vos dieron
       quando en la frontera   de Geón vos pusieron."

1370   Entendió Alexandre   que fablava follía
       e dizié vanedat   e non cavallería.
       Dixo entre su cuer: "Crïador, Tú me guía;
       devié a Ti pesar   esta sobrançería."

1371   Aventó un venablo   que tenié en la mano;
       asestól' a los dientes,   fuele dando de mano;
       diol' por medio la boca   al parlero loçano;
       non tragó peor huesso   nin moro nin cristiano.

1372   Geón perdió las bafas,   ca era mal colpado;
       si li pesó o non,   fue luego derrocado;
       fue todo fecho pieças,   en las lanças alçado,
       por verdat vos dezir,   de tal colpe me pago.

1373   Dexemos vos del rëy,   de los otros contemos:
       todos allí eran buenos,   nos de todos fablemos;
       pero, entre los otros,   Clitus non olvidemos;
       los buenos por los malos   dexar non los devemos.

1374   Rodeava los medos,   lidiava bien sin asco;
       mató un alto ome   que era de Damasco;
       tolliól' de la cabeça   el yelmo e el casco;
       mas mal galardón priso   del lazerio que trasco.

1375   Un hermano del muerto,   ome bien de prestar
       – Sanga era su nombre –,   cuidósele vengar.
       Mas quiso Dios a Clitus   valer e ayudar;
       que ovo de su mano   Sanga a finar.

1376   El padre de los muertos,   por su mala ventura,
       dexólo Dios bevir,   por la su grant rencura;
       vinié por acorrerles   a müy grant pressura;
       mas era, quand' él vino,   fecha la assadura.

1377   Quando los vío muertos,   paróse deserrado;
       estido un grant día   todo desacordado;
       non podié echar lágrema,   tant' era fatilado;
       si duras' en el siglo,   serié demuneado.

1369	I am one of the warriors who built the tower, who waged war against the Heaven-dwelling gods; your grievous sins dealt you a bad end indeed when they set you face to face with Geon."*
1370	Alexander understood that his words were folly, that his voice cried of vanity, not chivalry; he said in his heart, "Creator, be my guide; these arrogant words must weigh on You."
1371	He hurled a spear which he carried in his hand: he aimed it at his teeth and let it fly; it hit that brazen chatterbox full in the mouth; neither Moor nor Christian ever swallowed a worse bone.
1372	Geon ceased his mocking, for he was badly injured; like it or not, he was thrown at once to the ground, hacked all into pieces and raised up on lances: I tell you the truth, such a blow gives me pleasure.
1373	Let us leave the King and tell of the others; all men there were good; let us talk of them all; but, among the others, let us not forget Cleitus; we must not omit the good in favour of the bad.
1374	He was harassing the Medes and fighting with relish, and he killed a nobleman who came from Damascus; he removed from his head both his helmet and mail-cap; but he gained scant reward for the hardship he endured.*
1375	A brother of the dead man, a man of great worth, – Sanga was his name – intended to avenge him, but God willed to Cleitus His help and His support and it was the fate of Sanga to die there at his hand.
1376	The father of the dead men, through his ill fortune, was granted life by God, but to his great bitterness; he came with all haste to bring them assistance, but when he arrived, the deed had been done.
1377	When he saw they were dead, he stopped in dismay, and stood there for a long time, quite beside himself; in his distress he could not even bring himself to weep; had he continued in the world he would have turned quite mad.

1378   De que acordó Mega, començó de clamar:
"¡Ay sierpe enconada, mal passaste la mar!
Todo el tu venino yo lo he de tragar;
de que matastes los fijos, ven el padre matar.

1379   Sólo que a mí mates, avrás lo bien complido;
non avrá la condessa nin fijos nin marido;
verá duelo doblado, qual nunca fue veído,
¡qual lo vea aquella que te ovo parido!"

1380   Non quería el griego la cabeça tornar;
veyélo en grant cueita, queriélo escusar.
Dixo: "Id, don viejo, vuestros fijos plorar;
non quiero la mi lança en vos ensangrentar."

1381   Tanto lo pudo Mega a Clitus segudar
fasta que sele ovo mucho a acostar;
diole una lançada, fízolo ensañar;
ovo entre los fijos el padre a echar.

1382   Dexemos de Clitus, de Nicánor digamos;
non podriemos dezir de mejores dos manos.
Él e don Filotas amos eran hermanos,
fijos de don Parmenio, del que ante fablamos.

1383   El haz que él guïava mandávala en çierto;
como sierpe raviosa andava bocabierto.
Avién en los caldeos grand portillo abierto;
contra ésti non valen las yervas de mal huerto.

1384   Ovo de fincar ojo Dario a dó andava;
la resplandor del oro esso lo acusava;
dixo entre su cuer que mucho le pesava,
que aún la fazienda tan en peso estava.

1385   Aguijó contra él, dexó todo lo al;
querié a todas guisas quebrantar el real;
al que podié prender faziél' mala señal;
avié y de mejores pocos en el real.

1386   Rennón era de Dario amigo e pariente;
vínoli en acorro con mucha bella gente;
con mucho cavallero e con mucho sergente,
sobra bien adobados de oro e d'argente.

1378	When Mecha came to himself, he began to cry out: "Oh, you vile serpent, you crossed the sea to our ill, and it is my lot to swallow all your venom; as you have killed the children, come and kill the father.
1379	If only you kill me, your task will be well finished: the countess will have neither children nor a husband; she will meet with grief twice that ever known before; may the one who gave you birth know this too!"
1380	The Greek did not even want to turn his head to him; he saw his great distress and wanted to spare him; he said to him, "Old man, go and weep for your sons; it is not my wish to stain my lance with your blood."
1381	Mecha managed to ride towards Cleitus with such speed that he came within very close range of him; he dealt him a blow with his lance to provoke him; it was the father's fate to lie dead between his sons.
1382	Let us leave Cleitus and talk now of Nicanor: we could not tell of a finer pair of hands; he and Philotas, these two men were brothers, sons of Parmenion of whom we spoke before.
1383	The column he commanded he led with skill, roaming like a rabid snake, mouth ready for the kill; they had made a great breach in the Chaldean ranks; against him a rotten orchard's weeds are worth nothing.
1384	He chanced to set his gaze on where Darius stood, clearly marked out by the gleam of the gold; he said within his heart that it weighed heavy on him that the battle still hung so much in the balance.
1385	He spurred on towards Darius, abandoning all else, and sought his camp's destruction at whatever cost; on whoever he encountered he inflicted great harm; the camp did not hold many finer men than him.
1386	Remnon was a friend and kinsman of Darius and came in support of him with many fine men, with knights and vassals alike in large numbers, most richly adorned with silver and gold.

1387   Vío cómo Nicánor   a Dario aliñava;
       sallóle adelante,   allá onde estava;
       falló otro bien fiero,   si él fiero andava;
       todas gelas tenié   quantas él embidava.

1388   Allí fue grant la priessa   e firmes las feridas;
       fueron muchas cabeças   de los ombros tollidas,
       muchas lorigas buenas   rotas e descosidas,
       muchas buenas espadas   botas e cofondidas.

1389   Murién todos de buelta,   señores e vasallos;
       andavan con las siellas   vaçías los cavallos;
       non podién dar cuenta   las fadas a contarlos;
       avién a las vegadas   por fuerça a doblarlos.

1390   Pero como la cosa   que Dios quiere guïar
       nula fuerça del mundo   non la pued' emparar,
       ovieron los aláraves   la carrera a dar,
       ca eran enralidos,   non los podién durar.

1391   Estonç' asmó Nicánor   una bella razón:
       semejól' vera mente   esfuerço de varon;
       que, si de las sus manos   estorçiesse Rennón,
       non preçiarié lo al   todo un pepïón.

1392   Tanto pudieron ambos   su seso en es' andar,
       fasta que se ovieron   en uno a fallar;
       ovieron se entrambos   luego a devisar,
       a poder de cavallo   fueron se a colpar.

1393   Como quisieron ambos   ferirse a denodadas,
       las lanças de los puños   fueron luego peçiadas;
       diéronse los cavallos   tan firmes pechugadas,
       serién grandes dos torres   por ellas derrocadas.

1394   Cavallos e señores   cayeron embraçados;
       füe grant maravilla   que non fueron quebrados;
       pero fueron aína   en piedes levantados,
       que ya de cosimente   eran desfïuzados.

1395   Fuera mal quebrantado   Rennón de la caída;
       nin se podié mudar   nin dar firme ferida.
       Pudo más el de Greçia,   essa barva complida;
       óvolo a vençer,   destajóle la vida.

1387 He saw how Nicanor was making for Darius
and rode ahead to meet him on his path;
fierce though he was, he found his match in fury
and he received a blow for every one he dealt.

1388 There the conflict was intense and the blows were hard,
and many heads were sundered from their shoulders,
much fine chain-mail was broken and split open
and many good swords were blunted and cracked.

1389 They all died without distinction, lords and vassals,
and their horses galloped with their saddles empty.
The Fates were unable to keep up with the reckoning*
and at times they were compelled to double their count.

1390 But as an event which God wishes to guide
cannot be turned aside by any force in the world;
the Arabs had to turn to the path of flight,
for, reduced in number, they could not fight on.

1391 Then to Nicanor occurred a fine idea
which seemed to him a true feat for a man:
if Remnon were to escape from his hands,
he would not give tuppence for anything else.

1392 The two men both set their minds to this task
until they came to be in the same spot;
quickly they came to catch sight of each other
and made to do battle on horseback.

1393 As they were both intent on striking fierce blows,
the lances in their hands were quickly smashed to pieces;
so hard did the horses crash into each other,
they would have brought two massive towers to the ground.

1394 Both horses and knights fell down entangled
– it was a great wonder that their bodies were not broken –,
but they rose with all haste to stand on their feet,
for they had no faith in mercy being shown.

1395 Remnon had been terribly injured from the fall,
and could not move freely or strike a firm blow;
the Grecian was more able, that warrior of skill,
and managed to defeat him and cut short his life.

1396   Cavalleros ircanos   que a Dario guardavan
            – éstos eran mejores   de quantos y andavan –
            vieron que de Nicánor   tan grant daño tomavan;
            por poco, de despecho   que non se esguinçavan.

1397   Dieron todos en él,   que le tenién grant saña;
            çercaron lo en medio,   ca eran grant compaña;
            diéronle fiera priessa.   tanto que fue fazaña.
            El montón de las lanças   semejava montaña.

1398   Rebolviése Nicánor,   firié con amas manos;
            a diestro e siniestro   dava en los ircanos;
            los que prender podié   non li ivan muy sanos.
            A Rennón de Arabia   dávalos por hermanos.

1399   Que mucho vos queramos   la razón alongar,
            he voslo a dezir,   pero con grant pesar:
            eran muchos e buenos,   non los pudo durar;
            el buen muro de Greçia   ovo y a finar.

1400   Assí finó Nicánor,   un cuerpo tan complido;
            sano es el su nombre   maguer él es podrido;
            mas fizo tales daños   ante que fues' caído
            que será, mientre dure   el mundo, retraído.

1401   Ya passava medio día,   el sol torçié el peso;
            estava la fazienda   aún toda en peso;
            entendió Alexandre   qué daño avié preso.
            Por poco con rencura   non ixió de su seso.

1402   Tomóle con la ira   ravia al coraçón;
            mayores saltos dava   que çiervo nin león;
            non popó cavallero   nin escusó peón;
            iva dando a todos   muy mala maldiçión.

1403   Parmenio el dïoso,   que lo avié crïado,
            por poco non murié,   tant' era fatilado;
            de tres fijos tan buenos   uno l'era fincado;
            el, si non naçïesse,   fuera bien venturado.

1404   Los de parte de Dario,   la más mayor partida,
            querrién y más morir   que escapar a vida,
            ca veyén que la cosa   era toda torçida;
            querrién aventurarse   de voluntad complida.

1396	The knights from Hyrcania who stood in guard of Darius – the best of all those on the battlefield were these – saw that they were suffering such great harm from Nicanor and were nearly so bitter as to lash themselves.
1397	They all rushed upon him, for they bore him great anger, and encircled him, for they were many in number; they made a fierce attack on him, a feat worthy of heroes, and the mound of lances resembled a mountain.
1398	Nicanor spun round and fought with both his hands: to his right and his left he struck the Hyrcanian men; those he managed to strike came off ill indeed, and he held them to be brothers to the Arabian Remnon.
1399	However much we wish to extend the tale, I will tell you what happened, but my sorrow weighs heavy: they were many men and fine, and he could not hold out; the good wall of Greece there came to meet his end.*
1400	So died Nicanor, a man of great accomplishment; his name is in good health though his body decays; yet he brought his enemy such harm before his fall that his story will be told while the world endures.
1401	Midday was passing, the sun tipping its scales, and the battle was still hanging in the balance. Alexander understood that he had suffered a loss and very nearly went from his mind with grief.
1402	In his anger, great fury held sway over his heart and he gave greater bounds than a deer or lion; he showed no mercy to any knight or foot soldier and as he went he uttered cruel curses on them all.
1403	The aged Parmenion, the man who had raised him, was on the cusp of death, so great was his anguish; of his three fine sons, only one was left to him:* had he not been born it would have been his good fortune.
1404	Those on Darius' side, who were the greater number, were more willing to die there than escape to life, for they could see that events had reversed their course, and to make their venture now was all their hearts desired.

1405 El infante don Fidias   era de Orïente;
de linaje de Çiro,   niño barva poniente,
más blanco de color   que la nieve reziente;
querrié con Alexandre   justar de buena miente.

1406 Prometíale Dario,   a buena fe e sana,
si el campo rancasse,   de darle su hermana;
por end' querié fer nuevas   sobre feúza vana
ca vernié otro viento   otro día mañana.

1407 Eran de Alexandre   todos escarmentados;
eran, por foír d'él,   todos aconsejados;
baldonósili Fidias,   por sus grieves pecados;
mas después vino ora   que maldizié sus fados.

1408 Ya exié de galope,   querié con él juñir;
óvoli de traviesso   en siesto a sallir;
nin beldat nin linaje   non li pudo guarir;
cosiólo por el cuerpo,   ovo y a morir.

1409 Los griegos por Nicánor   fueron todos pesantes;
lidiavan con la saña   más afirmes que d'antes;
fazién muy grant carniça   en los pueblos persiantes;
los de parte de Dario   veyénse mal andantes.

1410 Andava Alexandre   como rayo irado;
querrié más seer muerto   que non seer rancado.
A Afrón e a Lisias   delibrólos privado
e otro más fuert' ome   que Melón fue llamado.

1411 Çenus e Eüménides,   Meleáger terçero,
rencuravan afirmes   el su buen compañero;
non le iva a Pérdicas   ninguno delantero;
todos eran estraños,   peón e cavallero.

1412 Que los queramos todos   por nombre ementar,
cada uno qué fizo,   cómo pudo lidiar,
¡mal pecado! la noche   podié ante uviar
que pudiéssemos sólo   el diezmo recontar.

1413 Mas, como diz' el sabio   – es verdad sin dubdança –
que en la fin yaz' todo,   el prez o mal estança,
non queramos seer   en luenga demorança;
vayamos a la fin   do yaze la ganançia.

1405	Prince Fidias, a man who hailed from the Orient, born of Cyrus' stock, and still in the flush of youth, whiter in colour than the newly-fallen snow, wished to meet Alexander in a full-blooded joust.
1406	Darius had promised him in good and full faith, if he won the day, to give him his sister; wherefore he wished to gain renown, vainly confident; for the next morning a new wind would be blowing.
1407	They had all been taught a lesson by Alexander and had made up their minds to flee from his presence. Fidias faced up to him, for his grievous sins, but later came the time when he cursed his fate.
1408	Now he went at a gallop to meet the King in combat, but the attack took a turn that was not in his favour: neither looks nor lineage afforded him protection; the King ran through his body and there he was to die.
1409	Grief for Nicanor weighed heavy on all the Greeks and they fought with fury, their resolve now heightened; they wrought great carnage among the Persian peoples, and Darius' men saw that their fortune was ill.
1410	Alexander moved like an angry bolt of lightning and would have rather died than suffer defeat; Affer and Lysias he quickly dispatched, with another strong man who was known as Amulon.
1411	Coenus and Eumenes, Meleager as a third, were in bitter lament over their good companion, and there was no man who approached Perdiccas in this; all felt a rare grief, both foot soldiers and knights.
1412	Even if we should seek to list them all by name and say what each man did and the skill with which he fought, – alas, what woe! – night may well fall upon us before we could include even a tenth of those men.
1413	But, as the wise man says – it is a truth beyond doubt – that it is at the end that all fame or failure lies, let us not delay and let a long time pass, but move on to the end, where the profit lies.

1414 Era más de nona, grant migero passado,
çerca era de viésperas, todo el sol tornado;
de los muertos el campo todo yazié cuajado;
don Alexandre mismo era fascas cansado.

1415 Los poderes de Dario eran fuert' enralidos;
los unos eran muertos e los otros fuïdos;
todas las pleitesías e todos los roídos
eran sobre las guardas de su cuerpo caídos.

1416 Ya lo veyé por ojo cóm' avié a seer;
veyé que de la muerte non podié estorçer;
querrié más seer muerto o estar por naçer
que tantas e tan grandes ocasiones veer.

1417 Aquellos que por quien él cuidava rancar
ya non veyé ninguno çerca de sí estar;
nin era por a fuir nin era por tornar;
yo he de la su cueita oy en día pesar.

1418 Pero aviá asmado de lidiando morir;
sus gentes eran muertas, él non querié bevir;
de que avié su regno todo a mal a ir,
él non querié del campo con la alma fuïr.

1419 Assí andava Dario su cueita comidiendo;
fueron seli las hazes poc' a poco moviendo;
fueron cuestas tornando, fuéronse desurdiendo;
fueron contra sus casas las cabeças corriendo.

1420 Quando cató Dario el su pueblo plenero,
veyése en el campo, fascas solo señero;
tirando de sus barvas, de todos postrimero,
desemparó el juego con todo su tablero.

1421 Assaz quisiera Dario en el campo fincar,
mas non gelo quisieron los fados otorgar;
ca era ya fadado, non podié al estar,
que Bessus e Narbázones lo avién a matar.

1422 Quand' sopo Alexandre que Dario era ido,
tovo de la fazienda que era mal sallido,
ca avié por él solo tal lazerio sofrido
e aviélo agora entre manos perdido.

1414	It was now a good time after the hour of None,* as Vespers drew near, the sun well in decline, and the field of battle lay thick with the dead; Alexander himself was now nearing exhaustion.
1415	Darius' forces were much reduced in number, some had met their deaths and others turned to flight; all of the fighting and all the roar of battle had fallen still over the protectors of his person.
1416	Now he saw with his own eyes how it was to be and saw that he could find no escape from his death; he would have rather longed to be dead or yet unborn than to see misfortunes so many and so great.
1417	Of those that he thought would bring victory to him he now saw none of them left standing nearby; he could not settle on flight or a return to the fray; sorrow still weighs on me today for his plight.
1418	But he had resolved to die while still in battle: his people were dead and he had no desire for life; and since now in his kingdom all was to be lost he wished not to flee the field with his soul intact.
1419	And so, as Darius took thought for his plight, his battle lines were slowly giving ground, turning in retreat and beginning to break up, those at the head making haste for their homes.
1420	When Darius had his whole people before his eyes, and saw himself on the field, near-deserted and alone, plucking at his beard, himself the last of all, he gave up the game, with no pieces on his board.
1421	Darius would much rather have remained on the field but the Fates were unwilling to grant this to him, for it was already ordained and could not be otherwise: Bessus and Nabarzanes were to be his assassins.*
1422	When Alexander learned that Darius had gone, he felt that he had emerged badly from the battle; since he had suffered such trials through that man alone, and now he had let him slip right through his hands.

1423 Iva vertiendo fuegos, a Dario encalçando,
como va la estrella por el çielo bolando
o como faz' el Ruédano que cae espumando,
do murió sant Mauriçio con muchos de su vando.

1424 Destajólos la noche, ovieron a quedar;
ovieron a las tiendas los griegos a tornar,
pero con grant rencura e con fiero pesar
por que mano en Dario non pudieron echar.

1425 Ante que fuessen ellos a las tiendas entrados
– de non aver rebuelta vinién assegurados –
salleron de traviesso dos reys apoderados
que querién más morir que bevir aontados.

1426 El rëy Alexandre fízos' maravillado;
por plazo non lo puso, maguer era cansado;
encubrió del escudo el su cuerpo lazrado;
delantero de todos salló luego al prado.

1427 Fue luego reçebido como él mereçié;
de porras e de lanças sól' cuenta non avié;
teniése por mejor qui primerol' firié;
de colpes en el cuerpo caber más non podié.

1428 Fue luego acorrido de las sus crïazones;
redráronlos a todos sobre los sus griñones;
davan malas pitanças, partién malas raçiones;
más afirmes lidiavan que non otras sazones.

1429 Luego de las primeras, como Dios lo querié,
murió el mayoral de quantos y avié;
plaziél' de coraçón al que morir podié,
mas a todo su grado bien vengado morié.

1430 Como querién morir, estavan denodados;
firiénlos e firién a dientes regañados;
ya dizién los de Greçia que eran enojados,
que la ira de Dios los avié deparados.

1431 Lisímacus, un griego, grant tuerto ha tomado,
ca en los más primeros devrié seer contado;
tant' y fue bien apreso e sobra bien guïado.
Mejoróse de quantos avié en el mercado.

1423   Flames poured from him as he went on Darius' heels,
        just like a shooting star when it flies across the sky,
        or like the River Rhône plunging down amidst the foam*
        – where Saint Maurice died with many of his legion.

1424   The night cut them short and they had to call a halt;
        the Greeks had to make their way back to their tents,
        though with great irritation and fierce displeasure
        since they had been unable to lay their hands on Darius.

1425   Before they had made their return to their tents,
        confident that they would meet no resistance,
        their path was crossed by two powerful kings
        who would die before they would live in shame.

1426   King Alexander, who was quite astounded,
        although he was tired, allowed no delay;
        he covered his ill-treated body with his shield
        and, before all his men, went at once into the field.

1427   He was at once given the reception he deserved;
        you could not even count the clubs and the lances;
        he who struck the first blow held himself the better
        and there was no more room for blows to his body.

1428   Immediately his vassals hurried to his aid
        and drove them all back in disarray;
        they served grim rations and food hard to stomach,
        fighting with even greater force than before.

1429   Right with the first blows, according to God's will,
        the leader of all those that were there met his end.
        The man who could find death was pleased in his heart,
        but to his great pleasure, he died well avenged.

1430   As they wished to die, they were bold in the fight,
        striking time and time again in their frenzy.
        Now the men of Greece said that their anger was stirred,
        that these men had been sent by the wrath of God.

1431   The Greek Lysimachus has been deeply wronged,*
        for his deeds must be recounted among the very first;
        he showed there such expertise and such great skill
        that he excelled all others who took part in those dealings.

1432 Sobre quantos y eran   encargóseles tanto
que tal daño les fizo   que avién grant quebranto;
los que estavan lueñe   avián ende espanto;
non semejava todo   depuerto nin disanto.

1433 Como trayén los griegos   esfuerço e ventura,
fizieron los lazrar   a la mayor mesura;
e los demás echaron   por esta sepoltura;
los otros dieron cuestas   con doblada rencura.

1434 Dario en es' comedio   non s'ovo de vagar,
por cuestas e por planos   cuitóse de andar;
fasta la media noche   tant' pudo caminar
que avrié otra guisa   tres días bien que far.

1435 Fue a la media noche   en un río uviado;
agua era cabdal   que non avié nul vado.
Asmó fer una cosa   de que füe passado;
si lo fecho oviesse   non fuera engañado.

1436 Asmava que fiziessen   la puente derrocar,
que los griegos por ella   non pudiessen passar;
mas asmó otra cosa: que serié mal estar
ques' perderién los suyos   que eran por llegar.

1437 Vençiólo p̈iedat   e non lo quiso fer;
púsolo en Dios todo,   morir o guareçer;
a r̈ey tan leal   e de tan buen creer
deviéra'l Cr̈iador   p̈iadat le aver.

1438 Dario, maguer rancado,   non se pudo morir
nin se pudo matar   nin del siglo sallir,
nin entrar en la tierra   nin al çielo sobir;
quando non pudo al,   óvolo a sofrir.

1439 Pero, que non toviessen   que era recreído,
atendié al su pueblo   que vinié desmarrido,
la una por saber   quánto avié perdido,
la otra por mostrarse   de esfuerço complido.

1440 Todos eran bien pocos   quando fueron venidos,
que más de las diez partes   allá eran perdidos.
Dario, con la rencura,   dava grandes sospiros;
querrié seer más muerto   que seer con los bivos.

1432	So intense was his attack on all who were near him and such harm did he cause them, that their distress was great; those who stood far from him were thrown into such terror that they did not think this festivity or sport.
1433	As the Greeks brought with them valour and good fortune, they made the Persians suffer to the highest degree; most of them they cast down into the same grave and those remaining fled with doubled rancour.
1434	Darius at this point allowed himself no rest and hastened to travel over hills and plains; by midnight, he had managed to ride so far as otherwise would have taken three full days.
1435	By midnight he had come to the edge of a river – a deep-flowing torrent with no place for crossing – and he thought to do something when on the other side; had he done it, he would not have been deceived.
1436	It occurred to him to have the bridge broken down, that the Greeks be unable to pass over it; but he also thought that it would be a misfortune that his troops who were still to arrive would be lost.
1437	Overcome by compassion, he would not do it; he set it all in God's hands, to die or be saved; to a king so loyal and of such firm belief the Creator in turn should show His mercy.
1438	Darius, defeated though he was, could not die, nor could he kill himself or escape the world, nor go down into the Earth or ascend to Heaven; since he could do nothing else, he was left to suffer.
1439	Yet, lest they consider that he had despaired, he attended to his people who arrived distressed, that he might both learn the size of his losses and also show that his spirit was undaunted.
1440	When they had all arrived, they were but a very few, for there more than ten parts of them had been destroyed. Darius was sighing deeply in his bitterness, keener to have death than the living's company.

1441 Encubrió su desarro   quando fueron llegados;
      refirió los sospiros   que tenié muy granados;
      començó de fablar   con los ojos mudados,
      ca entendié que todos   estavan deserrados.

1442 "Amigos," diz, "devémoslo   a los dios gradeçer
      que tan grandes quebrantos   nos dieron a veer;
      pero nos bien devemos   firme mente creer
      que merçet nos avrán   en cabo a aver.

1443 Somos mucho fallidos   contra el Crïador;
      non lo obedeçiemos   como atal señor,
      por end' somos caídos   en el su desamor,
      ca los yerros son grandes   e la culpa mayor.

1444 Mas es de tal natura,   esto es la verdat:
      maguer irado sea   non olvida piedat;
      fer nos ha en pues esto   tamaña caridat
      que aún bien deziremos   a la su magestat.

1445 Otra cosa nos debe   encara confortar:
      que sabemos por muchos   tales cosas passar.
      Çiro, tan poderoso   – com' oyestes contar –
      una muger lo ovo   en cabo a matar.

1446 El rey Sersis, que ovo   tan estraño poder
      ques' fazié por la mar   en los carros traher
      e podié en los campos   con las aves correr,
      abés pudo en cabo   una bestia aver.

1447 Si nos, que Dios lo quiso,   fuemos desbaratados,
      a varones conteçe,   ¡seamos esforzados!
      Vivo es vuestro rëy,   vos todos sodes sanos;
      creo que verná ora   que seremos vengados.

1448 Éssi sólo non cae   que non quiere luchar;
      éssi non fue vençido   que non quiso lidiar;
      todos los que quisieron   büen preçio ganar;
      siempre d'ellas e d'ellas   ovieron a tomar.

1449 Non vos vençió esfuerço   mas vençióvos ventura;
      quísovos dar por ellos   Dios mala majadura;
      que trayemos con nos   embargo e orrura:
      castrados e mugeres,   ésta fue grant locura.

1441	He hid his sorrow when they were arrived and suppressed the great sighs welling up. He began to speak with clouded eyes for he knew that all were in distress.
1442	"My friends," he said, "we must be grateful to the gods that they have granted us such great misfortune to endure, but we must, as well, be firm in our belief that in the end they will have mercy upon us.
1443	We have sinned greatly against our Creator, not obeying Him as we should do such a Lord; for this we have fallen into His disfavour, for our guilt is great and our error greater still.
1444	But He is of such a nature, and this is true indeed, that, though He may be angered, He does not forget mercy; after all of this He will show us such love that we shall yet bless Him in all His majesty.
1445	There is one thing more that must still bring us comfort, that we know such misfortunes befall many others: Cyrus, who was so powerful, as you have heard tell,* came in the end to be killed by a woman;
1446	King Xerxes, a man who possessed power so vast* that he had his chariots drawn over the sea and could take his ships across fields of battle, scarcely managed in the end to keep a single beast.
1447	If we have suffered defeat because it was God's will, that happens to men – let us be full of courage! Your King is alive and you are all still healthy and I believe the hour of our vengeance will arrive.
1448	He alone does not fall who does not wish to fight; he was never defeated who wished not to do battle. but all those who desired to win great renown had always to accept both victory and defeat.
1449	You were not defeated by valour but by destiny; God wanted to give you great torment at their hands; for we carried with us a burden of scum, of eunuchs and women – this was great folly.

1450 Desaquí otra guisa somos a aguisar;
      lleguemos quantas gentes pudiéremos llegar;
      dexemos estas nuevas que solemos llevar,
      ca por fierro se suele la fazienda rancar.

1451 Ellos en el enfloto de lo que avién fecho,
      ternán que lo fizieron por esfuerço derecho;
      pesará a los dios, aver les han despecho;
      perderán la ventura; nos cogeremos pecho."

1452 Como eran las gentes todas descorasnadas
      – non era maravilla ca eran malcuitadas –
      non les podié dezir palabras tan senadas
      que toller les pudiesse de los cueres las plagas.

1453 Veyén cosa mal puesta dende al otro día:
      que el rey Alexandre con su cavallería
      entrarié por la tierra a su plazentería,
      ca era de poderes e de gentes vazía.

1454 Cativarién las biudas que eran sin maridos;
      traerién a los fijos ant' las madres amidos.
      Mandarién los que eran nueva mente venidos;
      los otros andarién siervos e escarnidos.

1455 El rëy de los griegos de la buena ventura
      partió bien la ganançia a toda derechura;
      él non quiso end' parte nin ovo d'ello cura;
      dizién que era grant ganançia sin mesura.

1456 Fue todo en un rato fecho e delibrado;
      mandó luego mover el su real fonsado
      por conseguir a Dario que sel' era alçado,
      çercar a Babilonia, cabeça del regnado.

1457 Aviéla a Maçeo Dario acomendada,
      con el que ovo ante la fija desposada;
      era por defenderse la cosa bien guisada,
      mas a l'ira de Dios nos' li defende nada.

1458 Acordóse el rëy con toda la su gente
      por ir a Babilonia luego primeramente;
      sól' que éssa oviesse fecho el sagramente,
      luego vernién las otras todas a cosimente.

1450	Henceforth our tactics will be of different kind: let us muster all the men we can muster, and let us leave behind these ways which are our custom for battle is usually won by the sword.
1451	As the Greeks swell with pride in what they have done, they will hold that they performed a rightful act of valour; it will annoy the gods, who will bear them ill will; they will lose their good fortune and the profit will be ours."
1452	As all Darius' people were deeply disheartened – no cause for wonder, for they had suffered greatly –, he could not address them with words so apt that he could take away the wounds in their hearts.
1453	They saw the problem looming for another day, that King Alexander with his force of knights would enter their lands as and when he wished, for they were now empty of defences and troops.
1454	They would take captive the widows without husbands and drag away the children before their hapless mothers; command would lie with those who were newly arrived, and the others would suffer enslavement and scorn.
1455	The King of the Greeks, a man of good fortune, shared out the booty well with total fairness; he wished for no share, nor desired it at all; the booty was said to be vast beyond measure.
1456	In but a short time it was all done and set in order, and at once he ordered his royal army to move off, that they might seek out Darius, who had fled from him, and lay siege to Babylon, the kingdom's capital.
1457	Darius had placed it in Mazaeus' hands, to whom he had previously betrothed his daughter; the city was well prepared to defend itself, but against God's wrath there can be no defence.
1458	The King reached agreement with all of his people to go first of all, without delay, to Babylon: if just this city were to swear its loyalty, all the others would quickly choose to follow.

1459 Quando sopo Maçeo, que la villa tenié,
que el rëy Alexandre por a ella venié,
salló luego a él que mucho lo temié.
Rindióli la çibdat con quanto y avié.

1460 Quiérovos un poco todo lo al dexar;
del pleito de Babilonia vos quïero contar:
cómo yaz' assentada en tan noble lugar;
cómo es abondada de ríos e de mar.

1461 Yaze en lugar sano, comarca muy temprada;
nin la cueita verano nin faz' la invernada;
de todas las vïandas es sobra abondada;
de los bienes del siglo allí non mengua nada.

1462 Los que en ella moran dolor non los retienta;
pasan los mançebillos en dulçor su juventa;
el viejo la cabeça non l'ave tremolienta;
en ella son los árboles que llevan la pimienta.

1463 Allí son las espeçias: el puro galingal,
canela e gengibre, clavos e çetüal,
ençens e çinamomo, bálsamo que más val';
girofe, nuez moscada e nardo natural.

1464 De sí mismos, los árboles tanto han buen olor
que non avrié ant' ellos fuerça ningund dolor;
por esso son los omes sanos e de buena color;
bien a una jornada sienten el buen odor.

1465 Los quatro ríos santos todos los ha vezinos;
dizen que los dos fazen por ellas sus caminos.
Muelen solas espeçias más de quatro molinos;
más quatro muelen pebre e más quatro cominos.

1466 De ruedas de molinos que muelen las çiveras
e de ricas açeñas que las dizen traperas
avié grant abondança por todas las riberas;
eran dentro e fuera seguras las carreras.

1467 Rica es de pescados de ríos e de mar;
siempre los fallan frescos, non los quieren salar;
non d'uno mas de quantos omes podrién asmar;
son las aguas muy sanas por a bestias abevrar.

1459	When Mazaeus, who governed the city, found out* that King Alexander was coming against it, in his great fear he went straight out to meet him surrendering the city and all it held within.
1460	For a while I want to cease talk of all else;* I wish to give you an account of Babylon, how it lies set in a land of such splendour, and how it is favoured by rivers and sea.
1461	It lies in a healthy place, a temperate region: neither summer nor winter brings it trouble; it has a rich abundance of all kinds of food, lacking nothing of the riches of the world.
1462	Those who dwell there are assailed by no pain, and children pass their youth in sweet enjoyment; the old man never has a head that quivers, and in this city are the trees that bear pepper.
1463	Spices, too, are found there: pure galanga, cinnamon, ginger, cloves and zedoary, incense and cassia, balsam of greater cost, syzygium, nutmeg and spikenard.
1464	The trees in themselves have a scent so fine that no pain, in their presence, could have an effect, wherefore the men have such a healthy complexion, and the scent is perceived while a good day away.
1465	All four sacred rivers it has as its neighbours:* two of them are said to trace their paths through the city; there are more than four mills there to grind only spices, four more grind pepper and another four cumin.
1466	Of mill wheels which serve to grind the corn and powerful machines called fulling mills there was a great abundance all along the banks; within and without, the city's roads were safe.
1467	It is rich in fish from both rivers and sea, always fresh, for they have no wish to salt them – not in one kind, but in all that men could imagine –, the river-waters healthy for beasts to go to drink.

1468 Han essas santas aguas   otra mejor costumbre:
de piedras de grant preçio   han una muchedumbre;
unas que dan de noche   a luenga tierra lumbre,
otras que dan al flaco   salut e fermidumbre.

1469 El esmeraldo verde   allí suele seer
más claro que espejo   por ombre se veer;
el jaspis que es bueno   por ome lo traer:
nol' pueden a qui lo trae   yervas empeeçer.

1470 Allí son los gagates,   por natura ardientes,
que sacan los demonios,   segudan las sirpientes;
los magnetes, que son   unas piedras valientes:
éstos tiran el fierro,   si les metierdes mientes.

1471 Adamant', en que fierro   nunca fizo señal,
con sangre de cabrito   fiende se, non con al;
estopaçio, que es   de color comunal:
qual color tien' açerca   tórnas' ella en tal.

1472 Allí han la galaica,   assaz de buen mercado:
ésta tiene al ome   alegre e pagado.
Es en essa ribera   el meloçio trobado
que, por descobrir furtos,   es muy bueno provado.

1473 La piedra elitropia   allí suele naçer:
ésta es de grant preçio;   ¡quí la podiés' aver!
Ésta faz' a la luna   la claredat perder;
al ome que la tiene   non le pueden veer.

1474 Sagda, que las naves   faze a sí venir;
el coral, que los rayos   faze bien referir;
fázelo hematites   al ome salvo ir:
çelada nin engaño   nol' podrié nozir.

1475 Jaçinto, que se torna   de la color del día,
non dexa en el ome   ardor nin maletía;
por natura es fría,   end' ha tal valentía:
el adamant' lo taja,   non otra maestría.

1476 Margarita, que siempre   quiere yazer señera,
siempre la troban sola,   nunca ha compañera;
del roçío se cría   – palabra verdadera –,
que lo diz' sant Esidro,   que sopo la manera.

| 1468 | Those sacred waters have one virtue finer still:
they contain a wealth of very precious stones,*
some which by night give out light far around,
others which bring the frail health and strength. |
| --- | --- |
| 1469 | There the green emerald is often to be found,
clearer than a mirror for a man to see himself,
and jasper, which is good for a man to wear,
for poison is then powerless to harm him. |
| 1470 | Jet is to be found there, burning by nature,
which drives out demons and puts serpents to flight,
and magnets, too, which are stones of great worth;
these attract iron, if you observe them well. |
| 1471 | Diamond, on which iron never made its mark
and which nought but the blood of a baby goat can cut;
peridot, a stone which is of a common colour,
for it takes for itself whatever colour is nearby. |
| 1472 | Also there is turquoise, of high value in the market,
this stone keeps a man both happy and content;
and malachite, too, is found on those banks,
of proven worth for discovering thefts. |
| 1473 | Bloodstone often has its birth in that place;
its value is great – I wish I might possess it!
This stone makes the very moon lose its brilliance
and the man who wears it cannot be seen. |
| 1474 | Green sagda, which makes ships move towards it,
coral, which rejects and repels the sun's rays,
haematite, which allows a man to go in safety,
no trap or deception being able to harm him. |
| 1475 | Amethyst, which turns the colour of daylight
and leaves no fever or illness in man;
it is cold by nature and thus it has such strength
that diamond can cut it but there is no other way. |
| 1476 | The pearl, which wants always to lie by itself
– always found alone, it is never with another –,
and is born from the dew, I tell you in truth;
we are told by Saint Isidore, who understood its nature. |

1477   Pedorus, que tanto vale,   non es de olvidar:
        no es nado quil' pueda   la color terminar;
        de beldat nol' pueden   compañera trobar;
        las reínas la suelen   ésta mucho amar.

1478   Astrites es poquiella,   mas mayor que arbeja,
        pesada por natura,   más que ruvia bermeja;
        pareçe entre lumbre   que estrella semeja;
        dan por ella grant preçio,   maguer que es poquieja.

1479   Galatites es blanca   com' leche de oveja;
        faze a las nodrizas   aver leche sobeja;
        faze purgar la fleuma,   maguer sea aneja;
        regálas' en la boca,   que açúcar semeja.

1480   Galaçio es fermosa,   mas de fría manera:
        non podrié calentarse   por ninguna foguera;
        ámanla en verano   los que andan carrera,
        que non les faga mal   el sol en la mollera.

1481   Solgema echa rayos,   faz' lumbre sobejo:
        podrié a su lumbre   çenar un grant conçejo;
        creo que selenites   val' menos un poquillejo,
        ca mengua com' la luna   e creçe en parejo.

1482   Çinedia es longuilla,   piedra muy preçïada;
        en cabeça de pez   suele seer fallada;
        en ella lo entienden   los que la han usada
        si fará tiempo bueno   o tempestat irada.

1483   Achates es negrilla,   mas de grandes virtudes:
        refiere las tempestas   que vienen en las nuves.
        Faze quedar los ríos   que semejan paludes;
        otras y ha sin éstas   muchas buenas costumbres.

1484   Absicto, como dizen,   es negra e pesada;
        mas, quando una vez   es escalentada,
        fasta los siete días   non es esfrïada;
        serié por a enero   non mala dinarada.

1485   La santa dïonisia,   quando es bien molida
        e tornada en polvos,   e en agua metida,
        como si fuesse vino   faz' la tan saborida;
        nunca sintrié beudez   qui la oviés' tenida.

Book of Alexander

1477 Opal has worth so great it must not be forgotten
and there is no-one born who could determine its colour;
no other can be found as its partner in beauty
for this is a stone that queens are wont to adore.

1478 The sunflower opal is tiny, but larger than a pea,
heavy by nature and rather red than yellow;
it seems, when lit up, to resemble a star;
men pay a great price for it, so small though it be.

1479 Galactite is white as the milk of a goat
and ensures that a nurse's milk is abundant;
it purges of phlegm, even if it is very old,
and tastes like sugar, it is so sweet in the mouth.

1480 Rock crystal is beautiful, but in a cold fashion
and cannot be brought to heat by any fire;
it is loved in summer by those who walk outside,
that the sun might not do any harm to their heads.

1481 Sunstone gives out rays and creates a great blaze
such that a great gathering could dine by its light;
I believe that selenite is worth a little less
for it shrinks like the moon and grows as its twin.

1482 Cinaedia is a long and much-valued stone;
it is usually found in the head of a fish
and those who have used it have been able to see
if good weather will come, or an angry storm.

1483 Agate is black but it has great qualities;
it drives away the storms that are brewing in the clouds
and makes the rivers lie as still as marshland,
and it has many other fine traits besides these.

1484 The lignite apsyctos, they say, is weighty and black
and, after it has once been heated up,
in seven days' time it has still not grown cool;
it would bring no small profit in January.

1485 Holy dionysia, when thoroughly ground,
turned to dust and dissolved in water,
makes it taste as fine as if it were wine,
but none who had had it would ever feel drunk.

1486 Non es hexecontálito   de todas las peores,
que es entre mezclada   de sesenta colores.
El adamant' seguda   todos malos pavores:
qui la tiene consigo   non lo matan poçones.

1487 Irisius, si del rayo   del sol fuere ferida,
faz' la forma del arco   en la pared bastida.
Astrïón resplandeçe   como la luna complida,
pero a poco tiempo   es la su luz fallida.

1488 Electria hanla pocos,   ca es piedra preçiada;
en vientre de los gallos   suele seer fallada;
qui la toviés' consigo   en el cuello atada
nunca serié vençido   nin muerto a espada.

1489 Endros echa grant agua,   fría e bien sabrida;
semeja que tien' dentro   una fuent' escondida;
manternié doze omes   a larguera medida
si el agua que vierte   fuesse toda cogida.

1490 La virtud del cristal   todos nos la sabemos:
cómo salle d'él fuego   cutiano lo veemos;
mas nos por maravilla   esto non lo tenemos
por quanto cada día   en uso lo avemos.

1491 Safires e girgonças,   estas piedras luzientes,
en éstas ome bueno   sól' non y mete mientes;
mas las que por natura   son frías e calientes,
éstas tienen por buenas,   ca son senadas gentes.

1492 Más son de çient atantas   las piedras adonadas
mas son allí las gentes   de todas abondadas;
qui más quiere saber,   busque do son notadas,
ca quiero yo fincar   con las que he contadas.

1493 Son por la villa dentro   muchas dulçes fontanas
que son de día frías,   tibias en las mañanas;
nunca crían en ellas   nin gusanos nin ranas;
como son perenales,   son sabrosas e sanas.

1494 De panes e de vinos   es la villa abondada;
non podrién doze omes   comer la dinarada.
Yo leí – ¡assí aya   en Paraíso posada! –
que vendimian en el año   la segunda vegada.

1486	The opal sixty stone is far from the poorest, for it contains a mingling of sixty colours. Diamond chases all evil fears away and poisons cannot kill the man who bears it.
1487	The rainbow stone, which, if the sun's rays strike it, projects the form of the rainbow upon the wall; the moonstone is resplendent, just like the full moon, but in just a short time its light has faded.
1488	Few own alectorius, for it is a valued stone; it is usually found in the stomach of cocks; anyone who wore one tied round his neck would never be vanquished or killed by the sword.
1489	Water crystal gives off water which is cold and fine to taste, and it seems that it has a spring concealed within. It would sustain twelve men for a lengthy stretch if the water that it produces were all collected.
1490	Of crystal's quality we are all aware and each day from it we see fire emerge; but we do not consider this to be a wonder because we have it in use each day.
1491	Lapis lazuli and zircon, these radiant stones, to these the good man does not even pay attention, but the stones which by nature are hot and cold, these they hold to be good, being people of wisdom.
1492	The stones with special qualities are five times this number but the people there have a rich supply of them. Those who wish to know more, let them look where they are noted, for I intend to settle for those I have described.
1493	There are, within the city, many gentle fountains, which are cold by day, but, in the early morning, warm. In these springs neither worms nor frogs ever breed; since they are perennial, they are healthy and of sweet taste.
1494	The city is well stocked with breads and wines and twelve men could not eat one portion of the food. I have read – may I have such a resting place in Heaven! – that they make a second grape-harvest in a single year.

1495 Las florestas son grandes   redor de la çibdat;
y prenden los venados   a toda planidat;
los grandes e los chicos, los de media hedat,
assí s'ivan a ello   com' a su heredat.

1496 De gamos e de çiervos   e de otros venados,
de ossos e de ossas   e puercos mal domados,
de perdizes, de garças   e picos lorigados,
otros omes en el siglo   non son tan abondados.

1497 De estas avezillas,   ánades e çerçetas,
traen por la çibdat   plenas grandes carretas;
ruiseñores e gallos,   que son mas fermosetas;
por que cantan fermoso   éstas son mas caretas.

1498 Pero han muchas d'ellas,   e todas muy boniellas,
cad' uno a su puerta   tres o quatro çestiellas;
quand' empieçan sus sones   a fer las aveziellas,
las madres a los fijos   olvidarién por ellas.

1499 Y son los papagayos,   unas aves senadas,
que vençen a los omes   de seso a las vegadas;
y son las fieras tigres   – yazen encarçeladas –
non ha bestias en el mundo   que sean tan dubdadas.

1500 Las gentes son de preçio,   mayores e menores;
todos andan vestidos   de paños de colores;
cavalgan palafrenes   e mulas ambladores;
los pobres omes visten   xamit' e çiclatones.

1501 Que todas sus noblezas   vos queramos dezir,
antes podrián tres días   e tres noches troçir;
ca Galter non las pudo,   maguer quiso, complir.
Yo contra él non quiero,   nin podría venir.

1502 Pero y fincan cosas   que non son de dexar:
cómo vienen gananças   por tierra e por mar;
las más naves del mundo   y suelen arribar;
sola mente con esso   devrié rica estar.

1503 Embían pora África   e pora Eüropa
las naves cargadas   d'espeçias e de ropa;
por y traxo Antípater   en mal punto la copa
ond' priso Alexandre   en mal punto la sopa.

1495	The leafy glades that border the city are vast, and there they hunt game in great abundance; the old and the young, and those of a middle age, went about it as they would their own realm.
1496	Of deer and of stags and other game, of bears and she-bears and swine untamed, of partridges and herons and woodpeckers, no others in the world have such a wealth.
1497	Of ducks and teal and other small fowl they carry great carts through the city, filled full; nightingales and jays, which are more beautiful, for the beauty of their song are more highly valued.
1498	But they have many of them, and all are very fine, each with three or four small baskets on their door; and when the little birds begin to pipe their song they would make mothers forget their children.
1499	There are parrots there, birds of intelligence, which sometimes surpass men in good sense, and there, too, lie fierce tigers, held in cages; there are no beasts in the world that are so feared.
1500	The people are distinguished, both the elders and the young, and all go about dressed in richly-coloured clothes; they ride on palfreys and steady-moving mules; the poor men are dressed in silk and damask.
1501	If we wished to tell you of all its fine features three days and three nights would first pass by, for, though he sought to, Walter could not complete it, and I have neither wish nor power to rival him.
1502	But matters there remain that are not to be left: how great gain comes to the city by sea; most of the world's ships are wont to arrive there and with that alone it should be rich indeed.
1503	They send out to Africa and also to Europe ships heavily laden with spices and clothes; thence did Antipater, in ill moment, bring the cup* from which Alexander, in ill moment, did sup.

1504   Quiero fablar del sitio   e de la su grandez',
del alteza del muro   e de la su autez'.
De torres e de puertas,   quál a quál obedez';
serié pora Omero   grave, ca non rafez.

1505   Creo que bien podiestes   alguna vez oír
que quisieron al çielo   los gigantes sobir.
Fizieron una torre   – non vos cuido fallir –;
non ha quien la pudiesse   mesurar nin medir.

1506   Vío el Crïador   que fazién grant locura;
metió en ellos çisma   e grant mala ventura;
non conoçié ningund   ome de su natura;
ovo assí a seer   por su mala ventura.

1507   Fasta essa sazón   toda la gent' que era
fablavan un lenguaje   e por una manera;
en ebreo fablavan,   una lengua señera;
non sabién al fablar   nin escribir en çera.

1508   Metió Dïos en ellos   tamaña confusión
que olvidaron todos   el natural sermón;
fablavan sendas lenguas,   cad' una en su son;
non sabié un' a otro   quél' dizié o qué non.

1509   Si'l uno pedié agua   el otrol' dava cal;
el que pediá mortero   dávanli el cordal;
lo que dizié el uno   el otro fazié al;
ovo toda la obra   por ende ir a mal.

1510   Non se podién por guisa   ninguna acordar;
ovieron la lavor   por eso a dexar;
ovieron por el mundo   todos a derramar;
cad' un' por su comarca   ovieron a poblar.

1511   Assí está oy día   la torre empeçada,
pero de fiera guisa   sobra mucho alçada;
por la confusïón   que fue en ellos dada,
es toda essa tierra   Babilonia clamada.

1512   Setenta e dos fueron   los omes mayorales;
tantos son por el mundo   los lenguajes cabdales;
este girgonz' que traen,   estos lenguajes tales,
son se controbadiços   entre los menestrales.

1504	I wish to tell of the place and of its greatness, of the height of its wall and of its grandeur, of towers and of gates, and which of them is greatest; for Homer it would be a heavy task and far from easy.
1505	I think that you may well have heard on some occasion that the giants attempted to scale the heavens;* they built a tower – I do not think I mislead you –, and nobody could measure or calculate its height.
1506	The Creator saw them enacting great folly and set a rift among them, and great ill fortune; no man was able to understand his own people; and so it had to be to their ill fortune.
1507	Until that time all the people of the world spoke a single language and in the same way; they spoke in Hebrew, in a single tongue and could not speak or write on wax in any other.
1508	God set among those men such great confusion that they all forgot their natural form of speech; they spoke separate languages, each with its own ring, and could not tell what each other was saying or not.
1509	If one asked for water, the other gave him lime; and the man who asked for mortar was given rope; what each one said, the other did something else, and the whole building, therefore, was destined to fail.
1510	By no means were they able to reach an agreement, so they had to abandon the task they had in hand; they were all obliged to spread throughout the world and each one was to people his own region.
1511	So it is today, the tower has been started but in a bad way, and built too high. Through the confusion which was inflicted on them, all that land bears the name of Babylonia.
1512	Seventy-two in number were the leaders of those men,* as many as the world's major languages, for this gibberish they utter, these same languages, are now a source of confusion among the workers.

1513 Los unos son latinos, los otros son ebreos;
a los unos dizen griegos, a los otros caldeos;
a otros dizen áraves e a otros sabeos,
a otros egipçios, a otros amorreos.

1514 Otros dizen ingleses, otros son de Bretaña;
escotes e irlandos, otros de Alemaña;
los que biven en Galas favlan de otra maña;
non es con éstos Siria en lenguaje tal maña.

1515 Otros son los de Persia, otros son los indianos,
otros los de Samaria, otros los medïanos;
otros los de Panfilia e otros los ircanos;
otros son los de Frigia, otros los libïanos.

1516 Otros dizen partos e otros elemitanos,
otros son capadoçios, otros ninivitanos;
otros son çireneos, otros cananitanos;
otros los almoçones, e otros los çitanos.

1517 El ome que crïado fuesse en Babilonia
de duro entendrié la lengua de Iconia;
más son de otros tantos que cuenta la estoria,
mas yo por a saberlos de seso non he copia.

1518 Semíramis la buena, una sabia reína,
pobló a Babilonia por la gracia divina;
quando Dïos lo quiso, aguisólo aína,
pero antes despiso mucha buena farina.

1519 Tantas calles y fizo como son los linages;
fízolas poblar todas de diversos lenguajes.
Los unos a los otros non sabién fer mensajes;
los unos a los otros teniénse por salvajes.

1520 Qual quier' de todas ellas es sobre sí çibdat;
non sabrién contra otra aver comunidat;
la más pobre de todas serié grant heredat;
a un rëy podrié sacar de pobredat.

1521 Qui todos los lenguajes quisiesse aprender,
allí podrié de todos çertedumbre saber;
mas ante podrié viejo desdentado seer
que la terçera parte pudiés' él aprender.

1513	Some men are Latins and others are Hebrews, others call themselves Greeks and others Chaldeans; others they call Arabs and others Shebans, others Egyptians, and yet others Amorites.*
1514	Others call themselves English, others are from Brittany; there are Scots and Irish and others from Germany; those who live in Gaul speak in a different way; Syria is not similar to them in its language.
1515	Others are those from Persia and others are Indians,* others those from Samaria and others are Medes; others those from Pamphylia and others Hyrcanians; others are those from Phrygia and others are Libyans.
1516	Others call themselves Parthians and others Elamites; others are Cappadocians and others Ninivites, others are Cyreneans and others Canaanites, others are Amazons and others Scythians.
1517	A man who had been raised in Babylonia would find it hard to understand the Iconian tongue; but there are so many others of whom the story tells that I have not such ample wit as to retain them.
1518	The good Semiramis, a learned queen,* peopled Babylonia by divine grace; as God willed it, she accomplished it quickly, though first she was to squander much fine flour.
1519	She established as many streets as there were bloodlines and had them all peopled with men of different tongues; they did not know how to communicate with each other and so they reckoned each other to be savages.
1520	Any one of the streets is a city in itself and could not form a community with another. The poorest of all would be a great inheritance and could rescue a great king from poverty.
1521	Anyone who wanted to learn all the languages would be able there to learn them all with certainty, but he would come to be old and decrepit before he had managed to learn but a third.

1522 Por quanto es la villa   de tal buelta poblada
que los unos a los otros   non se entienden nada,
por tanto es de nombre   de confusïón honrrada,
ca Babilón *confusio*   es en latín clamada.

1523 La çerca es estraña,   en peña çimentada;
maguer yaze en peña   es bien carcaveada.
la cárcava es fonda,   de agua bien rasada;
naves traen por ella,   ca es fonda e larga.

1524 Un trecho de vallesta   es en alto el muro;
de biva argamassa   e de pedreñal duro;
en ancho otro tanto,   si mal non lo mesuro;
el que estoviés' dentro   devriá seer seguro.

1525 Las torres son espessas,   segund que aprendemos;
sobre guisa son muchas,   cuenta non les sabemos;
los días de un año   dizen que serién diezmos;
de qui las non vïesse   creídos non seriemos.

1526 Las demás son de canto   menudas e granadas;
las otras son de mármol,   redondas e quadradas;
mas éstas con aquéssas   son assí aferradas
que sean a aquéstas   aquéssas sobjudgadas.

1527 Ha y, sin los postigos,   treinta puertas cabdales;
guardan las sendos rëys,   que pocos ay de tales,
todos por natura   son rëys naturales;
dizen que todos tienen   regnos generales.

1528 El real es en medio,   fecho a maravellas;
y es el sol pintado,   la luna e las estrellas;
y están las colupnas,   los espejos en ellas,
en que se miran todas,   casadas e donzellas.

1529 Son dentro en la villa   los naturales vaños,
que les vienen las aguas   yus' la tierra en caños;
están aparejados   de ropas e d'escaños;
nunca y vino ome   a quien menguassen paños.

1530 Tiene en quatro cantos   quatro torres cabdales;
más claras son que vidrio   nin que finos cristales;
si fazen por la villa   furtos o cosas tales
allí lo veen luego   por çerteras señales.

1522	Since the city is populated with such a mixture that the people do not understand each other at all, for this very reason it boasts the name of confusion, for Babylon, in Latin, is called *confusio*.
1523	The city wall is astounding, its foundations in rock; though it sits on a crag, a fine moat surrounds it; the moat is a deep one and quite full of water; ships sail upon it, for it is deep and wide.
1524	The wall itself is a crossbow shot in height, formed of a mixture of fresh mortar and hard flint, and just as great in width, if I do not measure wrongly; whoever stood within it should indeed feel safe.
1525	The towers are thick, according to what we are told, and countless in number, too many to reckon: they say the days of the year would be a tenth as many; by whoever had not seen them, we would not be believed.
1526	The towers are mostly of stone, smaller ones and larger; others are of marble, both round and square; but these marble towers cling so firmly to the others that they seem to be completely overwhelmed by them.
1527	There are, besides the postern gates, thirty large gateways; a different king guards each, with whom few can compare; all of these are kings of royal birth and lineage; they say that they all have their own far-reaching kingdoms.
1528	The citadel is in the centre, a wonder of construction, and on it are depicted the sun, moon, and stars, and in it there are columns that are inset with mirrors in which, married or maiden, all women behold themselves.
1529	Within the city natural baths are to be found to which the water is piped beneath the ground; the baths are equipped with robes and with seats; no man ever came there and was lacking in clothes.
1530	On four rocks they have built four huge towers, shining more brightly than glass or fine crystal; if thefts or such crimes are committed in the city there they see it at once with total certainty.

1531   Nunca pudrién a ella   enemigos venir
        que bien de dos jornadas   se pudiessen cobrir;
        Nabucodonosor   allí solié dormir,
        el que se fazié dios   a los omes dezir.

1532   Non serié por asmar   la cuenta de las gentes;
        saldrién de cada cal   çient mill combatïentes.
        Éstos son cavalleros,   todos espada ciñientes;
        temo dirá alguno: "Calla, varón, que mientes."

1533   Fuera que la pudiessen   por espaçio veer,
        el bien de Babilonia   non lo podrián creer.
        ¡Busque otro maestro   qui más quisier' saber,
        ca yo en mi materia   quiero torno fazer!

1534   El rëy Alexandre   plógol' de voluntad
        quándol' besó la mano   el rëy de la çibdat.
        Vío quel' avié fecho   Dïos grant caridat
        ca non la ganara   menos de mortaldat.

1535   Mandó todas sus gentes   que fuessen allegadas;
        al entrar de la villa   fuessen hazes paradas;
        como pora batalla   fuessen todas armadas,
        que por traïción mala   non fuessen engañadas.

1536   El pueblo de la villa   fue todo acordado
        – non era maravilla,   ca era profetado –;
        salleron reçebirlo   al rey aventurado,
        ca veyén que de Dios   le era otorgado.

1537   Como las rúas eran,   ellos assí vinieron;
        todos por a.b.c.   con él cartas partieron;
        cad'uno sobre sí   omenajel' fizieron;
        de leal vassallaje   las verdades le dieron.

1538   Al entrar de la villa,   mugeres e varones
        salleron reçebirlo   con diversas cançiones;
        quáles eran las gentes,   quáles las proçesiones
        non lo sabrién dezir   loquelle nin sermones.

1539   Qui buen vestido ovo,   escusar non lo quiso;
        qui propio non lo ovo   emprestado lo priso;
        qui bella cosa ovo,   en la calle la miso.
        Nunca fue tan grant gozo   fuera de paraíso.

1531	Enemies could never come to the city who could keep themselves hidden at two days' distance; King Nebuchadnezzar used to spend his nights there,* the one who had his men address him as God.
1532	The number of the people could not be reckoned, for a hundred thousand warriors would come from each street; these are knights and men who gird on a sword for battle; I fear someone will say, "Hush, my man, you lie."
1533	Except those whose gaze had lingered upon it, none would be able to believe Babylon's wealth; let those who wish to know more seek another master, for I wish to make a return to my subject.
1534	King Alexander was filled with deep pleasure when the ruler of the city kissed his hand; he could see that God had done to him great mercy for he would not have taken it without great loss of life.
1535	He commanded his men all to gather together and form up their columns to enter the city and arm themselves, all of them, as if for battle, that they not be deceived by evil treachery.
1536	The people of the city were all in agreement – it was no wonder, for it had been foretold –; they went out to receive the King favoured by fortune, for they could see it had been granted him by God.
1537	As the streets were laid out, so they came to him; in documents by a.b.c. they fixed their accord;* each man paid Alexander full homage for himself and gave him his guarantee of loyal vassalage.
1538	As he entered the city, both women and men went out to receive him with various songs; what the people were like, and the processions, too, neither common speech nor sermons would know how to express.
1539	Those who possessed a fine garment did not spare it and those without their own put on one they had borrowed; those who owned something beautiful put it out in the street; there never was joy so great, outside of Paradise.

1540 Echavan los moçuelos ramos por las carreras,
cantando sus responsos de diversas maneras.
Bien pareçié que eran las gentes plazenteras,
que todos por sus puertas fazién grandes lumneras.

1541 Sacavan las espeçias, todas bien apiladas,
unas por destemprar, e otras destempradas;
pora temprar el aire todas bien aguisadas;
demás, eran las calles todas encortinadas.

1542 Ivan las proçessiones rica ment' ordenadas:
los clérigos primeros con sus cartas sagradas,
el rëy çerca ellos, que ordenaron las fadas,
el que todas las gentes avié mal espantadas.

1543 Vinién aprés del rëy todos sus senadores;
cónsules e perfectos vinién por guïadores;
después, los cavalleros que son sus defensores,
que los pueblos a éstos acatan por señores.

1544 Vinién más a espaldas, todos los del regnado;
como vinién de buelta era desbaratado;
mas, en cabo, las dueñas vinién tan aguisado
que les avié el rey Alexandre grant grado.

1545 El pleit' de los juglares era fiera rïota;
y avíe çinfoñas, farpa, giga e rota;
albogues e salterio, çítola que más trota,
guitarra e vïola, que las cueitas embota.

1546 Por amor de veer al rey de grant ventura,
por muros e por techos subién a grant pressura;
sedién por las finiestras gentes sin grant mesura;
algunos, como creo, sedién en angostura.

1547 Queremos d'este pleito delibrarnos privado:
fue el rey en las torres todas apoderado.
Sojornó en la çibdat fasta que fue pagado;
recabdó bien su pleito como ome venturado.

1548 Bien semejó en esto que fue de Dios amado.
Quando fue a su guisa el rëy sojornado,
mandó mover las señas, sallir fuera al prado;
¡Galterio, vé dormir, ca assaz has velado!

| 1540 | The children scattered the streets with branches,
singing their responses in many different styles;
the people had a look of tremendous joy
and they all lit great fires at their doors. |
|---|---|
| 1541 | They brought out the spices, all piled in heaps,
some still to be dried and others dried out,
all well prepared to give the air a sweet scent,
and all the streets were also adorned with hangings. |
| 1542 | There were processions drawn up with rich display,
the clergy at the fore with their holy Scriptures,
the King close behind them, whom the Fates ordained,
the man who had struck such fear into all peoples. |
| 1543 | After the King came all of his councillors,
consuls and prefects came as his protectors,
after them the knights who are his defenders
and on whom the people look as their lords. |
| 1544 | More towards the rear came all those from the kingdom,
arriving in disorder, as they all thronged together;
further back came the ladies, so elegantly dressed
that King Alexander was delighted by them. |
| 1545 | The minstrels' performance was one of wild merriment;
there were there pipes, harps, rebecs and lyres,
flutes and psalteries, fast-playing zithers,
guitars and viols, which ease men's cares.* |
| 1546 | In desire to see the King of great good fortune
they scrambled quickly up onto walls and roofs;
people beyond reckoning sat along the windows,
and some, I do believe, were cramped indeed. |
| 1547 | Quickly do we want to free ourselves of this account.
The King took possession of all the towers
and stayed in the city till his desire was sated;
rounding off his business as a man of good fortune. |
| 1548 | It seemed clear from this that he was loved by God;
and, when the King had stayed to his content,
he bade the standards be moved and the troops strike camp
Walter, go and sleep, you have stayed up long enough!* |

1549 Pero que por promessa   que por fuerça de dado,
     avién conseja fecho   que tañié en pecado;
     ivan por las aldeas   los cuerpos delectando;
     fazién bien a su guisa   de lo que ivan fallando.

1550 Mandó fincar las gentes   en un rico lugar;
     de fuentes e de prados   non podrié mejorar;
     metióles fueros nuevos   que non solién usar,
     que pudiessen las gentes   mas en çierto andar.

1551 Ordenó millenarios   por mandar mill varones;
     otros que guiassen çiento,   que son çenturïones;
     otros quinquagenarios,   otros decurïones;
     puso legïonarios   sobre las legïones.

1552 Por esso quiso fer   estos adelantados,
     por provar quáles eran   covardes o osados;
     ca muchos fazién poco,   que eran más nombrados
     que otros que fazién   los fechos muy granados.

1553 El querié que al bueno   la verdat le valiesse;
     non levasse soldada   qui non la mereçiesse;
     cada uno al suyo   tal silla le pusiesse
     e tal puesta de carne   por que lo entendiesse.

1554 Getró, con cuya fija   Moïsés fue casado,
     ovo a Moïsés   esti consejo dado
     onde bivió después   en paz e más honrado
     e el pleito del pueblo   fue mejor aliñado.

1555 Camió unas costumbres   que eran mal usadas;
     mas teniénlas por buenas   quando fueron mudadas.
     Como todas sus cosas,   eran bien adonadas;
     fueron todas las gentes   del su fecho pagadas.

1556 Las gentes otro tiempo   quando querién mover
     fazién cuernos e trompas   e bozinas tañer;
     luego sabién los omes   el signo entender,
     luego pensavan todos   las carreras prender.

1557 El rey Alexandre,   tesoro de proeza,
     arca de sapïençia,   exemplo de nobleza,
     que siempre amó prez   más que otra riqueza,
     mudó esta costumbre,   fizo grant sotileza.

1549   But, whether by a promise or the throw of a die,
        they had adopted a plan which amounted to sin:
        they went round the villages giving pleasure to their bodies,
        enjoying at will whatever they encountered.

1550   Alexander bade his men stop in a place of beauty
        – for springs and meadows it could not be bettered –
        and gave them new and unaccustomed codes of law,
        so that the people could live more properly.

1551   He established lords to govern groups of a thousand,
        others to lead a hundred, who were centurions;
        others commanded fifty, others were leaders of ten,
        and he set legionaries at the head of the legions.

1552   For this reason he sought to give these men authority,
        that they might show their true colours, cowardly or brave,
        for many men did little who were the most renowned
        and other men were those who carried out the greatest feats.

1553   He desired that the truth be of service to the good
        and that a man not deserving it should not receive pay,
        that each man should occupy the place most fitting
        and receive such a ration as he himself thought right

1554   Jethro, to whose daughter Moses was married,*
        had given to the prophet this very same advice,
        by which he lived afterwards in peace and greater honour
        and the lives of his people were better ordered.

1555   The King changed some customs which were ill suited
        – but they thought it good when the change was made –;
        like all he did, these matters were well thought out
        and the people were all pleased with what he had done.

1556   In other times, when his people wished to move out
        they sounded the call on horns, trumpets and clarions,
        and the men could understand the signal at once
        and all at once made ready to set out on their journey.

1557   King Alexander, the great treasure of prowess,
        ark of wisdom and exemplar of nobility,
        who always loved renown above all other riches,
        changed this custom, and this was a clever act.

1558   Las gentes eran grandes,   ca siempre le creçién;
       posavan a anchura   como sabor avién;
       quando tañián el cuerno   todos non lo oyén;
       por end' a las vegadas   grant engaño prendién.

1559   Mandóles, quand' oviessen   otro día a mover,
       fumo fuesse por signo   por fer lo entender;
       de noche, almenaras   por çerteras seer;
       otorgaron lo todos,   ovieron grant plazer.

1560   Quando ovo el rëy   sus cosas assentadas,
       sus fueros establidos,   sus lëys ordenadas,
       mandó luego mover   sus firmes mesnadas
       que, por que non movién,   eran ya enojadas.

1561   Fueron çercar a Susa,   una noble çibdat:
       serié grant xaramiello   fablar de su bondat.
       Como tierra sin rëy   e sin abtoridat
       reçibieron lo luego,   sin otra poridat.

1562   Assaz avié en Susa   que pudiessen prender;
       mas por que lo prisiessen   non lo podrién traer;
       en sacos nin en quilmas   non podién mas caber;
       aviénlo a dexar,   mas non en su querer.

1563   Quand' ovo Alexandre   a Susa sobjugada,
       firió sobre Uxión,   una villa famada;
       cuidóla entrar luego,   mas, por la mi espada,
       bien cara le costó   quan' la ovo ganada.

1564   Métades avié nombre   el rey que la tenié;
       del quebranto de Dario   sabet que nol' plazié.
       Amigos fueron amos,   ca bien lo conoçié;
       cuidólo él vengar,   lo que Dios non querié.

1565   Treviése en la villa,   que era bien çercada,
       e que era de dentro   de gentes bien poblada;
       estava en alto pueyo   en peña çimentada;
       tenié que por los griegos   non serié señorada.

1566   Quando sopo Alexandre   que en esso andava,
       dixo: "Dïos lo sabe,   que esto non cuidava;
       de la parte de Métades   esto non esperava;
       mas esti denodejo   non valdrá una fava."

1558	His forces were vast, for they were always growing, and encamped at will, as the desire took them; when they sounded the horn, not everyone heard it and therefore at times there was great confusion.
1559	He ordered that, when they had to move out in future, smoke should be the signal to convey the message, and fires should be the signal in the night-time, clear to see; they all approved of his idea, greatly pleased.
1560	When the King had set his affairs in good order, established his charters and set his laws in place, at once he commanded his stout troops to move out: they were already restless at not being on the move.
1561	They went to encircle Susa, a noble city;* to talk of its qualities would be a lengthy tale; as a city with no king nor authorities to govern they received Alexander with frankness and speed.
1562	There was plenty in Susa that they could have taken but, had they done so, it could not have been transported; in neither sacks nor bags could they hold any more and they had to leave it, though it was not their will.
1563	When Alexander held Susa beneath his control, he struck out against Uxion, a city of great fame.* He planned a quick entrance, but, by my sword, he had to pay a high price before taking it.
1564	Medates was the name of the King in power there* and I tell you that Darius' defeat did not please him; the two of them were friends, for he knew the man well and determined to avenge him – against God's will.
1565	He grew bold in the city with its fine walls and which held a large population within; it stood high on a hill with its foundations in rock and he did not believe it would be mastered by the Greeks.
1566	When Alexander understood that state of affairs, he said, "God knows that this is not what I planned; this is not what I was expecting from Medates, but this defiance will not be worth a bean."

1567 Uxïón fue çercada, Alexandre irado;
mandávala lidiar, que era ensañado.
Fazié en todo Métades razón e aguisado;
mas non valen escantos quando Dios es irado.

1568 Era de todas partes la cosa ençendida;
avién ellos e ellos la vergüença perdida;
la dubda de morir era toda fuïda;
non avién en ferir cosiment' nin medida.

1569 Vinieron en comedio la cosa assí yendo,
al rëy doze omes aprïessa corriendo.
Dixieron: "Rey, señor, ¿en qué estás contendiendo?
Tú mismo telo vees, quál daño vas prendiendo.

1570 Por ninguna batalla non la puedes prender;
antes puedes la media de las gentes perder.
Mas si a nos queredes escuchar e creer,
nos te daremos seso que la puedas prender.

1571 Nos somos de la tierra, sabemos las entradas,
sabemos las salidas, sí femos las passadas.
Si tú nos darás omes, nos les daremos gradas;
quando se catarán, dentro serán uviadas."

1572 Lamó luego el rëy a Taurón su privado,
que era de esfuerço muchas vezes provado.
Dixo: "Sepas, Taurón, en ti so acordado
que vayas con éstos recabdar un mandado.

1573 Pero quiero que lieves de mí esta señal.
Bien ten que yago muerto e que so con grant mal
si ante que tú seas en medio del real
en medio de Uxión non fuere Buçifal."

1574 Non lo dixo a sordo; pensó luego de ir;
entró en traspüesto por mejor s'encobrir;
mas ovieron los antes los otros a sentir:
fizieron los tornar, non pudieron subir.

1575 Quando vío Taurón que non podrién entrar,
fascas non querié menos en su tienda estar.
Dixo que más querié el alma y dexar
que con manos vazías a su señor tornar.

1567   Uxion was surrounded and Alexander, in a rage,
        ordered the attack be launched – for he was incensed;
        Medates' every action was prudent and appropriate
        but tricks have no value when God Himself is angry.

1568   On all sides the conflict raged in heated frenzy
        and both armies had shed any feeling of remorse;
        the fear of death had completely fled the field
        and they were without mercy or measure in their blows.

1569   At this point, with the battle reaching such a stage,
        twelve men ran up to the King in great haste
        and said, "Lord King, what are you striving for?
        You can see yourself what harm you are incurring.

1570   By no battle do you have the means to take the city;
        before you do, you may lose half of your troops;
        but, if you will heed us and believe what we say,
        we will give you a plan by which it can be captured.

1571   We are from this land and we know the ways in,
        we know the ways out, and are familiar with the paths;
        if you will give us men, we shall give them ladders
        and when they are discovered they will have come inside."

1572   The King at once called upon Tauron, his confidant,*
        whose valour had been many times proved, and said:
        "Tauron, I want you to know I have determined
        that you should go with these men to execute an order.

1573   But I wish you to take with you this pledge from me:
        consider it certain that I lie dead or gravely hurt
        if, before you reach the middle of the of the citadel,
        Bucephalus does not stand at Uxion's centre."

1574   It did not fall on deaf ears; Tauron went on his way;
        he entered in secrecy, to hide himself the better;
        but their enemies had perceived them beforehand,
        and made them turn back; they could not climb up.

1575   When Tauron saw that they could not get inside,
        he would almost have rather been back in his tent
        and said that he preferred to leave his soul behind there,
        rather than return to his lord with empty hands.

1576   Empeçóles a dar   una lit apressada,
       mas non querién por esso   dexar le la entrada;
       maguer que avié preso   mucha mala colpada,
       como querié morir   non lo preçiava nada.

1577   El rëy Alexandre,   de la otra partida,
       tenié bien la señal   que avié prometida.
       Avié a part' echada   mucha barva vellida,
       mas non podié por esso   entrar a la bastida.

1578   Pero tanto los pudo   ferir e acuitar
       que dieron a Taurón   un poco de vagar.
       Acreçiól' el esfuerço,   ovo ad abivar;
       oviéronle sin grado   la puerta a dexar.

1579   Tanto ovieron todos   en lo al que veer
       que mientes en Taurón   non pudieron meter;
       ovo seles en medio   del real a meter,
       ovo en lo más alto   el pendón a poner.

1580   Estava Alexandre   que la cosa veyé,
       catando a las torres   quándo assomarié;
       e quando fue asmando   que ya apareçié,
       mostró gelo a todos   quantos çerca tenié.

1581   Fueron los de Uxión   todos mal desmayados;
       quando el pendón veyeron,   fueron mal corasnados.
       Los griegos con grant gozo   fueron más esforçados;
       semejava que eran   nueva mente uviados.

1582   Métades e los otros   que eran de conçejo
       non sopieron de sí   mandado nin consejo;
       era a cada uno   angosto el pellejo;
       el castillo tan grande   faziés'les castillejo.

1583   Avié en la çibdat   una torre loçana,
       en cabo de la villa   de todas orellana;
       en altez' semejava   de las nuves hermana;
       era en el çimiento   firme e fuert' e sana.

1584   Métades con aquellos   que eran de su vando
       vieron que seles iva   su cosa mal parando.
       Fuéronse poc' a poco   a la torre llegando;
       dieron consigo dentro,   lo al desamparando.

1576	He started to launch a determined attack but that was not enough to force his way inside; although he had suffered many cruel blows, as he wanted to die, he thought nothing of it.
1577	King Alexander, in that other quarter, kept to the promise that he had made to Tauron: many fine warriors had he struck down but even so he could not breach their defences.
1578	But so great were the blows and the harm that he dealt that Tauron was given a little respite; his courage now swelled and his strength was restored; unwillingly, they had to yield the gateway to him.
1579	The men all had so many other concerns that they were unable to give thought to Tauron. He made his way into the citadel's middle and set his pennant on the very highest point.
1580	Alexander, who could see all that took place, was watching the towers to see when he emerged, and when he caught sight of him now coming into view, he pointed it out to all those that he had nearby.
1581	The men of Uxion were all filled with deep distress when they saw the pennant, and they were much disheartened; but the Greeks, in their joy, were strengthened in resolve and it seemed that they were fresh to the fight.
1582	Medates and the others who were in council did not have themselves either orders or plans to give, and each one felt that his skin was stretched tight; their huge castle was becoming a small fort.
1583	There was in the city a magnificent tower, at the edge of the place and far from the others; in its height it seemed to be a sister of the clouds but its foundations were firm, strong and very sound.
1584	Medates, with those who went at his side, saw that affairs were turning ill for them; little by little they made their way to that tower and took refuge within, forsaking all else.

1585   Los griegos en la villa   fueron apoderados;
ca eran los de dentro   todos desbaratados.
Fuera los que estavan   en la torre alçados,
todos yazién en fierros   e en sogas atados.

1586   Embió luego al rëy   Métades de paraje;
treinta de omes buenos   fueron con el mensaje:
quel' farién de grado   pleito e omenaje
de seer siempre suyos   de leal vassallaje.

1587   Tornaron les respuesta,   non qual ellos querían:
que por ninguna guisa   de muert' non estorçerían;
quando por lealdat,   ellos morir querían,
fallada avién ora   que lo recabdarían.

1588   En cueita eran Métades,   non sabié dó tornar;
pero ovo un seso   estraño a asmar:
embïó a la madre   de Dario a rogar
que rogasse por ellos,   fiziésselos quitar.

1589   Maguer querié, non era   Sisigambis osada
de demandar al rëy   cosa tan señalada.
Temiése la mesquina   que serié sossañada;
caerié en denodeo,   non recabdarié nada.

1590   Pero como el rëy   era de grant mesura,
aosóse por ende,   metiós' a grant ventura;
entró do 'stava él   con omill' catadura,
que perdonás' a Métades   ca fiziera locura.

1591   Entendió Alexandre   cómo avié dubdado;
fue contra la reína   un poquillo irado;
embïól' a dezir   que sí farié de grado,
mas, si jamás dubdava,   non serié su pagado.

1592   Perdonól' a Metades   con toda su çibdat;
otorgóles sus cosas   e toda su heredat;
mandóles que oviessen   complida egualdat.
¡Bendito sea rëy   que faze tal bondat!

1593   Nin de fijo la madre   nin de muger marido
non podrié acabar   tan granado pedido.
Darïo contra ella   non serié tan cosido,
mager ella lo ovo   de su vientre parido.

1585	The Greeks were in full control of the city for those within had all been defeated; except for those who had taken refuge in the tower, they all lay in irons or bound with ropes.
1586	Medates quickly sent nobles to the king: thirty good men went bearing his message, that they would gladly pay him the service and homage of being forever his loyal vassals.
1587	They were given a reply – not such as they sought – that by no means would they save themselves from death; since they had wished to die from a sense of loyalty, now had they found the time when they would achieve this.
1588	Medates was in trouble and knew not where to turn, but he managed to devise an unexpected plan: he sent out to Darius' mother with a plea that she beg for their safety and obtain their freedom.
1589	Willing though she was, Sisygambis did not dare* to ask of the King so conspicuous a favour; the poor woman feared that she would be rebuked, fall into ill favour and not achieve a thing.
1590	But, as the King was a man of great discretion, on that account she dared and took the chance: she came into his presence, with a humble look, and begged he pardon Medates his foolish conduct.
1591	Alexander realised how she had been in fear, and he was just a little angry with the Queen; he sent word to her that he would gladly do it, but if she ever feared him, she would not have his favour.
1592	He pardoned Medates, with all of his city, and ceded them their assets, their whole inheritance, ordering that they should have complete equality; blessed be a king who displays such goodness!
1593	Neither from a mother's son nor a wife's husband could so great a favour possibly be gained; Darius would not have shown such kindness to her, although she had birthed him from her own womb.

1594 El rëy Alexandre, maguer tanto ganava,
la pérdida de Dario non se li olvidava;
la su grant voluntad non se li amansava;
mas de día en día más se encorajava.

1595 Mandóle a Parmenio con muchos de poderes
ir por la tierras planas prometiendo averes
por saber de ti, Dario, en quáles tierras eres:
si finqueste en Persia o fuiste a los aires.

1596 Él con sus varones subié por las montañas,
do moran los serranos, essas gentes estrañas;
si fuesse por ventura Dario en las cabañas,
non le valiessen nada sus sesos nin sus mañas.

1597 Los passos eran firmes, angostas las carreras,
las gentes sobre guisa valientes e ligeras;
faziénle grandes daños de diversas maneras,
con cantos e con galgas e con lanças monteras.

1598 Antes que suso fuessen a las sierras sobidos,
ante ovieron muchos de los omes perdidos.
Los muertos de su grado non murién mal vendidos
pero fueron en cabo domados e vençidos.

1599 Deçendió de la sierra el buen rey acabado;
querié ir por a Persia, reino desamparado.
Fue luego a Persépolis, cabeça del regnado;
y falló a Parmenio, de ganançia cargado.

1600 Nunca tanto pudieron andar nin entender,
nunca tanto pudieron nin dar nin prometer
que pudiessen de Dario nul recabdo saber;
más querién a él solo que su regno tener.

1601 La çibdat non se pudo al rëy emparar;
como cosa sin dueño óvola a entrar.
Mandóla por çimiento destroïr e quemar;
nunca más la pudieron bastir nin restaurar.

1602 La çibdat de Persépolis, cosa tan prinçipal,
yazié sobre Atexin, una agua cabdal.
Assí fue estroída, toda ida a mal,
que non pareçe d'ella sola una señal.

Book of Alexander

1594   King Alexander, in spite of his great gain,
was not unmindful of Darius' escape,
and that great desire that he felt grew no gentler,
but day by day did his anger grow crueller.

1595   He sent out Parmenion with numerous troops
to go through the plains and promise gifts of wealth,
to learn of you, Darius, in what lands you are,
if you stayed in Persia or fled to the winds.

1596   Alexander and his men rode up into the hills,
where the mountain people dwell, that curious race;
if Darius, by chance, were among their dwellings,
all his tricks and artifice would not have availed him.

1597   The passes were hard and the pathways narrow,
the people exceedingly brave and swift of foot,
and they did them great harm in various ways,
with stones and with rocks and with hunting spears.

1598   Before they had made their way high into the mountains,
they had already lost a large number of their men;
the enemy who died willingly sold their lives dearly
but in the end they were defeated and tamed.

1599   The fine, accomplished King came down from the mountains,
he wished to move against Persia, an abandoned realm;
he went straight for Persepolis, the kingdom's capital,*
and there he met Parmenion, laden with his booty.

1600   Never were they able to travel or learn enough,
never were they able to promise or give enough
to manage to discover any news of Darius;
the King desired him alone more than all his realm.

1601   The city was unable to resist the King,
as it had no leader he came easily inside;
he ordered it be razed to the ground and burned
that it might never again be rebuilt or restored.

1602   The city of Persepolis, a place so fine,
lay on the Araxes, a deep-flowing river;
it was so utterly destroyed and brought to ruin
that today not a single trace of it remains.

| 1603 | Teniéle Alexandre saña vieja alçada,
ca los rëys de Persia, si fazién cavalgada,
allí tenién primero vigilia costumbrada,
ende llevavan todos armas d'obra esmerada. |

| 1604 | Dende sallïó Sersis cuando Greçia conquiso,
quando en subjecçión e en premia la miso;
soliénse de los griegos fer escarnio e riso,
por tanto Alexandre perdonar non le quiso. |

| 1605 | Fallaron en la villa averes muy granados,
ropas de grant valía, tesoros condesados;
ovo sobre la ropa muchos escabeçados;
los unos a los otros tolliénselo de manos. |

| 1606 | El menor al mayor nol' dava reverençia,
hermano a hermano nol' tenié obediençia;
grant el roído era, grant la desabenençia;
eran con la cobdiçia de mala continençia. |

| 1607 | Otra cosa fizieron por que fueron quemados:
falló y Alexandre tres mill de sus crïados;
cayeron en prisión, avién los desmembrados;
todos eran en miembros cabdales señalados. |

| 1608 | Non avié entre todos uno que fuesse sano,
que non oviesse menos el pïe o la mano,
el ojo o'l nariz o el labro susano,
o roxnado non fuesse en la fruent' con estaño. |

| 1609 | Ploró el rey de duelo, vençiólo pïedat;
mostró que le pesava de toda voluntad;
abraçólos a todos con grant benignidat;
olvidó con el duelo toda asperidat. |

| 1610 | Dixo el rey: "Amigos, esto en que estades;
non pesa más a vos que a mí, bien sepades.
Mas, qué queredes far quiero que lo digades;
otórgovos lo yo, que quiere que querades. |

| 1611 | Si avedes cobdiçia a la tierra tornar
o en esta provinçia queredes aturar,
aved vuestro consejo, sallid vos a fablar.
Lo que vos quisïerdes vos quiero otorgar." |

1603	Alexander bore against it a hatred of old, for the kings of Persia, if riding out on a raid, were first accustomed to keep a vigil there and thence to set out bearing finely worked arms.
1604	It was thence that Xerxes set out to conquer Greece when he set her beneath despotic oppression; they used to make ridicule and jest of the Greeks, wherefore Alexander would grant no pardon.
1605	They found in the city a very great wealth, clothes of great value and hidden treasures; the clothes led to many men losing their lives as they snatched them from each other's hands.
1606	The younger man paid no respect to his elder and brother did not show deference to brother; great was the uproar and great was the conflict; in their greed, their behaviour grew unruly.
1607	There was one other reason why the city was burned:* Alexander found there three thousand of his vassals who had been imprisoned and suffered loss of limbs; they had all undergone grievous mutilation.
1608	There was not a single one among them who was whole, who was not missing at least a foot or hand, an eye or his nose or his upper lip, or whose forehead burning metal had not branded.
1609	The King wept with grief, overcome with pity, and showed that he was filled with deepest sorrow; he embraced them all, with a great show of warmth, and forgot all harshness with the grief he felt.
1610	The King said, "My friends, the state that you are in grieves you no more than me, be sure of that; but what you wish to do, I wish for you to tell me: I grant to you whatever you desire.
1611	Whether you long to return to your homeland or whether you wish to remain in this province, take your own counsel and go aside to speak; my will is to grant you whatever you wish."

1612   Salleron consejarse   la compaña lazrada
por prender su acuerdo   de cosa destajada;
mas la desabenençia   fue entre ellos dada;
non podién entre sí   acordarse por nada.

1613   Querién los unos ir   e los otros fincar,
non se podién por nada   en uno acordar;
los unos a los otros   nos' querién escuchar;
nin aun razón por ren   non podién otorgar.

1614   Levantós' uno d'ellos,   un ome bien lenguado;
fue, como Galter dize,   Eütiçio clamado;
era sotil retórico,   non fue mal escuchado;
empeçó su razón   como buen advocado:

1615   "Quiero vos yo, amigos,   mío seso dezir;
si fuere vuestra graçia,   quem' querades oír:
que mucho nos queramos   contender e dezir,
es el mejor consejo   rafez de abenir.

1616   A ir con grant vergüença   alimosna pedir
non podemos agora   a ningund logar sallir;
yo non lo sé asmar,   non lo sé comedir,
con qué caras podamos   a nuestras tierras ir.

1617   Los que mal nos quisieren   avrán de nos vengança;
verán nuestros amigos   cada día grant lança;
avrán mala sabor,   nos nulla mejorança;
non se devrié nul ome   pagar de tal andança.

1618   Quando al ome viene   alguna ocasión,
de muerte o de pérdida   o de grant lisïón,
ploran lo los amigos   que han compassïón;
por esto sólo tienen   que le dan un grant don.

1619   Luego que de las lágremas   es ome alimpiado,
el clamor e el duelo   luego es olvidado;
d'éstas es el manar   muy aína quedado,
ca assoman aína   e secan se privado.

1620   Avrán nuestras mugeres   con nusco grant pesar,
que non avremos braços   con que las abraçar;
qui, quando era sano,   non me sabié amar
non me querrié agora   con el ojo catar.

1612	The wretched company went aside to take counsel, to form an agreement founded on a firm decision; but disagreement made its way in among them and in no respect could they reach an accord.
1613	Some wanted to leave and others wished to stay: they were completely unable to agree; they were unwilling to listen to each other and utterly unable to come to an assent.
1614	One of them got up, a man of clever tongue, a man, as Walter says, whose name was Euctemon; a subtle rhetorician, he gained their full attention; he began his speech as a good lawyer would.
1615	"My friends, I wish to explain to you my thoughts, if you are willing to listen to my words: however much we strive to argue and debate, the best plan is easy to arrive at.
1616	To go in great shame to beg for alms we cannot now leave for any place; I just cannot think, I just cannot imagine with what faces we can come to our own lands
1617	Whoever wills us ill will have their vengeance on us and every day our friends will meet great sorrow; they will come off worse and we shall not gain a thing; no man should be pleased with such a circumstance.
1618	When a man is struck by some misfortune, of death, or of loss, or of great injury, his friends shed tears for him in their compassion: in this alone they hold that they make him a great gift.
1619	As soon as a man has wiped away all his tears, the loud cries and sorrow are forgotten at once; the flowing of the tears is very quickly stopped for they well up rapidly and run dry just as fast.
1620	Our wives will have great sorrow from our presence, for we have no arms with which we might embrace them, and the one who could not love me when I was whole would not now be willing to set eyes on me.

1621 De solaz e de mesa   seremos desechados;
     darnos han, com' a gafos,   lugares apartados;
     serán por los parientes   los fijos denostados;
     ellos avrán grant cueita,   nos seremos lazrados.

1622 El ome que non ha   de cueita a sallir,
     quanto más pudïesse   se devié encobrir;
     al ome que non veen   non saben escarnir;
     es bien atales omes   solitarios bevir.

1623 Segund que yo entiendo,   el ome mal lazrado
     allí do lo coñoçen   es más embargado;
     do non saben quién es   non ha tanto cuitado;
     ave qual que refugio   contra el su mal fado.

1624 ¡Acordémosnos todos!   ¡Pidamos un pedido!
     Varones, nos dexemos   tod' aqueste roído;
     den nos en que bivamos,   nuestro vito complido;
     de Dios e de los omes   será por bien tenido."

1625 Fue luego en pie Reçeus,   Eütiçio callado;
     natural de Atenas,   ome bien razonado;
     contradíxolo todo   quanto avié fablado;
     non dexó un artículo   que non fues' recontado.

1626 Dixo: "Si me quisierdes,   señores, atender,
     quiero vos breve mente   esto contradizer;
     maguer que so de todos   de menor coñoçer,
     a quanto que él dixo   yo cuidol' responder.

1627 Todos nuestros amigos   nos a denostados:
     a mugeres e a fijos   a nos los mal pintados;
     si todos los amigos   son tan mal afeitados,
     todos, ellos e nos,   fuemos en fuert' dia nados.

1628 El amigo derecho,   que non es desleal,
     nunca es cambïado   nin por bien nin por mal;
     por ocasión quel' venga   non salle de señal;
     en cueita e en viçio   siempr' está en egual.

1629 Si ocasión nos vino   o ocasión prisiemos,
     non nos pararon tales   por que mal mereçiemos
     nin nos pararon tales   por mal que fizïemos,
     si non por que al rëy   nuestro señor sirviemos.

1621	From the bed and the table we shall be cast aside
	and we shall be sent to remote spots like lepers;
	sons will be insulted because of their fathers,
	great torment will be theirs, and we shall suffer.
1622	The man without means to escape his misfortune
	should conceal himself as far as he can;
	the man they do not see they cannot deride,
	and it is good for such men to live in solitude.
1623	As I understand it, the man beset by trials
	is most overwhelmed in the place where he is known;
	where they know not who he is, he endures less pain
	and he finds some refuge against his ill fate.
1624	Let us all agree and make our request;
	men, let us leave all this uproar behind;
	let them give us a home, a full portion of food,
	and by God and by men this will be held as right."
1625	Theteus arose the instant Euctemon fell silent;
	a native of Athens, he was a good speaker;
	he contradicted everything that man had said
	and did not leave a single point without rebuttal.
1626	He said, "If you are willing to heed me, my lords,
	I wish briefly to speak against what you have heard;
	although I am the one with least knowledge of all,
	I intend to respond to all that he said.
1627	He has spoken with insult of all of our friends
	and our wives and children he has painted ill;
	if all of our friends have a shine so dull,
	their birth and ours came on a grim day.
1628	The worthy friend, who shows no disloyalty,
	is never changed by triumph or disaster;
	whatever ill betides him, he strays not from his mark,
	in hardship and in pleasure, he always stays the same.
1629	If misfortune came upon us or if we have sought it,
	such things did not befall us because we deserved ill,
	nor did they befall us for ill that we have done,
	but because we were serving the King, our lord.

1630　El ome qu'en fazienda　e en lid va y cutiano
　　　pierde por aventura　ojo, nariz o mano;
　　　non lo tiene a onta　por que non sea sano;
　　　antes se preçia d'ello　e tienes' por loçano.

1631　Si nuestros enemigos,　a qui nos guerreamos,
　　　algunt mal nos fizieron　que non gelo buscamos,
　　　non nos cae en onta　que vergüença ayamos
　　　por que a nuestra tierra　sin dubda non vayamos.

1632　El ome en su tierra　bive más a sabor;
　　　fázenle, quando muere,　los parientes onor;
　　　los huessos e el alma　han folgança mejor,
　　　quando muchos parientes　están a derredor.

1633　Los omes de la tierra　al que es estraño
　　　en cabo del fossar　lo echan orellano;
　　　danle como a puerco　en la fuessa de mano.
　　　Nunca más dize nadi:　'Aquí yaze fulano.'

1634　Mas el ome que es　de cruda voluntad
　　　cúidase que los otros　son sines pïedat;
　　　como assí él es,　pleno de malvestat,
　　　tiene que en los omes　non a de caridat.

1635　Non serién las mugeres　tanto desvergonçadas
　　　que – por dubdo del siglo　non serién destemadas –
　　　non lieven a l'iglesia　candelas nin obladas
　　　e non fagan clamores　tañer a las vegadas.

1636　Los fijos e las fijas　dulçes son de veer;
　　　han de su compañía　los parientes plazer;
　　　encara non los pueden　tanto aborreçer
　　　que descubierta mente　los puedan falleçer.

1637　Amigos, quien quisiere　creer e escuchar
　　　non plantará majuelo　en ajeno lugar;
　　　buscará cómo pueda　a su tierra tornar;
　　　crudo es quien su casa　quiere desemparar."

1638　Finó su razón Reçeus;　quiso que se viniessen;
　　　mas pocos ovo d'ellos　que creer lo quisiessen;
　　　acordáronse todos　que esto le pidiessen:
　　　que les diesse consejo　por que allí biviessen.

1630	The man who goes daily into conflict or battle, perhaps loses an eye, his nose, or a hand; he does not think it shameful that he is not whole, but rather he is proud and thinks himself fine.
1631	If enemies of ours, against whom we fought, did us some harm that we did not seek, that does not bring dishonour to cause us such shame that we should not go to our own land without fear.
1632	Man lives with greater pleasure in his own land and when he dies his kinsfolk do him honour; both bones and soul find a happier rest when there are many relatives close by.
1633	The men of this land, for a man unknown to them, at the end of the burial cast him aside, and they toss him into the grave like a pig; nevermore says anyone, 'Here lies so-and-so.'
1634	But the man who is of a harsh disposition believes that others, too, are lacking pity; since such is his character, a man full of evil, he holds that in men there is no charity.
1635	Women would not be so devoid of shame that, in fear of being slighted by the world, they would not bring candles and offerings to the church nor sometimes have the bells ring out their cry.
1636	Sons and daughters are sweet to the eyes, and parents take pleasure in their company; moreover, they cannot feel such hatred for them as to be able to forsake them in the open.
1637	My friends, whoever will believe me and take heed will not put down new roots in a foreign land but seek out how he might return to his homeland; it is a harsh man who wants to abandon his home."
1638	Theteus ended his speech, his wish that they might leave, but there were few others present willing to believe him; they all came to a decision that they would ask the King to give them the means that they might make their life there.

1639 Consejóles el rëy que assí lo fiziessen;
dioles omes logados que allí los sirviessen,
heredades planeras de que se mantoviessen,
de oro e de plata quanto llevar pudiessen.

1640 Quando ovo el rëy todo esto librado,
deçendió por a India, un regno acabado,
por entender de Dario si era y tornado,
e conquerir las gentes, por complir su mandado.

1641 Dario en est' comedio, müy desolazado,
ya era en Ebráctana con poca gent' plegado;
çibdat de muy grant preçio, valiá un grant condado,
ond' prendié toda vía esfuerço acabado.

1642 Querié el ome bueno a los bractos entrar;
pueblos buenos e muchos, yazién çerca de mar;
queriéles su quebranto dezir e rencurar,
que salliesen con él el regno emparar.

1643 Estava aguisando por entrar en carrera;
vínole una carta, ençerrada en çera,
que prisiesse consejo por alguna manera
ca la huest' de los griegos dentro en Media era.

1644 Nol podié venir mensaje mas cuitado;
a quien gelo aduxo óvol' poco de grado;
ovo a demudar quanto tenié asmado,
desque non era ora de prender pan mudado.

1645 Plegó gentes sobejos, todos bien adobados,
más de çinquenta vezes mill omes bien armados.
Querié la vez terçera aún echar los dados,
mas era otra guisa escripto de los fados.

1646 Çerca vinié la ora del día maledito
en que non podié Dario de la muert' seer quito.
Un paxarillo que echava un grant grito
andava cada noche redor de la tienda fito.

1647 Çerca trayé de sí qui l'avié de matar,
del que él por derecho non se podié guardar;
mas lo que Dios ordena assí es a passar;
él mismo non se pudo de traïçión guardar.

1639	The King's advice to them was that they should do just that; he gave them paid servants to care for them in that place, estates of fine flat lands to sustain themselves and all the gold and silver they could carry.
1640	When the King had put all these matters to rest, he descended on India, a kingdom complete, in order to discover if Darius had gone there and conquer its people to conclude his undertaking.
1641	Darius, at this point, in deep desolation, was now in Ecbatana with a handful of troops* – a city of great wealth, and worth a large county –, where he still sought to gather well-equipped forces.
1642	The good man wanted to go to the Bactrians – a people good and numerous whose lands lay near the sea –; he wanted to recount and lament to them his sorrows, that they might go with him to defend his kingdom.
1643	He was making ready to ride on his way when a letter came to him sealed in wax telling him to form an alliance by some means, for the army of the Greeks was in Media.
1644	No more troubling message could have come to him, and he was not grateful to the man who brought it. He had to change all that he had planned to do, since this was not the time to take borrowed bread.
1645	He brought together many troops, all well equipped – there were over fifty thousand men, finely armed –, for he still desired a third roll of the dice, but it had not been so written by the Fates.
1646	The hour drew near on the accursed day when he would not be able to escape his death; a tiny bird, which gave out a piercing cry, fluttered unstintingly each night around his tent.
1647	He kept very near him the man who was to kill him, from whom he could not rightly protect himself; but what God ordains must thus come to pass; even He had no defence against treachery.

1648 En su casa trayé   los falsos traïdores,
los que avié de siervos   él fecho señores;
ya lo ivan asmando   entre sus coraçones.
Devrié quebrar la tierra   con tan falsos varones.

1649 ¡O tú, Dario mesquino,   tan mal seso oviste
el día que a éssos   tan grant poder les diste!
Al falso Narbazones   por tu mal coñoçiste;
mas, que mucho digamos,   en fado lo oviste.

1650 Libráronte los fados   de los tus enemigos,
diéronte a matar   a los falsos amigos.
Si quisiesses creer   los proverbios antiguos
non dariés tal poder   a villanos mendigos.

1651 Mandó ante sí Dario   sus varones venir.
Fizo cara fermosa,   queriése encobrir;
dixo el *bendicite*   por la orden complir;
respondieron "Dominus";   supieron recodir.

1652 "Amigos," diz, "est' siglo   e esti temporal,
siempre assí andido,   oras bien, oras mal;
suele en pues lo uno   siempre venir lo al:
el mal en pues el bien   el bien en pues el mal.

1653 La rueda de ventura   siempre assí corrió:
a los unos alçó,   a los otros premió;
a los mucho alçados   luego los deçendió;
a los que deçendió   en cabo los pujó.

1654 Assaz so deçendido   por mis graves pecados;
yazemos so la rueda,   yo e vos, mal fadados;
son los avenedizos   a los muros pujados;
somos de lo que fuemos   nos e ellos camiados.

1655 Pero cuido que la rueda   non podrá seer queda;
tornará el vissiesto,   mudará la moneda;
será nuestra ventura   pagada e más queda;
avrán los venedizos   a pechar nos la rienda.

1656 Por verdat vos lo digo,   assí vos lo convengo:
quando vos bivos sodes   e çerca mí vos tengo,
quanto de mi emperio   en nada non me tengo;
nunca seré vengado   si por vos non me vengo.

1648	In his very household he kept the false traitors, men that he had turned from serfs into lords; they were gradually forming their plans in their hearts – the earth should gape open with men so false.
1649	Oh, wretched Darius, you conceived a plan so ill the day you placed such power in those men's hands! You met lying Nabarzanes to your misfortune, though, whatever we may say, you had it in your fate.
1650	The Fates delivered you from your enemies but offered you to false friends to kill; were you willing to believe the ancient proverbs, you would not have given such power to vile beggars.
1651	Darius commanded that his nobles come before him, put on a cheerful front, and sought to hide his feelings; he spoke the *benedicite* to carry out the rite and they replied with "Dominus", knowing the response.
1652	"My friends," he said, "this world and this age have always been thus, now good and now bad, the one always comes just after the other, good after bad and then bad after good.
1653	The wheel of Fortune spun always like this, raising some men up and casting others down; those raised up on high it at once threw down and those it threw down it at last brought high.
1654	I have been cast down far enough for my great sins; I and you, ill-fated, lie at the wheel's nadir; the newcomers are those who are raised up high: our place and theirs have both changed from what they were.
1655	But I do not think that the wheel can be stilled, our luck will change and the coin spin over our fortune will be kinder and grow more clement, and the newcomers will have to pay us tribute.
1656	I tell you this in truth and this I can promise: while you are alive and I have you close at hand, I value as nothing the empire I possess; I shall never have my vengeance if not through you.

1657 La vuestra lealtat   que avedes complida,
      en omes d'esti siglo   nunca fue tan oída;
      del Crïador del Çielo   la ayades gradida,
      el que todo lo sabe   e nada non olvida.

1658 Por lealtat avedes   grant lazerio levado,
      los parientes perdidos,   el miedo olvidado;
      guardastes vuestro rëy,   muchas vezes rancado.
      ¡Del Crïador vos sea   esto galardonado!

1659 Si oviesse Maçeo   tal lealtat complida,
      non serié Babilonia   tan aína perdida;
      el que a su señor   da tan mala caída,
      ¡después aya mal siglo,   agora mala vida!

1660 Los que de nos sallieron,   a los griegos passaron,
      nunca en esti siglo   tan mal non barataron;
      el rëy Alexandre,   al que la mano besaron,
      non los preçiará nada,   que sabe que falsaron.

1661 Pero, con esto todo,   al vos quiero dezir;
      devemos envisar   lo que es de venir;
      nunca puede al ome   el mal tanto nozir
      si antes que avenga   lo sabe perçebir.

1662 Si non fïasse tanto   en vuestra compañía,
      de lo que dezir quiero   nada non vos diría;
      mas sé que sodes todos   omes sin villanía;
      de toda mi fazienda   ren non vos encobriría.

1663 Los griegos son venidos   por a mí conseguir;
      non es sazón nin ora   que podamos fuïr;
      más quiero esperarlos,   en el campo morir
      que con tan fiera onta   en esti siglo bevir.

1664 En el su cosimente   non quiero yo entrar;
      non quiero de su mano   benefiçio tomar;
      con la cabeça pueden   el emperio llevar;
      non pueden otra guisa   comigo pleitear.

1665 Los que fasta agora   me avedes guardado,
      guardat bien vuestro preçio   que avedes ganado
      faziendo com' el bueno   que muere aguisado;
      és' a acabada vida   e preçio acabado."

1657	The loyalty that you have maintained towards me is unheard of among men of this world; may the Creator in Heaven pay you thanks, He who knows all things, forgetting nought.
1658	For loyalty you have endured great trials, lost your kinsmen and forgotten your fear; you protected your King in his many defeats: may the Creator reward you for this!
1659	If Mazaeus had maintained such loyalty as this, Babylon would not have been so quickly lost; a man who allows his lord so great a fall should suffer after death and have a bad life now.
1660	Those men who left us and went over to the Greeks never in this world did such a bad piece of business. King Alexander, whose hand they kissed in homage, will think them worth nothing, knowing they deserted.
1661	But, with all this, I wish to tell you one thing more: we have to anticipate what is yet to come; evil can never do a man such great harm if he can foresee it before its arrival.
1662	If I did not have such trust in your company, I would tell you nothing of what I wish to say. But I know that you are all men without baseness and I would hide from you none of my affairs.
1663	The Greeks have come here to hunt me down; this is not the moment or the time to flee; I would rather wait for them and die on battle's field than live in this world and endure such shame.
1664	I have no wish to place myself at Alexander's mercy, nor desire to receive any favour from his hand; with my own head may they take away my empire and they cannot deal with me in any other way.
1665	Those of you who till now have stood by my side, keep a careful guard over the honour you have gained, acting as the good man who meets a fitting death; his life is full, his reputation untarnished."

1666 Nol' respuso ninguno   de todos los varones,
      ca eran espantados   de las tribulaçiones.
      Narbazones e Bessus   rebolvién los griñones,
      ca llenos de venino   tenién los coraçones.

1667 Respondiól' Atrabatus,   mas non fue todo nada.
      Dixo, "Señor, bien dizes,   es cosa aguisada;
      pésanos de la onta   que tú as tomada;
      o murremos nos todos   o será bien vengada.

1668 Los unos son tu sangre,   los otros tus crïados;
      todos por a servirte   somos aparejados;
      aún tan rafez miente   non seremos rancados.
      Ante que tú mal prengas   seremos nos dapnados."

1669 Levantós' Narbazones,   cuidó seer artero;
      fízosele el falso   a Dario consejero.
      "Oyas me," dixo, "rëy,"   el falso lisongero,
      "dart'e, como yo cuido,   un consejo çertero.

1670 Rëy, eres caído   en mal por tu ventura.
      Bolviste con los griegos   guerra en ora dura;
      es llegada la cosa   a fiera amargura
      e tú aún contiendes   en la mala tesura.

1671 Ate la ventura   a ti desamparado;
      al rëy Alexandre   sel' ha aporfijado.
      Es de tan fiera guisa   el vissiesto mudado,
      será tarde o nunca   en su lugar tornado.

1672 Maguer ome non pueda   la cosa acabar,
      non la devié por esso   tan aína dexar;
      debe muchos consejos   rebolver e buscar;
      Rëy, faz una cosa,   si querrás acordar.

1673 Da el regno a Bessus,   que es de grant natura;
      faga él la batalla   con aquesta gent' dura;
      como en Dios fío,   mudaremos ventura;
      tú fincarás honrado   e serás sin ardura.

1674 En cabo, quando fuere   la cosa acabada,
      tornarás en tu tierra,   la cosa amatada;
      si fuere por ventura   la tu gent' arrancada,
      la desonra a ti   non te cadrá en nada."

Book of Alexander

1666   Not one of all his men made him a reply,
being appalled at his tribulations.
Nabarzanes and Bessus tugged at their beards
for they had hearts filled full of poison.

1667   Artabazus replied, though his words proved empty,*
saying: "Lord, you speak truly and what you say is right;
we are filled with sorrow by the shame you have endured;
either we shall all die or it will be well avenged.

1668   Some of us are of your blood, others of your household,
and we are all ready to give you our service;
we shall still not be defeated with such ease;
before you come to harm, we shall meet our doom."

1669   Nabarzanes stood up, planning artful speech,
the traitor pretending to give Darius advice.
"Hear me, my King," said the traitorous flatterer,
"I shall give you what I think is sure advice.

1670   My King, you are fallen into ill through your misfortune;
you waged war against the Greeks at a cruel hour;
your affairs are now come to deep bitterness
and still you strive in this dangerous endeavour.

1671   You have been abandoned by your good fortune:
it has received King Alexander as a son;
luck has changed round to such a marked extent
that late or never will it turn to its old course.

1672   Even if no man can solve the problem completely,
it should not for that reason be so quickly abandoned;
it is vital to seek out and gather plentiful ideas;
my King, do one thing, if you are willing to agree.

1673   Give the kingdom to Bessus, who is of fine stock;
let him fight the battle against these tough people;
as I trust in God, we shall change our fortune
you will retain your honour and your troubles will end.

1674   Finally, when this business has come to its end,
you will return home, this affair now settled;
if your people should happen to suffer defeat,
none of the dishonour will fall upon you."

1675 El consejo a Dario   pesól' de coraçón;
entendió bien que ramo   era de traïción;
cuidól' dar del espada   e fiziera razón,
mas díxol' Atrabatus   que non era sazón.

1676 "Señor," dixo Atrabatus,   "al tiempo en que estamos
non es buena razón   que baraja bolvamos.
Entiendo bien que todos   con un cüer andamos;
fasta que Dïos quiera,   mejor es que suframos.

1677 Dexa correr la rueda;   da al tiempo passada;
encubre tu despecho   condesa tu espada;
quand' toda nuestra cosa   tenemos mal parada,
avrán los traïdores   encontra nos entrada.

1678 Los griegos andan çerca,   fiera ment' encarnados;
as los pueblos perdidos,   los barones menguados;
e si los que fincaran   ovieres despagados,
sepas, seremos todos,   nos e tú, afollados."

1679 Bessus, por encobrirse,   mostróse por irado;
rebtava a Narbazones   que dixo desguisado;
mas, por esso, si Dario   non s'oviesse callado,
fuera de tod' en todo   muerto e degollado.

1680 Non podién su nemiga   complir los perjurados;
vergüença más que miedo   los tenié embargados;
quando vinién ant' él   eran envergonçados,
ca ojos de señor   fuertes son e pesados.

1681 Asmaron un consejo   malo e algarivo:
por alguna manera   que lo prisiessen bivo;
metiéssenl' en cadena,   toviéssenlo cativo;
bien pareçié que era   el Crïador esquivo.

1682 Por amatar las bozes   e quedar los roídos,
vinieron ant' él rëy   los falsos desmentidos,
plorando de los ojos,   los cuerpos desguarnidos;
dizién que de todo   eran ya repentidos.

1683 Creyélo el buen ome   que dizién verdat;
entendió la palabra   mas non la voluntad;
ploró e perdonóles,   firmóles amistad.
¡Dios perdone al ome   de tan grant pïedat!

1675	This advice set great sorrow in Darius' heart: he knew well that the offer was born of treachery; he thought to put him to the sword – and he would have been right – but Artabazus told him that that was not the time.
1676	"My lord," said Artabazus, "at this present time it is not right that we become embroiled in disputes; I understand that we are all possessed of one mind and, until God wishes, it is better that we endure.
1677	Leave the wheel to spin round and let time pass, cover up your anger and sheathe your sword; when all our affairs are in such a bad way, traitors will have an opportunity against us.
1678	The Greeks are approaching, in a state of great fury, your people are lost and your men reduced in number, and should you displease the ones who remain, all of us, I tell you – we and you – shall be lost."
1679	Bessus, to conceal his true intent, feigned anger and rebuked Nabarzanes for speaking unwisely; but if Darius had not on that account stayed silent he would have been dead, his throat slashed wide open.
1680	The conspirators could not carry out their treachery, for shame – more than fear – made them hesitate; when they came before him they felt such guilt, for the eyes of a lord are hard and heavy.
1681	They devised a plan of evil perfidy: that in some way they should capture him alive, put him in chains and keep him as their captive; the Creator seemed indeed to be shunning him.
1682	To silence the voices and quell the rumours, the false perjurers came before the King, their eyes streaming with tears, their armour cast aside, saying that they had now repented of it all.
1683	The good man thought that they were speaking the truth; he understood their words but not their intent; he wept and forgave them, and affirmed his friendship – may God grant forgiveness to so merciful a man.

1684 Otro día mañana, la tierra alumbrada,
mandó mover el rëy Dario su albergada;
temiénse de los griegos, de la mala espantada;
queríen ir prender más segura posada.

1685 Ivan ya entendiendo todos la traïçión;
fablavan entre dientes todos una razón;
los unos dizién "sí", los otros dizién "non";
era entre los pueblos fiera la bulliçión.

1686 Un prínçip' de los griegos, ome muy venturoso
– Padrón era su nombre, al que dé Dios buen poso –
entendió el consejo malo e peligroso;
dixo: "Señor, Túm' valas, santo e poderoso."

1687 Acostóse al rëy quando vio aguisado,
ques' temié de los otros que serié barruntado.
Dixo: "Señor, merçed, non te sea pesado;
quiérote dezir cosa que non es a mi grado.

1688 Quiérente tus vassallos a traïçión matar;
oy ha de ser el día que lo as a provar.
Fuera Dios, non es ome que te pueda prestar;
sepas çierta mente: non puedes escapar.

1689 Narbazones e Bessus, traïdores provados,
ambos son sobre ti por matarte jurados;
andan con sus poderes sobre ti assemblados;
cuentan que son sobre ti quando serán çenados.

1690 Lo que yo mejor veo, quiero te consejar:
por nada tú non vayas con ellos albergar;
manda las nuestras tiendas çerca de ti sentar;
con la merçed de Dios te cuido emparar.

1691 Si yo non entendiesse la mala çalagarda,
sepas que non querría prenderte en mi guarda.
Mas si esto non fazes, por aquesta mi barva,
nunca viste tú noche en tus días más parda.

1692 Dexé a Alexandre e vin' a ti servir.
Señor, si a ti pierdo, non avré dó ir;
antes que tú muriesses, querría yo morir.
Rëy, yo non sabría otra cosa dezir."

1684   On the next morning, when light fell on the land.
King Darius commanded his army to set out;
they were afraid of the Greeks – they were in great terror –
and wished to go and occupy a more secure base.

1685   They were all now gradually learning of the treason
and all were muttering one thing through their teeth,
some saying "Yes" and others saying "No";
there was great agitation amongst his people.

1686   A prince of the Greeks, a man favoured by fortune,
Patron by name – may God grant him fine rest! –*
understood their evil and dangerous plan
and said, "Help me, holy and powerful Lord!"

1687   He approached the King when he saw his chance,
for he feared that the traitors would suspect him,
and said: "Forgive me, my lord, do not be disturbed,
but I wish to tell you something that troubles me.

1688   Your vassals wish to kill you in treachery;
this is to be the day that you will suffer it;
except for God, there is no man that can help you;
I tell you, it is certain that you cannot escape.

1689   Nabarzanes and Bessus, who are proven traitors,
have both sworn an oath that they will kill you;
and both have their forces assembled against you;
they intend to be upon you after dining.

1690   I want to advise you as to what I see as best:
on no account go and take lodging with them;
command that our tents should be pitched near to yours
and with God's mercy I intend to defend you.

1691   If I were not aware of their wicked trap,
I tell you I would not want you beneath my guard,
but if you do not do this, by this beard of mine,
never in your days will you have seen so dark a night.

1692   I left Alexander and I came to serve you;
my lord, if I lose you I shall have nowhere to go;
before you were to die, I too would wish for death,
my King, I could not say any more than this."

1693 Respondió con esto el buen emperador:
"Padrón," dixo, "gradéscotelo, téngotelo en amor;
assí como tú quieres guardar a tu señor,
assí seas guardado, siempre del Crïador.

1694 Más quiero yo morir o ocasión prender
que, ante que mal fagan, mis omes malmeter;
si de Dios es judgado, que assí ha de seer,
non podremos por seso ninguno estorçer.

1695 Yo los crïé a ambos de chiquillos moçuelos;
tan grant bien les quería como a mis fijuelos;
fize los poderosos, más que a sus avuelos;
non devrién contra mí echar tales anzuelos.

1696 En los que yo crïé non podría dubdar;
cuidaría en ello mortal mente pecar;
que quiere que me venga, quiérom' aventurar;
pero el tu consejo non podrié mejorar.

1697 Gradesco tu consejo, tu buena voluntat;
nunca podrié nul ome fer mayor lealtat;
debe seer contada siempre la tu bondat;
qui de ti mal dixiesse farié grant malvestat."

1698 A tan leal vassallo dél' Dïos paraíso,
que por salvar señor tan grant voluntad miso;
mas la virtud de Dios otra guisa lo quiso;
ovo a passar Dario lo que ovo promiso.

1699 Narbazones e Bessus – ¡non fuessen aparados! –
que en tan mal consejo son amos acordados;
cómo avién de fer estavan ya fablados,
del consejo primero un poco cameados.

1700 Luego l'ovieran muerto, mas pensaron al fer:
quando anocheçiesse, de bivo lo prender,
darlo a Alexandre por mejor lo aver,
si non seles pudiesse otra mient' defender.

1701 Quando vino la tarde que quisieron posar,
non se quisieron ellos al rëy acostar;
mandaron en su cabo las sus tiendas parar,
mas nunca se quisieron los falsos desarmar.

1693	The good Emperor gave him these words in reply: "Patron," he said, "I thank you and hold you with affection. Just as you wish to give protection to your lord, may you always be protected by the Creator.
1694	But I would rather die or come to harm myself than punish my men before they have done wrong; if it is judged by God that it must be so, by no wit shall we be able to avoid it.
1695	I brought them both up from tiny children and loved them as dearly as I did my own sons. I gave them power greater than their forbears' and they should not cast such hooks to catch me.
1696	Of those that I brought up I could feel no fear; I would think it a mortal sin against them; whatever should befall me, I want to take the chance, though I could not improve on your advice.
1697	I am grateful to you for your advice and good will; never could a man perform a greater act of loyalty; forever must men tell the tale of your goodness, any man who spoke ill of you would do a great wrong."
1698	May God grant Paradise to such a loyal vassal, who showed such great desire to save his lord. But God's authority willed it otherwise and Darius had to bear what He had determined.
1699	Nabarzanes and Bessus – oh that they had not conspired! – who were both agreed on such an evil scheme, had already spoken of how they would effect it, now a little changed from their original intent.
1700	They would have killed him quickly, but altered their plan: when darkness fell they would capture him alive and hand him to Alexander to win his good will, unless he could protect himself from them in other ways.
1701	When the evening came and they wanted to rest they had no wish to be near to the King; they had their tents pitched on the edge of the camp but never did the traitors wish to disarm.

1702 Coñoçiá ya por ojo   Dario la traïçión;
coñoció la palabra   quel' dixera Padrón;
veyé que nol' fincava   ninguna guarniçión;
alçó a Dios las manos,   fizo una oraçión.

1703 "Señor," dixo, "que sabes   todas las voluntades,
a qui non se encubren   ningunas poridades;
tuyos son los imperios   e todas las çibdades;
¡Señor, non pares mientes   en las mis malvestades!

1704 Bien sé que non Te fize   derecho nin serviçio;
segunt el que devía,   nin complí mi ofiçio;
so mucho pecador,   lleno de mucho viçio;
quando Tú me desamas,   yo bevir non cobdiçio.

1705 Pero, como yo creo,   segund mi conoçençia,
non deseredé huérfano   nin falsé convenençia;
siempre amé paz   e escusé entençia;
siempre esvïé guerra   e amé avenençia.

1706 Nunca fiz' adulterio   con mugeres casadas,
nunca desaforé   biudas nin maridadas;
Señor, las tierras yermas,   he todas bien pobladas,
e son todas las gentes   del pueblo mejoradas.

1707 Señor, si miento yo   en esto que Te digo,
derecho es que muera   como tu enemigo;
mas si yo fiz' justiçia   o tu mandado sigo,
Señor, derecho Tú   seas öy comigo.

1708 Si de Ti non les fuesse   a éstos ordenado,
non sería por ellos   oy tan mal desonrado.
Mas entiendo que so   de Ti desemparado;
morré de mala guisa,   como mal venturado.

1709 Qüando de la muerte   non puedo escapar,
quiero me yo mismo   con mi mano matar;
de mano de vil ome   non devo yo finar;
'rey mató a Dario',   dirán en el cantar."

1710 Fue prender un benablo   grand' e bien amolado:
oviéras'lo sin duda   por el cuerpo entrado.
mas seyé en la tienda   un moçuelo castrado;
dio grandes apellidos,   ca fue mal espantado.

1702	Now could Darius recognise the treachery with his eyes and he recognised the things that Patron had said to him; he could see that now he had no protection left; he raised his hands to God and spoke in prayer:
1703	"Lord," he said, "who know the desires of all men, the One from whom no secrets are concealed, who know what empires and all cities are like, Lord, do not give thought to my misdeeds.
1704	I know well that I did You neither justice nor service as I should have, and failed to fulfil my office. I am a man of great sin, I am full of much vice; while You do not love me, I have no wish for life.
1705	But I do believe that, as far as I know, I disinherited no orphan nor falsified agreements; I always loved peace and avoided conflict; I always shunned war and loved harmony.
1706	I was never an adulterer with women who were wed and I never harmed the rights of widows or wives; Lord, I have left the empty lands all well inhabited and improved the lives of all the nation's people.
1707	Lord, if I lie in what I say to You now, it is right that I should die as your enemy; but, if I acted justly or I follow your commands, Lord, it is right that You be with me today.
1708	If these men's conduct were not ordained by You, I would not suffer such dishonour at their hands, but I understand that I am forsaken by You; I shall die a bad death as a man of ill fortune.
1709	Since it is not possible for me to escape death, I want to deal it myself with my own hand; at a base man's hand I must not meet my end; 'A king killed Darius', they will say in the song."
1710	He went to fetch a long and sharp-pointed spear and would without doubt have thrust it through his body, but a young eunuch was present in the tent, who let out loud screams in his great terror.

1711   Como avié la cosa   estada retraída,
           tenién todos que era   la traïçión complida.
           Toda la gent' menuda   fue luego desmarrida;
           pensaron de fuïr,   cad'un' a su partida.

1712   Omes de su mesnada   fueron luego uviados,
           travaron del benablo   fiera ment' espantados;
           muerto seriá el rëy   si non fuessen plegados;
           por que fuera salleron,   teniénse por errados.

1713   Narbazones e Bessus   fueron luego venidos,
           espadas sobre manos,   de sus armas guarnidos.
           Fueron todos los otros   de la tienda tollidos;
           fazién los arredrar   a fuerça e amidos.

1714   Fue el rëy ligado   con muy fuertes dogales;
           metieron lo en fierros   los falsos desleales;
           tollieron le las pórporas,   vistieron le sayales.
           ¡Dios cofunda sïempre   tales serviçïales!

1715   Sabet, non lo dexaron   en la tienda estar;
           fizïeron lo ellos   a los otros levar;
           pero, por mayor ondra   e mayor bien estar,
           con cadenas de oro   le fizieron atar.

1716   El buen rëy en su casa   avié cabtividat;
           el justo de los falsos   aviá grant crüeldat;
           al ome pïadoso   falleçiél' pïedat;
           en lugar de justiçia   regnava falsedat.

1717   Narbazones e Bessus,   verament' dos pecados,
           quando en el buen rëy   fueron apoderados,
           de fincar en el plano   non fueron más osados.
           Fuéronse a las sierras   por seer más segurados.

1718   Los juïzios de Dios   assí suelen correr:
           quiere dar a los malos   e a los buenos toller;
           lieva todas las cosas   segund de su plazer
           por mostrar que ha   sobre todos poder.

1719   A los buenos da cueita   que bivan en pobreza,
           a los malos da fuerça,   averes e riqueza.
           Al fol da el meollo,   al cuerdo la corteza;
           los que non lo entienden   tienen lo a fereza.

1711	The people, as the plot had been made public knowledge, all thought that the treachery had been carried out; and all the lowly folk were immediately distressed and thought of flight, each one to his own region.
1712	Men of his army then promptly arrived and grabbed the spear from him, their terror great; the King would have died if they had not come but for leaving him they held themselves in error.
1713	Nabarzanes and Bessus immediately arrived, their swords in their hands, and bearing full armour; all the other men were made to leave the tent, driven away by force against their will.
1714	The King was bound up with very strong ropes and the false traitors put him in irons, took off his purple robes and dressed him in rough cloth – may God confound servants of this kind!
1715	I tell you, they did not let him stay in his tent but forced others to bear the good King outside; but for greater honour and greater well-being they had him imprisoned in chains of gold.
1716	The good King bore captivity in his own camp; the just man endured great cruelty from the false; the man of mercy found no mercy in others; and in place of justice, falsity reigned.
1717	Nabarzanes and Bessus, two true devils, now that they had the King in their power, no longer dared to stay out on the plain but made for the mountains for greater safety.
1718	Thus is it normal for God's judgements to be passed: He seeks to give to the bad and take from the good; He directs all things according to his will to show that He has power over all.
1719	To the good He gives troubles, that they live in poverty; to the bad He gives strength, possessions and wealth; He gives the fruit to the fool and the shell to the wise; those who lack understanding think it born of severity.

1720 El rey Alexandre, una barba fazera,
vínol' en est' comedio barrunte verdadera
que era en Baracta Dario, cosa çertera;
queriá lidiar con él aún la vez terçera.

1721 Maravillóse mucho, tóvolo a fazaña;
dizié que nunca fizo ome cosa tamaña;
dixo: "Non tien' aquél en los ojos lagaña
que de tal voluntad quiere verter su saña."

1722 Mandó mover las huestes, las tiendas arrancar;
avié puesto de ir por Baracta çercar,
la villa destroír, a Dario cativar,
desende adelante su guerra ençerrar.

1723 Vinol' un mensajero luego que fue movido,
que supiesse que Dario era dende sallido
e era sin dubdança a los bractos foído,
ca todos sus esfuerços le avién falleçido.

1724 Dixo: "Nin por aquesto non puede escapar;
do quiere que se vaya, yo lo iré buscar;
non se podrá en el siglo en tal lugar alçar
que por media la barva non sea a tomar."

1725 Subió por una sierra, por sallir a estajo,
lo que non podié fer si non con grant trabajo;
ca era el dïablo más duro que un macho,
non dava por lazerio quanto valié un ajo.

1726 Avié de la carrera un poco andado;
vínoli por ventura más çertero mandado
que Dario era preso, mala mente cuitado;
contógelo por orden cómo avié passado.

1727 Dïo una grant boz, alta como pavón:
"Crïador, ¡Tú vïeda tamaña traïción!
Deviés' fondir el mundo con quantos que y son
antes que fuesse fecha atal tribulación."

1728 Demandó a cabillo todas sus potestades:
"Oít," dixo, "amigos, quantos aquí estades.
Un mandado me vino, quiero que lo oyades;
como creo, non cuido que sabor end' ayades.

1720	King Alexander, an extraordinary warrior, received, at this point, information which proved true: that Darius was in Bactria – which was as sure as can be –, and wanted to fight with him still for a third time.
1721	He wondered greatly and considered it a marvel, saying that no man had ever done so great a thing; he said, "Darius has not the dust of sleep in his eyes, such is his desire to vent his anger."
1722	He bade his armies move out and camp be struck, and had resolved to go to lay siege to Bactria, to destroy the city and take Darius captive and from there on to put an end to his war.
1723	A messenger came to him the instant he moved out to tell him that Darius had left that place and had fled to the Bactrians – there was no doubt –, for now all his courage had deserted him.
1724	He said, "Not even in this way can he make an escape; wherever he might go I shall head in search of him. Nowhere in the world will he find a place to hide such that he cannot be taken fully by the beard."*
1725	He went up into the mountains to take a short cut, something he could not do without great effort; for the devil was harder than a warrior's mace and for suffering did not give the price of garlic.
1726	Alexander had already gone part of the way when a more certain message came to him by chance: that Darius was captive and in severe distress; he was told how it had happened, step by step.
1727	He gave out a great cry, as loud as a peacock: "Creator, may You forbid treachery so great! The world with all those in it ought to have been destroyed before such an act of cruelty were committed."
1728	He called to assembly all his men of power: "Today," he said, "my friends, all you who are here, a message has come to me; I want you to hear it. I do not believe that you will take pleasure from it.

1729 A Dario han traído   vassallos traïdores;
      yaze en grandes fierros,   sufre muchos dolores;
      han puesto por matarlo   por aver los onores,
      que sean, si pudiessen,   del emperio señores.

1730 ¡Valámosle amigos,   sí Dïos vos bendiga!
      Muy grant preçio nos cabe   vengar tan grant nemiga;
      nunca fue de los buenos   la traïçión amiga.
      ¡Valámosle amigos,   sí nos Dïos bendiga!

1731 Por valer tan grant cueita   es nos grant bien estança,
      más que si lo prisiéssemos   a escudo o a lança.
      ¡Por Dios que non fagades   ninguna demorança!
      Caer nos ha a todos,   si muriere, viltança."

1732 Movierons' a andar   a una grant pressura.
      Non avién de comer   nin de dormir ardura;
      quebrantavan los caballos   con la grant cansadura;
      non los podié vençer   frío nin calentura.

1733 De noche nin de día   vagar nunca se dieron
      fasta que en el término   do fue preso vinieron;
      pero un poquillejo   aquí se retenieron
      ca non podién saber   a quál parte fuyeron.

1734 Vinieron a pressura   al rëy dos varones;
      eran de los de Dario,   bien ricos infançones;
      querían de los griegos   más seer compañones
      que seguir la compaña   de tales traïdores.

1735 Reçibióles el rëy,   tornáronse sus vasallos,
      ca eran bien guarnidos   d'armas e de cavallos.
      Sabieron a los griegos   éstos tan bien guïarlos
      que fueron çerca de Dario   ante de medios gallos.

1736 Dixeron estos ambos,   como bien acordados:
      "Acojámonos, rëy,   vayamos cabdellados;
      los falsos traïdores   están aparejados;
      podemos rafez miente   seer engañados."

1737 "Otorgo", dixo'l rëy,   "que dizedes cordura.
      Vayamos nuestras hazes   paradas a ventura,
      ca el traïdor ome   es de mala natura;
      non ha entre las bestias   tan mala crïatura."

1729	Darius' treacherous vassals have betrayed him; he lies in heavy irons and suffers great pain. They are resolved to kill him to gain his honours in order, if they might, to be lords of his empire.
1730	Let us assist him, my friends, may God bless you! We gain great fame by avenging such a wrong; never was treachery a friend of good men; let us assist him, my friends, may God bless us!
1731	To give help in such distress is greatly to our credit, more than if we captured him by force of shield or lance. In God's name, let there be no cause for delay, for dishonour will fall on us all should he die."
1732	They set off on their march with the greatest haste and they felt no desire for food or sleep; they exhausted their horses with the tiring journey and neither cold nor heat could overcome them.
1733	By night and by day they allowed themselves no rest till they came to the spot where Darius had been seized; but for a short time they held back in that place, for they could not find out to where the traitors had fled.
1734	Two men hastened to come before the King, very wealthy nobles from Darius' side; they wanted more to be companions of the Greeks than to follow such a company of traitors.
1735	They were received by the King and became his vassals, for they were well equipped with both arms and horses; these men were able to guide the Greeks so well that they came near Darius by the early hours.
1736	These two men said, being firmly in agreement, "Let us ride together, King, formed up for battle for the false traitors are very well prepared and we could easily fall into an ambush."
1737	"I agree," said the King, "that what you say is right; let us travel with our lines correctly drawn up, for the treacherous man is of an evil nature, and there is no creature so evil among beasts."

1738 Ordenó bien sus hazes, ca lo avié usado;
en un poco de tiempo fue todo ordenado;
mas, ante que oviesse un migero passado,
fue el alva venida, e el día uviado.

1739 Narbazones e Bessus, quando la seña vieron,
de atender al rëy esfuerço non ovieron;
diéronse al guarir, esperar non quisieron.
Non era maravilla, ca negra la fizieron.

1740 Mandaron el cavallo a Dario cavalgar
por amor que pudiessen más aína andar,
maguer non lo querién de la prisión dexar
ca tenién que la cosa podrié en mal tornar.

1741 Dixo Dario: "Más quiero passión aquí prender
o del rey Alexandre en su prisión caer
que sólo una ora con vusco vida aver,
ca vos devié la tierra todos bivos sorver."

1742 De subir en cavallo nol' pudieron rancar;
cavalgarl' en azémilla temién mucho tardar;
de lexar lo a vida temiénse mal fallar.
Ovieron lo peor en cabo a asmar.

1743 Ovieron lo con saña lüego a çegar,
ovieron lo de colpes mortales a colpar;
dexaron lo por muerto, pensaron de andar;
non los podién cavallos ningunos alcançar.

1744 Narbazones e Bessus, ¡malditos vayades!
¡Por do quïer que fuéredes mal apresos seades!
¡El comer que comierdes con dolor lo comades!
¡Que per secula cuncta mal exemplo seades!

1745 Los falsos, por su cosa peor la acabar
mataron los cavallos que lo solién tirar;
desent' los carreteros que los solien levar.
Tenién que non avrié quien gelo rencurar.

1746 Quando ovieron los malos la traïçión complida,
fue luego entre ellos la discordia naçida.
Pensaron de fuïr cad'un' a su partida;
nunca jamás se vieron en toda la su vida.

1738	He drew up his columns wisely, for he was well practised; and in but a little time all was set in order; but even before a short while had elapsed dawn had come and the day had arrived.
1739	Nabarzanes and Bessus, when they saw the ensign, did not have the courage to await the King but sought to save themselves and did not wish to stay – it was no wonder, for they were ill served by fortune.
1740	They ordered that Darius should ride upon a horse, in their desire to travel as quickly as they could, although they did not want to free him from his chains, for they thought that things might take a turn for ill.
1741	Darius said, "I prefer to meet my death here or to fall into the prison of King Alexander than to spend just one hour of my life with you, for the earth ought to suck you all in alive."
1742	They were unable to compel him to mount a horse and feared to mount him on a pack-mule would cause long delay; they feared that leaving him alive would turn out ill and finally they came to decide on what was worst.
1743	In their anger they came to blind him at once and to beat him cruelly with deadly blows. Leaving him for dead, they rode on their way and no horses could manage to catch them.
1744	Nabarzanes and Bessus, a curse be upon you! May ill fortune pursue you wherever you turn! The food that you eat, may you eat it with pain! May you serve as an evil example for all ages!
1745	The traitors, to add even more wrong to their affairs, killed the horses that used to pull the royal chariot and then the charioteers who used to drive them on, thinking that no-one would seek vengeance for this.
1746	When the evil men had carried out their treachery, discord sprang up without delay in their midst; they decided to flee, each one to his own region, and they never met again in all their lives.

1747   Los unos de los otros   açerca se sedién;
          vino a Alexandre un ome, Letabien le dezién.
          Díxole que a Dario   aún bivo lo tenién,
          ca él non lo sabié   que muerto lo avién.

1748   Sallieron de galope,   dieron se a correr;
          mas, como diz' el vierso,   cuidar non es saber;
          todo era ya puesto   cóm' avié de seer,
          ca Dario de la muerte   non podié estorçer.

1749   Vino a poca d'ora   mensaje más çertero
          que muerto era Dario,   el su firme guerrero;
          quando ovo la cosa   dicha el mensajero,
          vidieron gelo todos   que non fue plazentero.

1750   Antuvióse el rëy,   cuidólos alcançar.
          Narbazones e Bessus   non lo podrién lograr;
          mas ovo un destorvo: quiérovos lo contar,
          ca non quiero que digan   que so medio juglar.

1751   De compañas de Dario,   omes de fuert' ventura,
          salleron cavalleros,   todos bien de natura;
          tres mill eran por cuento; fizieron todos jura
          de fincar en el campo,   perder toda rencura.

1752   Non querién a sus casas   sin lur señor tornar;
          quand' él era finado   querién todos finar,
          o sintién por ventura   que eran de rebtar;
          si ante fueron malos   queriénse mejorar.

1753   Pero pudieran antes   aguisarlo mejor:
          quando finar querién,   morir con su señor.
          Si lo oviessen fecho, non les fuera peor;
          mas era otra guisa   puesto del Crïador.

1754   Pero yo bien comido   que fueron engañados;
          non cuidaron que tanto   farién los endiablados,
          que, como eran ellos   de verbo abondados,
          con algunas guisas   los ternién amansados.

1755   Como quiere que sea,   ellos bien lo fazían,
          quando de traïçión   escusar se querían.
          Assaz lo demostravan   que culpa non avían;
          ca, si culpados fuessen,   con los otros irían.

1747	The two groups were now very near to each other; a man came to Alexander, Letabien by name, and told him that they still held Darius alive, for he did not know that they had killed him.
1748	They rode off at a gallop and went with all haste, but, as the saying says, "to think is not to know"; all was now disposed as it had to be, for Darius could not escape his death.
1749	A more accurate message came a short time later, that Darius, his determined foe in battle, was dead; when the messenger had given them this piece of news everyone could see that the King was far from pleased.
1750	The King rode out ahead, his intent to catch them up: Nabarzanes and Bessus would not get away with this; but there was an obstacle of which I wish to tell you, for I do not want it said that I am but half a minstrel.
1751	Among Darius' troops, men of great good fortune, there rode out knights, who were all of noble line; three thousand in number, they had all sworn an oath to remain on the battlefield and shed all their rancour.
1752	They had no desire to turn for home without their lord: since he had met his end they all wished to meet their own; or they felt perhaps that the blame should lie with them; if once they were bad men, they wished to be better.
1753	But they could have acted with greater wisdom before: since they wanted to die, they could have died with their lord. Had they acted thus, it would have been no worse for them, but the Creator had ordained it otherwise.
1754	But I firmly believe that they had been deceived; they did not think the Devil-guided men would go so far, for, since those men had such an ample gift for words, they must have found some means to win these men round.
1755	However that may be, they now were acting well in seeking to cast off the taint of treachery; they showed very clearly that they bore no guilt, for, were they to blame, they would have left with the others.

1756   Fueron a las feridas,   bolvieron el torneo;
non firié más afirmes   Judas el Macabeo.
Diz' el rey Alexandre: "Segund lo que yo creo,
de bevir estos omes   non han mucho desseo."

1757   Como todos avién   voluntad de finar,
firién entre los griegos,   fazién los ensañar;
los griegos fueron sañosos,   pensaron de tornar;
non dexavan las porras   seer de vagar.

1758   El ome porfidioso   que non quiere foïr
viene por penitençia   en el campo morir;
como non ha cobdiçia   ninguna de bevir,
non ha peor en mundo   bestia de referir.

1759   Aprissa murián ellos,   mas bien selo buscavan;
pero quanto podién   en balde non estavan;
dolavan en los griegos,   cabeças non tornavan;
todos murién de buelta;   sí murién que matavan.

1760   El rey Alexandre,   que tanto avié fecho,
en tan poco de rato   non fuera peor trecho;
vengaran por poco   los otros su despecho;
ovieran los de Dario   alcançado derecho.

1761   Pero non vos tengamos   en luengos xaramiellos:
fueron desbaratados   vassallos e cabdiellos;
fueron muertos e presos   viejos e mançebiellos;
avién grandes e chicos   caídos los martiellos.

1762   Quando fue la fazienda   fecha e delibrada,
la mesnada de Dario   fincó mal quebrantada;
pero con la vitoria   que les avié Dios dada
ovieron toda cueita   aína olvidada.

1763   El rey Alexandre,   maguer era irado,
non avié el dolor   de Dario olvidado;
andava el buen ome   doliente e aquexado,
que non podié saber   dó lo avién dexado.

1764   Folgaron tod' un día   que non podián andar;
avién mucho lidiado,   non se podién mudar;
mandó el rey a todos   desguarnir e folgar,
e mejar los plagados,   los muertos soterrar.

| 1756 | The first blows were struck and they began the contest;
Judas the Maccabean could not have struck firmer.*
King Alexander said, "As it seems to me,
these men do not have much desire for life." |
|---|---|
| 1757 | As these Persians all felt a desire to die,
they dealt the Greeks blows and drove them to anger;
the angry Greeks started returning their blows,
not allowing their clubs a moment's rest. |
| 1758 | The unyielding man, unwilling to flee,
comes to die on the battlefield as penance;
since he does not have any yearning to live,
no beast in the world is harder to repel. |
| 1759 | Their deaths came quickly – but they had sought them,
and as far as they were able they did not die in vain.
They struck at the Greeks and did not turn their heads,
and they all died together; they died as they killed. |
| 1760 | King Alexander, who had done so much,
never had worse treatment in such a short time:
the Persians very nearly avenged their anger;
Darius' men almost achieved victory. |
| 1761 | But let us not keep you with long explanations:
vassals and leaders both suffered defeat;
elders and youths were all dead or made captive
and men young and old had let their weapons fall. |
| 1762 | When the battle had been fought and brought to its end,
Darius' men were left firmly defeated,
but with the victory that God had granted them
the Greeks had quickly forgotten all their cares. |
| 1763 | King Alexander, angry though he was,
was not unmindful of what Darius had suffered;
the good man was stricken with grief and sorrow
at not knowing where he had been laid. |
| 1764 | They took a full day's rest, unable to move on:
they had had a hard fight and could not set out;
the King ordered them all to disarm and rest,
to heal the wounded and bury the dead. |

1765   Buscando por los muertos, tan espessos yazién,
la carrera de Dario   fallar non la podién;
por que non la fallavan   grant cordojo avién;
al que gela mostrasse   albriçias le darién.

1766   Todos ya enojados, yazién de cansadura;
fallóla Polistratus   en una val escura.
Buscando agua fría,   ca fazié grant calura,
óvola a fallar   por muy grant aventura.

1767   Los cavallos con cueita, que eran mal feridos,
andudieron musando   fasta que fueron caídos,
quando de tod' en todo   fueron ya enflaquidos;
cayeron ant' el rëy,   todos piedes tendidos.

1768   Por medio un vallejo   corrié un regajal;
naçié de buena fuente,   clara e perenal;
deçendié a fondón,   regava un pradal.
Por verdat vos dezir,   era fermoso val.

1769   Polistratus, buscando   la cabeça del río
– como siempre do nasçe   suele seer más frío –
en un campiello plano,   un agua manantío,
trobó las bestias muertas   e el carro vazío.

1770   Yazién çerca del rëy   muertos los carreteros;
yazién del otro cabo   muertos los escuderos;
yazié el ome bueno   entr' estos compañeros;
él yazíe en medio,   los otros orelleros.

1771   Como era el carro   rica ment' adobado,
como era Dario   de pareçer granado,
sópolo Polistratus,   fue dend' çertificado;
corrió ad Alexandre   luego con est' mandado.

1772   Fizo'l rëy grant duelo   por el emperador;
si fuesse su hermano   non lo fariá mayor.
Ploravan sus varones,   todos con grant dolor;
todos dizién: "¡Mal aya   Bessus el traïdor!"

1773   Tolléronle la sangre   e los paños untados;
vistiéronle vestidos,   valdoquis muy honrados;
calçáronle espuelas   con çapatos dorados;
non conprarién las luvas   aver de dos casados.

1765	As they searched among the dead – how thickly they lay! – they did not manage to find Darius' path; great was their regret as they failed to find it; to whoever revealed it they would give a reward.
1766	All now frustrated, they lay down exhausted, but Polystratus found it in a dark valley:* while seeking cold water – for the heat was great – he managed to find it by great good fortune.
1767	The horses were distressed, for they were dealt great wounds; whinnying in pain, they walked until they dropped; and when their strength had now been utterly spent they fell before the King, their legs fully extended.
1768	Through the middle of a little valley flowed a stream,* that was born from a fine spring, clear and never dry; it ran down into grassland and watered a meadow. It was indeed, I tell you, a valley of great beauty.
1769	Polystratus, while looking for the head of the river, – as it is always coldest at the point of its birth – in a little flat field, near the running water, found the dead horses and the empty chariot.
1770	Near to the King the charioteers lay dead and the squires lay dead on the other side; the good man lay in between these companions; he lay in the middle, the others at some distance.
1771	As the chariot was of enormous splendour and King Darius had a distinguished look, Polystratus realised and knew it was true, and ran to Alexander with this message at once.
1772	For the Emperor, the King made a great lament – had he been his brother he could have made no greater. His men all shed tears with the great grief, all saying, "A curse on Bessus the traitor!"
1773	They removed the blood and his dirtied garments and dressed him anew with noble baldachins, and fastened on spurs which had gilded shoes; the wealth of two dowries would not buy his gloves.

1774 Pusiéronle corona   clara e bien broñida
— en cabeça de ome   nunca fuera metida —
de fin' oro obrada,   de piedras bien bastida;
mejor non la toviera   en toda la su vida.

1775 El rey Alexandre   púsolo en el lecho;
púsol' çebtro en mano   e fizo grant derecho;
tornó en pïedat,   olvidó el despecho;
non le serié tan bien   si al oviesse fecho.

1776 Non podié con el duelo   las lágremas tener;
ívales a menudo   con el manto toller;
del cabeçal del lecho   non se querié bolver
si non a la sazón   que oviesse de comer.

1777 Plorando de los ojos,   començó de plañer,
diziendo "¡Ay Dario!   ¿Qué oviste d'aver!
Cuideste de mi mano   foír e estorçer;
oviste en peores   en cabo a caer.

1778 Si fuesse de ventura   e lo quisiés' el fado
que a cosiment' fuesses   de los griegos echado,
ovieras sines dubda   sabido e provado
que non ha señorío   en el siglo tan temprado.

1779 Avriás a mí señero   por señor catar;
podriás de mí ayuso   el imperio mandar;
yo a ti lo dïera   todo a ordenar;
de ti nunca querría   otra renta levar.

1780 Tu feziste el exemplo   que diz' de la cordera:
por miedo de los canes   sallió a la carrera;
fuyó contra los lobos,   cayó en la tordera;
tú fuste engañado   por esta misma manera.

1781 Nunca en Alexandre   tú devías dubdar;
si tú a él tornasses   él te sabrié honrar;
caíste en desierto,   en aviesso lugar;
oviéronte las bestias   todas a devorar.

1782 Escapeste de todos   los peligros del mar;
fuera, en el sequero,   oviest' a peligrar;
podist' el flumen todo   fast' en cabo andar;
en cab' dél en lo seco   ovist' a afogar.

1774	They gave him a crown, bright and well burnished, which had never been placed on the head of a man, worked in fine gold, adorned richly with gems; he had never worn better in the whole of his life.
1775	King Alexander lay him down on the bed, set a sceptre in his hand, and did him great honour. He was filled with compassion and forgot his anger. It would not have been right for him to act otherwise.
1776	In his grief he could not keep back his tears and repeatedly wiped them away with his cloak. He was not willing to leave the Persian's bed-side except at the time when he had to go and eat.
1777	Tears streaming from his eyes, he began to lament, saying, "Ah, Darius, what you had to endure! You thought that you would flee and escape my clutches but in the end came to fall among harsher men.
1778	If it were Fortune's wish and willed by fate that you had been thrown upon the mercy of the Greeks, you would doubtless have known and learnt from experience that there is no lordship in the world so mild.
1779	You would have had to look on me alone as your lord; and under me you could have commanded your empire. I would have allowed you to be master of it all never wanting to make any further charges.
1780	You followed the example men give of the lamb* that was afraid of the dogs and ran away: it fled straight to the wolves and fell into the trap; you were mistaken in the very same way.
1781	You ought never to have doubted Alexander: had you turned to him, he could have paid you honour; you fell into the desert, an evil place, and you were to be devoured by all the beasts.
1782	You made your escape from all the dangers of the sea but came to danger out of the water, on dry land; you were able to cross to the river's other side, but afterwards you drowned on reaching the bank.

1783   Darïo, ¡el tu preçio   siempre sea contado,
       sól' de lidiar comigo   tú fuste tan osado!
       Non te caya en onta   maguer fuste rancado,
       ca yo so Alexandre,   el del nombre pesado.

1784   Pero en una cosa   eres bien venturado,
       que fincó tu emperio   todo bien consejado;
       porfijaré, si bivo,   el tu fijo amado;
       buscaré a las fijas   casamiento honrado.

1785   Quanto yo te prometo,   bien lo cuido complir;
       si Dios me diere vida,   non lo cuido fallir;
       si esto non cumpliere,   quiérome mal dezir;
       ¡de qual muerte tu mueres,   me faga Dios morir!

1786   Assí me dexe Dios   mi voluntad complir:
       a Asia sobjudgar,   África conquerir;
       las torres de Marruecos   a mi mano venir;
       como de lo que digo   yo non cuido fallir.

1787   Desent' assí me dexe   a España passar,
       Sevilla e Toledo,   Galizia sobjudgar,
       Françia e Alemaña,   como passa la mar;
       como, si Dios quisiere,   yo te cuido vengar.

1788   En cabo, assí pueda   passar a Lombardía,
       la grant çibdat de Roma   meter en mi valía;
       entrar señor del mundo   en Corintio la mía;
       como de lo que digo,   falleçer non querría.

1789   Vassallos que tal cosa   fazen a su señor,
       en mí quando pudiessen   non farían mejor.
       ¡El que nunca oviere   merçed al traïdor
       nunca aver le quiera   merçed el Crïador!"

1790   Fazié sobejo duelo,   dizié buenas razones;
       fazié de fiera guisa   plorar a sus barones.
       Rogavan sobr' el cuerpo   muchas proçessïones;
       non serié más honrado   entre sus crïazones.

1791   Apelles, en comedio,   obró la sepultura:
       la tumba de primero,   después la cobertura;
       las basas en tres guisas,   de comunal mesura;
       tant' eran bien juntadas   que non pareçié juntura.

1783	Darius, may your fame be told of for ever, such was your bravery just in fighting with me! Let it not be to your shame that you were worsted, for I am Alexander, whose name is renowned.
1784	But in one thing do you have good fortune: that your empire was all left in good order; your beloved son I shall adopt, if I live, and seek marriages of honour for your daughters.
1785	All that I promise you, I intend to fulfil; if God grants me life I do not think I will fail; if I do not achieve it, I wish to curse myself, whatever death you die may God give to me, too!
1786	May God so allow me to fulfil my desire: to make Asia my subject, to conquer Africa, and to bring Morocco's towers within my grasp. In all that I say, I do not think I will fail.
1787	From there may he allow me to pass on to Spain and to master Seville, Toledo and Galicia, and France and Germany, just as the sea flows; if God wills it, I also intend to gain you vengeance.
1788	Finally may I also travel on to Lombardy, to set the great city of Rome beneath my sway, and enter my own Corinth as lord of the world; in all that I say I would not wish to fail.
1789	Vassals who act in such a way towards their lord would do no better for me, if they had the chance; anyone who ever shows mercy to a traitor,* may the Creator never have mercy on him!"
1790	He made a very great lament and spoke fine words and he caused his men to weep tears of bitterness; many processions offered prayers over Darius' body; among his own vassals he would not have been more honoured.
1791	Apelles, meanwhile, crafted his funerary monument, the tomb first of all, and the coverings to follow; the base was in three sections, all of like proportion, so cleverly joined that the join could not be seen.

1792   Debuxó el sepulcro   a muy grandes maraviellas:
        cómo corrié el sol,   la luna e las estrellas;
        cómo passan las noches,   los días en pues ellas;
        cómo fazen las dueñas   en mayo las corellas.

1793   Quáles tierras son buenas   de panes e de vinos,
        quáles pueblos son ricos   e quáles son mesquinos;
        de quál lugar a quál   responden los caminos,
        cómo han de andar   por ellos peregrinos.

1794   Y eran los grïegos,   qué fazién los latinos,
        e Saúl el vïejo   con todos sus vezinos;
        cómo yazién los mares   e los ríos vezinos,
        cómo sorben los ríos   los grandes a los chicos.

1795   Libia era de miesses   rica e abondada;
        la tierra de Amón,   de pluvia muy menguada.
        Rïégala Egibto,   tiénela muy bastada;
        el marfil es en India,   ende es tan nonbrada.

1796   Es de piedras preçiosas   África bien poblada;
        en ella yaz' Marruecos,   essa çibdat contada;
        Greçïa, por Atenas   de seso alumbrada;
        Roma yaz' sobre Tibre,   de buen muro çercada.

1797   Los pueblos de España   cómo son tan laugeros;
        pareçién los françeses   valientes cavalleros;
        Champaña, que aqueda   los vinos delanteros,
        Saba, do el ençenso   miden a sesteros.

1798   Cómo se preçian mucho   por Artús los bretones,
        cómo son los normanos   orgullosos varones;
        ingleses son fermosos,   de blandos coraçones,
        lombardos cobdiçiosos,   alemanes fellones.

1799   Allí escrivió la cuenta   ca de cor la sabié;
        el mundo quánd' fue fecho,   quántos años avié;
        de tres mil e nueveçientos   e doze non tollié;
        agora quatroçientos   e seis mill emprendié.

1800   Fízol' un petafio   escura ment' dictado;
        de Daniel lo priso,   que era y notado.
        Como era Apelles   clérigo bien letrado,
        todo su ministerio   tenié bien decorado.

1792	He designed the tomb to be full of great wonders, showing the movement of the sun, moon and stars, how the nights pass and the days which come after and how the ladies perform dances in May;
1793	which lands are fruitful for bread and for wine, which peoples have great wealth and which are poor, from where the roads start and where they have their end and how the pilgrims have to travel along them.
1794	The Greeks were there depicted and so too the Latins and Saul, the old man, with all his neighbours;* the position of the seas, where the nearby rivers flowed, and how the large rivers absorb the small.
1795	Libya was rich and abundant in its harvests, but the land of Ammon is sorely lacking in rain; its rich supply of water comes from Egypt's rivers. Ivory is from India, which wins great fame thereby.
1796	Africa has a great wealth of precious stones and there is found Morocco, that city of repute. Greece shines, through Athens, with the light of wisdom and Rome lies on the Tiber, a fine wall about it.
1797	He showed how the people of Spain were light of foot and the French appeared, too, warriors of valour; Champagne, which allows its best wines to rest, and Sheba, where incense is weighed in large measures.
1798	He showed how the Bretons draw great pride from Arthur* and how the men of Normandy are proud indeed; how the English are handsome, with gentle hearts, the Lombards greedy, and the Germans deceitful.*
1799	There he set down the account he knew by heart: when the world was created and how old it was:* three thousand nine hundred and twelve years old, no less, and now six thousand four hundred have elapsed.
1800	He produced an epitaph profound in expression – he took it from Daniel, for there it was recorded –; as Apelles was a man scholarly and learned, all the knowledge of his craft was firmly in his mind:

1801 "Hic situs est aries typicus, duo cornua cuius
fregit Alexander, totius malleus orbis;
duo cornua duo regna sunt,
persarum et medorum."

1802 "Aquí yaz' el carnero   de los cuernos del qual
quebrantó Alexandre,   de Greçia natural.
Narbazones e Bessus,   compaña desleal,
estos dos lo mataron   con traïción mortal."

1803 La obra fue complida,   el sepulcro alçado;
fue sobre los fusiellos   igual ment' assentado;
non pareçié yuntura,   tant' era bien labrado.
Tal cosa mereçié   rëy atán onrado.

1804 Fizo el rey demientre   el cuerpo balsamar;
quando fue balsamado,   al sepulcro llevar.
Fízolo a grant honra   cobrir e condesar.
Dios li preste el alma   si se quiere rogar.

1805 Nunca en esti siglo   devrié ome fïar,
que sabe a sus cosas   tan mala çaga dar;
a baxos nin a altos   non sabe perdonar;
non devriemos por esto   el otro olvidar.

1806 Anda como rüeda   que non quier' aturar;
el ome mal astrugo   non se sabe guardar;
trahe buenos falagos,   sábenos engañar;
nunca en un estado   puede quedo estar.

1807 Quand' ha el ome puesto   en algunt buen lugar,
dize: "Cede majori",   pénsal' de despeñar;
fáz'lo tal qual naçió   a la tierra tornar.
Va luego buscar otros   que pueda engañar.

1808 Qüando ha el ome   d'est' siglo a passar,
valía de un dinero   non li dexan llevar;
quanto gana el ome,   ha lo tod' a dexar;
hanlo sus enemigos   mortales a lograr.

1809 Tuelle con sus falagos   al ome el sentido;
lo quel' devriá membrar,   échalo en olvido;
es la carne señora,   el espíritu vençido;
faze barrer la casa   la muger al marido.

1801 "Hic situs est aries typicus, duo cornua cuius
fregit Alexander totius malleus orbis;
duo cornua duo regna sunt,
persarum et medorum."

1802 "In this place lies the ram whose pair of horns
was broken by Alexander, native of Greece;
Nabarzanes and Bessus, disloyal companions,
these two killed him in mortal treachery."*

1803 The work was completed and the tomb raised up
and balanced equally upon small columns;
the joins could not be seen, so fine was the work;
just as was deserved by so honoured a king.

1804 Meanwhile, the King had Darius' body embalmed
and, when it was embalmed, he had it taken to the tomb;
with great honour, he had it covered up and sealed within.
May God protect his soul, if He will hear our prayer.

1805 Man should never place his trust in this world,
which knows how to bring so grim an end to his affairs;
it knows not how to pardon any man, short or tall;
we ought not to forget the other world for this.

1806 It spins like a wheel which will not come to a halt
and the ill-starred man can find no protection;
it plies us with flattery and knows how to deceive us,
never able to be stilled and remain in one place.

1807 Once it has set a man in some favourable place,
it says "Cede to one greater" and looks to strike him down.*
It casts him back down to the ground, as at his birth,
and goes at once in search of others whom it may deceive.

1808 When a man comes to pass on from this world
he may not take with him the value of a penny;
whatever he wins, a man must leave it all behind
and it falls to his mortal enemies to gain it.

1809 With its flattery, it takes away man's good sense
and what he should remember is cast into oblivion;
the flesh is mistress and the spirit is servile;
it is the wife who makes the husband sweep the house.

1810 Encarna el pecado en el ome mesquino;
buélvelo con cobdiçia, sácalo de camino;
fázele olvidar la materia ond' vino;
el siglo por escarnio fázele el buçino.

1811 El ome, si quisiesse con recabdo andar,
devié entre su cuer la materia asmar;
como viene de tierra, a tierra es a tornar;
esto non puede fuerça ninguna estorvar.

1812 Dario, tan alto rëy, ome de tan grant conta,
en cabo abés ovo una foya angosta;
nol' valió su imperio quanto una langosta.
Quien en est' mundo fía él mismo se denosta.

1813 El ome dev' asmar lo que es por venir,
quál galardón espera en cabo reçebir;
si mala vida faze, mal ave a pedir;
el bueno verá gloria qual non sabrá pedir.

1814 Catando contra tierra como mal acordados,
olvidamos la forma a qui fuemos crïados,
cómo fuemos de Dios a su beldat formados;
andamos como bestias, de seso engañados.

1815 Quando nos de riqueza fazemos nos loçanos,
metemos la so tierra, ençerramos las manos;
más amamos a ella que a nuestros cristianos;
perdemos la en cabo como omes livianos.

1816 Plegamos con cobdiçia, olvidamos mesura;
nin a Dios nin a próximo non femos derechura;
desempara nos Dios, que non ha de nos cura;
veemos sobre nos mucha de grant rencura.

1817 Labradores non quieren derecha ment' dezmar,
aman unos a otros escatimas buscar;
buscan su día malo quand' están de vagar;
suele mucho cobdiçia entre ellos regnar.

1818 Anda grant falsedat entre los menestrales;
las obras fazen falsas, los puntos desleales;
perjúranse privado por ganar dos mencales;
pierden al Crïador por estas cosas tales.

Book of Alexander

1810   The Devil takes over the wretched man's flesh,
ensnares him with greed and lures him from his path;
he makes him forget from what matter he was born
and the world mocks him with its ridicule.

1811   A man, if he wished to conduct himself with care,
should turn his mind to that matter in his heart:
as he comes from earth, to earth he will return;
there is no force that can prevent this.

1812   Darius, a king so grand, a man of great renown,
in the end, all he had was a tiny grave;
his empire had not the value of a lobster;
he who trusts in this world condemns himself.

1813   Man must set his mind on those things that are to come,
the reward that he hopes to receive at his end;
if he leads an evil life, then evil will he suffer;
the good man will see glory beyond all he could request.

1814   Looking at the earth like those without sense,
we forget the form in which we were created,
how we were made by God in the beauty of His image,
and we move like beasts, deceived in our thoughts.

1815   When we become rich in worldly wealth,
we hide it under earth and close our hands;
loving it more than we do our fellow Christians
and we lose it in the end, like fickle men.

1816   We are filled with greed and forget all restraint
and do justice neither to God nor our neighbour.
God abandons us, as for us He has no care,
and we see very great anger weighing down upon us.

1817   Farmers are not willing to pay their tithes as due*
and love to seek disputes with one another;
when at rest, they go in search of their own perdition,
and it is usual that intense greed be their sovereign.

1818   Great falsity is abroad among the craftsmen:
they cheat in their work and in their stitches they deceive,
quick to commit perjury to gain two gold coins;
but they lose their Creator through such acts as these.

1819   Saben fer los bufones   muchas malas baratas;
buelven en sus mercaduras   muchas malas ratas;
non podrié dezir ome   todas sus garavatas;
morir quieren el día   que non ganan çapatas.

1820   Muchos con grant cobdiçia   tórnanse usureros;
dan dos e cogen quatro,   como de sus pecheros.
Venden los mal astrugos   las almas por dineros;
el día del Juïçio   non les valdrán bozeros.

1821   Los reyes e los prínçipes   con negra de cobdiçia
han a grant mercado   vendida la justiçia;
más aman fer tesoros   que vedar estultiçia.
Es el mundo perdido   por essa avariçia.

1822   Clérigos nin calonges,   çertas, nin las mongías,
non andan a derechura,   por las çapatas mías;
¡mal pecado! todos   andan con travessías;
por end' a derechura   non van las sermonías.

1823   Si los que son ministros   de los santos altares
sirviessen digna mente   cad'uno sus lugares,
non serién tan crüeles   los prínçipes seglares,
nin veriemos nos otros   tantos malos pesares.

1824   Somos los simples clérigos   errados e viçiosos,
los prelados mayores,   ricos e desdeñosos:
en prender somos agudos,   en lo al perezosos;
por ende son los santos   irados e sañosos.

1825   En las elecçïones   anda grant enconía;
unas vienen por premia,   otras por simonía;
non demandan hedat   nin sen nin cleriçía,
ende, non saben fer   nula derechuría.

1826   Como non han los omes   dubda de los prelados,
casan con sus parientas,   andan descaminados;
fazen malas rebueltas   casadas con casados;
somos por tales cosas   de Dios desemparados.

1827   Los que son assí fechos   exen después ladrones;
asman siempre nemigas,   fazen las traïciones;
dexan malos enxemplos   como malos varones;
recúdeles la sangre   a diez generaçiones.

1819	The traders know how to commit great deceptions and sell their wares for prices which are greatly unfair; no man could describe all their carryings on; they would die the day they fail to gain a pair of shoes.
1820	Many turn to usury in their great greed; giving two and taking four as though from taxpayers; the ill-fated wretches sell their souls for coins but lawyers will not help them on the Day of Judgement.
1821	Kings and princes, blinded by the blackness of greed, do a roaring trade in the sale of justice; they love to amass treasures more than outlaw folly; because of this avarice, the world is lost.
1822	Neither clergy nor canons nor – of course – nuns act as they rightly should, by my shoes! Through wicked sin they all fall into wrong, wherefore sermons do not reflect the truth.
1823	If those who are ministers of the holy altars each gave worthy service in their due place, the worldly princes would not display such cruelty and we would not see so many awful sorrows.
1824	We simple clergy are vice-ridden in error and the greater prelates are rich and disdainful: in taking we are sharp, but otherwise lazy; and so the saints are filled with wrath and anger.
1825	In the elections there is much injustice to be seen, some advance through power, others by simony.* Nothing is asked about age, knowledge or learning* and so they do not know how to act with any fairness.
1826	As men have no fear of the prelates of the Church, they marry their relatives and stray from the path, married women have evil affairs with married men; for reasons such as these we are abandoned by God.
1827	Those who have acted thus turn after into thieves, always planning harm and committing treachery and setting bad examples befitting men of evil; it lingers in the blood for ten generations.

1828 Qüando se bien catan   vassallos e señores,
     cavalleros e clérigos,   en buelta labradores,
     abades e obispos,   con los otros pastores,
     en todos ave tachas   de diversas colores.

1829 Por esso el pecado   ave tan grant poder;
     faze enamistades   a los omes bolver;
     hermanos con hermanas   fázenos contender;
     busca cómo nos pueda   peor escarneçer.

1830 Faz' contra los señores   los vassallos armar;
     lo que es fiera cosa,   faze los matar;
     del siglo que veemos   tan sin regla andar,
     quanto mejor pudiéssemos   nos devriemos guardar.

1831 Los griegos, quand' a Dario   ovieron soterrado,
     tovieron que avián   su pleito acabado.
     Todos querién tornar   a sus casas de grado,
     si del rey Alexandre   les fuesse otorgado.

1832 Movióse por la hueste   en este comedio un ruido
     que, desque Dario era   muerto e sobullido,
     el rey Alexandre,   que nunca fue vençido,
     querrié tornar a Greçia,   su lazerio complido.

1833 Las nuevas por la hueste   fueron tan abivadas,
     non serién más creídas   si fuessen pregonadas;
     fueron a poca de ora   las estacas rancadas,
     enselladas las bestias,   las troxeras guisadas.

1834 Entendiólo el rëy   e fue müy irado;
     quando murió su padre   non fue más cüitado.
     Demandó a capítulo,   el su noble senado;
     ante de media ora   fue todo aplegado.

1835 Quando fueron llegados,   empeçó de fablar:
     "Varones, ¿qué es esto   que vos quiere matar?
     En mal punto naçiemos   e passemos la mar
     si con tan mal recabdo   avemos a tornar.

1836 Nos agora tenemos   la cosa aguisada
     por a nuestro lazerio   dar büena finada;
     tolledes me la tierra   quem' avedes ganada;
     de la mi grant füerça   tornado so en nada.

| 1828 | When vassals and lords behold themselves with clear eyes, so too knights and clergy and farmers, besides, abbots and bishops, and the other ministers – on all of them are stains of different colours. |

| 1829 | For just this reason the Devil wields such power and makes men become each other's enemies, as he sets brothers in conflict with their sisters and searches out how he might mock us all the worse. |

| 1830 | He makes vassals take up arms against their lords, and even kill them, much to our amazement; from the world that we see in such lawlessness we should seek protection as best we can. |

| 1831 | The Greeks, when they had made burial of Darius, considered that their business was at an end, and they were all keen to return to their homes, if King Alexander were to grant them permission. |

| 1832 | At this point, a rumour ran through the army that, since Darius was now dead and interred, King Alexander, who had never been defeated, wished for a return to Greece, his trials at an end. |

| 1833 | The tale was so quickly spread throughout the army, as readily believed as if it had been announced; in but a little time the stakes had been pulled up, the animals saddled and the provisions made ready. |

| 1834 | The King learned of this and was filled with anger; he had been no more upset at his father's death. He summoned his noble council to a meeting and within half an hour they had all arrived. |

| 1835 | When they had all arrived, he began to speak: "My men, what is this that is eating at you? We were born and crossed the sea at an ill-fated moment if we are to return with such an ill gain. |

| 1836 | Now we have our affairs very well set to bring a fine conclusion to our trials; you are taking from me the land you won for me and from my great power I am reduced to nothing. |

1837　En lugar de victoria,　despreçio levaremos;
　　　en lugar de ganançia,　con pérdida iremos;
　　　quando en Greçia fuéremos,　varones, ¿qué diremos?
　　　De lo que conquisiemos,　¿qué recabdo daremos?"

1838　Dixeron los varones:　"¡Señor, non nos maltrayas!
　　　Nos todo lo faremos　como tú sabor ayas;
　　　nos seguirte queremos　do quiere que tú vayas;
　　　a todo nuestro grado　non querremos que cayas.

1839　Mas falaga los pueblos　ca ya quieren mover;
　　　faz lo que a nos dizes　a ellos entender.
　　　Todos querrán en cabo　complir el tu plazer,
　　　ca non querrán por ren　so serviçio perder."

1840　Mandó poner la cádera　en que sollié judgar
　　　en medio de la plaça,　en el mejor lugar;
　　　mandó grandes e chicos　a derredor posar.
　　　El buen emperador　empeçó de fablar:

1841　"Bien entiendo, amigos,　las vuestras voluntades:
　　　¡quánto tienpo ha passado　que comigo andades!
　　　Querriedes vos tornar　a vuestras heredades;
　　　¡sí Dïos me bendiga!　con derecho andades.

1842　Avedes vuestra tierra　quita de servidumbre;
　　　sodes bien alimpiados　de toda la calumbre;
　　　sodes vos demostrados　por de grant firmedumbre;
　　　más valen de vos pocos　que de otros muchedumbre.

1843　Más avedes de tierras　vos comigo ganadas
　　　que nunca otro rëy　ovo villas pobladas.
　　　Avedes rica mente　vuestras barvas honradas.
　　　Dario dirié las nuevas　sil' fuessen demandadas.

1844　Si esto que ganamos　fuesse bien recabado
　　　o de seer estable　fuesse yo segurado,
　　　lo que vos querrïedes　faría yo de grado,
　　　ca el sabor de Greçia　non lo he olvidado.

1845　Querría mis hermanas　e mi madre veer;
　　　avrién ellas comigo,　yo con ellas, plazer;
　　　mas veo dos contrarios　detrás remaneçer
　　　por do podriemos toda　la ganançia perder.

1837	In victory's place we shall carry back dishonour and in place of gains we shall return with losses. When we are in Greece, my men, what shall we say? What report shall we give of what we captured?"
1838	His men said, "Lord, do not criticise us! We will do everything that you desire and wish to follow you wherever you go; with all our hearts we do not want you to fall.
1839	But speak kindly to the people for they now want to leave, and make them understand what you are telling us. In the end they will all wish to carry out your will, for they will not be keen to lose what they have earned."
1840	He bade the chair on which he always sat in judgement be placed in a powerful position in the middle of the square; and that old and young alike should take their place around him; and, with this, the good Emperor began his address:
1841	"I understand well your desires, my friends: you have spent such a long time travelling with me! And you would like to return to your homelands. May God bless me! You have right on your side.
1842	You have released your land from enslavement, removed from yourselves any possible taint, and you have shown a great strength of purpose; a host of others are not worth a few of you.
1843	You have managed to win more lands with me than any other king ever founded cities; you have brought rich honour upon your persons; so Darius would testify were he asked.
1844	If what we have won were properly secured or if I were assured of its stability, willingly, then, would I do what you would like, for I have not forgotten the appeal of Greece.
1845	I would like to see my sisters and my mother; they would take pleasure in me and I in them; but I see two problems remaining behind us through which we could well lose all our gains.

1846   Buena es la conquista, mas non es bien finada;
        si vençida es Persia, aun non es bien domada;
        si a nuestras costumbres non fuere confirmada,
        contad que non tenemos nuestro fecho en nada.

1847   Vagar doma las cosas – díz'lo la escriptura –
        doma aves e bestias bravas por su natura,
        la sierva que es áspera espaçio la madura;
        entendet esto mismo de toda crïatura.

1848   Los que se nos rindieron por derecho temor,
        si entre nos e ellos non oviere amor,
        quando nos traspongamos avrán otro señor;
        seremos nos caídos en tan mala error.

1849   Vayamos con ellos, algunt poco faziendo;
        irán de nuestros lenguajes nuestro fuero sabiendo;
        de nuestra compañía irán sabor prendiendo;
        después, podremos ir alegres e ridiendo.

1850   La segunda contraria vos quiero demostrar,
        en que todos devemos mucho mientes parar:
        devemos nuestra cosa de tal guisa ligar
        que nuestros sucçessores non nos puedan rebtar.

1851   Maguer Dario es muerto, nos nada non ganamos,
        quando los traïdores a vida los dexamos;
        tornarán en el regno luego que nos vayamos;
        destrüirán los falsos los que nos escusamos.

1852   Como están las gentes de nos escarmentadas,
        non serán sola mente de contrastar osadas.
        Mandarán el emperio las manos perjuradas,
        las que ave diez años devián seer cortadas.

1853   Mas si vuestra fazienda queredes bien poner,
        fagamos lo que suele nuestro maestro fer:
        que quier' la carne mala de la plaga toller,
        que la que es büena non pueda corromper.

1854   Cortemos yerva mala que non faga raíz;
        fagamos que non pueda alçar la su çerviz;
        al ome traïdor, fijo de meretriz,
        merçed ha qui lo mata, el escripto lo diz'.

1846	The conquest is a fine one but not yet quite complete: though Persia has been routed it has still not been subdued; if it is not confirmed in the use of our customs, believe that we must rate what we have done as nothing.
1847	Time masters all things, so the text says: it masters birds and beasts wild by nature, and slowly it brings the bitter fruit to ripeness; understand this to be true of all creation.
1848	Those who gave us their surrender out of rightful fear, if there exists no love between us and them, when we depart they will take up a new lord, and we shall have fallen into grievous error.
1849	Let us keep working with them a little longer, they will gradually learn our language and our laws; gradually they will gain affection for our company and afterwards we shall have happiness and laughter.
1850	The second of the problems that I wish to point out, and to which we must all give a lot of thought, is that we have to settle our affairs in such a way that our successors might find no fault with us.
1851	Although Darius is dead, we have gained nothing when we have left the traitors behind us, alive. As soon as we leave, they will return to the kingdom, and the false men will destroy those we have spared.
1852	As the people have been taught such a lesson by us, they will not even dare to show resistance; the empire will be governed by traitorous hands, which ten years ago should have been cut off.*
1853	But if you wish to set your affairs to rights, let us do what is our master surgeon's custom, for he seeks to cut the bad flesh from the wound so that it may not corrupt that which is good.
1854	Let us pull up the weeds so that they may not root, let us make it that they cannot raise their heads; the traitorous man, the son of a harlot – his killer is pardoned, so the text says.

1855 Quando a ir oviéremos, vayamos segurados;
si non, seremos todos represos e rebtados.
si éstos destruïmos, iremos más onrados;
serán nuestros bernajes todos bien acabados.

1856 Vos nunca ovïestes voluntad nin sabor,
si aver lo pudistes, de parçir al traidor.
Pausona con los otros que mataron señor
dieron vos tal derecho que non podién mayor.

1857 Por lealtat büena que siempre mantoviestes
e que a traïdor parçir nunca quesiestes;
fuestes de Dios guïados mejor que non pidiestes;
devriedes aún fer lo que siempre feziestes."

1858 Recudieron le todos: "Rey, bien lo entendemos;
dizes grant derechura, nos complir lo queremos.
Do tú ir quisïeres nos contigo iremos;
mas a los traïdores espaçio non les demos."

1859 Entendió Alexandre que estavan pagados;
mandóles mover luego, ant' que fuessen esfriados.
Fueron luego movidos, en carrera entrados;
contra los traïdores ivan escalentados.

1860 Entraron en Hircania; fue luego conquerida;
pero fue en comedio mucha sangre vertida.
Al falso Narbazones prisieron lo a vida;
tovieron que avién fecha buena corrida.

1861 Avié y un ric' ome que non devié naçer.
Ovo con sus falagos al rëy a vençer;
com' al fierro el fuego físol' amolleçer;
ovo por él Narbazones de muert' a estorçer.

1862 Sabe Dios que me pesa de toda voluntat;
¡Dios al entre mediano nol' aya pïedat!
Segund mi conoçençia cuido dezir verdat;
menoscabó el rey mucho de su bondat.

1863 Allí vino al rëy una rica reína,
señora de la tierra quel' dizién Femenina.
Talestris la dixieron, desque fue pequeñina;
non trayé un varón, sólo por melezina.

1855   When we are to go, let us go in confidence;
        if not, we shall all face rebukes and accusations;
        if we destroy these men, we shall be more honoured;
        and our feats will all be brought to better end.

1856   You have never felt any wish or desire,
        if you could capture him, to spare the traitor.
        Pausanias, with the others who killed their lord,
        gave you this rule, which they could not have made firmer.

1857   For the fine loyalty you have always maintained
        and since you never wished to spare a traitor,
        by God you were guided even better than you asked;
        you should still act as you always have."

1858   They all replied, "Lord King, we understand well;
        all you say is right and we wish to comply.
        We shall go with you wherever you wish,
        but let us not now give the traitors respite."

1859   Alexander understood that his men were content,
        and bade them move out at once, before desire cooled;
        they all moved out from camp and took to the road,
        their anger against the traitors now inflamed.

1860   They entered Hyrcania, which was quickly conquered
        although much blood was spilt in the meantime;
        the traitor Nabarzanes they captured alive
        and they judged their expedition a success.

1861   There was a nobleman there who should not have been born*
        who managed to win the King round with his flattery;
        as fire does to iron, he made the King soften:
        through him, Nabarzanes was able to escape death.

1862   God knows that it makes me grieve with all my heart;
        may God have no pity on this go-between!
        According to my knowledge – I believe I speak the truth –
        in this way the King did great damage to his goodness.*

1863   A rich queen came to the King in that place,*
        who ruled the land that they called Femenina.
        Thalestris had been her name since she was very young,
        and she had a man's company only as medicine.

1864　　Trayá trezientas vírgines, en cavallos ligeros,
que non vedarién lid a sendos cavalleros;
todas eran maestras de fer colpes çerteros,
de tirar de ballestas e echar escuseros.

1865　　Las donas amazonas non biven con maridos;
nunca en essa tierra son varones caídos;
han en essas fronteras lugares establidos
do tres vezes en l'año yazen con sus maridos.

1866　　Si naçe fija fembra, la su madre la cría;
si naçe fijo masclo, al padre lo embía;
los unos a los otros sacan por merchandía
de lo que en la tierra ha mayor carestía.

1867　　Todas vinién vestidas de capas travesseras,
sus ballestas al cuello, turquesas e çerveras,
saetas e quadriellos de diversas maneras;
todas sabién ferir corriendo cavalleras.

1868　　Como avién su vida siempre de tal manera,
– avién de meter mano en toda fazendera –
la part' del lado diestro andava más soltera,
ca essa mano suele andar más correndera.

1869　　Fazen otra barata por mal non pareçer:
queman la teta diestra que non pueda creçer;
la otra por que puede más cubierta seer,
por crïar los infantes dexan la pobleçer.

1870　　Fasta la media pierna les da la vestidura;
non caerié en tierra por palmo de mesura;
calçan bragas muy prietas con firme ligadura;
semejan bien varones en toda su fechura.

1871　　Finque todo lo al, la estoria sigamos;
del pleito de la reina en esso entendamos;
merçed al Crïador, sólo dezir podamos,
assaz avemos rato e materia que digamos.

1872　　Venié apuesta mente Talestris la reína;
vistié preçiosos paños, todos de seda fina;
un açor en su mano, que fue de la marina:
serié a lo de menos de siet' mudas aína.

1864	She brought three hundred virgins on swift-footed horses, quite willing to do battle, each with a different knight; all of them were masters in striking true blows, in shooting a crossbow and setting an ambush.
1865	Amazon ladies do not live with husbands and never are men received into their lands. They have set up places on the frontiers of their realm where they lie with their husbands three times in a year.
1866	If a girl child is born, her mother brings her up, if a male child, she sends him to his father; each people take from the other in trade that of which their country has the greatest need.
1867	They all arrived wearing cloaks across their bodies, their crossbows slung at their necks, for hunting deer, with arrows, too, and darts of many different kinds, and they all knew how to strike a blow from horseback.
1868	As in their life they had to cope with great hardship and had to take part in all battles themselves, their right-hand side was allowed greater movement, for this is the hand that usually runs freest.
1869	They have another trick to give the right appearance: they burn their right breast so that it cannot grow; the other, because it can be more fully covered, they allow to grow, so they can suckle children.
1870	Their clothing covers half way down their leg but would not reach the ground by the measure of a palm; they wear very tight leggings, their fastenings firm; in all their appearance they are truly like men.
1871	Let all else be left, let us carry on our story, and bring our focus to the matter of the Queen. If we can but give thanks to the Creator, we have ample time and subject of which to tell.
1872	Queen Thalestris arrived, fine in appearance,* wearing beautiful clothes, all of fine silk, a hawk on her fist, which came from the sea and which had moulted at least seven times.

1873　　Avié müy buen cuerpo,　era bien estilada;
　　　　correa de tres palmos　la çiñía doblada;
　　　　nunca fue en el mundo　cara tan bien tajada;
　　　　non podrié por nul preçio　seer mejor poblada.

1874　　La fruente avié blanca,　alegre e serena;
　　　　plus clara que la luna　quando es düodena;
　　　　non avriá çerca d'ella　nul preçio Filomena,
　　　　de la que diz' Ovidio　una grant cantilena.

1875　　Tales las sobre çejas　como listas de seda,
　　　　eguales, bien abiertas,　de la nariz hereda;
　　　　fazié una sombriella　tan mansa e tan queda
　　　　que non serié comprada　por ninguna moneda.

1876　　La beldat de los ojos　era fiera nobleza;
　　　　las pestañas iguales,　de comunal grandeza;
　　　　quando bien las abrié　era fiera fadeza;
　　　　a cristiano perfecto　tolrié toda pereza.

1877　　Tant' avié la nariz　a razón afeitada
　　　　que non podriá Apelles　reprenderla en nada;
　　　　los labros abenidos,　la boca mesurada,
　　　　los dientes bien iguales,　blancos como cuajada.

1878　　Blanca era la dueña,　de muy fresca color;
　　　　avié y grant entrega　a un emperador;
　　　　la rosa del espino,　que es tan genta flor,
　　　　al maitín al ruçío　non pareçié mejor.

1879　　De la su fermosura,　non quiero más contar;
　　　　temo fer alguno　de voluntad pecar.
　　　　Los sus enseñamientos　non los sabriá favlar
　　　　Orfeüs, el que fizo　los árboles cantar.

1880　　El rëy Alexandre　sallóla reçebir;
　　　　muchol' plugo a ella　quando lo vio venir.
　　　　Estendieron las diestras,　fuéronselas ferir;
　　　　besaron s'en los ombros　por la salva complir.

1881　　El rey fue palaçiano,　prísola por la rienda;
　　　　por mejor ospedarla,　levóla a su tienda.
　　　　Después que fue yantada,　a ora de merienda,
　　　　entról' a demandar　el rey de su fazienda.

1873	She had a very fine body, tall and willowy; a belt of three palms' length twice girded her waist; never in this world was a face so finely formed: for no price could one more beautiful be found.
1874	Her brow was purest white, happy and serene, shining brighter than the moon in its fullest phase. She could not even be matched by Philomela, of whom Ovid tells at length in song.*
1875	She had eyebrows that were just like ribbons of silk, equal, well spaced, and set closely to the nose, forming a little shadow so gentle and so graceful that it could not be bought by any money on earth.
1876	The beauty of her eyes was of intense nobility, her eyelashes of equal and uniform length; when she opened her eyes it cast a powerful spell, enough to rouse from all torpor the most perfect Christian.
1877	Her nose was truly possessed of such beauty that Apelles could not have found a thing to fault; her lips in fine proportion, her mouth neatly-formed, and her teeth all equal-sized and white as whey.
1878	White was the lady's complexion, fresh of hue: she would be a great delight to an emperor; the rose that bears thorns, so lovely a flower would not seem finer in the morning dew.
1879	Of her great beauty I wish to tell you no more, for I fear I may make someone sin in their desire; to tell of her qualities would surpass even the powers of Orpheus who brought the very trees to sing.*
1880	King Alexander went out to receive her and she was delighted when she saw him approach. They held out their hands and clasped them together and kissed the other's shoulder to complete their greeting.
1881	The King acted nobly, took her horse by the reins, and to take better care of her he led her to his tent; once she had eaten, at the hour of refreshment, the King began to ask her of her business.

1882   "Quiero saber, reína,   ónd' es vuestra andada,
o por quál razón   sodes aquí uviada;
que quiere que pidades,   seredes escuchada;
vuestra petiçïón   non será repudiada.

1883   Si averes quisierdes,   grado al Crïador,
yo vos daré abondo,   mucho de buen amor.
Si de morar con nusco   ovierdes vos sabor,
honrar vos han los griegos   con su emperador."

1884   "Graçias," dixo Talestris   al rey "de la promessa;
non vin' ganar averes   nin soy juglaressa;
de bevir con varones   mi lëy non me lexa,
mas quiero responderte,   descobrirte mi quexa.

1885   Oí dezir tus nuevas,   que traes grant ventura,
grant seso e grant fuerça,   esfuerço e mesura;
teme te tod' el mundo,   es en grant estrechura.
Vin' veer de quál cuerpo   ixié tan grant pavura.

1886   Demás, quiero un dono   de tu mano levar:
aver de ti un fijo,   ¡nom' lo quieras negar!
Non avrá en el mundo   de linaje su par;
non te deves por tanto   contra mí denodar.

1887   Si fijo barón fuere   a ti lo enbiaré;
si Dios de mal me curia,   bien te lo guardaré;
fasta que nado sea,   nunca cavalgaré;
si fuere fija fembra   mi regno le daré."

1888   Dixo el rëy: "Plaz' me,   esto faré de grado."
Dio salto en la selva,   corrió bien el venado.
Recabdó la reína   rica ment' su mandado;
alegre e pagada   tornó al su regnado.

1889   Bessus, en est' comedio,   estava espantado;
avié por encobrirse   el nombre demudado.
En las tierras de Bactra   andava afotado,
pero trayé el miedo   al pescueço colgado.

1890   Avié grandes poderes   el falso assemblado;
por lidiar con los griegos   estava aguisado;
mas, quando a postremas   todo fue delibrado,
non ganó correduras   que fuesse bien pagado.

1882	"I wish to know, my Queen, from where you have come and for what reason you have arrived here; whatever you may ask for, you will be heard, and your request will not be rejected.
1883	If you wish for wealth – thanks be to the Creator – I shall most willingly give you an abundance. If it is your desire to remain here with us, the Greeks and their Emperor will all pay you honour."
1884	"I am grateful," said Thalestris, "to the King for his promise, but I came not to gain wealth, for no minstrel am I, and my law does not permit that I live among men; but I wish to reply and explain my concern.
1885	I have heard tell of you, that you possess great good fortune, great intelligence and strength, valour and restraint; the whole world fears you and lies in great disquiet; I came to see what person is the source of such terror.
1886	I wish to take away, besides, a gift from your hand: to bear a child by you – you must not refuse this; there will be no rival for bloodline in the world; but you must not on that account think ill of me.
1887	Should the child be a son, I shall send him to you; if God saves me from ill, I shall guard him well for you and until he is born I shall not mount a horse; but if it is a daughter I shall give her my realm."
1888	The King said, "I am delighted, I will willingly do it." He leapt into the forest, and gave the game good chase. The Queen carried out her business in very good measure, and, joyful and satisfied, returned to her kingdom.
1889	Bessus at this time was living in terror and had changed his name to conceal himself; in the lands of Bactria, he put on a bold front,* but he carried fear hanging round his neck.
1890	The traitor had brought together great forces and was prepared to fight against the Greeks, but, when in the end all reached its conclusion, he won no skirmish to give him satisfaction.

1891   Vino al rey barrunte, óvolo a saber;
           non ovo con mensaje nunca mayor plazer.
           Mandó cavalgar luego, las mesnadas mover;
           querrié vengar a Dario a todo so poder.

1892   Como avién las gentes fecha fiera ganançia,
           trayén oro e plata a fiera abondançia;
           dizién que verdat era, sin otra alabançia,
           non lo podrién mover los someros de Françia.

1893   La carga era grande, non la podién mover;
           avién la bien lazrada, non la querién perder;
           non podién las jornadas tan bien aproveçer;
           tanto como solién non se fazién temer.

1894   Asmó el rey senado entre su coraçón
           de llegar los averes todos en un montón;
           quando fuessen llegados ponelles un tizón
           que se fundiessen todos, tornassen en carvón.

1895   Fizo luego consejo con todo su senado.
           Díxoles que mostrassen quanto avién ganado;
           e él que sacarié lo suyo de buen grado.
           "Señor," dixeron todos, "faremos tu mandado."

1896   Sacó el rey lo suyo al almoneda primero;
           non quiso retener valía d'un dinero;
           desent' sacaron todos quis quier' de su çillero;
           quando fue allegado, fízose grant rimero.

1897   El rëy con su mano ençendió una faja.
           Diol' a todo fuego; nol' dolié nin migaja;
           non dexó de quemar una mala meaja;
           avié tan poco duelo como si fuesse paja.

1898   Pesávales a todos del daño grant que era;
           maguer eran pesantes, encubrién su dentera.
           Desque lo suyo mismo metié en la foguera,
           non le podién dezir una letra señera.

1899   En cabo confortaron se, tovieron lo por bien;
           coñoçieron que carga embargosa trayén;
           sólo que sanos fuessen, otro se ganarién;
           por mal aver buen preçio perder lo non querién.

1891	Word reached the King, and he came to learn the news: he was never so pleased at any message; at once he bade his men mount and his army move out; he wanted vengeance for Darius with all his might.
1892	As Alexander's men had made enormous gains bringing with them a great glut of gold and silver, they said it was true, with no exaggeration: it could not be moved by all the palfreys of France.
1893	The load was a great one and they could not move it; they had won it through great trials and did not want to lose it; they could not take such full advantage of the days and did not inspire fear as they had done before.
1894	The King then conceived a plan within his own mind: to gather all the booty in a single heap and, when it was assembled, to set a light to it, that it all be destroyed and turned to charcoal.
1895	Immediately he called all his council to a meeting and told them to show him all the gains they had made, and that he would most willingly bring out his own; "Lord," they all said, "we will do as you command."
1896	The King was first to set his possessions on the pile, and wished not to keep back the value of a penny; they all brought out whatever lay in their dwellings and when it had been gathered it made a great mound.
1897	The King with his own hand set a torch alight and set it all aflame without a crumb of sorrow; a paltry penny was not saved from being burned, and he felt as little grief as if it had all been straw.
1898	They were all distressed by the loss that was so great; but, though feeling great regret, they concealed their rage; since he had placed his own possessions on the fire there was not a single word that they could say to him.
1899	At last, they took comfort and saw that it was right; they realised that they had borne a troublesome burden; given but good health, they would win as much again; they wished not to lose their great repute for lowly gains.

1900 El pecado, que nunca se echa a dormir,
el que las malas telas suele siempre ordir,
la bestia maledita tanto pudo bollir
que basteció tal cosa ond' ovo a reír.

1901 Çerca era de Bactra el buen emperador,
do andava alçado Bessus el traïdor.
Oviera se por pocas preso mal baticor,
ond' él non se temié nin avié nul pavor.

1902 Fizieron le creer que lo querién matar
aquellos en qui él solié mucho fïar.
Maguer nos lo queremos encobrir e callar,
en Filotas es toda la cosa a quebrar.

1903 Filotas de esfuerço fue prínçip' acabado;
non ovo Alexandre un miembro más lazrado.
Pero, quanto en esso, fue pobre muy menguado:
non se sopo guardar del lazo del pecado.

1904 Omes de raíz mala asmaron malvestat:
por matar al bon rëy fizieron hermandat.
Sopo de Cabalino Filotas la verdat;
óvolo por tres días el fol en poridat.

1905 Como diz' el proverbio, que non ha encubierta
que en cabo de cosa a mal non se revierta,
supo por otras partes Alexandre la çierta;
parçir non gela quiso por boz nin por refierta.

1906 Pero, que non pudiessen dezir por aventura
que falsó Alexandre, por saña, derechura,
provógela por testes que feziera locura;
él negar non lo pudo por su mala ventura.

1907 Demandó a Filotas por seer lapidado;
non passó por mejor el su padre honrado;
maguer muchos lo salvan, que yo non les he grado,
qual fezieron tal ayan, ca non so su pagado.

1908 A cab' de siete dias, el duelo olvidado,
dio con sigo en Bactra el rey escalentado;
por caer sobre Bessus andava fazendado;
con ganançia del siglo non serié tan pagado.

1900	The Devil, who has never lain down to sleep, the one who unstintingly contrives evil snares, the accursed beast, busied himself to such effect that he created something that brought him to mirth.
1901	The good Emperor was now near to Bactria, where Bessus the traitor was hidden away; Alexander came close to sustaining great pain in a place where he felt neither fear nor dread.
1902	Men made him believe that some wanted to kill him – those men in whom he used to place great trust; though we wish to hide it and keep tongues stilled, the whole affair came crashing down on Philotas.*
1903	Philotas through his valour was a prince of distinction, and Alexander had no man more battle-scarred; but in just one respect he proved poor and bereft: he had no defence against the Devil's snare.
1904	Men of evil roots devised a foul crime and formed a conspiracy to kill the good King; Philotas knew the truth from Cebalinus, but the fool kept it secret for three days.
1905	As the saying goes: there's no thing concealed whose turn to ill's not in the end revealed; Alexander found out the truth by other means, and no words or argument could make him spare the man.
1906	But so that it could not be said by any chance that Alexander defied what is right in his rage, he had witnesses attest to Philotas' folly – who could not deny it, to his ill fortune.
1907	He cried for Philotas to be stoned to death: the victim's honoured father had no better fate; although many excuse him, I am not on their side: let their end match their conduct – I do not support them.
1908	After seven days, with the grief now forgotten, the King came to Bactria, his feelings aroused, and he was determined to fall upon Bessus: all the world's gains would not give him such pleasure.

1909 El falso non se pudo   ant' el rey contener;
     alçóse a las sierras   por mejor estorçer;
     mas tanto non se pudo   alçar nin esconder,
     en essa quinta ovo   en cabo a caer.

1910 Avié el rey consigo   un hermano de Dario;
     fïava en él mucho,   era su secretario;
     metiólo en su mano   por fer mayor escarnio,
     él selo justiçiasse   como a mal falsario.

1911 El alma fue mal dicha   e el cuerpo justiçiado;
     primero escarnido,   despues cruçificado;
     el alma fue perdida   el cuerpo desmembrado;
     yaz' dentro en infierno   con Judas abraçado.

1912 Bien avié guerreado   el buen emperador;
     érase bien provado   por buen batallador;
     vençiera e vengara   al buen emperador;
     mas del regno de Çitia   aún avié sabor.

1913 Luego movió desent'   sañoso e irado,
     como aguaducho   quando viene finchado.
     En ribera de Tanais,   un río señalado,
     mandó fincar las tiendas   al su pueblo lazrado.

1914 Tanais es de Çitia   e de Bactra mojón;
     Tanais las departe,   faze división;
     Europa e Asia allí   y fazen partiçión;
     agua es cabdal,   non le saben fondón.

1915 Fecho avién los griegos   puentes a maestría
     ond' passassen el flumen   a cab' de terçer día;
     mas, ante que sallesen   de la alverguería,
     vino a Alexandre   una mensajería.

1916 Viniéronle de Çitia   al rëy mensajeros;
     veinte eran por cuenta   e todos cavalleros;
     omes de santa vida,   simples e verdaderos;
     non sabié ningunt d'ellos   contar doze dineros.

1917 Quando fueron venidos   ant' el emperador
     empeçó a fablar   el que era mayor;
     todos lo escuchavan   ca end' avién sabor;
     era muy bien lenguado   e buen disputador.

1909	The traitor was not able to face up to the King and fled into the mountains to hide himself the better; but he could not flee or hide himself away so well as not to fall at last into the leader's share of booty.
1910	Together with the King was a brother of Darius;* he trusted him greatly – he was his secretary; to this man he gave Bessus for greater abasement, that he do justice to him as an evil traitor.
1911	The soul was cursed, the body brought to justice, mutilated first and then crucified;* the soul was damned, the body dismembered, and he lies in Hell in Judas' embrace.
1912	Well had the good Emperor fought his campaigns and he had proved himself to be a fine battler; he had both conquered and avenged the good Emperor but still had designs on the kingdom of Scythia.
1913	Immediately he pressed on, full of wrath and anger, like the current in a river's swollen flow; on the banks of the Tanaïs, a famous river,* he commanded his battle-worn troops to pitch camp.
1914	The Tanaïs marks the border of Scythia and Bactria; it separates the two, and marks out a division; there it makes a parting of Europe from Asia; it is a vast river whose depth cannot be known.
1915	The Greeks had constructed bridges with great skill on which to cross the river when the third day had passed; but before they had left their encampment and set out men came to Alexander with a message.
1916	Messengers came to the King from Scythia, twenty in number and all of them knights; men of holy life, they were simple and true, and none of them knew how to reckon up twelve coins.
1917	When they had come into the Emperor's presence, the eldest one of them began to speak; everyone listened, for he gave them great pleasure, an eloquent man, highly skilled in debate.

1918   Dixo: "Rey, si fuesse   tan grand el tu poder
       com' el coraçón has   e fazes pareçer,
       non te podrién los mares   nin las tierras caber;
       a Júpiter querriés   el emperio toller.

1919   Si toviesses la mano   diestra en Orïente,
       la siniestra en cabo   de todo Occidente,
       todo lo al yoguiesse   en el tu cosimente,
       tú non seriés pagado,   segund mío ençiente.

1920   Quand' oviesses los pueblos   todos sobjudgados,
       iriés çercar los mares,   conquerir los pescados,
       quebrantar los infiernos   que jazen sofondados,
       conquerir los antípodes   que non saben dó son nados.

1921   En cabo, si oviesses   liçençia o vagar,
       aún querriás de tu grado   en las nuves pujar;
       querriás de su ofiçio   el sol deseredar;
       tú querriás de tu mano   el mundo alumbrar.

1922   Lo que a Dios pediste   bien lo as acabado:
       de Dario eres quito,   de Bessus, bien vengado.
       Levántate del juego   mientras estás honrado;
       si se camia la mano   serás bien derribado.

1923   Conquistada as Persia,   Medïa e Caldea,
       África e Bactra, Libia,   Egibto e Judea;
       muchas otras provinçias   tienes en tu correa.
       Aún tú non te quieres   partir de la pelea.

1924   Quieres mucho sobir,   avrás a deçender;
       quieres mucho correr,   avrás tú de caher;
       semejas al idrópico   que muere por bever,
       quanto mas va beviendo   él más puede arder.

1925   El ome cobdiçioso   que nos' sabe guardar
       por una çeresuela   se dexa despeñar;
       çiégalo la cobdiçia,   faze lo assomar;
       faze lo de la çima   caer en mal lugar.

1926   Dezirt'he quét' contrá;   si nom' quieres creer,
       puedes por lo de menos   todo lo demás perder,
       lo que más te cuïdas   entre manos tener;
       sólo que te non vean,   hante de falleçer.

1918	He said, "My King, if your power were as great as the strength of heart you possess and display, the seas and the lands would be powerless to hold you and Jupiter's empire would you want to seize.
1919	If you had your right hand in Eastern lands and your left at the West's very edge so that all else lay within your possession, I believe that you would not be satisfied.
1920	When you had won dominion over all the world's peoples, you would go to besiege the seas and master the fish, and you would go to lay waste to the sunken depths of Hell and conquer the Antipodes, whose birth is known to none.
1921	In the end, if you had freedom or chance, you would still wish to soar up into the clouds: you would wish to overthrow the sun from its office, for with your own hand would you want to light the world.
1922	What you asked of God, you have brought to full conclusion: free of debt to Darius, you are well avenged on Bessus. Come away from the game, while you still have honour: if your hand changes you will be firmly cast down.
1923	You have conquered Persia, Media and Chaldea, Africa, Bactria, Libya, Egypt and Judea; your belt encircles many provinces more, but still you do not wish to leave the fight.
1924	You wish to climb up high – it is your lot to descend; you wish to run and run – it is your lot to fall; you are like the man with dropsy who is dying to drink but, the more he drinks, the more he burns with thirst.
1925	The greedy man, unable to protect himself, for a tiny cherry lets himself come crashing down; he is blinded by his greed which makes him climb to the top and makes him fall from the peak into a place of evil.*
1926	I shall say what will befall you; if you will not believe me, for the smallest part you can lose all the rest – what you are most confident of having in your grasp –; if they merely cannot see you, people will desert you.

1927   Los que tú as ganados, non tuyos naturales,
        tiénente grant despecho, non te serán leales;
        ca ya veen que han preso de ti muchos males;
        han su señor perdido e otras cosas tales.

1928   Rëy, esto te abonda, ¡quiéralo el senado!
        assaz ovist' contienda en lo que as ganado;
        si tú en al contiendes serás mal consejado,
        ca afogar te puedes con tan gruesso bocado.

1929   En guerrear con nusco non te ganarás nada;
        non ayas contra nos achaque nin entrada;
        non te faremos pérdida nin chica nin granada;
        non nos devriés tener rencura condesada.

1930   Rëy, si tú supiesses quál vida mantenemos,
        non avriás de nos cura, segundo que creemos;
        por los montes bevimos, que casa non sabemos;
        quanto val' un dinero de propio non avemos.

1931   Non es nuestra costumbre tesoro condesar;
        sól' nunca non nos miembra de lo de cras pensar;
        en nulla merchandía non sabemos andar
        si non quanto podemos de la tierra sacar.

1932   De la tierra sacamos nuestro vito cutiano;
        las sus tetas mamamos ivierno e verano;
        si non el que fiziere fecho fol o villano
        – non bivría con nusco aun que fues' nuestr' hermano.

1933   Si nos aviene pérdida, en paz nos la sofrimos;
        Dios lo da, Dios lo tuelle, nos esto comedimos;
        nos cosa sobejana a Dios nunca pedimos;
        que quier' que Él nos da nos essol' gradeçimos.

1934   Sobre nulla porfía nos puesta non tenemos;
        contienda nin porfidia nos nunca la queremos;
        a Dios sus derechuras todas gelas rendemos;
        nunca a nuestro próximo soberbia le fazemos.

1935   Nuestros anteçessores en tal vida bivieron;
        por buena e por santa ésta sola tovieron;
        nos éssa mantenemos que ellos mantovieron,
        ca veemos que vida perfecta 'stableçieron.

1927	Those that you have conquered, not those of your own country, bear you great resentment and will not be loyal to you; for they can see that through you they have borne many ills: they have lost their lord and suffered other such misfortunes.
1928	My King, this is enough for you; may your council will it! You have fought hard enough for what you have won; if you strive for more, you will be poorly advised; for you might choke on so hearty a mouthful.
1929	By waging war against us, you will not gain a thing; may you have no complaints with us or reasons to attack! We shall cause you no loss, neither great nor small; you should have no resentment stored up against us.
1930	My King, were you aware of the kind of life we lead, we do believe that you would not concern yourself with us; we live in the hills and know nothing of houses, and are without a penny's worth of assets of our own.
1931	It is not our custom to build up stores of treasure: we never even think to ponder what tomorrow will bring. We do not know how to trade in any merchandise except what we are able to take from the land.
1932	From the land do we take our everyday ration and we suckle at its breasts in winter and summer; except for any man performing base or foolish acts – he would not live with us even if he were our brother.
1933	If we should suffer loss, we endure it in peace: God gives, and God takes away, as we believe; never do we ask of God anything excessive; for whatever He gives us we are thankful to Him.
1934	We do not have any obduracy among us, we never wish for conflict or hostility and to God we render all His dues in full, never acting with arrogance towards our neighbour.
1935	Our ancestors lived in just such a way and held this life alone good and holy, which we now preserve just as they too had done; for we see that they established a perfect life.

1936 Aún con todo esto   al te quiero dezir;
somos gentes ligeras,   malas de conquerir;
somos bien aguisados   de tornar e fuïr;
de dardo e saeta   bien sabemos ferir.

1937 De embargo ninguno   non somos embargados;
de aver nin de ropa   non andamos cargados;
de morar non avemos   lugares costumbrados;
sabemos que del mundo   non seremos echados.

1938 El que perder non teme   nin cobdiçia ganar,
aquél puede sin miedo   e sin dubda lidiar;
que los que algo tienen,   cobdiçian condesar;
muchas cosas les pueden   a ellos embargar.

1939 Rëy, nos non queremos   contigo lidïar,
por do te rogamos   que nos dexes folgar;
contra nos non te quieras   por poco denodar;
pagamos nos si esto   quisieres otorgar."

1940 Calló el ome bueno,   que avié bien fablado;
de grado del conçejo   oviera recabado;
non dio el rey por ello   un puerro assado;
díxoles que por verba   non serié espantado.

1941 Entróles por la tierra,   fue los acometer;
priso mayores daños   que non cuidó prender,
pero non se pudieron   en cabo defender;
prendiendo malas pérdidas,   óvolos a vençer.

1942 Tornó el rey a Persia,   Çitïa sobjudgada;
la gent' brava e fiera   remansó bien domada.
El rey Alexandre   e la su gent' dubdada
grant sazón ha non fizo   tan fuerte cavalgada.

1943 Muchos pueblos estavan   por las tierras alçados
que nunca de los griegos   non serién ensayados;
mas quando a los çitos   vieron tan bien domados
vinién a la melena,   todos cabez' colgados.

1944 Era escontra todos   el rey tan atemprado
que non podrié ninguno   seer su despagado;
tanto avié con todos   en grant amor entrado
que, si su padre fuesse,   non serié más amado.

1936	Besides all this, I want to tell you one thing more: we are fleet-footed people, difficult to conquer, we are well prepared to turn our backs and flee, and skilled at striking with dart and arrow.
1937	We are not encumbered with any kind of burden and do not go laden with possessions or clothes; we have no customary places to dwell, knowing we shall not be cast out of the world.
1938	A man with no fear of loss nor desire for gain is able to fight without fear or terror, for those with belongings desire to store them away and there are many things that can weigh them down.
1939	My King, we do not want to wage war against you and so we beg of you to let us be at peace; do not grow angry with us for little reason; we are pleased if you are willing to grant this."
1940	The good man fell silent, having spoken well; he would have gained the council's willing agreement, but the King did not give for it a miserable roast leek and told them that he would not be terrified by words.
1941	He invaded their lands and launched his attack; he suffered greater harm than he planned to suffer but in the end they were unable to defend themselves: though he bore grave losses, he managed to defeat them.
1942	The King returned to Persia with Scythia subdued and the fierce and feisty people remained quite tamed. King Alexander and his band of dreaded men had not waged for a long time so fierce a campaign.
1943	There were many people taking refuge in their lands who had never been engaged in battle by the Greeks, but when they saw the Scythians so heavily overwhelmed they came with heads bowed to give their necks to the yoke.
1944	The King was so restrained in his treatment of them all that not a single one could be displeased with him; with all of them he had come into a friendship so close that if he were their father he would not have been more loved.

1945 El cabrón cornaludo   de la barva honrada
ya avié, *Deo graçias*,   la tierra ajuntada,
ca avié toda Asia   a su poder tornada;
fuera end' toda India,   non le fincava nada.

1946 Asmó ir veer India   cóm' era assentada,
buscar al rëy Poro   dentro en su posada,
en medio de su regno   fer le la salmorada,
de prender lo a vida   o matarlo a espada.

1947 Pero, ante que fuesse   en carrera entrado,
quiso complir a Dario   lo quel' avié jurado:
porfijarle el fijo,   el que avié crïado,
fer lo rëy de Persia   quando fuesse armado.

1948 Quando vío aquesto   la persïana gente,
que era Alexandre   de tan buen cosimente,
rindieron *Deo graçias*   al Rey Omnipotente;
tenién que era Dario,   el su señor, presente.

1949 Fizo mayor mesura   el cosido varón
ond' de todos los pueblos   ganó grant bendiçión:
quiso complir a Dario   la fecha promissión,
que non fuesse llamado   mintroso nin chufón.

1950 El mes era de mayo,   el tiempo glorïoso,
quando fazen las aves   un solaz deleitoso;
son cubiertos los prados   de vestido fermoso;
da sospiros la dueña   la que non ha esposo.

1951 Tiempo dulç' e sabroso   por bastir casamientos,
ca lo tempran las flores   e los sabrosos vientos;
cantan las donçelletas   sus mayos a convientos;
fazen unas a otras   buenos pronunçamientos.

1952 Caen en el sereno   las buenas ruçïadas;
entran en flor las miesses,   ca son ya espigadas;
fazen las dueñas triscas   en camisas delgadas;
entonç casan algunos   que pues messan las barvas.

1953 Andan moças e viejas   büeltas en amores;
van coger en la siesta   a los prados las flores;
dizen unas a otras   buenos pronunçiadores;
e aquellos más tiernos   tiénense por mejores.

1945	The great horned goat with the honoured beard*
	had now united the land, thanks be to God,
	for he had brought all Asia beneath his power
	and so, except all India, nothing remained.
1946	He planned to go to see India and how it was disposed,
	and to seek out King Porus within, in his own domain,
	and in his kingdom's middle to make him drink briny water:
	to take him alive or to kill him by the sword.
1947	However, before he set off on his way,
	he wished to fulfil what he had sworn to Darius*
	and adopt his son, the one that he had raised,
	and make him King of Persia when he was an armed knight.
1948	When the people of Persia beheld such a thing,
	that Alexander was a man of such compassion,
	they said "Thanks be to God" to the Almighty King
	and felt that Darius, their lord, was present.
1949	The kind man did one thing more of great wisdom,
	through which he won the blessing of all the peoples;
	he wanted to fulfil the promise made to Darius
	lest he should be labelled a liar or a braggart.
1950	It was the month of May, a time of glorious weather*
	when the birds create an air of gentlest pleasure,
	when the fields are draped with beautiful attire
	and the lady who lacks a husband sighs deeply.
1951	A time sweet and fragrant for the making of marriages,
	being scented by the flowers and the perfumed winds,
	when the groups of girls sing their May songs at gatherings
	and tell each other tales of pleasure.
1952	In the night's humid hours come pleasant falls of dew
	and the crops grow to flower, for now is their harvest;
	the girls frolic joyfully, lightly clad in shifts;
	then some men are wed who later pluck their beards.
1953	Both girls and old women, entranced by their love,
	in the afternoon, go to pick flowers in the meadows,
	telling each other of their suitors' loving whispers:
	those who are most tender are held to be the best.

1954   Los días son bien grandes,   los campos reverdidos;
        son los paxarïellos   de mal pelo sallidos;
        los távanos que muerden   non son aún venidos;
        luchan los moçuelos   en bragas, sin vestidos.

1955   El rëy Alexandre,   un cuerpo tan acabado,
        a la sabor del tiempo   que era tan temprado,
        fizo cort' general   con coraçón pagado;
        non fue varón en Persia   que non fues' y juntado.

1956   A menos que supiéssedes   sobre qué fue la cosa,
        bien podriedes tener   la razón por mintrosa;
        mas quiero vos dexar   toda la otra prosa;
        descobrir vos he'l testo,   empeçar vos la glosa.

1957   Quiero vos breve mente   dezir el brevïario;
        non vos quiero de poco   fer luengo sermonario;
        quiere casar el rëy   con la fija de Dario,
        con Roxana la genta,   fembra de grant donario.

1958   Las bodas fueron fechas   ricas e abondadas;
        andavan las carretas   de conduchos cargadas;
        sedién noches e días   las mesas aguisadas,
        de tovajas cubiertas,   de conducho pobladas.

1959   Avié grant abondançia   de carnes e pescados,
        de toros e de vacas,   de caças e venados;
        aduzién los conduchos,   todos bien adobados;
        cada uno con sus salsas   les eran presentados.

1960   Eran grandes e muchas   las mudas e los dones;
        non querién los juglares   çendales nin çiclatones;
        d'éstos avié y muchos   que fazién muchos sones,
        otros que meneavan   ximios e xafarrones.

1961   Duraron estas bodas   quinze días complidos;
        eran todos los días   los tablados feridos;
        teniénse los varones   de Persia por guaridos;
        tenién que de la guerra   non eran mal sallidos;

1962   Y fizo ad Apelles   tal tálamo obrar
        que el aver de Mida   non lo podrié comprar;
        tanto quiso el rëy   a la dueña honrar,
        serié dentro en Roma   honrado tal altar.

1954	The days are long and full, the fields clothed in green,
	the little birds have completed their moult,
	the horseflies that sting are not yet come,
	and the young boys wrestle in just their breeches.
1955	King Alexander, a man of distinction,
	in delight at the weather, come so gentle,
	convened his general court, with joy in his heart:
	there was no nobleman of Persia not present.
1956	Unless you knew what was the heart of the matter,
	you could easily take my words as false;
	but I want to omit all the rest of the story;
	I will show you the text for you to start on the gloss.
1957	I want to say the breviary to you with brevity,
	not preach a long sermon over a little:
	the King seeks marriage to Darius' daughter,
	to Rhoxane the beautiful, a woman of great charm.*
1958	The ceremony took place, rich and elaborate,
	and carts were heavily laden with provisions;
	the tables were laid ready by night and by day,
	covered with cloths and piled high with food.
1959	There was a great abundance of meat and of fish,
	of bulls and of cows, of venison and game.
	The food was brought in, all richly prepared,
	and each dish was served in its own sauce.
1960	The presents and gifts were great and many;
	the minstrels turned away fine silks and rich tunics;
	there were many of these there who made varied music
	and others there came bearing monkeys or masks.
1961	This ceremony lasted a full fifteen days,
	and every day the mock castles were attacked;
	the knights of Persia thought themselves to be safe;
	they felt that they had not emerged badly from the war.
1962	There he had Apelles craft such a marriage bed*
	that all Midas' wealth could not have bought it;
	such was the King's desire to pay the lady honour
	that such an altar would be honoured in Rome itself.

1963　　　Que vos quisiesse ome　　dezir la maestría,
　　　　　si non aquel quel' vío,　　semejarié follía;
　　　　　a los que lo solién　　mesurar cada día,
　　　　　en cara por a éssos　　serié sombrançería.

1964　　　Quando ovo el rëy　　las bodas çelebradas,
　　　　　las cartas fueron luego　　fechas e seelladas:
　　　　　todas las fazïendas,　　todas las cavalgadas
　　　　　fueron en essas cartas　　escriptas e notadas.

1965　　　Embiólas a Greçia　　a la su madre cara,
　　　　　a las sus hermanillas　　que él niñas dexara;
　　　　　al su maestro bueno,　　al de la barba sarra,
　　　　　el que muchos castigos　　buenos le enseñara.

1966　　　Quando fueron las cartas　　en Greçia arribadas,
　　　　　fueron bien reçebidas,　　fueron luego catadas;
　　　　　fueron madre e fijas　　alegres e pagadas;
　　　　　el maestro con gozo　　bien saltó tres passadas.

1967　　　Las dueñas greçïanas,　　con grandes alegrías,
　　　　　renovaron las bodas,　　otros tantos de días;
　　　　　metieron en cançiones　　las sus cavallerías,
　　　　　por que serán contadas　　fasta venga Elías.

1968　　　El rëy, maguer novio,　　non quiso grant vagar;
　　　　　calçóse las espuelas,　　pensó de cavalgar;
　　　　　deçendió por a India,　　fue a Poro buscar;
　　　　　maguer era cansado,　　non quiso detardar.

1969　　　El pecado, que nunca　　puede seer baldero,
　　　　　pora dapnar los buenos　　busca siempre sendero;
　　　　　como es longana,　　antiguo e artero,
　　　　　vertió y de su sal　　del su falso salero.

1970　　　Fiziéronle creer　　al rey grant falsedat:
　　　　　que Clitus e Ardófilo,　　leales por verdat,
　　　　　dizién en su persona　　cosa de liviandat;
　　　　　fizo matar ad ambos,　　mandó grant crüeldat.

1971　　　Amistat de los rëys　　non la tengo por sana,
　　　　　que creen rafez mente　　mucha palabra vana;
　　　　　regálase aína,　　de noch' a la mañana
　　　　　contra ome en balde　　por deslavar la lana.

1963	For a man to try to tell you of the craftsmanship, had that man himself not seen it, would seem folly; those who were accustomed to keep a daily reckoning – even for them it would be a source of wonder.
1964	When the King had carried out his wedding celebrations, letters were immediately written and sealed;* all the celebrations and all the processions were set in writing and noted in those letters.
1965	He sent them to Greece to his beloved mother, to the little sisters he had left behind as girls, and to his good master, the man of yellow beard, the one who had taught him many valuable lessons.
1966	When the letters had made their arrival in Greece, they were well received and immediately read; mothers and daughters felt delight and satisfaction and the master in his joy leapt three full paces.
1967	The women of Greece, in their great happiness, prolonged the wedding for as many days again and they set down Alexander's feats in songs, in which they will be told until Elijah is come.*
1968	The King, though newly wed, would not rest for long: he put on his spurs, and determined to ride off; going down into India, he went in search of Porus; although he was tired, he did not wish for delay.
1969	The Devil, who is never able to lie idle, ever searches for a path to damn the good; as he is very patient, ancient and artful, he poured in some salt from his cellar of deceit.
1970	The King was made to believe a great deception, that Cleitus and Ardophilus, truly loyal men,* had spoken shame-inducing things about his person; he had them both killed and ordered great cruelty.
1971	The friendship of kings I do not hold secure, for they easily believe many empty words. From night until morning it melts away when a man's conduct is doubted without reason.

1972 Ardófilo e Clitus, que ante terçer día
 eran de muy grant preçio e de grant valía;
 yazién mal esquivados sin nulla compañía;
 ¡Mala fue nado qui en este mundo fía!

1973 Fue luego el ruïdo por India levantado
 que era Alexandre en la tierra entrado;
 nol' plazió al rey Poro; fue muy mal espantado;
 súpole el mensaje áspero e pesado.

1974 Mandó por toda India los pregones andar
 – las cartas selladas por más los acuitar –
 que se llegasen aína todos a un lugar,
 ca menester les era de consejo tomar.

1975 Los pueblos con el miedo fueron luego plegados;
 temiendo lo que vino, fueron todos armados;
 trayén los elefantes, de castillos cargados,
 que son bestias valientes e muy apoderados.

1976 El elefant' es bestia de muy grant valentía;
 sobr' él arman engeños de muy grant carpentería:
 castillos en que puede ir grant cavallería,
 al menos treinta omes, o demás – non mintría.

1977 Sïempre ha sin grado derecho a estar:
 las piernas ha dobladas, non las puede juntar;
 por ninguna manera non se puede echar;
 si cae por ventura non se puede alçar.

1978 Quando quiere folgar, que es mucho cansado,
 busca un grant árvol que sea fortalado;
 pone y su çerviz, duerme assegurado;
 todos de su natura traen esti vezado.

1979 Si barruntar lo puede el ome caçador,
 corta con una sierra el árvol a redor;
 déxale un poquillo el ome sabidor,
 tanto que de su sombra non avriades sabor.

1980 Luego la bestia loca viene a su vezado;
 fírmase en el árvol, es luego trastornado;
 levantar non se puede, es luego degollado;
 fazen de los sus huessos el marfil esmerado.

1972	Ardophilus and Cleitus, who, three days ago, were men of very great standing and valour, now found themselves shunned and abandoned by all; he who trusts in this world had an evil birth!
1973	The rumour arose throughout India at once that King Alexander had entered the land; this did not please Porus but filled him with dread:* he found the message a harsh one and vexing.
1974	He ordered proclamations to be made through all India, the letters closed with his seal to give greater urgency, telling them all to gather quickly in one place, for it was necessary that they met in council.
1975	In their fear the peoples were quick to arrive and, fearing what came, they all went in armour, taking their elephants, with turrets on their backs; these are brave animals and of huge strength.
1976	The elephant is a beast of very great valour* upon which they mount cleverly built structures, turrets in which a great troop of knights can go, at least thirty men, or more, I would not lie.
1977	It always has, though unwilling, to remain on its feet: its legs are so thick that it cannot bend them, so that there is no way for it to lay itself down, and if it chances to fall it cannot rise again.
1978	When it is so tired that it wants to rest, it seeks out a tree that is large and sturdy, rests its head against it and sleeps secure; all beasts of this species have this custom.
1979	If the huntsman is able to spot such a tree, he cuts around its trunk with a saw; the clever man leaves just a little uncut, so little that you would not want its shade.
1980	As soon as the foolish beast comes, by its habit, and rests on the tree, it is at once brought down. It cannot rise up, its throat is cut at once, and from its bones polished ivory is made.

1981   De tales elefantes, con tales guarnimientos,
　　　　trayé en su compaña　Poro más de trezientos;
　　　　de tornos con foçijos, fuertes aguisamientos,
　　　　trayé catorze mill　e demás ocho çientos.

1982   De cavalleros solos, todos de buen derecho,
　　　　de treinta mill a suso　serién a un grant trecho;
　　　　más avrié de peones　por fazer todo fecho
　　　　que non fojas en monte　nin yervas en barvecho.

1983   Ovieron estas nuevas　al rëy a sonar
　　　　que querié con él Poro　batalla entablar;
　　　　con grant gozo que ovo　empeçó a saltar;
　　　　mandó al mensajero　rica albriçia dar.

1984   Mandó luego la carta　ditar al chançeller;
　　　　embïóla a Poro:　que avié grant plazer;
　　　　díxol' que grant lazerio　non quisies' él prender,
　　　　ca él selo irié　aina allá veer.

1985   El rëy Alexandre, un buen trasnochador,
　　　　de veer se en campo　avié grant sabor;
　　　　que non lo retenié　nin frío nin calor;
　　　　de todo dava poco, tant' era sofridor.

1986   Tant' avié grant cobdiçia　con Poro se fallar,
　　　　de día nin de noche　non quedó de andar;
　　　　al ome a que diera　la carta a levar
　　　　– lo que fue fiera cosa –　óvol' a alcançar.

1987   Los griegos por ventura　demás avrién andado,
　　　　mas fallaron un río,　Adapis es llamado;
　　　　verano e ivierno　nunca le fallan vado;
　　　　en ancho e en fondo　es grant desmesurado.

1988   Assí acaeçió, Dios lo quiso guïar;
　　　　quiso Dios muy aína　la cosa aguisar;
　　　　quando por la ribera　quisieron alongar,
　　　　vieron de part' d'allá　los de Poro estar.

1989   Firiera Alexandre　en ellos de buen grado,
　　　　mas non podién passar, ca non fallavan vado;
　　　　los labros se comié, tant' estava irado;
　　　　catando contra Poro, maldiziá al pecado.

1981	Of elephants like this, equipped in this way, Porus had over three hundred in his company; of chariots with scythes, a weapon of cruelty, he had fourteen thousand, and eight hundred more.
1982	Of horsemen alone, all of them of noble line, there would be a great number, above thirty thousand, and even more footsoldiers, for all kinds of tasks, than the leaves on the mountain or straws in the stubble.
1983	This news came to be given to the King that Porus desired to do battle with him;* Alexander started leaping with the great joy he felt and ordered that the messenger be given rich reward.
1984	He bade the chancellor compose a letter at once and sent it to Porus, saying he would be delighted; he said he did not want him to go to great trouble, but he would go with haste to meet him on his own ground.
1985	King Alexander, well versed in passing nights awake, had such strong desire to meet him on the battlefield that he was not held back either by cold or by heat; he cared little for anything, so great was his endurance.
1986	So great was his longing for his encounter with Porus that he did not break his journey by day or by night; the man that he had given the message to carry – a remarkable fact – was overtaken on the way.
1987	The Greeks would probably have travelled on further but they came upon a river, known as the Hydaspes; no crossing place is ever found in summer or winter, and in width and depth it is far beyond measure.
1988	And so it came to pass; God wished to guide it and chose to bring matters very quickly to a head: as they set about riding along the river bank, on the other side they saw Porus' army.
1989	Alexander would willingly have launched his attack but his army could not cross, for they found no ford; he gnawed on his lips, so great was his fury; as he looked towards Porus, he cursed the Devil.

1990 Maguer passar pudiessen por alguna manera,
 podriélos referir Poro de la ribera;
 nunca podrién asmar consejo nin carrera
 que llegassen a ellos por aver lit soltera.

1991 Estava una isla en medio levantada;
 era de todas partes de agua bien çercada;
 de fiera guisa era áspera la entrada,
 ca el río era fondo e luenga la passada.

1992 Non quiero de la isla agora mas favlar;
 otra vez avremos en ella a tornar;
 de dos amigos buenos vos quiero ementar;
 avremos a oír un poco de pesar.

1993 Avié entre los griegos dos mançebillos caros;
 al uno dizién Nícanor, al otro Simacos;
 eran de grant esfuerço, de linage muy altos;
 tal par de tales omes es en lugares claros.

1994 Fueron en una ora e un día naçidos;
 amos eran eguales, leal mente medidos;
 semejavan se mucho, vistián unos vestidos,
 por a bien e por a mal eran bien abenidos.

1995 Quando diziá el uno: "Fulán, fagamos esto",
 luego sedié el otro aguisado e presto;
 nunca fazié el uno tan poquillo de gesto
 que dixiesse el otro *"Non est in die festo"*.

1996 Si oviessen ellos algo a barruntar,
 o lengua aprender o conducho ganar
 o villa combater o las huestes velar,
 uno nunca sin otro non los verién andar.

1997 Demás, uno con otro tan grant bien se querién
 que el uno del otro partir non se podién;
 en uno comién ambos e en uno yazién;
 en cara los vestidos en uno los tenién.

1998 Quando querié el uno alguna ren dezir,
 presto era el otro por luego lo complir;
 más querié qual se quiere peligrar o morir
 que un fallimiento de su compañón oír.

| 1990 | Even if they could cross the river in some way,
Porus would be able to repel them from the bank;
never could they devise a plan or course of action
that they might reach them to engage in open battle. |

| 1991 | There was an island raised up in the middle of the river,
entirely surrounded by water on all sides;
the path of its approach was exceptionally hard,
for the river was a deep one and the crossing was long. |

| 1992 | I wish to talk no more of the island for now,
for we shall come once again to return to it;
I want to tell a tale of two good friends,
and we shall come to hear a little sorrow. |

| 1993 | Among the Greeks there were two dear young men,
they called one Nicanor and the other Symachus;*
they were of great valour and their lineage was high;
such a pair of men may be found in famous places. |

| 1994 | They were born at the same hour of the same day,
and were both of equal stature, identical in size;
their resemblance was close and their dress was alike;
for good or for bad these two men were of a kind. |

| 1995 | When one of them said, "My friend, let's do this!"
the other was immediately prepared and ready;
never did either of them make the slightest gesture
for the other to reply, "It is not the right occasion". |

| 1996 | If the two had a mission of espionage,
or information to discover, or provisions to obtain,
or a city to fight for, or the army to watch over,
you would never see the one without the other. |

| 1997 | Besides, they loved each other with such fondness
that the two of them could not be brought apart;
the two both ate together and together did they sleep,
and they even owned their clothes together, too. |

| 1998 | When one of them had something that he wanted to say,
the other one was ready to complete it at once;
either of them would rather have faced danger or died
than have heard any reproach from his companion. |

1999   Empeçó una cosa   Símacus ad asmar;
           entendiólo Nicánor,   mas non pudo folgar;
           estava barruntando   qué querié ensayar;
           queriél' la delantera   de buen grado furtar.

2000   "Dezirt'he," dixo Símacus,   "somos mal engañados,
           que nos e nuestro rëy   'stamos tan afrontados;
           valdriénos más que fuéssemos   en India soterrados
           si por quatro passadas   fuéremos mortiguados.

2001   Alguna maestría   avemos a buscar
           que podamos a Poro   de la riba redrar;
           si complir lo pudiéssemos   podemos nos honrar;
           podremos si muriéremos   con grant preçio finar.

2002   Si nos esti riviello   pudiéssemos passar
           e como se quïere   a la isla entrar,
           avriamos le a Poro   buscado grant pesar;
           nos avriamos más poco   después a trebejar."

2003   Aún non avié Símacus   el vierbo acabado,
           entendiólo Nicánor,   fue luego levantado;
           diz' "Yo te juro, Símacus,   mi amigo preçiado,
           que esso que me dizes   tenía yo asmado."

2004   Non posaron en tierra,   çiñieron las espadas;
           pusieron armas pocas,   mas non de las pesadas;
           metieron se a nado   por las ondas iradas;
           por entrar a la isla   fueron a denodadas.

2005   Quando esto vïeron   cavalleros de Greçia
           que fazién estos ambos   tamaña atrevençia,
           entraron en pues ellos   a müy grant femençia;
           non andava en medio   ninguna garridençia.

2006   Arribó a la isla   Símacus más primero;
           avién ya los de Poro   entrado el otero;
           firió luego en ellos   a guis' de cavallero,
           redrólos de la riba   más de medio migero.

2007   Fueron los indïanos   adiesso acorridos;
           mas de mientre los otros   fueron todos sallidos;
           allí fueron los colpes,   allí los alaridos;
           non valián guarniçiones   más que otros vestidos.

1999	Symachus began to conceive an idea and Nicanor understood, but could not wait; he was imagining what his friend wished to try, and he sought with all his will to take the lead.
2000	"I will tell you," said Symachus, "our error is grave, for we and our King are suffering disgrace; we would be better off buried in India, if we were mortified by four little paces.
2001	We must go in search of some skilful means so that we can drive Porus back from the bank; if we could achieve it, we can win honour, and if we die, we can do so with great glory.
2002	If we could manage to cross this little river and come to the island, in whatever way we could, we would have sought out a great sorrow for Porus, and after that the game would be nearly over."
2003	Symachus had not yet reached the end of his speech when Nicanor understood him and rose at once: he said, "I swear to you, Symachus, my valued friend, that I had also thought of what you say."
2004	They did not tarry on land but girded on their swords, arming themselves lightly and taking nothing heavy; they started to swim out across the angry waves, swimming furiously to get onto the island.
2005	When the knights of Greece saw what they were doing, that these two men were acting with such daring, they jumped in after them with unbridled zeal: there was no lack of commitment among them.
2006	Symachus was first to arrive at the island; Porus' men had already reached the hilltop; he went at once to strike them with knightly valour, and drove them over half a mile back from the bank.
2007	The Indian troops received very prompt support, but meanwhile the other Greeks had all arrived; there were the blows struck, and there were the screams, with armour worth no more than other clothing.

2008 Las nuves de los dardos   tan espessas corrién,
quebrantavan el aire;   tod' el sol tollién;
los de parte de Poro   de voluntad firién
mas los otros y todo   el belmez les tenién.

2009 Símacus – ¡que bien aya! –   que basteçió la cosa,
avié a part' echada   mucha barba cabosa;
su amigo Nicánor,   como sierpe raviosa,
quebrantava los cueres   de la gent' porfidiosa.

2010 Los griegos, maguer buenos,   non pudieron durar;
como eran poquillos,   ovieron a lazrar;
tanto se les pudieron   los otros encargar,
ovieron a Antígonus   el infant' a matar.

2011 Los griegos por Antígonus   fueron mucho irados;
por que lo avién menos,   teniénse por minguados;
fizieron se un cuño,   escudos embraçados;
bolvieron se con ellos   todos cabez' colgados.

2012 Mataron muchos d'ellos,   fizieron los quedar;
nunca mejor apresos   fueran en un lugar;
pudiéranse con tanto   bien honrados tornar,
mas óvolos esfuerço   loco a engañar.

2013 El ome estrevudo   que non trae cordura
pierde se rafez mientre   en una angostura;
non torna con ganançia   nin con nula presura;
dezir vos he lo mío: téngolo por locura.

2014 Todos en la fazienda   estavan ençendidos;
avián mucho lidiado,   estavan enflaquidos;
entraron los de Poro,   muchos omes guarnidos,
tres tantos que non fueron   de primero venidos.

2015 Luego que fueron suso,   pensaron de dolar;
murieron luego quinze   de omes de prestar;
fueras los dos amigos,   que oyestes contar,
non pudieron los otros   aver ningund vagar.

2016 Los amigos leales   solos eran fincados;
muertos eran los otros,   mas bien eran honrados;
sedién entr' ellos amos   solos, desamparados,
como entre los lobos   corderos reçién nados.

2008	The clouds of darts flew so thickly packed together, they tore the air asunder and obscured the whole sun; the men on Porus' side fought with all their courage, but their enemies kept them on a tight rein.
2009	Symachus – may he be blessed! – had forged the plan, and he had struck down many excellent warriors. His friend Nicanor, like a furious serpent, broke in two the hearts of those unyielding troops.
2010	The Greeks, although good men, could not hold out: as they were very few, they were to suffer harm; their foes were able to mount such an assault on them that they managed to kill Antigonus, the prince.*
2011	The Greeks were deeply angered on Antigonus' part and at his death they felt a deep sense of loss. They formed into a wedge, with their shields on their arms, and went back into battle, all their heads turned down.
2012	Many of them did they kill and make stay on the field: in no place had they ever enjoyed such fortune; with this much they could have returned with great honour, but thoughtless valour was to deceive them.
2013	A man who has daring but does not use wisdom is quickly lost in a thorny situation, and he does not return with profit or gain; I will tell you my opinion – I consider it folly.
2014	All those in the battle had their passions inflamed; they had battled hard and now they were tired. Porus' army arrived, a great troop of armed men, three times the number that had come at first.
2015	As soon as they had climbed up they started to strike and fifteen men of valour died at once: except for the friends, of whom you have heard tell, the other men could find no respite.
2016	The loyal friends were left on the battlefield alone: the others were dead, but they had won great honour; these two stood among them, alone, with no protection, like newly born lambs among the wolves.

2017 Bien estavan seguros   que non estorçerién,
ca acorro ninguno   otro non atendién.
Eran mucho cansados,   que lidiar nos' trevién;
aún por todo esso   tornar non se querién.

2018 Un pesar avién ambos   e un dolor señero;
temién ambos veer   la muert' del compañero;
ninguno por la suya   non dava un dinero;
entrariá qual se quiere   de grado delantero.

2019 Si querién a Nicánor   por ventura ferir,
adelantávas' Símacus   el colpe reçebir;
Nicánor esso mismo   más querié él morir
que un pesar de Símacus   veer nin oír.

2020 Mientre uno a otro   estavan aguardando,
vinieron dos venablos   por el aire bolando;
ambos cayeron muertos,   fue quedado el vando;
las indïanas yentes   non se fueron gabando.

2021 Mejores dos amigos   de mayor lealtad,
que assí fuessen ambos   de una voluntad,
nin naçerán nin naçieron,   cuido dezir verdat;
entre pocos cristianos   corre tal amistad.

2022 Por la huest' de los griegos   grand' era el dolor;
fiera era la pérdida,   el desarro mayor;
non prisieron un día   tan mala dessabor,
ca de la mançebía   éssos eran la flor.

2023 Poro con la vitoria   fízose muy loçano;
tenié que non avié   qui les tornasse mano;
mas, por toda la pérdida,   el rëy greçïano
tanto dava por ello   como por un tavano.

2024 Una cueita tenié   al coraçón fincada,
que por ninguna guisa   non podié fer passada;
ca fïava en Dios   e en la su espada
que, si passar pudiesse,   la cosa era librada.

2025 Poro era grant ome,   avié grant coraçón;
trayé un elefante   mayor que un durmón;
de los fieros gigantes   trayé generaçión;
era, sól' de veerlo,   una fuerte visión.

2017	They knew for certain that they would not escape, and that there was no help that they could expect; they were deeply tired and unable to fight on, yet despite all that they did not want to turn back.
2018	They both had one regret and one single sorrow: they were both afraid to see their companion die; neither for his own life would give a single coin and either would have gladly been the first to come to death.
2019	If by chance they tried to strike Nicanor, Symachus stepped forward to receive the blow; Nicanor likewise, had more desire for death than to see or hear any sorrow for Symachus.
2020	While these two were standing as each other's guards, two spears then came flying through the air; both fell dead and the force had been destroyed, but the Indian soldiers had no cause to boast.
2021	A better pair of friends, of greater loyalty, who, as these two men, were both of one single will, will not be nor have been born, I hold my words true: such friendship flows between few Christian people.
2022	The sorrow was great throughout the army of the Greeks; the loss was hard to bear and the grief even greater. They had never had a day of such bitter sorrow, for, of the Greek youth, those men were the flower.
2023	With the victory, Porus was filled with arrogance, and thought there were no troops who could attack them; but for all the loss that they had suffered, the Greek king cared as much for that as for a horsefly.
2024	He had one anxiety thrust into his heart: that by no means was he able to make a crossing, for he trusted in God and in his own sword that if he could cross, the matter was at an end.
2025	Porus was a huge man who had a great heart and was riding an elephant larger than a ship; he was descended from the ferocious giants: the very sight of him was an imposing vision.

Libro de Alexandre

2026   Como trayé consigo   muchos fieros gigantes,
       pavor avién los griegos,   estavan discordantes;
       teniénse por errados   que se non fueran antes;
       todos avién miedo   de seer mal andantes.

2027   Mas el rey Alexandre,   de lazerio usado,
       que por ningund peligro   nunca fue desmayado,
       andava bien alegre,   firme e esforçado;
       nunca dava un figo   por el afán passado.

2028   Como era de grant seso   e enviseça 'straña,
       sopo bien encobrir   su pesar e su saña;
       ovo a asmar   una cortesa maña;
       mientre omes oviere,   lo ternán por fazaña.

2029   Avié en su compaña   el rey aventurado
       muchos vassallos buenos,   mucho buen acostado,
       muchos buenos amigos   e mucho buen crïado;
       quales omes avié   assí era guardado.

2030   Entre los otros todos   avié un cavallero;
       fue de su crïazón,   era su mesnadero;
       semejávale tanto   al buen señor guerrero,
       como si lo oviessen   fecho los carpenteros.

2031   En cuerpo e en cara   e en toda fechura,
       en andar, en estar   e en cavalgadura,
       semejavan hermanos   en toda su figura;
       sól' por tanto en esso   avián buena ventura.

2032   Avié en Alexandre   Poro ojo fincado,
       a qual parte que iva   era bien aguardado;
       si quiere fues' en caça,   si quiere en venado,
       aguardávalo Poro,   el ojo remellado.

2033   Naves avién e barcas   en que podién passar,
       mas por ninguna guisa   non se supo furtar,
       ca, Poro lo veyendo,   podrié los trebejar;
       refiriéndolos él,   non podríen pasar.

2034   Quando vio que fuerça   nol' podíe prestar,
       oít el porfidioso   qué ovo ad asmar:
       mandó seer Atalaus   do él solié andar,
       con es' mismo adobo   que él solié parar.

2026	As he had many fierce giants about him, the Greeks were beside themselves with fear; they thought they were wrong not to have left before, and were all afraid that they would come to grief.
2027	But King Alexander, accustomed to hardship, who was never distressed by any danger, was full of good temper, determined and valiant and never gave a fig for the trials of the past.
2028	As he was of great good sense and rare sagacity, he was well able to conceal his sorrow and his rage, and he then managed to devise an ingenious scheme – as long as men live, they will think it a great feat.
2029	The fortunate King had with him in his army many fine vassals and many good men in his pay, many close friends and many faithful followers; as were the men he had, so was his protection.
2030	Among all of the others, there was a knight,* brought up in his household, who was in his close company: this warrior so closely resembled the good lord as if he were a copy that carpenters had made.
2031	In their body and their face and in all their appearance, in their gait, in their manner, and in the way they rode, they seemed like brothers in every aspect of their body, and in that alone were they men of great good fortune.
2032	Porus had kept his eyes trained on Alexander, and wherever he went he was closely observed; whether he was out hunting or whether after game, Porus was watching him, his eyes wide open.
2033	There were ships and boats in which they could cross, but in no way could it be done in secret, for, seeing them move, Porus could make play with them, and if he forced them back they could not pass.
2034	When Alexander saw that force could bring him no aid, hear what the tenacious man managed to devise: he ordered Attalus to go where he usually went* with that very same attire that he usually wore.

2035 Poro fue engañado, nol' sopo entender;
suvo en su atalaya como solié seer,
mas tan bien se sabié Atalaus componer
que nunca lo pudieron asmar nin coñoçer.

2036 Fues' de la almofalla el rëy escolando;
sallió de la ribera com' quis' va deportando,
con pocas de compañas, como qui va caçando;
assí le fue a Poro las pajuelas echando.

2037 Vino en est' comedio una niebla escura;
tanto era de çiega que non avié mesura;
pora'l rey Alexandre fue muy buena ventura,
ca encubrióle éssa toda su travessura.

2038 Atalaus redor sí mandó fer un ruïdo;
cuidó que fuessen beilas; fue Poro deçebido;
metióse en las naves el rëy perçebido;
ovo en poca d'ora ad Adapis troçido.

2039 Ovo luego con él tantos buenos passados
que non valién diez sueldos los que eran fincados;
estavan los varones de Poro desnudados;
yazién se desguarnidos e todos desarmados.

2040 El rëy Alexandre, quando fue arribado,
non les quiso dar plazo fasta otro mercado;
él movió delantero, com' era castigado,
pero de sus varones era bien aguardado.

2041 Aún sedié aguardando Poro la babusana;
sedié assegurado sobre feüza vana;
vínol' el mandadero a la meridïana,
que era engañado de la gente greçiana.

2042 Dende a poca d'ora fues' la niebla tolliendo,
fue la gent' assomando, las armas reluziendo;
fuéronsele a Poro albas negras faziendo;
lo que siempre dubdava ya lo iva veyendo.

2043 Fue con la sobre vienta Poro mal engañado,
estableçió sus hazes en un rato privado;
como antes estava todo bien recabdado
en un ratiello poco todo fue delivrado.

2035	Porus was deceived and not able to see through this: he was on his vantage point, as he was wont to be, but Attalus was able to comport himself so well that they could never work out or recognise who he was.
2036	The King gradually slipped away from the army and left the river bank like a man at leisure, with just a few companions, as if going hunting: so he pulled the wool over Porus' eyes.
2037	At just this moment there came down a dark fog; it was so blinding that it was beyond measure; for King Alexander it was a great stroke of luck, for that fog concealed his whole deceit.
2038	Attalus ordered that noise be made around him: thinking that they were sentinels, Porus was deceived; the King, the man of shrewdness, embarked on his ships, and in a little time he had crossed the Hydaspes.
2039	So many good men had crossed with him at once, and those left behind were not worth five small coins. The men on Porus' side had taken off their armour and now lay defenceless, and all without arms.
2040	King Alexander, when he too had arrived, wished to give them no rest before the next encounter; he advanced at his troops' head, as he had been taught, although he was well protected by his men.
2041	Porus was still watching over the substitute, basing his confidence on an empty belief, when the messenger came to him at midday to say that he had been tricked by the Greeks.
2042	A short while afterwards the fog slowly cleared, the men heaving into view, their arms gleaming, and a dawn black indeed was breaking for Porus, for what he always feared was now before his eyes.
2043	Porus was badly taken aback with the shock but rapidly had his battle lines drawn up; as everything had been well planned in advance, it was all made ready in a very short time.

2044   Dio en la delantera   quatro mill cavalleros,
        por carta escogidos,   sobra buenos braçeros;
        çiento carros bastidos   de buenos ballesteros,
        que fueron escogidos   por seer delanteros.

2045   Éstos solos pudieran   a todos defender
        que nunca Alexandre   los pudiesse romper;
        mas – la su mala ventura   que los suel' confonder –
        para carrera mala   ovieron a prender.

2046   Avié tan fiera pluvia   ante noche passada
        que la tierra en lodo   era toda tornada;
        los varones por ello   avién mala andada;
        non corrién suelta mente   e non les valié nada.

2047   El rëy Alexandre,   quando fue allegado,
        firió luego en ellos   como rayo irado.
        Buçifal por el lodo   non avié nul cuidado;
        fue de mala manera   rebuelto el mercado.

2048   Firié con él a una   la su bella mesnada;
        el señor era bueno   e ella esforçada;
        como avién los otros   la ora embargada,
        non podién rebolverse   nin fer espolonada.

2049   Las hazes eran bueltas,   los colpes abivados;
        grandes eran las bozes   e muchos los colpados;
        eran por a ferir   todos tan denodados,
        como si les echassen   perdón de sus pecados.

2050   Cuidóseles a todos   don Yulcos mejorar;
        en un elefant' fiero   vino al rey colpar;
        esperóle el rëy,   sópose bien guardar;
        nada de lo que quiso   non pudo recabdar.

2051   Tan bien sopo el rëy   la cosa aguisar,
        con Dios, que le querié   valer e ayudar;
        de la su mano ovo   don Yulcos a finar;
        en compaña de Poro   non remaneçió par.

2052   Toviéronse los griegos   por bïen estrenados,
        fueron por a lidiar   todos más abivados;
        davan e reçibién   como escalentados;
        soltavan les los sueños   que avíen soñados.

2044	He placed in the vanguard four thousand knights, chosen by lot and outstanding warriors, and a hundred carts full of fine crossbowmen, who had been chosen to go at the army's head.
2045	These men alone could have defended the whole force, for Alexander could never have broken through them; but his enemies' misfortune, men's habitual confounder, meant that their affairs were to take a wrong path.
2046	It had rained so heavily the night before that all the ground had been turned into mud; because of this, the knights found it difficult to move: they could not advance freely, and it availed them nothing.
2047	When King Alexander arrived in that place, he struck them immediately like angry lightning. Bucephalus was given no trouble by the mud, and affairs were thrown into total confusion.
2048	His fine army attacked with him as one; the lord was a good man and his army was brave; their enemies, as they had occupied the river bank, were not able to manoeuvre or launch a charge.
2049	The armies clashed and the blows were unleashed; great was the shouting and many blows were struck, and they were all so fervent in attack as if they had been offered pardon for their sins.
2050	To outdo all of them was Yulcon's intent: astride a fierce elephant, he came to strike the King. Alexander awaited him, knowing well his defence, and he could not achieve a thing of what he sought.
2051	The King knew so well how to deal with the matter, with the aid of God, who wished to help and support him, that Yulcon was to die at Alexander's hand; in Porus' army there remained no man to match him.
2052	The Greeks considered that they had begun well and were all feeling greater passion for the fight, giving and receiving blows like men who burned with fervour; the dreams that they had dreamed were turning true.

2053 Queriá ya Alexandre   a Poro allegar,
      que non querié cabeça   en ninguno tornar;
      pero en esse día   nol' pudo acabar;
      oviéronse con tanto   del campo a alçar.

2054 Otro día mañana,   el mundo alumbrado,
      tornaron al trebejo,   el campo fue poblado;
      empeçavan el pleito   do lo avién dexado;
      serié ningunt juglar   a duro escuchado.

2055 El rëy Alexandre,   a Poro demandando,
      metiése por las hazes,   ira de Dios echando.
      Poro a la siniestra   haz se fue acostando,
      do iva más afirmes   la lid escalentando.

2056 Astrio e Polidamas,   dos vassallos leales,
      aguardavan al rëy,   como sus naturales;
      eran en la fazienda   guerreros tant' mortales
      que desbalçaron muchos   de prínçipes cabdales.

2057 Rúbicus e Arístones   ovieron a justar;
      quebrantaron las lanças,   ovieron a dolar;
      sabié mejor Aristón   del espada colpar;
      fue engañado Rúbicus,   óvolo a lazrar.

2058 Cuidó a Polidamas   Cadaçenes ferir;
      treviése en su fuerça,   cuidólo destruir;
      mas ovo un griego, Gautus,   de cuesta a sallir;
      travessólo por guisa   ond' ovo a morir.

2059 En bien ivan los griegos   poniendo las feridas;
      avién de fiera guisa   las hazes arrompidas;
      los carros foçijados   con todas sus guaridas
      non le valién a Poro   tres arvejas podridas.

2060 Los griegos de los otros   trayén grant mejoría:
      cavallos bien ligeros,   uso e maestría;
      que si los elefantes   trayén grant valentía,
      non avién de correr   nula podestadía.

2061 Como trayén los griegos   los cavallos ligeros,
      firién los e tornavan,   faziénseles vezeros;
      los de los elefantes,   fuera los ballesteros,
      los otros non valién   todos sendos dineros.

2053	Alexander now wanted to come next to Porus, and so wished to turn his eyes upon no other man; but on that day he was not able to achieve it and therefore they had to leave the field of battle.
2054	The following morning, with the world bathed in light, they returned to their sport and the battlefield was peopled; they began the dispute just where they had left it; any minstrel would find it hard to be heard.
2055	King Alexander, as he went in search of Porus, made his way through the battle lines, breathing out God's wrath; Porus, in the left hand column, gradually drew near, where the battle was becoming most intense and heated.
2056	Ariston and Polidamas, two loyal vassals, were protecting the King as his kinsmen would. In battle, they proved such deadly warriors that they vanquished many princes of high rank.
2057	To Rubricus and Ariston did it fall to joust; they broke their lances and came to strike each other blows; Ariston was more skilled in handling the sword; Rubricus was outdone and came to suffer pain.
2058	Candaceus intended to strike Polidamas: he trusted in his strength and sought to kill him, but a Greek, Glaucus, stepped out from behind him and ran him through, dealing him a mortal wound.
2059	The Greeks were striking blows to great effect and had left the enemy columns quite destroyed; the scythed chariots, with all their protection, to Porus were not worth three rotten peas.
2060	The Greeks were much advantaged over their opponents, with their swift-footed horses, experience and skill; for if the elephants brought with them great courage, they were not able to run with any power.
2061	As the Greeks had with them fleet-footed horses, they struck their enemy and drew back, darting to and fro; of those on the elephants, except the crossbowmen, all the others were not worth a penny each.

2062 Como vinién los griegos   de despecho cargados,
      ivan por a ellos   a mantillos echados;
      como de tal non eran   los de Poro usados,
      fuéronse acogiendo   los que eran fincados.

2063 Poro, quando la cosa   vío ir tan a mal,
      fizo de elefantes   un tan fiero corral
      que non serié tan firme   de piedra nin de cal;
      el rëy era bueno   e bueno el real.

2064 Nunca de tantas guisas   lo podién ensayar
      que romper lo pudiessen   nin a Poro entrar;
      non lo podién prender   nin lo podién dexar,
      nin sabién qué se fer   nin sabién dó tornar.

2065 Vinián los elefantes   con sus lenguas barvadas;
      avién a Alexandre   muchas gentes dañadas;
      echavan les el boço   bien a quinze passadas;
      abatié uno d'ellos   quatro a las vegadas.

2066 Avremos – non vos pese –   la cosa a destajar:
      ovo esta fazienda   quinz' días a durar;
      avién todos los días   por coto a lidiar,
      pero al rëy Poro   non se podién llegar.

2067 Alexandre, de sesos   sossacador estraño,
      por a los elefantes   sossacó buen engaño;
      mandó fer ad Apelles   imágenes d'estaño;
      dos tantos que non ha   de días en el año.

2068 Éstas fueron aína   fechas e aguisadas;
      mandó las calentar,   implir las de brasadas;
      metieron las delante   en carretas ferradas,
      ca, si tales non fuessen,   serién luego quemadas.

2069 Fueron los elefantes   luego a su bezado;
      tenién que eran omes,   echavan el forcado,
      mas el que una vez   allá lo avié echado
      non tornarié a ome,   non serié tan cuitado.

2070 Demás, otra fazaña   oí ende dezir:
      que mandó Alexandre   los puercos aduzir;
      fuyén los elefantes   quand' los oyén gruñir,
      que nunca ante ellos   osavan refollir.

2062 As the Greeks were attacking filled full of fury,
they made for their enemy with standards unfurled;
as Porus' men were not used to such tactics,
those remaining moved steadily back in retreat.

2063 When Porus saw that things were going so badly,
he formed a great circle of elephants, so strong
that one of stone or lime would not be so secure;
the King was a fine man, and his fort, too, was fine.

2064 By whatever means the Greeks tried to attack,
they could not break the circle or get to Porus;
they could not take him captive, nor could they leave him:
they knew not what to do, and they could not retreat.

2065 The elephants were coming with their snouts –
they had done Alexander's men great harm;
they reached out with their trunks a full fifteen paces
and one of them struck down four men at a time.

2066 May it not grieve you – we must cut the matter short:
this battle was to last for fifteen days;
the Greeks were made to fight through all those days,
but they could not come close to King Porus.

2067 Alexander, a weaver of tricks of rare wiles,
wove a clever deceit for the elephants:
he commanded Apelles to make images of tin,
twice as many as the number of days in the year.

2068 These images were quickly made and prepared;
the King's orders were to heat them and fill them with coals;
they carried them forward in iron-clad carts,
for otherwise the carts would quickly have burned.

2069 The elephants immediately went to their custom:
they thought they were men, and extended their trunks;
but the elephant that had stretched his trunk there once
would turn on no other man, for fear of being burned.

2070 I have heard tell, too, of another of his tricks:
that Alexander ordered pigs to be brought,
and the elephants fled when they heard them grunt,
for they never dared to set themselves against them.

2071 Mandó luego entrar   delante los peones
con destrales agudos   e buenos segurones;
dar a los elefantes,   cortarles los jamones,
que abriessen carrera   sobre los sus griñones.

2072 El mandado del rëy   fue muy rica ment' tenido;
non quisieron los omes   echarlo en olvido.
Metieron se a ellos   de coraçón complido;
ovieron en un rato   grant portillo abrido.

2073 Firién todos en buelta   griegos e indïanos;
por mejor non passavan   medos e persïanos;
todos avién buen cuer,   todos trayén las manos;
de los que de Poro eran,   pocos andavan sanos.

2074 Ovo Alexandre   a Poro açechar;
en medio de la muela,   en un firme lugar,
en un tan grant bestión   como un castellar;
mas avié en comedio   grant muro a passar.

2075 Ellos por allegarse,   los otros por redrarlos,
estavan todos firmes,   señores e vassallos;
non podién entre muertos   meterse los cavallos;
avién los señores   sin grado a dexarlos.

2076 Fuelos el viento malo   a los indios firiendo;
sofrir non lo pudieron,   yas' ivan desordiendo;
fueron tornando cuestas,   los cavallos bolviendo;
nol' plogo ren a Poro   quando lo fue veyendo.

2077 Siempre esto solemos   de faziendas oír:
por pocos que se mueven,   han muchos a foír;
non los dexa el miedo   su derecho complir;
son, desque se müeven,   malos de referir.

2078 Fueron los indïanos   dura ment' descosidos;
avié los la vitoria   de su blasmo feridos.
Muchos avié que eran   sin feridas vençidos,
mas non podién quedar   desque eran movidos.

2079 Assaz entendié Poro;   cuidólos retener;
empeçó a altas bozes   a todos maltraer:
"Amigos, en mal preçio   vos queredes poner;
nunca en esti mundo   lo podredes perder.

2071 He ordered the footsoldiers to go forward at once,
bearing sharp hatchets and armed with strong axes,
to attack the elephants and hew off their legs,
that they might open a way through their midst.

2072 The command of the King was strictly obeyed
and the men did not wish to let it go unheeded;
they attacked the beasts with boldness in their hearts
and in a short time they had opened a large breach.

2073 Greeks and Indians all joined in the mêlée
and Medes and Persians met no finer fate;
all were of stout heart and they all fought well,
and few of Porus' men escaped unharmed.

2074 Alexander came to spy out Porus there,
on the top of a hill, in a well-defended spot,
upon a huge beast the size of a castle;
but in the meantime there was a high wall to pass.

2075 With one side seeking progress, their foes to drive them back,
everyone stood firm, both lords and their vassals;
the horses were not able to pass among the dead
and the unwilling knights had to leave them behind.

2076 The ill wind began to blow against the Indians;
they could not resist and were already losing order;
they began to retreat, turning back their horses;
Porus was far from pleased with what he saw.

2077 We are forever wont to hear this of battles:
for a few who give ground many have to flee.
Fear does not let them fulfil their rightful duty;
once they retreat, it is hard to turn them back.

2078 The Indian troops were cruelly dispirited
for victory had struck them with its curse.
Many had been defeated without suffering blows,
but once they had retreated, they could not stand their ground.

2079 Porus understood enough and tried to hold them back,
and he began to shout rebukes at all his men:
"My friends, you are keen to put yourselves in disgrace
which never in this world will you be able to lose.

2080   Amigos, ¡vuestro rëy non lo desemparedes!
Si Poro aquí finca, vos mal prez levaredes.
Tornat a la fazienda, ca rafez los vinçredes;
por quanto'l mundo dure, vos oy vos honraredes."

2081   Tanto non pudo Poro dezir nin predicar,
non los pudo por guisa ninguna acordar;
en cabo, quando vío que non querién tornar,
tornó él en el campo, empeçó de lidiar.

2082   Parientes e amigos quel' eran más carnales
– éstos eran al menos quinze señas cabdales –
más quisieron morir que seer desleales;
bien andant' fuera Poro si todos fuessen tales.

2083   Fincaron en el campo como firmes varones,
faziendo en los griegos daños e lisïones;
recudién firme mente a las sus qüestiones;
tanto que les pesava bien en los coraçones.

2084   Corrién ríos de sangre apriessa por el prado;
era de omes muertos rica ment' enfenado;
los bivos de los muertos non avién nul cuidado;
el que murié firiendo teniése por honrado.

2085   En cabo, non pudieron tanto se denodar,
que ovo el grïego su barba a honrar.
Ovieron a la seña de Poro a plegar,
ca avién a los otros tollidos del lugar.

2086   Fue toda la fazienda sobre Poro caída;
era en angostura, temié perder la vida,
ca avié el ome bueno toda su gent' perdida;
non veyé en el siglo nulla otra guarida.

2087   Muerto fuera o preso, ca era abatido,
el elefant' en tierra, mortal mente ferido;
mas fue en tal estorvo Alexandre caído,
nunca lo ovo peor después que fue naçido.

2088   Buçifal, el caboso de las manos ligeras,
que solié sin pereça delibrar las carreras,
avié mortales colpes por medio las çincheras;
ixién los estentinos, semejavan süeras.

2080	My friends, do not leave your king without protection: if Porus meets his end here, you will bear dishonour. Return to the battle, for you will beat them with ease; today you will win glory for the lifetime of the world."
2081	There was nothing that Porus could say or could preach: he could not return them to sense by any means; at last, when he saw that they would not turn back, he returned to the battlefield and started to fight.
2082	The kinsmen and friends who were closest to him – these were at least fifteen of the foremost knights – had more desire for death than to show disloyalty; Porus would have been fortunate had they all been thus.
2083	They remained on the battlefield like men firm of purpose, inflicting on the Greeks great harm and injury; to the taunts of the Greeks they gave a firm response, such as to cause them deep trouble in their hearts.
2084	Rivers of blood flowed swiftly through the meadow, which was richly strewn with the bodies of the dead. The living were not troubled by the dead men's presence, for the man who died in battle felt honoured.
2085	In the end they could not create enough resistance, for the Greek came to win honour for his person. They managed to fight their way to Porus' standard, for they had driven their opponents from the scene.
2086	The whole of the battle was fallen upon Porus; he was in distress, and feared he might lose his life, for the good man had now lost all of his troops and he saw no other protection in the world.
2087	He would have been captured or killed, for he had been felled: his elephant was on the ground, with a fatal wound, but Alexander had now fallen into such strife: he had never suffered worse since the day of his birth.
2088	The noble Bucephalus, his swift-footed horse, which never tarried on its way to journey's end, had been mortally wounded about its girth, and its intestines emerged, the colour of whey.

2089   Allegóse a Poro   Tráxillo, su hermano,
        vassallo d'Alexandre,   que besava su mano:
        "Rëy", diz', "seriá seso   e consejo muy sano
        que a merçet tornasses   del rëy greçïano.

2090   Es ome de mesura   e de grant pïedat;
        quien quiere se lo puede   vençer con humildat;
        dexarnos ha bevir   en nuestra heredat;
        rëy, si al fizieres,   será grant torpedat."

2091   Fue Poro contra Tráxillo   sañoso e irado,
        ca por lo que le dixo   era su despagado;
        remetiól' un benablo   que le avié fincado;
        echólo muerto frío   en la yerba del prado.

2092   Buçifal, con la muerte   ovo a recreer;
        entendiólo el rëy,   ovo a deçender;
        fue leal el caboso,   non se dexó caer
        fasta que vio al rëy   en sus piedes tener.

2093   Buçifal cayó muerto   a piedes del señor;
        remaneçió apeado   el buen emperador.
        Mintriemos si dixiéssemos   que non avié dolor;
        mandólo soterrar   a müy grant onor.

2094   Después fizo el rëy   do yazié soterrado
        poblar una çibdat   de muro bien obrado;
        dixéronle Buçífalia,   nombre bien señalado,
        por que fuera assí   el cavallo clamado.

2095   Mïentre el buen rëy   el cavallo camiava,
        Poro tomó consejo,   ca vio que mal estava;
        cavalgó un cavallo   que sobra bien andava;
        quand' el otro cató,   él bien lexos estava.

2096   Tóvose Alexandre   por muy mal escarnido,
        por que le era Poro   de las manos exido;
        ca tenié que su pleito   oviera bien complido
        si a Poro oviesse   consigo retenido.

2097   Pero en el poblado   non se osó fïar;
        alçóse a la sierra   por más salvo estar;
        mas el rey Alexandre   nol' quiso dar vagar;
        luego fue en el rastro,   queriégelo vedar.

2089	Taxiles now came up to Porus, his brother,* a vassal of Alexander, for he had kissed his hand: "My King," he said, "it would be wise and sound counsel for you to turn to the mercy of the Grecian king.
2090	He is a man of judgement and great compassion and any man can overcome him with humility; he will allow us to live in our homeland; my King, if you do otherwise, it will be great folly."
2091	Porus was furiously angry with Taxiles, bearing him resentment for what he had said; he let fly at him with a spear that still remained and laid him cold dead on the grass of the meadow.
2092	Bucephalus came to yield his spirit to death; the King understood this, and went to dismount; the fine steed was loyal and did not let himself fall until he saw the King standing on his feet.
2093	Bucephalus fell dead at the feet of his lord and the good Emperor stayed standing. We would lie if we said that he felt no grief; he bade him be interred with very great honour.
2094	Afterwards the King, where the horse lay buried, founded a city, with a finely built wall: they called it Bucephala, a name of great distinction,* after that which had been borne by the horse itself.
2095	Whilst the good King was changing his horse, Porus took advice, for he saw he was in trouble. He mounted a horse, a fine quality steed: when Alexander saw him, he was far in the distance.
2096	Alexander felt himself cruelly cheated because Porus had slipped through his hands, for he felt his business would have been well concluded if he had kept Porus within his grasp.
2097	But Porus did not dare to stay in a settled place: he took refuge in the mountains, to be safer; yet King Alexander would give him no respite: on his trail at once, he sought to halt his escape.

2098 Pero Galter el bueno   en su versificar
      sediá ende cansado   e queriá destajar;
      dexó de la materia   mucho en es' logar;
      quando lo él dexó   quiérolo yo contar.

2099 De Poro cómo fuyó   él non escrivió nada,
      ni cóm' fizo torneo   la segunda vegada;
      de muchas maravellas,   mucha bestia granada,
      que vençió Alexandre,   una lança provada.

2100 El rëy Alexandre,   que nunca falló par,
      quísolo su ventura   en todo acabar;
      quiso Dios por su ruego   tal virtud demostrar
      que serié a San Pedro   grant cosa a ganar.

2101 Tras unas altas sierras   – Caspïas son llamadas –
      que, fueras un portillo,   non avié mas entradas,
      falló muchas de gentes   en uno ajuntadas;
      fue tan grant muchedunbre   que non serién contadas.

2102 Todos en un lenguaje   fablavan su razón;
      trayén costumbres propias   todos en su missión;
      en contra Orïente   fazién su oración,
      pero bien semejavan   de flaca complexión.

2103 Demandó Alexandre   que querié entender:
      qué gentes eran éstas   o qué podién seer.
      "Rëy," dixo un sabio,   "¡non ayas qué temer!
      Non te puede por éstas   nul embargo naçer.

2104 Judíos son que yazen   en su cabtividat,
      gentes a qui Dios fizo   mucha de pïedat;
      mas ellos non supieron   guardarle lealtat,
      por ende son caídos   en esta mesquindat.

2105 Omes astrosos son,   de flacos coraçones;
      non valen pora armas   más que sendos cabrones;
      de suzia mantenençia,   astrosillos barones;
      cobdiçian dineruelos   más que gato pulmones."

2106 Contóle la estoria   e toda la razón:
      las plagas de Egipto,   la muert' de Faraón,
      cómo fue por la lëy   Moïsés el varón,
      en quál cuita tovieron   despüés a Arón.

2098	But Walter the good, as he wrote his poem,* was tired by now, and wished to be concise. At this point he omitted much of his subject, and, since he left it out, I wish to tell it.
2099	Of how Porus fled, he wrote nothing at all, nor of how he made a contest for the second time, nor of the many marvels and many great beasts that Alexander defeated, that worthy lance.
2100	For King Alexander, who never met his equal, his good fortune wished to complete him in all ways; in answer to his prayer, God wished to grant him such a power as would be a great gain to Saint Peter himself.
2101	Behind lofty peaks, called the Caspian Gates,* where there was no entry but a tiny pass, he found many people all gathered together,* a throng so great that they could not be counted.
2102	They all expressed their meaning in a single tongue and all had their own customs in their own land; while looking to the East they made their prayer, but they seemed of unhealthy complexion.
2103	Alexander asked, for he wanted to learn, what people were these, or what they might be. "My King," said a wise man, "you need not be afraid, for no harm to you can arise from these people.
2104	They are Jews who lie in their captivity, people on whom God showed great mercy, but they could not remain loyal to Him, through which they are fallen to this pitiful state.
2105	They are men in disgrace, with feeble hearts, their arms worth no more each than a goat; vile in what they eat, despicable people, they crave a little money more than a cat does lights."
2106	He told him the history and the whole explanation: the plagues of Egypt and the death of Pharaoh; how the noble Moses went for the Law and in what distress they then placed Aaron.

2107 Díxol' cómo entraron en tierra de promissión,
      cómo ovieron rëys de su generaçión;
      mas bolvieron en cabo con Dios dissençïón
      ond' ovieron a caer en la su maldiçión.

2108 En cabo cómo vino un rëy de Caldea;
      desbarató la hueste por destroír Judea;
      fizo la çibdat santa plus pobre que aldea;
      ixió a los judíos a mal essa pelea.

2109 Fueron los mal astrugos por sus grandes pecados
      los unos destroídos, los otros cativados;
      los que bevir pudieron, mesquinos e lazrados,
      fueron aquí metidos, que yazen ençerrados.

2110 Demás es les a todos por premia devedado
      – ca fue de los profetas assí profetizado –
      que muger nin varón non sea tan osado
      de passar esta foz, sól' non sea pensado.

2111 "Otorgo," diz' el rëy, "derecho es provado,
      pueblo sobre que fizo Dïos tant' aguisado
      e fue contra su lëy tan mal consejado
      fasta la fin del mundo devrié yazer ençerrado."

2112 Mandó con argamassa el portiello çerrar,
      que nunca más pudiessen nin sallir nin entrar;
      oviessen y las pasquas por siempre çelebrar,
      que los que lo oyessen dubdassen de pecar.

2113 Ovo un firme seso en cabo a asmar:
      rogó al Crïador que Él quisiesse dar
      consejo por que siempre oviesse a durar,
      qu'obra de mano fecha non podrié firm' estar.

2114 Quando ovo el rëy la oraçión complida,
      maguer era pagano fuele de Dios oída;
      moviéronse las peñas, cad'un' de su partida;
      soldáronse en medio, fue presa la sallida.

2115 Pero diz' el escripto, que bien es de creer,
      fasta la fin del mundo allí han de yazer;
      avrán çerca la fin ende a estorçer;
      avrán el mundo todo en quexa a meter.

2107	He told him how they entered the promised land, and how they had kings from among their own people; but in the end they came into dispute with God, wherefore they were to fall beneath His curse.
2108	Finally, how there came a king of Chaldea, who crushed their army and destroyed all Judea, and left the Holy City poorer than a village, and how that struggle went so badly for the Jews.
2109	Of the wretches, on account of their great sins, some were destroyed and others were imprisoned; those who could survive in poverty and suffering were sent to this place and they lie here enclosed.
2110	Besides, it is strictly forbidden to them all – for in this way it was foretold by the prophets – that any woman or man should have such daring as to pass through this cleft, not even in thought.
2111	"I grant," said the King, "that it is proven truth: a people against which God acted so justly, which went against His law, their counsel so ill, should be shut away until the end of the world."
2112	He ordered that the entry be sealed with mortar so that never again might they leave or come in; there should they have to hold their festivals forever that anyone who hears them should be in fear of sin.
2113	Finally he devised a plan of great wisdom: he prayed to the Creator to give him advice to ensure that this would endure for all time, for a work of human hand could not be secure.
2114	When the King had brought his prayer to its end, although he was a pagan it was heard by God; each one of the rocks moved inwards from its side and they were sealed in the middle, the exit closed.
2115	But the written text says – and it is to be believed –* that they are to lie there until the world's end, but as the end approaches they will make their escape, and they will bring affliction to all of the world.

2116 Quando Dios tanto fizo   por un ome pagano,
     tanto o más farié   por un fiel cristïano;
     por nos non lo perdamos,   d'esto so yo çertano;
     quien en Dios ave dubda   torpe es e villano.

2117 Encalçando a Poro,   que andava alçado,
     era de fiera guisa   el rey escalentado;
     com' un alán cadiello   que anda encarnado,
     teniendo la batalla   que faze el venado.

2118 Andava en su busca   en un rico lugar,
     falló los sus palaçios   do él solié morar;
     tal era su costumbre,   allí solié folgar
     la sazón que querié   su cuerpo deleitar.

2119 La obra del palaçio   non es de olvidar,
     maguer non la podamos   digna mente contar;
     por que mucho queramos   la verdat alabar,
     aún avrán por esso   algunos a dubdar.

2120 El lugar era plano,   rica ment' assentado,
     abondado de caça,   si quiere de venado;
     las montañas de çerca   do paçié el ganado;
     verano e ivierno   era logar temprado.

2121 Fueron de buen maestro   los palaçios sentados,
     fueron maestra mente   a quadra compassados;
     en peña viva fueron   los çimientos echados;
     por agua nin por fierro   non serién desatados.

2122 Eran bien enloçidas   e firmes las paredes;
     non fazién nula mengua   sávanas ni tapedes;
     el techo era pinto   a lazo e a redes,
     todo de oro fino,   como en Dios creedes.

2123 Las puertas eran todas   de marfil natural,
     blancas e reluzientes,   como fino cristal;
     los entalles sotiles,   bien alto el poyal.
     Casa era de rëy,   mas bien era real.

2124 Quatroçientas columpnas   avié en essas casas,
     todas de oro fino,   capiteles e basas;
     non serién plus luzientes   si fuessen bivas brasas,
     ca eran bien broñidas,   bien planas e bien rasas.

2116 Since God did all of this for a man who was pagan,
for a faithful Christian, He would do as much or more;
we must not lose Him – of this I am certain:
the man who doubts God is foolish and base.

2117 As he pursued Porus, who was in hiding,
the passions of the King were hotly aroused,
like a young mastiff which is roused to frenzy,
thinking of the fight that the game puts up.

2118 In his search, he came to a place of splendour:
he found the palace where Porus used to dwell.
Such was his custom: he would take his rest there
when he wanted to give pleasure to his body.

2119 The palace's adornment must not be forgotten,*
even if we can give no worthy account;
however much we desire to praise what is true,
for that very reason will some come to doubt.

2120 The area was flat, in a glorious setting;
it was rich in deer and in other kinds of game,
and there were mountains nearby, where flocks would graze;
in summer and winter it was a temperate place.

2121 The palace had been laid out by a fine master craftsman,
its masterful arrangement designed with precision.
The foundations had been set into living rock
and would not be destroyed by water or iron.

2122 Of fine decoration and of strength were the walls,
and there was no lack of coverings and rugs;
the ceiling was painted in entwining interlace,
all in fine gold, as you believe in God.

2123 The doors were all made of natural ivory,
with the whiteness and gleam of fine crystal;
the carvings were subtle, with mouldings high above:
it was a king's home, but it was royal indeed.

2124 There were four hundred columns in those buildings,
all of fine gold, both capitals and bases;
they would have shone no brighter had they been burning coals,
for they were finely burnished, quite flat and smooth.

2125   Muchas eran las cámaras, todas con sus sobrados;
de çiprés eran todos   los maderos obrados;
eran tan sotil mente   entre sí enlazados
que non entendié ome   do eran empeçados.

2126   Pendié de las columpnas   derredor de la sala
una muy rica viña,   de mejor non nos cala;
levava fojas d'oro,   grandes como la palma.
Querriá aver las mías   tales, ¡si Dios me vala!

2127   Las uvas de la viña   eran de grant femençia:
piedras eran preçiosas,   todas de grant potençia;
toda la peor era   de grant magnifiçençia;
el que plantó la viña   fue de grant sapïençia.

2128   Como entre las uvas   son diversas naturas,
assí eran las piedras   de diversas figuras:
las unas eran verdes,   las otras bien maduras;
nunca les fizo mal   gielo nin calenturas.

2129   Allí trobarié ome   las unas tardaniellas,
las otras migaruelas   que son más tempraniellas;
las blancas alfonsinas   que tornan amariellas;
las alfonsinas negras   que son más cardeniellas.

2130   Las buenas calagrañas   que se querién alçar,
las otras molejas   que fazen viejas trotar;
torrontés umorosa,   buena pora'l lagar;
quantas non podrié ome   dezir nin agrimar.

2131   Dexemos vos la viña   que era tan loçana,
que llevava vendimia   tardana e temprana;
digamos de un árbol   que sediá en la plaça,
que yazié y riqueza   fiera e adïana.

2132   En medio del enclaustro,   lugar tan acabado,
sediá un rico árbol,   en medio levantado;
nin era müy gruesso   nin era muy delgado,
de oro fino era   sotil mente obrado.

2133   Quantas aves en çielo   han bozes acordadas,
que dizen cantos dulces,   menudas e granadas,
todas en aquel árbol   pareçién figuradas,
cad' un' por su natura   de color devisadas.

2125	Many were the chambers, all with their dais, and the panels were all worked of cypress, the links with the others so subtly made that no man could tell where each began.
2126	There hung from the columns around the hall a magnificent vine, the finest in existence,* whose leaves were of gold, and a palm in length – I would like mine like that, may God help me!
2127	The grapes of the vine were rich indeed: they were precious stones, all with great powers; the poorest of all was truly exquisite: it was a great sage who planted the vine.
2128	As among grapes there are differing natures,* so too the stones were of differing forms: some were green, others of a riper hue; they never suffered harm from frost or heat.
2129	There a man would find some grapes appearing late, and others, "migaruelas", which are earlier; there are white "alfonsinas", whose colour turns yellow, and black "alfonsinas", more blue-black in tone.
2130	The fine "calagraña" which wants to be saved, the "moleja" which makes old ladies run, the juicy "torrontés", ideal for the press: so many that a man could not list or imagine.
2131	Let us leave that vine, of such luxuriant growth that bears a harvest in late and early season and speak of a tree which stood in the courtyard, for there lay there great and abundant wealth.
2132	In the middle of the cloister, so fine a spot, was a splendid tree, rising up in the centre: it was not very thick, it was not very slender, and it was subtly worked in fine gold.
2133	All the birds in the sky, with harmonious voices, that sing their sweet songs – birds large and small – all seemed to be there, depicted in that tree, the type of each distinguished by its colour.

2134
Todos los instrumentos   que usan los juglares,
otros de mayor preçio   que usan escolares,
de todos avié y   tres o quatro pares,
todos bien atemprados   por formar sus cantares.

2135
A la raíz del árbol   bien a quinze estados,
vinién unos cañones   que yazién soterrados;
eran de cobre duro   por en esso lavrados;
todos eran en el árbol   metidos e soldados.

2136
Sollavan con bufetes   en aquellos cañones,
luego dizián las aves   cada una sus sones;
los gayos, las calandras,   tordos e los gaviones,
el ruy señor que dize   las fermosas cançiones.

2137
Luenga serié la conta   de las aves contar;
la noche va viniendo   quiérovos destajar;
ya no sé quál quisiesse   de las otras echar
qüando la çigala   non quiso olvidar.

2138
Bolvién los estrumentos   a buelta con las aves;
modulavan a çierto   las cuerdas e las claves;
alçando e primiendo,   fazién cantos süaves,
tales que por a Órfeo   de formar serién graves.

2139
Allí era la música   cantada por razón,
las dulçes deballadas,   el plorant' semitón,
las dobles que refieren   cuitas del coraçón;
bien podién tirar preçio   a una prosiçión.

2140
Non es en este mundo   ome tan sabidor
que dezir vos pudiesse   quál era la dulçor;
mientre ome biviesse   en aquella sabor,
non avrié set nin fambre   nin ira nin dolor.

2141
Podedes vos por otra   cosa maravillar:
si quisiesse, las medias   solas farié cantar;
si quisiesse, la terçia;   si quisiesse, un par;
sotil fue el maestro   que lo sopo labrar.

2142
Óvolo Alexandre   por fiera estrañeza;
dixo que nunca viera   tan estraña riqueza.
Todos tenién que era   muy adaute nobleza;
nunca avién oído   de tan noble alteza.

2134	All of the instruments that minstrels use, and others of greater value used by scholars – there were three or four pairs of each in that place, all finely tuned to intone their songs.
2135	At the roots of the tree, at fifteen men's bodies' distance,* some pipes there emerged that lay beneath the ground; they were of tough copper, from which they were worked, and they were all fixed and welded to the tree.
2136	Men used bellows to blow down those pipes, and the birds each sang their own song at once, the jays, the larks, the thrushes and the swifts and the nightingale, which sings with great beauty.
2137	It would be a long tale to tell of all the birds; night is drawing in and I wish to cut it short for you; I know not which others I would wish to leave out, since the craftsman would not even omit the cicada.
2138	The instruments were mingled with the sound of the birds, the strings and the keys sure in their harmony; as they rose and fell, they made such sweet music: Orpheus would find it hard to form the like.
2139	There the singing and the music were in perfect proportion, the gentle cadences and the weeping semitone, the ballads which tell of the cares of the heart: these could well outdo the music of a procession.
2140	There is no man in all the world with such knowledge that he could describe to you what sweetness was there. As long as a man lived amidst that pleasure he would have not thirst nor hunger, rage nor grief.
2141	There is one thing more that may cause you to marvel: if it wished, it could make just half the birds sing, if it wished, a third, and if it wished, just two; it was a wise scholar who could create it.
2142	Alexander held it a remarkable wonder, and said that he had never seen such wondrous wealth. They all thought it of the most pleasing nobility, and had never heard of so noble an achievement.

2143 Por todas essas nuevas nin por essos sabores,
non perdiá Alexandre los malos baticores;
todas sus voluntades e todas sus sabores
yazién en sólo Poro e en sus valedores.

2144 Mientre que él estava en esti grant pesar,
non sabién a quál parte lo sallessen buscar;
ovo una barrunta çertera a llegar,
dixo que lo podié en Baracta fallar.

2145 Díxol' que adobava poderes e missiones
pora venir al campo lidiar con sus varones;
cuidava adozir tantas de legïones
que los ahontarié com' a malos garçones.

2146 Non priso ningund plazo, metióse en carrera;
avié con el sabor la voluntat ligera;
mas tanto quiso fer tesura sobrançera
que perdió de sus gentes muchas en la carrera.

2147 Luenga era la vía, avié muchas jornadas;
seca e peligrosa, avié malas passadas,
de serpientas raviosas e bestias entecadas
de que prisieron muchas de malas sorrostradas.

2148 Moviése, por amor de ante recabdar,
por tal tierra que ome adur podié passar;
tierra que non podrié ome tanto andar
que pudiesse un baso de agua limpia fallar.

2149 Quando fueron andando, cuitólos la fervor,
de la tierra el polvo, del çielo el calor;
si quiere los vassallos, si quiere el señor,
bevrién agua del río de müy buen amor.

2150 Ellos avién grant cueita, mas las bestias mayor;
faziéles mal la suya, mas las d'ellas peor;
bien avié de seer de juegos sofridor
el que non se quexasse de tan mala sabor.

2151 Los omes con la cueita lamién en las espadas;
otros bevién sin grado las orinas botadas;
andavan los mesquinos con las lenguas sacadas;
nunca fueron en mundo gentes tan quexadas.

2143	Not through all those novelties, nor through those delights had Alexander lost his painful anguish; all of his desires, and all his passions dwelt only on Porus and his protectors.
2144	Whilst he was suffering from this great sorrow and they knew not where to go in search of Porus,* he received information, known to be true: it said that he could find him in Bactria.
2145	It said he was preparing armies and resources to come to the battlefield to fight against the Greek's men; that it was his intention to bring so many legions that he would put them to shame like naughty boys.
2146	The King made no delay but set out on the path; his heart was light with the pleasure that he felt; but so great was his wish to perform a great feat that he lost a large number of his people on the way.
2147	The journey was an long one, lasting several days, enduring drought and dangers, with difficult stretches, encountering raging serpents and venomous creatures from which they suffered a great litany of harm.
2148	He was travelling, in his passion for quick success, through such land as no man ever managed to cross, land in which a man could never walk so far that he might find a glass of clean water.
2149	As they travelled along, the swelter struck them: the dust from the land, the heat from the sky; and not only the vassals but also the lord would have most willingly drunk water from a river.
2150	Their suffering was great, but the animals' greater; they were worried by their own, but more so by the beasts'. He would have to be most resilient to trials, the man who would not complain of such unpleasantness.
2151	The men in their distress licked their very swords; others unwillingly drank the urine they expelled; the poor wretches went with their tongues hanging out and never in the world had people suffered so.

2152   Falló en una piedra   Zoilus un pelaguiello;
        finchó de agua limpia   a penas un capiello.
        Diola toda al rey,   nol' fincó un sorbiello;
        nol' dava mal serviçio   al rey el mançebiello.

2153   El rëy, quando lo vio,   empeçó de reír;
        vertióla por la tierra,   non la quiso sorvir;
        dixo: "Con mis vassallos   cobdiçio yo morir;
        quando ellos murieren   non quiero yo bevir."

2154   Ovieron d'esti fecho   las gentes grant plazer;
        fueron tan confortadas   como con buen bever.
        Todos dizién: "¡Al rëy   fágalo Dios valer,
        que sabe a vassallos   tal lealtad tener!"

2155   Fallaron en comedio   muchas malas serpientes,
        unas con aguijones,   otras con malos dientes;
        unas vinién bolando,   otras sobre sus vientres;
        dañávanle al rëy   muchas de las sus gentes.

2156   Ovieron por ventura   un ome a fallar;
        mostróles una fuente   en un fiero lugar;
        mas dat quién se pudiesse   a ella aplegar:
        avié buenas custodias   que la sabién guardar.

2157   Muchas fieras serpientas   curiavan la fontana,
        onde diz' que non era   la entrada muy sana;
        non serié entradera   a la meredïana.
        ¡Qui quiere se la beva!   – yo non he d'ella gana.

2158   Quand' oyeron las gentes   de la fuent' retraer,
        fueron en tan grant quexa   que se querién perder.
        Movieron a la fuente   por amor de bever;
        non los podié el rëy   por nada retener.

2159   Faziéles la grant cueita   el miedo olvidar;
        fueron todas movidas   por ir al fontanar;
        quando vío el rëy   que podién peligrar,
        óvol' Dïos un seso   bueno a demostrar.

2160   Como era el rëy   sabidor e bien letrado,
        avié muy buen engeño,   maestro bien ortado,
        era büen filósofo,   maestro acabado;
        de todas las naturas   era bien decorado.

2152	Zoilus found under a stone a tiny pool:
	it scarcely filled a small cap with clean water;
	he gave it all to the King, and kept not a sip:
	the young boy was doing him no mean service.
2153	The King, when he saw it, began to laugh,
	and tipped it onto the ground, not wanting to sip.
	He said, "With my vassals do I desire to die,
	and when they are dead I have no wish to live."
2154	His people took great delight in this act
	and were just as comforted as by a good drink,
	all saying, "May God give strength to the King,
	who knows how to stay so loyal to his vassals."
2155	At this point they came across a mass of noxious snakes,
	some that had stings and others with vicious bites;
	some flew through the air, others slithered on their stomachs;
	many of the King's people did they harm.
2156	By good fortune they managed to find a man
	who showed them a spring in an unreachable place;
	but, even if someone were able to reach it,
	it had efficient guardians well able to protect it.
2157	Many fierce serpents were guarding the spring,
	wherefore they say that the entrance was not safe.
	At midday it would not be possible to enter –
	whoever wants to may drink it; I have no wish to do so!
2158	When Alexander's people heard tell of the spring,
	they were so troubled that they wished to be lost.
	They rushed towards the spring in their desire to drink;
	there was no way that the King could hold them back.
2159	Their desperation made them forget their fear
	and they had all set off towards the fount.
	When the King saw that they might be in danger,
	God came to reveal a shrewd plan to him.
2160	As the King was a man of knowledge and learning,
	of great intellect, too, and was a fine scholar,
	he was a good philosopher, his studies extensive,
	and he was well endowed with every quality.

2161 Sabié de las serpientas que traen tal manera
que al ome desnudo todas le dan carrera;
non avrién mayor miedo de una grant foguera;
en escripto yaz' esto; es cosa verdadera.

2162 Mandó el rey a todos tollerse los vestidos;
paráronse en carnes, como fueron naçidos.
Las serpientas davan silvos, muy malos percodidos;
teniénse por forçadas, fazién grandes ruïdos.

2163 El consejo del rëy de Dios fue embïado,
fue el pueblo guarido, de la sed terminado;
tovieron su carrera, qual avién empeçado;
fue tenido el rëy por ome más senado.

2164 Ovieron en un río amargo a venir;
non leemos su nombre, non vos lo sé dezir;
ancho era e fondo, non lo podién troçir;
todos pidién la muerte, non les querie venir.

2165 Yazién a todas partes, por todas las riberas,
montes grandes e fieros, de fieras cañaveras;
crïavan muchas bestias, de diversas maneras,
con quien ovieron muchas faziendas cabdelleras.

2166 Dieron salto en ellos unos mures granados;
eran los maleditos suzios e enconados;
tamaños como vulpes, los dientes regañados.
Los que prendién en carne luego eran librados.

2167 Ovieron los cavallos el miedo a sentir;
con coçes e con palmas tornaron a ferir;
fizieron los sin grado derramar e fuïr;
non osaron ningunos contra ellos sallir.

2168 Desent' salleron puercos de los cañaverales
que avién los colmillos mayores que cobdales;
a diestro e siniestro davan colpes mortales;
dañaron más de treinta, de prínçipes cabdales.

2169 Ovieron los maguera en cabo a vençer;
fizieron los fuïr, fuérons' a esconder;
si, por pecados malos, quisiessen contender,
ovieran se los griegos en cuita a veer.

2161	He knew about snakes that they had such a nature that they all make way for a man who is naked; they would have no more fear of a roaring fire – this lies in writing; what I say is true.
2162	The King ordered them all to take off their clothes and they stripped as naked as the day they were born. The snakes were hissing with evil and venom, and making a great din, knowing they were beaten.
2163	The advice of the King had been sent by God; the people had been saved, and released from thirst. They continued on their way as they had begun and the King was held a man of the greatest wisdom.
2164	They came to arrive at a hostile river; we can nowhere read its name, so this I cannot tell you. It was wide and deep and they could not cross; they all begged for death but it would not come.
2165	Everywhere, all along the river banks, there lay vast, wild and rough terrain with huge reed-beds, where there were reared many creatures of all kinds, against which they had many fearsome struggles.
2166	There were enormous mice that leapt upon them: the accursed creatures were foul and vicious; the size of foxes, they had their teeth bared, and whoever's flesh they bit was quickly dead.
2167	The horses came also to feel this fear, and went kicking and stamping to strike them; they made them unwillingly scatter and flee, and none of the mice dared emerge against them.
2168	Then there came swine from out of the reed-beds, which had tusks that were longer than a cubit. To the right and the left they struck deadly blows and injured over thirty princes of rank.
2169	Nonetheless, they managed at last to defeat them: the Greeks drove them to flight and they made for cover; had they tried to fight on, through their evil sins, the Greeks would have found themselves in adversity.

2170 A buelta de los puercos, salleron otros bravos;
avién, como conejos, de yus' tierra sus caños;
avié cad' uno d'ellos tres parejos de manos;
por tales dizen mostros los buenos escrivanos.

2171 El medio dia passado, fue la siesta viniendo;
fueron las moscas grandes e las bispas rugiendo;
fueron de fiera guisa las bestïas mordiendo,
tanto que a los omes se ivan cometiendo.

2172 Fueron de fiera guisa las bestias embravidas;
fazién las embravir las amargas feridas,
que eran de agujas tanto de percudidas
semejavan elosnas en alquitrán metidas.

2173 Al que una vegada firién los abejones,
non serié más cuitado si beviesse poçones;
sintién el mal sabor dentro los coraçones;
dizién: "¡Malditos sean atales aguijones!"

2174 Como non eran cosas que pudiessen colpar,
nin les podián foír nin les podián tornar;
ovo un buen consejo el rey a sossacar;
con Dios esso les ovo en cabo a prestar.

2175 Mandó a todos muchas de las cañas prender,
fer grandes manojos, quanto podián tener;
quand' los ovieron presos, mandólos ençender;
ovieron con aquello las moscas a vençer.

2176 De biésperas ayuso, las moscas derramadas,
cuidaron se las gentes seer aseguradas;
vinieron de murçiélagos mucho grandes nuvadas:
avezillas sin pluma, fiera ment' entecadas.

2177 Podién seer tan grandes com' unos gallarones;
alçavan e primián a vezes com' falcones;
davan grandes feridas, ca avién aguijones;
entrávales la ravia bien a los coraçones.

2178 Tornaron a las pajas quando la cueita vieron,
ca entendieron que antes provecho les tovieron;
quedaron los murçiélagos quando aquesto vieron;
las pajas esa noche ençendidas sovieron.

2170	Together with the swine, other fierce beasts emerged which, like rabbits, had their burrows underground, and each one of them had three pairs of hands: on such accounts the noble authors call them monsters.
2171	With midday past, and afternoon's heat approaching, huge flies and wasps went buzzing through the air, with fury did they set themselves upon the beasts, even to the point where these attacked the humans.
2172	The animals were raised to ferocious ire: it was the cruel bites making them irate, for they had stings so laden with poison they seemed like wormwood dipped in tar.
2173	Anyone stung once by the enormous bees would have suffered no more had he drunk poison. They felt the bitter taste deep inside their hearts and said, "Cursed be such hateful stings!"
2174	As these were not creatures that they could strike, they could not flee them or turn and attack, but the King managed to devise a good plan which brought them help in the end, with God's aid.
2175	He bade them all gather a large number of the reeds and bind into bundles all that they could collect. When they had been gathered, he commanded they be burned, and with this they managed to overcome the flies.
2176	After the hour of Vespers, with the flies now scattered, the people thought that they were in safety, but there arrived very great clouds of bats, little birds with no plumage, rife with disease.
2177	In size, they could be as large as a bustard, soaring and falling with a falcon's ease, inflicting grave wounds with the stings that they had; the very hearts of the men were filled with frenzy.
2178	They relit the reeds when they saw the danger, for they realised they brought them help before; when they saw this done the bats stayed away and the reeds were aflame for that night.

2179   De muchas otras bestias   vos podriamos contar
       que ovo Alexandre   en India a fallar;
       mas a esta sazón   queremos las dexar;
       queremos ir a Poro   conseguir e buscar.

2180   Pero de una bestia   vos quiero fer emiente,
       mayor que elefante   e mucho más valiente;
       era de raíz mala   e de mala simiente;
       venié bever al río   quand' el día caliente.

2181   Semejava cavallo   en toda su fechura;
       avié la tiesta negra   como mora madura;
       en medio de la fruente,   en la encrespadura,
       tenié tales tres cuernos   que era grant pavura.

2182   Los griegos de la bestia   ovieron grant pavor,
       mas dioles grant esfuerço   el buen emperador:
       "¡Esforçadvos, amigos!   Avedes buen señor;
       esta mala fantasma   non avrá nul valor."

2183   En la primera muepta   ovieron se guardar,
       mas ovo en la segunda   veint' e çinco matar;
       descalavró çinqüenta   aún a mal contar,
       pero en cabo óvola   el rey a delivrar.

2184   El rëy Alexandre,   guerrero natural,
       plus duro que un fierro   nin que un pedreñal;
       todo, viçio e cueitas,   preçiava por egual,
       ca, fuera por buen preçio,   non dava ren por al.

2185   Con todos los lazerios   nunca podié folgar,
       d'aquí a que se ovo   con Poro a fallar;
       lüego que en Bactra   uviaron assomar
       ellos fueron alegres,   Poro ovo pesar.

2186   Poro, quando los vío   tan irados venir,
       dixo: "¡Estos dïablos   non dubdan de morir!
       Nin serpientes nin omes   non les podrián nozir;
       non somos por a omes   si nos han a guarir."

2187   Movió luego sus gentes   que tenié aguisadas;
       paróseles delante   con sus hazes paradas;
       bien fazién pareçençias   amas a denodadas
       que se avién las treguas   un' a otra echadas.

2179 We could tell you tales of many other creatures
that Alexander was to find in India;
but at this point we want to leave them behind:
we wish to go in pursuit and search of Porus.

2180 But there is one beast I want to mention to you,
larger than an elephant and much more courageous;
it was of evil origin and born of evil seed,
and came to drink at the river in times of great heat.

2181 It resembled a horse in all its appearance,
its head the black colour of a ripened blackberry;
in the middle of its forehead, at the highest point,
it had three such horns as to inspire great terror.

2182 The Greeks were terribly afraid of this beast
but the good Emperor gave them great courage:
"Take heart, my friends, you have a good lord;
this evil apparition will have no strength."

2183 They managed to preserve themselves in the first attack,
but in the second it managed to kill twenty-five men,
splitting open fifty heads, even at a rough count;
but in the end the King managed to defeat it.

2184 King Alexander, a warrior by nature,
and hardier than an iron bar or piece of flint,
all suffering and hardships he valued as the same,
for he cared for nothing but his fine reputation.

2185 With all of his trials, he could never take rest,
from now until he came to track Porus down.
As soon as they managed to reach Bactria's edge
they were filled with joy but Porus was downhearted.

2186 When Porus saw them coming, filled with such rage,
he said, "These devils have no fear of death;
neither serpents nor men could bring them harm
and if our lives are in their hands, we shall not live

2187 At once he sent to battle the men he had ready
and set himself at the front with his columns drawn up.
Both armies put on a good show of hostility
for they had both rejected the chance of a truce.

2188   Los reys tenién sus hazes   firmes e cabdelleras,
       delanteras bien firmes   e buenas costaneras;
       gentes bien acordadas   que moviessen fazeras;
       qui quier' lo entendrié   que lo avién a veras.

2189   Non andavan en medio   nulos entremedianos;
       querién ellos e ellos   livrar lo por las manos;
       semejava lo al   trebejuelos livianos,
       como niños que juegan   pella por los solanos.

2190   El rëy Alexandre   ya los querié ferir,
       mas embïól' Poro   una razón dezir,
       que serié grant daño   tantas gentes morir;
       serié mejor que amos   lo fuessen desortir.

2191   El buen emperador,   que las sierpes domava,
       chico era de cuerpo,   maguer grande andava;
       end' se trevié d'él Poro   como él se asmava,
       mas nol' salló la cosa   como él se cuidava.

2192   Plaçiól' con estas nuevas   al natural guerrero;
       otorgó la batalla   e fue muy plazentero;
       non quiso plazo luengo,   nin dar otro manero.
       Mandó tornar aína   a Poro el trotero.

2193   Embiól' luego dezir   que quando puesto era
       pensasse de venir,   entrasse en carrera,
       ca él non tornarié   nin salirié del era
       fasta que bien oviesse   mondada la çivera.

2194   Poro, quando lo vío,   sallióle al sendero:
       "Digas me," diz', "Taxiello,   mio leal mensajero,
       qué nuevas tú me traes   d'aquel mio contrastero,
       que se preçïa mucho   por muy buen cavallero."

2195   Dixo el mensajero   la palabra çertera:
       "Señor, recabdo traigo,   palabra verdadera:
       el rëy Alexandre   en campo te espera;
       Señor, si por ti finca,   somos en grant dentera."

2196   Poro avié grant cuerpo   e muy grant valentía;
       non yazié en un ome   mayor cavallería;
       cuidó a Alexandre   meter en covardía,
       por ende avié dicho   tan grant sobrançaría.

2188	Both kings had steadfast and powerful columns, with strength in the vanguard and good troops on the flanks, their men well prepared to move forward for battle; anyone would understand they were in earnest.
2189	No intermediaries went between the armies: both sides sought to end this with their own hands; all else seemed to be sport of no consequence, like children playing ball games in the sun.
2190	King Alexander was now keen to strike them but Porus sent out to him to tell him his thoughts, that it would be a great shame for so many men to die: it would be better for the two of them to settle it.
2191	The good Emperor, the man who tamed the snakes, was small in body, though great in bearing; for this reason did Porus dare think to challenge him; but things did not turn out as he expected.
2192	The natural warrior was pleased at this news: he granted the combat with obvious pleasure. He did not want long delay, nor others involved, and bade the messenger go quickly back to Porus.
2193	He sent him the message that, when he was ready, he should ride out and set out on his path, for he would not turn or leave the threshing floor till he had rendered quite separate the wheat from the chaff.
2194	Porus, when he saw him, went out on the path and said, "Tell me, Taxiles, my loyal envoy,* what news you bring me from that opponent of mine, who rates himself highly as an excellent knight."
2195	The messenger gave him an accurate reply: "My lord, I bring an answer, it is the truth: King Alexander waits for you on the field of battle. My lord, if he defeats you, we are in great distress."
2196	Porus, strong of body, was a man of great valour, and no man was richer in the skills of knighthood. It was his intent to intimidate Alexander: and thus had he made such a daring proposal.

2197   Vío que, si tardasse   que le estariá mal;
echó la lança al cuello,   sallió al arenal;
ovieron a caer   entrambos en egual;
plogo a Alexandre,   a Poro otro tal.

2198   Las gentes, por veer   cosa tan missionada,
fazienda tan cabdal,   lucha tan guerreada,
estavan los catando,   cad'un' de su contrada,
ca era grant peligro   e cosa muy pesada.

2199   Cad'un' de su partida   fazién sus oraçiones,
fincavan los inojos,   prometién oblaçiones,
apretavan los puños,   primién los coraçones;
corrién las vivas lágremas   por medio los griñones.

2200   Ya eran ajuntados   amos los reys señeros;
ivan asaborgando   sus cavallos ligeros;
ivan se mesurando   como omes arteros,
ca preçiavan se ambos   por buenos cavalleros.

2201   Tornó Poro de cara   e fuelo a ferir;
entendiólo el otro   e fuelo reçebir;
dieron se tales colpes   al ora de venir
que farién a Sansón   de memoria sallir.

2202   Cad'un' en su derecho,   estos colpes sallidos,
cuitados de los colpes,   maguer eran guarnidos,
entre sus coraçones   ya eran repentidos
por que en tal porfaçio   eran entra metidos.

2203   Amos, uno con otro,   eran mal embargados;
los cavallos e ellos   eran escarmentados;
si fuessen los escudos   de fablar aguisados,
ellos sabrién dezir   los çerteros mandados.

2204   Fueron todas las gentes   de los colpes quexadas;
metieron grandes bozes   amas las albergadas;
querién ferir al çielo,   implién las vallejadas;
andavan por los montes   las bestias espantadas.

2205   Fue con las grandes bozes   Poro mal engañado;
tornó, que catarié   contra el su fonsado.
Alexandre por griegos   non ovo nul cuitado;
travessólo de cuesta;   fue Poro derrocado.

| 2197 | He saw that delay would be bad for him,
set his lance by his neck and rode into the arena.
The two men arrived there at just the same moment:
Alexander was pleased, and Porus just as much. |

| 2198 | The people, to see a confrontation so intense,
a battle so illustrious and a struggle so fierce,
were watching those two men, each from their own side,
for the danger was great and the matter of great moment. |

| 2199 | All the men, on both sides, were in prayer,
on their knees and promising oblations,
clenching their fists and with pounding hearts,
as the tears streamed down through their beards. |

| 2200 | Now the two kings had come together, alone;
they gave free rein to their swift-footed horses,
and weighed each other up, being men of great skill,
for both rated themselves as fine knights. |

| 2201 | Porus turned his head and went to strike his opponent,
and Alexander saw this and went to receive him.
Each dealt the other such blows when they met
as would have made Samson fall from memory. |

| 2202 | Each one for his part, when these blows had been struck,
was troubled by them, in spite of his armour,
within their own hearts they were now feeling regret
that they were embroiled in such a conflict. |

| 2203 | Both of these men were in deep discomfort;
their horses and they had learned a hard lesson;
if their shields had been able to speak out loud,
then they could have told the true story. |

| 2204 | All of the people were anxious with the blows,
and the camps of both men roared loudly;
they sought to strike the sky and fill the valleys with sound,
and up in the hills the beasts were terrified. |

| 2205 | Porus was completely deceived by the cries
and spun round to look upon his army.
Alexander remained unworried by the Greeks,
and ran him through his back; Porus was struck down. |

2206 Quando fue derrocado, compeçó de clamar:
"¡Merçed, rey Alexandre, non me quieras matar!
Tórnome tu vassallo en aqueste lugar;
quiero fer tu mandado, en nada non pecar.

2207 El tu buen cosimente que tú sueles aver,
mucho vales por ello, ¡non lo quieras perder!
Llévame a tu tienda, mándame guareçer;
cúidotelo con Dios aún bien mereçer."

2208 Ovo el rey camiada la mala voluntat;
olvidó el despecho, movióלo p̃iedat;
deçendió del cavallo con grant simpliçidat;
empeçó de dezir vierbo de amistat.

2209 "Poro, oviest' mal seso, feziste grant locura;
de meterte comigo a tan grant aventura;
bien te devriés membrar que diz' la Escriptura,
que desbuelve grant massa poca de levadura.

2210 Deviás me coñoçer e deviás me dubdar;
deviás aver vergüença de comigo te tomar;
qui te dio el consejo non te queriá vengar,
ca non es Alexandre tan rafez de domar."

2211 Respuso cuerda mente Poro, maguer colpado:
"Rëy," diz, "bien entiendo que era engañado;
fasta que vinïesses, bien tenía asmado
que non serié mi par en el mundo fallado.

2212 Mas so d'esta creençia movido e camiado:
si yo era fuerte, con más me so fallado;
qui a Poro creyere non será segurado
que a caer non aya e seer desguardado.

2213 A ti Alexandre, lo quiero esponer:
alto estás agora, en somo del clocher;
non seas segurado que non puedas caer,
ca son fado e viento malos de retener.

2214 Puede qui lo quisiere esto bien escrevir,
de Dario e de Poro enxenplo adozir:
ovieron de grant gloria a cuita venir;
natura es del mundo deçender e sobir."

2206 When he had been brought low, he began to shout:*
"Mercy, King Alexander, do not wish to kill me.
In this very place I will become your vassal;
I wish to do your bidding and fail you in nothing.

2207 The noble compassion you are wont to display,
it brings you great esteem; do not seek to lose it.
Take me to your tent, and bid my wounds be tended.
With God's will, I think I still deserve this of you."

2208 The King had abandoned his cruel intention;
he forgot his rancour and was moved by compassion.
He got down from his horse, the simplest of gestures,
and began to speak to him with words of friendship.

2209 "Your plan was bad, Porus, and you acted in great folly
in setting yourself against me in something so uncertain;
you really ought to have remembered what the Scripture says,
that just a little yeast makes a large amount of dough.

2210 You should have known me and you should have feared me;
you should have felt ashamed to challenge me.
Your advisers did not want to bring you redress,
for Alexander is not so easily tamed."

2211 Porus, though wounded, replied with wisdom:
"My King," he said, "I know well that I was wrong;
until you came, I believed it certain
that my equal would not be found in all the world.

2212 But I have now changed and abandoned that belief,
for if I was very strong I have met one stronger.
Anyone believing Porus will have no conviction
that he is not to fall and be left without protection.

2213 To you, Alexander, do I want to explain this:
you are now on high, at the top of the tower;
but do not be convinced that you cannot fall,
for fate and the wind are hard to hold back.

2214 Anyone who wishes can set this all in writing
and bring forward the examples of Darius and Porus
who had great glory, but were to come to suffer:
it is the nature of the world to rise and fall."

2215 Faziése Alexandre mucho maravillado:
      ome tan mal traído seer tan acordado.
      Asmó que, quando era alegre e pagado,
      de seso e d'esfuerço fue ome acabado.

2216 Fízolo el buen rëy aína guareçer;
      diole mayor emperio que non soliá aver;
      fueron tales amigos quales devián seer;
      otras cosas retraen que non son de creer.

2217 Avié toda su cosa el rey bien acabada;
      avié, maguer lazrado, a India sobjudgada;
      de los regnos de Asia non le fincava nada,
      fuera una çibdat que estava alçada.

2218 Sudraca era villa firme e bien poblada;
      yazié en lugar plano, mas era bien çercada.
      Cogió un mal enfoto: fizo jura sagrada
      que nunca de los griegos fuesse asseñorada.

2219 Tovo Alexandre que era grant escarnio
      ques' tovies' una villa más que Poro e Dario.
      Dixo: "Prometo e juro por éste mío gladio
      que non dexe en ella calleja nin nul barrio."

2220 Fue luego a lidiarla con muchas algarradas;
      çercóles las sallidas, tajóles las entradas;
      mas, como eran las torres firmes e bien labradas,
      sofrieron las feridas, estavan reveladas.

2221 Las puertas eran firmes, non las podién quebrantar;
      la paret era dura, non la podién cavar;
      nin la podién prender, nin la podién dexar;
      ovo bien quinze días en esso a durar.

2222 Dixo el rey por esto: "Non pued' assí seer."
      Mandó las escaleras en el muro poner;
      quiso la delantera él mismo prender;
      óvose en las menas someras a meter.

2223 Ya era el buen rëy en la tapia somera;
      subié en pues él mucha gente ligera.
      De la grant pesadura fallió la escalera;
      cayeron todos yuso, quebró mucha mollera.

2215	Alexander was struck with great wonder at this, that a man in such dire straits showed such wisdom. He reckoned that, when he was happy and content, he was a man of consummate wisdom and valour.
2216	The good King saw that he was quickly healed and gave him an empire richer than before, and they were good friends, just as it should be; other tales are told, which beggar belief.*
2217	The King had finely concluded all his business: although he suffered hardships, he had India subdued; nothing did he lack from all the kingdoms of Asia, except one city that had risen up against him.
2218	Sudracae was a powerful city, filled with people,* which lay on a plain but was ringed with strong walls. It became overconfident and swore an oath that it would never be mastered by the Greeks.
2219	Alexander took it as a great act of mockery that a city thought itself above Porus and Darius. He said, "I promise and swear by this sword of mine that no street or district shall I leave to stand within."
2220	He went at once to attack it with many siege engines; he surrounded their exits and cut off their ways in, but as the towers were solid and firmly constructed they bore the blows well, proving firm in defiance.
2221	The gates were sturdy and could not be broken down; the walls were unyielding and could not be undermined. They could not take the city nor abandon it, and so it remained for a full fifteen days.
2222	At this, the King said: "It cannot be so." He ordered the ladders to be placed against the wall; he wished to be the one to take the lead himself, and he managed to reach the highest battements.
2223	Now the good King was on the highest wall, many agile men climbing up behind him, but their weight was so great that the ladder was broken: they all crashed down, and many heads cracked in two.

2224 El rey fincó señero   en somo del castiello;
     sedié entre dos menas   en angosto portiello;
     tenié en el escudo   fito mucho quadriello,
     mas era la loriga   leal e el capiello.

2225 Los vassallos veyán   al señor mal seer;
     nol podián por manera   ninguna acorrer.
     Non tenián escaleras,   nin las podián aver;
     non se sabián por guisa   ninguna componer.

2226 Todos dizián: "Señor,   valer non te podemos;
     mas merçed te pedimos   los que bien te queremos:
     que salgas contra fuera,   que nos te reçibremos.
     Señor, si tú te pierdes,   nos todos nos perdemos.

2227 Por un mal castillejo   que non vale un figo
     mal es si tú te pierdes   e quantos son contigo."
     Respuso Alexandre: "Pues en esto vos digo:
     qui me da tal consejo   non m'es leal amigo.

2228 Non es pora buen rëy   tal cosa fazedera:
     podiendo entrar dentro   de sallir contra fuera.
     Sea como Dios quiera,   que biva o que muera,
     ca quiero dar batalla   a esta gent' guerrera."

2229 Dio salto en la villa,   su espada en mano;
     fue fiera maravilla   cómo escapó sano,
     mas, com' era en priessa   argudo e liviano,
     cobró en un ratillo   el buen rëy greçiano.

2230 El pueblo de Sudraca   quando fue acordado,
     fue el rey Alexandre   en piedes levantado;
     firieron en él todos   a coto assentado;
     non firrié mas apriessa   pedrisco en tablado.

2231 Estido el buen rëy   como buen sofridor;
     trayé a las vegadas   el braço en derredor;
     al que podié prender   faziél' mala sabor,
     d'éssa lo embïava   por a'l siglo mayor.

2232 Dios e la su ventura   que le quiso prestar,
     vïo un olmo viejo   çerca de sí estar;
     non le podién el tronco   diez omes abraçar;
     fuese a las espaldas   de él ad acostar.

2224	The King was left alone at the top of the castle, between two merlons, in a narrow doorway. A forest of arrows was fixed in his shield, but his coat and cap of mail were intact.
2225	The vassals could see their lord in his plight but had no means of being able to help him: they had no ladders nor could they obtain them. They knew of no way to set right their position.
2226	They all cried to him: "Lord, we cannot help you, but we who love you well do beg your mercy, that you might jump down so that we may receive you: lord, if you are lost, so are we all.
2227	For a wretched little castle that is not worth a fig, it is wrong if you are lost, and all those with you." Alexander replied, "Well, to this I say to you: he who gives me such counsel is no loyal friend.
2228	Such action as this is not fitting for a king, to flee outside when I might go within; let it be as God wills, that I live or die, for I wish to do battle with this warrior people."
2229	He leapt into the city, his sword in his hand; it was a great marvel that he escaped with his life; but as in battle he was sharp and fleet, the good Grecian king was quickly recovered.
2230	By the time that the people of Sudracae had realised, King Alexander was already on his feet. As one man did they all strike him blows: a stone would strike no faster on a target.
2231	The good King showed he was a man of resilience and at times he swung his sword around him; on any he could catch he inflicted deep pain, and with this he dispatched him to the greater world.
2232	Through God and his good fortune, which sought to bring him aid, he saw an old elm tree which stood close at hand. Ten men would not manage to link arms round its trunk. Alexander ran to set his back against the tree.

2233   Como de las espaldas   non avié qué temer,
        podié de los delante   mejor se defender;
        mas tan fiera prïessa   sabién en él poner,
        si çient manos oviesse   avrié pro que veer.

2234   Avié ante sí tantos   de los muertos echados,
        aviélos, maguer solo,   tan fuert' escarmentados,
        semejavan morruques   de çepos arrancados;
        d'apareçer ant'él   non eran osados.

2235   Ya era de la priessa   el rey tan enflaquido,
        aviá de la su fuerça   las tres partes perdido;
        non vinié de ninguna   parte el apellido;
        aviélo su ventura   en fuert' lugar metido.

2236   Vino una saeta   – ¡que sea maledita! –;
        quandos' cató, tenié la   al costado muy fita;
        por poco le fiziera   tal colpe la sagita
        qual fizo Fineás   en la medïanita.

2237   Sallé tanta de sangre,   ca fue grand' el forado,
        que podrié un cavallo   seer bien dessangrado;
        fuera que lo querié   otra guisa el fado,
        de bevir otra mente   non era aguisado.

2238   Quatro de sus vassallos: Timëus el braçero,
        segundo Peucestes,   Leonatus el terçero,
        el quarto fue Astrión,   un mortal cavallero;
        éstos por su ventura   le uviaron primero.

2239   Luego que allegaron,   non se dieron vagar:
        como qui fer lo quiere,   pensaron de dolar;
        fizieron los del rëy   un poquiello redrar;
        ovo ya quantïello   espaçio de folgar.

2240   Si, como eran quatro,   fuessen siete señeros,
        menester non avrié   el rey más compañeros;
        mas los proverbios viejos   siempre son verdaderos:
        que çient lobos rafez   comen a dos corderos.

2241   Lidiaron firme mente   quanto lidiar pudieron;
        por defender su rëy   todo poder metieron;
        mas, que mucho vos digamos,   tanto non contendieron
        que en cabo de cosa   a morir non ovieron.

2233	As he did not have to fear for what was at his back, he could protect himself better from those in front, but they managed to exert on him pressure so intense that had he a hundred hands, he would have used them all.
2234	There were so many dead men laid out before him, whom he, though alone, had taught such a hard lesson, they were like little shoots torn off from the vine and his foes dared not even stand before him.
2235	The King was now so weakened by the combat that he had lost three parts of his strength; from no side came the cry of battle to his aid: his fortune had placed him in a dire spot.
2236	He was struck by an arrow – a curse be upon it! –; when he saw it, it was fixed deep in his side. The arrow very nearly struck him such a blow as Phinehas' lance had dealt the Midianite.*
2237	So much blood flowed out, for the wound was deep, as would have left a horse quite bloodless. Had it not been that fate's will was different, he could not otherwise have continued his life.
2238	Four of his vassals, the warrior Timaeus,* second Peucestas, and third Leonnatus, with Ariston the fourth – a knight of deadly skill –, to his good fortune, these were first to bring him aid.
2239	As soon as they reached him, they did not delay but went to strike the enemy with all their hearts, driving them back a little way from the King: he now had a small amount of breathing space.
2240	If there had been just seven as those four were, the King would have needed no other companions; but the old sayings never fail to speak the truth: that a hundred wolves eat two lambs with ease.
2241	They fought staunchly for as long as they could fight and set all their strength to defending their King, but however much we tell you, they could not strive enough that in the end they did not come to meet their deaths.

2242 Lëy es bien usada   que debda de señor
non es en el siglo premia   tamaña nin mayor,
ond' ovieron los griegos   de retrecha pavor;
metiéronse a muerte,   olvidaron temor.

2243 Mientre los cuatro prínçipes   la grant priessa les dieron,
los otros en el muro   toda vía rompieron;
entraron a grant priessa   desque lugar ovieron;
a los que alcançavan   parçir non les quisieron.

2244 Non yaz' ningunt provecho   en alongar razón:
fue el rey acorrido   a estraña sazón;
fueron los de Sudraca   feridos a perdón;
non dexaron a vida   nin muger nin varón.

2245 Quando todo fue fecho,   la cosa aguisada,
non fallavan al rëy,   podién d'él saber nada;
era en fiera cueita   la greçisca mesnada:
tenién que su fazienda   era toda librada.

2246 Pero tanto ovieron   contender e buscar
fasta que lo ovieron   en cabo a fallar;
bien los veyá el rëy   mas non podiá llamar,
ca estava en ora   que se querié passar.

2247 Sacaron lo en braços   a un lugar çerçado,
ca es grant folgamiento   el çierço en verano;
él, maguer non favlava,   faziéles con la mano
que non oviessen cueita,   ca nunca fue más sano.

2248 Quando fueron catando   entre las guarniçiones,
fallaron de la sangre   muchos de cuajadones;
quebraron les a todos   luego los coraçones;
entró mal cuer de salto   entre los sus varones.

2249 Ovieron en todo esto   a fallar la ferida;
fallaron la saeta   que yazié escondida;
prometieron atanto   que non avié medida
al que les sopiés' dar   consejo de guarida.

2250 Cristóbolus, un mege,   era bien coñoscido.
Dixo, "Yo lo daré   a ocho dias guarido;
mas dubdo por que veo   que es muy enflaquido;
témome a ventura   de seer mal caído."

2242	It is a recognised law that a debt to one's lord is equalled or exceeded by no worldly obligation, on which account the Greeks were in dread of reproach and gave themselves up to death, their fear forgotten.
2243	While the four princes were waging battle so fierce, the others were still trying to break through the wall; when they had a place to do so, they rushed to come inside, and those that they caught they had no desire to spare.
2244	There lies no advantage in extending the account: the King was brought help at a crucial moment; the people of Sudracae were struck down, begging mercy, and the Greeks left alive neither women nor men.
2245	When everything was done and it had all reached its close, they could not find their king or learn anything about him. The army of the Greeks was in deep distress at this, feeling that their battle was completely lost.
2246	But so much did the Greeks strive and search until at last they managed to discover him. The King could see them clearly but could not call out, for he was now on the very cusp of death.
2247	They took him in their arms to a balmy space, for in summer, the north wind gives pleasant relief. Although he could not speak, he gestured with his hand not to be concerned, for he had never been more healthy.
2248	As they were looking at Alexander's armour, they found a large amount of clotted blood; their hearts were all instantly shattered with grief, and a shudder of fear ran through his men.
2249	Eventually they managed to find the wound and discovered the arrow lying hidden. They promised to give a reward without measure to the person who could tell them how to save him.
2250	Critobulus, a doctor who was well known,* said, "I will find a cure for him within eight days, but I am afraid, for I see him much weakened and I fear, by ill fortune, a very bad outcome."

2251 Cobró el rey su lengua e todo su sentido;
cató diestro e siniestro con su ojo vellido;
entendió que Cristóbolus estava desmarrido;
díxol' que semejava villano descosido.

2252 Díxol' que non dubdasse de fer su maestría,
que non morrié por esso antes del puesto día.
"Señor", dixo Cristóbolus, "volenter lo faría,
mas si a ti plaziesse una cosa querría:

2253 el fierro yaze fondo, en aviesso lugar;
la plaga es angosta, non lo podriá tirar;
avemos en la carne un poco a tajar,
que podamos el podre e el fierro sacar.

2254 Rëy, es buen consejo que te deves ligar,
que quando te tajare non te puedas tresnar,
ca podriá con la tresna ome rafez errar;
podrié poco de yerro la fazienda dañar."

2255 Diz' el rëy: "Seméjame cosa desaguisada
de yazer rëy preso con su barba ligada;
terniá mi fazienda toda por mal honrada
si mi poder perdiesse sola una vegada.

2256 Que quiere que tú fagas, bien lo cuido sofrir;
que tajes e que quemes, non me verás bollir.
Cristóbolus, ¿qué dubdas? ca rafez so de guarir;
avrás buen gualardón de mí a reçebir."

2257 El mege fue alegre, del rey assegurado;
buscó unas navajas de buen fierro temprado;
tajó a todas partes, enxampló el forado;
sacó fuera el fierro que yazié afondado.

2258 Sofriólo bien el rëy; estido bien quedado;
si yaziesse durmiendo non serié más pagado;
nin en nariz rugada nin en rostro camiado,
nunca lo entendió nul ome por cuitado.

2259 Ovo atán grant cueita, pero, a devenir,
que ovo de su seso sin grado a sallir;
cayó amorteçido, ovo a enflaquir,
tanto que a las bozes non sabié recodir.

2251	The King recovered his speech and all his wits and looked to left and right with his handsome eyes. He understood that Critobulus was distressed and told him he resembled a worthless, fearful man.
2252	He told him not to hesitate to use his skill for this would not kill him before the appointed day. "My lord," said Critobulus, "I would gladly do so, but if you were willing I would like one thing.
2253	The iron lies deep, and in an awkward place; the wound is narrow and I could not remove it; we have to make a small cut into your body to take out the rotten flesh and the iron.
2254	My King, it is sound advice that you must be bound so that, when I cut you, you cannot toss and turn, for a man could easily err with the writhing, and a small error could spoil the operation."
2255	The King said, "It seems an inappropriate thing for a king to lie captive with his person bound; I would hold that dishonour had been cast on all my deeds if I lost my power on one single occasion.
2256	Whatever you may do, I am sure I can endure it; whether you cut or you burn, you will not see me thrash. Why do you waver, Critobulus? I am easy to cure. You will come to receive a fine reward from me."
2257	The doctor was contented, reassured by the King, and he looked for knives of finely tempered iron. He cut all around and he widened the hole and extracted the iron which lay deep inside.
2258	The King endured it well and he remained quite still; he could not have been more still had he lain in sleep. Neither in a wrinkled nose nor any sign on his face could any man ever see that he was suffering.
2259	However, there was such great torment to come that against his will he came to fall from consciousness: he slumped back as if dead, losing all his strength, such that he could not reply to what was said to him.

2260 Fue por la albergada   el planto levantado;
      todos tenién del rëy   que era ya passado;
      quánta fue la tristiçia nunca serié asmado
      si non fuesse de ome   quel' oviesse provado.

2261 Cueita de buen señor, ¿qui la puede asmar?
      Quien una vez la gosta   siempre ha qué plorar;
      qui non la ha provada   devié a Dios rogar
      que nunca gela dexe   en esti mundo provar.

2262 El maestro al rëy   sópolo bien guardar;
      púsol' buenos emplastos   por la dolor temprar.
      Quiso Dios que la cosa   le ovo a prestar;
      con la merçed de Dios   ovo a mejorar.

2263 Quando vieron que era   el rey ya mejorado,
      el planto e el duelo   fue en gozo tornado;
      el que anda en mar   perdido e lazrado
      non serié más alegre   quando fues' arribado.

2264 Fue a pocos de días   el rëy bien guarido;
      demostrólo a todos   por seer más creído;
      estonz' dixieron todos: "Señor, seas gradido,
      que fezist' a Cristóbolus   maestro tan complido."

2265 El ome, qual vezado,   se veza a prender,
      si de mucho andar   si de mucho yazer;
      tómalo en natura,   quiere esso tener;
      todos biven en esso,   segund mi pareçer.

2266 El rëy Alexandre,   en vida aventurado,
      com' de chiqueza fue   de lazerio usado,
      aún sano non era   nin el colpe çerrado;
      por que non guerreava   estava enojado.

2267 Avié en essa quexa   muy grant mal enconía
      ond' avié grant pesar   toda su compañía;
      como non era sana   aún la maletía,
      tenién por aventura   que farié recaída.

2268 Tod' era ya guisado: naves e marineros,
      bateles e galeas   e conduchos pleneros.
      Poro e Abisario,   dos rëys cabdelleros,
      éssos avién de ir   en los más delanteros.

2260	The weeping spread throughout the camp of the Greeks, as everyone thought that the King was now dead. The strength of the sorrow could never be imagined except by a man who had experienced it there.
2261	The grief for a good lord – who can imagine it? Whoever tastes it once will weep for ever; the man who has not felt it should offer prayers to God that He will never let them endure it in this world.
2262	The master knew well how to care for the King and applied good dressings to ease his pain; it was God's will that the treatment prove of benefit, and with God's mercy he managed to recover.
2263	When they saw that the King had recovered the weeping and grief turned to joy; the man who sails the seas, lost and wretched, would be no happier on reaching land.
2264	Within just a few days the King had been cured: he showed this to everyone in order to convince them; and then they all said, "Lord, thanks be to You for making Critobulus so accomplished a master."
2265	Man grows accustomed to acting by his habit, whether to make great travels or lie much in repose; he chooses it by his nature and this is his desire; all men live by this pattern, as it seems to me.
2266	King Alexander, an adventurer in life, as from childhood he was accustomed to hardship, was not yet healthy and the wound had not closed, but he was now fretting because he was not at war.
2267	That anxiety produced very great ill-temper, from which his whole company felt deep sorrow; as he had not yet recovered from his illness, they thought there was a chance of a relapse.
2268	All now was ready, ships and their sailors, boats and galleys and plentiful supplies; Porus and Abisares, two powerful kings –* these men were to travel in the ships at the head.

2269   Asmava el buen ome   atravessar la mar,
         a la que nunca pudo   ome cabo fallar
         e buscar otras gentes   de otro semejar.
         por sossacar manera   nueva de guerrear;

2270   saber el sol dó naçe,   e el Nilo dó mana,
         el mar qué fuerça trae   quandol' fiere ventana;
         maguer avié grant seso,   acuçia sobejana,
         semejava en esto   una grant valitana.

2271   La gent' de Alexandre   era müy cuitada
         por que prendié carrera   que nunca fue usada;
         la plaga que non era   aún bïen sanada;
         por esto era en cueita   toda la su mesnada.

2272   Prisieron su consejo   todos los mayorales;
         dixeron le al rëy   palabras comunales:
         "Señor, mal nos semeja   buscar cosas atales,
         las que nunca pudieron   fallar omes carnales.

2273   Si de nuestro lazerio   tú non has nul cuidado,
         miémbrete de ti mismo   cóm' fuste mal colpado;
         si fazes recaída,   tente por afollado;
         non te valdrá un figo   quanto que has lazrado.

2274   La tu fiera cobdiçia   non te dexa folgar;
         señor eres del mundo,   non te puedes fartar.
         Nin podemos saber   nin podemos asmar
         qué cosa es aquésta   que quieres ensayar.

2275   Pero en todo esto   de ti non nos tememos;
         sól' que tú seas sano,   todo lo vençeremos;
         de bestias nin de sierpes   nos dubdo non avremos;
         a ti teniendo çerca,   a todo nos trevemos.

2276   Pero tan fieras cosas   sabes tú ensayar
         que non te podriá ome   ninguno aguardar;
         las cosas non recuden   todas a un lugar;
         el ome sabidor   deve se mesurar.

2277   Si meter te quisieres   en las ondas del mar,
         o en una foguera   te quieres afogar
         o de una grant peña   te quieres despeñar,
         en qual se quiere d'ellas   lo avrás a lazrar.

2269	The good man was intending to cross over the sea, of which none had ever managed to reach the far shore, and to seek out people of a different nature to devise a new way of waging war;
2270	and to learn where the sun rises and whence the Nile springs and what force the sea has when whipped up by the wind; although of great intelligence and exceptionally astute, in these plans he seemed a man of great presumption.
2271	Alexander's people were deeply anxious,* for he was taking a path never trodden before; he was yet to recover fully from his wound and for this reason his whole army was troubled.
2272	The senior commanders all met in council and spoke to the King with words that they shared: "It seems to us wrong, lord, to search for such things, as no men of flesh ever managed to find.
2273	If you have no concern for the suffering we bear, be mindful of yourself and your grave wound. Should you have a relapse, think yourself destroyed, and all that you have borne will not avail you a fig.
2274	Your burning desire does not let you rest: you are lord of the world and cannot be sated. We cannot know and we cannot imagine what thing that is which you wish to attempt.
2275	But with all of this, we have no fear on your account; provided you are healthy, we shall conquer all; we shall not be afraid of beasts or of serpents; having you close, we dare do anything.
2276	But you are prepared to undertake such strange things that no man would be able to protect you; things do not all come back to one place, and the man of wisdom must show restraint.
2277	If you wish to plunge into the waves of the sea or you wish to make yourself choke among flames or you wish to hurl yourself from a lofty crag, in any of these you will have to suffer.

2278 Los rëys has conquistos, las sierpes has domadas,
      las montañas rompidas, las bestias quebrantadas;
      quieres bolver contienda con las ondas iradas;
      de trebejo nin justa non son ellas usadas.

2279 Non es honra nin preçio pora ome honrado
      meters' a aventura en lugar desaguisado;
      non li cayera preçio a Éctor el famado
      de ir se abraçar con un puerco lodado."

2280 Quando ovo el prólogo Craterus acabado,
      otorgó Tolomeus que dezié aguisado;
      fue en essa boz todo el pueblo acordado:
      "¡Señor, por Dios que finques, fasta que seas sanado!

2281 Lo que dixo Craterus todos telo dezimos;
      ¡En pesar non te caya! Grant merçed te pedimos.
      Tú cata dó nos llevas, a quál siglo imos,
      ca nos a ti catamos e tu señal seguimos."

2282 Fue el rey alegre, tóvolo en grant grado;
      entendió de sus gentes que era much' amado.
      Respondióles fermoso, ca era bien lenguado;
      farié, si al fiziesse, tuerto e grant pecado.

2283 "Parientes e amigos, assaz lo demostrades,
      en dichos e en fechos, que mucho me amades;
      siempr' assí lo fezistes e oy lo afirmades;
      si non, non lazrariades assí como lazrades.

2284 Gradesco esto mucho que agora dixiestes,
      mas mucho más gradesco lo que siempre feziestes;
      los fijos e las mugeres por mí los olvidestes;
      nunca lo que yo quise non lo contradixiestes.

2285 Dexastes vuestras casas e vuestras heredades;
      passados ha diez años que comigo lazrades;
      mucho vos ha costado e cansados andades;
      por mi serviçio nada vos non menoscabades.

2286 Maguer a mí servistes quand' a Poro domastes,
      quand' a Dario vençistes e las bestias rancastes,
      la estoria troyana con esto la çegastes;
      honrastes a vos mismos, nuestro preçio alçastes.

Book of Alexander

2278 You have conquered kings and mastered serpents,
cracked open mountains and left beasts broken.
You now want to struggle with the angry waves
which are not used to sport or to jousting.

2279 It is no glory or fame for a man of honour
to give himself to fortune in an ill-fitting place;
the illustrious Hector would have won no glory
by going to wrestle with a muddy swine."

2280 When Craterus had brought this speech to an end,
Ptolemy agreed that he had spoken wisely
and the whole people were united in these words:
"Lord, by God may you stay until recovered!

2281 What Craterus has said do we all say to you;
do not be annoyed – we beg of you great favour!
Consider where you take us and to what world we go,
for we look to you and we follow your ensign."

2282 The King was filled with joy and took it in good heart:
he realised that he was well loved by his people.
His answer was handsome, for he was an eloquent man;
otherwise, he would have done wrong and greatly sinned.

2283 "My kinsmen and my friends, you show well enough
in words and in deeds that you love me from the heart;
you have always done so and today you affirm it;
otherwise, you would not bear the suffering you do.

2284 I am very grateful for what you have just said
but I am much more so for what you have always done.
For me you have put children and wives from your mind
and you have never contradicted what I sought.

2285 You have left behind you your homes and your inheritance
and for the past ten years you have suffered with me;
it has cost you dear and you are now exhausted
and in my service you have left nothing undone.

2286 Although you served me when you defeated Porus,
when you conquered Darius and overcame the beasts,
with this too you outshone the story of Troy,*
you won honour for yourselves and raised our reputation.

Libro de Alexandre

2287 Fazedes grant derecho   si de mí vos temedes,
      por algund mal achaque   que perder me podriedes;
      mas yo en mí non tengo   el cuer que vos tenedes;
      otro esfuerço traigo   el que vos non sabedes.

2288 Non conto yo mi vida   por años nin por días
      mas por buenas faziendas   e por cavallerías.
      Non escrivió Omero   en sus alegorías
      los meses de Aquiles   mas las barraganías.

2289 Dizen las escripturas   – yo leí el tratado –
      que siete son los mundos   que Dïos ovo dado;
      de los siete, el uno   abés lo he domado;
      por esto yo non conto   que nada he ganado.

2290 Quanto avemos visto   antes nos lo sabiemos;
      si al non apresiéssemos   en balde nos viviemos;
      por Dario e por Poro   que vençidos avemos,
      yo por esto non cuido   que grant cosa fiziemos.

2291 Embiónos Dios por esto   en aquestas partidas:
      por descobrir las cosas   que yazen sofondidas;
      cosas sabrán por nos   que non serían sabidas;
      serán las nuestras nuevas   en cántico metidas.

2292 Los omes que non saben   buen preçio aprender
      esto prenden por gloria: en balde se yazer;
      mas díz'lo el maestro,   mándalo retener:
      qui prodeza quisiere,   afán deve prender.

2293 Con todos vos a una   queriéndome seguir,
      buscaré los antípodes,   quiérolos conquerir;
      éstos son so la tierra,   com' oyemos dezir,
      mas yo non lo afirmo,   ca cuido de mentir.

2294 Por que vos me querades   en cara falleçer
      – lo que yo nunca cuido   oír nin veer –
      aquí son las mis manos   que me suelen valer,
      que se saben en priessa   fiera mente rebolver."

2295 Aún avié el rëy   mucho más que fablar;
      metieron todos bozes,   fiziéronlo callar:
      "Señor," dixeron todos,   "piensa de cavalgar;
      todos te seguiremos   por tierra e por mar."

2287	You are right if you feel fear on my account, that you may lose me by some ill occurrence, but I do not have within me the same heart as you. I have a different strength, and one you do not know.
2288	I do not count my life in years or in days but by great deeds and acts of chivalry. Homer did not set down in his allegories the months Achilles lived, but his acts of valour.
2289	So say the texts – I have read the treatise –:* that the worlds that God created are seven; of the seven, scarcely one have I conquered and therefore I count my gains as nothing.
2290	All that we have seen, we already knew before; if we learn nothing new, we have lived our lives in vain. As to Darius and Porus, whom we have defeated, I believe we have achieved nothing special.
2291	It was for this purpose that God sent us to these regions, in order to discover the things which lie buried; through us will things be known that would not have been discovered; the tale of our exploits will be recorded in song.
2292	Men who know not how to achieve great renown think that this is glory: to lie in idleness; but the master says, and commands us to remember, that only through effort can valour be achieved.
2293	With all of you wanting to follow me as one, I shall seek out the Antipodes – I want to conquer them;* they lie beneath the earth, or so we have heard tell, but I do not assert this, for I believe I might lie.
2294	Even if it happens that you still let me down – which I believe that I will never hear or see – here are my hands, which are wont to bring me help, and know how to act strongly in a difficult moment."
2295	The King still had a great deal more to say, but they all broke in and made him fall silent. "Lord," they all said, "take the decision to ride; we shall all follow you over land and sea.

2296   Mandó luego el rëy   los fuegos ençender,
fer fumos, como era   costumbre, de mover;
pensaron luego todos   las tiendas de coger,
aguisar sus faziendas,   sus troxas componer.

2297   Entraron por las naves,   pensaron de andar;
el mar era pagado,   non podié mejorar;
los vientos non podián   más derechos estar;
ivan e non sabián   escontra quál lugar.

2298   Aguisaron sus piértagas   bien derechas e sanas;
descogieron las áncoras,   alçaron las ventanas;
Eran con el buen viento   las naves muy livianas;
las gentes por el tiempo   tenién se por loçanas.

2299   Fueron a poca d'ora   en alta mar entrados;
andudieron grant tiempo   radíos e errados;
eran los marineros   fierament' embargados,
ca non sabián guïar   do non eran usados.

2300   Como rafez se suelen   los vientos demudar,
camióse el oraje,   ensañóse la mar;
empeçaron las ondas   a premir e alçar;
non las podiá el rëy   por armas amansar.

2301   Quanto ivan las naves   más a dentro entrando,
ívanse los peligros   tanto mas embargando.
"Señor," dizián las gentes,   "tanto irás buscando
que lo que te dixiemos   ir lo as ensayando."

2302   Todos estos peligros   non lo podián domar;
non se querié por ellos   repentir nin tornar.
Fizo Dïos grant cosa   en tal ome crïar
que non lo podián ondas   iradas espantar.

2303   Passó muchas tempestas   con su mala porfidia,
que las nuves avién   e los vientos enbidia;
dizién los marineros: "¿Cómol' fincara India
a esta cosa mala   que con las mares lidia?"

2304   Ulixes en diez años   que andudo errado
non víó más peligros   nin fue más ensayado,
pero, quando fue fecho   e todo delibrado,
salló como caboso   el rey aventurado.

2296	At once, the King ordered that the fires be lit and smoke be sent up, as was their custom, to move out. They all started instantly to take down their tents, make their preparations and load up their belongings.
2297	They embarked on the ships and began to sail. The sea was calm – it could have been no better. The winds could not have been more at their backs; they sailed, but knew not their destination.
2298	They made ready their oars, quite straight and firm, hauled in the anchors and hoisted the sails; with the following wind, the ships moved quickly and with such weather the men felt at ease.
2299	In just a little time they had reached the high sea; their course for a long time was errant and mistaken: the sailors found themselves in serious troubles for they could not navigate through unknown seas.
2300	As the winds so often change with great speed, the weather was transformed and the sea grew stormy and the waves began to surge up and plummet down; the King was not able to bring calm by force of arms.
2301	As the ships gradually came further out to sea the dangers grew steadily ever more hostile. "Lord," said the men, "you will go so far in searching that you will experience the things of which we told you."
2302	All of these dangers could not overwhelm him: they did not make him desire to repent or turn back. God did a great thing in creating such a man that he could not be frightened by the angry waves.
2303	He endured many storms through his rash insistence for he was envied by the clouds and the winds. The sailors said: "How could India have withstood this terrible force that fights with the seas?"
2304	Ulysses in the ten years that he wandered did not see more dangers or suffer more trials; but when it was done and everything was settled, the adventurous king emerged a noble hero.

2305 Una fazaña suelen las gentes retraer;
non yaze en escripto, es grave de creer;
si es verdat o non yo non he y qué fer,
maguer non la qüiero en olvido poner.

2306 Dizen que por saber qué fazién los pescados,
cómo bivién los chicos entre los más granados,
fizo arca de vidrio, con muzos bien çerrados,
metióse él de dentro con dos de sus crïados.

2307 Éstos fueron catados de todos los mejores,
por tal que non oviessen dono los traïdores,
ca que él o que ellos avrién aguardadores
non farién a su guisa los malos reboltores.

2308 Fue de buena betubne la cuba aguisada;
fue con buenas cadenas bien presa e calçada;
fue con priegos bien firmes a las naves pregada,
que fondir nos' podiesse e estoviés' colgada.

2309 Mandó que lo dexassen quinze días folgar;
las naves, con tod' esto, pensassen de andar;
assaz podrié en esto saber e mesurar
e meter en escripto los secretos del mar.

2310 La cuba fue echada en que el rey yazié;
a los unos pesava, a los otros plazié;
bien cuidavan algunos que nunca end' saldrié,
mas destajado era que en mar non morrié.

2311 Andava el buen rëy en su casa çerrada;
sedié grant coraçon en angosta posada.
Veyé toda la mar de pescados poblada;
non es bestia 'nel siglo que non fues' y trobada.

2312 Non bive en el mundo ninguna crïatura
que non cría la mar semejante figura;
traen enemistades entre sí por natura;
los fuertes a los flacos danles mala ventura.

2313 Estonçes vio el rëy en aquellas andadas
cómo echan los unos a los otros çeladas.
Dizié que ende fueran presas e sossacadas;
fueron desent' acá en el siglo usadas.

2305	Of one great exploit do people often tell* – it lies not in writing and is hard to believe –; if it is true or false I cannot determine, though I do not wish to let it be forgotten.
2306	They say that, to learn the activities of the fish, and how the small ones lived among those of greater size, he had a glass container made with tightly sealed entries, and went inside with two men of his household.
2307	These were selected from all the best men, that traitors might have no opportunity; for since both he and they would have protectors, those who sought trouble would not achieve their purpose.
2308	The container was coated with good bitumen and was fastened and tied with strong chains. It was secured to the ships with solid fixings so that it could not sink but stay suspended.
2309	He bade them let him stay there for fifteen days and that the ships should now set off to sail; thus he could well enough determine and measure and set down in writing the secrets of the sea.
2310	The container was cast overboard with the King inside: some it filled with sorrow, and others with joy. Some did not think that he would ever emerge from there, but it was ordained that in the sea he would not die.
2311	The good king was enclosed in his dwelling; his large heart was in just a small home. He could see all the sea inhabited with fish; there was no creature of the world not present.
2312	There is no living thing that exists in the world that the sea creates no image to resemble; there are hostilities among them by their nature and the strong bring ill fortune to the weak.
2313	Then the King saw, while he was on those travels, how some of them were laying traps for others; he said that thence had come tricks and deceptions that were used thereafter in the world of men.

2314   Tanto se acogián   al rëy los pescados
        como si los oviesse   por armas sobjudgados;
        vinién fasta la cuba,   todos cabez' colgados;
        tremién todos ant'él   como moços mojados.

2315   Jurava Alexandre   por el su diestro lado
        que nunca fue de omes   mejor acompañado;
        de los pueblos del mar   tóvose por pagado;
        contava que avié   grant imperio ganado.

2316   Otra fazaña vío   en essos pobladores:
        vío que los mayores   comién a los menores;
        los chicos a los grandes   tenién los por señores;
        maltrayán los más fuertes   a los que son menores.

2317   Diz' el rey: "Sobervia   es en todos lugares;
        es fuerça en la tierra,   e dentro en los mares;
        las aves, esso mismo,   non se catan por pares.
        ¡Dios confonda tal viçio   que tien' tantos lugares!

2318   Naçió entre los ángeles,   fizo muchos caer;
        derramó por tierra,   dioles Dios grant poder;
        la mesura non puede   su derecho aver;
        ascondió su cabeça,   non osa pareçer.

2319   Qui más puede más faze,   non de bien más de mal;
        qui más ha más quïere,   muere por ganar al;
        non verié de su grado   ninguno su egual;
        ¡mal pecado, ninguno   non es a Dios leal!

2320   Las aves e las bestias,   los omes, los pescados,
        todos son entre sí   a bandos derramados;
        de viçio e de sobervia   son todos entecados;
        los flacos de los fuertes   andan desafiados."

2321   Si, como lo sabié   el rëy bien asmar,
        quisiesse a sí mismo   a derechas judgar,
        bien devié un poquillo   su lengua refrenar,
        que tan fieras grandías   non quisiesse bafar.

2322   De su grado el rëy   más oviera estado,
        mas a sus crïazones   faziéseles pesado;
        temiendo ocasión   que suel' venir privado,
        sacáronlo bien ante   del término passado.

| 2314 | So much did the fish gather round the King
it was as if he had subdued them by arms;
they came to the container and all had their heads bowed,
all trembling before him like children who were wet. |

| 2315 | Alexander swore by his right-hand side
that he was never better served with companions.
He felt great satisfaction at the races of the sea,
and considered that he had won a great empire. |

| 2316 | He saw another striking feature of those who dwelt there:
he saw that the larger ate those smaller than them;
the smaller ones thought of the larger as their lords
and the stronger ones ill-treated all those of lesser size. |

| 2317 | The King said, "Pride exists in every place;
it is a force on earth and within the seas;
likewise, birds do not see themselves as equals.
May God confound a vice that so many places have! |

| 2318 | It was born among the angels and made many fall.
It spread over the earth and God gave it great power.
Moderation is not able to take its rightful place:
it has hidden its head and it dares not appear. |

| 2319 | He who can do more does more, not good but ill;
he who has more wants more and dies for more still;
no man would willingly see any as his equal;
it is a wicked sin: there is none loyal to God. |

| 2320 | The birds and the beasts, the men, the fish,
are all divided into bands among themselves.
They are all afflicted with vice and with pride
and the weak are oppressed by the strong." |

| 2321 | If, just as the King was well able to see this,
he were willing to pass judgement rightly on himself,
he would certainly have to hold back his tongue a little
for he would not wish to utter such conceited words. |

| 2322 | It would have been the King's wish to stay there longer
but his vassals were beginning to grow concerned;
fearing misfortune, which comes often with speed,
they took him out well before the due time had passed. |

2323   Fueron con su señor   alegres las mesnadas;
vinieron todas verlo,   menudas e granadas;
besavan le las manos   tres o quatro vegadas;
dezién: "Agora somos,   señor, resuçitadas."

2324   Quiero dexar el rëy   en las naves folgar;
quiero de la su sobervia   un poquillo fablar;
quiero vos la materia   un poquillo dexar,
pero será en cabo   todo a un lugar.

2325   La Natura que cría   todas las crïaturas,
las que son paladinas   e las que son escuras,
tuvo que Alexandre   dixo palabras duras,
que querié conquerir   las secretas naturas.

2326   Tovo la rica dueña   que era sobjudgada,
quel' querié él toller   la lëy condonada;
de su poder non fuera   nunca deseredada
si non que Alexandre   la avié aontada.

2327   En las cosas secretas   quiso él entender,
que nunca ome bivo   non las pudo saber;
quísolas Alexandre   por fuerça coñoscer;
nunca mayor sobervia   comidió Luçifer.

2328   Aviéle Dïos dado   los regnos en su poder;
non sele podié fuerça   ninguna defender;
querié saber los mares,   los infiernos veer,
lo que non podié ome   nunca acabeçer.

2329   Pesó al Crïador   que crïó la Natura;
ovo de Alexandre   saña e grant rencura.
Dixo: "Este lunático,   que non cata mesura,
Yol' tornaré el gozo   todo en amargura.

2330   Él sopo la soberbia   de los peçes judgar;
la que en sí tenié   non la sopo asmar;
ome que tantos sabe   judiçios delibrar,
por qual juiçio dio   por tal debe passar."

2331   Quando vio la Natura   que al Señor pesava,
ovo grant alegría,   maguer triste andava;
movióse de las nuves   de do siempre morava
por mostrar su rencura,   quál quebranto tomava.

2323	The men of the army were delighted with their lord, and all came to see him, young and old alike; they planted three or four kisses on his hands, saying, "Now, lord, our life has been restored."
2324	I want to leave the King relaxing in his ships: I want to talk a little of his pride; I want to leave my subject, for a little while; but in the end it will all come to one place.
2325	Nature, which is nurse to every living creature,* those which shine brightly and those which are dark, thought that Alexander had said harsh words and that he wanted to master her mysteries.
2326	The fine lady felt that she had been overcome and that he wished to seize her given law. Never would she be deprived of her power, but Alexander had brought shame upon her.
2327	He wished to gain an understanding of the secret matters that no living man had ever managed to learn before. Alexander wanted to discover them by force: Lucifer himself never conceived of greater pride.
2328	God had granted him kingdoms under his sway, and no force could defend itself against him; he sought to know the seas and see the infernal depths, things which no man could ever manage to achieve.
2329	It troubled the Creator who had created Nature: He bore for Alexander great rancour and rage. He said, "For this lunatic who shows no restraint, I shall turn all his joy into bitterness.
2330	He knew how to judge the pride of the fish, but he could not make out the pride he had within. A man who knows how to pass so many judgements must undergo such judgement as he gave."
2331	When Nature saw that the Lord was troubled she was overjoyed, although she had been sad. She came down from the clouds, where she always dwelt to set forth her anger and the offence she had taken.

2332 Bien veyé que por ome   nunca serié vengada,
      ca moros e judíos   temién la su espada;
      asmó quel' echassen   una mala çelada,
      buscar cómo le diessen   collaçión enconada.

2333 Pospuso sus lavores,   las que solié usar,
      por nuevas crïaturas   las almas guerrear;
      deçendió al infierno   su pleito recabdar,
      por a'l rey Alexandre   mala carrera dar.

2334 De la cort' del infierno,   un fambriento lugar,
      – la materia lo manda –   quiero ende fablar:
      mal suelo, mal poblado,   mal techo, mal fogar;
      es dubdo e espanto,   sólo de començar.

2335 El Crïador que fizo   todas la crïaturas,
      con diversos donaires   e diversas figuras,
      ordenó los lugares   de diversas naturas,
      do reçiben las almas   lazerios e folguras.

2336 Fizo por a los buenos   que lo aman servir,
      que su aver non dubdan   con los pobres partir,
      el santo paraíso   do non pueden morir,
      do non podrán un punto   de lazeria sofrir.

2337 Allí serán en gloria   qual non sabrián pedir,
      qual non podrié nul ome   fablar nin comedir;
      metrán toda su fuerça   en a Dios bendezir,
      al que fue e al que es,   al que a de venir.

2338 Nunca sintrán tiniebra   nin frío nin calentura;
      verán la faz de Dios,   muy dulçe catadura;
      non se fartarán d'ella,   tant es la su dulçura;
      qui allí eredare   será de grant ventura.

2339 Para los otros malos   que tienen mala vida,
      que han la carrera   derecha aborrida,
      fue fecho el infierno,   çibdat mala complida,
      assaz mal aforado,   sin ninguna sallida.

2340 Fondo yaz' el infierno,   nunca entra y lumbre;
      de sentir luz ninguna   non es su costumbre;
      los muros son de sufre,   presos con tal betumbre;
      que non los derromprié   ninguna fortidumbre.

2332	She saw well that she would never be avenged by a man, for both Moors and Jews were afraid of his sword. She planned that she would lay for him an evil trap, and seek out how he might be given poisoned food.
2333	She put aside her tasks, to which she was accustomed, to find other creatures who could make war on souls; she went down into Hell, to deal with her business, and set an evil path before King Alexander.
2334	Of the court of Hell, a place fraught with hunger, do I want to speak, for my subject dictates it: an evil land, evil dwelling, evil house, an evil place, there are qualms and terror in merely setting out.
2335	The Creator, who made every creature with differing graces and differing forms, did ordain places of differing kinds where souls receive suffering or pleasures.
2336	He made for the good men who love to serve Him, and do not wait to share their wealth with the poor, the Holy Paradise, where they cannot come to death, and will not be able to feel the slightest pain.
2337	There will they have glory such as they could not seek, and such as no man could speak of or imagine; they will put all their strength into the blessing of God, who was, who is now, and who shall be.
2338	They will never feel darkness, cold, or heat and will see the face of God, a delightful countenance; they will never tire of it, so great is its delight: who inherits that place will be blessed indeed.
2339	For those other evil men who lead an evil life and have abhorred the straight path of Right, Hell was created, a city of utter evil, under evil jurisdiction, and with no way out.
2340	Hell lies deep and there no lustre ever enters: it is not their way to be aware of any light. The walls are of sulphur, held fast with such bitumen that no force could ever break them down.

2341   Silvan por las riberas   muchas malas sirpientes;
están días e noches   aguzando los dientes;
assechan a las almas,   non tienen a al mientes;
por esto peligraron   los primeros parientes.

2342   Quando veen venir   las almas pecadrizes,
trávanles de los labros,   préndenlas de las narizes;
fázenles encorvar   sin grado las çervizes;
las que allí non fueren   tengan se por felizes.

2343   Nunca fartar se pueden,   están muertas de fambre;
están todas cargadas   de mala vedegambre;
non apretarián tanto   cadenas de arambre.
¡Dios libre tod' cristiano   de tan mala pelambre!

2344   En todas sus comarcas   non naçen nunca flores
si non espinas duras,   e cardos poñidores;
tovas que fazen fumos   e amargos pudores;
peñiscales agudos   que son mucho peores.

2345   Dexemos de las islas,   digamos del raval;
aún después íremos   entrando al real.
Avié poblaçión suzia   fuera al mercadal:
los siet' viçios cabdales   que guardan el portal.

2346   Morava Avariçia   luego en la frontera;
ésta es de los viçios   madrona cabdellera;
quant' allega Cobdiçia,   que es su compañera,
estálo escondiendo   dentro en la puchera.

2347   Quanto doña Cobdiçia   podié ir aportando,
ívalo Avariçia   so tierra condesando;
quando le pidién algo,   querié quebrar jurando;
muchos son en el siglo   que tien' en el su vando.

2348   Han una crïadella   estas malas serores:
Ambiçio es su nombre,   que muere por onores;
trae malos sossacos,   encubiertas peores;
non bivrián de su grado   amigos nin señores.

2349   Avién estas fambrientas   compañas desleales:
logros, furtos, rapinas   e engaños mortales;
éstos mandan las rúas,   yazen por los ravales;
andan a las vegadas   vestidos de sayales.

2341	Many evil serpents hiss along the banks, which are day and night sharpening their fangs; they spy out for souls, and think of nothing else: on this account our eldest forbears fell to danger.
2342	When they see the sinful souls make their arrival, they tear at their lips and seize them by the nose; they make them twist their necks round against their will; may those that do not pass there hold themselves favoured!
2343	They can never eat their fill but are dying of hunger and are all weighed down with a poisonous burden; chains of wire would not bear on them so cruelly; may God free any Christian from such evil harm.
2344	Flowers never grow in any of its districts, but sharp thorns and thistles with a sting; here are stones which belch out smoke and bitter smells, and sharp rocks which are far more unpleasant.
2345	Let us leave the single houses and talk of the outskirts, and afterwards we shall make for the citadel; there was a filthy population outside, in the market, and the Seven Deadly Sins were guarding the gateway.
2346	There dwelt Avarice, right out at the front: this is the mother and leader of the sins and everything that Greed, her companion, brings, she is hiding and storing away in the pot.
2347	Everything that Greed was able to heap up, Avarice would hide it all beneath the ground; when asked for something, she wished to burst, full of oaths; there are many in this world who are in her company.
2348	These two vices have a little serving-girl: she is called Ambition and she dies for honours; she devises evil schemes and even worse traps and neither friends nor lords could live at ease with her.
2349	These hungry wretches have disloyal companions: gain, thefts, pillage, and deadly deceptions; these rule the streets and lie throughout the town, and sometimes go about dressed in rough tunics.

2350 Aven por concosina   una mala vezina:
      Enbidia, la que fue   e siempre será mesquina;
      un viçio que non sana   por nula melezina,
      ques' prende con quis quiere   por cabellos aína.

2351 Quando vee al próximo   bien aver o litiçia,
      matarse quiere toda   con derecha maliçia;
      mas si vee algunos   que caen en tristiçia,
      esto ha por gozo,   ca nunca al codiçia.

2352 Toda cosa derecha   razona ella mal;
      delante dize bien,   de çaga dize al;
      pésal' com' puerco gruesso   en ajeno corral;
      si matarlo quisiesse,   non le prestarié sal.

2353 Escontra la Cobdiçia   está cabez' tornada;
      tiene de mal corage   la voluntad tornada;
      por lo que ella puede   está desaborada;
      si la quemasse fuego,   serié ella pagada.

2354 Como de mala çepa   naçen malos gromones,
      naçen de esti viçio   viçiosas crïazones:
      maldiçiones, tristiçias   e otras traiçiones;
      despiertas' cada día   con malos aguijones.

2355 Quando vee buen fecho,   quiérelo encobrir;
      si encobrir nol' puede,   quiérelo destroír;
      faze a muchos omes   mala vida bevir;
      por onde ovo'l diablo   en Saúl a venir.

2356 Mantiene dona Ira   la terçera posada;
      con coraçón ravioso,   de refiertas cargada,
      royendo las estacas,   la su visión turbada;
      non querié quel' dixesse   ome ninguno nada.

2357 Está tanto de çiega   que non sabe ques' diga;
      diziendo villanía,   alueyas e nemiga;
      como se acaeçe   si algunt la castiga,
      tórnal' como si fuesse   su mortal enemiga.

2358 Estával' a los piedes   Herodes su crïado,
      el que ovo con ira   a los niños matado;
      dával' muy grandes muessos   al siniestro costado
      don Lamet, el que ovo   a su guión matado.

2350   As their relative, they have a wicked neighbour:
       Envy, which was and always will be full of spite.
       This is a vice which is cured with no medicine
       and is quick to grab anyone by the hair.

2351   On seeing that her neighbour has possessions or joy,
       she longs to kill herself with the deep malice in her;
       but if she sees others who are falling into sorrow
       this is her source of joy, for it is all she ever desires.

2352   She finds cause to criticise anything that is right,
       and openly says one thing, behind your back another.
       She is upset to see a fat pig in another's yard;
       if he wanted to kill it, she would lend him no salt.

2353   She has turned her head to look towards Greed
       and her heart has been turned by evil temper.
       She feels irritation at what gives her comrade pleasure;
       if the fires consumed her, it would please her.

2354   Just as a bad vine produces bad shoots,
       from this vice is born a vicious progeny:
       curses, unhappiness and other treacheries;
       she awakens every day with sharp stings.

2355   When she sees a good deed she wishes to conceal it;
       if she cannot conceal it she wishes to destroy it;
       she causes many men to lead an evil life,
       and thus did the Devil manage to enter Saul.*

2356   The third dwelling place belongs to Anger,
       with a rabid heart and laden with conflicts,
       gnawing at stakes with her vision clouded;
       she wanted no man to speak a word to her.

2357   She is so blind she does not know what is said,
       she says foul things, cries out and utters insults;
       and so it happens if someone reprehends her:
       she turns on them as if a mortal foe.

2358   At her feet was her servant Herod,*
       who had killed the children in anger;
       biting deeply into her left-hand side,
       was Lamech, who had killed his guide.*

2359 Quiere la cosa mala   quebrar por el despecho,
que aquel barón bueno,   don Job, le ovo fecho.
Qui se desdiz' atanto,   non cadrá otro pecho.
Nunca contendrá tanto   que aya end' derecho.

2360 Un enxemplo vos quiero   en esto adozir:
cómo sabe Envidia   a ome deçebir,
e cómo en sí misma   querrié grant mal sofrir
por amor que podiesse   al vezino nozir.

2361 Diz' que dos compañeros   de diverso semblante,
el uno cobdiçioso,   el otro enbidiante,
fazián amos carrera   por un monte verdiante;
fallaron un ric' ome,   de cuerpo bien estante.

2362 Díxoles grant promessa   ante que se partiesse:
que pidiesse el uno   lo que sabor oviesse;
a ésse darié tanto   quanto que le pidiesse,
al otro doble tanto   que callando 'stoviesse.

2363 Calló el cobdiçioso;   non quiso dezir nada,
por amor que llevase   la raçïón doblada;
quando entendió'l otro   esta mala çelada,
quiso quebrar d'enbidia   por medio la corada.

2364 Asmó entre su cuer,   pidió un fuerte pedido,
qual non fue en el siglo   nin visto nin oído:
"Señor," diz', "tú me tuelle   el ojo más querido;
dobla al compañero   el don que yo te pido."

2365 Fízos' el ome bueno   mucho maravillado;
del ome enbidioso   fue muy despagado;
vido que la Enbidia   es tan mortal pecado
que non es por nul viçio   ome tan mal dapnado.

2366 Clérigos e canonges   que fazen simonías
non serán ende menos   por las çapatas mías;
el plomo regalado   bevrán todos los días;
non creo que gusanos   críen en las enzías.

2367 Pare esta diablessa   un fijo traïdor:
Odio, el que vieda   Dïos, Nuestro Señor;
de todos los pecados,   ésti es el mayor;
el que muere con él   contéçel' grant error.

2359	The evil creature wants to burst with the malice that the good man Job had caused her to feel.* One who has such bluster will bring down no other heart: she will never strive so much as to gain satisfaction.
2360	At this point, I wish to bring before you an *exemplum** which shows how Envy can deceive a man, and how she would be willing to endure great hurt herself in the desire that she might harm her neighbour.
2361	They tell of two companions, their characters different, one full of greed, and the other full of envy: the two of them were walking across a green hillside when they met a nobleman of fine appearance.
2362	Before he left them he made them a great promise: that one of them should ask for what he wanted, and he would give that man all that he requested, but the other, who stayed quiet, twice as much.
2363	The greedy man was silent, wanting to say nothing, out of his desire to take a double share; and when the other understood his unfair trick he felt as though his insides would burst with envy.
2364	He thought it over and then made a strange request which had never in the world been seen or heard. "My lord," he said, "take away the sharper of my eyes, and give my companion twice the gift I ask of you."
2365	The good man felt great amazement at these words and was greatly displeased with the envious man; he saw then that Envy is so mortal a sin that by no vice is man so evilly damned.
2366	Clergy and canons who commit simony* will be damned no less than these, by my shoes! Every day will they drink down molten lead, and I do not think that worms will grow in their gums.
2367	Envy, this she-devil, had a treacherous son: Hatred, which the Lord our God forbids. Of all of the sins, this one is the greatest; the man who dies through this is in great error.

2368 Éste faz' a los omes   omezidios obrar;
     fázeles a las madres   a los fijos matar;
     éste faz' las iglesias   sagradas vïolar;
     sabe a los perlados   de mesura sacar.

2369 Quand' a otri non puede   ferir nin alcançar,
     quïere a sí misma   con su mano matar;
     ¡De tan mal enemigo,   tan malo de rancar,
     El que salvó el mundo   nos deñe a emparar!

2370 Assí quiso don Pluto   su palaçio complir
     que non podié ome   por nulla part' fuïr;
     paró otras barreras   por ome embaír,
     que d'una o de otra   non pudiesse guarir.

2371 Muchos son que Cobdiçia   non los puede vençer;
     encara non los puede   Enbidia corromper;
     de Ira non se temen,   sábense defender,
     mas puede los en cabo   Luxuria cofonder.

2372 Por ende el pecado,   sabidor de todo mal,
     pobló a Luxurïa   en el quarto fastïal;
     suzia e descarnida,   más ardiente que cal;
     con su poder corrompe   todo el mercadal.

2373 Sedié acompañada   de suzias crïazones:
     forniçios, adulterios   e otras poluciones;
     el viçio sodomítico   con sus abusïones,
     muchas otras orreças,   tan malas o peores.

2374 Como son los viçïos   de diversas maneras,
     arden en sus posadas   otras tantas fogueras;
     fierven sobre los fuegos   otras tantas calderas
     en que arden e cuezen   las almas forniqueras.

2375 Saco end' los casados   que son a bendiçión,
     que lealtad mantienen   fembra con su varón;
     allí queman e tribulan   quantas fallidas son,
     si non las que escusa   la vera confessión.

2376 Otro viçio que llama   San Paulo Inmundiçia,
     éste prende del fumo   déçima e promiçia;
     aún de lo que finca   que non toma Cobdiçia,
     prende raçión doblada   a plenera justiçia.

2368	This sin makes men commit murders and leads mothers to kill their children; it brings the desecration of holy churches and can drive prelates from prudence.
2369	When he cannot strike or reach another, he seeks to kill himself with his own hand. From such an evil enemy, so hard to defeat, may He who saved the world deign to free us.
2370	Pluto wished his palace to be built in such a way* that there be no place where any man could flee. He set up other barriers to hold men prisoner that from one or another they could not escape.
2371	There are many men that Greed cannot overcome, and that Envy, too, is unable to corrupt; they have no fear of Anger and are safe from its attack, but in the end, Lust is able to confound them.
2372	And therefore the Devil, an expert in all evil, placed Lust in the fourth part of his edifice: dirty and gaunt, quicklime burns not so hot; with her power she corrupts the whole market square.
2373	She was accompanied by her filthy offspring: fornication, adultery and other corruptions; the vice of Sodom, with all its perversions, and many abhorrent ways, just as bad or worse still.
2374	As the vices are all of differing natures, there are just as many fires burning in their dwellings, with just as many cauldrons seething on the flames, in which the fornicating souls boil and bubble.
2375	Excluded are those couples legitimately married who maintain fidelity between woman and man; but there do writhe and burn all those fallen into sin, except those who are excused by true confession.*
2376	Another vice, that Saint Paul calls Uncleanness, takes the tithes and the first fruit from the smoke, and still from the remnant left untouched by Greed takes a double ration which it holds as its due.

2377 Están y rostri tuertas   rica ment' afumadas,
muchas barvas que fueron   tenidas por honradas;
otras están desnudas   que fueron perjuradas;
éstas tienen las lenguas   de gusanos cargadas.

2378 Tienen el lugar quinto   Gola e Glotonía;
éstas fazen al ome   fer mucha villanía;
han con la Luxuría   éstas su cofradía,
las unas sin las otras   abés bivrián un día.

2379 Gola está en medio,   sus dedos relamiendo,
allent' la Glotonía,   regüeldos revertiendo,
allende la Beudez,   tornando e beviendo,
los miembros con vergüença   descubiertos yaziendo.

2380 Toda su mantenençia   traen con los garçones,
con mugeres livianas   que non aman sermones,
comiendo a escuso   de noch' a los tizones,
yaziendo por tavernas,   tastando los tapones.

2381 Non llamo glotonía   comer ome fartura
en oras convinientes   por tener la natura,
mas comer sobejano   e bever sin mesura;
éstos dizen los físicos   que dañan la natura.

2382 Si Adam non oviesse   estado tan glotón,
non oviera Mesías   presa tal passïón;
si Lot tanto beviesse   como manda Catón,
non ferié en sus fijas   fijos tan sin razón.

2383 Los omes que se vezan   tal vida mantener
son malos ganadores,   non lo han do aver;
tórnanse a furtar,   iglesias derromper;
han por tal manera   las almas a perder.

2384 Aman mucho los dados   e han a descreer;
nunca van a iglesia   penitençia prender;
mucho mas les valdrié   que fuessen por naçer
o seer bestias mudas   que tal vida fazer.

2385 Otros son por el mundo   que son tan venterneros
que por comer a solas   entran en los çilleros;
non parten con los pobres   nin con los compañeros;
alçan lo que sobra   fuerte en los bolseros.

2377	There, with faces contorted, and engulfed in smoke, are many gentlemen once held in honour; others who were perjurers are now stripped naked, and their tongues are heaving with their load of worms.
2378	The fifth place is occupied by Appetite and Gluttony, which cause man to commit many acts of evil. These two sins form their brotherhood with Lust, and none could live a day without the others.
2379	In the centre is Appetite, licking its fingers, on one side the belching figure of Gluttony, and on the other Drunkenness, vomiting and drinking, with its members lying shamefully exposed.
2380	They have all their dealings with youthful men and fickle women with no love of sermons, eating secretly at night by the light of a torch, lying in the taverns, and drawing from flagons.
2381	I do not call it gluttony when a man eats enough, at times that are appropriate, to meet his natural needs, but eating to excess and drinking without measure – as the physicians tell us – harm his natural state.
2382	If Adam had not had such a gluttonous desire, the Messiah would not have suffered such a Passion. If Lot had drunk only the amount that Cato orders,* he would not have fathered sons with his daughters in such folly.
2383	Men who are accustomed to lead such a life are poor at earning and know not where to gain more; they turn to theft and to crimes against churches: in such a way they come to lose their souls.
2384	With great love for dice-games, they come to disbelieve, and never go to church to do their penance; it would serve them far better not to have been born, or to be mute beasts, than to have such a life.
2385	There are others in the world who are so voracious that they shut themselves away in their rooms to eat alone; they share nothing with the poor or with their companions and what they have left over they stow away in bags.

2386 Éstos son con el *Dives* en infierno fondidos;
teniendo agua çerca yazen de set perdidos;
veyendo los comeres están muy desfambridos,
que querrién seer muertos más que seer naçidos.

2387 De viçios tan villanos devémosnos guardar:
Acçidia es su nombre, suele mucho dañar;
ésta suele al ome venir con grant pesar;
por tal duelo que faze, ha ome a errar.

2388 Veemos muchas vezes esto acaeçer
que, quando ome pierde pariente o aver,
ome que bien lo quiere tantos' quiere doler
que viene a sazón que quiere recreer.

2389 Derraiga e descree e déxase morir;
presto es el dïablo, viénelo reçebir;
liévalo al infierno, mándalo bien servir:
faz'lo en la resina e en plomo bollir.

2390 Miémbrame que solemos leer en un actor
que tornó Nïobé en piedra por dolor;
Felis tornó en árvol por el su buen señor;
semejan me errados de Dios Nuestro Señor.

2391 Mas asmo otra cosa, que cueido y pecar;
otra guisa se debe esto interpretar:
que yo creer non puedo que pudiesse estar
que pudiessen los omes en tal cosa tornar.

2392 Non quiso el actor dezir que son dapnados,
que los que a infierno son una vez levados
dixo por encubierta que son en al tornados;
assaz puede el ome dezir que son dapnados.

2393 Sé que querrá alguno darme un estribot';
querráme dar enxenplo de la muger de Lot;
assaz es pora esso un contrarïo mot',
mas podriá determinarlo un cativo arlot.

2394 Sobre todos del siglo, nos devemos guardar
del que sabe sin lança e sin espada matar;
quando ome se cuida más seguro estar,
entonçe suele él las sus redes gitar.

2386	These men are with Dives, sunk deep in Hell;* they have water nearby yet are lost with thirst; they have food in sight yet they ache with hunger; they would rather be dead than ever have been born.
2387	We must keep ourselves free from vices so foul: Indolence is its name, its way to do great harm and to come upon a man who bears the deepest sorrow: through the grief that he endures, he falls into error.
2388	With great regularity we see this come to pass: that when a man loses his kinsman or his wealth, a man with great love for them has such desire to grieve that he comes to such a time when he begins to lose his faith.
2389	He declines and disbelieves and descends into death; the Devil is ready and comes to take him in: he carries him to Hell and sees he is well served, and he has him boiled in resin and in lead.
2390	In an author, I remember we are wont to read* that Niobe turned into a stone in her grief, and Phyllis became a tree, on her good lord's account. It seems to me that they erred against the Lord our God.
2391	But something else occurs to me, which I hold at fault, that this must be interpreted in a different way: for I cannot believe that it could indeed be true that men might be able to turn into such things.
2392	The author did not wish to say that they had been damned, for those who have once been carried into Hell, disguisedly, he said, are turned into something else, and man is clearly able to conclude that they were damned.
2393	I know that someone will wish to answer me back, and quote me the example of the wife of Lot;* sufficient for that is one contrary word,* but that could be pronounced by any wretched scoundrel.
2394	Above all those in the world, we must protect ourselves against the one who can kill without lance or sword; at the point when a man believes that he is safest, that is when the Devil is wont to cast his nets.

2395   Muchos son que se suelen   de los viçios guardar;
en fechos e en dichos   se guardan de pecar;
non los podrié en nada   ome escatimar;
mas suele Vana Gloria   en ellos habitar.

2396   Son pocos que la sepan   sentir nin coñosçer;
son pocos que en ella   non hayan que veer;
sabe con los mayores   sus cubiertas traer,
ca en los viles omes   nunca puede caber.

2397   Si un poco quisierdes   saber mi entender,
mejor vos lo querría   dezir e esponer;
saben lo por ventura   algunos entender,
por onde nos devemos   algunt poco retener.

2398   El dïablo antiguo,   que nunca puede dormir,
sienpre anda bullendo   por a nos deçebir;
quantas trae de redes   podistes lo oïr
si quisiestes en ello   las orejas abrir.

2399   Aguisa a los unos   que sean cobdiçiosos;
faz' los otros irados,   los otros enbidiosos,
los otros venterneros,   los otros luxuriosos;
embébdalos e mátalos   con tales açedosos.

2400   Los buenos e los santos   que non quieren fallir,
que oran, alimosnan   e piensan de servir,
saben con sus sermones   los otros convertir;
pésal' tanto con éstos   que se quiere morir.

2401   Sabe un letüario   a éstos bien guisar:
pégaseles quedillo   al siniestro quexar;
faz' al que es buen ome   del buen fecho membrar,
tanto que se deleita   en ello glorïar.

2402   Fázelo a los pueblos   bendezir e laudar;
muévelo el mal viento,   fázelo levantar;
fázelo el dïablo   en sequera nadar;
piensa cómo lo faga,   si pudiesse, pecar.

2403   Por esta vía era   Zózimas engañado
quando tenié que era   en bondat acabado;
fuera que lo querié   Dios tornar en su estado,
si non, tod' su lazerio   avrié mal embregado.

2395	There are many who routinely keep themselves from vices
and who keep themselves from sinning in deeds and words.
In nothing would a man be able to reproach them,
but within them Vainglory is wont to abide.
2396	There are few who can feel or recognise it,
yet few, too, who are free from its touch.
It can weave its deceptions with people of stature,
for among common men it can never find its home.
2397	If you wished, for a moment, to learn my meaning,
I would like to tell you and expound it better;
some by good fortune can already understand,
wherefore we must restrain ourselves a little.
2398	The aged Devil, never able to sleep,
is always scheming to lay his hands upon us;
of all the snares he brings you have been able to hear,
if you were willing to open your ears to it.
2399	He induces some men to lead a life of greed;
he makes other men angry and others envious,
other men gluttonous and still others lustful:
he makes them drunk and kills them with such poisons.
2400	The good men and the holy, who do not want to err,
they who pray, who give alms, and who seek to serve,
know how to convert other men through their sermons:
he is so troubled by these that he would willingly die.
2401	He knows well how to make an electuary for these men,
and gives it to them drop by drop on the left side of their jaws;
he makes the good man call to mind his good deeds,
so much that he delights and glories in them.
2402	He makes people bless and praise the good man
and the ill wind moves him and makes him grow proud.
The Devil makes him try to swim while on dry land,
and devises ways of making him sin.
2403	It was in this way that Zosimas was deceived,*
when he thought that he had reached the height of goodness;
had not God wished to return him to his place,
then all his trials would have been squandered.

2404 Este dïablo suele   al ome embeudar,
que non ha nul poder   escuentra Dios tornar;
ésti fizo al rëy   de Babilón errar,
por ond' ovo grant tiempo   con las bestias andar.

2405 Éstos son siete viçios   que dizen prinçipales;
éstos son los pecados   que dizen criminales;
estos siete por el mundo   fazen todos los males;
muchas barbas honradas   lievan en sus dogales.

2406 E todos éstos tiene   la Soberbia ligados;
todos son sus ministros,   que traen sus mandados;
ella es la reína,   ellos son sus crïados;
a todos siet' los tiene   rica ment' doctrinados.

2407 Por esso en la cuenta   non es ella echada,
por que es de los viçios   emperadriz llamada;
ella les da a todos   gobierno e soldada;
por egualar con éstos   es cosa desaguisada.

2408 Sobre todos los otros   puja el su ostal;
tiene que en el mundo   non puede aver egual;
anda en grant cavallo   por medio del mercadal,
desdeñando a todos   e diziéndoles mal.

2409 Ándase alabando   si non fues' por ella
que Dios nunca oviera   de Luçifer querella;
Adam tan mal metido   non seriá a la pella,
nin tan bien non serié   de Ester la punçella.

2410 A omes e a ángeles   está dando refierta;
tiene con grant corage   la fruente descubierta;
non sabe su desdén   sobre qui lo revierta;
empeitra su cavallo   a qui quier' que açierta.

2411 Que mucho yo vos quiera   de los viçios dezir,
podedes lo todos   vos mismos comedir.
Quïero, si queredes   atender e oïr,
dexar de lo de fuera,   del real escrevir.

2412 En medio del infierno   fumea el fornaz;
arde días e noches,   nunca flama non faz';
allí está el rëy,   enemigo de paz,
faziendo a las almas   juegos que non les plaz'.

2404	This Devil is accustomed to inebriate man such that he has no power to turn back to God; it was he who brought the King of Babylon to sin,* for which he had to spend a long time with the animals.
2405	These are the seven vices which they call capital,* and these are the sins which they call deadly. These seven are the cause of all evils in the world, and lead many men of honour by their halters.
2406	All of these vices are held bound by Pride; all are her ministers, who carry out her orders. She is the Queen and they are her servants; she has thoroughly taught all seven of them.
2407	For that reason she is not included in the count, since she is known as the Empress of the vices; to all of them she gives their commands and pay, and it is wrong to place her on their level.
2408	She raises up her dwelling above all the others and believes that in the world she can have no equal. She rides around the market place on a great horse, scorning everyone and speaking ill of all.
2409	She delights in the fact that, were it not for her, God would never have had quarrel with Lucifer, Adam would not have been so evilly set in shame, nor the girl Esther have met with such success.*
2410	She is always making discord for men and angels and in her great pique she has her brow uncovered; she does not know on whom to cast her disdain and her horse tramples on whoever comes near.
2411	However much I wish to tell you of the vices you can all think this out for yourselves; I wish, if you are willing to give ear and listen, to leave the outer districts and write of the citadel.
2412	In the middle of Hell smokes the furnace which burns day and night and never with a flame; there is the King, the enemy of peace, playing tricks on the souls, which do not please them.

2413 Allí arden las almas   por el mal que fizieron,
unas más, otras menos,   segunt que mereçieron;
sienten menos de pena   las que menos fallieron;
sufren mayor lazerio   las que peor bivieron.

2414 Una cosa es fórnaz   que siempre es ardiente,
mas non sienten sus penas   todas igüal mente;
cunte como a los omes   con el sol muy caliente:
unos han con él quexa,   otros non han y miente.

2415 Ardiendo en las flamas,   triemblan de grant frïura;
yaziendo en las nieves,   mueren de calentura;
non han en los infiernos   ninguna tempradura;
tiene cada rincón   abondo de rencura.

2416 Dizen que yaze Tiçio   en essa cofradía,
al que comen los buitres   doze vezes al día;
doze vezes lo comen   e doz' vezes se cría;
si una vez finasse   avrié grant mejoría.

2417 Podrié más rafez mente   essas penas sofrir
si sopiesse en cabo   que podrié de y exir,
mas ésta es la cueita: que non podrá morir
nin podrá de las penas   nunca jamás sallir.

2418 Estas nuestras fogueras   amargan como fiel;
serién contra éssas   mas dulçes que la miel.
Devrié ome por Dios   dar la una pïel
quel' fuesse rogador   el señor san Miguel.

2419 Arden días e noches   maldiziendo su fado.
Él que les da las penas   con esto es pagado;
las mesquinas que arden   avriénle muy grant grado
sólo que las dexasse   tornar del otro cabo.

2420 Las almas de los niños   que non son bateadas,
que son por el pecado   original dapnadas,
non arden con las otras,   están más apartadas,
pero en grant tiniebra,   de luz desfeüzadas.

2421 Assaz es fiera pena,   non coñosco mayor,
de nunca veer ome   la faz del Crïador;
como al que la vee   es gloria e dulçor,
assí es a los otros   pena e grant dolor.

2413	There the souls burn for the evil that they did, some more, and others less, as they deserve; those who were less sinful feel less pain, but those who lived worse bear greater torment.
2414	The furnace is something that is constantly burning, but the souls do not all feel its pains in equal measure; it happens as to men beneath the burning sun: it causes some discomfort; others feel nothing.
2415	Burning in the flames, they tremble with great cold and lying in the snow they are dying of heat; in the regions of Hell there is no temperance, and in every corner bitterness abounds.
2416	They say that Tityus lies amidst that brotherhood,* twelve times a day being eaten by the vultures; twelve times they eat him and twelve times he grows: if he could ever die, he would much improve his lot.
2417	He could endure those sufferings more easily if he knew that at the end he could escape them; but this is the torment: that he will not manage death, nor evermore be able to emerge from his tortures.
2418	The fires of our world burn as bitterly as gall; compared to those, they would be sweeter than honey; a man should be prepared to give up his skin for God so that Saint Michael might intercede for him.
2419	Day and night do they burn as they curse their fate: with this, the one who torments them is satisfied; and the wretched, burning souls would be very grateful if he would only let them turn onto their other side.
2420	The souls of the children who were never baptised, which have been damned through original sin, do not burn with the others, but are to one side, and held in deep darkness, with no hope of light.
2421	It is a bitterly cruel torment – I know none greater – that a man should never see the Creator's face; as it is glory and sweetness to the man who sees it, so to the others it is torment and great pain.

2422   Los justos, otros tiempos, yazién en es' lugar,
       ante que los uviasse   Jhesu Christo salvar;
       mas quiso - ¡aleluya! –   entonçes ençerrar;
       nunca más lo esperen,   ca pueden y badar.

2423   Que mucho vos queramos   del infierno dezir,
       non podriemos el diezmo   de su mal escrevir;
       mas devemos a Dios   la su merçed pedir
       que nunca nos lo dexe   ensayar nin sentir.

2424   Tant' avemos, señores,   la razón alongada;
       dexamos la Natura   sola, desamparada;
       mas tornemos en ella,   fagamos la pagada;
       entendamos en ella   fasta ont' sea tornada.

2425   Deçendió al infierno   recabdar su mandado;
       el infierno con ella   fue luego espantado;
       paróse a la puerta,   su boço emboçado,
       que non la embargasse   el infierno enconado.

2426   Mandó luego la dueña   a Belçebut llamar;
       fue aína venido,   non lo osó tardar;
       pero camió el ábito   con que solié andar,
       ca temié que la dueña   poders' iá espantar.

2427   Priso cara angélica,   qual la solié aver
       quando enloqueçió   por su bel pareçer.
       "Señora," diz', "¿qué puede   esta cosa seer?
       Yo nunca vos cuidava   en est' siglo veer."

2428   Mas d'aquesto non quiso   escuchar la reína,
       ca querié recabdar   e tornarse aína;
       non querié luenga mente   morar en la sentina,
       ca era toda llena   de mala calabrina.

2429   "Cueita me faz' prender   a mí esta carrera;
       cueita es general,   ca non una señera.
       Si fuere la menaza   de Alexandre vera,
       non vale nuestro reino   una vil cañavera.

2430   El rëy de los griegos,   un soberbio varón,
       ave'l siglo echado   en grant tribulaçión;
       vençió al rey de India   e al de Babilón,
       a Media e Asïa   con su subjeçïon.

2422	The just in other times used to lie in that place, before Jesus Christ came to bring them salvation; but then – Hallelujah! – he chose to seal it shut; nevermore may they await him: they can wait in vain.
2423	However much we desire to tell you of Hell, we could not write a tenth of its evil; but we are compelled to ask God for His mercy, that He never allow us to feel or endure it.
2424	My lords, so far have we extended our account that we left Nature alone and abandoned; but let us turn to her and give her satisfaction, and stay at her side till she has made her way back.
2425	She went down into Hell to perform her errand: Hell was in terror at once at her coming; she stopped at the gateway with her face covered up so as not to be choked by Hell's filthy fumes.
2426	At once the lady bade that Beelzebub be called: he came with haste for he dared not delay; but he changed from his customary appearance for he feared lest the lady be afraid.
2427	He wore the face of an angel, such as he once possessed at the time when he grew mad through the beauty of his looks. "My lady", he said, "what can this matter be? I never expected to see you in this place."
2428	The Queen had no desire to hear any more of this: she wished to carry out her business and return in haste. She did not wish to make a long stay in this sewer, for it was filled throughout with an evil stench.
2429	"Anxiety makes me undertake this journey, an anxiety that all share: it is not mine alone; for if the threat that Alexander poses is true, our kingdom is not worth a common reed.
2430	He is King of the Greeks, a man of great pride, and has cast the world into great tribulation; he conquered the kings of Babylonia and India and brought Media and Africa to subjection.

2431 Non lo osan los rëys en campo esperar;
non le pueden las bestias nin las sierpes durar;
temen la su espada todos de mar a mar;
non es ome naçido quel' pueda contrastar.

2432 Non se tovo por esto en cara por pagado;
el secreto del mar ave escodriñado.
Por todos los peligros non fue quebrantado;
en cara en India oy está más apagado.

2433 Quando non falla cosa quel' pueda contrastar,
dize que los infiernos quiere escodriñar;
todos los mis secretos quier' despaladinar;
a mí e a vos todos en cadenas levar.

2434 Tu pudiest' los parientes primeros deçebir
por ond' en tu cadena ovieron a morir.
Si éste vençïere lo que cuida complir,
de la tu ocasión avremos qué dezir.

2435 Quando fust' por tu culpa de los cielos gitado,
non aviés do entrar, estavas desirado.
Yo te di est' lugar por que eres dubdado;
por vengar mi despecho deves seer pagado."

2436 Don Satanás non quiso la voluntat tardar;
batió amas sus manos, pensóse de tornar;
por ond' nunca passava mandava pregonar
que pensassen las lëys sus casas aguardar.

2437 Non echó Satanás la cosa en olvido;
demudó la figura, echó un grant bramido;
Fue luego el conçeio del infierno venido;
el que vinié mas tarde teniése por fallido.

2438 "Quiero vos yo, conçejo, unas nuevas contar,
en las quales devedes todos mientes parar;
fazienda vos acreçe, quieren vos guerrear;
si mientes non metiéredes, pueden vos quebrantar.

2439 El rëy de los griegos es muy fiero sallido;
omes, sierpes e bestias, todo lo ha vençido;
con el poder agora es tanto enloquido
que miedo e vergüença todo lo ha perdido.

2431	Kings dare not await him on the field of battle, nor can beasts or snakes endure against him; from sea to sea all men are in fear of his sword and there is no man born who can oppose him.
2432	Not even with this did he think himself satisfied: he has pried into all the secrets of the sea and was never brought to harm by any of its perils. What is more, he is today in India, elated.
2433	As he can find nothing that can resist him, he says he wants to spy into the depths of Hell; he desires to lay open all of my secrets and to carry off the two of us in chains.
2434	You were able to deceive mankind's first forbears wherefore it was their lot to die in your fetters. If this man conquers you, as he intends to do, we shall have much to say of your misfortune.
2435	When, for your crime, you were cast down from Heaven and had nowhere to enter, thrown into exile, I gave you this place, through which you are feared; you must now be content to avenge my anger."
2436	Satan did not wish to cause delay to her desire: Nature clapped her two hands, and went to turn away. Even where she never went, she bade it be proclaimed that her subjects must take care to respect her laws.
2437	Satan did not let the matter be forgotten; he changed his appearance and let out a huge roar. His council came at once from the depths of Hell and the last to arrive held himself as lost.
2438	"I want, my council, to give you some news, to which you must all pay close attention. Trouble is brewing, they want to make war on you; if you do not take care, they may bring you destruction.
2439	The King of the Greeks has proved very fierce, and has conquered all: men, serpents and beasts. With power he has now so far lost his mind that he has shed all sense of fear and shame.

2440 Non le cabe el mundo   nil' puede abondar;
dizen que los antípodes   quiere venir buscar;
desent' tiene asmado   los infiernos proiçiar,
a mí con todos vos   en cadenas echar.

2441 Pero en una cosa   prengo yo grant espanto:
cantan las Escripturas   un desabrido canto
que parrá una virgen   un fijo müy santo
por que han los infiernos   a prender mal quebranto.

2442 Si es ésti o non,   non vos lo sé dezir,
mas valiente contrario   nos ha a devenir;
tollernos ha las almas,   est' non puede fallir;
robarnos ha el canpo   – nol' podremos nozir.

2443 Como quiere que sea,   devemos aguisar
cómo carrera mala   le fagamos tomar;
quisequiere que esto   pudiesse acabar,
gualardón le daría   que non sabriá asmar."

2444 La corte fue amargada,   empeçó de reñir
como canes que quieren   uno a otro sallir;
pero non le sabiá   ninguno recodir;
non respondió ninguno   que lo quisies' complir.

2445 Levantóse en medio   una su crïadiella;
Traïçion la llamaron   bien de chiquiella,
nombre de grant color   e de mala manziella.
Ésta lo trastornó   de la çelestial siella.

2446 Andava por la casa   mucho entrametida;
tiene cara alegre,   la voluntad podrida;
mas la mano siniestra   tiénela escondida,
de medezinas malas   tiénela bien bastida.

2447 "Conçejo," diz' la mala,   "quiero que me oyades:
quiero vos escusar   a todos, bien sepades.
¡Nunca essa cueita   vos nada non ayades!
Yo lo porné de guisa   que pagados seades.

2448 Esto cuido aína   complir e aguisar,
ca yo le sabré tal salsa   bastir e destemprar
que, sólo que la uvie   de los rostros tastar,
nin a sí nin a otri   non podrá consejar.

2440	The world is not able to contain him or sate him:
	they say that the Antipodes he wants to come to find;
	he intends then to drive out the inhabitants of Hell,
	and cast me, with all of you, into chains.
2441	But there is one thing that causes me great fear:
	the Scriptures have a troubling song to sing
	that a virgin will give birth to a very holy child
	through whom Hell is to be deeply shaken.
2442	If this is he or not, I am unable to tell you,
	but a valiant opponent is to come to us;
	he will snatch the souls from us, this cannot fail to be;
	he will take the field from us, powerless to harm him.
2443	However it may be, we must prepare a way
	that we can make him take a troubled path;
	to whoever might be able to bring this about
	I would give a prize that he could not imagine."
2444	The court grew bitter and began to squabble,
	like dogs that are eager to attack each other,
	but none of them knew how to give him an answer;
	no-one replied that they wished to undertake this.
2445	In the midst of this arose a hireling of his,
	known as Treachery right from her earliest days
	– a name full of colour and one of wicked shame –:
	it was she who made him fall from his celestial seat.
2446	She traversed the dwelling, the meddlesome thing,
	with a joyful face and a rotten heart;
	but she kept her left hand hidden away,
	and she kept it well supplied with evil medicines.
2447	"Council," the evil creature said, "I want you to hear me;
	I want to save you all, as you must be well aware;
	may you never have a part of that misfortune:
	I will see to it that you may rest at ease.
2448	I intend to arrange and plan for this quickly:
	I shall be able to concoct and brew such a poison
	that should he but come to get a taste on his lips
	he will not be able to advise himself or others.

2449 Tengo todo mi pleito rica ment' acabado:
al alcaide Antípater, mi amigo afiado
téngolo rica mente de soldada cargado;
fer lo ha volenter, que lo tien' ya asmado.

2450 Tenía ya sus cartas so sello çerrado;
el rëy Alexandre por él a embïado;
ca es ome de días, teniá lo por senado;
queriál' por a consigo, ont' es mal engañado.

2451 Ya está en carrera, de su casa sallido;
será en Babiloña en tal tiempo venido;
verná luego el rëy ardient' e ençendido:
será al quinto día todo su pan molido."

2452 Fue Belçebus pagado, plaziól' de su crïada;
de todo el conçejo fue müy alabada.
Rogóla que le diesse de temprano çivada,
que fuesse recabdando de buena maitinada.

2453 Movióse la maliella, non lo quiso tardar;
metióse en carrera, pensó de aguijar;
ovo en la posada del conde a entrar.
¡Del Crïador que pueda mal siglo alcançar!

2454 Aún la ora era de gallos por venir;
el traïdor velaba, que non queriá dormir;
tanto pudo la mala basteçer e bollir
fasta que lo fizo en ello comedir.

2455 Demostróle la suzia toda la maestría,
quál espeçia le diesse, quál ora, en quál día;
firieron se las palmas por firmar pleitesía;
él fincó como malo e ella fue su vía.

2456 ¡Ay conde Antípater, non fuesses pareçido!
As mal pleïto fecho, mal seso comedido;
será fasta la fin el tu mal retraído;
más te valdriá a ti que non fuesses naçido.

2457 Quieres toller del mundo una grant claredat;
quieres tornar a Greçia a grant tenebredat.
Traïdor, ¿por qué amas tan fiera malvestat?
¡Guárdate que non fagas con Bessus hermandat!

2449	All of my scheme I have fully worked out: my faithful friend, the Count Antipater,* whom with lavish gifts I have kept in my pay, will willingly do it, for he already has it planned.
2450	He already has the letter, closed with his seal, for King Alexander has sent for that man. As he is a man of age, the King thought him wise and wanted him with him: here was his grave error.
2451	Gone from his home, he is already on his way and will have come to Babylonia by the appointed time; straight to the King will he come, aflame with passion and on the fifth day all his meal will be ground."
2452	Beelzebub was delighted and pleased with his servant, and she won great acclaim from the whole assembly. He asked her to be prompt in giving fodder to her mount, that she might go about her business in the early hours.
2453	The wicked creature departed, with no wish to delay, and undertook her journey and spurred on her way; she came to make her way into the lodgings of the Count, – may the Creator see that he meets an evil end!
2454	The hour of the cock-crow had still not arrived, but the traitor was awake, with no desire to sleep; so much could the evil creature scheme and intrigue that there did she implant the idea in his mind.
2455	The foul creature showed him the whole of the craft, what spice to give him, at what hour and on what day; they shook hands with each other to confirm their agreement; he was left full of evil and she went on her way.
2456	Oh, Count Antipater, that you had never appeared! You have made an evil pact and devised an evil plan; your evil will be told of till the end of the world; you would have been better served not to have been born.
2457	You wish to take away a great light from the world, and you wish to plunge Greece back into deep darkness. You traitor, why do you love such great wickedness? Beware lest you find yourself a brother to Bessus!

2458   El rëy Alexandre, cuerpo tan acabado,
       avié en es' comedio todo el mar buscado;
       cabo non le fallava, era se ya tornado;
       ya lo yva trayendo el poder del pecado.

2459   Ordenó sus faziendas con sus buenos varones;
       compassó todo'l mundo: cómo son tres quiñones,
       cómo son cada uno de diversas regiones,
       de diversas maneras, de diversos sermones.

2460   Asmó de la primera – mas non le valió nada –
       tornar en Babiloña, essa çibdat famada,
       ordenar toda Asïa, la que aviá ganada,
       que, si se fuesse ende, estodiés' recabdada.

2461   Troçir luego ad África, conquerir essas gentes:
       Marruecos con las tierras que le son soyaçientes;
       ganar los Montes Claros, lugares convinientes,
       que non son mucho fríos nin son mucho calientes.

2462   Desque oviesse África en su poder tornada,
       entrar en Eüropa, toda la mar passada,
       empeçar en España, una tierra señada,
       tierra de fuertes gentes e bien encastillada.

2463   Desent' conquerir Françia, una gente loçana;
       ingleses, alemanes, lombardos con Toscana;
       fer se llamar señor en la çibdat romana,
       tornarse por a Greçia, con voluntat bien sana.

2464   Bien dixo el salmista, en esto grant verdat,
       que lo que ome asma todo es vanidat;
       asma ome grant salto entre su voluntat;
       quanto cata, non puede sallir a la meitat.

2465   Si quanto ome asma oviesse a complir,
       non podrié Alexandre más que yo conquerir;
       mas, como es grant salto por a'l çielo sobir,
       tan grant ribaço cae entre fer e dezir.

2466   Ya avié el buen rëy la cosa estajada;
       avié en su talento la cosa compassada;
       mandó alçar los fumos, mover el albergada,
       ir pora Babiloña en ora entecada.

2458	King Alexander, a man of such distinction, in the meantime, had searched the whole sea. He had found no end and had now turned for home; the power of the Devil was now drawing him on.
2459	He set in order his affairs, together with his fine knights, mapping out the whole world and how there are three portions, how each one of them is made up of differing regions, with differing customs and differing speech.
2460	He thought first – though it was of no profit to him – of returning to Babylon, that city of fame, and bringing order to all Asia, which he had won, so that, if he were to leave, it would remain secure;
2461	of crossing straight to Africa to master those peoples, Morocco and the lands which lie below it; of winning the Shining Mountains, a place of comfort,* for they endure neither great cold nor great heat;
2462	and – when he had brought Africa into his power – of coming into Europe, after crossing all the seas, and beginning with Spain, an illustrious land, of powerful peoples and well endowed with castles;
2463	and then of conquering France, with its proud people, and the English, the Germans, the Lombards and Tuscans, of having himself declared lord in the city of Rome,* and returning to Greece with a healthy heart.
2464	The Psalmist spoke well and in this spoke great truth:* that everything a man plans is vanity; a man within his own heart plans a great leap, but when he looks, he cannot jump half the distance.
2465	If men were to accomplish all that they imagine, Alexander could not conquer any more than I, but as it is a great leap to rise to the Heavens, there is just as great a climb between actions and words.
2466	The good King had now taken his decision and mapped out his course of action in his heart. He ordered smoke to be sent up and camp to be struck and that they march to Babylon, at an ill-fated hour.

2467   Dïez años avié en Asïa estado,
mas avié, *Deo graçias*, su pleito acabado;
avié ricas çibdades en comedio poblado,
Alexandria la buena, do él fue trasladado.

2468   Si quisiesse el fado prestar le mayor vida,
poblara por aventura Troya la destroída;
mas sabe Dios los omes tener en tal medida
que non da a ninguno prosperidat complida.

2469   Ant' que a Babilonia por ojo la veamos,
ante que en conpaña del traïdor cayamos,
de las cosas que vío que escriptas fallamos,
maguer que non de todas, en algunas digamos.

2470   Non podriemos contar todas las sus visiones,
todas las que vïeron él con sus varones;
serié luenga tardança, ca son luengas razones;
non cabríen en cartas de quinze cabrones.

2471   Non podriemos de todas las bestias ementar
con quien muchas de vezes ovieron a lidiar;
podriamos muchos días en poca pro andar;
querríavos de grado la cosa estajar.

2472   Entre la multedunbre de los otros bestiones,
falló omes montesas, mugeres e barones;
los unos más de días, los otros moçajones;
andavan con las bestias, paçiendo los gamones.

2473   Non vistié ninguno ninguna vestidura;
todos eran vellosos en toda su fechura;
de noche, como bestias, yaçién en tierra dura;
qui los non entendiesse avrié fiera pavura.

2474   Ovieron con los cavallos d'ellos a alcançar;
ca eran muy ligeros, non los podién tomar;
maguer les preguntavan non les sabién fablar,
que non los entendián e avián a callar.

2475   Falló el avezilla que Fenis es llamada;
sola es en el siglo, nunca será doblada.
Ella mesma se quema de que es medïada;
de la ceniça muerta naçe otra vegada.

| 2467 | Ten years now had Alexander been in Asia,
but, thanks be to God, he had completed his business;
in that time he had founded prosperous cities,
like fine Alexandria, where he was taken.* |
|---|---|
| 2468 | If fate had been willing to grant him longer life,
he would perhaps have peopled the remains of Troy;
but God knows how to keep men within such bounds
that he grants to none absolute prosperity. |
| 2469 | Before we set our eyes upon Babylon,
and before we fall into the traitor's company,
of the things that he saw, that we have found in writing,*
let us talk now of some, though not of all. |
| 2470 | We could not tell of all that passed before his eyes,
all of those that were seen by him and his men;
it would be a long delay, for they are long accounts:
they would not fit on the parchment of fifteen rams' skins. |
| 2471 | We would not be able to mention all the beasts
with which they had to fight on many occasions;
we might spend many days in making little progress:
I would gladly like to cut the matter short for you. |
| 2472 | Among the multitude of other creatures,
he found mountain-dwelling people, men and women;
some were more advanced in years, others were still youthful;
they went among the beasts, and were grazing on the plants. |
| 2473 | Not one of them wore a single piece of clothing:
they were all hairy all over their bodies;
they lay on the hard ground at night, like the beasts,
and would terrify whoever did not know them. |
| 2474 | They had to ride on horseback to catch those people,
for they could not be captured, being very fleet of foot.
Though they questioned them, they were unable to speak,
for they did not understand them and had to stay silent. |
| 2475 | The King found the bird that is known as the Phoenix,*
which is alone in the world, there will never be a second:
the very bird burns itself in the middle of its life,
and from the dead ashes it is born anew. |

2476 Quando se siente vieja, aguisa su calera;
ençiérrase e quémase dentro en la foguera;
finca el gusanillo, como grano de pera;
cría como de nuevo; ésta es cosa verdadera.

2477 Fue yendo el buen rëy, teniendo su camino,
rico de buen esfuerço, pobre de pan e vino;
fallaron grant abondo de venado montino.
¡Qui con tal señor fuesse nunca serié mezquino!

2478 Fallaron un palaçio en una isla plana;
era dentro e fuera de obra adïana;
oviéronlo poblado Febus e su hermana,
a la que los actores suelen llamar Dïana.

2479 Fallaron un buen ome que la casa guardava;
reçibiólos fermoso, levantós ond' estava;
priso al rey por la mano, demandól' cóm' andava,
de quál parte vinié o quál cosa buscava.

2480 Comié el buen ome ençenso, ca non al;
guardava un buen templo, en medio del corral;
era todo obrado de oro natural;
çercávalo una viña que era otro tal.

2481 "Rey," dixo el fraire, "si me quisieres oír,
quiero te una cosa demostrar e dezir:
des que acá te quiso tu fado aduzir,
podes de tu ventura con çertedumbre ir.

2482 Yo te sabré dos árboles en est' monte mostrar
que non puedes tal cosa entre tu cuer asmar;
que ellos te non digan en qué puede finar;
si en plazer te cabe, puedes lo ir provar.

2483 El uno es el sol, es assí adonado;
el otro es la luna, es assí encantado
que pronunçia al ome quanto tiene asmado;
y verá que traen ambos lenguaje devisado.

2484 Mas si ir quisïeres en esta romería,
mester ha que seades limpios de terçer dia.
Descalços vos conviene d'entrar en esta vía,
ca es grant santidad e grant podestadía."

2476	When it feels that it is ageing it prepares its furnace; it shuts itself away and burns itself in the fire; there remains a little worm like the pip of a pear, and it grows as if anew; this is the true account.
2477	The good King kept travelling, keeping to his path, rich in noble endeavour and poor in bread and wine. They found a great abundance of mountain game; one who was with such a lord would never be in need.
2478	They found a palace upon a low-lying island, a work of excellence inside and out; there had dwelled Phoebus and his sister, whom the authors are wont to call Diana.*
2479	They found a good man who watched over the dwelling: he welcomed them handsomely and rose from where he sat; he took the King by the hand and asked him how he fared, from where he had come and what it was he sought.
2480	The good man ate incense and nothing besides that; he minded a fine temple in the courtyard's middle: it was all finely built and made of pure gold, and around it ran a vine, whose nature was the same.
2481	"My King," said the friar, "if you are willing to hear me, I want to explain and point out to you one thing: since your fate has chosen to bring you to this place, you can go from here certain of your fortune.
2482	I shall be able to show you two trees on this mountain, and you cannot conceive of any matter in your heart that they cannot tell you what ending it might have; if you so please, you can go and test it out.
2483	One is the sun, which has received such gifts, the other is the moon, which has been so enchanted, that they tell a man all he has imagined; then will it be seen how each has a twofold tongue.*
2484	But should you wish to go on this pilgrimage you must have purified yourselves for three days; you have to go barefoot to set out on this path, for it is of great sanctity and potency."

2485   Diz' el rëy al fraire: "Capellán, bien sepades
        que bien limpios andamos   d'esso que vos cuidades,
        mas si vos nos guïardes   a essas santidades,
        dar vos emos ofrendas   que mañas vos querades."

2486   Príso'l rey paños viles,   como de romero.
        Guïándolos el fraire,   metiólos en el sendero;
        pero levó consigo,   por non andar señero,
        Pérdicas e Antígonus,   Tolomeus el terçero.

2487   Entraron por los montes,   pensaron de andar,
        fasta que a las árvoles   ovieron de llegar;
        pero ante ovieron   las vides a fallar
        que saben ençenso   e bálsamo levar.

2488   Quando fueron llegados   a la grant santidat,
        predicóles el fraire   de la proprïedat;
        díxoles que asmassen   entre su voluntat;
        de quál cosa quisiessen   sabrién çierta verdat.

2489   Compeçó Alexandre   entre su cuer asmar
        sil' podrié en el mundo   nulla cosa 'scapar,
        si podrié con victoria   a su tierra tornar;
        cómo era puesto,   cómo avié d'estar.

2490   Respúsol' el un árvol   muy fiera razón:
        "Rey, yo bien entiendo   la tu entencïón;
        señor serás del mundo   a poca de sazón,
        mas nunca tornarás   en la tu regïón."

2491   Fabló el de la luna,   el sol estido callado;
        "Matart' han traedores,   morrás apoçonado.
        Rey," diz, "sé firme;   nunca serás rancado;
        el que tiene las yervas   es mucho tu privado."

2492   Díxo'l rey al árvol: "Si me quieres pagar,
        demostra me su nombre,   de quien me debe matar.
        Si non, si me dixiesses   sola ment' el lugar,
        per alguna manera   me podría guardar."

2493   "Rëy," dixo el árvol, "si fuesses sabidor,
        fariés descabeçar   luego el traïdor;
        el astre del fado   non avrié nul valor;
        avría grant rancura   de mí el Crïador."

2485	The King said to the friar, "Chaplain, be assured that we are quite clean of what causes you concern, but, if you would guide us to those holy places, we shall give you offerings as great as you wish."
2486	The King put on lowly clothes, like a pilgrim and the friar set them on the path, as their guide; but the King took with him, so as not to walk alone, Perdiccas, Antigonus, and Ptolemy as a third.
2487	They entered the hills and set about walking until they came to arrive at the trees; but before that they managed to find the vines which can produce incense and balsam.
2488	When they had come to the place of great sanctity, the friar preached to them on its properties; he told them that they should think within their own hearts of any thing of which they wished to know the certain truth.
2489	Alexander began to wonder in his heart if anything in the world could escape him, if he could return to his land in victory, how things were determined and how they were to be.
2490	One tree replied to him with very hard words: "King, I understand your meaning well; you will very soon be lord of the world but you will never return to your region."
2491	The moon's tree spoke, with the sun's fallen silent: "Traitors will kill you and you will die of poison. King," it said, "stand firm, you will never be defeated; the man who has the potion is very close to you."
2492	The King said to the tree, "If you wish to please me, show me the name of the one who is to kill me; if not, if you were only to tell me the place, in some way I could protect myself from it."
2493	"King," said the tree, "if you had this knowledge you would have the traitor beheaded at once, and so the star of your fate would have no force, and the Creator would bear me much anger."

2494 "Rëy," dixo el fraire, "assaz avedes oído;
si más te contendieres serás por fol tenido."
Fue luego el consejo del fraire reçebido;
tornaron a la casa onde avién sallido.

2495 Teniendo su carrera que avién empeçada,
fallaron los açephalos, la gent' descabeçada;
traen ante los pechos la cara enformada;
podrién a sobrevienta dar mala espantada.

2496 Alexandre el bueno, potestat sin frontera,
asmó una cosa andando por la carrera:
cómo aguisarié poyo o escalera
por veer todo'l mundo cóm' yazié o quál era.

2497 Fizo prender dos grifos, que son aves valientes;
abezólos a carnes saladas e rezientes;
tóvolos muy viçiosos de carnes convinientes
fasta que se fizieron gruessos e muy valientes.

2498 Fizo fer una capa de cuero muy sovado,
quanto cabrié un ome a anchura posado;
ligóla a los grifos con un firme filado
que non podrié falsar por un ome pesado.

2499 Fízoles el comer por tres días toller
por amor que oviessen talento de comer;
fízose él demientre en el cuero coser,
la cara descubierta, que pudiesse veer.

2500 Priso en una piértega la carne espetada,
en medio de los grifos pero bien alongada;
cuidavan se çevar, mas non les valió nada;
los grifos por prender la dieron luego bolada.

2501 Quanto ellos bolavan él tanto se erçía;
el rey Alexandre todavía sobía:
a las vezes alçava, a la vezes premía;
allá ivan los grifos do el rëy quería.

2502 Cuitávalos la fambre que avién encargada;
corrién por çevarse, mas non les valié nada;
bolavan todavía e cumplién su jornada;
era el rey traspuesto de la su albergada.

2494	"King," said the friar, "you have heard enough: if you insist further you will be held a fool." The counsel of the friar was accepted at once, and they returned to the dwelling from which they had set out.
2495	As he kept to the journey which he had begun they met the acephali, a headless people,* whose face was formed at the front of their chest; through surprise they could give a terrible shock.
2496	Alexander the good, a power without limits, conceived an idea as he travelled his route: how he would build an embankment or a ladder to see the form and the nature of all the world.
2497	He had his men catch two gryphons, worthy birds,* and accustomed them to salted and fresh flesh; he had them addicted to flavourful meat until they became stout and full of strength.
2498	He had a pouch made of well softened leather, big enough to hold a man lying full length, and tied it to the gryphons with a strong thread that a heavy man's weight could not break.
2499	He had their food be taken away for three days, in his desire that they be eager to eat; meanwhile he had himself sewn into the pouch with his face exposed, so that he could see.
2500	He placed the meat, which had been skewered on a pole, in between the gryphons but well ahead of them; they sought to feed on it, but it was to no avail, and, to seize it, the gryphons at once took flight.
2501	As high as they flew, just as high did he rise: King Alexander made his way ever upwards; sometimes he soared up, and sometimes he swooped, and the gryphons went where the King wished.
2502	They were gnawed by the hunger that they had endured and pressed on to feed themselves, but to no avail. They continued to fly until the end of their voyage, and the King was hidden from the sight of his army.

2503   Alçávales la carne   quando querié sobir,
       iva la abaxando   quando queriá deçir;
       do veyán ir la carne,   allá avien de ir.
       Non los riebto, ca fambre   mala es de sofrir.

2504   Tanto pudo el rëy   a las nuves pujar:
       veyé montes e valles   de yus' de sí estar;
       veyé entrar los ríos   todos en alta mar,
       mas cóm' yazié o non,   nunca lo pudo asmar.

2505   Veyé en quáles puertos   son angostos los mares,
       veyé grandes peligros   en muchos de lugares;
       veyé muchas galeas   dar en los peñiscales,
       otras sallir a puerto,   adobar de yantares.

2506   Mesuró toda África   cómo yaz' assentada,
       por quál parte serié   más rafez la entrada;
       luego vio que por Siria   avié mejor passada,
       ca avié grant sallida   e larguera entrada.

2507   Luengo serié de todo   quanto que vio contar;
       non podrié a lo medio   el día avondar;
       mas en una ora   sopo mientes parar
       lo que todos abades   non lo sabrián asmar.

2508   Solemos lo leer   – diz'lo la escriptura –
       que es llamado mundo   el ome por figura;
       qui comedir quisiere   e asmar la fechura
       entendrá que es bien   razón sin de presura.

2509   Asïa es el cuerpo,   segunt mi oçïente,
       sol e luna, los ojos,   que naçen de oriente;
       los braços son la cruz   del Rëy Omnipotente
       que fue muerto en Asia   por salut de la gente.

2510   La pierna que deçende   del siniestro costado
       es el reino de África,   por ella figurado;
       Toda la mandan moros,   un pueblo renegado,
       que oran a Mahómad,   un traïdor provado.

2511   Es por la pierna diestra   Eüropa notada:
       ésta es mas católica,   de la fe más poblada;
       ésta es de la diestra   del Obispo santiguada;
       tienen Petrus e Paulus   en ella su posada.

Book of Alexander

2503   He raised the meat before them when he wanted to rise
and lowered it when it was his wish to descend;
where they saw the meat go, there they had to follow
– I do not blame them, for hunger is hard to endure.

2504   The King was able to soar so high into the clouds
that he saw mountains and valleys lie below him;
he saw the rivers all flow out into the high seas,
but their extent he could never imagine.

2505   He saw in which harbours were the sea's waters narrow;
he saw great dangers which lay in many places;
he saw many galleys be wrecked on the rocks
and others come to port and make ready for the feast.

2506   He gauged the way in which all Africa was laid out,
and where it would be easiest to enter;
he saw at once that through Syria the route was best,
for it had a wide exit and the entry was large.

2507   It would be a long tale to tell all that he saw:
the whole day would not allow for half of it;
but in a single hour he managed to take in
what all the abbots are not able to imagine.

2508   We are used to reading – and the writings say it –
that the world is known as an image of Man;*
whoever wants to think and reflect on its form
will understand with no trouble that this is quite true.

2509   As I see it, Asia is the body of the man;
the sun and moon are the eyes, which are born in the East;
the arms are the cross of the Almighty King,
who died in Asia for the people's salvation.

2510   The leg that hangs down from the left-hand side
is the kingdom of Africa, which it represents;
it is all ruled by Moors, a renegade people,
who pray to Mahomet, a proven traitor.*

2511   It is Europe that is depicted by the right leg:
this is the most Catholic, most peopled with believers,
and it is blessed by the right hand of the Bishop:
there it is that Peter and Paul have their dwellings.

2512 La carne es la tierra,   espessa e pesada;
      el mar es el pellejo,   que la tiene çercada;
      las venas son los ríos, que la tienen temprada;
      fazen diestro e siniestro   mucha tornaviscada.

2513 Los huessos son las peñas   que alçan los collados;
      cabellos de cabeça   las yerbas de los prados;
      crían en esta tierra   muchos malos venados
      que son por majamiento   de los nuestros pecados.

2514 Desque ovo el rëy   la tierra bien asmada,
      que ovo a su guisa   la voluntat pagada,
      abaxóles el çevo,   guïólos de tornada;
      fue en poco de rato   entre la su mesnada.

2515 La ventura del rëy,   que lo querié guïar,
      ante que d'esti mundo   oviesse a pasar,
      en el poder del mundo   quísolo acabar;
      mas ovo assaz poco   en esso a durar.

2516 Grand' era la su fama   por el mundo sallida,
      que era toda África   en grant miedo metida;
      teniése Eüropa   mucho por falleçida
      que la obedïençia   non avía complida.

2517 Acordaron se todos   – plaçió al Crïador –
      por reçebir al rey   de Greçia por señor;
      embïáronle luego   al buen emperador
      parias e omenajes,   e signos de pavor.

2518 Embiáronle parias,   ruegos multiplicados,
      de cada una tierra   presentes señalados;
      los que ivan con ellos   eran omes honrados;
      omes eran de seso   e muy bien razonados.

2519 Embiaron de Marruecos   un yelmo natural,
      en el yelmo escripto   vassallage leal;
      ca el rey Alexandre   non cobdiçiava al
      si non el señorío   con poca de señal.

2520 Embïól' España   ofreçer vassallage;
      embïól' por parïas   un potro de liñage,
      que avié esta manera   el rey de grant corage:
      tomarles poca renta   sil' fazién omenage.

2512	The flesh is the land, which is thick and heavy,
	and the sea is the skin by which it is enclosed;
	the veins are the rivers which keep it temperate
	and which made great meanders left and right.
2513	The bones are the rocks which raise up the hills,
	and the hairs of the head are the grass of the fields;
	in this land are bred many evil wild beasts,
	and these serve as punishment for our sins.
2514	Once the King had fully surveyed the land
	and had sated his longing as he wished,
	he lowered the food and directed them back,
	and in a short time he was among his men.
2515	The King's good fortune, which wished to be his guide,
	before that man was to pass from this world,
	wished to make his worldly power complete,
	though he was to keep it for a short enough time.
2516	Great was his fame which had spread throughout the world,
	so great that Africa was plunged into the depths of fear.
	Europe felt that it had made a grave error
	by not paying full obedience to the King.
2517	They all were agreed, it pleased the Creator,
	to accept the King of Greece as their lord;
	immediately they sent out to the good Emperor
	tribute and homage and tokens of fear.
2518	They sent to him tribute, many supplications*
	and extraordinary gifts from each of the lands;
	those accompanying these were men of honour,
	intelligent men, highly skilled in speech.
2519	They sent a helmet from Morocco of their own native type,
	with a pledge of loyal vassalage written on it,
	for King Alexander desired nothing else
	except lordship and sought few material gifts.
2520	Spain sent him her offer of vassalage
	and sent a pedigree colt as tribute,
	for this was the way of the valiant King:
	to demand little payment if they paid him homage.

2521 Non se tovo por esso França por aontada:
embïól un escudo en funda bien obrada.
Alemaña, sobre escripta, e fue bien acordada,
embïól por parïas una rica espada.

2522 El señor de Seçilia – ¡que Dios lo benediga! –
embïól' por parïas una rica loriga;
los que ivan más tarde, creo que verdad diga,
tenién que avién fecho fallimient' o nemiga.

2523 Por estos çinco regnos que avemos contados,
devemos entender los que non son notados;
todos eran en esta manera acordados
que sólo de la nuevas eran mal espantados.

2524 Como son muchas tierras – contar non las podría –
ivan con estas parias mucha cavallería;
nunca passó un tiempo tan fiera romería
que más gent' non passava en esta legaçía.

2525 Levavan con las parias, por seer más creídas,
todos cartas çerradas por *a.b.c.* partidas;
tantas fueron las gentes a los puertos venidas
que eran sobre mucho las naves encaridas.

2526 Fueron en Babilonia las gentes allegadas;
la villa, maguer grande, adur avié posadas.
Las moças e las viejas sedién maravilladas
de tan estrañas gentes que eran ajuntadas.

2527 Allegaron las nuevas al rey aventurado
que era en su busca el mundo ajuntado,
quel' querién fazer todos omenaje de grado,
ofreçerle las parias e jurar su mandado.

2528 El rëy con las nuevas ovo grant alegría;
ovo luego movida la su cavallería;
non cuidava veer la ora e el día
que oviesse ganado toda la monarchía.

2529 Fue pora Babilonia a müy grant pressura
por reçebir grant gloria e grant buena ventura;
dávale la cobdiçia alas e calentura;
non sabié quál çelada le tenié la Natura.

2521	France did not feel herself shamed by this, and sent him a shield in a richly worked case; with a written document and with full agreement, Germany sent him a costly sword in tribute.
2522	The Lord of Sicily – may God give him blessing! –* sent to him in tribute a rich coat of mail. Those last to arrive – I believe I tell the truth – felt that they had acted in error or enmity.
2523	After these five kingdoms that we have mentioned, we must understand those not in our list: all the dominions were agreed in this matter, that they were filled with terror just by his renown.
2524	As the lands are so many that I could not count them, with these tributes there went a great force of knights; there never was a time with a pilgrimage so great that more people did not take part in this ceremony.
2525	With the tributes, in order to be fully believed, they all brought sealed letters, divided by a.b.c., and there were so many people who came to the ports that the ships bore a very heavy burden.
2526	In Babylon had all the people arrived: though the city was great, the dwellings were scarce; the women young and old were all struck with wonder that people so extraordinary were gathered there.
2527	The news came to the king that fortune favoured that the world had assembled to seek him, and all were gladly willing to pay him homage, to offer him tribute and swear him allegiance.
2528	The King was greatly delighted at the news and immediately formed up his force of knights. He had not thought that he would see the hour and the day when he had won a sovereignty complete.
2529	In very great haste did he make for Babylon to accept great glory and fine and great good fortune; his desire gave him wings and the heat of passion, but he did not know what trap Nature had for him.

2530   ¡El rëy Alexandre,   cuerpo tan acabado,
       vas a reçebir grant gloria,   mas eres engañado!
       ¡Tal es la tu ventura   e el tu prinçipado
       como la flor del lirio   que se cae privado!

2531   Esta set que te faz'   acuitar el camino,
       toda te la estaja   un mal baso de vino;
       desque el tu Antípater   en Babilonia vino,
       siempr' en tu muerte anda   con Jobas, mal vezino.

2532   Quando fueres en somo   de la rueda alçado,
       non durarás un día   que serás trastornado;
       serás entre la rueda   e la tierra echado;
       lo que viste en Dario   será en ti tornado.

2533   Avié el rey venido   çerca de la çibdat;
       sallólo reçebir   toda la vezindat.
       Llegáronse de gentes   una infinidat;
       semejava por poco   el val de Josafat.

2534   Finchiánle las carreras   de ramos e de flores,
       de blancas, de bermejas   e de otras colores;
       muchos eran los cantos,   muchos los cantadores,
       muchos los instrumentos,   muchos los tocadores.

2535   Non eran los adobos   todos d'una manera;
       gentes de muchas partes   trayén mucha venera.
       El rey, con la priessa,   non podié ir carrera;
       plaziél' al que uviava   besar la estribera.

2536   Cad' un' en su lenguaje   diziá al Crïador:
       "¡Loado sea Dios,   que nos dio tal señor!"
       Los que bien lo amavan   avián end' grant sabor,
       mas non sele camiava   el cuer al traïdor.

2537   Entró por la çibdat,   fue por a la posada.
       ¡Si entrado non fuesse   fascas non perdrié nada!
       Mas ante fueron bísperas,   la siesta bien quedada,
       que toda la gent' fuesse   en la villa entrada.

2538   Otro día mañana,   fuera al mercadal,
       mandó fer el buen rëy   conçejo general;
       mandó posar la cátedra   en un alto poyal,
       en un lugar çerrado,   so un rico çendal.

2530	King Alexander, you who are so fine a warrior,
	you are going to receive great glory, but you are deceived;
	your good fortune and your princely sway
	are like the flower of the lily which is quick to drop.
2531	This thirst which makes the journey cause you anguish
	will all be quenched by a vile glass of wine;
	ever since your Antipater came to Babylon,
	he has plotted your death, with Iolaus, an evil neighbour.*
2532	When you are raised up to the height of the wheel,
	you will not last a day but be sent cast down;
	you will be thrown down from the wheel to the ground:
	what you saw in Darius will be turned on you.
2533	The King had arrived a short distance from the city
	and all those in the area went out to receive him.
	An infinite number of people flocked around him:
	it was much like the Valley of Josaphat.*
2534	For him the roads were strewn with branches and flowers,
	of white and red and a variety of colours;
	many were the songs and many were the singers,
	many were the instruments with many there to play them.
2535	The adornments were not all of the same kind:
	people of many regions brought many scallop shells;*
	the King, with the throng, could not travel on his path,
	and it pleased those arriving to kiss his stirrup.
2536	In their own tongue, they each said to the Creator,
	"Praise be to God who gave us such a lord!"
	Those who loved him well took great pleasure in this,
	but no change took place in the heart of the traitor.
2537	He entered the city and made for his dwelling
	– had he not entered, he would scarce have lost a thing;
	but Vespers had come with the hour of Sext well past
	before the people were all inside the city.
2538	The next morning, outside in the market square,
	the good King convened a general council:
	he bade his throne be set on a raised up spot,
	in a place enclosed beneath a rich silk canopy.

2539 Ante que a las parias   entremos reçebir,
quiérovos de la obra   de la tienda dezir.
Segunt que lo entiendo   cuídolo departir;
qui mejorar pudiere   avrél' qué gradeçir.

2540 Larga era la tienda,   redonda e bien tajada;
a dos mill cavalleros   darié larga posada.
Apelles el maestro   la ovo debujada;
non farié otro ome   obra tan esmerada.

2541 El paño de la tienda   era rico sobejo;
era de seda fina,   de un xamit vermejo;
com' era bien texido   egual mente parejo,
quando el sol rayava   luziá como espejo.

2542 El tendal fue de boiri,   sotil mente obrado,
de pedaços menudos   en torno compassado;
como era bien preso   e bien endereçado,
nol' devisarié ome   dó era ajuntado.

2543 Guarniólo el maestro   de alto a fondón
de piedras de grant preçio,   todas bien a razón;
non falleçiá ninguna   de las que ricas son;
toda la plus sotil   era de grant missión.

2544 Tenié en la cabeça   tres pomas de buen oro;
qual se quiere de todas   valié un grant tesoro;
nunca tan ricas vío   nin judío nin moro.
¡Si en el mundo fuessen   saberlas devrié Poro!

2545 Non querría el tiempo   en las cuerdas perder,
ca avría grant rato   en ellas a poner:
eran de fina seda;   podián mucho valer
las lazadas de oro   do avién a prender.

2546 Las estacas cabdales,   que las cuerdas tiravan,
toda la otra obra   éssas la adobavan;
las unas a las otras   en ren non semejavan;
como omes espessos   tan espessas estavan.

2547 Las de la otra orden,   que tiran las ventanas,
de todas las mejores   semejavan hermanas;
de oro eran todas,   de obra muy loçanas;
tenién todas en alto   sendas ricas mançanas.

2539	Before we come to the receiving of the tributes,
	I want to tell you of the tent's decoration:*
	as I understand it, I intend to pass it on;
	whoever can do better I shall have cause to thank.
2540	The tent was extensive, round and well proportioned,
	and would give ample room for two thousand knights;
	the master craftsman Apelles had been its designer:
	no other would have fashioned a work of such elegance.
2541	The fabric of the tent was truly exquisite:
	it was of fine silk, the cloth red in hue;
	as it was well woven, even and smooth,
	when the sun shone, it gleamed like a mirror.
2542	The tent-post was cleverly worked with ivory,
	and embellished all around with tiny pieces.
	As it was well joined and elegantly fastened
	no man could have told where the links were made.
2543	The master adorned it from top to bottom
	with stones of great value, all set in proportion.
	None of the most precious was missing from there,
	and that which stood out least was of great price.
2544	It had at its top three apples of fine gold,
	and any of these was worth a great treasure;
	neither Jew nor Moor ever saw one so rich;
	if the world had any, Porus should know them.
2545	I would not wish to lose time on the ropes
	for I would have to spend a long while on them;
	they were of fine silk; there must have been great value
	in the fastenings for them, which were made of gold.
2546	The principal stakes which held fast the ropes
	embellished all the rest of the tent;
	they did not resemble each other at all,
	and their thickness was like that of stout men.
2547	Those of the other kind, that held the windows tight,
	seemed to be the sisters of all the larger ones;
	they were all of gold and very handsomely worked
	and each one had a priceless apple atop it.

2548   Querría a la obra　de la tienda entrar;
　　　　　en estas menudençias　non querría tardar;
　　　　　avemos y un rato　assaz que deportar;
　　　　　ir se nos ha guisando　demientre la yantar.

2549   Bien pareçié la tienda　quando era alçada;
　　　　　suso era redonda;　a derredor quadrada;
　　　　　de somo fasta fondo　era bien estoriada:
　　　　　qué cosa conteçió　o en quál tenporada.

2550   Era en la corona　el çielo debuxado,
　　　　　todo de crïaturas　angélicas poblado;
　　　　　mas el lugar do fue　Luçifer derribado
　　　　　todo estava yermo,　pobre e deshonrado.

2551   Crïava Dios al ome　por enchir es' lugar;
　　　　　el malo con enbidia　óvogel' a furtar;
　　　　　por el furto los angeles　ovieron grant pesar;
　　　　　fue judgado el ome　por morir e lazrar.

2552   Çerca estas estorias　e çerca un rincón,
　　　　　alçavan los gigantes　torre a grant missïón;
　　　　　mas metió Dios en ellos　atal confusïón
　　　　　por que avién de ir　todos en perdiçión.

2553   Las ondas del diluvio　tanto querién sobir,
　　　　　por somo de Tiburio　querién fascas complir.
　　　　　Noé bevié el vino,　non lo podié sofrir;
　　　　　yazié desordenado,　queriénlo encobrir.

2554   En un' de los fastiales,　luego en la entrada,
　　　　　la natura del año　sedié toda pintada;
　　　　　los meses con sus días,　con su luna contada,
　　　　　cad' uno quál fazienda　avié acomendada.

2555   Estava don Janero,　a dos partes catando,
　　　　　çercado de çeçinas　çepas acarreando;
　　　　　tenié gruessas gallinas,　estávalas assando;
　　　　　estava de la percha　longanizas tirando.

2556   Estava don Febrero　sus manos calentando;
　　　　　oras fazía sol,　oras saraçeando;
　　　　　verano de ivierno　ívalos desemblando;
　　　　　por que era más chico　sediése querellando.

2548	I would like to come to the tent's decoration, and not delay over such details as these; we still have a long enough time for entertainment whilst in the meantime our meal is prepared.
2549	The tent had a fine look when it was erect, round at its height and with four straight sides; from the top to the bottom it was covered with stories of what events took place and in what times.
2550	Heavens was depicted on the crown, all thronging with angelic creatures; but the place where Lucifer had been cast down was desolate, poor and full of dishonour.
2551	It was to fill that place that God created Man, but the Evil One with envy came to steal it from him; on account of the theft, the angels bore great pain, and Man was condemned to suffer death and hardship.
2552	Near to these stories and near to a corner, with great endeavour, the giants raised a tower, but God set among them such great confusion by which they all came to fall into perdition.
2553	The waters of the flood sought to rise so far that they almost wished to come above the peak of Mount Tabor.* Noah drank the wine, and it was more than he could manage:* he lay in a sprawl, while they tried to cover him.
2554	On one of the panels, which was right by the entry, all the nature of the year was depicted:* the months with their days and their phases of the moon, and the tasks with which each one was entrusted.
2555	There was January, who looked in two directions, surrounded by cured meats and carrying vines; he had two fat hens which he was roasting and was carrying sausages on a pole.
2556	There was February, warming his hands; now the sun shone, now it was snowing; he was separating summer and winter, and, because he was shortest, was complaining.

2557 Março avié grant priessa de sus viñas labrar,
      priessa con podadores e priessa con cavar;
      fazié aves e bestias ya en çelos andar,
      los días e las noches faziélos egualar.

2558 Abril sacava huestes por a ir guerrear,
      ca avié ya alcaçeres grandes por a segar;
      fazié meter las viñas por a vino levar,
      creçer miesses e yerbas, los días alongar.

2559 Sedié el mes de Mayo coronado de flores,
      afeitando los campos de diversas colores,
      organeando las mayas e cantando d'amores,
      espigando las miesses que siembran labradores.

2560 Madurava don Junio las miesses e los prados;
      tenié redor de sí muchos ordios segados,
      de çerezas maduras los çerezos cargados;
      eran al mayor siesto los días allegados.

2561 Sedié el mes de Julio logando segadores;
      corriénle por la cara a priessa los sudores;
      segudavan las bestias las moscas mordedores;
      fazié tornar los vinos de amargas sabores.

2562 Trillava don Agosto las miesses por las eras;
      abentava las parvas, alçava las çiveras;
      yva de los agrazes faziendo uvas veras;
      eston' faziá atupno sus órdenes primeras.

2563 Setiembre trayé varas, segudié las nogueras;
      apretava las cubas, podava las mimbreras,
      vendimiava las viñas con falçes podaderas;
      non dexava los pássaros llegar a las figueras.

2564 Estava don Otubre sus miéssegos faziendo;
      ensayava los vinos que yazién ferviendo;
      iva como de nuevo sus cosas requiriendo;
      iva pora sembrar el ivierno viniendo.

2565 Noviembre segudié a los puercos las landes;
      cayera de un robre, levávanlo en andes;
      empieçan al cresuelo velar los abezantes,
      ca son las noches luengas, los días non tan grandes.

2557	March was in great haste to tend to his vines, in haste with the pruning and in haste to dig; he made birds and beasts now full of desire and made the days and nights of equal length.
2558	April sent out armies to go and make war, for now there were great castles to be reaped; he had the vines tended, so that wine be produced, and made the crops and grass grow, the days lengthen.
2559	The month of May was crowned with flowers, decking the fields in manifold colours, intoning the spring songs and singing of love, bringing to ear the crops that the farmers sow.
2560	June brought the crops and the meadows to ripeness, and had around him many harvested fields; the cherry trees were laden with ripe cherry fruit; and the days had now reached their greatest length.
2561	Now the month of July was hiring reapers and sweat streamed swiftly down his face; the flies, with their bites, pursued the beasts; and he made the wine take a bitter taste.
2562	August beat the harvest on the threshing floor, winnowed the corn and carried off the grain; He gave sour-tasting grapes their true taste and Autumn then performed its first tasks.
2563	September with his staffs shook the walnut trees, sealed the casks tight and pruned the osiers. He harvested the vines with his pruning sickle and kept the birds from coming to the fig trees.
2564	October was engaged upon blending the wines, and he tried those which were fermenting; once more he went seeking out his tools, and went out to sow, for winter was coming.
2565	November shook down the acorns for the pigs: he felled them from the oak, and they were carried on trays. Students begin to keep their vigil by lamplight, for the nights are long, but the days not so.

2566 Matava los püercos   Diziembre por mañana,
       almorçava los fígados   por amatar la gana;
       tenié niebla escura   siempre por la mañana,
       ca es en essi tiempo   ella muy cutïana.

2567 En el segundo paño   de la rica lavor,
       las estorias cabdales,   fechas de buen pintor:
       la una fue de Hércules,   firme campeador,
       la otra fue de Paris,   un buen doñeador.

2568 Niñuelo era Hércules,   assaz poco moçuelo;
       adur abrié los ojos,   yazié en el berçuelo.
       Entendió la madrastra   que era fuerte niñuelo;
       querriá fer a la madre   veer del fijo duelo.

2569 Embïava dos sierpes;   queriénlo afogar;
       perçibiólas el niño   que lo querién matar.
       Ovo con sendas manos   a ellas allegar;
       afogólas a amas;   ovo ella pesar.

2570 Desent' ivas' crïando,   sintiése muy valiente;
       vençié muchas batallas,   conquirié mucha gente;
       echava ad Anteon   muy aviltada mente;
       plantava sus mojones   luego en occidente.

2571 Paris rabió a Elena,   fizo grant adulterio;
       reçibieron lo en Troya   mas fue por su lazerio;
       non quisieron los griegos   sofrir tan grant contrario;
       juraron de vengarse   todos en el salterio.

2572 Vinién çercar a Troya   con agüeros catados;
       estavan los de dentro   firmes e aguisados.
       Eran de todas partes   represos e lazrados,
       pero ellos e ellos   estavan esforçados.

2573 Los diez años passados   que la çerca durava,
       avié a morir Éctor   – Aquiles lo matava –
       pero aún la villa   en duro se parava,
       ca el término puesto   aún non se llegava.

2574 Avié aún Aquiles   en cabo a morir,
       ond' avién el cavallo   los griegos a bastir;
       avién con grant engaño   Troya a conquerir;
       oviéronla por suelo   toda a destroír.

2566	December slaughtered the pigs in the morning and lunched on figs to deaden his hunger; always did the morning bring a thick fog, for it comes very often at that time.
2567	Upon the second panel of the rich creation, of the momentous scenes, which a fine painter rendered, one was that of Hercules, who was a stout battler, and the other was of Paris, the fine gallant.
2568	A little child was Hercules, not even yet a boy;* his eyes he scarcely opened and he lay in his cradle; his stepmother saw that he was a strong child, and wished to make the mother feel grief for her son.
2569	She sent two serpents, which tried to strangle him, but the child realised that they wished to kill him: he managed to take hold of them, one in each hand, and he strangled them both, to her sorrow.
2570	Then he grew older and felt full of courage, he won many battles and conquered many people. He inflicted on Antaeus a most shameful death, and he set down his markers on reaching the West.*
2571	Paris stole Helen, in a great act of adultery, and was welcomed into Troy, but to their misery; the Greeks were unwilling to suffer such an insult, and they all swore vengeance on the psaltery.
2572	The auguries consulted, they went to besiege Troy, but those within were firm and well prepared; everywhere men were being driven back and wounded, but the armies of both sides were of great valour.
2573	With the ten years that the siege lasted now passed, it was Hector's fate to die at Achilles' hands; but the city still continued its bitter resistance, for the appointed time had still not arrived.
2574	Achilles still had to meet his end, at last, on which account the Greeks were to build the horse, and through a great deception they were to conquer Troy and leave it razed completely to the ground.

2575 Quando el rey Alexandre estas gestas veyé,
creçiél' el coraçon, grant esfuerço cogié;
dizié que por su pleito un clavo non darié;
si non se mejorasse, morir se dexarié.

2576 En el paño terçero de la tienda honrada
era la mapamundi escripta e notada;
bien tenié qui la fizo la tierra decorada
como si la oviesse con sus piedes andada.

2577 Tenié el mar en medio a la tierra çercada;
contra la mar, la tierra non semejava nada;
era éssa en éssa más yerma que poblada;
d'ella yazié pasturas, d'ella yazié labrada.

2578 Las tres partes del mundo yazién bien devisadas;
Asïa a las otras aviélas engañadas;
Eüropa e África yazién muy renconadas;
deviendo seer fijas, semejavan anadas.

2579 Assí fue el maestro sotil e acordado,
non olvidó çibdat nin castillo ortado,
nin río, nin otero, nin yermo nin lavrado;
non olvidó emperio nin ningunt buen condado.

2580 Tajo, Duero e Ebro, tres aguas son cabdales;
Cogolla e Moncayo, enfiestos dos poyales;
en España ave estos çinco señales
con mucho buen castillo e villas naturales.

2581 ¿Qué mejores querades que Burgos e Panplona,
Soria e Toledo, Leon e Lisbona?
Por Gascoña corre el río de Garona;
en éssa yaz' Burdeu, vezino de Bayona.

2582 La çibdat de Paris jazié en media Françia:
de toda clereçía avié y abondançia.
Tors yazié sobre Leire, villa de grant ganançia;
más delant' corrié Ruédano, río de abondançia.

2583 Yazién en Lombardía Pavía e Milana;
pero detrás dexamos Bergoña e Vïana;
Boloña sobre todas pareçe palaçiana;
de leyes e decretos éssa es la fontana.

2575	When King Alexander saw these exploits, his heart swelled up and he took great courage. He said that he would not give a nail for his cause; if he did not do better, he would let himself die.
2576	On the third panel of the celebrated tent was set out and represented a map of the world. Its maker had depicted the earth with skill, as if he had walked it upon his own feet.
2577	The land was in the middle, surrounded by the sea and, compared with the sea, it was as nothing; the land, within the sea, was more deserted than peopled; and here there lay pastures, and there ploughed land.
2578	The three parts of the world were clearly divided: the other two of them had been deceived by Asia, and Europe and Africa were deeply enraged: though they ought to be daughters, step-children they seemed.
2579	The master craftsman was so subtle and sure of mind that he forgot no city and no castle of note, no river, no hill, no land barren or worked; he forgot no empire or any fine county.
2580	Tagus, Douro and Ebro, three major rivers, Cogolla and Moncayo, two towering peaks:* in the country of Spain there are these five landmarks, with many fine castles and native cities.
2581	What better could you want than Burgos and Pamplona, Soria and Toledo, León and Lisbon?* Through Gascony there runs the River Garonne; on this lies Bordeaux, a neighbour of Bayonne.
2582	The city of Paris lay in the middle of France, with a rich abundance of all kinds of learning.* Tours lay on the Loire, a city of great profit; further on ran the Rhône, a river of bounty.*
2583	In Lombardy were to be found Pavia and Milan, but others we have left behind: Burgundy and Vienne; Bologna seems outstanding above all others* and it is the fount of all laws and decrees.

2584   En cabo de Toscana,   Lombardía passada,
en ribera de Tibre   yazié Roma poblada;
yazié el que la ovo   primero çimentada,
de su hermano mismo   la cabeça cortada.

2585   Si quisiéremos todas   la tierras ementar,
otro tamaño libro   podríe y entrar;
mas quiero en la cosa   a destajo andar;
ca so yo ya cansado,   querría me folgar.

2586   Los castillos de Asia   con todas sus heredades
ya nos fablamos d'ellos,   si bien vos acordades;
los tribus, los linajes,   los tiempos, las hedades,
todos yazién en ella   con sus propïedades.

2587   Alexandre en ella   lo podié perçebir:
quánto avié conquisto,   quánto por conquerir;
non sele podié tierra   alçar nin encobrir
que él non la supiesse   buscar e combatir.

2588   Escrivió el maestro   en el quarto fastial
las gestas del buen rëy,   súpolas bien contar:
de quántos años era   quand empeçó reinar,
cómo supo el cuello   de Nicolao domar;

2589   quál muerte fizo dar   al falso de Pausón,
el que al rey Felipo   mató a traïción;
cómo destruyó Tebas   e sobre quál razón;
cómo ovo a Atenas   pïedat e perdón;

2590   cómo passó a Asia   a Darïo buscar,
cómo a Troya ovo   en Frigia a fallar;
la fazienda de Tiro   non la quiso lexar
– cómo sopo su onta   el rëy bien vengar –;

2591   el torneo de Ménona,   que valié lit campal,
que duró tres días,   fazienda fue cabdal;
cómo a los judíos   otorgó su señal,
cómo desvolvïó   la laçada real;

2592   la fazienda de Dario,   el buen emperador:
quáles fueron en ella   muertos por su señor;
cómo murió cascuno,   quál fue el matador,
la prisión de los fijos   e de la su uxor;

2584	At Tuscany's end, having passed through Lombardy, on the banks of the Tiber lay the city of Rome; in it lay the man who had been its first founder and cut off the head of his very own brother.*
2585	If we were to seek to mention all of the lands another book of equal size could begin there; but I want to come to an end in this matter; for I am tired now and I would like to rest.
2586	The castles of Asia together with their lands – we have talked of them already, if your recall is sound – and the tribes, the families, the times, and the ages, were all to be found there, with their many features.
2587	On his tent, Alexander could have sight of it all: all that he had conquered and all he might still. No land could rise against him or hide itself away so that he could not find it and engage it in war.
2588	The master recounted upon the fourth panel the deeds of the good King, elegantly told: how old he was at the inception of his reign and how he managed to make Nicolao bow his head;
2589	the death that he inflicted on Pausanias, the traitor, the man who treacherously murdered King Philip; how he destroyed Thebes and the reason that he had, and how he showed mercy and pardon to Athens;
2590	how he went to Asia to seek out Darius, and how when in Phrygia he came to find Troy; he wished not to omit the battle for Tyre and how the King was well able to avenge his shame;
2591	the contest with Memnon, a pitched battle's equal, which lasted for a full three days, a mighty feat; how he gave his sign of protection to the Jews and how he undid the royal knot;
2592	the battle against the good Emperor Darius, and those who died there in the service of their lord; how each one died and at the hands of what man, and the capture of Darius' children and wife;

2593   la grant emperadriz   cómo fue soterrada
e la su sepoltura   cómo fue debuxada;
cómo rancó a Dario   la segunda vegada,
cómo fue Babilonia   conquista e poblada;

2594   la traiçión de Dario,   cómo murió traído,
cómo fue soterrado   e Bessus escarnido.
Fue el su casamiento   mas aína metido;
el campo de la tienda   con esto fue complido.

2595   Non quiero de la tienda   fer grant alegoría;
non quiero detener   en palabra el día;
quánto podié valer   preçiar non lo podría;
non la podriá comprar   el aver d'Almaría.

2596   Quando fue el buen rey   a la tienda entrado,
paróse en la cátedra,   lugar tan honrado;
mandó traer las parias   quel' avién mandado
e leer por conçejo   las cartas del ditado.

2597   Quando fueron las cartas   abiertas e leídas,
los omenajes fechos,   las parias reçebidas,
alçó a Dios los ojos   e, las manos tendidas,
dixo unas palabras   fermosas e sabridas:

2598   "Rëy de los rëys,   que non conoçes par,
en tu mano yaze   el toller e el dar,
el alçar e premir,   el ferir e sanar;
Señor, ¡laudado seas,   que lo deves estar!

2599   Señor, siempre Te devo   bendeçir e laudar
que tan bien me dreçeste   mi cosa acabar;
que por pavor, Señor,   sin otro mal llevar,
vienen todas las tierras   la mi mano besar.

2600   Non Telo devién menos   las tierras gradeçer
por que non ensayaron   quál es el mi poder;
si en otra porfidia   se quisiessen meter,
non se podrián por guisa   ninguna componer."

2601   Quando fue la fazienda   toda bien delibrada,
fue bien ora de nona,   medio día passada,
emperador del mundo,   a proçessión honrada,
con *Te Deum laudamus*   tornó a su posada.

2593	the manner in which the great Empress was interred, and the decoration that was given to her tomb; how he routed Darius for a second time and how Babylon was captured and re-peopled;
2594	the betrayal of Darius, how he died betrayed, how he was entombed and how Bessus was shamed; Alexander's wedding was more briefly described and with this the expanse of the tent was completed.
2595	I do not wish to make a great allegory of the tent, and I do not wish to hold the day back with my words; I could not set a value on what it might be worth, but the wealth of Almería could not buy it.*
2596	When the good King had come into the tent, he sat on his throne, a place of such honour; he ordered that the tribute sent to him be brought in, and that the official letters be read out in council.
2597	When the letters had been opened and read, the homage had been done and the tributes received, he raised his eyes and his outstretched palms to God, and spoke words of great beauty and charm.
2598	"King of all kings, You who know no equal, in whose hand it lies to take and to give, to raise up and cast down, to wound and to heal, Lord, may You be praised, for thus You should be!
2599	I must give You forever, Lord, blessings and praise, for so well did You guide me to achieving my end that simply out of fear, Lord, without further sanction, do the lands all come to kiss my hand.
2600	The lands should be no less grateful to You that they have not known the extent of my power, for, if they sought further engagement in conflict, there is no way in which they could endure."
2601	When his business had all been fully completed, it was the hour of None, and midday had passed; the Emperor of the world in an honoured procession spoke the *Te Deum* and returned to his quarters.

2602 Fue la noche venida, mala e peligrosa;
amaneçió mañana, çiega e tenebrosa;
vinié robar el mundo de la su flor preçiosa
que era más preçiada que lirïo nin rosa.

2603 Las estrellas del çielo, por el día tardar,
andavan a pereça, davan se grant vagar;
tardava el luzero, nos' podié espertar;
apenas lo pudieron las otras levantar.

2604 Essa noche vidieron – solémoslo leer –
las estrellas del çielo entre sí combater,
que, como fuertes signos ovo en el naçer,
vïeron a la muerte fuertes apareçer.

2605 Antípater el falso, ministro del pecado,
essa noche lo puso, quando ovo çenado,
que en el otro día, quando fuesse yantado,
con el primer bever fuesse empoçonado.

2606 Fue el sol levantado triste e doloriento;
tardarié, si pudiesse, de muy buen talento;
forçólo la Natura, siguio su mandamiento;
amaneçió un día negro e carboniento.

2607 El rëy, con la gloria e con el buen plazer,
mandó que adobassen temprano de comer;
querié los omes nuevos por huéspedes aver;
querié de cada uno las mañas entender.

2608 Fue ant' de medio día el comer aguisado,
el palaçio muy limpio, rica ment' enfenado;
fue el pueblo venido, por orden assentado,
el rëy sobre todos, como bien enseñado.

2609 Metió en todo mientes de müy grant femençia;
entendió de cada uno toda su mantenençia;
quando vino en cabo, terminó su sentençia
que eran españoles de mejor cabtenençia.

2610 Jobas el traïdor, que non devriá naçer,
súpose en serviçio mucho entrameter;
ovo todos los otros ministros a vençer,
tanto que Alexandre avié grant plazer.

2602	The night had come, full of evil and danger, and morning dawned, which was gloomy and blind; it came to rob the world of its precious flower, more highly prized than any lily or rose.
2603	The stars of the sky, to hold back the day,* moved round sluggishly, making no haste, and the morning star delayed, unable to wake: the others could scarcely rouse it from its slumbers.
2604	That night men saw – as we are used to reading – the stars in the heavens do battle with each other, for, as powerful signs appeared at his birth, so others of power were seen at his death.
2605	Antipater the false, the Devil's minister, decided on that night, once he had dined, that on the next day, when the King had eaten, he would be poisoned with the first drink he took.
2606	Saddened and grief-stricken, the sun had risen: if it could, it would have been delighted to delay, but Nature forced it, and it followed her command, and the day dawned black and carbon-grey.
2607	The King, with his glory and with his good temper, ordered food to be prepared for an early meal. He wanted to have the new arrivals as his guests and he wished to learn the customs of each one.
2608	The food had been made ready before midday, the palace brilliantly clean and richly perfumed. The people had come and were seated in order, with the King above them all, as was fitting.
2609	Very carefully, the King turned his mind on it all, and learnt of all the ways that each one had; when he came to the end he pronounced his judgement: that the Spaniards were of the greatest excellence.
2610	Iolaus, the traitor who should never have been born,* was able to gain a high position in his service; he managed to outdo all the other ministers such that Alexander was greatly pleased with him.

2611   Por ocasión del mundo, que avié a prender
       la copa con que siempre solié el rey bever;
       óvola por ventura en el puño coger;
       nunca dexarla quiso a otri a tener.

2612   Quando vino la ora que querién dormir,
       ca ovieron grant día passado en dezir,
       mandó el rey del vino a Jobas adozir;
       plaziól' al traïdor e gozólo oír.

2613   Deslavó bien la copa e finchóla de vino;
       rebolvió como pudo en ella el venino;
       vestido d'escarlata, sobre paños de lino,
       presentóla al rey con el inojo enclino.

2614   La ora fue llegada, non podiá al seer;
       querié la fortedupne la cabeça torçer;
       priso el rey la copa – non la deviá prender –
       avié los días fechos, compeçó de bever.

2615   Abés uvió la copa de los rostros toller,
       luego sintió la ravia que lo quiso prender.
       Demandó una péñola por vómito fazer,
       que, si tornar pudiesse, cuidava guareçer.

2616   El falso traïdor, alma endïablada,
       avié esto asmado, teniéla erbolada;
       pusógela en mano de mal fuego cargada.
       Tan bien podrié el malo darle grant cuchillada.

2617   Metió el rey la péñola por amor de tornar;
       non podrié peor fuego en su cuerpo entrar;
       enveninó las venas que pudo alcançar;
       en lugar de guarir, fízolas peorar.

2618   ¡Maldito sea cuerpo que tal cosa faze!
       ¡Maldita sea alma que en tal cuerpo yaze!
       ¡Maldito sea cuerpo que d'aquello le plaze!
       ¡Dios lo eche en lazo que nunca se deslaze!

2619   Fue la dïablería luego escalentando,
       por las venas del cuerpo fuese apoderando;
       ívasele el alma en el cuerpo angostando,
       ívasle la memoria fiera ment' apretando.

2611	To the world's misfortune, Iolaus came to hold the cup from which the King always used to take his drink; by good fortune he was able to take it for himself, never willing to let it go or hand it to another.
2612	When the hour came at which they wished to sleep, for they had passed a long time in talking, the King bade Iolaus bring him wine, which the traitor was pleased and delighted to hear.
2613	He washed the cup well and filled it full of wine, stirring in the poison as well as he could; dressed in crimson over linen garments, he presented it to the King on bended knee.
2614	The hour had come, it could not be otherwise, and his failing strength wished to let his head loll. The King took the cup which he should not have taken; his days were at an end: he began to drink.
2615	He had hardly come to take the cup from his lips, and felt at once the burning pain which sought to seize him; he asked for a feather to induce him to vomit, for, if he could bring it up, he thought he could recover.
2616	The false traitor, a soul possessed by the Devil, had thought of this and coated it with poison. He placed it in the King's hand, charged with evil fire – the evil man could equally have stabbed him.
2617	The King used the feather to make himself vomit: no worse fire could have entered his body. It poisoned the veins it was able to reach: instead of curing them, it made them grow worse.
2618	Cursed be a body that does such a thing! Cursed be a soul that lies in such a body! Cursed be a body that delights in such a thing! May God trap it in a snare that is never undone!
2619	At once, the devilry was stoked to greater heat and gradually took hold of the veins of the body; steadily the soul shrank back within his body and his memory rapidly ebbed away.

2620 Como Dios non queriá, nol' podiá res valer;
nol pudïeron físicos ningunos acorrer;
entendió el buen rëy qué avié de seer;
mandóse sacar fuera, en el campo poner.

2621 Grand' era la tristeza entre las crïazones;
andavan mal cuitados todos sus varones;
llegávales la ravia bien a los coraçones;
nunca fueron tañidos de tales aguijones.

2622 Esforçóse el rey, maguer era cuitado;
pósose en el lecho, paróse assentado;
mandó posar a todos por la yerba del prado;
fízoles buen sermón e bien adeliñado:

2623 "Parientes e amigos, que redor mí seedes,
quiérovos bien e preçio, ca vos lo mereçedes;
por vos gané imperio, vos me lo contenedes;
lo que me prometistes complido lo avedes.

2624 Con omes e con bestias avedes campeado;
nunca fuestes vençidos, ¡Dios sea end' laudado!
A tal señal avedes a vuestro rey llegado
a qual nunca llegó ome de madre nado.

2625 Los que vos apremiavan avedes los premiados;
los que se vos alçaron avedes los baxados;
avedes de los otros recabdos recabdados,
parias e omenajes e escriptos notados.

2626 Grado al Crïador e a vuestras sudores,
sodes del mundo todo cabeças e señores.
De quantos nunca fueron vos sodes los mejores;
nin fueron nin serán tales guerreadores.

2627 Desque esto he visto, que en el tiempo mío
fue el mundo todo en nuestro señorío;
desaquí por que muera – será como yo fío –
non daría por ende un baso d'agua de río.

2628 Ante tengo de Dios que me faz' grant amor,
que, estando honrado, en complido valor,
assí quiere que vaya por a'l siglo mayor,
ante que pesar prenga nin ningún dessabor.

2620	As God was unwilling, nothing could help him; no physicians were able to come to his aid; the good King, who understood what was to be, bade he be taken outside and laid in the open.
2621	Great was the sadness among his vassals and his men were all sunk in deep distress; their anger dug down deep into their hearts; they had never been struck by so harsh a goad.
2622	The King struggled hard, although he was in pain, set himself on his bed, and sat himself up. He bade them all sit on the grass of the field and spoke to them a fine and well-composed sermon:
2623	"Kinsfolk and friends who are gathered around me, I love you well and dearly, for this you deserve; through you I won empire and you guard it for me: that which you promised me you have fulfilled.
2624	You have fought campaigns against men and beasts, and never been defeated, may God be praised! You have brought your King to a position of renown such as none of woman born has ever achieved.
2625	Those who oppressed you, you have overthrown; those who lorded it above you, you have brought down; from the other peoples you have acquired profit, tributes and homage and written undertakings.
2626	Thanks to the Creator and to your own sweat, you are the leaders and lords of all the world. Of all there have ever been, you are the finest; there never were nor will there be such warriors.
2627	Since I have seen this: that in my own time the whole world has come under our authority, henceforth, for my death – of which I am sure – I would not give a glass of river-water.
2628	Rather I consider that God shows me great love, for, being honoured and with valour absolute, He wants me to go thus to the greater world before I suffer sorrow or any setback.

2629　　Suélense en un rato　las cosas demudar;
　　　　el cavallo ligero　suele entrepeçar.
　　　　Si sola una onta　oviesse a tomar,
　　　　avrié todo mi preçio　en nada a tornar.

2630　　Del ome que se passa　mientre está honrado,
　　　　ésse dizen los sabios　que es aventurado.
　　　　Si se va acostando,　trastórnase privado;
　　　　tod' va agua ayuso　quanto que ha lazrado.

2631　　Seré del Rey del cielo　alta ment' reçebido;
　　　　quando a mí oviere,　teners'a por guarido;
　　　　seré en la su corte　honrado e servido;
　　　　todos me laudarán　por que non fui vençido.

2632　　En otra cosa prengo　esfuerço e pagamiento:
　　　　farán sobre mí todos　duelos e plañimiento;
　　　　todos vistrán sayales　por fer su complimiento;
　　　　quando me ementaren　avrán confortamiento.

2633　　En cabo, quando fueren　a sus tierras tornados,
　　　　demandarles han nuevas,　dirán estos mandados;
　　　　serán fechos los duelos,　los plantos renovados;
　　　　todos dirán: '¡Señor,　avedes nos dexados!'

2634　　Quiero mi firmamiento　ante todos poner,
　　　　que después non ayades　sobre qué contender,
　　　　ca sé que abenençia　non podredes aver:
　　　　podriedes en pelea　en un rato caer.

2635　　Quiero partir mi regno　mientre con vusco seo:
　　　　Greçïa do a Pérdicas,　ca sé que bien la empleo;
　　　　comiendo le mi madre,　servir l'a como creo;
　　　　el regno de Egibto　do lo a Tolomeo.

2636　　Pero en todo esto　meto tal condiçión
　　　　que, si de mi Roxana　naçier' fijo varón,
　　　　suyo sea el regno,　ca esto es razón;
　　　　qui lo non obedeçiere　fará grant traïçión.

2637　　Si fuere fija fembra,　buscarle casamiento,
　　　　obedeçerla todos,　complir su mandamiento.
　　　　Simeón, mi notario,　prenga aguisamiento
　　　　e meta en escripto　todo mi testamento.

2629	In just a short time things are given to change and the fleet-footed horse often stumbles; if I were to suffer one single act of shame all my renown would turn to nothing.
2630	Of the man who passes on whilst he is in honour, the wise men say that he enjoys good fortune. If he begins to decline, he is quickly brought down, and all that he has suffered is carried downstream.
2631	I shall be warmly received by the King of Heaven, and when He has me, He will feel Himself protected. In His court, I shall be honoured and well served, and all will praise me, for I suffered no defeat.
2632	In one thing more I take courage and contentment: that over me will everyone lament and grieve. All will dress in sackcloth to pay their respects, and in saying my name they will have solace.
2633	When finally they have returned to their lands they will be asked for news and will give this account; grieving there will be, and laments will be renewed, and all will say: 'Lord, You have forsaken us!'
2634	It is my desire to set my will before you all, so that afterwards you might have no cause for dispute, for I know that you will not be able to agree, and that in a short time you might fall into conflict.
2635	I wish to divide up my realm while I am with you: Greece I give to Perdiccas, for I know I use it well; I commend to him my mother, whom he will serve as I believe; and the kingdom of Egypt I give to Ptolemy.
2636	But upon all this I place this condition, that if Rhoxane should bear a son by me,* let the kingdom be his, for this is how it should be; whoever fails to obey him will commit great treachery.
2637	Should the child be a girl, then seek marriage for her; all are to obey her and fulfil her commands. Let Simeon, my notary, take careful heed and set down all my testament in writing.

2638　　Demás, por el serviçio que a mí a metido,
　　　　do le a Capadoçia, regno grand' e complido;
　　　　Felipo, mi fraire, non tenga quel' olvido:
　　　　pora en Pentapolis lo tengo esleído.

2639　　Otorgo a Antígonus Libia e Panfilïa;
　　　　dole en atenençia encara toda Frigia;
　　　　a mi amo Antípater mando toda Çiliçia,
　　　　a Jobas e Cassánder fasta'l río de Libia.

2640　　Sin esto, a los otros – que ayan egualdat –
　　　　ellos prendan señor segunt su voluntat;
　　　　mando a Meleáguer Siria por heredat;
　　　　en Ponto a Limacus pongo por potestat.

2641　　El otro Tolomeo, que dizen el menor,
　　　　dole Siria la magna que sea end' señor.
　　　　Babilonia, con todas las tierras derredor,
　　　　mando que caten todos por rey a Nicanor.

2642　　Todas las otras tierras que por sí se rindieron,
　　　　suéltolos que se bivan como antes bivieron;
　　　　quando en contra mí tan bien se mantovieron,
　　　　de merçed les aver grant carga me pusieron.

2643　　Do por mi sepulcro de oro çient talientos;
　　　　bien pueden ende fer todos sus conplimientos;
　　　　por a los saçerdotes e por a los convientos,
　　　　de oro fino mando dos vegadas quinientos.

2644　　Quiero en Alexandria aver mi sepultura,
　　　　la que fiz' en Egibto rica sobre mesura;
　　　　creo que Tolomeo averlo ha en cura;
　　　　téngase si lo cumple por de buena ventura."

2645　　Fue el rey en todo esto la palabra perdiendo,
　　　　la nariz aguzando, la lengua engordiendo;
　　　　dixo a sus varones: "Ya lo ides veyendo:
　　　　arrenunçio el mundo, a Dios vos acomiendo."

2646　　Acostó la cabeça sobre un fazeruelo;
　　　　non serié ome bivo que non oviesse duelo.
　　　　Mandó que lo echassen del lecho en el suelo,
　　　　ca avié ya travado del alma el anzuelo.

2638	In addition, for the service that he has given me,
	I give him Cappadocia, a great and fine kingdom.
	Philip, my brother, should not feel that I forget him:*
	I have him marked out for Pentapolis.
2639	I grant to Antigonus Pamphylia and Libya
	and I grant him in friendship all Phrygia, too;
	to my lord Antipater I give all of Cilicia
	and to Iolaus and Cassander as far as Libya's river.*
2640	Besides this, let the others have an equal share,
	and let them choose a lord according to their will.
	To Meleager I entrust Syria as his realm,
	and set Lysimachus in command in the Hellespont.
2641	To the other Ptolemy, known as the younger,*
	I give Greater Syria for him to be its lord.
	Babylon and all of its surrounding lands
	I bid all look on Nicanor as king.
2642	All the other lands that of their own accord surrendered,
	I release them to live as they lived before;
	since they conducted themselves so finely towards me
	they placed on me a great charge to show them mercy.
2643	For my tomb I give a hundred talents of gold,*
	with which they can well make all due payments;
	and for the priests as well as for the convents
	twice five hundred I bequeath, of fine gold.
2644	In Alexandria I wish my tomb to be,*
	which I set up in Egypt, rich beyond measure.
	I believe that Ptolemy will have this in his care;
	let him think himself of fortune if he effects this."
2645	Amidst all this, the King was losing his speech,
	his nose growing tight and his tongue swelling up.
	He said to his men: "Now you can see:
	I renounce the world and commend you to God."
2646	Now he laid his head to rest upon a pillow;
	there could be no man alive who felt no grief.
	He ordered them to move him from his bed to the ground,*
	for the hook had now taken hold of his soul.

2647   Non pudo el espíritu   de la ora passar;
       del mandado de Dios   non pudo escapar;
       desemparó la carne   en que solié morar.
       Remaneçió el cuerpo   qual podedes asmar.

2648   El gozo fue tornado   en bozes e en planto.
       "Señor," dizién los unos,   "¿quién vio atal quebranto?
       A vos aviamos todos   por saya e por manto.
       Señor, ¡maldito sea   quien nos guerreó tanto!"

2649   "Señor," dizián los otros,   "¿dó iremos guarir?
       Quando a ti perdemos,   más nos valdrié morir.
       Señor, agora eras   en sazón de bevir,
       quando el mundo todo   te avié a servir."

2650   "Señor," dizián los otros,   "¿agora qué faremos?
       Tornar en Europa   sin ti non osaremos.
       Señor, los tus crïados   oy nos departiremos.
       Quanto el mundo sea   non nos ajuntaremos."

2651   Dizián del otro cabo: "¡Ay, emperador!
       ¿Cómo lo quiso esto   sofrir el Crïador,
       por dar tan grant poder   a un mal traïdor,
       por fer tantos huérfanos   de tan gentil señor?"

2652   "Señor, " dizián los otros,   "mala fue tal çelada,
       que valer non te pudo   toda la tu mesnada;
       anda con el tu duelo   toda muy desarrada;
       nunca prendieron omes   tan mala sorrostrada."

2653   Dizién los omes buenos   que las parias traxeron:
       "Señor, ¡çiegos se vean   quantos mal vos fizieron!
       Quando nos preguntaren   los que nos esleyeron,
       ¿qué respuesta daremos   de lo que nos dixeron?

2654   Señor, por estas nuevas   que nos les levaremos
       nin nos darán albriçias   nin grado non avremos.
       Vevir tan sin ventura,   señor, nunca sabemos:
       quand' ayer te ganamos   e oy te perdemos.

2655   Non deviá este día,   señor, amaneçer,
       que nos faze a todos   tan buen padre perder.
       Señor, la tu ventura   que tú soliás aver
       mal te desamparó   por a nos cofonder.

2647   His spirit could not pass the appointed hour
and it could not escape what God had determined;
it abandoned the flesh in which it was used to dwell
and the body was left, as you can imagine.*

2648   The joy was transformed into cries and laments:
"Lord," some said, "who has seen such sorrow?
We all took you as our tunic and our cloak
cursed be he, lord, who has attacked us so!"

2649   "Lord," said others, "where shall we go to be safe?
Death would have been better for us, since we lose you.
Now was the time, lord, for you to be alive,
when the whole world was to serve you."

2650   "Lord," said others, "what shall we do now?
We shall not dare return to Europe without you.
We, lord, your vassals, shall all part today,
and while the world endures we shall not meet again."

2651   They said, on the other side, "Alas, our Emperor!
How has the Creator been willing to suffer this,
to give such great power to an evil traitor,
and to make so many orphans of such a noble lord?"

2652   "Lord," said others, "evil was such deception
that all of your army could bring you no aid;
it is all distraught with sorrow at your loss;
no men ever suffered so harsh an affliction."

2653   The good men who had brought him tribute said,
"Lord, may all who did you harm be struck blind!
When we are asked by those who selected us,
what answer shall we give of what was said to us?

2654   Lord, for these tidings that we shall bear to them
we shall be given no reward and receive no thanks;
we know not how to live so forsaken by fortune
when yesterday we gained you and today we bear your loss.

2655   This day, lord, ought never to have dawned,
which makes us all lose a father so good;
lord, the good fortune that you used to possess
deserted you cruelly to confound us.

2656 Viniemos a tu corte   alegres e pagados;
     partirnos hemos ende   tristes e desmayados.
     Señor, mal somos muertos   e mal somos cuitados;
     en mal tiempo nos dieron   salto nuestros pecados.

2657 Señor, con la tu muerte   más gentes as matadas
     que non matest' en vida   tú nin tus mesnadas.
     Señor, son todas las tierras   con tu muert' fatiladas
     ca eran con ti   todas alegres e pagadas."

2658 Por toda la çibdat   era grand' el dolor.
     Los unos dezián "¡Padre!",   los otros "¡Ay, señor!".
     Otros dezián "¡Rey!"   otros "¡Emperador!";
     todos, grandes e chicos,   fazién muy grant dolor.

2659 Roxana sobre todos   era muy debatida;
     a los piedes del rëy   yaziá amorteçida;
     teniélo abraçado,   yazía estordida;
     avía mucha agua   por la cara vertida.

2660 Maguer que non podiá   la cabeça alçar,
     bien fazié demostrança   que lo querié besar;
     non la podién del cuerpo   toller nin despegar.
     Quando ome asmasse,   non era de rebtar.

2661 "Señor," dizián las dueñas,   "nos somos mal fadadas,
     ca fincamos señeras   e desaconsejadas;
     non somos cavalleros   que prendamos soldadas;
     avremos a bevir   como mal aventuradas.

2662 Señor, tú nos honravas   por sola tu bondat;
     non catavas a nos   mas a tu pïedat.
     Señor, non fue en ome   nunca tal caridat
     por fer sobre cativas   tamaña egualdat."

2663 Dexemos nos del planto,   ca cosa es passada.
     Quiero ir destajando   por ir a la finada;
     tengo la voluntad   con el duelo turbada;
     maguer que me estudio,   non puedo dezir nada.

2664 Como diz' el Escripto   de Dios, Nuestro Señor,
     que mal tienen en uno   ovejas sin pastor,
     entró en los varones   çisma e mal fervor:
     queriá ir cada uno   basteçer su onor.

2656	We came to your court full of happiness and joy but we shall take our leave sad and in despair; we bear a harsh death, lord, and suffer deep distress; in a bitter moment did our sins assail us.
2657	Lord, in dying you have brought death to more people than you and your armies killed during your life; lord, with your death all the lands are distressed, for with you, they would all have had pleasure and joy."
2658	Throughout the whole city, great was the grief, some saying, "Father!" others "Alas, lord!", others saying "King!", and others, "Emperor!"; all, great and small, were deep in grief.
2659	Rhoxane above all was brought low by this and lay close to death at the feet of the King. She held him in her arms and lay there stunned, as the tears went streaming down her face.
2660	Although she was unable to raise his head she showed clearly that she longed to kiss him; she could not be taken or parted from the body; no man who thought rightly could blame her.
2661	"Lord," said the ladies, "fate has treated us ill, for we are left alone, women unprotected; we are no knights who gain reward for their service; we shall have to live a life of misfortune.
2662	You paid us honour, lord, just by your goodness, looking not upon us, but to your mercy. Lord, there never was such charity in a man, that he treated captive women with such justice."
2663	Let us leave the lament, for it is now passed; I wish to cut my story short, to reach the end. My heart is troubled by the sorrow I feel, and for all that I try, I have no words.
2664	As the Scripture of the Lord our God tells us, sheep get on badly without their shepherd; schism and unrest came among the knights* as each sought to increase his own honour.

2665   Entendió Tolomeo   de qué pie cosqueavan;
            pareçié bien por ojo   que movidos andavan;
            fízolo soterrar   mientre llegados estavan,
            ca el cabdal sepulcro   aún non lo labravan.

2666   Estió en Babiloña   gran tiempo soterrado
            fasta que ovïeron   el sepulcro labrado;
            mas fue en Alexandria   en cabo trasladado;
            metiólo Tolomeo   en el sepulcro honrado.

2667   Non podriá Alexandre   tal tesoro ganar;
            por oro nin por plata   non lo podrié comprar.
            Si non fuesse pagano   de vida tan seglar,
            deviélo ir el mundo   todo a adorar.

2668   Si murieron las carnes,   que lo han por natura,
            non murió el buen preçio: öy en cara dura.
            Qui muere en buen preçio   es de buena ventura,
            ca lo meten los sabios   luego en escriptura.

2669   ¡Grado al Crïador,   que es rëy de gloria,
            el que bive e regna   en complida victoria!
            Acabada avemos,   señores, la estoria
            del buen rëy de Greçia,   señor de Babilonia.

2670   Señores, quien quisiere   su alma bien salvar,
            debe en esti siglo   assaz poco fïar;
            debe a Dios servir,   dévelo bien pregar
            que en poder del mundo   non lo quiera dexar.

2671   La gloria d'esti mundo,   quien bien quiere asmar,
            más que la flor del campo   non la debe preçiar;
            ca, quando ome cuida   más seguro estar,
            échalo de cabeça   en el peor lugar.

2672   Alexandre, que era   rëy de grant poder,
            que mares nin tierra   non lo podién caber,
            en una foya ovo   a cabo a caer
            que non podié de término   doze pïes tener.

2673   Quiérome vos con tanto,   señores, espedir.
            Gradéscovos lo mucho   quem' quisiestes oïr.
            Si fallesçí en algo,   devedes me parçir:
            so de poca çïençia,   devedes me sofrir.

2665	Ptolemy understood the way they were inclined and it was clear to his eyes that they were restive; he had the King buried while they were together, for the building of the great tomb was not yet begun.
2666	For a long time he was buried in Babylon until the working of the tomb was complete; but at last he was transferred to Alexandria where Ptolemy set him in his honoured vault.
2667	Alexandria could not have won such a treasure, nor have bought it for gold or for silver. Were he not a pagan, of so worldly a life, all the world should go to pay him reverence.
2668	Although his flesh perished, as it must do by nature, his honour did not die, for it still endures today; a man who dies with honour enjoys good fortune, for at once wise men set his deeds down in writing.
2669	Thanks be to the Creator, who is King of glory,* who lives and reigns in perfect victory, we have reached, my lords, the end of the story of Greece's good king and Babylonia's lord.
2670	My lords, one who seeks salvation for his soul must place little trust in this earthly life, but he must serve God and say prayers to Him not to forsake him in the grip of the world.
2671	The glory of this world one who seeks right thought must value no higher than the flower of the field, for at the time when a man believes himself safest, it casts him down head first into the foulest place.
2672	For Alexander, who was a king of great power, and could not be contained by seas or by land, in the end it was his lot to fall into a grave which could not have been twelve feet in length.
2673	With this much, my lords, I wish to take my leave of you: I pay you great thanks that you were willing to hear me. If I erred in anything, you must grant me pardon: I am of little knowledge, you must be forgiving.

2674 Pero pedir vos quiero, çerca de la finada,
– quiero por mi serviçio de vos prender soldada –
dezir el *Paternoster* por mí una vegada;
a mí faredes pro; vos non perderedes nada.

2675
P
Si queredes saber quién fizo esti ditado,
Gonçalo de Berçeo es por nombre clamado:
natural de Madrid, en Sant Myllán crïado,
del abat Johán Sánchez notario por nombrado.

2675
O
Se quisierdes saber quién escrevió este ditado,
Johán Lorenço, bon clérigo e ondrado:
natural de Astorga, de mañas bien temprado;
el día del jüyzio Dios sea mío pagado.

Amen
Finito libro reddatur cena magistro.

Book of Alexander

2674	But I wish to ask you, as we are near the end, – I seek some payment from you for my service – to say a *Paternoster* for me, just once. You will do good to me and not lose a thing.
2675 P	If you wish to know who wrote this composition,* he bears the name of Gonzalo de Berceo, a native of Madrid, and raised in San Millán, appointed notary of Abbot Juan Sánchez.
2675 O	If you wish to know who wrote down this composition, he was Juan Lorenzo, a fine and honoured cleric, a native of Astorga, of well tempered habit; on the Day of Judgement, may God be my friend.

Amen
Now that the book is finished, let dinner be given to the master.

NOTES

2b A craft without fault ...: the Spanish text plays on the double meaning of *pecado* (= 'sin' or 'error') in connection with both the metrical regularity of the poem and the conduct or scholarship of the clergy. For an analysis of the opening stanzas of the poem, see Introduction, Section 2.

5a I want to read a book ...: this could be an allusion to reading as a public performance. It could also (as line d suggests) allude to the author's task in following and elaborating on his principal source and model, Gautier de Châtillon's *Alexandreis*; see Introduction, Section 5.

6c Porus is the official, rather than the personal, name of the warrior-king who ruled Paurava from 340 to 317 BC. Porus was the most powerful of the Indian rulers against whom Alexander fought and, when they encountered each other in battle, his territories extended from Gujirat to the Punjab. **Darius III** (ca. 380–330 BC) was the last king of the Achaemenid Empire of Persia which he ruled from 336 to 330 BC. In spite of the harsh verdict of posterity, he was a skilled military commander and he was clearly a tougher figure than the *Libro de Alexandre* makes him appear. He was deposed during Alexander's conquest.

8ff. Great prodigies occurred ...: the account of these events and of Alexander's childhood is based principally on the *Roman d'Alexandre* (Willis 1935, 6–11). In the *Alexandreis*, the description of the prodigies is included towards the end of the poem, as Alexander's death approaches (in the *Libro de Alexandre*, see stanzas 2602–2604). There are well-known biblical parallels, too, for some of these prodigies, such as the hailstones in *Revelation* 16:21.

13c Philip and Olympias: Philip II of Macedon ruled from 359 to 336 BC, dominating his times by virtue of his military and political skills. He had several wives and in 357 he married Olympias (originally Polyxena and then Myrtale) of Epirus, sealing a political alliance. Their son Alexander was born in 356 and she also bore Philip a daughter, Cleopatra. Olympias was a powerful figure (see Introduction, Section 5). Green (1991, 30) tells us that "[o]ur sources, ... while admitting Olympias' beauty, describe her variously as sullen, jealous, bloody-minded, arrogant, headstrong and meddlesome. To these attributes we may add towering political ambition and a literally murderous temper."

15d He resembled Hercules: The royal house of Macedon claimed descent from Hercules and Alexander saw himself as a heroic figure in the mould of this semi-divine ancestor (Hercules was the son of Zeus). He consciously sought to emulate Hercules' achievements and to draw attention to his connection with the hero (for example in the resemblance to the figure of Hercules evident in coins that he minted).

17a He studied the arts: Alexander's education is based on the "Seven Liberal Arts", the *Trivium* and the *Quadrivium*, the basis of the programme of education in the medieval university and whose importance to the author of the *Libro de Alexandre* is emphasised on a number of occasions. See also stanzas 39–45. Although the picture of the prince's education is clearly one adapted to the medieval world, the historical Alexander certainly received a full academic education which was to colour his interests and attitudes in later life (see Introduction, Section 5 and Green 1991, 55–62).

19b they said that he resembled Master Nectanebo: Nectanebo II, the last of the Egyptian Pharaohs, was driven from his throne in 343 BC. Legend, incorporated in the *Alexander Romance* (see Introduction, Section 5), held that he was a great magician and that, taking on the form of a snake, he had slept with Olympias on the night that she conceived Alexander, having convinced her that her serpentine partner was the God Ammon. Our poet follows the *Roman d'Alexandre,* criticising those who believe the rumour about Alexander's paternity, and recounts the death of Nectanebo. At the same time, he does seem in stanza 19d to admit some possibility that the rumour is true, and interpretations differ as to who is the father alluded to in stanza 20d.

22b tributary vassals of the King of Babylon: although the Persian empire still constituted a powerful and constant threat, in Alexander's lifetime the Macedonians had in fact long ceased to pay it tribute. On the other hand, since the second half of the fifth century, the Great King of Persia had claimed as his own all of Asia up to the Aegean coastline of Anatolia in the west and Darius still maintained control over a number of Greek states through what were essentially puppet regimes, exacting payment in money or in kind. Under the Achaemenid rulers, **Babylon** was the administrative capital of the Persian empire and it was situated about eighty-five kilometres south of the modern city of Baghdad. In Alexander's time it was probably still the largest city in the world. For a description of its splendours, see note to stanzas 1460 ff.

25a my good master: the master of whom Alexander is so greatly in awe is Aristotle, the eminent Greek philosopher who, in about 342 BC – before he had earned the outstanding reputation that he was later to enjoy – was invited by Philip to act as tutor to Alexander (who was then 14, rather than 7 as suggested in 38c). At the time he was 42, much younger than the description of him in the *Libro de Alexandre* would suggest. He fulfilled his role for two years, at Mieza, a relatively secluded village in the foothills of the Bermius mountains where he taught Alexander together with a select group of his contemporaries, including his lifelong friend Hephaestion. Although there is no evidence that Alexander was considered an exceptional scholar, Aristotle does seem to have helped to inspire in him an enduring interest in literature and science (see also Introduction, Section 5); he is also said to have produced for him an edition of the *Iliad*. The title that Aristotle is repeatedly given in the poem (master or *maestro = magister*) was applied in the Middle Ages to a person possessing a licence to teach from a university.

30c the Medes: these were an ancient Iranian people, who lived in the northern, western, and north-western areas of present-day Iran. The creator of the Median kingdom is traditionally held to have been Deioces, whom Herodotus says ruled for 53 years (Herodotus 1.102), probably around 728–625 BC. The Persian king Cyrus the Great is said to have led a revolt against his grandfather, Astyages, who at that time ruled over the Medes; Cyrus defeated him (Herodotus 1.123–30). The Persians thus became rulers of Asia in place of the Medes.

32c he had formed a syllogism ...: Aristotle's theory of the syllogism is a crucial part of his contribution to western thought; our poet knows at least enough about Aristotle's work to make this association.

33a the hour of None: one of the canonical hours of prayer in the Church day, and originally appointed for about 3.00 in the afternoon. Its name comes from the Latin *nonus*, ninth: according to Roman custom, the day began at sunrise and ended at sunset, and this period was divided into twelve hours (their lengths varying with the time of year). Thus the ninth hour will fall in mid-afternoon.

40b the figures: the figures, or "colours", a wide range of ornamental stylistic devices, are explained and codified in the rhetorical and grammatical treatises of Antiquity and of the Middle Ages (see also Introduction, Section 6). In the thirteenth century any educated person would, at an early stage in their training, have learned to recognise and use them in any form of Latin composition.

43a I learnt all about medicine: Medicine or Natural Sciences was not normally considered part of the Quadrivium, although by the end of the twelfth century its study was becoming quite prominent (particularly so, for example, in centres such as the southern Italian town of Salerno). On the other hand, we would have expected to find Geometry among the disciplines included by Alexander in his list of the Seven Liberal Arts.

45c the signs of the sun ...: the study of Astronomy would have included that of Astrology.

47d against Porus and Darius: there was no association between these two figures and there is no reason why Alexander should have any knowledge of Porus' existence at this stage.

48ff. a few words of guidance: Aristotle's words of advice are based on the equivalent passage from the *Alexandreis* (Townsend 2007, 35 ff.).

70a Hector in the *Iliad* is the most prominent warrior on the Trojan side, leading the defence of the city, marked out among the Trojans for his prowess on the battlefield (see Helenus at *Iliad* 6.77–9). He was the eldest son of Priam and Hecuba, brother of Paris, husband to Andromache and father to Astyanax. He dies outside Troy at Achilles' hands (*Iliad* 22). **Diomedes** was the son of Tydeus and Deipyle, and King of Argos. He is one of the most powerful of the Greek warriors to fight at Troy, after Achilles, and is feared accordingly (see, for example, *Iliad* 6.98–100, where he is even said to be more fearsome than Achilles). He is also praised for his wise counsel by Nestor in *Iliad* 9 (his name itself means "counselled by Zeus").

70c Achilles is the central character and the greatest warrior of the *Iliad*. He was said to be the son of the mortal Peleus, king of the Myrmidons, and the sea nymph Thetis. According to some legends, he was invulnerable on all parts of his body except for his heel, a protection he gained after his mother dipped him in the waters of the Styx; she held on to him by the heel, so this remained his one area of weakness, as the waters never touched this place, and he died after an arrow shot by Paris pierced this spot.

88a   the Tower of Babylon: although there is no firm factual basis for the geographical identification of the Tower of Babel (see *Genesis* 11) with the Kingdom of Babylonia, it is considered likely that the huge ancient Babylonian Ziggurat (a stepped construction consisting of seven storeys and rising to a height of 270 feet and topped by a small temple) inspired the story of the Tower. The Ziggurat dated from the seventh century BC and came in historical tradition to be identified with the biblical story of the attempt to build a tower so high that its top would reach into the heavens. The Spanish poet, who makes extensive use of this story as an *exemplum* to demonstrate the futility and destructiveness of human pride, exploits its coincidence with the political and moral significance of Alexander's Babylonian conquest.

88b   the land of Sion: Mount Sion (or Zion) is a hill in Jerusalem, but the name has been used in Jewish writing in various ways: to designate the mount on which the Temple was built, the Temple itself, Jerusalem as a whole and even the entirety of the land of Israel.

88d   all that belonged to Charles …: the allusion is to Charlemagne (ca. 742–814 AD), King of the Franks and Emperor of the West (800–814). Having defeated the Saxons and the Lombards and fought the Arabs in Spain, Charlemagne assumed control of most of Christian Europe, seeking to consolidate order and Christian culture among the nations of the West. The Spanish poet sees Charlemagne as the embodiment of power and dominance and is clearly untroubled by the anachronistic comparison that he is attributing to Alexander.

90b   three thousand marks: the mark was equivalent to 8 oz. of gold or silver, though there were considerable fluctuations in its value throughout the Middle Ages.

90c   Pisa: the Tuscan city power of Pisa acquired great fame as one of the four main historical Marine Republics of Italy. It became a very important commercial centre and controlled a significant Mediterranean merchant fleet and navy.

91c   Lombardy: this extensive region in northern Italy was famed for its wealth. Taking advantage of its highly developed agriculture, industry and commerce during the Middle Ages, it became an extremely important economic centre and its trade and banking activities were extended well into northern Europe. The name "Lombardy" came to be used to designate the whole of northern Italy.

94b   Lord Vulcan: in Roman mythology, Vulcan is the god of fire, the son of Jupiter and Juno. He is also a manufacturer of arms: in *Aeneid* 8, he creates new armour for Aeneas, as his Greek equivalent, Hephaestus, does for Achilles at *Iliad* 18 – Alexander's desire to compare himself to such figures as these is not a passing one.

98c   Apelles: Apelles (born ca. 370 BC) is considered to have been the greatest of the Greek painters and his works included paintings of both Philip and Alexander, as well as of several of the latter's generals. Allegedly, Alexander allowed no other artist to paint him and paid Apelles immense sums for some of his work. In the *Libro de Alexandre* the production of several important artefacts, requiring detailed and highly skilled work, is attributed to Apelles, who thus becomes an extremely important figure within the poem in his role as commentator on its characters. See Introduction, Section 7.

104b Xerxes: this seems to be an allusion to Xerxes I (the Great), a Persian emperor who reigned from 485 to 465 BC and took part in ultimately unsuccessful wars against Athens and other Greek states. Any association of this figure with Alexander's father is clearly anachronistic.

108a The merits of the horse ...: Bucephalus, whose Greek name means "ox-head", was to become probably the most famous horse of antiquity, serving Alexander in almost all of his battles before dying at the age of almost thirty. The earliest account of Alexander's acquisition of Bucephalus is by Plutarch, who tells how at the age of ten he amazed his father by taming this seemingly wild beast, but other versions emphasise the animal's mythic attributes. The *Alexander Romance* already tells us that Bucephalus had horns and ate human flesh.

111a A king of Cappadocia – whose name I have forgotten –: Cappadocia was an extensive inland district of Asia Minor (modern Turkey). The poet's source, the *Historia de Proeliis*, does not give the name of the king who made the gift. Demaratus of Corinth is named as the donor by Diodorus in his *Bibliotheca historica* (17.76.6).

129a an audacious king: this king, in a passage which is based on the *Historia de Proeliis* (Willis 1934, 94), is a fictitious character. On the other hand, we can see in the episode an echo of the early campaigns in which the young Alexander – appointed as Regent of Macedonia at the age of sixteen – gave an impressive display of military prowess in firmly suppressing an uprising by the Maedi, a hostile tribe who lived on the borders of Thrace and Paeonia.

142a messengers from Darius: the source of the following fictional episode is the *Historia de Proeliis* (Willis 1934, 94). There was no question of the Persians demanding tribute of the Macedonians (see note to 22b, above). The aim of Alexander's venture into Asia was in fact to impose Macedonian control over the Greek cities which were currently tributaries of the Persian empire. Moreover, the enterprise had already been conceived by King Philip, with the aim of encouraging the Asiatic Greeks to transfer their allegiance (Cartledge 2004, 87 ff.).

146c Arsanes' son: Darius was the son of Arsanes (or Arsames or Arsham). His mother was Sisygambis, who seems to have been a sister of Arsanes.

160c Armenia rose up: there is no historical source for this episode. At this stage, Armenia was still part of the Persian empire and it was only to come under Alexander's control after his victory over Darius at Arbela in 331 BC, five years after he became King of Macedonia. Again, the immediate source is the *Historia de Proeliis* (Willis 1934, 94).

168b having won himself great honour: the Spanish text says literally that he had gained honour for his beard. In medieval Spain the beard was an important symbol of virility, dignity and honour and it is mentioned on a number of occasions in the *Poema de Mio Cid* (see, for example, Such and Hodgkinson 1987, 58 and 208).

169a A nobleman: literally "a wealthy man"; in the Spain of the Middle Ages and beyond the phrase "rico ome" denotes a specific social category, a member of the upper nobility. Pausanias was the man who carried out the assassination, in full public view, of Philip in 336 BC. One of the king's intimate bodyguards, he was said by official sources to have been motivated by a personal grudge, but there are strong arguments for suspecting that there were political motives and that Olympias and probably Alexander himself had some responsibility for the murder; see Introduction, Section 5 and Green 1991, 91–110. Pausanias was pursued and promptly killed by three of Alexander's close friends, who thus prevented further investigation. It was Alexander who had most to gain through the death of his father, but once he was installed on the throne any suggestion of his guilt was quickly silenced. The picture of Pausanias as a powerful rebel, driven by lust for the queen, is to be found in the *Alexander Romance* and in the *Historia de Proeliis*.

195b and was taken to Corinth to be with the other kings: in fact Philip was buried in Aegae, the royal capital of Macedon. He and Alexander were, however, closely associated with Corinth: in 338/337 BC, following his defeat of an alliance of Theban and Athenian forces, Philip had created a federation of Greek states to assist his struggle against Persia; the federation's congress of representatives was to meet at Corinth (modern historians have coined for it the title "the League of Corinth") and Philip was declared commander of its army. Following Philip's death, Alexander marched south to Corinth and obliged the League's Greek representatives to confirm him as its hereditary leader or *hegemon,* and it is this event that is reflected in stanza 197.

211a Athens at this point took a very bad decision: in 338 BC Alexander's father had won a decisive victory at Chaeronea over the allied forces of Thebes and Athens. In 336, when they received news of Philip's assassination, the Thebans were quick to think of throwing off Macedonian domination, and in 335, on hearing a rumour that Alexander had been killed, they moved into open defiance, supported by Athens and some other Greek states. Alexander marched rapidly against Thebes and the Athenians failed to provide relief or reinforcements for their allies. Following the fall of Thebes, it was the council of the League of Corinth which, in theory at least, determined that every trace of the great city of history and legend was to be destroyed. In the short term, the Athenians were quick to return to compliance and Alexander's punishment of their city was slight, amounting to an insistence that one prominent general be sent into exile. Nevertheless, the Greek states were deeply shocked by the fate of Thebes and their hatred of Alexander was to prove enduring.

Demosthenes (384–322 BC), the prominent Athenian statesman and orator, was renowned for his opposition to Alexander. He had previously played an important part in forging an alliance against Philip and in the year after Philip's death he famously ridiculed Alexander's Homeric pretensions. He was instrumental in persuading the Thebans to embark on their ill-judged defiance of Alexander's power. Once the Athenians had agreed to accept Macedonian hegemony, Demosthenes was effectively silenced as an opponent to Alexander. It was after a further rebellion, following Alexander's death, that Demosthenes was to commit suicide in order to avoid capture.

216c   and thus Alexander was at odds with Thebes: the Spanish poet presents this episode in terms of the relationship between a king and a treacherous vassal. There is no historical basis for the assertion that Thebes and the other Greek city states were in alliance with Darius, and Alexander was in no sense the king of a united Greece. Nevertheless, the young king had taken over from his father dominance over the League of Corinth, from which the Thebans (in alliance with the Athenians – see note to 211a) were now struggling to free themselves; it was crucial that he demonstrate his single-mindedness and his military control, and the exemplary punishment that he meted out to Thebes had an evident political purpose: to put an end to any potential Greek opposition to his power and thus to prepare the way for his Persian campaign.

229c   the Greeks: our poet consistently describes Alexander's principally Macedonian forces as "Greeks", confusingly in this case, since that term could more appropriately be applied to the people of Thebes. In fact, Alexander's forces can never be accurately described as Greek. During his Asian campaigns the Greek states contributed less than a fifth of his troops and only a tenth of his cavalry. Athens, for example, in spite of the number of ships that she had available, contributed only twenty vessels to Alexander's navy, and in fact far more Greek troops fought for – and remained loyal to – Darius than ever formed part of Alexander's army.

238a   Hercules, Diomedes, Achilles, Bacchus: in mentioning these four figures, Cleadas attempts to tighten the association between the city of Thebes and Alexander himself. **Hercules** (see also note to stanza 15d) was the son of Zeus and Alcmene, the Theban queen. He defended Thebes in battle from the kingdom of Orchomenus, and subsequently married Megara, eldest daughter of Thebes' ruler, Creon. **Diomedes** (see also note to 70a) was the son of Tydeus, one of the warrior-kings who fought in the expedition known as the "Seven Against Thebes" (see *Iliad* 4.370–400). Diomedes himself, along with other sons of fathers who fell in that expedition (the "epigonoi", offspring), later fought in a second, successful, expedition against Thebes. **Achilles** (see also note to 70c) has no direct association with Thebes, but his link is with Alexander himself, who claimed descent from him through his mother Olympias, and cultivated the association with the Homeric hero. See also the note to stanzas 332 ff. The god **Bacchus** (Greek: Dionysus) was said to be the son of Zeus and the priestess Semele, daughter of Cadmus, King of Thebes. His link with Thebes is strong: in Euripides' *Bacchae*, it is Thebes first of all that he excites with his Bacchic cries (ll. 23–4). He had strong northern Greek links (he is most often represented as a Thracian, outside of Euripides); Alexander consciously associated himself with him, and particularly with Dionysus' fabled expedition to India (see also, for example, 256c below). There is possibly another link here with Alexander himself in that his mother Olympias was devoted to the orgiastic rites of Dionysus.

243cd   a Theban came there ...: this is Cleitomachus, a Theban athlete particularly famed as a boxer; the story appears in the *Alexander Romance*. In fact, the city was rebuilt at the instigation of Cassander, king of Macedonia from 305 to 297 BC who was acting out of his hatred for Alexander, conceived during his visit to Babylon just before the Emperor's death (Green, 1971, 473).

247c   as the poet Walter tells us in his verse ...: in fact, our poet's figures do not coincide with those of Gautier de Châtillon, who gives a figure of 182 ships.

256a   If Hercules had not travelled across to Spain, ...: Hercules' tenth labour was to bring back to Greece the cattle of the giant Geryon, who dwelt in Erytheia, a region which scholars have associated with Tartessus in southern Iberia. On the way to Spain he is said to have set up the Pillars of Hercules in Gibraltar and Ceuta.

258cd   If Jason had not opened the ways overseas...: the story of Jason's quest to retrieve a golden ram's fleece is best known to us from the *Argonautica* of Apollonius Rhodius, which was composed in the third century BC. The story, however, is much older than this, and its setting is contemporary with other poems of the Epic Cycle, of which only the *Iliad* and *Odyssey* survive in anything but fragmentary form. There is a reference to the saga in *Odyssey* 12.69–72.

259a   two good sisters ...: in fact, Alexander had only one sister (Cleopatra) by Philip and Olympias. He had a number of other half-sisters fathered by Philip.

276–294   here we have to include a digression: The world map or *mappa mundi* described in these stanzas is based principally on a passage from the *Alexandreis* (1. 396–426), but our poet has also drawn on San Isidoro's *Etymologiae* (XIV, 1–5) as well as the Bible. The *Etymologiae* was the work of St Isidore of Seville (600–636 AD) and its twenty books sought to constitute a summary of the knowledge accumulated by early seventh-century Christendom. In Book XIV, Isidore enumerates and briefly describes the political divisions of the world. A map design commonly associated with Isidore of Seville is a survival of the ancient Greek tripartite division of the world into Asia, Africa and Europe, surrounded by the ocean. This simple scheme of a world divided into the three known major land masses is represented essentially by the form of a T within an O, and was to continue to form the basis of most subsequent medieval cartography. The map is, therefore, essentially cruciform and in its more sophisticated versions the shape of the cross is marked by the sea (see stanza 280d). Jerusalem occupies the central position in the map. For one such medieval map of the world, see the illustration on page xvii. In practical terms, Alexander's geographical ideas were very vague. He had no idea at all of the existence of the main part of the Indian sub-continent, or indeed of the immense land-mass from China to Malaysia, and he was convinced that the Ocean could be seen from the summit of the Hindu Kush (Green 1991, 379).

279d the Moors hold the others, to our great sorrow: this would seem to be an allusion to the fact that at the time of the poem's composition Jerusalem was in Moslem hands. This had been the case since its capitulation to Saladin in 1187, and, in spite of the campaigns of 1202–1204 and 1217–1221, it was only in 1229 that the Sixth Crusade, led by Holy Roman Emperor Frederick II, led to its recovery. It was to be captured by Moslems once again fifteen years later.

287a The four holy rivers ...: see *Genesis* 2:10–14. The river systems of the Tigris and the Euphrates watered the lands around Babylon. The other two rivers mentioned in Genesis are the Pishon and the Gihon (possibly the Nile and the Ganges respectively).

298a Now Aurora made ready to unlock her doors: Aurora (Greek: Eos) is the dawn goddess, and her coming heralded the arrival of the new day. The doors mentioned here refer to her task of opening the gates of heaven so that Phoebus Apollo, the sun god, could ride his chariot across the sky every day.

301d Festinus, his squire: the historical Hephaestion was much more than a squire to Alexander; he was a childhood – and, indeed, lifelong – friend, his closest confidant and in due course one of his principal commanders. Utterly devoted to Alexander, he was to play a particularly important part in his Indian campaigns.

311b Cleitus and Ptolemy, two loyal men: Cleitus, known as "the Black", commanded Alexander's Royal Squadron from the beginning of the expedition. He was killed by Alexander in a drunken rage in 328 BC. **Ptolemy**, or Ptolemaeus, son of Lagus, first emerges as an independent commander in late 331, well into the Persian campaign. He seems to have risen through the ranks. A sign of his growing importance is the fact that he was given the responsibility for bringing in the traitor Bessus. His prominence continued to increase and after Alexander's death he was given Egypt as his satrapy. He was one of the key figures in the struggle for power in the final years of the fourth century BC and he established a kingship in Egypt in 306/5. Ptolemy composed a *History of Alexander*, used by both Arrian and Curtius.

311ff. The source for this episode, in which Alexander agrees to appoint a council of twelve trusted men, is a literary one, the *Roman d'Alexandre* (Casas Rigall, ed. 2007, 214). However, the historical Alexander did surround himself with a small personal guard and a contingent of companions (*hetairoi*). There are also echoes of medieval epic – such as the role of the Twelve Peers in the *Chanson de Roland* – as well as obvious biblical and ecclesiastical parallels, as is pointed out in stanza 319d. Significantly, perhaps, in 1242 King Fernando III himself created a Council of Twelve for the administration of justice (Casas Rigall, ed. 2007, 214).

317a Elier: neither manuscript gives a reading clear enough to enable this figure to be identified. Casas Rigall (ed. 2007, 215) suggests that the equivalent figure in the *Alexandreis* may be Tauron – a commander who figured in Alexander's Persian and Indian campaigns.

317d Parmenion: Parmenion had been a senior and influential general in the years preceding Philip's death, and was identified with the "old guard", from whose influence Alexander increasingly sought to free himself. As a commander, although he continued to play a prominent role and to exercise considerable power, he enjoyed mixed success in Asia Minor. Quite often he was given difficult tasks and limited resources, and, on a number of critical occasions (as is reflected in the *Libro de Alexandre*) his advice was rejected by Alexander. It is clear that Callisthenes takes every opportunity in his official record of the campaigns to comment on occasions when Parmenion supposedly gave bad advice and there is a strong sense of a personal vendetta between Alexander and Parmenion (Green 1991, 339). Very soon after his son Philotas had been notoriously put to death, Parmenion was himself murdered.

318a–d   Eumenes and Samson: the Thracian **Eumenes** was secretary successively to Philip and Alexander. In the division of power at Babylon after Alexander's death, he was appointed satrap of Paphlagonia and Cappadocia. The name of **Samson** seems to be based on that of Sanses in the *Roman d'Alexandre* (Casas Rigall, ed. 2007, 215). For **Festinus** (Hephaestion), see note to stanza 301d. **Philotas** was the son of Parmenion and an early friend of Alexander. By the beginning of the Asiatic expedition he was in charge of the highly prestigious Companion Cavalry, and he played a vital role in the Battle of the Granicus. He seems, however, to have been arrogant, high-handed and generally unpopular, and an error of judgement provided a pretext for his execution in 330 BC. **Nicanor** was another son of Parmenion and brother to Philotas. He probably owes his early prominence to the services done by Parmenion. In the Battle of the Granicus, he too occupied a very important position in the Macedonian line in charge of the *hypaspists* or footguard. He died of illness in 330 BC. Both manuscripts give as the eleventh peer Clitus (Cleitus), but this is clearly an error, this individual was mentioned in 311b. Most scholars accept that the name given here should be **Antigonus**. Antigonus commanded 7000 Greek Hoplites in 334 BC, when Alexander's army crossed into Asia. See also note to stanza 979c. **Perdiccas** was a loyal supporter of Alexander. He occupied key positions at the Granicus, Issus and Gaugamela and at the Hydaspes he commanded the main striking force against Porus. After the death of Hephaestion, Perdiccas succeeded him as the commander of the Companion Cavalry. He was the most powerful of the generals in Babylon at the time of Alexander's death and it is reported that Alexander on his death bed gave Perdiccas his signet ring. As commander-in-chief of the army, he subsequently fought to hold Alexander's empire together under his own control.

322ff.   Next he came to Troy, the city of ill fortune: Alexander did, indeed, make for Troy at the beginning of his Asian expedition in order to honour Achilles' tomb. In his youth had been deeply imbued with the tales of Troy and the exploits of the Greek heroes (see, for example, Lane Fox 2004, 47–49). Through his mother he was considered to be a descendant of Achilles and Alexander came to identify closely with the Greek hero. His father had been compared with Agamemnon and his close friend Hephaestion was often likened to Achilles' intimate companion Patroclus. Aristotle taught Alexander the works of Homer and prepared for him a text of the *Iliad* on which, during his campaigns, he was said to rest his head when he slept. Alexander's own historian emphasised the parallels between his campaigns and Homer's account of the Trojan War and contemporary artists also sought to draw attention to the connection by portraying Alexander in coins and statues as Achilles.

323c   Homer: for the account of the Trojan War (stanzas 417–719), the *Libro de Alexandre* does not draw directly on the works of Homer but on the *Ilias Latina* or *Homerus Latinus*, a version of the story condensed into 1070 Latin hexameters, probably written by Baebius Italicus during the reign of Nero. It was this work, rather than Homer's, which was known in western Europe during the Middle Ages. Our poet has also drawn (stanzas 335–416 and 720–761) on the *Excidium Troiae*, a school text which seems to be a condensed version of a more lengthy epitome of the story of Troy, running through to the founding of Rome by Trojan descendants (the focus of the *Aeneid*).

324a   the young Ganymede: Ganymede, a beautiful Trojan, was held to have been abducted while tending a flock of sheep upon Mount Ida in Phrygia. Zeus either sent an eagle or transformed himself into one, on which Ganymede was borne to Olympus, where he served as cupbearer to the gods, and was later set in the sky as the constellation Aquarius, the water-carrier. The abduction is referred to at *Iliad* 5.265–273, where Diomedes talks of Aeneas' horses, of the stock that Zeus gave to Tros, Ganymede's father, in payment for his abduction.

327c   where Oenone composed a fine pair of verses: in Greek mythology, Oenone was the first wife of Paris, whom he abandoned for Helen. She was an Oread, a mountain nymph, of Mount Ida in Phrygia, and Paris fell in love with her when he was a shepherd; they married, and had a son. After Paris' judgement that Aphrodite (Venus) was more beautiful than Hera (Juno) or Athena (Minerva), he left her for Helen of Troy, as Aphrodite promised him the most beautiful woman in the world if he chose her. It was Paris' theft of Menelaus' wife Helen that caused the Trojan War. Oenone is said to have told Paris as he left to come to her if he was injured, but later, overcome with jealousy, refused to help him with a wound that proved fatal. She relented too late: he was dead when she came to help him, and she committed suicide, overcome with grief. The **fine pair of verses** is in fact composed by Paris, not by Oenone, at *Heroides* 5.29–30, pledging his love for Oenone, and this is referenced at *Alexandreis* 1. 457–460.

330d   his few words: the Spanish text uses the word *dictado*, a technical term for an elegant piece of composition, linked to the Latin *dictamen*: the art of letter writing. The teacher of this art had come in the twelfth century to be known as a *dictator* (Murphy 1974, 212–213).

333   They laid out great offerings ...: in fact the tone of Alexander's homage was slightly different from this. He and his companion Hephaestion laid wreaths on the tombs of Achilles and Patroclus respectively and then ran a race round them, naked and anointed with oil (Green 1991, 167).

368c   a book from Ovid's hand: this book has been variously identified (see

Casas Rigall, ed. 2007, 228) as Ovid's *Ars Amatoria*, the *Metamorphoses* and the *Fasti*, but it has also been argued (Arizaleta 1999, 52, 57, 101) that the Spanish poet did not have first-hand knowledge of the text.

373ab   I am known as Proserpina...: Pallas Athena, sister of Phoebus Apollo, was the goddess of both war and wisdom. The Romans knew her as Minerva. Her identification with Proserpina (Persephone) and with Diana (Artemis) is, however, erroneous.

376a   Venus then leapt up: the *Excidium Troiae*, our poet's source for this passage, adds that she was naked. It is, perhaps, typical of the Spanish poet's heavily moralising approach throughout the poem that he removed this detail.

381b   when Jupiter struck the blow against his father: here there is confusion of two mythological scenes: the overthrowing by Zeus (Jupiter) of his father Cronus (Saturn), and the castration by Cronus of his own father, Uranus (Caelus). While the text refers to Jupiter's action, Venus (Aphrodite) had her birth after the castration, when Uranus's genitals were thrown into the sea, and foam formed around the immortal flesh; from this, Aphrodite, whose name derives from *aphros (*foam), was born, by the island of Cyprus (see Hesiod, *Theogony* 178–200).

388b   Menelaus' wife: Helen was herself depicted in Greek mythology as being of divine parentage. She is said to have been the child of Zeus (who had taken on the form of a swan: see Euripides, *Helen* 17–21) and Leda. When still a child, she was abducted by the Athenian Theseus (see stanza 389b, and, for example, Plutarch, *Theseus* 31), and subsequently rescued by her brothers, Castor and Pollux, and returned to Sparta. She was famed for her beauty (see note to 327c): in one tradition, she attracted many suitors, who all swore an oath to support her eventual husband against anyone who should quarrel with him. She came to marry Menelaus, and thus the Greeks raised an enormous army, in accordance with this oath, to go and lay siege to Troy after Paris stole her away.

405c   that they would have to stay there into the eleventh: this (a campaign lasting into the eleventh year) is the duration of the siege in the account given in the *Excidium Troiae*, whilst in the Homeric version and in the *Ilias Latina* the period is ten years. The Spanish poet is inconsistent in the version that he adopts (see, for example, stanza 729).

410ff.   There are various accounts (in post-Homeric sources) of the ways in which Achilles' mother (Thetis) sought to keep him safe from the war. In a commonly known version, she sent him to the court of Lycomedes, in Scyros, where he was concealed and disguised as a young girl. During his stay he had an affair with Lycomedes' daughter, who had a son by him. Achilles was finally discovered by Odysseus (Latin: Ulysses), who, pretending to be a pedlar, tricked him into revealing his martial instincts, just as he does in the *Alexandre* version.

417ff.   He had a friend whom he greatly loved...: the outline of this episode is the same as that in the *Ilias Latina*, but the Spanish poet clearly mistakes the timescale, leading to confusion at a later stage in his narrative (see note to stanza

607d). In both the *Iliad* and the *Ilias Latina*, Achilles' quarrel with Agamemnon occurs when nine years of the siege have passed. The friend whom Achilles is said here to have loved was Briseïs, a girl who was given to him as part of his spoil for his role in the capture of a Trojan town before the events of the *Iliad* begin; Agamemnon, the leader of the expedition, takes her for himself when forced to give up his own prize of honour, Chryseïs (see *Iliad* 1).

435ff. I would like to tell you of the names of the princes: the list of the Greek warriors, including several minor figures, poses many problems in the establishment of the text. Names (and numbers) may have been distorted (see Casas Rigall, ed. 2007, 242) by the copyists of the Spanish poem, by the poet himself, or even in the manuscript that he was using of his Latin source. Our practice, as throughout the text, has been to produce a reading which seems likely to correspond as closely as possible to what our poet actually wrote. Clearly, however, there will in several cases be a difference between the name used in the Spanish text and the Latin or anglicised form used in the translation.

We have restricted the scope of these notes to the most famous and significant members of the Greek and Trojan forces who appear in the list and have not attempted to produce a catalogue of the relatively minor figures.

437a Agamemnon: Agamemnon was the son of Atreus and Aerope, and brother of Menelaus. He is represented variously as the king of Mycenae (including by Homer) or of Argos. He was the overall commander of the Greek forces during the Trojan War. He married Clytemnestra, who bore him four children: Orestes, Iphigenia, Electra, and Chrysothemis, but was to bring about his death on his return from Troy.

441c Ajax: this seems to be the first of the four warriors of the same name to be mentioned in this section of the Spanish text. However, he is in fact the same individual (Ajax Locros) that is mentioned in 449ab. The other figures by the name of Ajax that appear here (444c and 449ab) both correspond to the more famous Ajax son of Telamon also known as the "Greater Ajax"; in Homer's *Iliad* he is described as being of colossal stature, the tallest and strongest of all the Greeks and outstanding among them for his military skill.

441d Ulysses' son: the reading of the text is unclear here; the son of Ulysses would be Telemachus, although at the time he would have been still a young child. The alternative reading would be "el fidel Ulixero" ("the faithful Ulysses").

491c but another came to Paris' aid: in Homer's narrative and in the *Ilias Latina*, Paris is saved by the intervention of Venus (see, for example, *Iliad* 3.373–82). Typically, the Spanish poet rejects such an explicit reference to the involvement of a pagan deity and produces a more rational explanation for Paris' escape from death.

535a Aeneas: the Trojan hero Aeneas was the son of Anchises and Venus, husband to Creusa (and, later, in Italy, to Lavinia), and father of Ascanius (Iulus). His father was a cousin of King Priam of Troy. The escape of Aeneas with his band of Trojans from Troy, their long journey to Italy, and the war they fought there with the native

Italians is the subject of Virgil's *Aeneid*: from this mixture of Trojan and Italian stock will come the mighty race of Romans.

550d Bellona was an ancient Roman war deity, possibly predating Mars in this role.

561a Sarpedon, a newly dubbed Trojan knight: Sarpedon was a son of Zeus (Jupiter) and Laodamia, and King of Lycia. He fought on the side of the Trojans, and was one of Troy's greatest allies. He dies at the hands of Patroclus, who has donned Achilles' armour (see *Iliad* 16).

568d sang Kyries: a short petition, often set to music, used in the Eastern and Roman Churches, especially at the beginning of the Mass.

569a Andromache: Andromache was the daughter of Eëtion, King of Cilician Thebes; she was the wife of Hector and mother of Astyanax (Scamandrius was his name, but the people of Troy called him Astyanax, "lord of the city", for it was his father, Hector, who defended Troy: see *Iliad* 6.402–03). Her father and brothers were killed by Achilles during the Trojan War and her mother died in Troy before its fall (see *Iliad* 6.414–28). After Hector's death and the fall of Troy, as we read in the *Aeneid*, Andromache became the slave and concubine of Neoptolemus (Pyrrhus), Achilles' son. She bore him a son, and in due course was given to another of his slaves, Helenus, Hector's brother. At Pyrrhus' death, some of his kingdom came into Helenus' hands, and the two ruled over the imitation of Troy that they had built (*Aeneid* 3.320–43). The form of Andromache's name that appears (here and elsewhere) in the manuscripts is corrupt, although it may well be that the shortened form was introduced by the poet himself, probably for metrical convenience.

607d Achilles who gave so little help: there is no indication in the *Libro de Alexandre* that Achilles is still in conflict with Agamemnon (their dispute seems to have been settled in stanza 422). On the other hand, according to the *Ilias Latina*, which the poet seems to be following here, Achilles has not yet been reconciled with his fellow Greeks and (e.g. in stanza 610) is continuing to refuse to take part in the war against the Trojans. Thus, he is finally won round in stanza 614, even though, as recounted in the Spanish poem, the dispute had been settled long before. The confusion seems to result from a misunderstanding on the part of the Spanish poet (see also note to lines 417 ff.).

629d all of them kinsmen: In view of the difficulty of identifying with clarity the figures and relationships mentioned in his source, the Spanish poet opts for this phrase, which must be understood loosely as applying to close relatives.

636a An officer of Achilles, Patroclus by name…: Patroclus is said to be Achilles' "dear companion" at *Iliad* 9.205, but the nature of the relationship is far from uncontroversial: Plato (*Symposium* 179e-180b) holds that they were lovers, and says that Aeschylus did too (see fr. 134a), though with their roles reversed. This is not so apparent in the *Iliad*, but the bond between the men is clearly immensely strong, and it is his grief over his companion's death that rouses Achilles to furious anger against Hector, Patroclus' slayer, and brings him back into the battle, after Patroclus had donned

Achilles' armour and gone out to the battlefield, to help the ailing Greeks, but met his death at Hector's hands. Alexander's relationship with Hephaestion was often likened to that of Achilles with Patroclus (see note to stanzas 322 ff.).

651c with the week of prayer over ...: the Spanish text uses the term *setenarios* for the funeral celebrations, implying a period of seven days. It is an ecclesiastical term applied to a cycle of seven days of prayer to God, the Virgin and the Saints.

655c the tower built by those treacherous people: this is one of several allusions to the biblical Tower of Babel (*Genesis* 11) made in the Spanish poem (see, for example, note to 88a and also Introduction Sections 6 and 7). It is significant that here the detail was added by the Spanish poet.

658a There were the sun's twelve signs in harmony: the twelve signs are those of the zodiac, the twelve main constellations. This stanza is original with the Spanish poet, who repeatedly seeks to emphasize the natural order and harmony of God's creation, against which Alexander ultimately offends. For the significance of the details included in this description of Achilles' arms, see Introduction, Section 7.

711c hurling forth his lance and striking the mock castle: the detail seems inappropriate as Achilles is still on the field of battle and such an action – belonging to a time of entertainment, relaxation and celebration – would be much more likely to take place later, back in the Greek camp. Casas Rigall, ed. (2007, 307–308) speculates that this stanza may have been displaced. On the other hand, battle scenes elsewhere in the *Libro de Alexandre* take on the character of a medieval joust or mêlée, with appropriate breaks and presided over by judges; we should not be too surprised that Achilles' celebrations are depicted in this way.

737a He thought of building a horse ...: although the account of the capture of the city is based on the *Excidium Troiae*, the Spanish poet has adapted this part of his source freely. Instead of a wooden horse left as a gift (as a defeated general might commonly surrender his horse as a token of respect), he here describes a large siege castle in the form of a horse. The deception which brings about the fall of Troy depends not on tricking the Trojans into taking the horse into the city but on luring them out in search of booty (see stanza 751).

759c We have no way of knowing what became of Helen: indeed, this is not mentioned in either the *Ilias Latina* or the *Excidium Troiae*. The *Odyssey* does, however, make it clear that after the war she returns to Sparta with her husband Menelaus (Telemachus finds her there with him in *Odyssey* 4).

760–761 In *Manuscrito O* these lines are accompanied by a miniature which depicts Alexander standing between Achilles' tomb and a lectern, addressing his soldiers. See illustration on p.xv. Casas Rigall, ed. (2007, 318) points out that in this miniature Alexander's right eye is red (see stanza 150a).

798b King Alexander, son of the god Ammon: see also note to stanza 1168b Ammon was an oracle god, whose oracle was situated in the Siwah oasis, about 500 kilometres to the west of Memphis, the capital of ancient Egypt. He is commonly represented as having the horns of a ram. He may have been related to Baal Hammon a god venerated by the Semitic peoples, but his cult was taken over by the Egyptians, who identified him with their supreme god Amun. One of the new centres of the cult was Athens, where a temple was built in the harbour of Piraeus, and another centre was to be found in the Macedonian town of Aphythis where Alexander will certainly have come across the statue of the god. Indeed, the Greeks identified Ammon with Zeus, king of their own gods (see note to 1168b). In February 331 Alexander visited the Siwah oasis (see the account in stanzas 1166–83), according to some sources, because he wanted to imitate his ancestor Hercules. There is no doubt that Alexander preserved a particular devotion to Ammon (see Cartledge 2004, 209–210, Green 1991, 217–273) and a silver coin issued in Alexander's lifetime shows him wearing the horns of Ammon (Cartledge 2004, 222). Moreover, the close identification with Ammon can be seen as part of the process by which Alexander encouraged and even, ultimately, ordered his own deification.

802c   it was sealed with wax and fastened with thread: repeatedly our poet emphasises the practical and bureaucratic details of correspondence, as he does, for example, when he draws attention to the role of the chancellor (810c). In the present passage, the detail is based directly on the *Alexandreis* (2. 43–44) where the king sets his image in wax: that is, he uses the royal seal.

816b   and he wrote a letter with blood-coloured ink: in contrast with 810c, here Alexander writes the letter himself (as he is certainly capable of doing, given the emphasis in the text on his education). The detail of the blood-coloured ink is original with the Spanish poet.

820c   Just as Xerxes had done: this is Xerxes I of Persia (see note to stanza 104b). Xerxes had assembled a vast force for an invasion of Greece and the Greek historian Herodotus numbered his troops in millions (Herodotus 7.186). They did have some success, but following major Greek victories at Salamis and Plataea, the Persians were eventually cleared from Europe and the Aegean coasts.

822b   the warrior Memnon: Memnon of Rhodes was the highly skilful commander of the Greek mercenaries fighting in the service of Darius, who as a reward had named him satrap of Asia Minor. Memnon intelligently warned that it was impossible for the Persians to defeat the Macedonian army in a set-piece confrontation, and called for a strategy of scorched earth, advice which was rejected. He also suggested trying to stir up a revolt in Greece itself, having first wrested control of the most important Aegean islands. Memnon died during the siege of Mytilene in August 333, probably of illness, and not at this early stage in Alexander's campaign. He had no connection with Media (see stanza 823a).

826b   this battle lasted for three full days: according to the *Historia de Proeliis*, which does not mention Memnon, this initial battle between Alexander and the Persians lasted from dawn to midday. The first historical clash with the Persians was in fact the Battle of the River Granicus, where the Macedonians fought against an army commanded by Darius' nobles and including 15,000 Greek mercenaries. This was considered to be a relatively small-scale encounter but, although the Macedonians' casualties were light, those of the Persian forces (including mercenaries) were reckoned to have numbered 22,500.

828c   a city that bore the name of Sardes: Sardes or Sardis, the modern Turkish city of Sart, was the capital of the ancient kingdom of Lydia. It was under Persian domination until it surrendered to Alexander in 334 BC.

829c   the Sangarius: in the winter of 334 BC, Alexander rapidly reached Gordion (Gordium), the capital of Phrygia and an ancient city on the banks of the river Sangarius. In fact he was joining Parmenion, who had recently captured the city. Its historical wealth was famous: Phrygia and its capital had reached the height of its prosperity under the legendary King Midas who had ruled in the late eighth century BC (see stanza 830d). On the acropolis was to be found the chariot of Gordio, the first Phrygian king. Its yoke was bound with the bark of a cornel tree. According to tradition, the person who could untie the knot would become ruler of Asia. Plutarch's version of the events cites Aristobulus, who says that Alexander solved the problem by pulling out the wooden pole pin (Plutarch, *Alexander* 18), but it is more generally stated that he sliced the knot in two with his sword. Alexander's subsequent conquest of Asia seems to have fulfilled the prophecy. Weiss (2006, 130) examines the symbolism of the episode: "The knot can be understood on various levels. Explicitly, it represents all the intricacies of Asia, the greatest empire on earth (831). As such it stands for a problem that is central to the political concerns of the poem, for this empire, like all empires, is made up of multitudinous strands miraculously intertwined to create what seems like a seamless whole. ... The knot is in one respect a trope for unity in diversity …".

838c   Ancira is the present-day Turkish city of Ankara.

860d   Damietta was an important port in lower Egypt, situated close to the Nile estuary. It was the focus of the Fifth Crusade in 1219, when it was captured by forces under the leadership of the Spanish papal legate Cardinal Pelagius, only to be lost again to the Moslems in 1221. It was again briefly in Christian hands from 1249 to 1250, during Louis IX's Seventh Crusade. Damietta was seen as the key to the Nile and thus to the wealth of Egypt, and it was particularly famous for its linen cloth. This allusion has been the subject of some discussion for the dating of the *Libro de Alexandre*, but the balance of opinion is that there is no reason to suppose that it could not have been made before the capture of Damietta in 1219. Certainly, it does seem significant that, at the time when the poem was composed, Damietta was famous enough for the poet to choose to use it as a byword for wealth.

863b   the three heavens: Casas Rigall, ed. (2007, 343–344) points out that this reference may be biblical (see II Corinthians 12:2) and that it could also be related to the concept of the heavens accepted in the Ptolemaic system, whose authority was accepted throughout the Middle Ages: the heavens were divided into three parts: the sphere of the fixed stars, the *primum mobile*, which communicates motion to the lower spheres, and the Empyrean or seat of the deity and angels.

867a   Near to the King went his wife and queen: this was Stateira, wife and (probably) half-sister of Darius. It was indeed the tradition of the Achaemenids that members of the royal household, including the women and children, should accompany the armies on their campaigns.

878a how they had set Tarsus aflame: the Persian commander Arsames had been present when Memnon had proposed the scorched earth policy (see note to stanza 822b) and, after the disaster at the Granicus, was attempting to put such a policy into operation. He began to evacuate Tarsus with the intention of looting the city of its treasure and burning it to the ground.

882c Cilicia: a large region on the south-eastern coast of Asia Minor (modern Turkey).

884ff. But something so awful very nearly occurred there: the episode of Alexander's illness was historically of great significance: while Alexander lay ill (in fact in Tarsus) from July to September 333, Darius' army had been summoned, organised and led out from Babylon. There were also fears of attacks on the Greek coastline. Darius duly arrived on the plains of Syria with an army estimated at 600,000 men, outnumbering Alexander's forces ten to one. Alexander's troops marched 70 miles in two days to the shores of the Gulf of Issus, but Darius (perhaps assuming that Alexander was actually afraid to fight him) had already moved on.

905b he was of great distinction, whose name I would conceal: in spite of the intention which the poet expresses on this occasion, Parmenion's name is disclosed shortly afterwards in 912c, a revelation which, as Casas Rigall, ed. (2007, 353) suggests, is justified by the logic of the narrative. The allusion in 912cd is to Parmenion's murder which took place at Alexander's command following the execution of the general's son Philotas in September 330. It is highly unlikely that Parmenion's eventual death would have had any direct connection with the time of Alexander's illness. Nevertheless, it certainly seems to be true that there were tensions between Parmenion and Alexander, in spite of the important military role that the former continued to play in the campaigns.

914c Issus: a city in Cilicia (see note to 882c) on the Gulf of Issus (Iskenderun). This is the rapid march mentioned in the note to stanzas 884 ff.

917a because he said nothing: our poet has changed the emphasis from that to be found in his source, the *Alexandreis* (2. 269–271), where there is a suggestion that Sisenes has kept a treacherous matter secret. Gautier de Châtillon, like Quintus Curtius, his own source, considers the execution unjust, but the Spanish poet at this stage refrains from making any criticism of his hero.

918 One other prince ...: Timodes was the nephew of Memnon (see note to 822b), after whose death he assumed command of the Greek mercenaries fighting in Darius' army. There is no mention in our poet's sources of a disagreement with Alexander or a change of sides.

935–940 this was indeed a most beautiful spot: here the poet includes a classic example of a *locus amoenus*, a literary topic very common in both classical and medieval literature and one whose use was strongly recommended by the literary theorists. The passage has its source in the *Alexandreis*, but there is a strong contrast between the highly ornate Latin version and the simple beauty of the passage from the *Libro de Alexandre*. There is, of course, an ironic contrast between the emphasis on peace and harmony in this description and the savagery of the battle scene to which it is about to give way.

948a   The huge-bodied giants ...: see also notes to stanzas 88b and 655c. Our poet follows Gautier de Châtillon (*Alexandreis* 2. 498–503) in identifying the biblical tribe of Nimrod who constructed the Tower of Babel (*Genesis* 6:4, 11) with the giants of classical mythology who sought to climb up into heaven in their revolt against Zeus, which was put down with the help of the other gods and with the aid of Hercules. The identification of these classical and biblical traditions seems to have been quite common and already appears, for example, in the work of the sixth-century Byzantine chronicler John Malalas.

979c   Antigonus: Antigonus Monophthalmus ("the one-eyed") was appointed satrap of Greater Phrygia by Alexander. He three times saved Alexander's life in military encounters. A huge and towering man, he was a powerful – and ruthless – figure. He played a major part in the wars which followed Alexander's death until his death at the Battle of Ipsus in 301 BC.

979d   Craterus: Craterus was appointed by Alexander to command a battalion at Granicus and he then commanded the entire infantry at Issus; in some later campaigns he was given supreme authority over the army whilst Alexander occupied himself with special missions. It seems that before Alexander's death Craterus had been appointed to replace Antipater in authority in Greece. He died in battle in 321 BC.

991b   Nebuchadnezzar who conquered Judea: Nebuchadnezzar II was a ruler of Babylon in the Chaldean Dynasty, who reigned from about 605 BC to 562 BC. He is famous for his monumental building within his capital of Babylon, and known for his conquests of Judah and Jerusalem and for the deportation of a large part of the Jewish population of Judah to Babylon. He is said to have had the Jewish king Sedecias blinded, placed in fetters and taken to Babylon. As a result of his destruction of temples in Jerusalem and the conquest of Judah he is vilified in the Bible. The account of his madness is given in *Daniel* 4.

995a   ... the treacherous son: Amel-Marduk, known in the Hebrew Bible as Evil-Merodach, was Nebuchadnezzar's son and successor. He was said to have dismembered the dead body of his father and fed it to vultures, a detail which the Spanish poet would have found in the *Alexandreis*. Amel-Marduk reigned for only a year, before being murdered by his brother-in-law.

996c   The hand which wrote the obscure message: *Daniel* 5: 1–4 recounts how, as the Persian armies were closing in on Babylon, Nebuchadnezzar's descendant Belshazzar gave a feast at which the sacred vessels of Solomon's Temple, which had been brought to Babylon by Nebuchadnezzar, were profaned by those present. During the festivities, a hand was seen writing on the wall of the chamber an incomprehensible sentence. When the Hebrew Daniel was called in, he explained that the mysterious words expressed a divine judgement. Belshazzar was killed that same night, and the city fell to the invading armies.

997a The story of Cyrus: Cyrus the Great of Persia, who reigned from 559 to 530 BC, was the founder of the Persian Empire. He conquered the Medes (see note to 30c) and his empire eventually included most of south-west Asia and much of central Asia, from Egypt and the Hellespont in the West to the Indus River in the East. He ruled over his empire until his death in 530, following a campaign in central Asia.

997d Croesus: King Croesus of Lydia was the brother-in-law of Astyages, the last king of the Median empire. In about 547 BC he attacked Persia, laying siege to the city of Pteria. Cyrus levied an army and marched against the Lydians. After the Battle of Pteria, Croesus retreated to Sardis. He sent out requests for his allies to send aid, but, before the allies could unite, Cyrus pushed the war into Lydian territory and besieged Croesus in his capital. In the final Battle of Thymbra between the two rulers, Cyrus defeated and captured Croesus, though, according to Herodotus (1.85–89, especially 1.86) he spared his life and kept him as an advisor.

998a how Cyrus was secretly raised in the hills: Herodotus' account of Cyrus' early life (1.107–113) gives us the following picture: he was the son of Cambyses and Mandane, daughter of Astyages, the ruler of the Medes. But Astyages had had visions, seeing a great flood flow from Mandane and engulf Asia, and seeing a vine grow from her womb and overshadow all Asia. Fearing that the offspring of his daughter would rule Asia in his stead, he stole the child away at his birth and gave him to Harpagus, telling him to kill and bury the child. Harpagus could not bring himself to do so, and gave Cyrus to a herdsman, Mithridates, to leave out, exposed, in his fields, that he might die. Mithridates' own wife, as he was called away, had a child too, but the baby was still-born. They decided to set their own, dead, baby on the hillside, exposed to the wild beasts, and raise Cyrus as their own: thus Cyrus was brought up in secret, being thought dead.

998d it was a woman who killed him in battle: in Herodotus' account (1.214), Cyrus met his death in a ferocious battle with the Massagetae, a tribe from the southern deserts of Kharesm and Kizilhoum. The queen of the Massagetae, Tomyris, led the attack. The Persian forces suffered heavy casualties, including Cyrus himself. After the battle, Tomyris ordered the head of Cyrus to be dipped in blood in order to emphasize her vengeance for the death of her son at his hands.

1002ff. The account of the Battle of Issus, like those of all the other battles described in the *Libro de Alexandre*, is presented as a series of individual hand-to-hand combats. In this, the poet follows his sources but also the convention followed in medieval (and, indeed, classical) narrative poetry. No clear picture of the development of the battle emerges from the Spanish poem, but essentially, the key to the Macedonians' early success was the charge of the Companion Cavalry that Alexander himself led on the right. He managed to hold his forces together and, with his central phalanx holding firm and with the Persian left wing destroyed, he then turned his cavalry charge inwards towards Darius' Greek mercenaries in the centre. On the left, Parmenion's forces were under pressure, but, when the Persian right wing saw that their centre and left had collapsed, they took to flight. Darius had fled in his chariot after the success of the early Macedonian cavalry charge.

1009b   a man called Arethas: this individual, like nearly all of Darius' warriors who are named, is a literary creation: in this case, it seems, of Gautier de Châtillon. Some of the members of Alexander's army named in this and other battle scenes (e.g. Helim, Dolit and Hermogenes in stanza 1034) likewise have no historical counterparts.

1017c   Mazaeus: this is a clearly identifiable – and prominent – historical figure. He was a Persian nobleman who was appointed to the office of satrap possibly as early as 361 BC and seems to have been promoted under the rule of Darius. He took part in the crucial battle of Gaugamela and it is thought that he may already have been satrap of Babylonia. Mazaeus entertained Alexander in Babylon and gave him advice. In return, Alexander appointed him as satrap of Babylonia, an unusually important office for a Persian in Alexander's empire.

1032a   Nineveh: this city had been the capital of the Assyrian empire at its height. Situated on the eastern bank of the Tigris next to the modern-day Iraqi city of Mosul, Nineveh was an important junction for commercial routes crossing the Tigris and it became one of the greatest of all the region's ancient cities. However, its sacking by the Babylonians and Medes in 612 BC effectively put an end to the Assyrian Empire, and Nineveh never regained its former importance. By the age of Alexander it would have sunk into obscurity.

1045a   The Fate who severs the threads of life: in Greek mythology, the white-robed Moirae (Fates) were the personifications of destiny, known to the Romans as the Parcae. They are Lachesis ("disposer of lots"), Clotho ("spinner") and Atropos ("inflexible"), with charge of the past, present, and future respectively. They control the metaphorical thread of life of every mortal: Clotho spins the thread of life from her distaff onto her spindle; Lachesis measures the thread of life with her rod; and Atropos cuts the thread at a person's death. Their Roman names are Nona, Decima, and Morta. For an example of a classical account of the Moirae, see Plato, *Republic* 617b–e. Atropos is the subject of this stanza.

1049c   a brother of Darius: Oxathres and other Persian nobles are recorded as fighting valiantly against the Macedonian cavalry.

1063d and 1064c   born of adultery and of lowly origin / who brought death to his father in secret... : see notes to 19b and 169a. The detail of Alexander's responsibility for his father's death is not to be found in the *Alexandreis* and the Spanish poet's likely source is the *Roman d'Alexandre*.

1068a   Meleager: there were two Macedonian warriors by this name. One, the son of Neoptolemus, played a major part in Alexander's campaigns (and in the struggle for power which followed his death); he is known to have fought at Issus and Gaugamela. The other, a member of an aristocratic family, led a squadron of the Companion Cavalry at Gaugamela.

1083c and honoured them as much as if he were their father: Alexander's treatment of his royal captives was, indeed, exemplary; he granted them royal status and continued to treat Darius' wife, Stateira, as a queen. They were allowed to receive whatever allowances Darius himself had granted them. They were allowed private quarters, received gifts, and were never used for political bargaining (see Lane Fox 2004, 163–164 and Green 1991, 234–235).

1085 The lord of Damascus devised a wicked scheme: since the capture of the city in 538 BC, Damascus had been the capital of the Persian province of Syria. This account of how the unnamed satrap of Damascus sought to betray Darius by handing his wealth over to Alexander is found in the *Alexandreis* and in Quintus Curtius.

1090d that they be well prepared to lay siege to Sidon: Sidon had enjoyed great wealth as a Phoenician city state. However, it had suffered greatly at the hands of invaders. In 351 BC, unable to resist the forces of Artaxerxes III, the Sidonians had locked their gates and set fire to their own city. More than 40,000 had died in the conflagration. Under twenty years after such a disaster, the city was still too weak to oppose Alexander and it was quick to sue for peace.

1092a they brought siege to Tyre: the name of this historic Phoenician city and enormously wealthy commercial centre means "rock". Tyre stood on an island 730 metres off the coast and in order to besiege the city Alexander had to build a causeway to bridge the divide. This he did, using stone from the walls of the old city and the labour of local villagers. The Macedonians attacked Tyre on several fronts, including a naval assault. After a siege that lasted seven months, Alexander was able to lead his troops over the walls and into the city. 6,000 Tyrians were killed and 30,000 enslaved. Angered by the murder of the envoys that he had sent before the start of the siege, Alexander crucified 2,000 Tyrian troops along the coast.

1118b Agenor: Agenor was a Phoenician king of Tyre, said to be the son of the god Poseidon.

1118c but it was later restored in the time of Christ: Tyre was to remain an important trading centre and it retained much of its independence when the area became a Roman province. In the Christian era it was to achieve prominence: Paul of Tarsus spent a week in conversation with the disciples there. It was recaptured by the Crusaders from the Moslems in 1124 and it became one of the most important cities of the Kingdom of Jerusalem.

1119a The good King Hiram: Hiram I was king of Tyre and Byblos from 969 to 936 BC, and he seems to have developed Tyre from a satellite of Sidon into an extremely important Phoenician trading centre. Hiram allied himself with King Solomon of Israel and thus ensured himself access to the major trade routes. He sent Solomon architects, workmen and cedar wood to build the First Temple in Jerusalem.

1119d Melqart: for this interpretation of the reading of the Spanish text, see Nelson, ed. (1978, 409) and Casas Rigall, ed. (2007, 401). The god Melqart was venerated in Phoenician and Punic cultures from Syria to Spain and was the tutelary god of the city of Tyre. He is often represented in a form indistinguishable from that of Hercules, with whom he was commonly identified in mythology and cult.

1120b   Gaza: strategically situated on the Mediterranean coastal route, two miles from the sea, Gaza was a prosperous centre of trade and a stopping point on the caravan route between Egypt and Syria. The siege of Gaza gave Alexander his second opportunity in a short period to demonstrate his remarkable skill in countering major technical difficulties. Its inhabitants prided themselves on their steep fort and Alexander countered this by building a mound on which to site catapults and siege towers. Under pressure from these, the defenders held out for only two months. Alexander was wounded twice during the siege, once quite seriously when his shoulder was pierced by an arrow and once when he was wounded by an artillery stone. When the city was taken, all the male inhabitants were killed and the women and children were enslaved.

1134a   Jadus: the High Priest of Jersualem is mentioned by name in the *Historia de Proeliis* (Casas Rigall, ed. 2007, 405).

1138d   All the Jews: the term *aljama*, which is used in the Spanish text, was applied in medieval Spain to self-governing Jewish communities under Christian rule. There is a clear sense here that Alexander's relationship with the people of Jerusalem is, in the poet's mind, essentially that of a medieval monarch with the Jewish inhabitants of a Christian city.

1145a   He read in a prophecy from the Book of Daniel: this prophecy in *Daniel* 8 and 11:2–3 is mentioned in the *Historia de Proeliis*.

1155a   He had four characters drawn on his forehead: this is the Tetragrammaton, the Hebrew name of God, transliterated in four letters as YHWH. Compare the description of Jadus in stanza 1139.

1164a   Samaria: in fact, following a rebellion in the north of the region, Alexander destroyed the main town of Samaria and slaughtered the rebel leaders.

1165d   to the Jews alone: in the Spanish poet's source, ultimately, but probably not directly, Josephus' *Antiquities of the Jews* (*Antiquitates Judaicae*) (Casas Rigall, ed. 2007, 411), the Samaritans claim to be Hebrews but not from Judea; here, Alexander is unconvinced by their request but defers his decision.

1166b   and he entered Egypt: Alexander now moved south to Egypt, where he spent about six months. For the future this region would give him a strong coastal base and in a personal sense the time that he spent there was to mark an important psychological turning-point in his life. This was in no real sense a conquest, for Egypt's satrap – who had no resources with which to offer resistance – instead offered Alexander a warm welcome and gifts. For almost two hundred years Egypt had been occupied and exploited by the Persians, who were deeply unpopular, and so Alexander was now hailed as a liberator and offered the crown of Upper and Lower Egypt.

1167d   to go on a pilgrimage: Alexander is presented here as a medieval pilgrim, the kind of figure who would be associated with the pilgrimage to Santiago de

Compostela; see also the note to stanza 2535b. For Alexander's connection with the shrine of Ammon, see note to 798b.

1168b   Libya: this means Libya Cyrenaica, Eastern Libya, centred on the Greek colony of Cyrene. It would have been through the nearby Greek colony (with close links to Sparta) that the fame and worship of Ammon had spread to Greece long before Alexander paid his famous visit to the oracle. Indeed, the Greeks explained this highly honoured figure of Ammon as a form of Zeus, king of their own Olympian Gods (and thus the equivalent of the Roman god Jupiter). In Cyrene a temple was built to the horned figure of Zeus Ammon. It is not surprising that Alexander chose to pay this visit to the oracle at Ammon, in spite of the practical disadvantages of the detour, which involved considerable loss of time and allowed Darius an important opportunity to regroup after his defeat, for it was "the last available oracle of Greek repute before Alexander led his troops inland into Asia, and Alexander wished to consult him for this simple reason alone." (Lane Fox 2004, 194) Alexander was, moreover, highly superstitious and "there was also a powerful streak of the religious mystic in him." (Cartledge 2004, 209) During the visit, he asked a question of the god and we are told that he received the answer that he desired; we do not know what that was. What is undoubtedly true, however, is that after the visit to the Siwah oasis Alexander considered himself to be not just descended from Zeus but in some way his son.

1169a   In other times, when Bacchus had mastery of India: for Bacchus (Dionysus) see note to 239a. The most famous part of Dionysus' wanderings as a young man was his expedition of conquest to India, taking with him, among other things, the vine (his expedition is the subject of the *Dionysiaca* of Nonnus of Panopolis). Dionysus had returned to Greece in triumph. Fifteen generations later, according to tradition, Alexander's ancestor Hercules was also to travel to India, siring a line of Indian kings. Alexander was to make much of the parallel between this and his own achievements and was determined to outshine both of his illustrious predecessors, perhaps in this way giving proof of his own divine nature (see Green 1991, 380).

1170c   Bacchus begged Jupiter to show them ...: Casas Rigall, ed. (2007, 412) suggests that this story of the origin of the temple is drawn from an annotation to the manuscript of the *Alexandreis*.

1189cd   Bactrians: Bactria is the Greek name of the country between the range of the Hindu Kush and the Amu Darya (Oxus) river; its capital, Bactra (now Balkh), was located in what is now northern Afghanistan. Bactria had been conquered by Cyrus the Great in the sixth century BC, and since then it had formed one of the satrapies of the Persian empire. The **Scythians** were a people of horse-riding nomadic herdsmen who dominated the vast steppe lands stretching from the north of the Black Sea to the east of the Caspian Sea. They were famed for their independent and warlike nature.

1190   Canaan is an ancient term for a region approximating to present-day Israel and the West Bank and Gaza, together with adjoining coastal lands and parts of Lebanon and Syria. Casas Rigall, ed. (2007, 417) suggests that, as this region was already in the hands of Alexander and seems not to fit with the other more exotic ones mentioned, the poet originally included a different name. The **Chaldeans** were a Semitic people of Arabian origin who settled in southern Mesopotamia in the early part of the first millennium BC. After the conquest of Babylonia by the Persians in the sixth century BC, the Chaldeans had disappeared as a separate people. For the **Medians**, Medes or Midianites, see note to stanza 30c. **Sheba** (or Saba) was the powerful incense trading kingdom where the fabled Queen of Sheba is said to have resided. With its capital at Maryab (later known as Marib), it was the oldest and most important of the South Arabian kingdoms.

1191 The two lesser Indies, with the third and the greatest ...: the "third and greatest" corresponds to Indostan (essentially most of the Indian sub-continent together with the areas bordering it to the north-east) and the "lesser Indies" are on the one hand Indochina and on the other the area stretching from Iran to East Africa. For **Porus** (or Puru) see note to stanza 6c. This powerful ruler is famed for his immense physical stature and for his courage in battle. After his defeat by Alexander at the battle of Jhelum/Hydaspes River, he was released back to his kingdom and actually given the land of a neighbouring ruler who had fled. Porus is reported to have participated in Alexander's later conquests further east in India.

1196d the heads of the serpent: in Greek mythology, the Lernaean Hydra was an ancient serpent-like chthonic water beast, that possessed numerous heads and poisonous breath. To kill it was the second of Hercules' Twelve Labours, a task particularly hindered by one curious property of the beast: whenever one head was severed, two grew back in its place. This was overcome by scorching the stumps each time a head was cut off.

1198a Antaeus: this is another allusion to Alexander's supposed ancestor Hercules. The giant Antaeus would compel all strangers passing through his country to wrestle him. He was extremely strong, as long as he remained in contact with the ground (his mother, Earth); his strength was thus renewed when he was thrown to the ground, but if he was not in contact with the earth he grew very weak. Hercules, realising the source of his strength, crushed him to death whilst holding him aloft.

1199b Arbela: this was a town in ancient Assyria (now known as Arbil or Erbil, north-east of Nineveh, which Darius used as his base before he marched to do battle at Gaugamela).

1201ff. they saw that the moon was changing in colour: there was, indeed, a full lunar eclipse on the night of the 20th–21st September 331 BC, under two weeks before the battle of Gaugamela, which took place on 1st October.

1209b Aristander: Aristander of Telmessus had accompanied King Philip as early as 357/6 and during Alexander's campaigns he interpreted various omens for the King. The role that he played before the battle of Gaugamela is well documented. He seems to have died during the campaigns through illness or old age.

1210ff. He began to speak and held everyone's attention: Aristander's explanations draw not only on the *Alexandreis* (3. 463–543) but also – seemingly among other sources (Casas Rigall, ed. 2007, 424–428) – on St Isidore's *Etymologiae* (see note to stanzas 276–294). The *Etymologiae* give a broadly correct explanation of a lunar eclipse (the basis of stanza 1228) and one of a solar eclipse, which Aristander also includes (1224–25). The idea that the sun is seven times the size of the earth (stanza 1222c) seems to be original with the Spanish poet. Aristander does offer alternative explanations and takes from the *Alexandreis* the idea that the proximity of the sun robs other heavenly bodies of their light (1215–1217, 1226–1227). Stanzas 1229–1231, in which rational explanation gives way to superstition, seem out of keeping with the remainder of Aristander's speech.

1241c Shem, Ham and Japheth, each in his own land: according to *Genesis* 10, the whole population of the earth was to be descended from Noah's three sons, and writers such as Josephus and, through him, Saint Jerome and Saint Isidore, attempted to assign ethnicities to the offspring of each of them. In broad terms, Shem, Ham and Japheth have been identified with Asia, Africa and Europe respectively.

1242b and all the twelve tribes, the sons of Israel: *Genesis* tells how the descendants of the twelve sons of Jacob (whose name was changed to Israel) were to be identified as the twelve tribes, which initially bore their names.

1242cd the plagues of Egypt and the cruel angel; / the Tau on the doors, in lamb's blood marked ...: the allusion here is to tenth and final plague of Egypt: the death of all Egyptian first-born males. God told Moses to order the Israelites to mark their doorpost with lamb's blood, in order that the plague of death would pass over them, and at midnight the Angel of Death passed through the country to take the life of all the Egyptian first-born, including Pharaoh's own son. *Tau* is the last letter of the Hebrew alphabet and refers here to the bloody mark.

1243b and how the peoples asked for Aaron as their king: Aaron was Moses' brother. During Moses' long absence on Mount Sinai the people of Israel asked Aaron to give them a visible God that they could carry with them. His response was to have made the golden calf, which God destroyed during their idolatrous celebration.

1243d how Dathan and Abiron were swallowed up: while on Mount Sinai, Dathan and Abiron (together with Core) led a rebellion against Moses and Aaron. We are told (*Numbers* 27) that the earth opened up and swallowed Dathan and Abiron and their households.

1247 David (who reigned from approximately 1000 to 970 BC) was the second King of Judah and Israel. Most of the psalms of the Old Testament are attributed to him and for this reason he is commonly depicted in medieval art holding a psaltery (a stringed musical instrument of the harp or the zither family). **Solomon**, David's son, is believed to have ruled from about 970 to 928 BC and is famed for his ability as a judge and for the construction of the Temple of Jerusalem. Under his rule the country reached the height of its civilisation. **Rehoboam**, son and successor to Solomon, as King of Judah (until about 917), was an ultimately unsuccessful ruler and his reign saw the northern part of his kingdom seize independence as the Kingdom of Israel. Weiss (2006, 139) points out how these three men were all powerful figures whose reigns ended in conflict and rebellion, such as to serve as a warning to Alexander himself.

1290d   I shall make him take this kitten to the river: Alexander, using one of the colourful popular expressions in which the poem abounds, makes it clear that Darius will have to deal with an unpleasant task – face up to his responsibilities and confront a harsh future.

1332c   the hour of Terce: the third hour of prayer (see note to stanza 33a), corresponding to about 9.00 a.m.

1338ab   It was the month of May: as in the account of the Battle of Issus, this conflict is preceded by an allusion to the beauty of nature, a comment on the horror of what is to follow. In fact the battle of Gaugamela took place not in May but in October. Later in the poem there is a more extended and more lyrical passage in which the description of the delights of May is not set in an ironic context and sets the scene not for battle but for Alexander's marriage (see note to stanzas 1950–1954).

1339   Daniel ... had made the prophecy: Daniel's prophecy is also mentioned in the *Alexandreis*: as is explained in *Daniel* 8: 20, the he-goat destroys the two-horned ram (Darius, with the two horns symbolising Persia and Media). It is also very tempting to see in the description of Alexander as an "untamed goat" an allusion to the identification of Alexander with the horned god Ammon. See also stanzas 1801–1802.

1348ff.   The Battle of Gaugamela (sometimes known as Arbela) was fought between Darius' massive forces, drawn from many parts of the Persian empire, together with a large contingent of Greek mercenaries, and Alexander's army which was made up of Macedonians and other troops provided by his Thracian allies and members of the Corinthian League. Modern estimates (more conservative than the figures in contemporary accounts) suggest that Darius had an army of about 100,000, including 12,000 cavalry, 200 scythed chariots and even some war elephants, whilst the forces at Alexander's disposal were under half that size (about 40,000 infantry and 7,000 cavalry). Alexander's strategy was to draw as much of the Persian cavalry as possible to the flanks so as to create a gap within the enemy line where a decisive blow could then be struck at Darius in the centre. A further valuable tactic was the method of dealing with the potentially devastating chariots: to move aside and create a gap within which they would eventually be trapped. As the Persians moved towards the Macedonian flanks in their attack, Alexander formed his units into a giant wedge and himself led the charge. Alexander with most of his cavalry moved parallel to Darius' front lines, heading away from the prepared battlefield. A gap opened in the Persian forces and a large force then smashed into the weakened Persian centre, destroying Darius' royal guard and the Greek mercenaries. Darius was in danger of himself being cut off, and the generally held modern view, based on Arrian's account, is that he now broke and ran, with the rest of his army following him. Alexander did not set off after Darius at this point for he received desperate messages from Parmenion on the left and, in order to give support here, he delayed his pursuit. There were further complications to follow as Alexander's forces collided in the central plain with Persian and Indian cavalry who were seeking to withdraw after looting the Macedonians' baggage camp. A furious conflict ensued, in which Alexander himself was for a time in serious danger, but finally those Persians who survived fled in disorder from the battlefield. Alexander hoped to capture Darius in the town of Arbela, but by now his adversary had fled. It is estimated that almost a third of the Persian army was killed in the battle and subsequent pursuit, with about as many again captured.

1354c   the Philistine: the allusion here is clearly to Goliath and thus to a man of huge size and strength. See also stanza 1364 and note to 1364d.

1364d   a full thirty cubits: there are various figures for the size of the cubit, a measure employed by various ancient peoples and still in use in the Middle Ages. It relates to the distance from the tip of the fingers to the elbow and is generally considered to equate to about 18 inches. This would give this giant a height of over 45 feet.

1369d   Geon: the name is derived from that of Gaia, or Ge, the Greek earth goddess and mother of the giants who attacked the heavens.

1374d   but he gained scant reward for the hardship he endured: see also note to stanza 311b. Cleitus had played an important military role throughout the campaigns and at the Granicus he had saved Alexander's life. However, he seems to have been a critic of Alexander's orientalising tendencies (Cartledge 2004, 72) and, possibly for this reason, in autumn 328 they became involved in a violent argument during a drinking bout. Alexander ran him through with a lance and the army now retrospectively judged Cleitus guilty of treason. The comment made in this stanza is a significant one in that the poet, whose attitude to his hero has so far been one of unwavering admiration and approval, now alludes for the first time to the darker side of Alexander's conduct.

1389cd   the Fates: see note to stanza 1045a.

1399d   came to meet his end: there is confusion here, originating in the *Alexandreis*, for Nicanor was to die of illness in the year following this battle (see also note to stanza 318).

1403cd   of his three fine sons, only one was left to him: the youngest of Parmenion's three attested sons was Hector. He held no military office but he was drowned in the Nile in 332/1. For the circumstances surrounding the death of Philotas, see note to stanza 1902d.

1414ab   the hour of None: see note to stanza 33a; **as Vespers drew near:** Vespers is the evening prayer service in the Roman Catholic, Eastern (Byzantine) Catholic, and Eastern Orthodox liturgies of the canonical hours; its mention here is a further example of the christianisation and medievalisation of the narrative.

1421d   Bessus was the satrap of Bactria and relative of Darius who, after the battle of Gaugamela – in which he had himself played a prominent part, in charge of the left wing of the Persian army – conspired against and murdered Darius and seized power, assuming the title of Artaxerxes V. **Nabarzanes** had commanded the Persian cavalry at Issus. He was involved in the plot against Darius, fled to Hyrcania and, after surrendering to Alexander, was, in the short term, pardoned.

1423cd The **River Rhône** and **Saint Maurice** are both mentioned by Gautier de Châtillon. St Maurice was a Roman solider who was executed for refusing to fight to put down a Christian rebellion in Gaul.

1431a The historical figure of **Lysimachus** is in fact not mentioned until 328 BC, well after the battle of Gaugamela. In the battle of the Hydaspes against the forces of Porus, however, he is known to have fought in the immediate vicinity of Alexander. After Alexander's death, he was given control of Thrace and in 306 or 305 he assumed the title of "King". He did not die until 282/81.

1445cd Cyrus: for the death of Cyrus I, see note to stanza 997a.

1446 King Xerxes: see notes to stanzas 104b and 820c. Herodotus tells how Xerxes achieved two major feats of technology in the course of his wars against the Greek states: he had a pontoon bridge of boats constructed to cross the Hellespont (1446b: Herodotus 7.36), and had a ship canal dug through the neck of the Athos peninsula in Chalcidice (1446c: Herodotus 7.22–24). In stanza 1446d our poet seems to have misinterpreted his source in the *Alexandreis*, which in fact mentions a ship rather than a beast.

1459a For **Mazaeus**, see note to stanza 1017c.

1460ff. I wish to give you an account of Babylon: Babylon, situated on the river Euphrates, south of the modern Baghdad, was the finest city in Darius' empire. "Babylon", it has been commented, "marked the first and most important step in his [Alexander's] progress to becoming the richest man in the world." (Lane Fox 2004, 237). It had been built on an almost unimaginable scale, with its huge walls, towering sacred Ziggurat, immense stone viaduct bridging the river Euphrates, vast palaces and famous Hanging Gardens. In 539 BC, serious damage had been done to the city by Xerxes' troops in punishment for a nationalist rebelion, including the demolition of the Ziggurat and the temple which stood on it. Nevertheless, to the war-weary Macedonians it must have seemed an earthly paradise. It was two hundred years since the ancient city had fallen to the Persian king. From the plains of Babylonia (Lower Mesopotamia), characterised by their rich and productive soils, the court drained the considerable resources on which it depended and Iranian dignitaries enjoyed a magnificent way of life. The warm welcome that Alexander undoubtedly received on arriving before the walls of Babylon marked an extremely important moment in his career. It was explained largely by fear and the desire to appease so powerful a conqueror, though the gestures towards the city's priesthood and temple communities were also extremely important. It seems, indeed, that Alexander had promised to restore the Ziggurat and the shrine which stood on it (Green 1991, 303). Our poet has based this extensive description principally on the *Roman d'Alexandre*, adapting his source freely and weaving in material from a number of other texts, including the *Alexandreis*, the *Etymologiae*, the *Epistola Presbiteri Iohannis* and seemingly *Floire et Blancheflor*, a French romantic idyll written in the third quarter of the twelfth century (Casas Rigall, ed. 2007, 476). It is an outstanding example of his desire – and his ability – to assemble and integrate into an effective whole material taken from a range of sources, in order to enrich his narrative and to develop and comment on the underlying themes of his poem.

1465a   All four sacred rivers: See note to stanza 287a.

1468–1492   a wealth of very precious stones: This list of precious stones is based on the *Etymologiae*, which associates them mainly with Asia; however, on a number of occasions the account of the properties included in the *Libro de Alexandre* is at odds with the information given in our poet's source. Several of the names are distorted, but it is difficult to tell at what stage this distortion took place; see Casas Rigall, ed. (2007, 478), who also points out that the names given to the stones in the *Etymologiae* and in the *Libro de Alexandre* do not today always relate today to the same minerals.

1503c   Antipater (Antipatros) was a Macedonian nobleman who had risen to prominence by the time that Alexander's father acceded to the throne of Macedonia and under Philip he achieved a position of considerable power. He played an important part in securing the throne for Alexander after Philip's assassination. When Alexander embarked for Asia in 334 BC, he left Antipater as his Macedonian regent, effectively his viceroy in Europe. Antipater put down the uprising of Peloponnesian states headed by the Spartan king Agis III, a victory which left him in a position of supreme power in Greece. There is no firm evidence that he had any involvement in any plot against Alexander but a rift does seem to have opened up between the two men. Alexander openly asserted that Antipater had regal aspirations, whilst on the other hand Antipater became highly critical of the Emperor's desire for deification. It seems that in 324 Alexander decided to replace Antipater as regent of Macedonia with Craterus and it is not surprising that after Alexander's death stories quickly began to circulate that Antipater and his sons had been involved in a plot to murder the King. It may well be that Alexander in fact died of illness rather than as the result of any such act of treachery. Following Alexander's death, Antipater rapidly became involved in a war with the Greek states which ended in the re-establishment of Macedonian dominance. He died of illness in 319.

1505ff.   the giants attempted to scale the heavens: this is the longest of the passages in the *Libro de Alexandre* which develop the story of the Tower of Babel. For the question of its relationship with Babylon, see note to stanza 88a. Here again the poet blends the biblical account of the events leading to the creation of the many languages (*Daniel* 11:1–9) with elements taken from the myth of the war of the Giants against the gods (see note to 948a). The false etymology of *Babel* given in stanza 1522 comes ultimately from *Genesis* 11: 9.

1512a   Seventy-two in number: the origin of this figure is the list of the male offspring of the sons of Noah, given in *Daniel* 10.

1513d The **Amorites** were a Semitic people who dominated Mesopotamia from about 1900 to 1600 BC, with Babylon as their capital.

1515–1517 **Samaria** is the central region of the Biblical land of Israel. For the **Medes** and the **Canaanites** (1516c), see notes to stanzas 30c and 1190. **Pamphylia** is a southwestern region of Anatolia (Asia Minor). **Hyrcanians:** Hyrcania was situated between the Caspian Sea, which was previously called the Hyrcanian Ocean, in the north and the Alborz mountains to the south and west. **Phrygia** was a kingdom in the west central part of the Anatolian Highland, part of modern Turkey. It was briefly conquered by its neighbour Lydia, before passing into the Persian Empire. The **Parthians** were to become an extremely powerful people in the century following Alexander's death. From the early second century BC and for a period of some 400 years, they extended their power from an area corresponding to north-eastern Iran, conquered most of the Middle East and south-west Asia, controlled the Silk Road and built Parthia into a vast empire which proved a counterbalance to that of Rome in the West. Parthia at one time occupied areas which now form part of Iran, Iraq, Turkey, Armenia, Georgia, Azerbaijan, Turkmenistan, Afghanistan, Tajikistan, Pakistan, Syria, Lebanon, Jordan, Palestine and Israel. The **Elamites** called their country *Haltamti*, later rendered as *Elam*, which means "highland"; Elam, lasting from around 2700 BC to 539 BC, is one of the oldest recorded civilizations, centered in the far west and south-west of modern-day Iran. For **Cappadocia** see note to stanza 111a and for the **Ninevites**, see note to stanza 1032a. The **Cyreneans** were inhabitants of the north African Greek colony of Cyrene (see note to stanza 1186b). For the **Amazons**, see the note to stanza 1863 and for the **Scythians** the note to 1189cd. **Iconia** was the capital of Lycaonia, a large region in the interior of Asia Minor, north of Mount Taurus, which was bounded in the east by Cappadocia and in the west by Phrygia and Pisidia.

1518a **Semiramis** was an Assyrian queen around whom many legends have grown. Believed to be the daughter of a goddess, she became the wife of Ninus, with whom she is said to have founded Babylon. Significantly, perhaps, Semiramis has been connected with the biblical character of Nimrod, who built the Tower of Babel. She is also sometimes identified with the historical figure of Shammuramat, the Babylonian wife of Shamshi-Adad V (who ruled from 811 to 808 BC).

1531 King Nebuchadnezzar: see note to stanza 991b; **the one who had his men address him as God:** Casas Rigall, ed. (2007, 594) points out that this is in fact not the Babylonian King Nebuchadnezzar who figures in *Daniel* but the Assyrian ruler of the same name, who is mentioned in *Judith* I (although he is often identified with the Babylonian king). Of Nebuchadnezzar's palaces in Babylon, one alone contained some six hundred rooms.

1537b **in documents by a.b.c:** these were legal documents in which two copies were made on the same parchment with, in the centre, an inscription, which was usually in the form of a sequence of letters. The document (and the set of letters) was then divided into two and the authenticity of one of the copies could be demonstrated by showing that the two parts matched exactly.

1545d   guitars: Casas Rigall, ed. (2007, 496) questions this reading, which he suggests is a later scribal insertion, and prefers *cítara*, a kind of lyre.

1548d   Walter, go and sleep, you have stayed up long enough: this line is one of the most enigmatic in the poem and has long perplexed scholars (see Introduction, Section 3). In this text and translation we have opted for the suggestion made by Michael (1986): that here the Spanish poet apostrophises his source, the book that he has open on his desk, as though he were speaking to its author, Gautier de Châtillon, in person. The tone is gently humorous. The subsequent uncertainty over the name and the introduction by copyists of other and more confusing versions can be explained as the result of a misreading of Gautier's name.

1554   Jethro ... had given to the prophet this very same advice: the advice of the priest Jethro was that Moses should choose wise and trustworthy representatives from among all the leaders of Israel and appoint them as "rulers of thousands, of hundreds, of fifties, and of tens" (*Exodus* 18:18–27).

1561a   Susa was an ancient city of the Elamite, Persian and Parthian empires of Iran, located about 150 miles east of the Tigris River. In Alexander's day it was a rich and highly impressive city, said to be twenty kilometres in circumference, having been built under Darius I two centuries previously. Its satrap formally made over to Alexander more than 50,000 talents of gold and silver and, given that a talent was equivalent to at least 25 kg., the value of such a hoard would have been immense.

1563b   Uxion is not mentioned in any of the major historical sources or in the *Alexandreis*, but the attack on a town of the Uxii in late 331 BC is clearly documented.

1564a   Medates was the satrap of the region, who, according to the *Alexandreis*, was married to a niece of Darius' mother Sisygambis (see Casas Rigall, ed. 2007, 502).

1572a   Tauron first appears in historical records in late 331, when he is sent by Alexander to attack the Uxian town. He is not mentioned again until 326, when he took part in the battle with Porus.

1589a This is the first mention by name of **Sisygambis**, the mother of Darius.

1599c In late April or May 330 Alexander burned to the ground the ceremonial capital of the Achaemenid Empire at **Persepolis**, with its vast and imposing palace built and decorated by Darius I and his successors. This may have been a calculated act to demonstrate the power of Alexander to punish those who opposed him, similar to the destruction of Thebes. It may also have been, as stanzas 1603–1604 suggest, a symbolic act of vengeance for what Alexander saw as many years of repression. He is said to have told his troops that Persepolis was "the most hateful city in the world" (Lane Fox 2004, 248). It also possessed enormous wealth. It has been calculated that the fortune that Alexander carried off from the treasure vaults of Persepolis was equivalent to the national income of the Athenian empire at its height for nearly 300 years (Green 1991, 316).

1607ff.   There was one other reason why the city was burned: this episode is reported by Quintus Curtius and included in the *Alexandreis*. Elsewhere it is reported that on his way to Persepolis Alexander met with the families of Greeks who had in the past been deported to Persia and that he honoured them with gifts, a free passage home and exemption from taxes (Lane Fox 2004, 248).

1641b The Greeks considered **Ecbatana** to have been the capital of Media, and attributed its foundation to Deioces, who was said to have surrounded his palace with seven concentric walls of different colours. Under the Persian kings, Ecbatana, situated at the foot of Mount Elvend, was a summer residence. Later, it was to become the capital of the Parthian rulers.

1667a Artabazus, grandson of the Persian Artaxerxes II, had rebelled against royal authority and fled to the court of Philip where he lived in exile until the mid 340s BC. A firm supporter of Darius, in 330 he tried to reduce the hostility between his king and Nabarzanes and Bessus. Having failed to prevent Bessus from imprisoning Darius, he and his followers set off and sought refuge in the mountains, before eventually surrendering to Alexander. In due course he was appointed satrap of Bactria, but a year later he asked to be excused from his position because of old age (see Heckel 2006, 55).

1686b Patron was a mercenary in Darius' service and commanded the Greek mercenaries who remained loyal to the Persian king after the defeat at Gaugamela. After the death of Darius, 1,500 of the mercenaries agreed to surrender unconditionally.

1724d In medieval Spain to pull or pluck a man's beard was the most deadly form of insult. The law codes considered it to be an assault of equivalent seriousness to castration.

1756b Judas the Maccabean or *Judas Maccabeus* was a Jewish guerrilla leader who played an important part in the revolt (which began in 167 BC, headed initially by his father Mattathias) against the Seleucid empire under King Antiochus IV Epiphanes, with the aim of preventing the imposition of Hellenism upon Judea and of preserving the Jewish religion.

1766b Polystratus is generally recorded as the Macedonian soldier who found Darius when he had been left to die. He may have been a historical figure, but there is no other evidence of his existence.

1768 Through the middle of a little valley ...: this is another example (see also stanzas 935–940 and 1338ab) of how our poet uses the description of a *locus amoenus* or scene of great natural beauty as a contrast to the awful events for which it is the setting.

1780a You followed the example: see note to stanza 2360a.

1789cd anyone who ever shows mercy to a traitor: it is ironic, in the light of this curse, that Alexander does go on to pardon Nabarzanes (stanzas 1860–1862; see also notes to stanzas 1421d and 1861a), an act for which, in the light of this stanza, his own death at the hands of traitors can be seen as punishment.

1794b Saul, in the final years of the eleventh century BC, was the first King of Israel. He enjoyed an uneasy relationship with David, his son-in-law, became engaged in a feud with the priestly class, and eventually died in battle with the Philistines on Mount Gilboa. His fall from power and the nature of his death provide an appropriate parallel with Darius.

1798a   The legends of **Arthur** were widely known by the beginning of the thirteenth century. Geoffrey of Monmouth's *Historia Regum Britanniae* and other works had done much to structure and shape the myths of Arthur and Merlin; and between 1170 and 1190 Chrétien de Troyes, who for some years served at the court of his patroness Countess Marie de Champagne, wrote his extremely influential series of Arthurian courtly romances.

1798d   The **Lombards** were seen as the embodiment of greed because of their immense commercial success (see note to stanza 91c).

1799   when the world was created: for the significance of this much debated stanza and the light that it sheds on the date of composition of the *Libro de Alexandre*, see Introduction, Section 3. Essentially, 1799c gives the date of Darius' funeral and 1799d should allow the date of the poem's composition to be calculated; following the reading in *Manuscrito P*, this would appear to be 1203–4, although the validity of this conclusion is far from being universally accepted.

1801–02   *Hic situs est aries typicus* ...: the first two lines of the epitaph are two Latin hexameters quoted from the *Alexandreis* (7. 423–424). The remaining Latin is not of Latin metre and is in origin taken from *Daniel* 8:20 as a gloss to explain the symbolism of the ram's horns. The stanza translates as follows: "here lies the symbolic ram, whose two horns Alexander broke, the hammer of all the world; the two horns are the two kingdoms, of the Persians and the Medes". Stanza 1802 is the Spanish poet's loose translation of the lines quoted from the *Alexandreis*, but it does not include the gloss, in whose place lines c–d are included, giving prominence to the role of the traitors.

1807b   Cede to one greater: Arizaleta (1999, 101) points to the source of this quotation in the *Disticha Catonis*, a collection of proverbial wisdom and morality composed by the otherwise unknown Dionysius Cato in the 3rd or 4th century AD. Also known as *The Cato*, this work was an extremely popular medieval schoolbook for teaching Latin, valued not only as a Latin textbook but also as a moral guide. It consists of a short preface (*epistola*); a group of rules for living, expressed in prose (*breves sententiae*); and four books of moral aphorisms. In the second half of the thirteenth century this work also gave rise to a Spanish text, the *Castigos y ejemplos de Catón*, composed in the *cuaderna vía* verse form.

1817ff.   For possible parallels between this section and the conclusions of the Fourth Lateran Council, see Introduction, Section 3.

1825b   others by simony: this is the ecclesiastical crime of paying for or selling offices or positions in the hierarchy of a church. It is perhaps significant that there are a number of sections dealing with simony, specifically among monks, nuns and clerics, in the report of the Fourth Lateran Council of 1215. See also note to stanza 2375d.

1825c   Nothing is asked about age: the career of a son of Fernando III illustrates very well the abuses which were clearly rife. Don Felipe at the age of 12 was named a canon of Toledo and shortly afterwards of Burgos and Valladolid, and he was also appointed Abbot of Castrojeriz in Burgos. At 16 he was also elected Abbot of Santa María de Valladolid, at 18 or 19 he became Bishop of Osma (although the legal requirement was a minimum age of 30) and by the age of 25 he was Archbishop of Seville. He later abandoned the priesthood and twice married, proceeding to take part in the rebellions against his brother Alfonso X (Álvarez Borge 2003, 306).

1852d   ten years ago: almost certainly this has no more specific sense than "a long time ago".

1861a   There was a nobleman there ...: this is an allusion to Bagoas, a good-looking eunuch of Darius III. Bagoas surrendered to Alexander along with Nabarzanes and, rapidly becoming a favourite and flatterer of the Macedonian king (there were some accusations, too, that they were sexually intimate), he managed to save Nabarzanes' life with his persuasive charms.

1862d   in this way the King did great damage to his goodness: the Spanish poet here expresses open and direct criticism of Alexander for the first time, thus beginning a significant new stage in the poem's development.

1863   A rich queen: according to Greek legend, the Amazons were a race of female warriors, unusually fierce, who lived without male company. Herodotus follows the geographical theory of the Epic Cycle, and places their home on the banks of the River Thermodon. He tells, too, at 7.110–117, of Amazon intermarriage with Scythians. The attempt at geographical fixity and the tale of marriage with a real race both indicate, for the historian, a genuine belief in their existence, although the tradition is not constant and seems to assign the Amazons variously to three centres, one in western Asia Minor, one in Pontus, and one in Scythia. This home that Herodotus gives them is in a region bordering Scythia in Sarmatia, and it is possible that the tales of them may be based on the warrior women among the Sarmatians who fought alongside men. Hercules' Ninth Labour was to retrieve the girdle of the Amazon warrior queen Hippolyte, which she was willing to give him, but Juno is said to have convinced the Amazons that he was trying to kill their queen, denying any chance for the labour to be completed peacefully. The account of Alexander's encounter with Thalestris can be seen as a deliberate parallel with the legend of Hercules' marriage to a local goddess (Stoneman 2008, 130); for the account of Hercules and the goddess, see Herodotus 4.8–9). The *Alexander Romance* records how Queen **Thalestris** of the Amazons brought 300 women to Alexander the Great, hoping to breed a race of children as strong and intelligent as he, and how she stayed with the Macedonian king for 13 days and nights in the hope that he would father a daughter by her. There are numerous authorities for the visit to Alexander by the queen of the Amazons, but it is certainly fictitious: several of Alexander's biographers, including Plutarch, dispute the truth of the story. Casas Rigall, ed. (2007, 560) points out that the name **Femenina** (or some variant) is commonly used in medieval texts to denote the land of the Amazons.

1872–1879 Queen Thalestris arrived, fine in appearance: the classic portrait of female beauty was a topic much exploited in narrative poetry of the twelfth and thirteenth centuries. Its use was recommended by the literary theorists such as Geoffrey of Vinsauf, but there are many examples in texts likely to have been known by our Spanish poet, such as French *romans d'antiquité* like the *Roman d'Eneas* and the *Roman de Thèbes*. For the most part, the approach to this portrait and the details included are conventional, but the detail of the hawk (suggesting, perhaps, Thalestris' warlike nature) is a significant individualising feature.

1874cd Ovid includes in the *Metamorphoses* (6.424–674) the account of the transformation of **Philomela**, daughter of Pandion I, King of Athens. Philomela's sister Procne was married to King Tereus of Thrace and had a son, Itys, by him. Tereus raped Philomela, and then cut her tongue out and imprisoned her. However, Philomela wove a tapestry which revealed the crime to Procne. In order to take vengeance, Procne killed Itys, cooked him, and served him to Tereus, who then pursued both women wishing to kill them. All three were transformed into birds and Philomela into a nightingale. Casas Rigall, ed. (2007, 560–561) points to parallels with the version of the story composed by Chrétien de Troyes (see note to 1798a).

1879d **Orpheus** was called by Pindar the "father of songs" (*Pythian* 4. 177), and was revered as a master among poets and musicians; for a passage similar to our present bringing the trees to sing, see Euripides, *Bacchae* 560–564. A famous version of Orpheus' story is told at Virgil, *Georgics* 4. 450–527: deprived of his lover, Eurydice, by death, Orpheus goes down into the Underworld and by the power of his song convinces the infernal gods to allow him to take Eurydice back to the realm of the living. Proserpina sets the condition on this that he may not look back at Eurydice until they completed the path out of the Underworld. However, when he comes back to the breezes above, he cannot help himself, and looks back; Proserpina's condition is broken, and Eurydice is taken back down to the shades below. Bereft once more, and stricken with grief, nothing can turn Orpheus from his sorrow, and he is killed by Thracian women in a state of Bacchic frenzy, angered at his neglect of them, as he thinks only of Eurydice. Ovid (*Metamorphoses* 10.1–85) also tells of Orpheus' descent to the Underworld to retrieve Eurydice along similar lines (though here Pluto gives the condition), and Orpheus' song is so powerful in this account that it even brings a pause to the eternal torments (such as the vultures pecking Tityus' liver: see note to 2416a).

1889c **Bactria:** See note to 1189cd.

1902d **the whole affair came crashing down on Philotas:** Arguably, this affair is best seen as conspiracy not *by* but *against* Philotas and it demonstrated the extent to which Alexander was prepared to act ruthlessly to ensure his complete dominance (see Cartledge 2004, 67 ff.). Philotas was the eldest son of Alexander's senior general, Parmenion, and, as commander of the prestigious Companion Cavalry, he was an extremely important figure in his own right. Information against Philotas had clearly been collected over an extended period, and one point of conflict may have been his objection to Alexander's process of orientalisation. Late in 330 it was alleged that a Macedonian called Dimnus had been hatching a plot against Alexander's life and that Philotas, although he had been informed of this plot, had failed to report it. Philotas was accused of treason, brutally tortured (a detail omitted in the *Libro de Alexandre*) and tried by the army. Although he had no involvement in the plot, he was convicted and stoned to death. Shortly afterwards, his father was murdered at Alexander's command. These were sordid political acts; in Cartledge's words (2004, 69) "Philotas's end may be described as judicial murder. That of his father was undisguised assassination." Our poet is unusual in his unswerving defence of Alexander's conduct, emphasising as always the need for total devotion to one's lord and king.

1910a   a brother of Darius: this is Oxathres (see note to line 1049c), who is recorded as joining Alexander's forces after Darius' death and who became one of his close-knit circle of advisers.

1911b   mutilated first and then crucified: according to Arrian's explanation, the mutilation of the traitor Bessus, according to oriental tradition, meant the slicing off of his nose and ears before his execution. Although we are told that Alexander had handed Bessus over to Oxathres for punishment, the nature of his treatment was such as to make a specific point: according to Cartledge (2004, 72), it served "to demonstrate especially to his [Alexander's] Iranian subjects that Alexander was now in effect Great King and that any oriental rebels would be put down in the symbolically appropriate oriental fashion."

1913c   The Greeks gave the name **Tanaïs** to the River Don, one of the most important rivers in Russia and a major trade route. They also established a settlement of the same name.

1925d   a place of evil: this phrase (in Spanish "mal lugar") is commonly used in medieval Spanish texts to denote Hell.

1945a   The great horned goat with the honoured beard: Daniel's prophecy (*Daniel*, 8) has now been fulfilled (see note to stanza 1339). The mention of the beard is related to an epithet commonly applied to epic heroes; it is much used, for example, in the *Poema de Mio Cid*, where the beard is an important motif associated with the theme of honour. See also note to stanza 1724d. Ian Michael (1961, 38–39) points out that there appears to be an echo here of Alexander's title in Arabic literature: "Dhu 'l-Karnain" ("the two horned"), one explanation for which is that he ruled both the Eastern and the Western horns of the world.

1947b   what he had sworn to Darius: this relates to the promise made in stanza 1784.

1950–1954   It was the month of May...: Casas Rigall, ed. (2007, 576) reviews various suggestions for the origin of this passage, both in the Spanish poet's sources and in popular tradition. The spring description was also a topic commonly dealt with in medieval Latin lyrics, where poets displayed a knowledge and mastery of rhetorical techniques which may have had their origin in study under the grammarians.

1957d **Rhoxane** was wrongly identified in the *Alexander Romance* as a daughter of Darius, and it is from here – through the *Historia de Proeliis* – that our poet adopts the error about her origin. She was the daughter of a Bactrian nobleman and was about fourteen when she was encountered by Alexander, among thirty maidens introduced to him at a banquet. She was famed for her beauty, but the chief reason for the marriage will have been political: the marriage helped to end opposition to Alexander in the north-eastern part of his territories. Rhoxane bore her husband a son, who was either still-born or died shortly after birth, and she was again pregnant when Alexander died (see note to stanza 2636).

1962–1963 **There he had Apelles craft such a marriage bed:** the absence of a set-piece description here seems surprising, and it is possible that the account of Alexander's tent, eventually situated at the end of the poem, was originally intended for inclusion here. There is evidence within that section (stanzas 2539–2595), such as the list of lands still to be conquered, which suggests that it is indeed more appropriate to an earlier stage in Alexander's career.

1964b **letters were immediately written and sealed:** the apocryphal letters from Alexander to his mother and to Aristotle were widely considered as authentic in the Middle Ages. Prose versions of two letters to his mother were included in the *Manuscrito O* of the *Libro de Alexandre*.

1967d **until Elijah is come:** according to II *Kings*, Elijah raised the dead, brought fire down from the sky, and ascended into Heaven on a whirlwind. Jesus and John the Baptist are sometimes identified with Elijah. Based on a prophecy in *Malachi*, some Jews still await his return as a sign of the coming of the Messiah.

1970b **Cleitus and Ardophilus:** for **Cleitus** see notes to stanzas 311b and 1374d. The name **Ardophilus** (which coincides with that of a Persian killed by Cleitus in stanza 1014) seems to be used here to denote a combination of the figures of Hermolaus and Callisthenes. Hermolaus, involved in the "Conspiracy of the Pages" against Alexander, was executed in 327. Callisthenes is never mentioned by name by the Spanish poet and his death receives this one disguised mention. However, Alexander's treatment of him is generally viewed as very significant: a relative of Aristotle, he was appointed Alexander's official historian, but, despite considerable flattery in his writings, he seems to have fallen out with him over the question of *proskynesis*, in Persian terms an act of obeisance towards a superior but for the Greeks a religious gesture performed in honour of the gods. Callisthenes was executed for alleged treason, though as to the exact nature of his unpleasant death there is considerable debate (see Cartledge 2004, 263–265).

1973c **Porus:** see notes to stanzas 6c and 1191. Gautier de Châtillon rightly depicts Porus as a regional ruler, albeit a very powerful one. In the *Libro de Alexandre*, however, he is presented as an emperor as powerful and influential as Darius himself.

1976–1980 **The elephant is a beast of very great valour ...:** both Michael (1970, 8–9 and 272–273) and Bly and Deyermond (1972, 171–74) point to the parallels between this passage and the depiction of the elephant in Bestiary tradition, showing how, by presenting it as the embodiment of the sin of pride, the Spanish poet is offering a further comment on the conduct of Alexander himself. The Bestiary text that the poet seems to have known is the *Physiologus,* a book written or compiled in Greek by an unknown author, probably in the second century AD; it was translated into Latin in about 400 and later into many European and Middle-Eastern languages.

1983ff. that Porus desired to do battle with him: what was to ensue was the battle of the Hydaspes or Jhelum, the last of Alexander's great set-piece victories during his campaigns, fought in May 326 BC. When Alexander reached the river Hydaspes (the Greek name for the river Jhelum) King Porus' large army was already drawn up on the opposite bank. The armies were visible to each other, but the river was broad, swift and turbulent and there was no crossing point. The main body of Porus's army is reckoned to have numbered between 20,000 and 50,000 infantry, with between 2,000 and 4,000 cavalry and up to 200 elephants and 1,000 chariots. Alexander's army is unlikely to have numbered more than 40,000. Porus, making full use of the elephants, guarded carefully all the river crossings, but, after some weeks of diversionary tactics Alexander successfully made a night crossing some eighteen miles upstream from the base camp, in spite of a mishap caused by mistaking an island for a promontory of the opposite bank. Porus now marched at once to meet Alexander's army. The battle opened with Alexander's bowmen raining arrows on the Indian cavalry in the left wing, who were then attacked by the Companion Cavalry. Alexander's officer Coenus led a cavalry charge which caught the Indian right wing in the rear, and the Indian cavalry were forced back among the elephants, with resulting confusion. In the battle and pursuit, 20,000 Indian infantry were killed and about 3,000 cavalry were lost. The Indian chariots were wrecked and the surviving elephants were taken as booty.

1993 Nicanor and **Symachus** are literary creations; the account in our poet's source, the *Alexandreis,* is at 9.77–147. Here the two young men, of one mind, seek to cross a river at which their forces are stuck, and to drive back their foes from the other bank, but they die in the attempt. They bear resemblance to two characters in the *Aeneid,* namely Nisus and Euryalus, who share a deep, loving bond. In the *Aeneid,* during the funeral games of book 5, Nisus is winning the foot race, only to slip on a patch of blood; he does not forget Euryalus, and throws himself in Salius' path, tripping him and leaving the way clear for Euryalus to win (5.315–39). Book 9 (9.176–502) sees the pair make a daring raid on the Rutulian camp at night and slaughter their sleeping enemies. Daylight draws near, and Nisus realises, but allows Euryalus to put on armour plundered from the dead, including a helmet with gorgeous plumes. He is seen by a passing cavalry detachment and captured; Nisus sees him taken and tries to distract their foes, but Volcens kills Euryalus before his eyes. The tremendous bond of love, which is the core of the similarity between these pairs of characters, in sundered in death.

2010d Antigonus: see note to stanza 979c.

2030a a knight: both manuscripts of the *Libro de Alexandre* mention four knights. The *Alexandreis* tells of just one knight and the evidence suggests that the multiplication of the number of Alexander's doubles is the result of a misreading by the Spanish poet: see Casas Rigall, ed. (2007, 591). The plural forms in stanza 2031 clearly relate to Alexander and his double. In both our text and our translation we have followed the sense of the passage as reflected in the *Alexandreis*.

2034c Casas Rigall, ed. (2007, 592) suggests that the name **Atalaus** could relate to a figure of that name who was accused of complicity in the conspiracy that led to Philotas' death but was subsequently absolved.

2089a Taxiles: this is a historical figure, but he was not Porus' brother. Taxiles was the name given by the Greeks to the prince or king who reigned over the region between the Indus and the Hydaspes rivers in the Punjab. His real name was Ambhi and the Greeks appear to have called him Taxiles or Taxilas, after the name of his capital city of Taxila. He seems to have been on hostile terms with his neighbour Porus, who ruled the area east of the Hydaspes.

2094c Bucephala was the city founded by Alexander and named in honour of his horse, Bucephalus. Bucephala lay on the west bank of the Hydaspes river and it is believed to correspond to modern-day Jhelum in Pakistan. We are told that Alexander was plunged into grief by Bucephalus' death. He had ridden this mount during all of his great victories, although as the horse had aged he had started to use it sparingly in battle, saving it for the final victory charge.

2098–2099 But Walter the good ... was tired by now: the Spanish poet marks clearly for us the point at which he departs from the narrative of the *Alexandreis* and exploits material to be found in other Alexander texts, notably the *Historia de Proeliis*. He is to return to the line of his main source for what he presents as Alexander's second combat with Porus in stanzas 2186 ff. His purpose is to produce a comprehensive and encyclopedic account, including material which he considers will be informative and colourful, and also shed important light on the nature and conduct of his hero. Some of what follows is an expression of wonder at the natural marvels believed to exist in virtually unknown regions, whilst some of the episodes that the poet incorporates attribute to Alexander superhuman and at times almost divine powers. Where he doubts their plausibility (for example, in stanza 2305), he tells us so clearly. The account, taken as a whole, is to give a full picture of what was known and believed about Alexander, with all his strengths and weaknesses.

2101a Behind lofty peaks, called the Caspian Gates: this name was originally applied to the narrow region at the south-eastern corner of the Caspian Sea, through which Alexander in fact marched in the pursuit of Bessus. It is, however, transferred in some Alexander texts, including those followed by our poet, to the passes through the Caucasus, on the other side of the Caspian Sea. The nature of the pass is never very clear; some sources say it is a pass between mountains while others say it is a pass between the peaks and the Caspian Sea.

2101c ff. he found many people all gathered together: Michael (1982) has shown that this episode fuses two biblical episodes: the story of the Ten Lost Tribes of Israel and that of the enclosure of the cursed tribes of Gog and Magog. The author of the *Libro de Alexandre* was certainly not the first to make this identification (it is also found, for example, in Peter Comestor's twelfth-century sacred history the *Historia Scholastica*, which includes an account of Alexander's deeds). The ten ancient tribes disappeared from the biblical narrative after the Kingdom of Israel was enslaved and exiled by ancient Assyria; they were gradually assimilated into other peoples but nevertheless a belief persisted that one day they would be rediscovered. On the other hand, the tradition of Gog and Magog begins with the reference to Magog in *Genesis* and continues with cryptic prophecies in *Ezekiel*, with echoes in the *Book of Revelation*. According to *Revelation* (20.7–8) "and when the thousand years are expired, Satan shall be loosed out of his prison, and shall go out to deceive the nations which are in the four quarters of the earth, Gog and Magog, to gather them together to battle." Gog and Magog generally appear together representing Satan in the final conflict against God's people, but they occur widely and in various guises in mythology and folklore. In the *Alexander Romance*, Alexander defends the world against them by constructing the Gates of Alexander, an immense wall between two mountains that will stop the invaders until the time of the Final Judgement. In the *Romance*, these gates are built between two mountains in the Caucasus known as the "Breasts of the World". Surprisingly, perhaps, the story of Alexander's enclosure of the "Unclean Nations" was adopted directly into the Qur'an, although here no specific race is mentioned. For an analysis of the heavily anti-Semitic aspects of the Spanish poet's depiction of this episode, see Weiss (2005, 134–138).

2115a   But the written text says: The texts in question are likely to be *Ezekiel* 38–39 and, particularly, *Revelation* 20:7–8, which tells of Gog and Magog, the servants of Satan, preparing to do battle against the saints (see note to stanza 2101c).

2118–2142   The palace's adornment must not be forgotten: the source of this description is in the *Historia de Proeliis*, though the Spanish poet has eleborated on this source extensively (Casas Rigall, ed. 2007, 607). The historical basis for some of the wonders that are described here seems more likely to be the Persian city of Persepolis (see Green 1991, 316).

2126b   a magnificent vine: in origin, this seems to relate to the jewelled golden vine which Alexander carried off from the Great King's bedchamber at Persepolis: a symbolic Tree of Life, representing unbroken Achaemenid government (Green, 1991, 316). The vine is first mentioned by Alexander's chamberlain, Chares, and the historian Amyntas emphasises the detail of bunches of grapes "composed of most valuable precious stones" (Stoneman 2008, 45).

2128ff.   As among grapes there are differing natures: some of the grape varieties mentioned in the following stanzas can be quite easily identified; these might include the term *tempraniellas* (translated here as **earlier**), which – if meant here as a noun

– would relate to the variety most closely associated with La Rioja; **calagrañas**, originally associated with La Rioja, are known as being more suitable for eating than for making wine; **molejas** are literally "soft" grapes and could actually mean raisins; the **torrontés** grape is known for producing a crisp, aromatic white wine and today is very common, for example, in Argentina; **migaruelas** and **alfonsinas** have defied editors' attempts to identify them, though Casas Rigall, ed. (2007, 610), makes some tentative suggestions.

2135–2141 **At the roots of the tree, at fifteen men's bodies' distance:** Michael (1997, 278) explains that "It is clear that the Spanish poet understood his sources to be describing a cleverly designed pneumatic device, similar to a pipe organ, by which compressed air from bellows was forced through copper pipes hidden in the trunk of the tree." However, the mechanism described in these stanzas does not figure in our poet's source, the *Historia de Proeliis*. Michael (*ibid.*, 285–86) suggests that the source could be an illumination that the poet encountered in a manuscript of the Latin text. Certainly, such automata were not the preserve of fiction: based on the engineering principles of Heron of Alexandria, they became quite widespread in Byzantium (Stoneman 2008, 48).

2144b **and they knew not where to go in search of Porus:** in fact there was no need for such a search; after the defeat, the historical Porus surrendered to Alexander, who retained him in his service. Alexander would at a later stage, however, have to put down a rebellion led by his ally's nephew and namesake. Nevertheless, after a month's rest in Porus' territory, the performance of funeral rites and the holding of traditional games, Alexander continued to plan for the future. He was determined to press on to the waters of the "Endless Ocean", though his troops were more and more affected by exhaustion, particularly in the months after the Battle of the Hydaspis/Jhelum, by disease and as a result of the extreme weather conditions in which their campaigns were carried out. More and more these factors were to have an effect in sapping morale.

2155–2163 **At this point they came across a mass of noxious snakes:** this episode serves to display Alexander's knowledge as a scholar and natural scientist, but in representing nakedness (a sign of humility) as a way of repelling the serpent – associated with the Devil or with temptation – it provides a counterbalance to the depiction of the elephant as a representative of pride. The source could be the *Etymologiae* or a Bestiary such as the *Physiologus* (see note to stanzas 1976–1980).

2194b **Taxiles:** there seems to be an error on the part of the poet here, as the death of Taxiles was described in stanza 2091.

2206–2207 **When he had been brought low:** these stanzas mark the end of the section based principally on the *Historia de Proeliis*, which narrates the death of Porus. As was seen above (see notes to stanzas 1191 and 2144d), far from meeting his death either in pitched battle or in a duel, Porus was actually rewarded by Alexander for the valour that he had displayed in battle – and this is here reflected in the account given in both the *Alexandreis* and the *Libro de Alexandre*.

2216d other tales are told, which beggar belief: this is probably an allusion to the account of the extensive travels which, according to some branches of Alexander tradition, Alexander and Porus undertook together, and possibly to the story, present in both the *Historia de Proeliis* and the *Roman d'Alexandre*, of Porus' later death at the hands of Alexander.

2218a Sudracae was a powerful city, filled with people: this city was situated on the alluvial plains in the central Punjab, on the banks of the River Hydraotes (Ravi). It may possibly correspond to the modern Multan. It belonged to the Malli people (Malavas) who ruled the Punjab in the fourth century BC and offered stiff resistance to Alexander, who is known to have been seriously wounded in the course of taking the town. This episode came at a low-point in the campaigns, for historically the attack on the Malli took place in the winter of 326/25 BC, on the way back from the River Hyphasis (Beas), where the exhausted and demoralised Macedonian troops had effectively mutinied and refused to trek any further east.

2236cd as Phinehas' lance had dealt the Midianite: *Numbers* 26:6–8 recounts that when Phinehas, grandson of Aaron the priest, saw that one of the people of Israel had brought a Midianite woman into his family, he brought a spear and ran both the man and the woman through the body. "Thus", we are told, "the plague was stayed from the people of Israel."

2238 Timaeus was a minor figure of whom little is known; the historical **Peucestas**, on the other hand, first appeared as a commander in the Hydaspes fleet and later, in reward for his bravery during the Mallian campaign, was assigned the satrapy of Persis; he became the first Macedonian known to speak the Persian language. He was in Babylon at the time of Alexander's death and it has been suggested that he was involved in the conspiracy against the Emperor. As a very popular figure in the East, he became deeply involved in the conflicts which marked the following years. **Leonnatus** was a prominent figure throughout the campaigns. He was awarded a golden crown for his courage in India and a later victory over the *Oreitae*. After Alexander's death he was given the satrapy of Phrygia, but became involved in intrigues and, in the course of a subsequent campaign, died in battle. There are a number of historical figures who are known by the name of **Ariston**. One of them is a Thessalian *hetairos* (companion) of Alexander who was (probably falsely) to be associated with the conspiracy to poison him. Another prominent Ariston was a member of the Paeonian royal family who played an important part early in Alexander's campaigns, for example as a commander in the Battle of Gaugamela.

2250 Critobulus seems to have been not only a physician but also a *trierarchos* (trireme-commander) among the Hydaspes fleet (see Arrian, *Indica* 18). He can be identified with the doctor who had pulled an arrow from the eye of Alexander's father some 28 years before.

2268c Abisares: This was an Indian king also known by the Greeks as Embisarus, who ruled mountainous territories beyond the river Hydaspes and had sent embassies to Alexander both before and after the victory over Porus. As in the case of Porus,

Alexander not only allowed him to retain his kingdom but also increased its extent, and on his death he allowed him to be succeeded by his own son.

2271ff. Alexander's people were deeply anxious ...: This debate relates to the so-called "mutiny" of the Hyphasis or Beas river, an episode which in fact occurred before the campaign against the Malli people (see note to stanza 2218a). In his desire to press on to find the shores of the "Endless Ocean", Alexander had miscalculated the mood of his men, who for eight years had struggled not only against hostile and powerful enemies but also against extreme climatic conditions and a range of other natural dangers (there was now real fear, for example, of an encounter with fabled giant elephants). In the foothills of Kashmir the troops effectively refused to go any further or to cross the Hyphasis / Beas. It was the senior general Coenus who spoke on their behalf. Alexander eventually agreed to turn back, thus leaving the Beas river as the marker of the eastern frontier of his empire. Unlike his historical counterpart, the Alexander of the Spanish poem is able to persuade his men to carry on with the conquest.

2286c with this too you outshone the glory of Troy: in fact, we feel the story of Troy quite forcefully in these lines, with a collocation of material to evoke it. Hector (see note to stanza 70a), Troy's leading warrior, is mentioned at 2279c. The mention of Alexander's men suffering for ten years at 2285b recalls the ten years of siege necessary before the Greeks could take the city of Troy. Homer and his account are then explicitly mentioned at 2288c. It is in this stanza, 2288, that the Trojan reference reaches its climax with the mention of Achilles (see note to 70c). Interestingly, however, our poet mentions specifically Homer's recording of Achilles' acts of valour over his months of life. In fact, Achilles has to choose between these, between returning to his home to live a long, peaceful life, and remaining at Troy to fight, where he will win great honour but also meet his death (for his awareness that to fight on at Troy means his death, see, for example, his conversation with his mother, Thetis, at *Iliad* 18.70–137, especially 94–100). Alexander seeks often to draw parallels between himself and the heroes of mythic past, and Achilles' choice of the path that brought renown for his deeds over that of simple long life offers him a striking example for this, even allowing for the importance of Achilles' grief and desire to gain vengeance for his fallen companion Patroclus in his decision. Certainly Alexander is seen in our poem to value reputation above all else (see, for example, stanza 2184).

2289 So say the texts – I have read the treatise –: the treatise in question is probably the *Etymologiae*, although the reference may be to an annotation to a manuscript of the *Alexandreis* (Casas Rigall, ed. 2007, 639). The **seven worlds** are the Earth, the Moon and the five planets known at that time.

2293b I shall seek out the Antipodes – I want to conquer them: the poet mentions the Antipodes three times (see also stanzas 1920 and 2440), presenting them as a people who are to be found in the depths of the earth and, specifically, in the vicinity of Hell. Deyermond (2002) hypothesises from a number of parallels with the *Divine Comedy* that Dante, directly or indirectly, had knowledge of such details of the *Libro de Alexandre*.

2305 Of one great exploit do people often tell: Alexander's submarine exploits are not included in the *Alexandreis* but they do figure in both the *Historia de Proeliis* and the *Roman d'Alexandre*, though Casas Rigall, ed. (2007, 642) suggests that the poet was working from memory of them when he wrote this passage. After the withdrawal from the Hyphasis/Beas river, the historical Alexander marched to Nicaea and Bucephala, settlements founded earlier that year, where his shipwrights were at work on a fleet of ships intended to sail to the Indian Ocean. By early 326 BC the fleet was ready to sail to the Ocean by way of the Jhelum and Indus rivers. It was in the course of this voyage that the encounter with the Malli people and Alexander's near-fatal wound occurred. By mid-July 325 the end of the river voyage was in sight as the fleet reached the head of the Indus estuary. Sacrifices were carried out on islands at the mouth of the river and plans were made to construct a boat-house and leave a garrison. Alexander's plan was for the ships to leave the mouth of the Indus, turn through the Indian Ocean and enter the Persian Gulf. Alexander himself, however, far from taking part in marine, or submarine adventures, was to march by land – and the new expedition was to prove both gruelling and hazardous.

2325ff. Nature, which is nurse to every living creature: the source for this account of the intervention of Nature is to be found in the *Alexandreis*, but crucially the Spanish poet introduces a change by showing her to be clearly subordinate to God's will: see Casas Rigall, ed. (2007, 646).

2355d and thus did the Devil manage to enter Saul: according to I *Samuel*, King Saul became increasingly jealous of David's growing success and popularity to the extent of trying in a number of ways to kill him. Saul became increasingly irrational and eventually committed suicide.

2358a Herod: Herod I or Herod the Great was a Roman client king of Judea. In Christian scripture, Herod is known for his role in the Massacre of the Innocents, described in *Matthew*, 2, where he is enraged at being outwitted by the *Magi*.

2358d Lamech: Lamech is the sixth-generation descendant of Cain (*Genesis* 4:18) who tells his wives of vengeance that he has exacted: "I have slain a man for wounding me; / a young man for striking me." He is also the subject of an apocryphal *Book of Lamech* of which only the name is known; Jewish sources, seemingly derived from this, recount how, as an old man with failing eyesight, he killed – while out hunting – both his ancestor Cain and his own son. (See Bañeza Román 1994, 145–146.)

2359ff. the good man Job: The *Book of Job* describes how, in spite of all the afflictions which have been heaped on Job, he refuses to question divine providence or to curse the name of God.

2360a At this point, I wish to bring before you an *exemplum*: together with the tale of the lamb and the wild dogs in stanza 1780, this is the only set-piece *exemplum*, or moralising anecdote, to be used in the *Libro de Alexandre*. It is a well known story and its use is documented in the work of several thirteenth-century writers. What is strikingly typical of our poet's practice, however, is the use of the technical term to designate such exploitation of the device. The *exemplum* was an important feature of the preacher's art: the subject matter could be taken from fables, folktales, legends or real history, and collections of *exempla* (such as that of Jacques de Vitry, ca. 1160/70–1240) were produced as an aid to preachers. The literary theorists of the twelfth and thirteenth centuries, such as Geoffey of Vinsauf, also recommended the use of *exempla* to adorn a literary work.

2366a   Clergy and canons: both manuscripts contain the reading "clerics and knights", but we have followed Nelson's reconstruction of this line, with the more logical "clérigos y canonges" denoting the more secular and regular clergy.

2370a   Pluto: Pluto is another name for the Greek god Hades, the lord of the underworld; the obvious similarities with Satan mean that in the Christian world he comes to be associated with evil. His name is probably derived from *ploutos* (wealth), and originally he is not linked with the underworld but, as the "Wealth-giver", he enriches men with the fruits of the earth. By the 5th century BC, however, Pluto has become a common name used to refer to Hades in myth and in cult (see *Oxford Classical Dictionary*, 661). Pluto is not mentioned in the account of this episode in the *Alexandreis*.

2375d   true confession: Franchini (1997) evaluates the significance of the allusion to the *vera confessio* and the corresponding emphasis on this at the Fourth Lateran Council of 1215, arguing that this detail could be a factor in the dating of the *Libro de Alexandre*. Casas Rigall, ed. (2007, 657) urges caution. See also, however, the emphasis on performing the penance imposed by the priest in 2384b, and for further possible evidence of the influence on the poet of the conclusions of the Fourth Lateran Council, see Introduction, Section 4.

2382c   If Lot had drunk only the amount that Cato orders: *Genesis* 19:30–38 tells of how, taking refuge with their father in a cave, Lot's daughters, incorrectly believing they were the only females to have survived the destruction of Sodom and the surrounding area, assumed it was their responsibility to bear children. On two successive nights, they got their father drunk enough to abandon his judgement completely and have sexual intercourse with them. Each became pregnant. For the allusion to Cato, see note to stanza 1807b.

2386a   Dives: There are different possible interpretations of this allusion. In Latin, the meaning is "rich" or "rich man" and the word is used in the Latin Vulgate Bible in the parable of the rich man and Lazarus, at *Luke* 16:19–31. Others – including Cañas ed. (1988, 532) – interpret it as an allusion to Pluto, or Hades, lord of the underworld, via the probable etymology of his name; see note to 2370a.

2390a   In an author, I remember we are wont to read: A fundamental part of the study of Grammar in the Middle Ages related to the analysis of literary texts which served as a model of good writing. There was an accepted corpus of texts which formed the core of this part of every student's education, known in Latin as the *auctores* (hence, for example, the Spanish term *actorista* used in stanza 1197a to denote a teacher of grammar). In this case, the author in question is Ovid, although it is possible that the stories will have been encountered in a commentary or in an anthology or *florilegium*. **Niobe**'s story is told in the *Metamorphoses* (6.146–312): she boasted of her superiority to Leto because, while the goddess only had two children, she had fourteen (though the story is an old one, and the numbers vary: see, for example, *Iliad* 24.602–617, where the number is twelve, six sons and six daughters). Leto's son Apollo killed her seven sons with his arrows, and her daughter Artemis killed Niobe's seven daughters, leaving her childless. Niobe fled into the mountains and turned into stone as she wept. The story of **Phyllis** and Demophon is told in *Heroides* 2, an imaginary letter which Phyllis, Queen of Thrace, writes to Demophon, with whom she fell in love when he stayed at her court on his return from the Trojan War. Demophon has to sail to Athens, but he promises to return to her soon. He does not return, however, and in some versions of the myth (though this is not in the *Heroides*), Phyllis is turned into an almond tree, which remains leafless; it is to this that our poet alludes here. The link between the two stories and our text here is that in the poet's eyes the fact that both women succumb to their grief means they fall prey to the vice of Accidy.

2393b The wife of Lot: Lot was the nephew and brother-in-law of Abraham. *Genesis* 19 tells how, as Lot and his wife (who is not named) fled from Sodom, "his wife looked back from behind him, and she became a pillar of salt."

2393c sufficient for that is one contrary word: the meaning here is that the explanation – probably that, unlike the pagan texts, the biblical episode has a clear moral framework and purpose – should be self-evident.

2403a Zosimas: This is most likely to be Zosimas of Palestine, also called Zosima, commemorated as a saint in the Eastern Orthodox and Greek-Catholic churches. Saint Zosimas was born in the second half of the fifth century. He became a monk in a monastery in Palestine, gaining a reputation as a great elder and ascetic. At the age of fifty-three, he moved to a very strict monastery located in the wilderness close to the Jordan River, where he spent the remainder of his life, and is reputed to have lived to the age of almost one hundred. He is best known for the tale of his encounter with St Mary of Egypt – recounted, for example, in French and Spanish poems of the thirteenth century. Casas Rigall, ed. (2007, 664) also suggests a possible identification with Saint Zosimus who was pope from March 18, 417 to December 26, 418 and whose savage temper coloured all the controversies in which he took part.

2404c it was he who brought the King of Babylon to sin: This is Nebuchadnezzar – see note to stanza 991b.

2405a These are the seven vices: more than seven figures have been described, but the following are those on which the poet has sought to concentrate attention as the "prinçipales" or capital vices: Avarice (stanzas 2346 ff.), Greed (2346 ff.), Anger (2367 ff.), Lust (2371 ff.), Gluttony (2378 ff.), Indolence (Accidy) (2387 ff.), Vainglory (2395 ff.).

Notes

2409d **Esther** is the heroine of the Biblical Book of *Esther* which is named after her. As a result of Esther's intervention and influence, her husband Ahasuerus followed in the footsteps of his maternal grandfather, Cyrus the Great, in showing mercy to the Jews of Persia. Esther, characterised by her humility and her faithfulness to God, is used as a counter to the other examples given in stanza 2409.

2416a **Tityus** in Greek mythology was a giant, a son of Gaia, Earth, who tried to rape Leto. His slayer is variously said to be either Zeus, Apollo, Artemis, or these last two together, who are Leto's children. As punishment, he is stretched out in the underworld and vultures feed on his liver (see, for example, *Odyssey* 11.576–81), which was said to regenerate, so that the torment was eternal: this aspect lies behind our present lines.

2449ff. **Antipater:** For this important figure – widely held to be involved in the assassination of Alexander – see note to stanza 1503c.

2461c **the Shining Mountains:** These are the Atlas Mountains which stretch across north-west Africa, extending about 2,400 kilometres through Morocco, Algeria, and Tunisia. The term *Montes Claros* is also used in the *Poema de Mio Cid*, a text more or less contemporary with the *Libro de Alexandre*, to denote the Atlas range.

2463c **having himself declared lord in the city of Rome:** the parallel here is clearly with the coronation of the Holy Roman Emperor in Rome, as in the case, for example, during the poet's lifetime of Otto of Brunswick in 1209 and Frederick II of Sicily in 1220. Stanza 1788b contains a similar possible allusion.

2464a **The Psalmist:** the poet is alluding to Solomon, to whom has been attributed the composition of some of the Psalms and also – according to its opening two chapters, but not according to most modern scholars – the Book of *Ecclesiastes*. The second verse of *Ecclesiastes* declares: "Vanity of vanities! All is vanity ..."

2467d **like fine Alexandria, where he was taken:** the *Libro de Alexandre* has not previously mentioned the founding of Alexandria in 331 BC on the coast of north-central Egypt. After Alexander's death his remains were indeed taken to Alexandria, but this was essentially a political ploy by its ruler Ptolemy (see Introduction, Section 5 and note to stanza 2644a).

2469c **of the things that he saw, that we have found in writing:** as we have already seen, our poet is keen to make his account a comprehensive one and he sees any written source (here the *Historia de Proeliis*) as an authority to be taken seriously. Nevertheless, he rejects some of the more far-fetched elements and incorporates others of his own in his evident desire to produce an account which, in his view, is plausible and ultimately truthful.

2475a **the bird that is known as the Phoenix:** the Phoenix is in origin a sacred firebird (the Bennu bird) in Egyptian mythology. At the end of its life-cycle the Phoenix builds itself a nest and then ignites, with both the nest and the bird burning fiercely and being reduced to ashes, from which a new, young Phoenix rises. It is incorporated, too, into classical mythology (see, for example, the elegiac poem

De Ave Phoenice, and accounts at Herodotus 2.73 and Tacitus, *Annales* 6.28). Its life being eternally renewed through death, it became a powerful symbol for both pagans and Christians, the latter using it as a symbol, in art and literature, for the resurrection of Christ.

2478cd There is no mention of **Phoebus** and **Diana** in the poet's source for this episode, the *Historia de Proeliis*, but they relate to the trees of the Sun and the Moon mentioned in stanzas 2482 ff. Phoebus is the sun god, and Diana, among her other characteristics, is a moon goddess.

2483d then will it be seen how each has a twofold tongue: according to the *Historia de Proeliis*, each of the trees gave part of its prophecy in each of two languages.

2495b the acephali: these curious beings are described in the *Historia de Proeliis*, though not by this name. Otherwise known as Blemmyes, they figure quite widely in classical and medieval texts, for example in Pliny the Elder, *Naturalis historia* 5.46, which says that the Blemmyes are said to have been without heads, with their eyes and their mouth fixed in their chests. Their name here is derived from Greek *akephalos*, headless. These creatures appear quite commonly in manuscript illuminations and are represented on a twelfth-century *mappa mundi*.

2497a two gryphons: the use of gryphons is mentioned in both the *Historia de Proeliis* and the *Roman d'Alexandre*. The gryphon is a legendary creature with the body and hind quarters of a lion and the head and wings of an eagle.

2508ff. the world is known as an image of Man: In his *De natura rerum*, Saint Isidore explicitly describes man as a microcosm of the world (Casas Rigall, ed. 2007, 686). Various parallels have been noted in both Christian and non-Christian texts, but there are particularly interesting parallels with some Hebrew writings, for example with the comparison between Man and the Universe made by Joseph ben Jacob ibn Tzaddik. This Spanish rabbi, poet, and philosopher lived in the early twelfth century and held office in Córdoba jointly with Maimon, the father of the great scholar Maimonides. In his *Olam Katan* he analyses in detail the parallels between Man and the world around him, for example between his hair and the grass and vegetation, his veins and arteries and the rivers and canals, and his bones and the mountains.

2510cd it is all ruled by Moors...: The two manuscripts have markedly different readings for these lines. The reading on which the translation is based represents the version to be found in *O*, but *P* describes the Moors as "greatly feared" and Mahomet as an "honoured prophet".

2518ff. They sent him tribute: Casas Rigall, ed. (2007, 688) points out that, surprisingly, perhaps, this episode does seem to have a firm historical basis.

2522a The Lord of Sicily: Frederick II of Sicily, of the Hohenstaufen dynasty, was Holy Roman Emperor from 1220 until his death in 1250. He led the Crusade in 1228 which brought about the restitution to Christendom of Jerusalem. He was also famous for his scholarship and – said to speak nine languages – he was known as "stupor mundi" ("the wonder of the world"). He founded the University of Palermo in 1224. Frederick was known to have an interest in the career of Alexander, with whom he was often compared. He was even represented as having horns, a feature clearly intended to associate him with Alexander, and material from the *Alexander Romance* is known to have been in the hands of scholars connected with his court (Stoneman 2008, 205–206). Scholars have been inclined to disregard the value of the present passage as evidence for dating the composition of the *Libro de Alexandre* (Arizaleta 1999, 22–23 and Casas Rigall, ed. 2007, 689), arguing that Sicily is mentioned in an equivalent passage in the *Alexandreis* and that the poet seems not be aware of Frederick's dual role as ruler of Sicily and of much of Germany. However, these arguments do not entirely convince: it is surely significant that the poet moves from a general allusion to the Kingdom of Sicily (effectively equivalent to southern Italy) in his source, replacing it by praise for a particular ruler; and Frederick was most closely identified with Sicily, where he was raised and spent most of his life, whilst his power in Germany was tenuous until after the defeat in 1215 and eventual death in 1218 of his rival Otto of Brunswick.

2531d   Iolaus was the youngest son of Antipater and probably served Alexander during the later stages of the Asiatic campaigns. He was given the title of "wine-pourer" and there were later to be rumours that he had actually committed the act of poisoning Alexander. Apart from this, nothing is known of his career until after the King's death, when he appears to have returned to Macedonia.

2533d The **Valley of Josaphat** is mentioned in *Joel* 3, where Jahveh announces that He will gather together all nations, and enter into judgement with them. It seems, then, that Jahveh's judgment on the Gentiles will take place in the valley where, in the presence of Josaphat, King of Judah, He had annihilated the coalition of the enemies of the Hebrew people. There is a clear suggestion here that a time of judgement for Alexander is about to arrive.

2535b   people of many regions brought many scallop shells: the scallop shell was the emblem of the pilgrim to Santiago de Compostela. This city's cathedral was the destination of the important medieval pilgrimage route, the Way of St James (in Spanish the *Camino de Santiago*). Following the purported discovery in the early ninth century of the tomb of St James the Apostle, the cousin of Christ, his shrine achieved a massive popularity as a centre of pilgrimage, to the extent that, at the height if its popularity in the eleventh and twelfth centuries, more than half a million travellers each year are said to have used the road to Santiago de Compostela. The *Camino* continues to be much travelled today. The most important route ran from the Pyrenees, across northern Spain, and it is highly likely that the author of the *Libro de Alexandre* will have had a good deal of contact with pilgrims. By including this detail, he is endowing the gathering to pay homage to Alexander with some of the spiritual significance of the pilgrimage.

2537c   the hour of Sext: another of the canonical hours of prayer in the Church day (see note to stanza 33a), which would fall at about midday.

2539–2595   I want to tell you of the tent's decoration: it seems likely that the

.ection which follows was originally composed for inclusion at an earlier point in the poem (see note to stanzas 1962–1963) but that, because of the powerful part that it plays in resuming and reinforcing important themes of the poem, it was later reinserted at this crucial stage in the narrative.

2553b Mount Tabor: the reference in the Spanish text could be to the Italian Mount Tibur in the central Apennines, but a more appropriate spot would be Mount Tabor, situated in Lower Galilee, at the eastern end of the Jezreel Valley, 17 kilometres west of the Sea of Galilee. It is believed by many to be the site of the Transfiguration of Christ.

2553cd Noah drank the wine, and it was more than he could manage: *Genesis* 9: 20–27 tells how, after the flood, Noah became a tiller of the soil, planted a vineyard and drank the wine to excess. Like Alexander he is a man who has known a great success but errs through his lack of self-control.

2554–2566 all the nature of the year was depicted: there were numerous examples in both literature and the visual arts on which the Spanish poet could have based this passage. Probably the most famous Spanish example of the depiction of the labours of the months is to be found on the ceiling of the Pantheon of Kings in the Real Colegiata de San Isidoro in León. The correspondence between the activities depicted there and those described in the *Libro de Alexandre* is not very close, but it is interesting to note how this element stands out as the only part of the extensive paintings which are not explicitly biblical and moralising in content. Mâle (1972, 67–75) analyses the carvings on the cathedrals of Paris and Chartres which treat the same theme. The subject is a common one, but the poet has a specific purpose in including this detail at a critical stage in his narrative. The theme is, of course, the natural cycle (although war intrudes – 2558ab), with its progress through the seasons which brings constant change but whose course cannot be stopped or altered; and it is precisely Nature who has been offended by the excessive conduct of Alexander.

2568–2569 A little child was Hercules, not even yet a boy: there have been repeated allusions to Alexander's supposed link with Hercules (see, for example, the note to stanza 15d). This passage complements the account given in stanza 27: Juno seeks to take vengeance on Jupiter and the woman he lay with, Alcmene, by sending two serpents to kill their child, Hercules, but Hercules, from his cradle, strangles them both.

2570d and he set down his markers on reaching the West: this is an allusion to the "Pillars of Hercules"; see note to stanza 256a.

2580b Cogolla and Moncayo: Moncayo (altitude about 2000 metres) is situated on the limits between the provinces of Soria and Zaragoza whilst Cogolla (in the western part of La Rioja) is really little more than a hill. The fact that these two features are mentioned as outstanding among the peaks of Spain would seem to give some indication of the region with which the poet was most familiar, and the association with the important monastery of San Millán de la Cogolla, with its known connection with Gonzalo de Berceo, is an intriguing one (see Introduction, Section 3).

2581b Soria: *Manuscrito O* gives Sevilla, but this is an improbable reading, given that the city was not reconquered from the Moslems until 1248. Particularly in view of the possible connections with northern Spain suggested above (see note to 2580b and Introduction, Section 3), it seems sensible to follow Casas Rigall's argument (2007, 704) in favour of Soria. Burgos, Pamplona and León are all situated on the pilgrim route to Santiago de Compostela.

2582a–b The city of Paris: the University of Paris was one of the great centres of learning of medieval Europe. It grew up in the latter part of the twelfth century, with four faculties: Arts, Medicine, Law and Theology, and its students were divided into four *nationes* according to regional origin or language. Among the many Castilian students to attend the University of Paris were Sancho and Felipe, sons of Fernando III and destined for ecclesiastical careers (González Jiménez 2004, 16).

2582d the Rhône, a river of bounty: the River Rhône is mentioned twice in the *Libro de Alexandre*; see note to stanza 1423cd.

2583 Bologna seems outstanding above all others: the law school at **Bologna** was established by the early twelfth century and by the latter part of the century it had become an important centre attracting law students from all over Europe. It has been argued that there was already a school at **Pavia** in the late eleventh century. Although we have opted for the reading of "Burgundy" in 2583b, *Manuscrito O* gives "Tolosa", presumably Toulouse: the University of Toulouse was founded in 1229 and one of its earliest teachers was John of Garland, a prominent grammarian and literary theorist.

2584d and cut off the head of his very own brother: the allusion is to Romulus and Remus, brothers, sons of Mars and mythical founders of Rome. Romulus is said to have killed his brother, Remus, giving his own name to the city that the two had founded.

2595d the wealth of Almería: when the *Libro de Alexandre* was composed, the city of Almería was still part of Moslem Spain. The city was founded by Abd ar-Rahman III of Córdoba in 955 as an important port, both commercial and military. Its *alcazaba* is the second largest among the Muslim fortresses of Andalusia. A silk industry supported Almería in the 11th century and made its strategic harbour even more important. Almería suffered many sieges, notably a crusade directed against this famously wealthy Moslem city in October 1147. Within a decade it had passed to the control of the Almoravid emirs, and its prosperity continued. Only at the end of 1489 did it fall into Christian hands.

2603–2604 The stars of the sky: these stanzas are clearly intended to form a contrast with the accounts of the prodigies which preceded Alexander's birth (see stanzas 8–10).

2610a Iolaus, the traitor ...: for Antipater's son Iolaus, see note to stanza 2531d. The *Libro de Alexandre* does not mention the relationship between them.

2636 if Rhoxane should bear a son by me: Rhoxane did indeed bear Alexander a son, with whom she had become pregnant in December 324 BC. The status of this child – who was to be known as Alexander IV – would become a highly contentious matter. Caught up in the ensuing conflicts, they were eventually both murdered some seven years later.

2638   Philip, my brother: the man who was to become Philip III of Macedon was a son of King Philip II by Philinna of Larissa, allegedly a Thessalian dancer, and a half-brother of Alexander. Originally named Arrhidaeus, he took the name Philip when he ascended to the throne. He was apparently "mentally retarded", though, according to the rumour reported by Plutarch, he became weak-minded and epileptic following a poisoning attempt by Olympias. Alexander was fond of him and took him on his campaigns, though probably for political reasons. After Alexander's death, Arrhidaeus was proclaimed king by the Macedonian army in Asia. However, he was a mere figurehead and he was eventually murdered in 317 BC. **Pentapolis**: literally "five cities". This name was in fact applied to various groupings of five cities, one of which was the "cities of the plain" (Sodom, Gomorrah, Admah, Zeboim, and Zoar) and another the cities of Cyrenaica, in north Africa (Berenice, Arsinoe, Ptolemais, Cyrene and Apollonia).

2639d   Cassander was a son of Antipater. Known to have been a frail youth (he suffered from a long-term illness later in life) he appears not to have played a part in Alexander's campaigns. In 324 he was dispatched to Babylon, seemingly to answer charges against his father. Popular belief widely associated him, together with his father and brother, with the poisoning of Alexander. After the death of Alexander, Cassander returned to Macedonia, but he was to play an extensive part in the intrigues and conflicts of the following years. His conflict with Queen Olympias was particularly bitter and he was also responsible for the murder of Rhoxane and Alexander IV (see note to stanza 2636). His long-lasting hatred of Alexander seems to have originated in the treatment that he received from the Emperor while in Babylon (see Green 1991, 472). **Libya's river** is the Nile.

2641a   the other Ptolemy: there is no clearly identifiable "other Ptolemy" among Alexander's forces. The introduction of this figure may be the result of a misreading, as in Alexander's source this region is given to Phitonus.

2643a   a hundred talents of gold: this means something in excess of 2,500 kg of gold, worth an immense sum.

2644a   In Alexandria I wish my tomb to be: after Alexander's death, the regent Perdiccas kept his body in Babylon, where it was embalmed and lay in state; the body was an important symbol of power and authority and this may well explain why, as in 321 BC it was eventually being transported with great ceremony back to Aegae, the Macdeonian capital, Ptolemy seized it and had it taken to Egypt – where, he argued, Alexander had desired to be buried (perhaps because of the connection with Ammon). Work began on a mausoleum in Alexandria, but it was not until 293 BC that Alexander's body was finally laid to rest in it. Two hundred years later the sarcophagus was melted down to produce coinage and, though the body was re-interred, the tomb may finally have been destroyed during riots in the late third century AD. Today, the whereabouts of the tomb are a mystery.

2646c He ordered them to move him from his bed to the ground: some scholars argue that the manner of Alexander's death demonstrates a humility which is evidence that in the poet's eyes he achieved salvation, but Michael (1970, 107–111) argues that this detail simply reflects the action of some medieval Christian kings.

2647   Alexander died in June 323 BC.

2664c schism and unrest came among the knights: those who struggled for power after Alexander's death were known as the *Diadochoi* (literally meaning "successors") and the conflicts following his death are sometimes known as the *Wars of the Diadochoi*. Alexander left a huge empire composed of many essentially independent territories and there was almost immediately a dispute among his generals as to who his successor should be. As a compromise, Alexander's mentally defective half-brother Arrhidaeus was to become King (as Philip III), and rule jointly with Rhoxane's child, assuming that it was a boy. Arrhidaeus, Rhoxane and her son Alexander were all in due course to be murdered. Perdiccas, who had been Alexander's second in command and received from him his signet ring, became Regent of the entire Empire, effectively assuming full control and rewarding the other generals who had supported him with satrapies in various parts of the Empire. Ptolemy, for example, received Egypt. A concerted revolt was put down in Greece, but soon further conflict broke out, and Perdiccas himself was murdered by some of his own officers during an invasion of Egypt which had in effect been provoked by the theft of Alexander's body. Alexander's empire was already well on the way to fragmentation. The conflicts were to drag on well into the following century and it was only with the deaths of the last of the successors that a "workable balance of power" was achieved, with Egypt, Africa and Asia remaining as three distinct corners of the old empire. For a full account of the struggles which marked these years and the following two centuries, see Green (2007).

2669ff.   In the final section of the *Libro de Alexandre*, the poet includes all the elements recommended by the literary theorists for concluding a poem, such as a brief summary of the theme of the work, an expression of humility and a request for some kind of reward, although he seeks not the glory of recognition but a prayer for his soul. Casas Rigall, ed. (2007, 724) points to close parallels between the phrasing of the request in stanza 2674 and the concluding stanza of Berceo's *Del sacrificio de la misa* and also the more down-to-earth pleas for a glass of wine in Berceo's *Vida de santo Domingo* and in the *Poema de Mio Cid*.

2675 P & O   The role as copyist of **Juan Lorenzo of Astorga** (Astorga is a small town situated very close to the city of León) is consistent with the presence of numerous Leonese characteristics in *Manuscrito O*. The stanza which attributes the *Libro de Alexandre* to Gonzalo de Berceo is generally regarded as apocryphal, although the information which it contains tallies closely with that given in the strikingly similar) final stanza of Berceo's *Vida de san Millán*. The request for the master to be given dinner appears only in *Manuscrito O*.